KEN SCHULTZ'S

Fishing Encyclopedia

Worldwide Angling Guide

VOLUME 5

KEN SCHULTZ'S
Fishing Encyclopedia

Worldwide Angling Guide

Ken Schultz

IDG Books Worldwide, Inc.
An International Data Group Company
Foster City, CA • Chicago, IL • Indianapolis, IN • New York, NY • Southlake, TX

IDG Books Worldwide, Inc.
An International Data Group Company
919 E. Hillsdale Boulevard
Suite 400
Foster City, CA 94404

Copyright © 2000 by Ken Schultz

All rights reserved. No part of this book shall be reproduced, stored in a retrieval system, or transmitted by any means, electronic, mechanical, photocopying, recording, or otherwise, without written permission from the publisher. No patent liability is assumed with respect to the use of the information contained herein. Although every precaution has been taken in the preparation of this book, the publisher and author assume no responsibility for errors or omissions. Neither is any liability assumed for damages resulting from the use of the information contained herein.

Webster's New World is a registered trademark of Macmillan General Reference USA, Inc., a wholly owned subsidiary of IDG Books Worldwide, Inc.

The IDG Books Worldwide logo is a registered trademark under exclusive license to IDG Books Worldwide, Inc., from International Data Group, Inc.

For general information on books from IDG Books Worldwide's in the U.S., please call our Consumer Customer Service department at 800-762-2974. For reseller information, including discounts and premium sales, please call our Reseller Customer Service department at 800-434-3422.

For information on a multimedia version of this book, available from Tricom Intrtactive, Inc., please go to this Web site: intellipedia.com

To contact the author, please visit: www.kenshultz.com

Library of Congress Cataloging-in-Publication Data

This edition of *Ken Schultz's Fishing Encyclopedia*, which is published in 7 volumes, contains the entire contents of the work as previously published in a single volume: *Ken Schultz's Fishing Encyclopedia*, ISBN 9780028620572

This is Volume 5 of 7

Schultz, Ken, 1950–
Ken Shultz's fishing encyclopedia: worldwide angling guide/ Ken Schultz. — 1st ed.
  p. cm.
ISBN 0-02-862057-7
Volume 5: ISBN 9781684427710 (hardcover) | ISBN 9781684427727 (paperback)

1. Fishing—Encyclopedias. 2. Fishes—Encyclopedias. I. Title.
SH411.S38 2000
799.1'03—dc21 99-033719
CIP

Manufactured in the United States of America

First Edition

Trademarks

All terms mentioned in this book that are known to be trademarks or service marks have been appropriately capitalized. IDG Books cannot attest to the accuracy of this information. Use of a term in this book should not be regarded as affecting the validity of any trademark or service mark.

Table of Contents

Introduction
vii

Acknowledgments
ix

Photo Credits
xix

Fishing Encyclopedia Entries

N
1

O
105

P
133

Q
233

R
245

Appendix: Conversion Charts for Weights and Measures
297

Introduction

"Ah, the gallant fisher's life! It is the best of any;
'Tis full of pleasure, void of strife, And 'tis beloved by many."
—IZAAK WALTON

"All men are equal before fish."
—HERBERT HOOVER

WHILE PRODUCING THIS FISHING ENCYCLOPEDIA I SPOKE TO MANY HUNDREDS OF informed anglers. Nearly all of them thought the compilation of all things piscatorial was too overwhelming to contemplate because the angling universe is so enormous and diverse.

Certainly a modern fishing encyclopedia—if it truly provides a full field of knowledge—runs counter to the short and specialized tenets of today's journalism. Yet it is precisely because there is so much to the sport of fishing, plus an increasing profusion of specialized equipment and confusing terminology, that it was necessary to bring order and perspective to all of this in one definitive book.

Ken Schultz's Fishing Encyclopedia & Worldwide Angling Guide has been a long time in the making. I started thinking about it in 1991. Since work began in earnest in 1995, the project became even more expansive than expected, and indeed there were times when it was nearly overwhelming. As a result, the book grew much bigger than originally planned, becoming 50 percent larger than any fishing encyclopedia that has heretofore been published.

As a result, however, this encyclopedia contains the equivalent of thirty standard-length books, meaning that there is ample space to devote to the species, equipment, techniques, locations, and ancillary matters that encompass the angling universe. Consider that nearly one-third of the encyclopedia is comprised of the most comprehensive information on worldwide angling opportunities ever assembled. There is absolutely no place to find these details together; indeed, some elements of the *Worldwide Angling Guide* cannot be found anywhere else at all.

Likewise, the coverage of angling methods and equipment has never been addressed more comprehensively between the covers of any other book. In fact, *Ken Schultz's Fishing Encyclopedia* contains the most modern, illuminating, and extensive dis-courses on the basic elements of fishing tackle—baitcasting, big-game, conventional, flycasting, spinning, and spincasting—ever found in one place. Each of these entries undoubtedly contain more than all but the most scrupulous person will want to know.

Great lengths were also taken, however, to make sure that the less obvious subjects in the angling universe were included and reviewed in comprehensive fashion. For example, nowhere else is there a more extensive review of the principles, methods, and pros and cons of catch-and-release—perhaps the most important angling conservation development of the twentieth century.

Topics like fisheries management, angling-related travel, choosing guides and charter boats, and the care and preparation of fish for consumption, which are among many unglamorous subjects taken for granted elsewhere, receive complete explanation and review here. Likewise the otherwise oft-ignored subjects of ethics and etiquette—increasingly important issues as human pressures increase—are included.

Although there's an enormous amount of information in this book, every topic was approached with the intent to take nothing for granted and to present information in straightforward language. Angling is not like nuclear physics, and if it was half as complicated as some people try to make it, no one would enjoy it or have success. The extensive insertion of cross references is thus intended to direct you through a continuing stream of appropriate topics, so you can take any subject as far as you want to go. Some cross references appear within entry text next to topics that are more thoroughly reviewed elsewhere; many cross references appear at the end of entry text, either to direct you to the appropriate subject entry or to note related topics.

We've tried to make things easy to find and to place subjects where you're most likely to look for them, even if you're unsure of the proper terms or spelling. As an example, you'll find rainbow trout under the "T" entries (trout, rainbow) rather than under the "R" entries. Also, at the back of the book is a weights and measures conversion chart; this will be convenient for many readers since there's a liberal mix of metric and U.S. customary weights and measures throughout this book, just as there is at boat docks, fish camps, and tackle shops throughout the world.

Because the text is encyclopedic in format, however, it does not provide a full sense of the joy or spirit of sportfishing—the pleasure that makes it "beloved by many," as Izaak Walton said. Perhaps the accompanying photos help convey this. Photos and line art, incidentally, were planned and selected to reflect the broad, eclectic places and situations that so many anglers experience, as well as to reflect the great diversity of its participants. Angling is a very democratic recreation; as the quotation from President Hoover implies, the fish don't care who hooks them.

It is a special delight to publish this encyclopedia at the close of the twentieth century—a period with the most phenomenal sportfishing growth in the history of mankind—and at the advent of a new millennium. Knowing that the decades ahead will require proper stewardship of aquatic resources—something that anglers in particular have always demonstrated personal and financial support for—this text has been written and edited with sensitivity to conservation issues while also being realistic about the role that humans play as the highest predators and the diverse motivations they bring to angling.

In a sense, the sport of fishing is like a book with as many footnotes as main text. It is full of variables, especially individual skills, weather issues, peculiarities among species, habitat differences, and so forth. You may notice that the words "usually" and "generally" occur often in portions of the text. This isn't meant to be vague; it's because there are often no hard-and-fast rules in catching fish, no matter what you may have heard to the contrary. There are norms, but straying from norms is common for one reason or another, as any angler who has been humbled at a "hot" site at the "best" time of the season can attest.

While there is a wealth of reliable information here, a caveat is in order with regard to the contents of the *Worldwide Angling Guide*. Many of the countries profiled have not in the past provided, or do not currently provide, or may not in the future provide stable travel environments, especially to tourists of certain nationalities. Jungle fishing opportunities are especially among those that may present danger. Angola, Colombia, and Zambia come immediately to mind in this regard. Civil unrest can likewise make travel in certain places dangerous; recent troubles in Kenya, Indonesia, Russia, Uganda, and the Balkans serve as examples. The adventurous angler needs to use good judgment.

Things change the environmental order and aquatic resources, too. Yugoslavia hadn't been wrecked by bombs when that entry was written; Nicaragua and Honduras were leveled by Hurricane Georges right after those entries were written. Environmental changes sometimes radically alter the presence or availability of certain gamefish species, and in the more remote pockets of the world only native people and intrepid explorers are likely to know it.

On a final note, it is tempting to say, as marketers and publicists are wont to do, that this book contains everything an angler will ever need to know about fish and fishing. But new developments in fishing tackle will surely come along, changes in some habitats or in fish populations will alter the techniques and equipment used, and certainly natural changes will take place in some of the world's best angling spots. However, a lot of the fundamentals—the underlying principles of fish behavior, the function of basic equipment, and angling methodology—will be constant, making most of the information in this book relevant to the discerning angler even in years to come.

I expect to add to this body of knowledge in time, so if you think there's something that should have been included, if you have knowledge about fishing in a country that wasn't covered, or if you can suggest an improvement to any aspect of this book, please visit my website—www.kenschultz.com— and post a message about it.

Now, turn to any page and become absorbed.

—Ken Schultz

"If I fished only to capture fish, my fishing trips would have ended long ago."

— ZANE GREY

Acknowledgments

Producing a book of this magnitude required the involvement of a tremendous number of people and a great array of talents. This encyclopedia would not have gone beyond a mere suggestion, however, had it not been for the endorsement and encouragement of Natalie Chapman, a former publisher at Macmillan General Reference, now IDG Books Consumer Reference, whose confidence and vision made this book possible, and who gave me free rein to produce it as necessary. I'm also indebted to publisher Marie Butler-Knight, who took this project over in mid-stream, marshaled all the resources, and fervently shepherded the book to completion. Sincere appreciation is also extended to Renee Wilmeth and Kristi Hart, who directed the publisher's nitty-gritty editorial and production work with outstanding dedication and professionalism, plus a reassuring enthusiasm; to Pamela Benner, who paid excellent attention to details in the copyediting process and made good suggestions; and to many other directly involved personnel, particularly Beth Jordan, Faunette Johnston, and Jeanine Bucek.

This book could also not have been completed without the special assistance of my wife, Sandy, and my daughters, Alyson, Megan, and Kristen. They each helped in a variety of ways, especially by being patient. Sandy's assistance with a host of matters was very beneficial, and Kristen was particularly vital, pitching in for a second time during a desperate period with important research and writing assistance.

In order to make this encyclopedia truly comprehensive and of worldwide significance it was imperative to involve a host of contributors with expertise in technical fisheries matters, regional angling opportunities, and specialized sportfishing topics. I'm grateful for their participation and excellent contributions, the bulk of which made up the *Worldwide Angling Guide*. In particular, appreciation is extended to the incomparable Ed Migdalski, who provided technical scientific fisheries advice and vetted all of the fish art.

I'm also indebted to the late, and incomparable in his own right, A. J. McClane. His fishing encyclopedia of 1965 and 1974, though now outdated, was not only a phenomenal reference work, but a monumental achievement in an era before personal computers, electronic mail, fax machines, scanners, laser printers, and the various modern technology that made putting this book together far easier than it was in his time. Unlike me, he was unable to write and edit on a laptop computer in cars, planes, airports, hotel rooms, and other places, or receive electronically transmitted text. More significantly, McClane set a very high bar for what a real fishing encyclopedia ought to be, and provided a template for such a book for the twenty-first century. Without his accomplishment, it would have been much more difficult to plan and publish this book. (Aside to historians: four contributors to this project—Ed Migdalski, George Reiger, Jack Samson, and Bill Scifres—were also contributors to McClane's encyclopedia.)

Just as McClane, the contributors to this book, and the people at IDG Books Worldwide are the best in their fields, so is *Field & Stream* the largest and best fishing and hunting magazine in the world, and I've been privileged to be part of this publication continuously since 1973. I appreciate the confidence and opportunities provided me over that time by its editors. Those opportunities laid the groundwork for this encyclopedia. I'm especially grateful to Editor Slaton White and Managing Editor Mike Toth for allowing me leeway over the last several years that I've been working on this project.

Information, suggestions, encouragement, technical advice, reference paraphernalia, reviews and critiques, and assorted material assistance were received from so many individuals and organizations that some will likely be overlooked in these acknowledgments, for which I apologize.

I'm very grateful to the following individuals:

Blaine Anderson
John Anthon
Dick Ballard
Ron Ballanti
LaVerne Barnes
Cameron Baty
Susan Baumgartner
Gene Bay
Dick Bengraff
Virginia Benoit
Walt Boname
Toby Bradshaw
Eric Burnley

Cyril Calendini
Bill Chapman, Jr.
Jim Chapralis
Larry Columbo
David Cosby
Gary Dollahon
Lou Duarte
Todd DuPuis
Jack Erskine
Mike Fine
Paul Fuller
Riccardo Galigani
Ken Gangler

Acknowledgments

Guy Geffroy
Lois Gerber
Alessandro Giangio
Barry Gibson
Gary Giudice
Fred Golofaro
Jerry Gomber
George Gowen
Garry Gurke
Judy Hammond
Bill Hilts, Jr.
Bruce Holt
Dr. James Imai
Jimmy Kano
Nick Karas
Glenda Kelley
Gary King
Jason Klein
Bob Lang
Steen Larsen
Mike Leech
Bill Liston
Chun Liu
George Loechl
Paulo Loes
Frank Longino
Jim Matthews
John Mazurkewicz
Tom Melton
Paul Merzig
Ed Mesunas
Bill Miller
Gail Morchower

András Nagy
Andy Newman
Stuart Newman
Donald J. Orth
Tom Pagliaroli
Sheldon Pasternack
Dennis Phillips
Stanko Popovic
Norville Prosser
Jim Reist
Al Ristori
Milt Rosko
Gail Ross
Sharon Rushton
Pat Salimeno
Marty Salovin
Glenn Sapir
Christine Moore Serrao
Vin Sparano
Ron Speed, Sr.
Roy Stiner
Mick Thill
Roger Tucker
Jerry Valentine
Mike Walker
Ben Wechsler
Mark Weintz
Fenner Weller
Jim White
Anthony M. Williams
Dick Wood
Peter Yaskowski

I'm also grateful to the following companies and organizations (and specific people where noted in parenthesis):

American Sportfishing Association (Mike Hayden)
American Wire (Michael Shields)
Arkie Lures
The Atlantic Salmon Federation
Bay de Noc Lure Co.
Bead Tackle (Peter Renkert)
Bear Advertising (Dick Bear, Mark Malkin)
Big Jon (Jerry Livingstone)
Bullet Weights (Douglas Crumrine)
Bushnell Sports Optics (Barbara Mellman)
Cabela's Inc. (Tony Dolle)
Classic Fishing Products (Mike Richards)
C-Map USA (Pam Oldham)
Computrol, Inc.
Cossack Bait Products (Garry Shaw)
Cuba Specialty Mfg. Co. (Craig Osterhus, Dana Pickup)
Daiwa Corp.
Earie Dearie Lure Co. (Helen Galbincea)
EZE Lap Diamond (Donna Long)
Fin-Nor (Niels Stenhoj)
Flambeau Products Corp. (Jason Sauey)
Florida Keys and Key West Visitors Bureau
Flow-Rite of Tennessee (Don Zielinski)
Furuno
Future Fisherman Foundation
Garmin International (Steve Featherstone)
G. Loomis (Gary Loomis, Steve Rajeff)
Gudebrod
International Game Fish Association (Jim Brown)
Hudson River Foundation
Interphase Technologies
K-C Tackle (Raymond Packer)
L. L. Bean (Mary Rose MacKinnon)
L&S Bait Co. (Eric Bachnik)
Lowrance Electronics (Darrell Lowrance, Steve Schneider)
Luhr Jensen & Sons (Phil Jensen, Barry Ternahan)
Magellan Systems Corp. (Don Meyer)
Mann's Bait Co.
Marado Inc.
Old Town Canoe (Jim Kaiser)
O. Mustad & Sons USA (John DeVries)
National Freshwater Fishing Hall of Fame
Nomadic Expeditions (Denise Gogarty)
Normark Corp. (Ron Weber, Craig Weber)
The Orvis Company
Outdoor Technologies
Owner America Corp. (Kat Shitanishi)
Penn Fishing Tackle
Pradco (Joe Hughes, Bruce Stanton)
Scientific Anglers
Shakespeare Fishing Tackle (Mark Davis)
Sheldon's Inc.
Shimano American Corp.
Si-Tex Marine Electronics
Storm Lures (Sharon Andrews, John Storm)
Sufix USA, Inc.
Techsonics Industries
Len Thompson Lures (Richard Pallister)
Top Brass Tackle (Eric Cosby)
Tru-Turn Hooks (Wes Campbell)
Wisconsin Pharmacal
H. D. Wood Advertising
Worden's Lures
The Worth Co.
Wright & McGill Co. (George Large)
Yakima Bait Co. (Rob Phillips)
Zebco Corp. (Jenni Foster)

Gratitude is also due the following government agencies and government-funded programs (and the people noted in parenthesis), which provided research and reference materials, and, in some cases, other forms of assistance:

Alabama Cooperative Extension Service (Richard Wallace)
Alabama Department of Conservation and Natural Resources (Stan Cook)
Alabama Sea Grant Extension Program
Alaska Department of Fish and Game (Jon Lyman)
Alaska Sea Grant College Program (Kurt Byers)
Alberta Department of Environmental Protection

Acknowledgments

Arizona Game and Fish Department
Arkansas Cooperative Extension Program, Univ. of Arkansas (Nathan Stone)
Arkansas Game and Fish Commission (Keith Sutton)
Auburn University Marine Extension (Richard Wallace, William Hosking, Stephen Szedlmayer)
Brazil Embratur
British Columbia Ministry of Environment, Fisheries Branch
California Department of Fish and Game (A. Petrovich)
Canada Department of Fisheries and Oceans
Canadian Consul General
Cayman Islands Department of Tourism
Colorado Department of Natural Resources
Connecticut Department of Environmental Protection
Delaware Division of Fish and Wildlife
Florida Department of Environmental Protection, Marine Research Institute and Division of Marine Resources (Jim Lewis)
Florida Game and Freshwater Fish Commission, Division of Fisheries (Henry Cabbage)
Georgia Department of Natural Resources (Chris Martin)
Great Lakes Fishery Commission
Guam Department of Agriculture (Gerry Davis)
Hawaii Department of Land and Natural Resources, Division of Aquatic Resources
Idaho Department of Fish and Game (Jack Trueblood)
Illinois Department of Natural Resources
Indiana Department of Natural Resources (Jon Marshall)
International Center for Living Aquatic Resources Management/Food and Agriculture Organization of the United Nations
Iowa Department of Natural Resources (Steve Suman)
Kansas Department of Wildlife and Parks (Mike Miller)
Kentucky Department of Fish and Wildlife Resources (J. Beth Garland)
Louisiana Department of Wildlife and Fisheries
Louisiana Sea Grant College Program
Maine Department of Inland Fisheries and Wildlife (V. Paul Reynolds)
Manitoba Department of Natural Resources, Fisheries Branch (Carl Wall)
Maryland Department of Natural Resources (Eugene Deems, Jr.)
Maryland Sea Grant College Program (Jack Greer)
Massachusetts Division of Fisheries and Wildlife
Michigan Department of Natural Resources, Fisheries Division
Michigan Sea Grant College Program (Martha Walter)
Minnesota Department of Natural Resources (Tom Dickson)
Mississippi Department of Wildlife, Fisheries and Parks (Jim Walker)
Missouri Department of Conservation (John McPherson)
Montana Division of Fish, Wildlife, and Parks
Nevada Department of Conservation and Natural Resources
New Brunswick Department of Economic Development and Tourism
New Brunswick Department of Natural Resources, Fish and Wildlife Branch (Peter Cronin)
Newfoundland Department of Natural Resources
New Hampshire Fish and Game Department (Patricia Fleurie)
New Jersey Division of Fish, Game and Wildlife (Dave Chanda)
New Mexico Department of Game and Fish (Ruth Anderson)
New York Department of Environmental Conservation (Robert Brandt)
New York Sea Grant Program (David MacNeill, Mark Malchoff)
NOAA/Gray's Reef National Marine Sanctuary (Beth Kostka)
NOAA/National Marine Fisheries Service
NOAA/National Weather Service
North Carolina Division of Boating and Inland Fisheries (Fred Harris)
North Carolina Sea Grant
North Dakota Game and Fish Department (Terry Steinwand)
Nova Scotia Department of Fisheries (Murray Hill)
Nova Scotia Department of Lands and Forests (Barry Sabean)
Ohio Department of Natural Resources
Ohio Sea Grant College Program
Oklahoma Department of Wildlife Conservation (Nels Rodefeld)
Ontario Ministry of Economic Development, Trade & Tourism (Tom Boyd)
Ontario Ministry of Natural Resources
Oregon Department of Fish and Wildlife (Randy Henry)
Oregon Sea Grant (Pat Kight)
Parátur, State of Pará, Brazil
Pennsylvania Fish and Boat Commission
Portuguese National Tourist Office (Maria Joáo Ramires)
Prince Edward Island Department of Environmental Resources
Quebec Department of Recreation, Fish and Game
Rhode Island Division of Fish and Game
Rhode Island Sea Grant
Saskatchewan Department of Environment, Fish and Wildlife (Bruce Howard)

South Carolina Department of Natural Resources (Greg Lucas)
South Carolina Sea Grant Consortium (John Tibbetts)
South Dakota Department of Game, Fish and Parks
Spain Ministry of Commerce and Tourism
Tennessee Wildlife Resources Agency (Dave Woodward)
Texas Parks and Wildlife (Steve Lightfoot)
Tourism British Columbia
Tourism New Brunswick
Tourism Newfoundland and Labrador
Tourism Nova Scotia (Randy Brooks)
Tourism Prince Edward Island (Carol Horne)
Tourism Quebec (Siegfried Gagnon)
Tourism Saskatchewan (Gerard Makuch, Nadine Howard)
Travel Alberta (Peter Gregus)
Travel Manitoba (Dennis Maksymetz, Colette Fontaine, Gord Richardson)
University of Connecticut Sea Grant Marine Advisory Program (Nancy Balcom)
University of Delaware Sea Grant College Program
University of Florida Cooperative Extension Service
University of New Hampshire and University of Maine Sea Grant College Program
U.S. Fish and Wildlife Service
Utah Department of Natural Resources (Gerry Schlappe)
Vermont Department of Fish and Wildlife (John Hall)
Virginia Department of Game and Inland Fisheries (Mitchell Norman)
Washington Department of Fish and Wildlife (Nina Carter, James Chandler)
Washington Sea Grant Program (Kris Freeman)
West Virginia Division of Natural Resources (Hoy Murphy)
Wisconsin Department of Natural Resources (David Kunelius)
Woods Hole Oceanographic Institute (Tracey Crago)
Wyoming Game and Fish Department
Yukon Territory Department of Renewable Resources (Susan Thompson)

Finally, I'm also grateful to four student interns, whose early work compiling and organizing research materials was of much help—Kristen Schultz of Oberlin College, Alyson Schultz of Boston University, Mathew Kane of Hamilton College, and John Kuhner of Princeton University—and to Megan Schultz of Ithaca College, for Web site development and advice.

—Ken Schultz

About the Author, Artists, and Contributors

PRINCIPAL AUTHOR AND EDITOR

Ken Schultz has been a staff fishing writer and editor for *Field & Stream* since 1973. His feature articles and columns for that publication appear monthly, and he contributes to the magazine's nationally syndicated weekly radio show and to its Web site. Schultz is a frequent author of the outdoors column of the *New York Times*, and he previously was a syndicated newspaper columnist for Gannett. He has authored a dozen books on sportfishing and angling travel topics, has been a featured guest on CNBC, ESPN, and The Nashville Network, and appears regularly in assorted fishing segments for the Outdoor Life Network. A widely traveled angler, Schultz is a former holder of seven line-class world records and was inducted into the Fishing Hall of Fame in 1998. He lives in Forestburgh, New York.

THE ARTISTS

Steve T. Goione is a rising star in the world of fishing and boating art, working in mixed mediums to present his lifelong passion for angling in a dynamic and realistic style. Although he drew the distinctive pen-and-ink illustrations for this book as well as the dust-jacket cover, Goione is primarily a creator of fine art. From his studio in Toms River, New Jersey, he produces commissioned fishing scenes for private collections and limited-edition prints, and he has created original artwork for Sea World in Florida. Goione has also made a mark among boat builders and owners for commissioned renderings of big-game sportfishing craft, and he recently created original artwork for the latest products of Hatteras Yachts. A frequent guest artist on the big-game fishing tournament circuit, Goione appears at exclusive contests each year from Nantucket to Venezuela, and his work is regularly featured at fund-raising events for prominent conservation organizations.

David Kiphuth, whose renderings of fish appear in this book, has had a varied career in the field of art, having been a professional illustrator since 1969. His work has included portraiture, architectural renderings, maps, and book illustration. Kiphuth has created archaeological and scientific book and exhibit renderings for the Yale Peabody Museum, the Yale Department of Anthropology, and Yale University Press. He formerly maintained a studio and gallery in Branford, Connecticut, where he created and sold wildlife and nature art and animal portraits. Since 1989, he has been the staff illustrator for the *Gazette Newspapers* in Schenectady, New York. He lives in Saratoga Springs, New York.

THE CONTRIBUTORS

Brett Albanese of Virginia is a Ph.D candidate at the Department of Fisheries and Wildlife Sciences at Virginia Polytechnic Institute; he formerly worked at the Mississippi Museum of Natural Sciences.

Ken Allen of Maine is Associate Editor of *Maine Sportsman* and a prolific writer, photographer, newspaper columnist, book author, and guide.

Michael Babcock of Montana is Outdoors Editor of the *Great Falls Tribune*.

Ken Bailey of Alberta is Manager of Field Operations in central Alberta for Ducks Unlimited Canada; he is a prolific writer and President of the Outdoor Writers Association of Canada.

Dick Ballard of Missouri is President of Dick Ballard's Fishing Adventures and a foremost authority on Amazonian angling; he's sent anglers fishing around the world for 18 years, and established the first travel service for Bass Pro Shops.

Scott Bannerot of Pennsylvania and Florida has a Ph.D. in fisheries science and has worked in marine biological research and consulting; he is a photojournalist and a charter boat captain.

John A. Barnes of Bermuda is the Director of Agriculture and Fisheries for Bermuda; he authors a weekly fishing column in the Bermuda *Mid Ocean News*, and is an IGFA representative.

Rob Barraclough of Indonesia and England works in the oil industry and is a charter boat captain and freelance writer.

Carlos M. Barrantes of Costa Rica established the first two sportfishing camps in Costa Rica; he is an IGFA representative and was the first President of the Costa Rican Fishing Federation.

Cody Beers of Wyoming works for the Wyoming Game and Fish Department as Associate Editor of *Wyoming Wildlife* magazine and Editor of *Wyoming Wildlife News and Wild Times*; he is also a freelance writer and photographer.

Bob Berry of California is one of the world's top fish carvers and sculptors, and swept all divisions of the 1986 world championship of fish carving; he is a foremost competition judge, a former professional taxidermist, and author of the book *Fish Carving*.

Mike Bleech of Pennsylvania is a writer and photographer whose work has appeared in most major U.S. fishing and hunting magazines.

Larry Blomquist of Louisiana is Publisher of *Breakthrough*, the world's largest taxidermy trade magazine, and one of the top competition judges in North America; he is a retired award-winning taxidermist, and former President of the National Taxidermists Association.

Fred Bonner of North Carolina is Editor of *Carolina Adventure* magazine; he is also a syndicated newspaper columnist, fisheries biologist, and an IGFA representative.

Judith Bowman of New York has been a foremost sporting books dealer for over twenty years; she produces two sporting book catalogs a year, with special emphasis on fishing.

John Brownlee of Florida is Senior Editor of *Salt Water Sportsman* and a former charter boat captain; he has served on the South Atlantic Fishery Management Council, is former Chairman of the Florida Conservation Association, and is an IGFA representative.

Eric B. Burnley of Virginia is the author of *Surf Fishing the Atlantic Coast* and a radio show host; he is a charter boat captain and Regional Editor of both *Salt Water Sportsman* and *The Fisherman* magazines.

Erwin Bursik of South Africa is Publisher of *Ski-Boat* and *Flyfishing* magazines of Durban, a member of the executive board of the South African Deep Sea Angling Association, and an IGFA representative.

Mac Campbell of Great Britain works for *Angling Plus*, a match fishing magazine, and has previously worked for *Sea Angler*, *Trout Fisherman*, and *Angling Times*.

Jim Casada of South Carolina is the author of many books, including *Modern Fly Fishing*; he is Senior Editor of *Sporting Classics* magazine, and outdoor columnist for the Rock Hill *Herald* and Greensboro *News and Record*.

Göran Cederberg of Sweden has been Editor of several international fact-packed large-format angling books, including *The Complete Book of Sportfishing*; he contributes regularly to north-European publications and has been chief editor of a Swedish sportfishing magazine.

Matthew D. Chan of Virginia is a Ph.D candidate at the Department of Fisheries and Wildlife Sciences at Virginia Polytechnic Institute; he formerly worked as a fisheries biologist for the U.S. Army Corps of Engineers.

Dawn Charging of North Dakota is Outdoors Director for the North Dakota State Tourism Department; she is also a writer and photographer whose family owns a successful fishing resort on Lake Sakakawea.

Homer Circle of Florida has been Angling Editor of *Sports Afield* magazine for 34 years; the dean of American outdoor writers, he is the recipient of numerous media and achievement awards, a former member of the Arkansas Game & Fish Commission, and a renowned television and video host.

Barry Ord Clarke of Norway is a professional photographer and writer and the author of several books on fly fishing and fly tying; he contributes regularly to most European fishing magazines, and is fishing consultant to Norway's largest private sporting estate.

Soc Clay of Kentucky is an accomplished and prolific fishing writer and photographer whose work has appeared in every major outdoor periodical in North America.

Angelo Cuanang of California is a Pacific Regional Editor for *Salt Water Sportsman* and a freelance writer and photographer.

Paula J. Del Giudice of Nevada is Outdoor Columnist for the *Las Vegas Sun*; a freelance writer, photographer, and book author; and former President of the Nevada Wildlife Federation.

Arthur De Mello of Uganda is a representative for the IGFA in Uganda.

Hansjörg Dietiker of Switzerland is Editor of the Swiss Anglers Magazine *Petri-Heil*, and an IGFA representative.

Philippe Dolivet of France is the Chief Editor of the French fly fishing magazine *Plaisirs de la Pêche* and a professional photographer; he is a fly fishing instructor and competitor, an ichthyologist, and an IGFA representative.

Gary Edwards of Wyoming is a longtime fishing guide and a television show host; he is the former Editor and Publisher of *Salmon Fever* magazine, and a former fly rod world record holder.

D'arcy Egan of Ohio has been a sportswriter for *The Cleveland Plain Dealer* for over 20 years; he authored the book, *Guide to Ohio Fishing*, and is host of the American Outdoorsman Radio Network.

Bill Ensor of New Brunswick works for the Fish & Wildlife Branch of the New Brunswick Department of Natural Resources; he was formerly marketing manager of fishing and hunting for the New Brunswick Department of Tourism, and is a longtime fishing guide.

Jack Erskine of Australia is a foremost big-game tackle designer and technical innovator who has helped design many of the modern rods, reels, and drag systems in use today.

Stan Fagerstrom of Oregon is one of the world's best known trick and accuracy casters, and has been featured at sport shows worldwide for half a century; he is also a book, magazine, and newspaper writer.

Jan Fogt of Florida is Editor of *The Bahamas Sportfishing Guide* and was the founding editor of

Bahamas Blue Water Magazine; she is a contributing editor for *Sport Fishing* and *Marlin* magazines, and is also a book author.

Frank Fry of the Yukon Territory has worked with the Yukon Territory's Department of Natural Resources on various fishing projects.

Mike Garzillo of New Hampshire has been a newspaper columnist for 24 years; he is a regular contributor to various publications and a former regional editor for *Outdoor Life*.

Alessandro Giangio of Italy writes for Italy's premier fishing magazine, *Pesca in Mare*, and has been published worldwide; he has authored five books, is owner and master instructor of the Fishbuster Trolling School and Sportfishing Travel, and has a charter boat in Huatulco, Mexico.

Jerry Gibbs of Vermont is Fishing Editor of *Outdoor Life*, where his career as a staff writer has spanned three decades and made him one of North America's most respected angling authors; he has written several books and has been inducted into the Fishing Hall of Fame.

Barry Gibson of Massachusetts is Editor of *Salt Water Sportsman* and a longtime Maine charter boat captain; he is a former member of the New England Fishery Management Council, and former advisor to the International Commission for the Conservation of Atlantic Tunas.

Jerry Gomber of New Jersey has over twenty-five years of experience in design, development, and marketing of fishing rods and reels; during that period he has been responsible for several successful product innovations.

George Gruenefeld of Quebec and Saskatchewan is Editor of *Canadian Outdoor Publications*; he has written for many magazines in Canada and the U.S., is a book author, and was formerly Outdoors Editor for the *Montreal Gazette*.

Chris Hanks of the Northwest Territories is an anthropologist, freelance writer, and author of the book *Fly Fishing in the Northwest Territories*.

Steve Harper of Kansas is the Outdoors Editor of the *Wichita Eagle* and author of the book *Kansas Day Trips*; in 1995 he was named Conservation Communicator of the Year by the Kansas Wildlife Federation.

Dan Heiner of Alaska is an advertising agency executive and former editor and writer for *Alaska Outdoors* magazine; he is the author of four books on Alaska fishing, including *Fly Fishing Alaska's Wild Rivers*.

Bob Hodge of Tennessee is the Outdoors Editor of the *Knoxville News-Sentinel*; he was named the state's Best Outdoor Writer for 1996-97 by the Tennessee Sportswriters Association.

Grant Hopkins of Ontario is the outdoor columnist for the *Ottawa Citizen*, a frequent contributor to *Ontario Out of Doors*, and retired from the Royal Canadian Air Force.

John Husar of Illinois is the longtime outdoors columnist and general sportswriter of the *Chicago Tribune* and co-host of a Chicago radio show; he has worked for newspapers in Kansas, Texas, and New Mexico, and has covered the last nine Olympics.

Jim Imai of California has a Ph.D in physics and is Professor of Physics at California State University, Dominguez Hills; he is a Consulting Physicist for the Daiwa Corporation, and a leading authority on the design and performance of fishing reels and rods.

James Kano of Ontario is the Marketing Director of Japan Communications in Toronto and Outdoor Coordinator for the Press and Tourism division of the Ontario government; his articles have appeared online and in newspapers, guide books, and magazines.

Nick Karas of New York is the retired outdoor columnist for (New York) *Newsday* and a charter boat captain and ichthyologist; he has written for many national magazines and authored a dozen books, including *The Striped Bass* and *Brook Trout*.

Lee Kernen of Wisconsin is the retired Director of Fisheries for the State of Wisconsin; he is also a writer, fishing guide, and fisheries consultant.

Ronnie Kovach of California is a radio and television show host, educator, magazine writer, guide, and author of five books, including *Bass Fishing in California*, *Trout Fishing in California*, and *Saltwater Fishing in California*.

Steen Larsen of Denmark is one of Europe's leading sportfishing writers and photographers; he is a book author and lecturer, and contributes widely to many European angling publications.

Dick Lewers of Australia is Technical Editor of *Encyclopaedia of Australian Fishing*, author of seven books on angling, a former IGFA representative, 35-year columnist for *Modern Fishing Magazine*, and past President of the Australian National Sportfishing Association.

Bill Loftus of Idaho is the Outdoors Editor of the *Lewiston Morning Tribune* and the author of two guidebooks to Idaho.

Maurice Loustau-LaLanne of Seychelles is the Principal Secretary in the Ministry of Tourism and Transport for the Seychelles, and an IGFA representative.

Carl. F. Luckey of Alabama is a writer specializing in antiques and collectibles; he has authored ten books, including his best-selling, 618-page work, *Old Fishing Lures and Tackle*.

Joe Macaluso of Louisiana is an award-winning outdoors sportswriter/editor for the *Baton Rouge Advocate*; his weekly fishing reports have appeared in Louisiana newspapers since 1976.

Rosanne Macfarlane of Prince Edward Island recently received her Masters degree in Biology at

Acadia University; she works for the Department of Fisheries and Environment.

Dennis Maksymetz of Manitoba is Manager of Tourism Marketing for the Industry, Trade and Tourism division of the Manitoba government.

Don Mann of Florida is a longtime contributor to *Florida Sportsman*, a record-holding big-game angler, and book author; his articles and photographs have appeared in many publications.

Al Marlowe of Colorado has written numerous articles for outdoor magazines; he authored a trail guide for the Flat Tops Wilderness area and a fly fishing guide for the Colorado River.

Peter B. Mathiesen of Missouri is Executive Editor and Producer of the *Field & Stream Radio Hour*; he is also a magazine writer, photographer, and video and television show producer.

John McCoy of West Virginia is Outdoors Editor for the *Charleston Daily Mail*, Regional Editor for *Field & Stream*, and a frequent contributor to regional and national magazines.

Tom Meade of Rhode Island writes about the outdoors for the *Providence Journal-Bulletin*; he is the author of *Essential Fly Fishing*, and writes for various magazines.

Ed Migdalski of Connecticut is the retired Director of Yale University's Outdoor Education and Club Sports Programs, retired Ichthyologist for the Yale Peabody Museum, and holder of the current world record for the largest strictly freshwater fish (pirarucú) ever caught on rod and reel.

Kent Mitchell of Georgia has covered outdoor sports for the *Atlanta Journal-Constitution* for three decades; he has received the Communicator of the Year Award from the Georgia Wildlife Federation, and has authored three books on martial arts.

Bill Monroe of Oregon has covered the outdoors for his state's largest daily newspaper, *The Oregonian*, for 18 years.

Gary W. Moore of Vermont is a freelance writer and photographer; he is former Commissioner of the Vermont Fish and Wildlife Department and former Chairman of the Vermont Water Resources Board.

Sam Mossman of New Zealand is Special Projects Editor for *New Zealand Fishing News* magazine; he is the author of three books and hundreds of magazine articles, and has held five world and numerous New Zealand fishing records.

Perry Munro of Nova Scotia is a writer and artist who contributes to *The Atlantic Salmon Journal* and various other magazines; he is also an outfitter, master guide, operator of Maple Mountain Lodge, and a Director of Trout Unlimited Canada.

Iain Nicolson of Angola is an IGFA representative and has a Ph.D. in molecular genetics; he and his family pioneered fishing for blue marlin in Angola and collectively established six world fishing records.

Chris Niskanen of Minnesota is the Outdoors Editor of the *St. Paul Pioneer Press*.

Donald J. Orth of Virginia is a Professor of Fisheries Science in the Department of Fisheries & Wildlife Sciences at Virginia Polytechnic Institute.

Tom Pagliaroli of New Jersey is an advertising agency executive, freelance writer, and photographer whose work has appeared in various regional and national publications.

Ali Pasiner of Turkey is an attorney, the author of two fishing books, and a consultant to the Turkish version of the *Encyclopaedia Britannica*; he is also a writer, editor, and representative of the IGFA.

C. Boyd Pfeiffer of Maryland is a longtime journalist and photographer, a regular columnist for many angling magazines, and the author of numerous books on fishing topics, the latest of which is *Fly Fishing Salt Water Basics*.

Larry Porter of Nebraska has been on the sports staff of the *Omaha World-Herald* for over three decades and their outdoors writer since 1990; he has been named Nebraska Sportswriter of the Year three times, and is a former professional tournament angler.

Steve Price of Texas is a longtime Senior Writer for *Bassmaster* magazine and contributor to a wide variety of national sporting magazines; he is an accomplished photographer and author of several books.

Gareth Purnell of England is Editor of Britain's leading angling magazine, *Improve Your Coarse Fishing*, and former News Editor of *Angling Times*; he has fished annually in the World Freshwater Angling Championships since 1993.

George Reiger of Virginia is Conservation Editor of *Field & Stream* and *Salt Water Sportsman* magazines and the most widely respected conservation writer in North America; he has been a staff writer for *Field & Stream* since 1972, is the author of seven books on angling and marine ecology, and the recipient of numerous honors and awards.

Tim Renken of Missouri has been the outdoors writer for the *St. Louis Post-Dispatch* since 1963; he previously worked for the Nebraska Game Commission.

Len Rich of Newfoundland is the author of two books and many outdoor magazine articles; he operates Awesome Lake Lodge in Labrador, is a former Hunting and Fishing Development Officer for Newfoundland and Labrador, and is a past representative of the Atlantic Salmon Federation.

Tom Richardson of Massachusetts is Managing Editor of *Salt Water Sportsman* magazine, as well as a freelance writer and photographer.

Al Ristori of New Jersey is Saltwater Fishing Editor of the *Newark Star-Ledger*, Regional Editor of *Salt Water Sportsman*, Conservation Editor of *The Fisherman* magazine, and the author of several books; he is also a charter boat captain and has served on the Mid-Atlantic Fishery Management Council.

Jim Rizzuto of Hawaii is Hawaii Editor for *Salt Water Sportsman* and *Western Outdoors*, a longtime columnist for *West Hawaii Today* and *Hawaii Fishing News*, and the author of the books *Modern Hawaiian Gamefishing* and *Fishing Hawaii Style*.

Nels Rodefeld of Oklahoma is an avid angler and hunter who frequently covers Oklahoma's hunting and fishing scene.

Milt Rosko of New Jersey is a writer for *Big Game Fishing Journal* and various other publications and a longtime authority on saltwater sportfishing; he is a photographer, book author, magazine feature writer, and lecturer.

Terry Rudnick of Washington has been writing articles on Northwest fishing subjects for more than 25 years; he is the author of the book *Washington Fishing, the Complete Guide*, and co-author of *How to Catch Trophy Halibut*.

Bob Sampson, Jr. of Connecticut is a writer, photographer, science teacher, and fisheries biologist; his work has appeared in numerous national and regional magazines.

Jack Samson of New Mexico is the retired Editor-in-Chief of *Field & Stream* and a former Associated Press columnist; he is Saltwater Editor of *Fly Rod & Reel* magazine, author of twenty books, and the first angler to catch both Atlantic and Pacific sailfish and all five species of marlin on a fly.

Ray Sasser of Texas is the Outdoor Editor of *The Dallas Morning News* and a freelance contributor to various magazines; he has been writing about outdoor sports for over 25 years.

Carl Werner Schmidt-Luchs of Germany is a contributor to *Blinker*, the largest angling magazine in Europe; he is a photographer, writer, and author of a dozen angling books.

Kristen Schultz of Massachusetts is a writer who recently graduated from Oberlin College; she works for an engineering consulting firm.

Bill Scifres of Indiana has been the Outdoor Editor of the *Indianapolis Star* since 1953; he is a book author, freelance writer, and photographer.

Eric Sharp of Michigan is Outdoor Editor of *The Detroit News*, and was formerly Outdoor Editor of *The Miami Herald*.

Luis Sier of Argentina is a newspaper columnist, a former magazine publisher, and an outfitter who operates several Argentinian fishing camps.

Jeff Simpson of South Dakota is an information officer for the State of South Dakota, a book author and freelance magazine writer, and former project developer for Cowles Creative Publishing.

DeWayne Smith of Arizona is an information officer for the Maricopa County Parks and Recreation Department; he covered the outdoors for over 30 years for *The Phoenix Gazette*.

Ryan Smith of Virginia is a research assistant with the Department of Fisheries and Wildlife Sciences at Virginia Polytechnic Institute.

Michael Snook of Saskatchewan is a freelance writer, conservationist, outdoor educator, and television producer.

Frank Sousa of Massachusetts is a writer for the *Springfield Sunday Republican* and the *Union News*, Editor/Publisher of *Northeast Woods and Waters*, and a freelance writer and photographer.

Vin T. Sparano of New Jersey is Senior Field Editor and retired Editor-in-Chief of *Outdoor Life*, for whom he worked for over three decades; he is a former syndicated columnist for *Gannett Newspapers*, and the author/editor of fourteen books, including *The Complete Outdoors Encyclopedia*.

Vladimir Stakic of Yugoslavia is Deputy Editor-in-Chief of the Yugoslavian angling magazines *Ribolovacka Revija* and *Ribolovacke Novine*, a freelance writer, and the author of three books of short stories.

Bob Stearns of Florida has been the staff boating/saltwater fishing writer of *Field & Stream* for 20 years and is the Electronics Editor of *Salt Water Sportsman*; the author of two books, he is a renowned fly fishing and light tackle expert, and has held two fly rod world records for sailfish.

Larry Stone of Iowa has been a writer and photographer for over three decades, and writes about the outdoors for the *Des Moines Register*.

Keith Sutton of Arkansas is Editor of *Arkansas Wildlife magazine*, a conservation publication of the Arkansas Game & Fish Commission, and a prolific freelance writer and photographer.

Ferenc Szalay of Hungary is Editor-in-Chief of *Magyar Horgász*, Hungary's premier fishing magazine; he is also President of the Hungarian National Committee for Match Fishing and Executive Board member of the Federation Internationale de la Pêche Sportive en Eau Douce.

Allan Tarvid of Texas is a contributing editor for *Sport Fishing* magazine and has authored hundreds of articles on electronics for sporting and commercial fishing and emergency service use; he has been a fishing guide and search and rescue diver.

Rikk Taylor of British Columbia is Editor and Publisher of *British Columbia Sport Fishing* magazine.

Mick Thill of Illinois and England is one of the world's top professional match fishing anglers and the first and only person to medal in the open water and ice fishing World Freshwater Fishing Championships; he is also a prominent float designer, and coach of the U. S. World Championship fishing teams.

Albert A. W. Threadingham of Fiji is an IGFA representative for the Fiji Islands and Governor of the Hawaiian International Billfish Association and the Pacific Ocean Research Foundation; he is a former world-record fish holder.

Raj Tilak of Maryland and India is co-author of the book *Game Fishes of India and Angling,* and author of more than 200 research publications; he is experienced in fisheries and wildlife management, with extensive knowledge of gamefishes and their ecology in India.

Anssi Uitti of Finland works for the Finnish outdoor magazine *Metsästys ja Kalastus*, and his articles have appeared in *Urheilukalastus* (Sportfishing) and *Perhokalastus* (Flyfishing) magazines.

Luis Umpierre of Puerto Rico is a physician, Editor of *Notipesca* (Fishing News), President of the Puerto Rico Sportfishing Association, and advisory member of the Caribbean Fishery Management Council.

Rudy Van Duijnhoven of Holland is a freelance photographer and author; his work appears monthly in *BEET-Sportvissers* magazine, and he is European Correspondent for Fly Fishing in *Salt Waters* magazine.

Carlo Vernocchi of Italy and Zanzibar introduced modern big-game fishing to the Zanzibar archipelago of Tanzania in 1992; he is an IGFA representative and charter boat captain.

Victor Villavicencio of Manila is a representative for the IGFA in the Philippines.

Tsutomu Wakabayashi of Japan is the General Manager of the Japan Game Fish Association; he has written for several Japanese fishing magazines, and is an IGFA representative.

Steve Waters of Florida is the outdoors writer for the *Fort Lauderdale Sun-Sentinel* and occasionally writes for national magazines; he was formerly a newspaper writer and video executive in New York.

Tom Wharton of Utah has been Outdoor Editor of the *Salt Lake Tribune* since 1976; he has co-authored five books, and is past President of the Outdoor Writers Association of America.

Jesse E. Williams of New Mexico is the retired Chief of Public Affairs for the New Mexico Department of Game and Fish, and a former Colorado wildlife manager and environmental education supervisor.

Juergen Willms of the Yukon Territory has worked with the Yukon Territory's Department of Natural Resources on various fishing projects.

Jorge Xifra of Paraguay operates El Pescador, a sportfishing outfitting service; he is a writer, television show host, IGFA representative, and holder of four world fishing records.

Photo Credits

ALL PHOTOGRAPHS BY KEN SCHULTZ EXCEPT FOR THE FOLLOWING:

Barry Ord Clarke 93
Daiwa 285
Grady White Boats 79

Nick Karas 293
Al Ristori 137, 221, 246
Tourism PEI 225

Rudy van Duijnhoven 13
Dick Wood 144

NAIL KNOT
A fishing knot for line-to-line connections.

See: Knots, Fishing.

NAMIBIA
This southwestern African nation, bounded by Angola to the north, South Africa to the south, and primarily Botswana to the east, is something of a study in contrasts. Its entire coastal region is low lying and marked by the 60- to 100-mile-wide Namib Desert, which faces the South Atlantic Ocean. Here, these waters are cooled by the northerly flowing Benguela Current. Farther inland, Namibia's terrain is mountainous, and the important permanently flowing rivers are primarily at its extremities, forming boundaries. Relatively few traveling anglers visit Namibia. Those who do are mostly from South Africa and focus their attention along its nearly deserted, vast coastline. One gets the feeling that no one has been here before.

Coastal Fishing
For the first-time visitor, the endless expanses of beaches fringing the Namib Desert are eye-opening, and a party of anglers seldom will encounter others throughout an entire day's fishing. These areas are a great distance from anywhere—it is roughly 2,000 miles from Pretoria, South Africa, to Terrace Bay—and along the coast itself, local ingenuity has devised a road built from salt. It does not break up easily and manages to ward off the ravages of the desert climate to provide a smooth, tarlike surface that is dangerous only when moistened by sea mist.

Along the coast the cold Atlantic provides a belt of cool air that seldom exceeds 18°C. Anything above this is regarded as hot. In winter months, however, a dreaded wind comes off the desert, turning the length of the coast into a furnace, with temperatures reaching 40°C. The wind starts at dawn and lasts until 2 P.M., almost to the minute. Mornings are thus spent in protected environs. No one dares travel against this wind, as it is a veritable sandblaster that quickly peels paint off vehicles and scars windscreens.

Although coastal fishing throughout the year is good, December through April is the prime period, and the most sought-after species include kob, steenbras, blacktail, and galjoen for lighter-tackle anglers, and bronze whaler, gulley, and cow sharks for heavy-tackle artists. Caught by the thousands every year is the saltwater silver catfish. Normally frowned upon by visiting anglers, this species is eagerly sought by local anglers, who regard smoked catfish as a delicacy.

Three significant fishing regions define this coast. The first is called Long Beach and stretches from Walvis Bay at midcoast to Swakopmund some 19 miles north. Local anglers just about always make good catches there. The second is some 40 miles north of Swakopmund at Henties Bay, which owes its existence to visiting anglers, who either rent a cottage or stay in the hotel there.

The third is the so-called Public Recreational Area, which is the region from Henties Bay north to Mile 108 (various locations are marked according to their distance from Swakopmund). Each year it attains the status of a "holy fishing pilgrimage" for thousands of anglers. Here, people are at liberty to do more or less what they like, and this must be the last true wilderness left in southern Africa. Only the salt road to Terrace Bay cuts across the Public Recreational Area, and 4×4 vehicles are necessary when traveling off it. There are no telephones, no lights, no doctors: in short, nothing. Self-sufficient camping, some of it at various caravan parks, is the norm.

Beyond Mile 108 lies Skeleton Coast National Park. A ranger's post is established at the Ukab River, and only those with a firm booking at Terrace Bay (or Tora Bay during December) are allowed in. Terrace Bay's fishing lodge, about 250 miles north, was converted from an old mining enterprise and accommodates only 48 guests.

All along the coast, the most popular species is the galjoen, mainly caught on red baits, which wash ashore during high tides. The surf line is filled with sea bamboo and seaweed, and anglers land galjoen by casting into this. Some years the galjoen are found in more open water.

Blacktail is popular and is also caught with red baits. Bronze whaler sharks are targeted in the summer with traditional sardine baits. Gully sharks are pests that break up the light galjoen tackle. Galjoen of 10 to 12 pounds are taken during mid- to late winter. They are the fattest fish here and, when barbecued over an open fire, are delicious.

The usual route anglers take in Namibia begins with a week at Terrace Bay, catching galjoen and blacktail. Then, they move down the coast in search of kob and steenbras. Baits for the latter two are white mussels dug from the beaches, sardines, chokka, and red baits. When kob and steenbras are running, it's difficult to stop angling.

After fishing the Public Recreational Area, many anglers spend a few days at Henties Bay or Swakopmund, whereas others visit a famous spot south of Walvis Bay—the vast lagoon area of Sunwich Harbour.

Recreational boat fishing was unknown in Namibia until a few enterprising individuals began to operate a ski boat out of Henties Bay. Their catches, however, are not greater than that of the beach anglers. Boat fishing is more popular from the harbors at Swakopmund and Lüderitz. The lagoon at Lüderitz is famous for its cow sharks (weighing 150 pounds and more).

When anglers have had their fill of these favored species, they turn their attention to sharks, particularly during the summer months. Heavy tackle notwithstanding, some anglers have enjoyed tremendous battles with big bronze whalers that frequent the inshore line.

Inland Fishing

Few traveling anglers think of fishing in Namibia's freshwater impoundments, even though coarse fishing for bream, catfish, and yellowfish is quite good. The most notable freshwater opportunity is in the Caprivi Strip, a panhandled piece of land northeast of Namibia and possibly one of the best wildlife areas in southwestern Africa. There are three main rivers in the Caprivi Strip: the Zambezi, on the border with Zambia; the Kwando; and the Okavango, which originates in Angola and forms a border with that country, then enters Botswana to reach the world-renowned Okavango Swamp. All three rivers have the best angling for tigerfish and bream that Namibia can offer.

The Zambezi River tigerfish has lured many an angler to the Caprivi. Living as they do in fast-flowing water, these fish are fit and very strong. The speed at which they leave their lairs, which are in the eddies and the lee of channel walls in the vast sandbanks, to hit trolled spoons, launches them into the air like missiles. Thereafter, provided the hook stays embedded in the tiger's armor-plated jaw, a long and spectacular fight ensues.

Another favorite lair of the Zambezi tiger is slightly downstream of a herd of wallowing hippos, where small bream—the tigerfish's main food source—are attracted by the stirred-up detritus of the riverbed.

Fishing the hippo herds can be an exciting way to catch tigerfish; it's necessary to get a boat close enough to the herd to find the fish, yet be nimble enough to maneuver away quickly should an irate bull take exception to your presence.

The meandering Zambezi allows anglers to travel for many miles downstream from Katima Mulilo, fishing the quieter deep-water eddies or the fast-flowing sections over sandbanks, at the same time enjoying the river's beauty and harshness. Excellent light-tackle bream fishing is possible where the river slows down in deep channels, and between reed-lined banks. To end a perfect day on the river, a toast to the setting sun over one of Africa's mightiest rivers is a haunting, unforgettable experience.

NATIONAL FISHING LURE COLLECTORS CLUB

An organization of fishing tackle collectors.
See: Antique Fishing Tackle.

NATIONAL MARINE FISHERIES SERVICE

Founded in 1871 as the United States Commission of Fish and Fisheries, the National Marine Fisheries Service (NMFS) is the federal agency charged with managing and sustaining most living marine resources and their habitats in U.S. waters. These resources include many species of fish, lobster, shrimp, crabs, clams, whales, dolphins, seals, and sea turtles, as well as the environment where these animals live, feed, and breed.

The agency is part of the National Oceanic and Atmospheric Administration (NOAA) within the U.S. Department of Commerce, where it was placed in 1970 after previously being known as the Bureau of Commercial Fisheries, a part of the U.S. Fish and Wildlife Service. Its jurisdiction is federal waters, which start 3 miles from shore and extend 200 miles into the ocean, although seaward boundaries of Texas, Puerto Rico, and the Gulf Coast of Florida extend 9 miles from shore.

The mission of NMFS is to build sustainable fisheries, recover protected species, and sustain healthy coasts. It has the responsibility of protecting endangered and threatened marine species and their habitat, and conducts cooperative marine research with other federal agencies, state fisheries agencies, universities, and other organizations. It also measures the economic effects of fishing practices and fishery regulations, enforces federal fisheries laws, and plays a role in managing fish and marine mammals that swim between waters of the United States and other countries.

NMFS has the obligation to work with eight Regional Fishery Management Councils (see: fisheries management council), created by the Magnuson Fishery Conservation and Management Act (see: Magnuson Act) and responsible for managing marine fish stocks. This brings together many parties, but recreational anglers largely feel it is heavily biased toward commercial fishing interests.

Other responsibilities of NMFS are derived from such federal laws as the Endangered Species Act, which protects species that are threatened or endangered; the Marine Mammal Protection Act, which regulates interactions with marine mammals; the Lacey Act, which prohibits fish or wildlife transactions and activities that violate state, federal, native American tribal, or foreign laws; the Fish and Wildlife Coordination Act, which authorizes

---

Fish that live in Arctic and Antarctic waters produce their own antifreeze.

NMFS to collect fisheries data and to advise other agencies on environmental decisions that affect living marine resources; and the Federal Power Act, which allows NMFS to minimize effects of dam operations on anadromous fish, such as prescribing fish passageways that bypass dams.

NMFS is not involved with the management of strictly freshwater fish, which falls under the jurisdiction of respective state fish and wildlife agencies and the Fish and Wildlife Service *(see)*, which is part of the Department of the Interior.

NATIVE

A species of fish that is endemic to a region, watershed, or specific body of water. A native species is distinguished from an introduced or exotic species *(see)*, which occurs outside its endemic range and has been placed there by unnatural means (usually deliberate but sometimes accidental planting by humans). The term "native" is particularly applied in North America to endemic trout, especially brook trout.

NATURAL BAIT

Live or dead organisms that occur in nature and which are used to attract and catch fish. The term natural bait is used to differentiate such items from artificial baits, which are technically lures *(see)*; from processed baits *(see)*, which are food items (corn, cheese, bread, etc.); and from chum *(see)*.

Natural bait is used popularly in both freshwater and saltwater around the world, and includes a wide array of items. These include, but are not limited to, alewives, anchovies, ballyhoo, bunker (mossbunker or menhaden), butterfish, chubs, clams, corn, crabs, crayfish, crickets, eel, eggs, frogs, grubs, grasshoppers, hellgrammites, herring, killifish, leeches, mackerel, maggots, minnows, mullet, mussels, pilchards, pinfish, porgy, salamanders (waterdog), sand eels, sardines, sculpin, seaworms, shad, shiners, shrimp, silversides, smelt, spearing, squid, suckers, sunfish, waxworms, whiting, and assorted earthworms. Brief categorical reviews follow.

Freshwater Natural Bait

Prominent freshwater natural bait includes the following.

Earthworms/nightcrawlers. These are used in whole or in parts, on one or more bait hooks, and are tipped onto jig hooks, crawled behind spinner harnesses, and weighted and fished under a float. They are especially used in fishing for such panfish as bluegills and perch, as well as walleye, bullheads, stream trout, and river steelhead, primarily with No. 6 or 8 hooks. Nightcrawlers are generally preferred, but small and lively anglerworms are also used, though primarily for panfishing.

Crayfish. Also known as crawfish or crawdads, and fished in both hard-shell and soft-shell

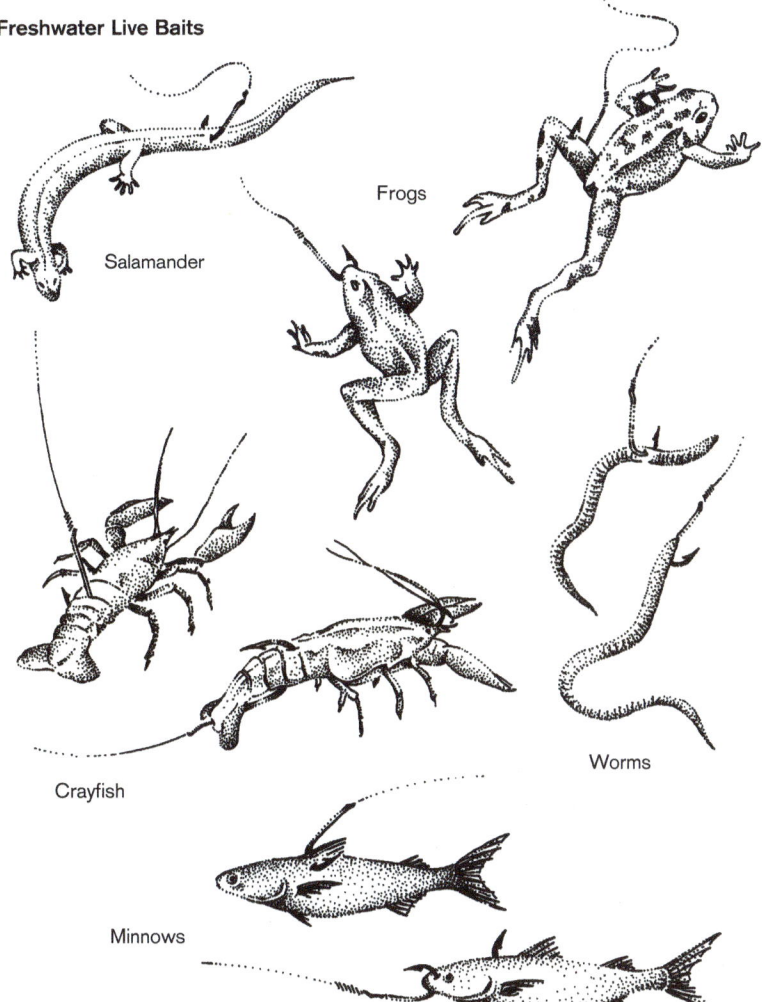

Freshwater Live Baits

versions (the latter preferred but not always available), crayfish are hooked through the tail with a long-shanked hook. They are primarily used for smallmouth bass fishing. Tails and pieces of the tail are used for other fish, however, most notably for steelhead drift fishing.

Minnows/shiners. There are numerous species and sizes of these baitfish (including fathead minnow, dace, Arkansas shiner, golden shiner, and chub) used primarily as live bait for a host of large and small fish. Smaller bait may also be hooked through the lips to adorn the hook of a jig or jig-spinner combination. Small minnows are used for crappies, ice fishing, bass, walleye, and trout. Very large shiners are popularly used in Florida for big largemouth bass, and large baitfish (including suckers) are fished for such species as pike, muskellunge, and lake trout.

Leeches. These are used whole primarily for walleyes and smallmouth bass. They are rigged similarly to worms, and when cast or trolled are hooked through the sucker with a No. 6 or 8 hook.

Waterdogs. Also known as mud puppies, these salamanders are not available everywhere but are used for a variety of gamefish, including striped bass.

Crickets, grasshoppers, and hellgrammites. These delectables are used for many small fish. Hellgrammites attract stream trout and smallmouth bass; grasshoppers and crickets are good for various panfish species as well as crappie and stream trout. Hellgrammites should be hooked under the collar with a No. 6 or 8 hook, and the others through the body with a long-shanked light-wire hook.

Frogs. Live frogs are quite popular in some Canadian and northern U.S. locales and rather ignored most everywhere else. The prime quarry is bass, followed by pike. They can be hooked through the lips or thigh.

Salmon eggs. Salmon eggs are popularly used for drift fishing for trout and salmon. Rainbow trout and steelhead, in particular, are major quarries. These are fished singly with small salmon egg hooks, or as a group in an unwrapped cluster or in a nylon mesh spawn bag (called a spawn sack). Imitation eggs and egg sacks are quite popular as well. The natural eggs are cured and preserved for fishing applications.

Herring. Included here are such fragile baitfish species as alewives, which are also called sawbellies and found in northern climes where they are popularly used alive for trout in lakes; shad (primarily gizzard but also the threadfin variety), which are found in southern U.S. climes and fished live or as dead or cut bait; and herring, which are coastal, river-run fish used alive or dead for stripers and various catfishes on the East Coast and for salmon (via lift-and-drop mooching) on the West Coast.

Chum. Most of the chumming *(see)* done in freshwater is not with natural baits, although there are opportunities for this if you can procure enough bait economically to be able to chum. An angler who cast-nets for shad, for example, might be able to procure enough bait to dispense live shad as chum for largemouth bass or stripers. Saving old bait and using it to lightly chum in chunks is a possibility when fishing for catfish and stripers in big reservoirs and rivers.

Others. Some miscellaneous baits include caddis larvae for stream trout; mayflies for trout, crappies, etc.; bluegills for striped bass (where legal); grass shrimp for panfish; perch eyes for tipping on a jig when ice fishing for yellow perch; cisco, whitefish, and other large species fished alive for northern pike; and chunks or strips of fish meat, for tipping on a jig, especially for lake trout, or behind a spoon for pickerel or pike, or in some instances, dead-bait bottom fishing for assorted species (pike, lake trout, catfish, sturgeon).

Saltwater Natural Bait

Prominent saltwater natural bait includes the following.

Marine worms. Worms such as sandworms, clamworms, and bloodworms are used whole or in parts, on one or more hooks, or behind a spinner rig for stillfishing, trolling, or drifting for a variety of small inshore fish, as well as blackfish, flounder, and others.

Eels. Eels are a hardy bait, primarily used in inshore drift fishing and casting. They are fished on jigs as well as lip-hooked on a bottom rig, and are a top live bait for striped bass.

Shrimp/crabs/crayfish. Live shrimp are a highly popular bait for a wide variety of coastal fish. They can be hooked through the top of the head for free swimming, or threaded on a bait hook or jig head. Live blue crabs are also used for many species of fish; smaller versions take tarpon and permit, while larger ones are fished deep for snapper, grouper, redfish, and others. They are hooked through the tip of the shell, often with claws removed. Fiddler crabs, which are abundant in many tidal areas, are used for snappers, groupers, sheepshead, and other fish. Saltwater crayfish, which are quite large, are used in southern marine waters for cubera snapper and large groupers.

Assorted live fish. You name the fish, and if it is the right size, it can probably be used as live bait for some saltwater predator. Depending on locale and availability, of course, such species as pinfish, blue runner, anchovy, menhaden, grunts, sardines, pilchards, mackerel, and herring are favored. These fish are hooked through the lips or back, sometimes with a double-hook setup, or through the eyes (soft-fleshed fish).

Offshore baits. An assortment of natural baits is used in offshore trolling situations for billfish, tuna, dolphin, wahoo, king mackerel, and so forth. Squid, ballyhoo (balao), mullet, mackerel, and bonito are the main baits, usually fished whole, but sometimes in strips. Many of these baits are purchased frozen, then thawed in water and rigged with wire and thread on stainless steel hooks and wire leaders *(see: bait rig)*.

Chum. A good deal of chumming *(see)* is done in saltwater, especially for tuna, shark, and

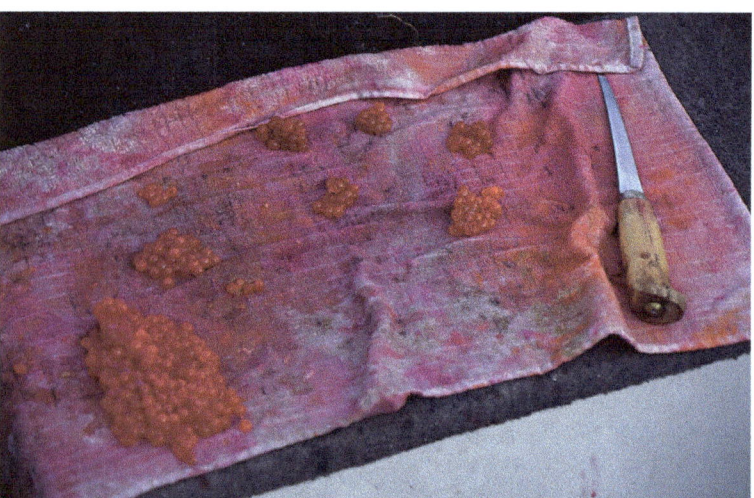

A skein of preserved salmon eggs is cut into chunks for direct use on a hook or as part of an egg sack.

Saltwater Live Baits

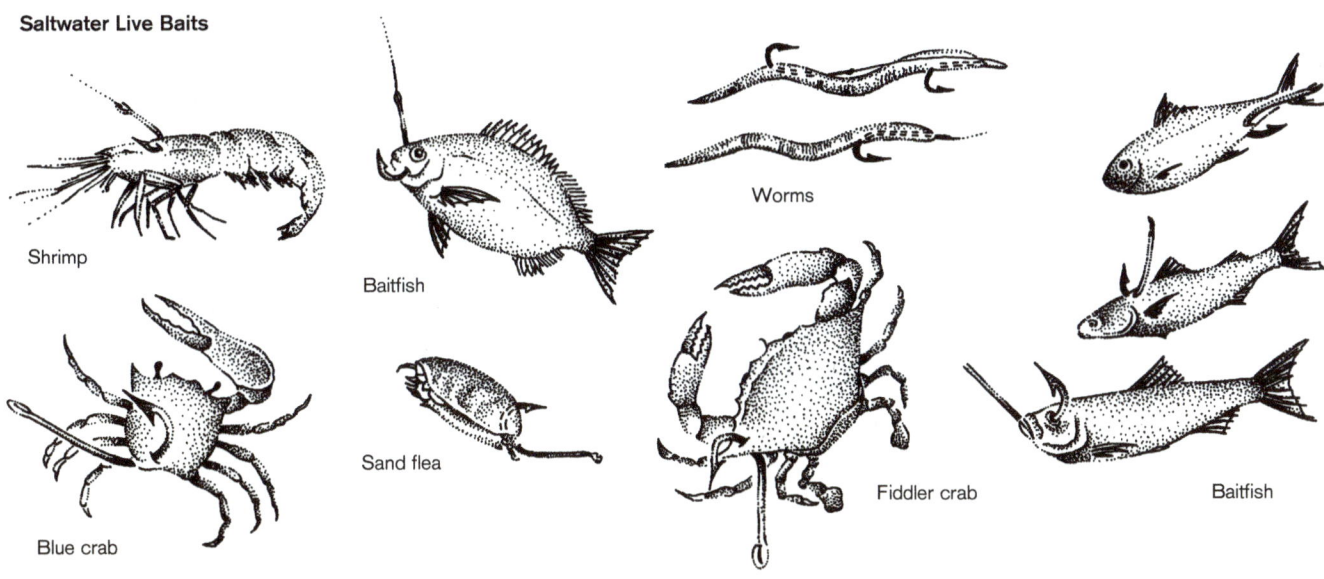

reef species. It is done inshore as well as offshore by small private boat anglers as well as party and charter boat anglers. The same species that are used as live bait, as well as smaller fish that are ground up (like menhaden), are used as chum, and also as cut or strip bait that is placed amidst the chum.

Others. Other morsels used for various saltwater fish include sand fleas, which are used by surf and pier anglers for pompano; cut plug baits, used for mooching (trolling with cut herring for Pacific Northwest salmon) or bottom fishing; octopus chunks for drift fishing or stillfishing; and dead baits, including clams, mussels, snails, fish chunks/strips/heads, used for drifting or stillfishing.

A dead bait rig that is very effective for bottom fishing for tarpon can be made by tying a 10/0 hook to one end of a 6-foot 120-pound-test monofilament leader and a barrel swivel at the other end. Behead a mullet and attach a bait needle with an open eye to swivel. Then pull the leader through the bait and out the tail until the hook is placed as shown in the following illustration.

Dead Bait Rig

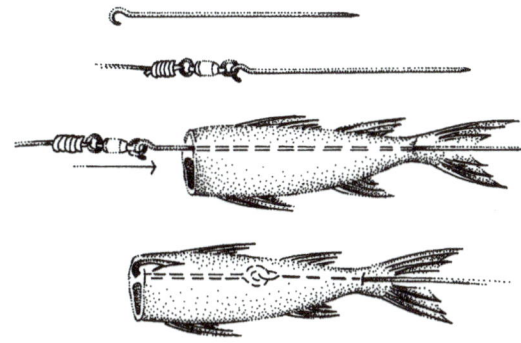

General Tips

Most live baits are hooked through the head or lips (tail for crayfish) for casting and free-lining, but through the midsection for stillfishing with or without a float.

Bait has to be presented properly to be effective. This includes the physical appearance as well as the movement, or in some cases, lack of movement. Natural bait is generally fished in a more passive manner than lures, because the target fish have time to watch it, smell, it, and perhaps touch it before striking. If it moves in a swift or unnatural manner, it may cause alarm, although a natural bait that appears to be struggling, as many do when hooked, can in itself be attractive to a predator because it appears more vulnerable and easier to capture. There are some exceptions to this slow-fishing mantra, however, such as when live bait is trolled below the surface or when rigged dead bait is pulled over the surface for pelagic species, although these tactics are still designed to represent natural prey actions. Another exception is when a live natural bait is hooked on a jig and fished more actively than it would be if fished alone.

Where live bait is used, liveliness is vital. Many fish aren't interested in inactive or dead bait, so it's important to keep your bait as fresh and vigorous as possible. Change live bait whenever the current offering seems to be losing its vitality, and make sure that it acts naturally. A crayfish that rolls instead of crawls, for example, or a minnow that doesn't swim energetically, lessens the chance of success.

The water that bait is kept in ideally should be oxygenated or changed periodically to keep it healthy for the fish. Pay close attention to the freshness of the water, as well as the temperature, to ensure that bait remains in good condition. Some bait, such as alewives and herring, can only be kept in circular or oval baitwells or livewells *(see)*; they bunch into the corners of other wells and die, so the method of retaining them is important.

It is helpful to hold your line when live-lining bait. When fishing with a float or bobber, it's easy to tell if a fish is mouthing your live offering. But that isn't the case when letting bait run freely. Then, it is often difficult to know if a fish has

Different fish require different rigging; a butterfish (top) is hooked through its belly, while a ling is hooked through its head.

picked up your offering or if your bait is hung on brush, rock, or grass. Keep a light hold on the line to detect gentle strikes, and when in doubt, pull ever so softly on the line. If it moves off vigorously, you've got a fish.

Unless a fish has savagely attacked your bait offering and run off with it, it may be necessary to wait before setting the hook. For some fish, it does not pay to be in a rush to set the hook when live-bait angling. Certain fish need time to consume their quarry because they grab the bait crosswise in their mouth and swim a short distance away before swallowing the fish. By waiting a short time, and by not putting tension on the line during this period, you stand a better chance of hooking such fish.

This is not always the best move for all fish, however, and it can lead to deep hooking of some specimens that you must or want to release unharmed. Considering the type and size of bait used, the kind of hook, and the tendencies of the targeted fish, striking fairly quickly after the take may be better to minimize deep hooking. When you do have a deeply hooked fish, be especially careful about handling and unhooking it. There's a good chance that a fish released with a hook in it will survive if it is not bleeding. More about this issue is discussed in the entry on catch-and- release (see).

NAVIGATION

From a boating perspective, navigation is the act of steering a boat, plotting a course, and/or determining boat position. Every angler who uses a boat is a navigator, most to a very minor degree, some to a major degree. The extent to which anglers are familiar with navigation is largely influenced by the waters on which they boat and the type of vessel employed. The principles of navigation should be familiar to anyone venturing on big waters—whether ocean, lake, or river—or likely to boat in the dark or fog or in inclement weather, or likely to travel in any locale featuring official aids to navigation such as buoys.

No matter where an angler boats or what craft is used, the safety of the operator, the occupants, the boat, and others is a primary concern. Moving a boat necessarily entails avoiding hazards and obstructions that may be visible or out of sight; negotiating current, wakes, and waves; piloting under changing and sometimes severe weather conditions; encountering other boats; and maneuvering in and around docks, harbors, canals, and other areas. Piloting any type of boat is a serious responsibility, and the operator should be able to navigate safely under all circumstances.

In addition to being able to properly steer and maneuver a boat, anglers should be familiar with various tools used in navigating. These include a compass (see), electronic navigation devices such as Loran (see) and GPS (see), navigational charts and maps (see), and sonar (see).

Sonar is not actually a navigational tool, but it is probably more widely used during the act of navigating by fishing boat operators than any other instrument. This is because many angler-boaters (the majority in freshwater) rely heavily on sonar for bottom-depth information while fishing and while moving from one place to another. Although bottom depth has only minor value in determining position, it has obvious value in helping to avoid running aground. Likewise, radar has some value in determining position, and more value in avoiding running aground or preventing collision, but only the largest sportfishing boats are equipped with it. It used to be that only midsize and larger fishing boats used electronic navigational devices, especially Loran, but that has completely changed. Today, many freshwater and saltwater boats in the 16- to 21-foot range are equipped with such devices, primarily GPS, although handheld GPS units make

One of the most embarrassing navigational errors is running aground; hopefully this happens on a sandbar, as here, where no damage is done.

navigation via that instrument easy for any anglers in any vessel. Navigational charts or maps are used by many anglers not just for their value in showing the proper routes to take on a given body of water, but also for locating suitable fish habitat.

Navigation can be made more difficult by adverse weather, so it is advisable for anglers to keep an eye on weather conditions and be alert to changes that may signal a storm.

Anglers and boaters have become increasingly reliant on electronic devices to give them information relevant to fishing, boating, navigation, and the weather. But if the electronic devices on a boat fail, which they sometimes do, and there is no quick way to determine depth, course, position, or speed, an angler who can't make adjustments could be in a very serious situation. There have long been ways to determine this information without electronics, including dead reckoning *(see)*, and anglers are advised to become acquainted with these through boating and piloting literature.

With or without electronic devices, angler-boaters need to use common sense and good judgment whenever they are boating, especially in difficult circumstances or on unfamiliar waters. Unfamiliar waters, especially those likely to have unmarked obstructions (rock reefs, sandbars, trees, etc.), require special attention. On large and un-familiar bodies of water, consider using various launch sites to minimize distance traveled. Studying a good map, preferably a navigational chart, is important, and it's a good idea to ask local boaters, marina operators, and tackle shop personnel about hazards to avoid. Whenever you enter a new part of that body of water, do so carefully, operate your boat slowly, watch your sonar, and observe the water and shoreline closely. In tidal waters, be attentive to water level changes, and don't take risks.

NAVIGATIONAL CHART
A chart depicting hydrographic information and significant detail regarding depth, obstructions, and navigational aids.
See: Maps; Navigation.

NEAP TIDE
See: Tides.

NEARSHORE
The shallow portion of inshore saltwaters adjacent to the shoreline. In fishing parlance, inshore is a more common term than nearshore, and they are generally interchangeable, although nearshore is more specific.
See: Inshore; Inshore Fishing; Onshore.

NEBRASKA
Because Nebraska is a prairie state, few fishing opportunities exist that are not the result of man-made reservoirs. Notable exceptions are the hundreds of small, shallow, natural lakes that dot the Sandhills in the north-central region.

Nebraska anglers long have been accustomed to traveling in order to pursue their favorite species. Four-fifths of the population lives in the eastern third of the state, and there are no major reservoirs in that region. The Missouri River, which marks the state's eastern boundary, is that area's most important body of water. But the river is channelized below Gavins Point Dam at Yankton, South Dakota, and is not much more than a water chute for barge traffic from Sioux City, Iowa, to where it empties into the Mississippi River near St. Louis.

The majority of big reservoirs are in the southwest, including Lake McConaughy, the state's largest impoundment. Big Mac, as it is known, covers roughly 35,000 surface acres and is nearly 20 miles long.

Nebraska boasts several distinct geological features, including the Sandhills, and fishing opportunities vary accordingly. All of the state's coldwater trout streams are in the northwest and north-central regions, which include the Panhandle's canyon-laced Pine Ridge County. The midsection is flat and accommodates the Platte River, which each spring and fall lures millions of waterfowl in a spectacular migration through a narrow Central Flyway opening roughly from Grand Island west to North Platte.

Most of the state's reservoirs are showing signs of aging as siltation and shoreline degradation suffocate the habitat. But in 1997, the Nebraska legislature took a unique and important step in the rehabilitation process by requiring anglers to purchase an annual $5 aquatic habitat stamp along with a fishing license. Money generated by the sale of the stamp can be used only to enhance and restore aquatic habitat in Nebraska's reservoirs, lakes, and streams. Nebraska's commitment to the future was assured when it became the first state to require such a stamp.

The importance of habitat to Nebraska's fisheries was brought sharply into focus during a five-year (1988 to 1992) drought that left moisture-starved reservoirs at or near all-time low-water levels. Harlan County Reservoir, the state's third-largest reservoir, was so depleted that most biologists didn't expect it ever to fill again. But it did fill, miraculously almost overnight, and most of the other reservoirs were in flood pool as well by the spring of 1993.

All the vegetation and trees that grew along the shorelines during the low-water years were then covered by water. The nutrient-rich mix provided food, spawning habitat, and cover, and many species pulled off fantastic hatches. The good old days returned, and the size of walleye caught in McConaughy in the latter 1990s rivaled that of Lake Erie's western basin and Lake Huron's Saginaw Bay. Proof of this is evidenced by the results of a two-person team, two-day walleye tournament held on Big Mac in 1997, when the winning team posted 20 fish that weighed a phenomenal 5.72 pounds on average.

Nebraska is the crossroads of the United States—where east meets west, and where north meets south. As a result, a rich biological diversity exists within its borders. Hunters have long taken pride in Nebraska's reputation as the mixed-bag capital of the nation. It's the same for anglers, who somewhere in the state can catch everything from chinook salmon to paddlefish, trout to flathead catfish, bluegills to walleye, and hybrid stripers to muskies.

Channel catfish, because they are available in nearly all Nebraska waters, likely are the most popular fish. Walleye are a close second.

Northeast

This region relies on agriculture, and its rolling hills make the land highly readable. It contains several small reservoirs—most of which cover fewer than 250 acres—and Lewis and Clark Lake, a Missouri River impoundment above Gavins Point Dam that is the state's second-largest reservoir and shared with South Dakota.

Upper Missouri River. A 45-mile-long unchannelized portion of the Missouri River is tucked away between Fort Randall and Gavins Point Dams. This scenic area is particularly productive. The upper Missouri is wider here than anywhere below Gavins Point Dam. It contains quite a few sandy islands and many oxbows, and the depth usually averages between 5 and 10 feet.

This is the state's top smallmouth bass spot, but largemouth bass also linger far back in the oxbows. Northern pike, walleye, sauger, crappie, and bluegills, along with flathead and channel catfish, are available, too. Because they must fight the current, the walleye here are more trim than their bulkier reservoir brethren.

Lewis and Clark Lake. Lewis and Clark produced a 101-pound blue catfish in 1990. The Nebraska jug fisherman who caught it missed a chance at the state record (100 pounds, 8 ounces from the Missouri River near Wynot in 1970) when he cleaned the fish after weighing it on an uncertified scale. The 30,000-acre reservoir is slightly smaller than Lake McConaughy and is the last impoundment on the Missouri River. Most anglers seek its walleye and sauger.

Gavins Point Dam tailwaters. The tailwaters of Gavens Point Dam on the Missouri is the only area in the state where paddlefish are allowed to be snagged. The paddlefish season annually runs the full month of October, and only those who have special permits are allowed to pursue the filter-feeding fish. At times, especially during the spring and fall, paddlefish crowd into the area below the dam in such numbers that anglers jigging for walleye or sauger routinely snag them. The state-record paddlefish weighed 91 pounds, 8 ounces and was landed in 1978. Although anglers prefer to catch walleye and sauger, they catch all species of fish, including rainbow trout and smallmouth bass, below the dam. The smallies and trout come from South Dakota reservoirs upstream.

Willow Creek Lake. Located 2 miles south of Pierce, Willow Creek Lake is a 700-acre impoundment. It is the largest in the northeast region with the exception of Lewis and Clark. Although it contains walleye, largemouth bass, northern pike, and tiger muskies, its worth as a panfish lake surfaces during the winter months, when ice anglers drill for bluegills and crappie.

Fremont State Lakes. The thirst for fishable water by eastern Nebraskans is evidenced by the popularity of the Fremont State chain—20 sandpit lakes that cover 280 acres in all. These small lakes draw about 800,000 visitors a year, making them the second most popular destination for water recreation in the state. Largemouth bass, panfish, and channel catfish are targets of anglers who crowd onto these small bodies of water.

Southeast

Several small flood-control reservoirs have been built near Omaha and Lincoln. Branched Oak and Pawnee are among a series of Salt Valley reservoirs that were constructed near Lincoln during the 1960s and 1970s. All these metropolitan reservoirs receive extremely heavy fishing pressure, but Branched Oak (1,800 acres) and Pawnee (740 acres) are in a league of their own in terms of drawing power. They rank first and third, respectively, among the state's reservoirs in the number of visitors each year.

Branched Oak. Branched Oak used to be one of the state's premier walleye fisheries, but an infestation of white perch has whittled down the walleye population. Little if any natural recruitment is occurring, and stockings of fingerlings have failed because the young walleye are either eaten by the white perch or are unable to compete with them for food. Crappie are beginning to rebound, and the lake is loaded with channel and flathead catfish. Biologists, however, say that the only way to make this a viable fishery once again is to apply rotenone, eradicate all the fish, and start over. Those in power are reluctant to do this because the water level would have to be drawn down before the rotenone could be applied. Emptying the state's most popular lake among pleasure boaters might be too much of a political hot potato, and these issues could prevent biologists from restoring this once excellent fishery.

Burchard Lake. The Salt Valley reservoirs had life expectancies of 100 years when they were built. Burchard, only 7 miles from the Kansas border, is not a Salt Valley impoundment. But it sets a standard for clean water and good watershed that biologists want to duplicate in all other eastern Nebraska reservoirs. The clean water enables weeds to grow. This in turn creates excellent habitat, which provides for good populations of bluegills and largemouth bass, along with some crappie. This 150-acre lake will become a model for all rehabilitation projects using money generated by the sales of aquatic habitat stamps.

Missouri River. Wing dams and river bends offer about the only habitat along the channelized portion of the river. Flathead and channel catfish are available for the few river rats who know how and where to catch them. But change is in the wind. There is a movement to restore more natural conditions—opening up some oxbows and reconnecting them to the river, giving it more of a natural meander. As the natural conditions are reestablished, fishing for additional species will improve, and more people will look to the river as a fishing destination. It's unlikely that federal funds will ever become available to construct a large reservoir in eastern Nebraska. But the river already is there, and its restoration one day will provide a vibrant fishing opportunity for the water-starved residents of eastern Nebraska.

South-Central

Interstate 80 lakes. Motorists traveling on Interstate 80 between Grand Island and Sutherland can observe what have become important fisheries to Nebraskans. A series of 41 borrow pits located along I-80 were created in the 1960s when dirt was taken from those pits to build the interstate highway. Because of the high water table along the Platte River, the pits quickly filled, and the state initiated stocking programs.

Most are small pits—only three are larger than 30 acres—and few have good access for boats. The majority of anglers either fish from shore or use small boats, canoes, or tubes. Those who do manage to launch larger boats do so for the comfort, not the added horsepower, as only electric motors are allowed. Although some receive fairly extensive fishing pressure, as a whole the lakes are overlooked by hard-core anglers, who drive right by them en route to much larger reservoirs.

The small lakes primarily offer largemouth bass, bluegills, and channel catfish. Some have rock bass, a few have yellow perch or northern pike, and a couple contain walleye. Smallmouth bass initially were stocked in many of the lakes, but largemouth bass eventually found their way into the lakes, where they were better able to compete for food. The smallmouths have slowly gone by the wayside.

Harlan County Reservoir. Traditionally, the state's third-largest reservoir (13,500 acres) has been an excellent walleye fishery. But a gradual decline in the fishery is in progress, and the walleye catch in the late 1990s was very poor. The recruitment has been very weak the last several years. The species of choice now seems to be white bass. The crappie population has increased dramatically in the aftermath of high water levels, and the number of channel catfish has improved. Biologists are hoping to make this an excellent fishery for hybrid striped bass, which are known as wipers here.

Sherman Reservoir. A 2,600-acre impoundment, Sherman is the state's most consistent crappie fishery. It has numerous coves and consistent water levels each year. About two-thirds of the crappie anglers fish from boats, but the many coves allow bank anglers easy access to the fish, too, especially during the May spawning period. A 10-inch minimum length limit for crappie went into effect in 1998. Walleye also attract attention, and there's an 18-inch minimum size limit. White bass success varies from good to excellent.

Johnson Reservoir. Walleye and white bass help make Johnson, a 2,800-acre lake, a strong magnet for anglers. Crappie are also beginning to draw attention, and the lake had a good number of crappie more than 10 inches long in the late 1990s. Numbers of channel catfish are low, compared to those in other reservoirs.

Elwood Reservoir. Elwood is one of three state reservoirs that utilize alewife as a food source, and this 1,200-acre impoundment is considered among the best walleye producers in the state. The lake level, however, is subject to extreme changes in water elevation because of irrigation demands. This fluctuation causes a loss of shoreline vegetation and apparently hampers panfish recruitment. Reproduction of channel catfish also is restricted, but there are good numbers of big channels.

Southwest

Nebraska's big reservoirs are in this region, and all are established walleye and white bass fisheries. But there are bonus fish, too, such as the state-record 64-pound, 15-ounce striped bass caught from Sutherland Reservoir in 1993. Biologists believe the huge striper initially was stocked in McConaughy and made its way down the canal system to Sutherland. That canal also produced the state-record 14-pound, 2-ounce rainbow trout in 1975. Other Platte Valley reservoirs—Maloney and Jeffrey—along with Medicine Creek and Enders, all produce good numbers of 15- to 18-inch walleye. Medicine Creek also can be exceptional for white bass and crappie.

McConaughy Reservoir. Nebraska's largest reservoir was a world-class walleye fishery in the latter 1990s, when it experienced the best years for walleye in its history. Five-fish limits of between 8- and 10-pounders were not uncommon in 1997, which prompted the Nebraska Game and Parks Commission to lower the state's walleye limit to four and to allow anglers to keep only one walleye a day longer than 25 inches. The state-record walleye of 16 pounds, 2 ounces was caught in 1971, long before alewives became the primary prey fish. Alewives produce big walleye, and the state's top

The method of angling with a fly developed earlier and faster than any other type of artificial lure fishing—perhaps because early anglers were concerned mostly with trout in rivers and streams.

three walleye fisheries—Big Mac, Merritt, and Elwood—are the only alewife-based reservoirs.

There is a trade-off, though. The alewife population at McConaughy has exploded, and walleye eggs or small fry are being eaten by them at such a pace that there is little if any natural recruitment occurring. Stocking of fingerling walleye appears to be the only way to beat the alewife. Biologists also plan to stock chinook salmon and brown trout in an attempt to reduce alewife numbers.

Lake Ogallala. Although Lake Ogallala covers only 590 acres, this small reservoir, which lies beneath Big Mac's Kingsley Dam, is the state's most important trout fishery. Biologists are managing this as a trophy lake for rainbow trout, brown trout, and chinook salmon.

Red Willow Reservoir. A 1,630-acre lake, Red Willow might be the state's best all-around fishery, barely edging Merritt and Elwood for that honor. It has become the premier wiper lake, but an angler never really knows what might gulp a lure. A guide and his client once stayed in one spot long enough to catch five Master Angler (the state's large-catch recognition program) species—channel catfish, largemouth bass, walleye, wipers, and northern pike. It yields lots of white bass, and the crappie population is building up once again.

Swanson Reservoir. Wipers in Swanson Reservoir are beginning to put on bulk and could one day rival those in Red Willow if anglers release this sterile hybrid cross between a white bass and a striped bass. This 5,000-acre lake has mostly a flat bottom and is essentially void of structure, yet it still manages to produce good classes of walleye, white bass, and crappie. This might be the state's best lake for flathead catfish.

Panhandle

Most of the state's coldwater trout streams are in this region, but a vigorous stocking program is necessary due to the decline of Lake McConaughy as a rainbow trout fishery. A breed of rainbow trout known as the McConaughy strain flourished in Big Mac until the late 1970s. Most trout anglers blame the decline of rainbows on the stocking of stripers. The stripers are about gone now, and the Nebraska Game and Parks Commission has ordered that no further striper stockings can take place in the state. Biologists, however, still can't revive the rainbow trout population, even though federal fish hatcheries have maintained the McConaughy strain. It's believed alewives are outcompeting the rainbows for the small food that once was available.

The McConaughy strain is unusual. These rainbows have an inclination to migrate out of the lake and to travel far up the coldwater streams to spawn. In the glory days of McConaughy as a trout fishery, most of the fish migrated from the west end of the lake up the North Platte River. When they ran into a tributary they liked, they left the river and headed up the creek to spawn.

Many of the streams run through the Pine Ridge, which stretches from north of Rushville to the Wyoming border, a distance of more than 80 miles, and varies in altitude from 3,100 feet to just over a mile high. Pine forests stretch as far as the eye can see, and the cool, gravel-bottomed streams are stocked with brook, brown, and rainbow trout. Public access is available on many of the streams, such as Soldier, Squaw, Chadron, Nine-Mile, Pumpkin, and Otter Creeks. But they and other streams meander mostly on private ground, and obtaining permission to fish is a necessity. A few reservoirs also are available, along with some Sandhill lakes. A sandpit near Scottsbluff in 1997 yielded the state-record northern pike, a 30-pound, 1-ounce specimen.

Box Butte Reservoir. Box Butte is a 1,600-acre lake that is subject to severe irrigation drawdown each summer, yet it still produces decent panfishing for yellow perch, crappie, and bluegills. It has a good population of northern pike, and some walleye and largemouth bass also inhabit the lake.

Lake Minatare. Lake Minatare is the largest impoundment, at 2,300 acres, in the Panhandle region. It is closed during the fall/winter waterfowl migration because it harbors so many waterfowl during that period. The good news for western Nebraska anglers is that it's beginning to rebound as a walleye fishery. Also available are small-mouth bass, channel catfish, wipers, white bass, and perch.

North-Central

The Sandhills, one of the geological wonders of the world, cover one-fourth of Nebraska. A satellite picture of the Sandhills taken from 500 miles up shows that the hills lie in a diagonal pattern, running northeast to southwest. All are steep on the southeast side because they are wind-blown dunes; it appears the predominant wind was out of the northwest when the Sandhills were formed. This was once a largely bare sand system, but a growth of grass that anchored the dunes was likely triggered by increased rainfall and perhaps decreased temperature.

This is range country, and the native grasses are grazed by cattle. Large ranching operations and a few small villages dot the Sandhills. The region has a high water table, and hundreds of shallow lakes are interspersed among the stabilized sand dunes, some of which rise to a height of 400 feet.

Sandhill lakes. The Sandhill lakes are shallow and average between 6 and 10 feet in depth. Many are so saline that they can't support fish, but those that have freshwater are very productive. Most have abundant aquatic vegetation—unless they have a high population of carp—and they become weed-choked and difficult to fish during the summer. The best time to fish is in the spring and winter. Some, such as Pelican Lake in the Valentine National Wildlife Refuge, offer world-class ice fishing opportunities for bluegills that run 2 pounds and larger. Northern pike, largemouth bass, and perch also are sought by many Sandhill lakes anglers.

Merritt Reservoir. A 2,900-acre lake, Merritt is a premier Nebraska fishery for a variety of species. It is the state's top water for channel catfish and muskellunge. The state record for both species was set here, and each weighed 41 pounds, 8 ounces. The channel was caught in 1985 and the muskie in 1992. The lake is best known for its walleye, even though there is little if any natural recruitment. Stockings preserve its status as a walleye fishery. Good populations of bluegills, crappie, and perch make it the state's best panfish lake.

Calamus Reservoir. Nebraska's newest reservoir is showing signs of finally becoming a viable fishery after 18 years of Dead Sea status. It was among the nation's best lakes for northern pike during its early years. Panfish and largemouth bass are other shallow-water species that flourished when it was first flooded. But when the flooded habitat decayed, the shallow-water species crashed. Now, some open-water species have finally begun to emerge. Walleye fishing was excellent in the latter 1990s, and a huge population of small fish has been building. Wipers and white bass are improving, too. The reservoir finally is able to sustain fish populations that biologists thought it could when it was built. The future looks bright for this 5,200-acre lake.

NEEDLEFISH

There are 32 species in the Belonidae family of needlefish, many of which are also known as longtoms or sea gar. Most live in tropical seas, a few inhabit cooler waters of temperate regions, and some stray occasionally into freshwater. They are often observed by coastal anglers, and some are caught frequently.

The most distinguishing feature of these fish is their elongated upper and lower jaws, which have numerous needlelike teeth. The upper jaw is shorter than the lower jaw; however, in two species the lower jaw is shorter. They have slender elongate bodies that are silver on the flanks and bluish or dark green along the back, and also feature small scales and a wide mouth. In most species, both the bones and the flesh are greenish, but they make good eating. Some species are pursued commercially, with Europeans and Scandinavians exhibiting the most interest in this species as a food fish.

Garfish

Atlantic Needlefish

Needlefish commonly skip across the surface when hooked on rod and reel, when alarmed, and when attracted to lights. They leap from the water and hurtle through the air like an arrow. Since they have a habit of leaping toward lights at night, they present a serious hazard to night anglers and people on low well-lit boats. People who have been struck or impaled have been badly injured, and in rare cases killed. Beneath the surface, these fish swim very rapidly. Plugs, streamer flies, spoons, jigs, and live baits will all catch needlefish. Light tackle ensures a good fight.

Species

One of the most widely dispersed species is the houndfish *(Tylosurus crocodilus crocodilus)*, which is found nearly worldwide in tropical and warm temperate waters. It is common in the western Atlantic, ranging from New Jersey southward through the Caribbean to Brazil. In the eastern Atlantic it ranges from Cameroon to South Africa; in the Indian Ocean it occurs in South Africa; in the western Pacific it ranges from Japan to Australia. In the eastern Pacific it is replaced by *T. c. fodiator*, the Mexican houndfish.

The houndfish averages 2 feet or less in length but occasionally attains a length of 4 to 5 feet. It is also known as hound needlefish, crocodile needlefish, and crocodile longtom, and the all-tackle world record is 6 pounds, 11 ounces (the record for Mexican houndfish is 21 pounds, 12 ounces). Compared to other, generally smaller members of the family, houndfish have a relatively short, stout beak. They are found singly or in small groups, readily strike artificial lures, and are exciting to take on rod and reel.

The Atlantic needlefish *(Strongylura marina)* is a smaller species that inhabits coastal areas and mangrove-lined lagoons and also enters freshwater. It occurs in the western Atlantic and ranges from the Gulf of Maine to Brazil. It is absent from the Bahamas and Antilles. It grows to 31 inches and can weigh slightly more than 3 pounds.

Similar in size is the garfish *(Belone belone belone)*, which occurs in the eastern Atlantic from Norway and south Iceland to the British Isles, including the Baltic Sea, with related species (or subspecies) present from France to the Canary Islands, including the Mediterranean. The garfish has considerable commercial interest and is known as *hornfisk* in Denmark, *orphie* in France, *agugila* in Italy, *horngjel* in Norway, *agulha* in Portugal, *aguja* in Spain, *hongädda* in Sweden, and *zargana* in Turkey.

NEOPRENE

A prominent wader *(see)* material that provides warmth in cold water.

NEST

A visible bed, often circular, made by egg-laying fish on the bottom of a body of water for spawning. Eggs are laid in the nest, and sometimes they are guarded by one or more of the parents.

NET

A mesh bag mounted on a wooden or metal frame with one or more handles. Used for capturing individual hooked fish, this device is also known as a landing net to distinguish it from a seine or commercial fishing net. Landing nets are an important and regularly used accessory for freshwater anglers, from stream trout waders to big water boaters. They are less frequently used by saltwater anglers, mostly for smaller fish in bays and shallows.

Nets should be suited to the kind of angling being done and the fish anticipated. Stream nets for trout have a short handle and small hoop diameter (12 to 14 inches) for use with small fish while boat nets have longer handles (perhaps collapsible) and larger hoops. The further one has to reach (from boat or pier), the longer the handle needed; however, the heavier the fish you may catch, the sturdier the handle necessary (usually reinforced). Pier and bridge anglers use a large, handleless net that is lowered and raised on a rope. A few nets incorporate a scale into the handle in order to weigh a fish that has been netted.

With all nets, the larger the fish, the bigger the hoop and the deeper the bag necessary. Although it seems foolish to net small fish with big nets, it's worse to be caught with a net that can't fit the fish. For small-boat fishing, a net that is at least 4 feet long from net rim to handle butt, with a wide rim and a deep net bag, is a popular choice. For very big fish in big water and boats with high freeboard, a 6-foot handle is better. Most nets feature aluminum handles and frames. Mesh bags are rubber, polyethylene, nylon, or cotton, although cotton tends to rot. All nets should be rinsed after use to increase their longevity.

Mesh bags with wooden side handles, called cradles, have been used by fisheries technicians and some anglers to support fish without handling, but they are cumbersome and difficult for a lone angler to use. With help from a companion, however, they're very good for landing long fish that are to be released, and make a good net for long toothy species like pike and muskie.

See: Cast Net; Catch-and-Release; Landing Fish.

NETHERLANDS

Upon landing at Schiphol Airport near Amsterdam, few people realize that they are at that moment not only near some good fishing areas, but also several meters below sea level, a situation that also exists throughout much of the western and northern provinces of the Netherlands. Should the sea level rise considerably in the next century, as has been forecast by some scientists, and if not enough is done to avert these problems, many people in the Netherlands will have serious problems. Still, lighthearted Dutch anglers say that angling from the bedroom window has certain charms.

Also known as Holland, the Netherlands covers just 41,526 square kilometers and is bordered on the west and north by the North Sea, on the east by Germany, and on the south by Belgium. With a population of more than 15 million, it is one of the most densely populated countries in the world. Most of its residents live in the relatively small delta area of rivers like the Maas, Rijn, and Schelde.

Those rivers and deltas transport water to the sea near the port of Rotterdam and between the islands of the southwestern province of Zeeland. The Rijn once held one of the world's largest stocks of Atlantic salmon, a unique run of fish almost completely extinct since World War II. These fish started to reappear a few years ago, however, due to the improvement of fish habitat, stocking programs, and the construction of fish ladders. Holland is, and probably always has been, a passageway for fish like Atlantic salmon and sea trout, and even the water in small creeks in the east and south holds too much sand for these fish to deposit their eggs with any chance of success. The total number of mature salmon going upriver was very small in the late 1990s, offering only a slight chance to hook one, but there may be a viable fishery for salmon someday if the numbers improve.

Other species, of course—including pike, pikeperch (zander), and trout, which are tops among freshwater gamefish—draw the attention of resident and visiting anglers. Interest in eels, perch, carp, bream, and roach is high as well. In saltwater, mackerel, cod, whiting, and assorted flatfish are the main species.

Freshwater

Freshwater fish in Holland inhabit a network of canals, lakes, and rivers. Significant Dutch rivers include the Rhine, which flows from Germany, and its tributaries; the Maas, which is an extension of the Meuse from Belgium; and the Schelde, which also enters from Belgium. Many small lakes grace the northern and western regions. The world-renowned Dutch delta redevelopment and reclamation program has created numerous freshwater lakes, the largest of which is the IJsselmeer in the central part of the country; this is the former Zuiderzee, which was created after being diked by the Afsluitdijk.

Club and organized match fishing are major activities throughout the country. As in the rest of western Europe, roach and bronze bream are the most common and favorite species. Pole fishing for these fish is how most anglers begin, and if they master this method up to championship level, they will eventually use take-apart poles up to 12 meters in length.

Coarse species in canals and rivers that are continually fished for matches are very difficult to catch, and this has become a challenge that Dutch anglers thrive on. They must continually improve their delicate floats, rigs, and chum recipes to outwit the fish and other anglers. They have done this successfully enough for the country to have won a pair of world titles and individual championships. Incidentally, the challenge of catching big carp (more than 25 pounds), which started in England, has caught on lately in Holland.

Rivers. The first part of the river Maas, the Grensmaas, is shallow and runs with considerable speed. It is ideal habitat for coarse species like barbel, carp, and chub, which are sought with match rod, feeder rod, pole, and fly tackle. This area also contains sea-run trout.

In general, match rods are between 3.3 and 4.5 meters long and are used with spinning reels to fish floats at considerable distances from shore. Feeder rods are equipped with delicate tips to telegraph the light take of a fish. The "feeders" are wire or plastic cages, weighted with lead, that are filled with groundbait before being cast to the spot to be fished. A short, light length of nylon monofilament line with a hook is connected somewhat above the feeder. Dutch anglers use poles in lengths from 5 to more than 14 meters. To improve control over a drifting float, the line is often considerably shorter than the rod, and the pole is taken apart when a fish is landed and/or new bait is put on the hook. The natural and processed baits used most often when fishing these types of tackle include maggots, casters, worms, bloodworms, bread, hemp, and corn.

Numerous gravel pits have been created along the rivers, and these range from just a few acres to thousands of acres. These are often much deeper than the rivers to which they are connected—down to 20 meters in some cases—and are frequented by anglers for coarse species and zander.

Fishing with jigs equipped with shad bodies and other soft plastics straight below a boat or float tube—a method called *vertical fishing* in Holland—can produce zander up to 100 centimeters in length and 20 pounds in weight, although smaller zander around 50 centimeters are the norm. Perch and pike are a much appreciated bycatch of this method. In winter these gravel pits host match anglers who fish for roach with wagglers at depths of between 5 and 15 meters.

Where canals enter the rivers, and on a larger scale upstream from where the river IJssel flows into the IJsselmeer, there is an annual "spring run" in April and May of great numbers of roach and bream (and to some extent ide), which move upriver to spawn. Exceptional catches are possible during this period on pole, feeder rod, and match rod.

Fly anglers along the river IJssel have developed a style of nymph fishing suited to these conditions. A 4- to 5-meter-long leader, heavy nymphs with fluorescent materials incorporated into the body, and a clearly visible strike indicator are the main tools of the trade. Good-size roach and bream take a well-bent fly rod to pull them from the main flow of the river.

Another fish regularly inhabiting Dutch rivers is the bleak, a small silvery fish found and pursued in the top layers of the water. They take small dry flies well, but their speed in taking these, as well as their small mouths, makes them hard to hook.

The asp is a fish that has entered Holland's waters in recent years, originating in Germany and evidently washing downstream during high water periods. Ten years ago this fish was unheard of in Dutch rivers but is now an exciting prospect for anglers using flycasting and spinning tackle.

River anglers also have an opportunity to pursue zander. During the long summer evenings, many fly anglers cast fast-sinking lines and 10-centimeter-long streamers for zander. The take on a streamer can be hardly noticeable, just a little increased resistance, so anglers set the hook when they feel this, and a good-size zander could be heading for deeper water in the next instant.

In the saltwater or brackish water of harbors close to where main rivers enter the sea, anglers

An angler fishes for coarse species in a Dutch canal.

have challenging sport catching mullet. It's impressive to see these torpedo-shaped fish 'sunbathing' in summer months, and some can be 80 to 100 centimeters long. Catching them is not too easy, as they mainly feed on weeds, but anglers who use bread or small parts of herring do catch mullet.

Lakes. The shallow waters of Holland's *polders,* or sections of land reclaimed from the sea and protected by dikes, provide diverse fishing opportunity. The oldest polders are found in the provinces of Utrecht, Zuid-Holland, Noord-Holland, Friesland, and Overijssel. Many of these waters badly need to be restored to their former depth, whereas others suffer from the inflow of manure and pesticides. A good polder water is gin clear (even though it appears otherwise because of the dark bottom) and filled with numerous aquatic plants.

The polder canals and lakes are hunting grounds for anglers who cast unweighted spinners, little wobblers, and spoons for pike and perch. Ultralight-tackle enthusiasts cast maggots or bread in search of rudd. Fly anglers catch rudd as well as roach and perch on dry flies and nymphs, and northern pike on streamer flies. Carp anglers have success in polder waters by sneaking along and dropping a bait in likely looking places, or by baiting certain areas and fishing over this chum until their electronic strike indicators go off.

Another member of the cyprinid family, the tench is an inhabitant of waters that are crowded with plants. Some anglers will first clear a few square meters of aquatic plants, drop some groundbait (with worms added) there, and await the arrival of the tench.

Until mid-1998 it was legal to fish for pike, perch, and zander with live baits, but new legislation stopped this popular and successful technique. In discolored waters, dead fish used as baits can be as successful as live baits; anglers use roach, herring, sprat, or mackerel to attract pike in particular.

Zander and big pike inhabit the larger lakes scattered throughout Holland, and these include the Vinkeveense, Nieuwkoopse Plassen, and the Friese Meren. Trolling lures and baits is a popular method for pike, whereas vertical fishing with jigs or using small dead baits is popular for zander. Drifting along the shoreline while casting jerkbaits, minnow plugs, and spoons is also popular.

Wherever there is access along the shoreline of these lakes, anglers pursue perch and zander using assorted methods with baits and jigs. Anglers fishing from belly boats cast either flies or pieces of bread toward the reeds and other vegetation along the shore. The float tube has firmly established itself in Holland as an excellent device for fishing waters that are otherwise difficult to access. Still, rowboats are available for rent on all the established waters.

Wels have been inhabitants of a small number of waters in Holland for a considerable time, and in recent years they have spread to other sites as well, like those connected with the river Maas. Most wels are hooked and lost by anglers fishing for zander or pike, but in late 1997 a wels of more than 45 kilograms was caught in the Biesbosch. Wels are a protected species in the Netherlands and must be returned to the water immediately.

The trout fisheries Eemhof, Kempervennen, Berenkuil, and Baggelhuizen are four examples of popular daily-fee privately operated fisheries. These are rather large natural or man-made lakes where fly anglers have room to enjoy their sport and where newcomers can get casting and fishing instruction if needed. A fee for the day or several hours is charged, and the waters are stocked primarily with rainbow trout, and sometimes brown trout; these may be released if handled with great care, or they may be kept for an additional fee. They are similar to commercial fishing preserves in the United States. Other, usually smaller, trout fisheries are managed as strictly put-and-take waters, and may be fished with various tackle and methods. The rainbow trout caught here are plate-size, but some waters are stocked with larger specimens.

For sea-run trout, the Veerse Meer and Oostvoornse Meer, especially the latter, have in recent years gained international recognition as two of the best sea trout fisheries of Europe. The Oostvoornse Meer is situated just below Rotterdam; the Veerse Meer lies farther south, near Veere in the province of Zeeland.

Both lakes are brackish, and their great supply of baitfish, saltwater scuds, and shrimp means plenty of food for trout. In the Oostvoornse Meer, trout have been known to grow up to 2.5 centimeters per month. The largest trout to come out of these lakes are well over 20 pounds.

In the Oostvoornse Meer, all trout have to be returned to the water, no motorboats are allowed, and one can only fish with a fly or an artificial lure. Fly anglers must use at least a 2X tippet to cope with the fish that can be expected here. The shallow water between shore and the many dams in the Oostvoornse Meer are prime feeding grounds for these trout, and easier for most anglers to fish. Beyond the dams, the water gains depth rapidly.

Saltwater
The coastline of the North Sea in the Netherlands consists mainly of dunes, but in the southwest there are gaps formed by river mouths, which forged an expansive delta of islands and waterways. In the north, the dunes were broken through by the sea, creating the West Frisian Islands; behind these is a tidal sea called the Waddenzee, which is popular for anglers seeking flatfish. Some areas of this beautiful seascape produce mackerel, garfish, bass, and sea trout.

Surf casting for flounder, whiting, cod, and bass is a common activity along the coast, using weights from 80 to 200 grams and baited hooks that are cast with long rods great distances from the

---

If the salt in the sea could be removed and spread evenly over the Earth's land surface, it would form a layer more than 500 feet thick—about the height of a 40-story building.

shoreline. A wind blowing toward shore is usually preferred; summer is the best time for bass, whereas cod move in closer to land in the colder months.

Piers and dams like those near IJmuiden, Hoek, Scheveningen, Haringvliet, and Zierikzee are popular fishing sites, too. Garfish are caught here close to the surface. Bass are hooked here but are often lost among the rocks by shore-based anglers. Casting toward shore from a drifting or anchored boat results in more bass landed. These are caught by various means, but fly tackle, using heavy sinking lines to fish down to 8 meters, has earned a place for this species in recent years as well.

Hundreds of small boats also set out to sea regularly from a number of harbors when the conditions and weather are right. Fishing over shipwrecks in late autumn, winter, and early spring often produces large cod, up to 40 pounds on some occasions. In summer, the same boats are on the hunt for bass. Party boats are also available from many ports along the coast, and some fish all year. Mackerel are the main pursuit from June through September, and cod during winter. Whiting and flatfish are also caught.

Licenses and Regulations

Licenses and regulations are a complex matter in Holland. Two types of licenses are needed for most Dutch waters, although none is needed for sportfishing in saltwater. *Sportvisakte,* the national license, is a yearly one available from post offices, tackle shops, and some fishing clubs. This license gives anglers the right to fish with a maximum of two rods, one of which has to be devoted to predator species (i.e., equipped with an artificial lure or streamer).

The second license is one that allows an angler to fish a particular waterway. Depending on the specific watercourse, one has to be a club member, have a weekly ticket or daily tickets, or be covered by the *Grote Vergunning* (large license), which covers a lot of water across Holland. The *Grote Vergunning* is offered by the national federation of anglers (NVVS, in Holland); most fishing clubs in Holland belong to this organization and only their members can receive the license. It cannot be bought in a shop (although one can purchase a membership to some fishing clubs in a large number of fishing tackle stores). The Oostvoornse Meer and Veerse Meer are just two examples of waters covered by the *Grote Vergunning.*

A number of public waters exist in Holland for which the *Sportvisakte* is the only license needed if you do not fish for pike, perch, or zander. A membership for one year in a fishing club varies in cost depending on the number of members and the number of waters to which they have fishing rights. Some have no more than twenty-five members; the biggest ones have thousands of members.

In the Netherlands, closed seasons are enforced for certain species of fish, and some regulations cover bait types, as well as special considerations for certain waters. Minimum size limits apply to most species, with the exception of carp, garfish, and twaite shad *(Alosa fallax),* although many Dutch anglers practice catch-and-release in freshwater. Nearly all fishing clubs have their own regulations in addition. These may pertain to an extended closed season for pike, prohibition of treble hooks, or the prohibition of night fishing. Ask about these issues when you buy a license or decide to become a member of a club.

NET KEEPER

A device that tethers a landing net to the body of a wading angler so that it is out of the way when fishing yet easily accessible. Net keepers are fastened to a retractable chain or string, or to a quick-release clip.

NETTING

See: Landing Fish; Catch-and-Release.

NEVADA

Nevada's fishing opportunities are surprisingly abundant and widely varied, particularly since the state receives less precipitation than any other state in the United States.

In its northwestern corner, Nevada has an abundant lake trout population in forested Lake Tahoe; at the opposite end of the state, it has the Colorado River, which winds across the Mohave Desert, forming canyonlike Lakes Mead and Mohave and boasting famous largemouth bass and striped bass fisheries. In between are numerous natural lakes and man-made reservoirs—mostly used as storage for flood control or irrigation—that also provide terrific fisheries for stocked and wild trout.

Nevada has approximately 535 fishable streams with nearly 3,000 miles of habitat, mostly in the northern two-thirds of the state, that are underutilized; most anglers head for the larger rivers and more developed lakes and reservoirs. Yet these flowages possess reproducing populations of brown trout, brook trout, Lahontan cutthroat trout, redband trout, bull trout, mountain whitefish, and other species.

Northern Region

Wildhorse, Wilson Sink, and South Fork Reservoirs. Wildhorse, Wilson Sink, and South Fork are all in the northeastern corner of Nevada and are "put-grow-and-take" trout fisheries. They are primarily stocked with rainbow trout, but also with browns and rainbow-cutthroat hybrids. They have secondary opportunities for such warmwater species as smallmouth and largemouth bass, yellow perch, crappie, and channel catfish. Additionally, South Fork has wild brown trout and native Lahontan cutthroat trout.

Wildhorse is a 2,830-acre irrigation storage reservoir on the East Fork of the Owyhee River. It's about 60 miles north of Elko, with good year-round access via Route 225. Located off Route 226, nearby Wilson Sink Reservoir is small at 800 surface acres. Access at Wilson is less dependable in the winter when the dirt road thaws enough to become mud. South Fork Reservoir, which covers 1,650 surface acres and is 3 miles long, is 20 miles southwest of Elko off Route 228 on the South Fork of the Humboldt River. Access is good year-round.

All three reservoirs are stocked with 8- to 10-inch trout, mostly rainbows, in the spring and fall, which quickly grow to 13 to 17 inches if they're not caught first. Fishing off the bottom from shore with worms and prepared baits is popular during spring and fall, as is casting spinners and spoons. Boaters troll with small spoons and spinners. Float-tube anglers like fishing the "no wake" zone in the willows at the south end of South Fork for bass and trout. The rock dam face and rocky points, especially those jutting out on either side of the dam, are good places to fish for smallmouth bass in April, May, September, and October.

Ice fishing for trout is popular at these reservoirs during the winter, from late December through much of February. Yellow perch are a welcome winter bonus at Wildhorse. Smallmouth bass, crappie, and catfish also inhabit Wildhorse, and Wilson has largemouth bass. Spring and early summer are the best times for these species.

Fishing beneath the dams at both Wildhorse and South Fork can be good when high flows have washed fish into the rivers.

Ruby Mountains and East Humboldt's lakes and streams. The Ruby Mountains and East Humboldt Mountains are among the most scenic and glacier-carved in Nevada. Twenty high-mountain lakes and dozens of streams provide angling opportunities to backpackers searching for wild brook trout and native Lahontan cutthroat trout. The only stream stocked with rainbow trout is Lamoille Creek in Lamoille Canyon, which receives more fishing pressure than any other stream in Elko County. Much access to other fishable streams in the ranges is blocked by private property, although the upper reaches of many streams are accessed downslope from the Ruby Crest Trail.

Ruby Lake National Wildlife Refuge. Located 65 miles southeast of Elko, the 37,632-acre Ruby Lake National Wildlife Refuge consists of marshes, open ponds, and islands bordered by wet meadows and grass- and sagebrush-covered uplands.

Fishing for abundant, but usually small, largemouth bass is popular throughout the marsh area. The Collection Ditch flowing on the west side of the North and East Sump units is a favorite among fly anglers because it can be fished only with artificials. Anglers can catch rainbows and 5- to 10-pound brown trout here.

Rye Patch Reservoir. Located 22 miles north of Lovelock and 50 miles southeast of Winnemucca, Rye Patch Reservoir is an impoundment on the Humboldt River. Built for irrigation storage and flood control, it provides good habitat to walleye, spotted bass, white crappie, hybrid stripers, yellow perch, channel catfish, black crappie, bluegills, and green sunfish.

The Pitt-Taylor Arm at the upper end of the 22-mile-long reservoir has many islands with rocky shorelines that hold walleye and crappie, as well as brushy areas that hold spotted bass. Angling for walleye up to 12 pounds begins late in March and extends through mid-May, then picks up again in September. Anglers use deep-diving plugs and yellow or white crappie jigs on the windswept shorelines in 8 feet of water over structure. Fishing for walleye below the dam is good when that structure is spilling water.

A deep-spawning fish, spotted bass are caught in typical largemouth bass habitat. The spotted bass on average here are small but can run up to 5 pounds. Catfish up to 27 pounds have been caught at Rye Patch and are mainly landed on stinkbaits fished in areas where fresh water flows. Hybrid striped bass, locally called wipers, are caught up to 8 pounds and provide excitement in open water from June through September.

Smaller waters. Excellent stream fishing opportunities exist throughout many of the mountain ranges in northern Nevada. The East and West Forks of the Jarbidge, Bruneau, and Mary's Rivers in northeastern Nevada offer excellent opportunities to catch native wild trout. Bull trout in the 6- to 10-inch range inhabit the East Fork of the Jarbidge River or the upper stretches of the West Fork. The East Fork is rather remote, offering little access but excellent fishing. Due to aggressive conservation measures, fishing is excellent on the Bruneau River, primarily for redband trout. The Mary's River and its tributaries are under extensive management to restore Lahontan cutthroat trout. The upper stretches of the Mary's River offer the best fishing.

Notable small reservoirs and lakes include: Squaw Creek, Chimney, Knott Creek, Onion Valley, Big Springs, Dry Creek, Crittenden, and Dorsey Reservoirs, as well as Blue Lakes and Angel Lake.

Central Region

Pyramid and Walker Lakes. Pyramid and Walker Lakes are two premier Lahontan cutthroat trout lakes. They are dependent on good flows of high-quality water to sustain fish populations; otherwise, they would become too alkaline. Both are also at the end of closed basins; the Truckee River flows into Pyramid, and the East Fork and West Fork of the Walker River join to flow into Walker Lake. Because flows from the Truckee River have been committed to Pyramid Lake to protect the endangered cui-ui, a native sucker that also inhabits the large desert lake, Pyramid's fishery seems to hold up better than Walker Lake's, which receives less dependable flows from the Walker.

Just 30 miles northeast of Reno on the reservation of the Pyramid Lake Paiute Tribe, Pyramid Lake is 26 miles long, up to 11 miles wide, and 350 feet deep in spots. It is open to trout fishing from fall through spring. The best times to catch trophy Lahontan cutthroat are November through April; flycasting big woolly-looking flies or fishing deep from boats with spoons are common tactics at this artificials-only site. Boaters should be cautious of quick-changing weather conditions that can make this lake treacherous.

The entire west shore of Pyramid Lake between Warrior Point on the north and Popcorn on the south is good for shore fishing and trolling. Trolling is popular on the eastern shoreline between Hell's Kitchen and Anderson Bay. The western shoreline of Walker Lake produces cutthroats in the 1- to 4-pound range. Sportsman's Beach and the Cliffs are particularly popular with shore anglers.

Spawning Sacramento perch (not a perch but a sunfish) at Pyramid can be caught by jigging off the rocky shorelines during May or June.

Lake Tahoe. Lake trout, known here as mackinaw, filled the niche in Lake Tahoe left by the demise of Lahontan cutthroat trout, a species that once migrated into the lake on their spawning runs up the Truckee River from Pyramid Lake.

Although most of Lake Tahoe lies in California, plenty of action still exists along the northern and eastern shores for those fishing on the Nevada side. Lake trout here are found in 100- to 400-foot depths, and successful deep fishing for them requires heavy, specialized equipment. Boaters here troll with downriggers or lead-core line, whereas others jig with heavy spoons.

Fishing year-around is good, although dedicated Tahoe anglers prefer the colder months of November through March. Mackinaw in the 5- to 15-pound range are common, and fish in the 20-pound class are available.

From Sand Harbor to Cave Rock, anglers can also fish shallow near the surface with lighter gear for native rainbows (reared in Marlette Lake for return to Lake Tahoe) and browns, and can occasionally pick up a lake trout. Shore fishing at Cave Rock for brown trout and stocked rainbows is also popular.

Truckee, Carson, and Walker Rivers. Western Nevada's largest rivers are the Truckee, East Carson, Carson, and East and West Forks of the Walker. These are only small streams by some standards, but they all offer good fishing for stocked and wild rainbow trout, as well as a diversity of other wild, and some native, species.

The Truckee River, which flows out of Lake Tahoe, down through the mountains, through the middle of Reno, then east and north to Pyramid Lake, is a premier trout stream of the West. The section from the California line down to the Interstate 80 bridge (upstream from Crystal Peak Park) is designated for artificial lures only and is managed as a wild trout area. This section offers a little bit of every kind of water a fly angler could want.

Anglers can catch stocked rainbow, cutthroat, and brown trout throughout the trophy section and down through the cities of Reno and Sparks and beyond. Brown trout populations increase in those areas where the river is warmer because they tolerate changes in water temperature better. Mountain whitefish are caught upstream from Reno. When water flows are high, the fishing can be excellent east of town downstream to Wadsworth.

The Carson River and the East Fork of the Carson offer good fishing for 12- to 15-inch stocked brown, rainbow, and cutthroat trout near Carson City on the Carson River, and above Dresslerville on the East Carson.

The West Walker flows out of Topaz Lake as the Topaz Canal and offers good fishing in Wilson Canyon for 12- to 15-inch stocked rainbows, browns, and cutthroats in the late fall and winter, when irrigation seasons are over and water flows are reduced.

The first 15 miles of the East Walker in Nevada offers excellent fishing for wild browns and rainbows up to 3 pounds. The catch-and-release area once known as the Rosaschi Ranch, and now managed by the Forest Service, is 2 miles from the California border and extends 7 miles. This catch-and-release area has become crowded because of attention to its special designation; however, the adjoining stretches offer fishing that's just as good.

Lahontan Reservoir. With 10,000 surface acres, 17 miles of length, and nearly 100 miles of shoreline, Lahontan Reservoir is one of the state's top warmwater fisheries. Approximately 20 miles from Fallon, this impoundment has white bass, hybrid stripers, walleye, channel catfish, white catfish, bullhead, yellow perch, largemouth bass, spotted bass, and the occasional rainbow trout.

White bass and 3- to 4-pound wipers concentrate on the confluences of water inflows such as the Truckee Canal and the Carson River at the end of March, and can be caught from shore on a jig or minnow. Popular areas are the No. 9 and 11 beaches. Fish become more widely distributed as the season progresses.

Walleye range up to 14 pounds and are caught where sandy and rocky bottoms combine with emergent vegetation. The end of May signals the beginning of walleye season.

Topaz Lake. Fishing the January 1 opener at Topaz Lake is a good way to celebrate the new year for many anglers. This popular reservoir offers good boat and shore fishing for stocked rainbows. Boaters troll the rocky eastern shoreline to the mouth and then back up the center of the lake.

Smaller reservoirs. Central Nevada has numerous other small lakes and reservoirs that offer

It has been reported that the first tagging of fish in the United States occurred in 1873, when an angler tagged Atlantic salmon in the Penobscot River in Maine.

anglers good opportunities to catch stocked rainbows and some warmwater species, particularly bass. Trout fisheries include Illipah Reservoir, Cave Lake, Groves Lake, and Eagle Valley Reservoir. Trout and bass can both be found at Echo Canyon Reservoir and the reservoirs at Kirch Wildlife Management Area—Adams-McGill, Cold Springs, and Haymeadow. The ponds at Mason Valley Wildlife Management Area offer bass and panfish.

Southern Region

Lake Mead. Located on the southern border of Nevada and Arizona on the Colorado River, Lake Mead was formed when Hoover (now Boulder) Dam was completed in 1935. When full, the water rises to a maximum depth of 590 feet, creating an impoundment that is 110 miles long with 550 miles of shoreline and 162,000 surface acres.

Soon after the dam's completion, the lake was stocked with largemouth bass, black crappie, bluegills, green sunfish, and threadfin shad for forage. To enhance the fishery, biologists tried stocking different species, including striped bass in 1969, although it was not expected that stripers would reproduce in the Colorado system. Reproduction was documented, however, in 1973. Now, the striped bass is the premier gamefish in the reservoir.

The best areas to fish for all species in Lake Mead are in Las Vegas Bay, Calville Bay, and the upper Overton; feeder streams and washes at these sites add nutrients to the lake and enhance the production of forage fish.

Anglers jig cut bait, like frozen anchovies, or troll shad-imitation lures to catch stripers that average 2 pounds. Fish in the 20- to 30-pound range are possible, more commonly in the fall and usually on shad imitations. Beginning in July and continuing through much of the rest of the year, anglers can take striped bass using a variety of topwater lures, often by fishing early and scouting for surface activity.

Largemouth bass are popular at Lake Mead, too. Bass from 4 to 8 pounds are available in addition to smaller specimens. Las Vegas Bay produces good-size bass because of the available nutrients and forage fish.

The Overton Arm is a top spot to fish for black crappie, some of which range up to 3 pounds. Channel catfish up to 8 to 10 pounds are taken on cut anchovies or stinkbaits. Anglers have landed tilapia and smallmouth bass in Lake Mead, although there is no fishery for either, and the lake has a big population of carp.

Lake Mohave and the Colorado River. When Davis Dam, above Laughlin on the Nevada side of the river, was completed in 1951, it formed narrow 67-mile-long Lake Mohave.

The upper 15 miles of the reservoir, where trout are stocked regularly, provides the best fishing for striped bass, which were first found in Mohave in 1980 after being washed over Boulder Dam in high-water years. While most of the stripers in Mohave are less than 14 inches, some weigh up to 60 pounds or more. The best time to pursue them is at night or on slightly breezy days from September through November, on cut anchovies, squid, or large shad-imitating lures.

Striped bass in the Colorado River beneath Davis Dam range from 10 inches to 20 to 30 pounds. Late spring and early summer are good times to fish the river for stripers that have moved up from Arizona's Lake Havasu to spawn.

Anglers can catch stocked trout in the Willow Beach area or below Davis Dam, where there's good access for shore fishing.

Largemouth bass up to 9 pounds inhabit most Mohave coves that have weedbeds, except the cold upper 15 miles, in the spring. When water levels decline in the fall and weedbeds are uncovered is another good time.

Channel catfish up to 15 or 20 pounds are caught throughout the summer on cut bait or stinkbait fished on the bottom. Bluegills are caught throughout the lake below the upper 15 miles.

NEW BRUNSWICK

The largest of the three Maritime Provinces of eastern Canada, New Brunswick is best known for its Atlantic salmon fishing. The province contains several rivers that are among the more renowned and important Atlantic salmon fisheries in North America. In recent years, however, nonresident anglers are also traveling in increasing numbers to this coastal province for smallmouth bass fishing, as New Brunswick has excellent fishing for this species in rivers and lakes.

New Brunswick's inland fishery resource includes 46 freshwater, anadromous, and catadromous fish species. Approximately 90 percent of sportfishing efforts are directed at brook trout, Atlantic salmon, smallmouth bass, landlocked salmon, white perch,

Early summer mornings find Lake Mead's stripers active.

yellow perch, and chain pickerel. Only 5 percent of angling effort is directed at coastal species. This is spread among striped bass, American shad, mackerel, cod, flounder, and pollock, and these species are greatly underutilized.

New Brunswick attracts many American anglers because of its proximity to the eastern United States; these anglers are primarily interested in salmon and bass. It attracts other Canadian visitors because of its Atlantic salmon. The catch and effort overall for Atlantic salmon have increased in recent years, despite a decline in the total Canadian salmon abundance and catch since 1970. The Miramichi watershed supports 60 to 70 percent of the provincial angler effort for Atlantic salmon. Angling restrictions have been placed on many New Brunswick salmon rivers with insufficient juvenile and adult populations.

Brook trout are the most popular species among resident anglers and are widely available in the province. Effort and catch per day for this species, however, have decreased in recent years, primarily due to overfishing, habitat degradation, and introduction of competitive fish species.

Smallmouth bass angling continues to increase in popularity in southwestern New Brunswick waters. The overall catch of these fish doubled between 1990 and 1995. According to creel surveys, more than 95 percent of bass are released. Other warmwater fish—particularly white perch, yellow perch and chain pickerel—are significantly less popular than the aforementioned species. Ice fishing, which is legal from January 1 through March 31, is permissible in selected waters for all species; this method is not especially popular, although ice fishing in frozen estuaries for smelt has a good following.

Catch and effort for coastal species such as flounder, mackerel, and pollock have remained relatively constant for several decades. Recreational fisheries for striped bass have declined, and highly restrictive harvest limits have been imposed.

Nonresidents are required by law to be accompanied by a licensed guide when angling in New Brunswick's designated Atlantic salmon waters. A licensed guide is not required when angling in other waters for landlocked salmon, brook trout, or smallmouth bass; however, there is no substitute for local knowledge, and the services of a licensed guide are recommended for visitors, at least in the short term.

Atlantic Salmon

Atlantic salmon are locally considered the "king" of sportfish, a reputation derived from their strong fight and acrobatics when hooked. They are the fish most sought after by nonresident anglers.

New Brunswick rivers currently produce 80 percent of the Maritime Provinces' overall Atlantic salmon fishery. In the past, when the commercial fishery was operating, Canada harvested about 17 percent of the world's Atlantic salmon, of which 25

Anglers fish the Miramichi River for Atlantic salmon.

percent were fish originating in New Brunswick.

Atlantic salmon inhabit nearly every stream with unrestricted access to the sea. Adult salmon are known to frequent 100 streams and rivers, and approximately 50 of these support an angling fishery. The best known salmon waters in New Brunswick are the Miramichi, Restigouche, Saint John, and Tobique Rivers. The Main Southwest Miramichi, which is extremely popular, is a lovely, long, winding, generally shallow river with many bars and pools, and it is an easy river to wade under most circumstances. It is wide by the standards of most trout anglers, and its regular visitors are known for long casting, although that is not an absolute necessity.

New Brunswick offers 2,528 kilometers of fishable salmon waters, of which 850 kilometers provide unrestricted public access. Approximately 45 percent of the salmon water is adjacent to private or freehold property, and landowner permission is required to angle there. The province leases about 7 percent, or 182 kilometers, of good salmon water to clubs and corporate interests. Another 205 kilometers of Crown Reserve water is available exclusively to residents fortunate enough to have their applications drawn from a lottery-type process.

On the Miramichi system, access to private waters is readily available through several lodges catering to visiting anglers. Guests at these operations enjoy exclusive angling on the waters controlled by the host lodge. The Restigouche system is accessible only to anglers invited as guests of the controlling club or corporate interests. The Saint John and Tobique Rivers are public domain and readily accessible.

Angling for Atlantic salmon in New Brunswick was first recognized as sport in the 1850s, but took on a modern popularity only after World War II. Since the 1920s, Atlantic salmon abundance has declined substantially. Although Atlantic salmon returns from the ocean have been declining, most juvenile populations in New Brunswick's rivers appear reasonably healthy. Anglers remain optimistic that improvements in salmon returns to the rivers and to the recreational fishery will occur.

Fly fishing is the only legal method of angling for Atlantic salmon in this province. Atlantic salmon angling has historically been that of catch-and-retain, yet hook-and-release regulations for all large salmon greater than 63 centimeters (25 inches) in total length were implemented in New Brunswick in 1984. The province has a season-total bag limit of eight grilse (fish less than 63 centimeters in total length). Nonresident anglers require a guide when angling for salmon. Angler catches have averaged 41,645 grilse (42 percent released) and 14,800 multi-sea-winter fish (100 percent mandatory release) during the period 1987 to 1995. This is for combined kelt and bright fish.

Nonresidents continue to go to New Brunswick to angle for salmon regardless of the requirements for guides or the lower catches in the past few years. Angler and nonangler alike recognize the importance of the fishery to the economy of the province, especially to the smaller communities along the rivers. More than 100 businesses provide outfitting services to salmon anglers.

Atlantic salmon season opens annually on April 15; this includes the time frame referred to as kelt fishing, as there is no longer a distinct kelt season. Actual angling opportunity begins when the rivers are ice-free.

New Brunswick has two distinct Atlantic salmon fisheries, the kelt, or "spring," fishery and the summer, or "bright," fishery.

The kelt fishery is primarily focused on the Miramichi system and runs from opening day until late May. This fishery focuses on Atlantic salmon that are descending the river, having spent the winter under the ice. Local terminology describes these as "black" salmon; however, this is clearly a misnomer, as fish regain their bright ocean camouflage immediately upon starting their descent. This is the only time when Atlantic salmon actively feed while in freshwater and are therefore eager to take a fly. Angling for kelts is almost entirely done from a boat, in high, coldwater conditions. The most common tackle is 8- or 9-weight full-sink or sink-tip lines, 9- to 10-foot rods, and large, brightly colored streamer flies.

The bright fishery is focused on the timing of runs, and the timing varies from river to river. The earliest fish show up in the Restigouche system in early June, in the Saint John in mid-June, and in the Miramichi in early July. Peak timing on all systems is the first three weeks of July. The Miramichi system receives a second important run in mid-September, and enjoys excellent angling from then until the season closure in mid-October; the availability of these fish is subject to annual variation, depending on water levels, rainfall, and temperatures.

Most angling on the Restigouche is from long motorized canoes, whereas on the other rivers it is by wading. In all cases, the most common tackle is 8- or 9-weight floating lines, 9- to 14-foot leaders (8- to 12-pound tippets), reels that hold 150 yards of 25-pound backing, 9- or 10-foot rods, and both wet and dry flies in sizes 2 to 10.

The importance of Atlantic salmon angling to New Brunswick is reflected in the province's decision to proclaim an Atlantic salmon fly as an official symbol in 1993. The symbolic salmon fly was designated as the "Picture Province" and designed by Warren Duncan. It comprised the following: a tag of gold symbolizing the value of Atlantic salmon to New Brunswick; a butt of green floss honoring the fiddlehead; a tail of red goose fibers to match Canada's flag, indicating New Brunswick's ties with the nation; a body of cranberry, as cranberry is one of New Brunswick's official colors; a rib of medium oval gold tinsel; a hackle of lemon yellow, which is the background color of New Brunswick's flag; and a wing of hair from the black bear, which roams widely in the province.

Landlocked Salmon

Landlocked salmon are managed in approximately 40 lakes and two rivers, all located in the Saint John, Musquash, Magaguadavic, and St. Croix watersheds in New Brunswick. Landlocked and sea-run salmon have similar life cycles, except adult landlocked salmon substitute freshwater lakes for the ocean. The importance of landlocked salmon to the recreational fishery has increased substantially over the past decade with the implementation of an effective stocking program that produces native strains of fish. Restrictive daily catches and minimum length limits have also improved the quality of the fishery.

Lakes that support landlocked salmon have basically clean, cool, well-oxygenated water. Other physical and biological requirements include adequate forage species and access to suitable spawning/nursery grounds. Sixteen lakes, notably East Grand, Chamcook, Magaguadavic, Digdeguash, Oromocto, Loch Alva, Crystal, and Sisson, currently provide the majority of the landlocked salmon fisheries in New Brunswick. River fisheries occur in the St. Croix and Magaguadavic Rivers.

The present landlocked salmon distribution is heavily weighted toward the southwestern portion of the province. The remaining populations are randomly scattered throughout northwestern and southeastern New Brunswick. In total, New Brunswick's landlocked salmon lakes cover less than 150,000 acres, with the southwest having more than three-quarters of the provincial total.

The best landlocked salmon fishing occurs in the four- to five-week period following ice out and again in September. Trolling with tandem streamer flies or minnow-imitating plugs is the most popular and productive technique.

The demand on landlocked salmon continues to increase, although effort is light in comparison with

---

Thanks to high rates of evaporation, the Red Sea and the Persian Gulf have the saltiest water in the world.

many other jurisdictions in eastern Canada and the U.S. Fishing pressure has especially increased on the prime landlocked salmon waters. Landlocked salmon angling, to many anglers, offers a suitable alternative to brook trout and sea-run Atlantic salmon fishing, and with ample opportunity to harvest fish for the table as well.

Brook Trout

As the most abundant coldwater gamefish in New Brunswick, the brook trout has always been, and still is, the most sought-after species by resident anglers. Brook trout are found virtually everywhere in the province, with the exception of acid peat moss lakes in the eastern region. This includes many coastal rivers and streams. Most bodies of water, with the exception of a few in the north-central region of the province, are now accessible to the brook trout angler.

New Brunswick contains approximately 40,000 kilometers of streams that are suitable habitat for brook trout, and more than 2,000 lakes that contain this species. The most productive brook trout lakes are small, less than 80 hectares. The biggest concentration of lakes under 80 hectares is in the northern and western portions of the province, while the largest lakes are in the southern portion. The absence of predatory species such as chain pickerel and smallmouth bass in northern and western drainages benefits brook trout production.

The average size of brook trout in the province is 5 centimeters by the end of the first growing season, 10 to 13 centimeters after the second, and 20 to 25 centimeters after the third. Brook trout older than five years are rare, with two- and three-year-olds constituting the bulk of the catch. Brook trout in certain lakes have reached 2 to 3 kilograms.

Some New Brunswick brook trout migrate to saltwater or brackish water, where they put on extra growth and become known locally as "sea trout." Virtually all coastal rivers and streams once had sea-run fish; however, sea-run populations of brook trout have been declining due to increased pre-dation by seals and overexploitation by anglers. The Miramichi River system offers excellent opportunity for angling. Stems of note include Cains River, North Branch Main Southwest Miramichi River, Beadle Brook, Dungarvon River, and the Northwest Miramichi River. The Tabusintac River is another excellent river for sea-run brook trout.

Migratory behavior is variable from river to river, but in all cases, growth in the estuary and marine environment is rapid. Returning fish may weigh as much as 3 kilograms, although the average is considerably less.

New Brunswick waters still provide good-quality brook trout fishing, although the number of larger fish available has decreased. In some waters, recreational angling has contributed to reduced stocks. In recent years, however, effort for this species has been reduced overall, partly as a result of a shift in angler preference to smallmouth bass angling and of the introduction of competitive fish species.

Most of New Brunswick's trout lakes have natural or wild fish. The lakes with the best wild specimens tend to occur in waters that are distant from major population centers, and many are in geologically elevated areas.

Generally the best fishing is from mid-May through late June. After this time, brook trout congregate in coldwater spring holes; at this time, intimate local knowledge is required for success. The most popular method of fishing for brook trout is with live worms and a small spinner. Fly anglers use standard streamer patterns in the early season and match the hatch as the season wears on.

The stocking of 120 lakes with up to 190,000 brook trout per year has resulted in the creation of additional angling opportunities for fish of 20-centimeters and larger. Hatchery releases, however, account for a minute portion of the total brook trout catch.

Smallmouth Bass

Although smallmouth bass are not native to the province, increased interest and enthusiasm have been demonstrated by anglers, and this species now ranks second in popularity with nonresidents. Smallmouth bass were introduced into New Brunswick about 1870, and have become established throughout southwestern New Brunswick in the Saint John, Magaguadavic, and St. Croix drainages.

Self-sustaining populations of smallmouths are known to inhabit 40 lakes, which range from shallow mesotrophic ponds to deep, clear oligotrophic lakes having both warmwater and coldwater fisheries. The provincial government has taken a cautious approach in establishing smallmouth bass populations outside its present range. The geographical range of the smallmouth bass has been extended in recent years through the good intentions but illegal actions of individual anglers. Bass are opportunistic, competitive, and hardy, and in some instances are responsible for the decline of brook trout populations.

The most obvious of New Brunswick's smallmouth bass waters is the massive (60-mile-long) lake just north of the capital city of Fredericton, locally called the Mactaquac Headpond. This is an impoundment of the St. John River and it has plentiful, and large, smallmouths. Most of the other rock- and boulder-laden smallmouth lakes in southwestern New Brunswick are easy to find and cool enough to provide good angling throughout the summer. Among the more notable ones are Harvey, Oromocto, East Grand, Little Magaguadavic, and George. These are places where you can fish with a guide or on your own (if the latter, be extremely careful, as some are tricky to navigate), and they hold enough bass to provide reasonable success even when angling conditions aren't prime.

Some good river fishing is possible as well. One of the most notable waters is the Meduxnekeag River from Jackson Falls to Woodstock (which also has nice brown trout). A wide range of tackle choices makes fishing suitable to anglers of all interests, but fly and spinning gear are favored, especially early in the season.

Natives of New Brunswick have only recently recognized the social and economic benefits of smallmouth bass, as bass fishing increased dramatically in the 1980s and 1990s. Catches increased approximately eightfold. One unique aspect of this fishery is the ability of bass to be successfully hooked and released. This provides an opportunity to increase angling effort without greatly affecting total mortality.

The spawning period in New Brunswick is from mid-May to mid-June but varies slightly from year to year and area to area depending on water temperature and spring freshet. The best angling also occurs from mid-May to mid-June and picks up again from late August through the season closure in mid-October. Although smallmouth bass weighing more than 5 pounds have been caught in New Brunswick, most bass average $1^1/_2$ to 2 pounds.

Other Species

Brown trout/lake trout. New Brunswick has a limited brown trout population. These fish occur in the Loch Lomond Lakes, Meduxnekeag River, and the lower Digdeguash River system, and are most popular with a handful of anglers from those areas. The average size is 1 pound, with specimens in the 3- to 5-pound range not uncommon.

Lake trout inhabit 12 lakes in the province. The most notable of these are Long and Serpentine Lakes in the north, and Chamcook Lake in the south. To most provincial anglers, fishing for lakers is strictly an ice-out fishery, enjoyed by trolling with assorted lures and tandem streamers. The average size is 2 to 5 pounds, with an occasional fish over 10 pounds.

American shad. Shad are a virtually overlooked fishery in New Brunswick. They are most abundant in the Saint John and Miramichi Rivers, and angling effort is concentrated predominantly in the latter. In the vast lower reaches of the Saint John River, concentrations of shad are difficult to locate and are not normally a targeted species. Because the Miramichi is a designated Atlantic salmon river, fishing for shad there is with flies only. The best fishing is during the first three weeks of June. Suggested tackle is an 8- or 9-weight outfit, with sinking-tip lines, 4- to 8-foot leaders, and unweighted white or yellow flies.

White perch. The white perch is known to inhabit 28 lakes in New Brunswick, all but one in the southwestern region. This species is also found in the St. Croix, Bocabec, Gaspereau, Miramichi, and Saint John Rivers. Lakes known to have good angling populations include North, McAdam, Bolton, and Second Eel.

New Brunswick anglers catch a fair number of these good table fish annually. The largest recorded fish taken from freshwater weighed 4.75 pounds and was 19 inches long— several times larger than the average catch. Most white perch are caught in freshwater, but some are taken from waters in the upper estuaries. Saltwater populations along the New Brunswick coastline are scattered and of small size.

The best white perch angling occurs just after ice out and again in mid-September, primarily with spinning gear and angle worms or small plastic jigs and grubs.

Yellow perch. Yellow perch exist throughout the province and are treated as coarse fish by most anglers in New Brunswick, although some angle for them as table fare. Endemic to many waters in New Brunswick, yellow perch are found in all counties except Albert and are particularly abundant in the southwestern region. The species is documented in 82 lakes and several streams, and has been found in the Miramichi River estuary. The highest catches occur in the Saint John watershed followed by the St. Croix and Miramichi drainages.

Yellow perch reach 38 centimeters in length in the Canaan River, but in most waters they average 17 to 23 centimeters. They are caught quite shallow here in the summer. There are no creel limits or minimum length limits for the yellow perch, which does not have sportfish status. Angling for yellow perch in inland waters is restricted to those seasons that are open for sportfish.

Saltwater and Estuarial Fisheries

The New Brunswick coastline is irregular, possessing deep bays, inlets, and estuaries. It is distinguished by its border with the 160-mile long Bay of Fundy, which is narrow in the headwaters region and produces remarkable 30- to 50-foot variations between high and low tides. Lower estuarial and coastal species in New Brunswick include smelt, striped bass, American shad, mackerel, cod, flounder, pollock, and dogfish sharks. Guide or charter boat services are minimal at best. Visitors are best advised to consult with locals at the wharves in the numerous fishing communities along the coast.

The majority of angling effort occurs in Passamaquoddy Bay, Bay of Chaleur to the northeast, and Northumberland Strait, which separates New Brunswick from Prince Edward Island. Striped bass, cod, and mackerel are angled in northern coastal or estuarial waters, whereas cod, flounder, and pollock are caught primarily in Bay of Fundy waters to the south. Striped bass are taken primarily in Tabusintac, Richibucto, Kouchibouguac, Nepisiguit, and Miramichi estuaries, and to a lesser extent the lower Saint John River.

New Brunswick has two distinct populations of striped bass. One is that of the most nortern strain of this species in the southern Gulf of St. Lawrence. These fish primarily spawn in the Miramichi estuary and migrate locally in the southern Gulf of St. Lawrence. They average 2 to 3 pounds; 20-pounders are considered trophy size. Overexploitation by both commercial and sportfishing interests has contributed to declining numbers. The commercial fishery, including the sale of bycatch, has been stopped. Angling for these fish is restricted to catch-and-release only. Most angling effort occurs in the Miramichi, Tabusintac, and Nepisiguit estuaries.

The other striped bass population is a migratory one that spawns in rivers of the Bay of Fundy. It is part of the same population that migrates through American coastal waters south to Florida; New Brunswick waters are the extreme northern edge of its range. The average size of these stripers is 6 to 8 pounds, but some are in the 30- to 40-pound class. Anglers are permitted to retain one fish (check the size limit) per day, with a minimum size restriction. The decline in population is attributable to man-made structures, such as the Mactaquac Dam on the Saint John River and a municipal causeway across the Petticodiac River in the Moncton/Riverview area, which prohibit these fish from reaching their spawning grounds. Most angling effort is concentrated in the estuaries of the Saint John, St. Croix, and Magaguadavic Rivers.

The potential for saltwater angling expansion along the province's extensive coastline is huge, as hundreds of thousands of angler days could be supported without overexploitation of prolific species, especially mackerel, flounder, dogfish, and pollock.

NEWFOUNDLAND AND LABRADOR

Canada's easternmost province comprises two geographically separate and distinct areas: Newfoundland, a large island of more than 42,000 square miles situated off Canada's east coast, and Labrador, a much larger landmass of nearly 115,000 square miles lying to the northeast of Quebec. Each boasts a wide variety of freshwater, as well as limited saltwater, sportfishing opportunities.

In Newfoundland, the major interests are rainbow trout, brown trout, brook trout (locally called Eastern brook trout), anadromous (sea-run) brown and rainbow (steelhead) trout, sea-run brook trout, arctic charr, and Atlantic salmon. In Labrador they are Atlantic salmon, brook trout, ouananiche (landlocked Atlantic salmon), sea-run brook trout, northern pike, whitefish, burbot, arctic charr, lake trout, landlocked charr, and splake.

Salmon are of special interest in this province. About 60 percent of North America's Atlantic salmon rivers exist here. More than 180 waterways have been identified as rivers with significant migrations of salmon. Several smaller flowages sustain small annual salmon runs. The major streams are called "scheduled" rivers and are restricted to fly fishing during the short summer season between early June and early September. Two rivers—the Humber and Gander—have later runs and also offer an extended period of catch-and-release angling lasting through the end of September.

In freshwater, the majority of river angling is restricted to fly fishing and casting techniques; in most large lakes and ponds, various methods are permitted, including trolling or angling with lures and baits.

Saltwater angling is generally confined to stream estuaries, where sea-run brown, rainbow, or brook trout prepare to migrate upstream. Local anglers occasionally pursue mackerel by lure and spinning rod, and a fledgling shark fishery with heavier tackle is gaining popularity among tour boat owners.

The giant bluefin tuna fishery that once existed in eastern Newfoundland disappeared with declines in such food fish as capelin and herring. Collapse of northern cod stocks due to overharvesting has virtually eliminated the commercial cod fishery. "Cod jigging," a traditional method of snagging codfish with a strong waxed-cord line and heavily weighted hook, has been a mainstay of the resident food fishery for centuries, but even this practice is under strict control and annual review. The need to rebuild stocks has put any permanent recreational saltwater fishery for groundfish, especially cod and halibut, on the back burner for the immediate future.

Newfoundland

A large, sparsely populated island, Newfoundland is about equal in size to the combined states of Maine and New Hampshire and has a surprising 8,498 miles of rugged coastline. About one-third of the island's population of 500,000 resides in the capital city of St. John's and surrounding communities on the east coast's Avalon Peninsula.

Although Newfoundland has a modern highway system, it is accessible to nonresidents only by air or sea. Four airports serve the island portion of Newfoundland: Deer Lake and Stephenville on the west coast, Gander near mid-island, and St. John's on the east coast. Major carriers fly into these, and smaller regional airlines service outlying areas. Large, oceangoing ferries transport vehicles and passengers from North Sydney, Nova Scotia, to Port aux Basques, Newfoundland, on a year-round basis, a 90-mile jaunt that lasts about 6 hours. During summer months an alternate service lands on the southeast coast at Argentia, site of a former U.S. naval base. This crossing takes about 16 hours and is available twice weekly. Anglers wishing to spend some time in Newfoundland with their own vehicles have these choices; in both instances, reservations are recommended.

The Trans-Canada Highway runs across Newfoundland for 540 miles, from Port aux Basques to St. John's, with paved secondary roads opening access to coastal communities. Modern lodging, restaurants, and other facilities across the

One Russian Beluga sturgeon was weighed in at 3,359 pounds.

island provide a variety of services and amenities for the traveling angler, the majority of whom are interested in salmon.

Thanks largely to a moratorium on commercial salmon nets and a buyout of most commercial salmon licenses imposed by the Canadian government in 1991, Atlantic salmon stocks have made a strong recovery. This political decision was hailed by many anglers as one of the most significant conservation actions of the twentieth century. The vast majority of commercial fishermen relinquished their salmon licenses, and wild Atlantic salmon are now free to enter streams directly from their ocean feeding grounds without encountering gill-net obstructions.

All rivers on the island are considered "public" water. Although all of the scheduled salmon rivers are open to nonresident anglers, they must employ local guides or outfitters. Many government-inspected and -licensed outfitters and guiding services offer packages in various locations across the island. Facilities range from rustic to resort class.

For those seeking privacy and an undisturbed wilderness setting, some outfitters provide access to remote rivers inland or along the island's south coast, where there are no (or very few) roads. Tourists are able to fish within a half mile (800 meters) of a provincial highway for trout only, without hiring a guide, which offers family recreational opportunities.

Salmon populations in most rivers are dominated by grilse—salmon that have been at sea only one year before returning to spawn. These fish generally measure under 26 inches and weigh 6 pounds or less. With escapement of large salmon from commercial nets and an increase of repeat-spawning grilse, the relative mix of larger salmon to grilse has increased significantly.

In addition to salmon, the island of Newfoundland contains some of the world's most productive, and interesting, trout waters. Sea-run brook trout, brown trout, and rainbow trout enter many of the island's rivers at various times of the spring and summer. Visitors to St. John's might consider bringing along a fly rod, as some of the best brown trout angling can be found on several streams weaving through the city.

Most small ponds or lakes contain populations of small, wild resident Eastern brook trout, called "mud trout" by residents. In the more remote areas of the island that have limited access, 2- or 3-pound brook trout can be caught on occasion.

Near L'Anse aux Meadows, a UNESCO World Heritage site where Vikings landed and settled in North America long before Columbus, lies Pistolet Bay and its rivers. Here, wild arctic charr can be attracted by skilled fly anglers.

Arctic charr that escaped an aquaculture-rearing project inhabit Grand Lake on the west coast. At 87 miles long, Grand is the island's largest lake. Another product of aquaculture escapement, the rainbow trout, is found in the Bay d'Espoir area of the south coast, where large specimens may be taken below the hydrogenerating plant.

Western region. The west coast of Newfoundland has some of the finest salmon rivers in the province. Typical rivers are spate streams—crystal clear and icy cold—which peak during the spring breakup and become more logy as summer progresses. They are fed from the Long Range Mountain highlands, a plateau that rises majestically some 2,000 feet from the coast and extends from Port aux Basques to the tip of the Great Northern Peninsula. The Trans-Canada Highway and other roads in the provincial network pass over many of these rivers, providing ready access to nearby salmon pools.

Angling pioneer Lee Wulff made many of these rivers well known in his writing and films. They include the Grand Codroy, Serpentine, Harry's, River of Ponds, Portland Creek, Lomond, and the mighty Humber. Other rivers of interest include Crabbes, Robinsons, Southwest Brook, Bottom Brook, Sop's Arm, Main River, Fishell's, St. Genevieve, Castors, Big East, and Torrent, although these are just a few. Numerous opportunities to pursue Atlantic salmon exist on this coast.

The dominant waterway is the Humber River, which begins high in the mountains behind Gros Morne National Park and, after flowing nearly 90 miles, exits into the Bay of Islands near the modern city of Corner Brook. The Lower Humber is known for its genetic strain of large salmon that can tip the scales at more than 50 pounds, and each season experienced veterans are able to subdue and release salmon in this weight class.

One mecca for resident salmon anglers on the Upper Humber River is Sir Richard Squires Park. This site is accessible by road and lies to the northeast of Deer Lake via the community of Cormack. The river here is wide and shallow, and dominated by Big Falls, a natural barrier that temporarily slows fish migration. Peak runs usually occur here in early July and last for three to four weeks.

Popular salmon flies are the Blue Charm, Thunder & Lightning, Orange Puppy, Green Highlander, and many more that are variations of classic British patterns. The original complicated feather wings are generally replaced with a thatch of black moose hair, which is plentiful on the island. Productive locally tied flies are readily available at area stores.

As noted, Pistolet Bay at the top of the Northern Peninsula has small runs of arctic charr, while Eastern brook trout may be found in numerous lakes and ponds throughout the west coast. Sea-run brook trout can be caught later in the summer at most estuaries. The Cloud River is a popular sea trout river on the northeast side of the peninsula. The Cloud also contains Atlantic salmon and is accessible primarily by boat from the community of Roddickton.

Grand Lake, and interconnecting Sandy and

Birchy Lakes, contain landlocked salmon, known here as ouananiche, as well as trophy-size brook trout and aquaculture-raised charr escapees. Spring season, just after ice-out, is the best time to pursue these species, usually with spinning tackle or live bait. Access to Grand Lake is in the community of Howley, which is about 20 road miles east of Deer Lake.

Several ponds in the interior of the Great Northern Peninsula are accessible by a series of woods roads and offer casual fishing for brook trout. Many of the larger or more remote watersheds such as Bluey, Adies Lake, Star Lake, Cat Arm Reservoir, Ten Mile Lake, and Southwest Pond once held trout in the 5-pound class, and a few such specimens are still taken from time to time, although the relative size declined as woods-road construction provided ease of access.

Gros Morne National Park near Bonne Bay manages its own salmon rivers and resources, and requires a special park fishing license for angling. These are available at park offices.

South coast. Most salmon rivers of the south coast are isolated and difficult to access, and these conditions have preserved excellent angling for Atlantic salmon. Rivers such as the Garia, LaPoile, and Grey are accessible only via a boat trip on saltwater from small communities, or by helicopter.

A partially paved road system leads from the Trans-Canada Highway through a rugged landscape to Burgeo, once a prosperous south coast fishing community, and the site of Grandy's Brook. The road also provides access to interior lakes and ponds that provide recreational angling for trout and landlocked salmon. It is a popular jumping off point for canoeists.

Due to their isolation, most south coast rivers receive low resident pressure, and the quality of angling is excellent, although a high percentage of salmon here are grilse. Outfitters provide nonresident access to these remote areas.

The Conne River, in addition to salmon angling, sustains a limited food fishery for the Conne River Indian Band, Newfoundland's only status band with a reserve located in Baie d'Espoir. A major attraction here is the river below the Baie d'Espoir hydroelectric facility, where escaped pen-raised rainbow trout are plentiful and can be taken readily by lure or fly throughout a long season.

Interior region. In central Newfoundland, the Exploits and Gander Rivers, and their tributaries, dominate the much flatter landscape. Both rivers were monitored for several years by counting fences and showed significant increases in salmon populations following the moratorium. By the late 1990s, the runs on each had increased from an average of 5,000 to 7,000 fish in previous years to more than 25,000. The Exploits watershed, including connecting lakes and ponds, is the island's longest at more than 200 miles.

The lower portion of the Exploits is readily accessible and is most popular with resident anglers, as it flows near the communities of Bishops Falls and Grand Falls–Windsor. At peak times, hundreds of anglers can be observed from the Exploits bridge near Bishops Falls as they fish local pools by wading or from boats.

A project completed in the late 1990s at the Exploits River near Grand Falls-Windsor is a migration bypass route and Salmon Interpretation Centre. Spearheaded by the Environment Resources Management Association volunteer group, the complex provides a glass-walled viewing area for visitors to watch salmon on their way upstream. The fish ladder provides an unobstructed path for salmon to reach spawning areas farther upriver.

A hidden gem of the Exploits is Great Rattling Brook, a small, intimate tributary that contains a high percentage of large salmon. Accessible by a gravel woods road and short hike, or with the aid of a local outfitter, the stream contains numerous small pools and excellent dry-fly water.

Farther east, the main stem of the Gander River is roughly 32 miles long as it exits from Gander Lake near the community of Appleton and enters saltwater at George's Point in Gander Bay. The river is shallow and contains four ponds, or "steadies" as they are known locally, connected by intimidating rapids and narrows. There are numerous pools on this river, and the ratio of salmon to grilse is good. The Northwest Gander is a major tributary that wanders through a remote wilderness area as it nears headwaters.

Much of the main river is accessible only by boat, and a unique river craft has been developed over decades to navigate the shallow and often narrow access points. The Gander River boat is a 25-foot-long freighter canoe built from locally cut and seasoned spruce planks and juniper ribbing. A typical craft is powered by a 20-horsepower outboard. Intimate knowledge of the river is a must, and local guides have passed this information down from generation to generation.

The Gander River Management Association secured approval from the provincial government to initiate a pilot project in a specific watershed management scheme. Begun in 1997, it was the first for the province and included a special Gander River license to fish these waters. The permits are available at local stores and through any of several outfitters.

In a similar pilot project, regeneration of the Indian Bay watershed near Gander began in the early 1990s and was designed to rebuild populations of the trophy brook trout that were once plentiful in this series of interconnected ponds and streams. Positive achievements have resulted, and large trout stocks there have been rebuilding.

Other salmon rivers of interest in the central region include the Indian River located near

> The existence of rods for fishing dates back to 2000 B.C. in Egypt, but the use of rods for more than just an extension of the line didn't come about until the advent of flycasting in the eighteenth century.

Springdale, the Gambo River to the east of Gander, and the Terra Nova River, a popular cottage area where a successful rebuilding of salmon stocks was achieved in a project led by the local rural development association.

Eastern region. The eastern region as described here excludes the Avalon Peninsula but does include several salmon rivers located on the Burin Peninsula and watersheds. These are within the Bay du Nord Provincial Wilderness Reserve.

The most significant waterway here is Long Harbour River, with lesser streams including Bay d'Loup, Piper's Hole, North Harbour, and Northwest. Many rivers are accessible by road or a short hike.

Terra Nova National Park lies between Glovertown and Port Blandford, and, as in the case with Gros Morne, a special park license is required to fish on salmon rivers within park boundaries.

There are many secondary streams on the Bonavista and Burin Peninsulas that have small runs of Atlantic salmon and sea-run trout. One such stream near Clarenville, the Shoal Harbour River, is unique due to a resource mix that includes sea-run and resident brook trout, brown trout, rainbow trout, Atlantic salmon, and the remnants of an experimental Pacific pink salmon introduction from the 1960s.

Rivers in this area generally have earlier migrations of salmon than west coast or central rivers and are populated primarily by grilse. Most interior areas offer angling for brook trout and landlocked salmon. A handful of outfitters provide access to the few salmon rivers lying within boundaries of the Bay du Nord Wilderness Reserve.

Avalon Peninsula. The Avalon Peninsula, which is as far east as you can go in North America, contains the highest density of human population and the widest diversity of salmonid species on the island. Rainbow, brook, and brown trout, as well as Atlantic salmon, can all be caught on rivers of the Avalon.

Visitors to St. John's are often surprised to learn that excellent brown trout angling is available on streams that flow through the city center and border on busy thoroughfares or meander through residential areas. The Waterford River, Quidi Vidi, and Long Pond are among the best bets for quick, casual fly fishing.

Indigenous species are highlighted in a glass-walled fluvarium at the Freshwater Resource Centre, where visitors may see fish in their natural habitat. This site on Long Pond is a stone's throw from Confederation Building, the seat of government; across the pond are the grounds of Memorial University. Brown trout are plentiful in Long Pond and connecting streams.

Large anadromous brown trout of more than 20 pounds have been caught within a half-hour drive of the capital at other parts of the Avalon Peninsula. Sites include Renews River estuary, Cape Royal, Bay Bulls, Manuels River, Kelligrews River, and Topsail Beach, to name but a few.

Rainbow trout inhabit several rivers and ponds between St. John's and Portugal Cove, including Three Island Pond, Ocean Pond, Great Cove, and Gallow's Cove Pond.

The Avalon's top salmon river is the Salmonier. Other salmon streams include the Renous, Biscay Bay, Northwest Trepassey, Branch, and Little Salmonier. The Rocky River and Colinet River, virtually destroyed by commercial overfishing, have slowly recovered thanks to projects by local conservation organizations.

Small brook trout are found in most ponds of the Avalon Peninsula, especially within boundaries of the Avalon Wilderness Reserve, where access is limited. Other productive ponds are located near the Witless Bay line and St. Mary's Bay.

Many Avalon-area salmon anglers, however, prefer a trip to less-populated regions of the province, where abundance and choices of rivers may be greater and crowding less a problem.

Labrador

For a genuine wilderness experience and quality of angling equal to the world's top exotic locales, Labrador still ranks among the best. There are few remaining pristine wilderness areas in eastern North America that contain such a diversity of resources as Labrador, and there is plenty of elbow room. This huge landmass contains a population of only 35,000 people; this distribution is akin to spreading the population of Bangor, Maine, over an area as large as all of the New England states. To say it is underpopulated is a gross understatement.

This enormous region is dotted with hundreds of pristine lakes and raging rivers, expansive forests of fir and spruce, and some of eastern North America's highest mountains. Labrador has a diversity of landscapes, ranging from breathtaking fiords rising from the sea to giant icebergs floating south on the Labrador current, resembling a fleet of white sailing ships on the horizon.

Several species inhabit the waters of Labrador, including northern pike, lake trout, splake, landlocked salmon, brook trout, landlocked charr, and whitefish in the south and west; Atlantic salmon in coastal rivers; and sea-run arctic charr in the northern areas.

Dozens of government-inspected and -licensed outfitters provide access to nonresident anglers, who are required by provincial regulation to hire outfitter services above 52° north latitude. This includes most of Labrador. Facilities vary from simple and efficient to opulent and luxurious, and a range of creature comforts is offered. Most of the fishing camps are fly-in operations, and pressure on their resources is minimal.

The majority of outfitters impose catch-and-release restrictions; retention of one or two trophy fish enables them to preserve the quality of the

Excellent brook trout fishing exists in streams like this in Labrador.

fishery. Fly fishing for trout and salmon is particularly popular, but casting with spinning gear and some trolling are also practiced. Atlantic salmon are enticed to any of the normal hair-wing patterns and to large Bomber dry flies constructed of spun and clipped deer hair and a bright orange palmered hackle. The Bomber and smaller Orange Bug are also good for taking large trout.

Fishing with large flies for big brook trout (and to some extent northern pike), especially surface products such as hair mice, is a Labrador phenomenon that has to be seen to be believed. One reason why large surface flies work so well, sometimes drifted freely and sometimes skittered or riffled across the surface, is that brook trout here include lemmings in their diet. It is not unusual to capture a trout with a belly containing one or more of these creatures. Although mouse imitations work on these fish, such large flies as the Bomber, Muddler Minnow, and Woolly Worm are also effective.

In addition to lemmings, Labrador is known for its large hexagenia hatches, although other natural insect foods include stoneflies, mayflies, caddis, and sedges. Good trout flies here include stimulators and enticers, Stoneflies, Irresistibles, Muddlers, Wulffs, and most of the insect simulations. Charr are normally taken on lures and spinning tackle but provide an excellent challenge for fly fishing. Small, dark nymphs or brightly colored streamers are good choices for charr. Lake trout and pike are caught on a wide range of offerings, as are landlocked salmon.

Roads are few in Labrador, and travel to the vast interior has been limited to float-equipped aircraft or helicopters. This isolation has helped in part to preserve Labrador's fabulous angling resources and pristine wilderness. The Trans-Labrador Highway has opened road access to towns such as Happy Valley-Goose Bay, but is normally under construction or repair due to extreme weather conditions, and motorists should exercise caution. A road is planned along the east coast to connect the communities of Red Bay and Cartwright. Once a link is completed between Cartwright and Happy Valley-Goose Bay, road access to much of Labrador will be a reality.

One railway operates within the province and connects Sept-Iles, Quebec, with Shefferville, Quebec, in the north and has a spur line running to Wabush-Labrador City. Passengers and vehicles are carried on this, but its primary role is to transport iron ore pellets from mine to market.

There is scheduled air service from mainland points to airports at Happy Valley-Goose Bay, Churchill Falls, and Wabush-Labrador City. Smaller airlines connect with most coastal communities and to points within the province. Most visitors arrive by air to these sites, then connect with their outfitter for further travel, especially by floatplane.

Western region. In western Labrador, the iron ore mining towns of Wabush-Labrador City are step-off points to access interior lakes and streams via float-equipped aircraft. Most watersheds here are affected by the enormous Smallwood Reservoir and its series of electronically operated dams, which control water flow through giant turbines at the distant Churchill Falls.

The Ashuanipi River system connects two large watersheds, Menihek Lake to the North and Ashuanipi Lake to the south. Lac Joseph and Atikonak Lake are two enormous watersheds that lie to the southeast of Labrador City-Wabush; lakes to the north and east include Shaw, Dyke, Crossroads, Ashtray, Albert, Woods, Lobstick, Gabbro, and Andre. Fly-in outfitting camps are located on many of these waterways. These lakes and numerous others are affected by energy needs at Churchill Falls, one of the world's largest hydroelectric-generating facilities, and they are all a part of the massive Smallwood Reservoir system.

The fish species of this region include northern pike, lake trout, splake, brook trout, whitefish, burbot, and ouananiche (landlocked salmon). The 22-pound, 11-ounce world-record landlocked salmon was caught on Smallwood Reservoir at Lobstick Dam in 1983, and several more have come close to breaking that record.

Lake trout to 40 pounds, and northern pike in the 20- to 30-pound range, have been caught in the reservoir, although lakers in this region are usually in the 8- to 15-pound class and pike are in the 5- to 12-pound range. Really big specimens are rare; however, in some places you can catch lakers one right after the other, and in other places plenty of pike, although there's not much in the way of traditional weedbed fishing. Whitefish and trophy-size brook trout favor the rapids below the various dam structures, where water is normally cold and highly oxygenated. These have high concentrations of whitefish, a plentiful food base that attracts the other, larger species. Indeed, whitefish are plentiful enough to be caught on spinners and plugs as one fishes for other species.

Accessed only by floatplane, and primarily from Wabush-Labrador City, this region sees few visitors each year, and then only from late June through early September. The better fishing for landlocked salmon occurs in June and again in late August and September. Smaller fish are available all summer long in the rivers, especially in the pools and quick water between lakes. They are typically caught on spinners, spoons, and flies.

Although this is not the heart of Labrador's brook trout fishery, this species is plentiful in certain places in the region and can be had up to 7 pounds. Some sections of this area rival the better-known brook trout waters in the central part of Labrador, and 4- and 5-pounders are regularly caught. The Ashuanipi and McKenzie Rivers produce many trout in the 3- to 5-pound class, which is outstanding by any standards, as well as the occasional larger fish. Murray River and the outflow of Crossroads Lake are also very good, and undoubtedly many locales produce great results at certain times, especially if the water is not too low.

These fish can be caught all season long and on various lures.

The preferred method of angling in this region is with spinning or baitcasting tackle and lures or baits, although fly fishing is productive for brook trout and whitefish. Ouananiche often take large streamers, lake trout prefer large lures trolled deep, and pike strike a variety of offerings, but there is room for all types of fishing, depending on the location and time of year.

Burbot, a freshwater cousin of the cod, are found in cold lakes, usually at extreme depths, and are receptive to baits, although there is little interest in these fish among visiting anglers. Splake, a cross between lake and brook trout, inhabit some western Labrador watersheds and will strike a lure or large fly under varying conditions.

Central region. East of Smallwood Reservoir, the central region features Happy Valley-Goose Bay as the primary hub for visiting anglers. This region is known to generations of fly anglers for its superb resource of large brook trout (in the 4- to 8-pound class). To the southwest of Goose Bay is an area with several lakes containing trophy-size brookies, including the famed Minipi Lake, Little Minipi, Anne Marie, and Minonipi watersheds. Landlocked charr are also taken in this system, generally in early autumn as water cools and spawning time approaches.

Several outfitters provide access to the southeast interior, which contains a portion of the Eagle River headwaters, including Igloo Lake, Park Lake, Osprey Lake, Eagle Lake, and Crook's Lake. Awesome Lake and English River lie farther east at the edge of the Mealy Mountain range. These watersheds, with the exception of Awesome Lake, also contain northern pike in addition to a trophy brook trout resource. Giant brook trout have been caught in the English River, which flows out of Awesome Lake, and at several of the inlets that leave the mountains and flow over waterfalls to enter the lake. Awesome Lake is ringed on the west by mountains, including two reaching to 3,500 and 3,800 feet, making for an inspiring angling backdrop. Snow remains on the slopes throughout the season.

Peripheral lakes that offer outfitter camps and contain a mix of brook trout, lake trout, and northern pike include Night, Shapio, Border, and Double Mer.

No roads exist in this wilderness region, so access to these remote outfitter camps is provided via floatplane or helicopter. The combination of distance and difficulty of access has helped preserve these unique brook trout resources and a high quality of angling.

South coast region. Road access is available to the Straits area in the far southeastern corner of coastal Labrador, where two well-known salmon rivers—the Pinware and the Forteau—are easily accessible from the island of Newfoundland via a 90-minute ferry ride from St. Barbe, Newfoundland,

Ice anglers take note: the thickest ice on record was measured by echo soundings at 2.97 miles off the coast of Antarctica.

to Blanc Sablon, Quebec. Scheduled airline services carry passengers and freight to nearby Blanc Sablon airport.

These two rivers receive significant resident pressure, but there is an outfitter camp on the Forteau, and several outfitters provide service on the Pinware. Facilities are comfortable, and local guides have firsthand knowledge of these important streams.

Road access disappears at Red Bay, a few miles farther north along the south coast. A road system to connect Red Bay to Cartwright, a major settlement at the mouth of the Eagle River, is planned.

This isolated coast contains four rivers with runs of Atlantic salmon, and small communities lie at the base of each. These include Port Hope Simpson at the Alexis River, Mary's Harbour at the St. Lewis River, Charlottetown at the Gilbert River, and Norman Bay at the Hawke River. A fishing camp sits at the base of the Gilbert River, and farther north are lodges at the more remote Sandhill River.

The renowned Eagle River is the favored salmon stream on this part of the coast. It empties into Sandwich Bay near Cartwright, and there are outfitter lodges and private camps in operation on the Lower Eagle. Nearby rivers with good salmon runs but limited access include North, White Bear, and Paradise Rivers. Sea-run brook trout of significant sizes are taken from all these rivers during early summer.

Labrador has experienced a reduced commercial fishery for salmon, but a strict quota has been in effect in this area—designated by the federal Department of Fisheries & Oceans as Salmon Fishing Area (SFA) 2—and farther north, above Lake Melville, in SFA 1.

North coast region. The coastal area and interior region above Lake Melville, identified as the north coast, is isolated except for scheduled air service and a shipping route in summer. A mix of Atlantic salmon, arctic charr, and sea-run brook trout are taken at outfitter lodges located at Michael's River, Big River, Adlatok River, Voisey's Bay, and Flower's River. Northern pike and lake trout are found in lakes at the lower extremes of this vast area.

The facilities vary from basic to semiluxurious, and fishing is excellent during the peak, from mid-July through late August. This region is dotted with numerous lakes and rivers, some of which hold a mix of fish species. Access is extremely limited, however, and the terrain is generally unfriendly to the unprepared. As in much of Labrador, outfitter lodges are a necessity.

Above the northernmost community of Nain are several rivers offering excellent arctic charr angling. Outfitter camps operate in this area at Tasiuyak Lake and Umiakovik Lake during the short summer season. Even farther north, near the site of a former U.S. radar installation, is a charr and caribou camp at Saglek Bay.

NEW HAMPSHIRE

Between the Canadian border in the north and the Atlantic Ocean in the south, New Hampshire has diverse fishing opportunities, probably more than the average angler can sample in a lifetime of trying. More than 4,000 miles of trout and Atlantic salmon streams and in excess of 200 coldwater lakes and ponds in New Hampshire hold brook, brown, rainbow, and lake trout as well as landlocked salmon. The warmwater fishery consists primarily of roughly 1,200 bodies of water located chiefly in the south. Although the coastline is relatively short, an abundance of striped bass draws anglers from far inland to the marine fishery.

The coldwater resource is the focus of the majority of management efforts and programs. Bass anglers, however, are increasing in number, and as they voice their expectations the warmwater fishery is receiving more attention from state agencies. Trout and salmon management still relies on hatchery and stocking programs, but the objective of providing anglers with a quality experience supersedes any put-and-take philosophy.

Major Rivers

In the northern half of the state, the Connecticut, Pemigewasset, Androscoggin, and Saco River basins are the major watersheds and provide classic mountain-stream trout fishing.

Connecticut River. The Connecticut River rises just below the Canadian border in Pittsburg and flows south into Massachusetts, forming the New Hampshire and Vermont border along the way. From its headwaters down to Lancaster, the Connecticut offers anglers some of the best public waters in the East. Brookies and rainbows averaging 10 to 12 inches are the mainstay, but there's always the chance of hooking a huge brown. Every season, local youngsters fishing the town pool haul in brown trout weighing in the double digits.

In the special regulation sections of the river between Second Connecticut Lake and Lake Francis, landlocked salmon are a spring and fall wild card. Fly anglers new to this portion of the river should bring caddis and stonefly patterns in black, brown, tan, and olive.

From Pittsburg to just north of Lancaster, the water is a mixture of rapids, riffles, pockets, long glides, and occasional deep pools formed by bends in the river where it flows through flat farmland. This stretch gets fished hard, but it is productive all season long. To avoid crowds, move downstream, below Colebrook, where the pressure is considerably lighter and the fishing often is even better.

Below Lancaster, the stream widens, deepens, and gets much bigger. This section is good trout water, but there is much more of it. Noteworthy is the brown trout tailwater fishery below Moore Dam in the Littleton area. Downstream of Lebanon to Massachusetts, the river changes into big, slower-flowing water that provides excellent fishing for bass, and the occasional northern pike in the setback sloughs. The lower half of the Connecticut is generally boating water.

Five Connecticut River tributaries merit specific recognition: the Ammonoosuc River at Woodsville, the Mascoma at Lebanon, the Sugar at West Claremont, the Cold at Actworth, and the Ashuelot at Hinsdale. Each is a good trout fishery in its own accord.

Pemigewasset and Merrimack Rivers. The second most significant north-to-south watershed in New Hampshire is comprised of two rivers. The Pemigewasset rises in the northern reaches of the White Mountains and joins the Merrimack River at Franklin. The Merrimack flows southward from Franklin into Massachusetts.

Gin clear and gravel-bottomed, the Pemi looks like a trout angler's dream stream, and often it lives up to those expectations. Route 3 runs beside the Pemi for much of its length, and stream access is easy. Fly anglers especially favor the Pemi because its technical fishing aspects test them thoroughly over the course of the season.

At Franklin, the Pemi and the Winnepesaukee Rivers merge to form the Merrimack River. The upper Merrimack sustains a trout and salmon coldwater fishery through much of the summer, and the stretch from Concord to the Massachusetts border has outstanding smallmouth bass fishing.

Particularly noteworthy are the Atlantic salmon brood stock fishery and access opportunities along the Merrimack and lower Pemigewasset Rivers. In conjunction with an Atlantic salmon restoration program, surplus adult fish weighing up to 15 pounds and more are released into these rivers, providing a first-class salmon fishery rivaling that found in famous streams. For a fishing license and a salmon permit, anglers can experience sport that would cost big bucks elsewhere.

Portions of the Merrimack and Pemigewasset Rivers and their tributaries to the first upstream bridge are subject to special regulations, some of which require fly fishing only, or the use of artificial lures only, with one hook point.

Androscoggin River. Located in east-central Coos County between Errol, New Hampshire, and Gorham, Maine, the Androscoggin River is New Hampshire's version of a "western" trout stream. This is big water that holds plenty of big fish all year long. Two-pound brookies, 5-pound rainbows, and log-length browns can come at any time and virtually anywhere. The occasional landlocked salmon hooked in swift water makes things even more interesting. Most anglers find the river productive throughout the season, even in the dog days of summer. Fly anglers mark their calendar for the third week in June, when the alderfly hatch triggers a trophy-trout feeding frenzy.

Saco River. In the Mount Washington valley, a network of feeder streams joins the Saco River. From the Conway area and downstream about 20 miles into Maine, the Saco is a first-class trout stream. This section of the river lies amidst many tourist attractions, so it gets heavy pressure from visiting anglers seeking the big browns and rainbows that give the river its reputation. Savvy local anglers tend to give more play to Saco feeder streams, such as the Ellis and the Swift.

North Country Lakes and Ponds

Lakes and ponds in the northern half of the state generally tend to be coldwater fisheries, whereas those in the southern half typically are either warmwater or two-tier fisheries.

In Pittsburg, near the Canadian border, Lake Francis and First, Second, and Third Connecticut Lakes fall into the big-water category, best fished from a seaworthy boat. Brook, rainbow, and brown trout share the waters with landlocked salmon and lake trout. Whether the fishing is trolling for salmon and lakers during the day, or casting a fly to visible trout cruising the surface film and sipping evening-hatch caddisflies, these lakes offer good, consistent fishing from ice out in May through October.

Among the best northern trout ponds are the following: Boundry Pond (covering 18 acres and also called Mountain Pond) in Pittsburg, Lower Trio Pond (68 acres) in Odell, Little and Big Greenough Pond (303 acres) in Wentworth Location, Nathan Pond (26 acres) in Dixville, Little and Big Diamond Pond (230 acres) in Stewartstown, Connor Pond (86 acres) in Ossipee, and Big Dan Hole Pond (408 acres) in Tuftonboro.

Lakes Region

The Lakes Region in the midsection of the state gets its name from several famous fishing lakes. Chief among these is Lake Winnipesaukee, New Hampshire's angling crown jewel and largest body of water. It has 44,586 surface acres, hundreds of islands, underwater structure that drops off to depths exceeding 100 feet, and grassy or sandy shallow bays. Winnipesaukee gets its well-deserved angling reputation from lake trout and landlocked salmon; but among bass anglers, the big lake is also acclaimed for superb smallmouth bass action.

From ice out in late April to roughly Memorial Day, anglers take landlocked salmon on the surface by trolling lures and flies that imitate smelt, the lake's primary forage fish. As the water warms and gives up its oxygen, salmon retreat to the colder water in the 20- to 40-foot depths. Salmon prefer temperatures in the mid-50s; during July and August this means they'll be in the 40- to 70-foot depths in this big lake. Many salmon anglers think that a brisk trolling speed is best for salmon; however, maintaining a slower speed—as close to 1.8 miles per hour (mph) as possible—is consistently most productive for Winnipesaukee salmon.

In spring, just after ice out, lake trout may be taken in the shallows on light-tackle rigs, such as live smelt fished under a bobber. In summer, lake trout seek their preferred 50°F water temperature

Squam Lake is noted for its smallmouth bass as well as lake trout and salmon.

in the 40- to 100-foot depths. This means slow, deep trolling. A rule of thumb for summertime Winnipesaukee lakers is to troll the 55-foot contour at less than 2 mph. Trolling lures work well, but the old standby here of trolling sewn-on bait, such as jack smelt, is tough to beat.

From spring through fall, Winnipesaukee's smallmouth bass fishery is as good as any other in the Northeast. Bass boats are now as numerous there as other types of craft, especially when there's a fishing tournament in progress. The old-time technique of using crayfish or hellgrammites for baits is still a good bet here for anglers who want to tie into a 5-plus-pound smallmouth bass.

In late September and October, smallmouth bass in Winnipesaukee and other waters in the Lakes Region return to the shallows and indulge in a feeding binge. The fishing can be truly terrific during this time.

In winter, ice anglers take over the lakes, and colonies of ice fishing shacks—locally called "bobhouses"—dot the prime areas. The main species of interest to ice anglers are lake trout, rainbow trout, pickerel, bass, yellow perch, and white perch. Salmon are protected during the ice fishing season.

The large-lakes rainbow trout program is a key component of Lakes Region fisheries management. To mitigate fishing pressure on lake trout and provide a high-quality alternative, the state stocks rainbow trout. Rainbows in Winnipesaukee can exceed 5 pounds. No fail-safe tactic has yet been developed, however, for targeting and catching these fish locally. In most instances, large lake rainbows are caught by chance, not by design.

Year-round, Lake Winnipesaukee incurs heavy fishing pressure, but the fisheries are closely monitored and aggressively managed because they are among the state's most valuable recreational and economic resources.

Much of what pertains to Winnipesaukee is generally true for the other Lakes Region waters. Squam and Winnisquam Lakes offer smaller versions of Lake Winnipesaukee's fisheries. Newfound and Sunapee Lakes no longer merit their former reputations for lake trout and salmon, but the state Fish and Game Department is trying to restore them to their former glory.

Squam Lake, which at 6,764 acres is the second-largest lake in New Hampshire, deserves special note because it is one of the unsung jewels of New England. This predominantly deep body of water has numerous islands and rocky shoals. The water is pure and crystal clear, and you can watch a lure drift off to the bottom in depths twice your body length and then some.

Located near Holderness in the foothills of New Hampshire's White Mountains, Squam is a premier New England smallmouth bass fishery. It also offers fine landlocked salmon angling, harboring larger landlocks on average than its much bigger nearby sister lake, Winnipesaukee. Lake trout thrive here, too, although these favor deep water and are tough to come by most of the year. The lake has been noted for large white perch in the past.

The finest time for smallmouth fishing is in the spring, from early June through the fourth of July. Once the weather sets in and the surface layers warm up, bass retreat to the areas around deep, rocky shoals. Some great fishing can be had at Squam in midsummer, if you locate these spots and work them carefully, using jigs, live crayfish, and perhaps surface plugs in the evening.

For landlocked salmon, the months of April and May, when the fish are closer to the surface and near shore in pursuit of spawning smelt, are the best times to fish. There is little nonfishing boat traffic at that time, and the salmon are plentiful. Most anglers fish traditionally, trolling streamer flies on a fly line or lead-core line. Later, the fish move deeper and are harder to locate.

Warmwater Fisheries

Although there are roughly 1,200 bodies of warm water in the Granite State, only a third of them are managed to any extent by the New Hampshire Fish and Game Department. Most of these waters are located south of the White Mountains. In New Hampshire, ponds and lakes are categorized according to the fish species inhabiting the waters, and the warmwater/coldwater distinction is fuzzy in instances where waters that contain bass are stocked with trout to provide a seasonal put-and-take trout fishery.

It is common here for a given body of water to hold and sustain both trout and bass, a situation known as a two-tier fishery. For example, 707-acre Spofford Lake, located in Chesterfield, not only has trout and bass, but it also produced a state-record northern pike that weighed 21 pounds, 4.6 ounces.

Where waters tend to be on the warm side, brook trout don't fare well; rainbows and browns adapt moderately well among the largemouth and smallmouth bass that may be there. Massabesic Lake in Auburn is a 2,512-acre site that does an acceptable job of supporting both trout and bass. Depending on tackle and technique, anglers here can take rainbow trout, brown trout, largemouth and smallmouth bass, white perch, and bluegills.

New Hampshire does possess pure, classic largemouth bass waters, mostly in the southern end of the state. About 10 miles southwest of Concord, in the Weare and Hopkinton area, is a loosely connected network of water between Hopkinton and Everett Lakes. When fish biologists studied these waters, they found big bass and plenty of them in the midst of extensive reaches of flooded standing timber. This ideal bass habitat produces big fish and good fishing. Anglers have landed largemouths up to 8 pounds in these waters, and fish in the 4- to 5-pound class are definitely possible.

Largemouth bass may not readily come to mind when one thinks of New Hampshire, but the bass fishery is extensive enough to keep a plethora of bass clubs and bass anglers happy.

Saltwater

New Hampshire's coastline is short, about 15 miles as the crow flies, but its marine resources are varied and the saltwater fishing grounds are well known. Offshore structures like the Isles of Shoals have been drawing anglers since the Vikings found and harvested an abundance of cod, haddock, pollock, and flounder. These groundfish species have declined in number, as is true all along the Atlantic coast, but striped bass and bluefish provide an exciting recreational fishery. From May through October, the Great Bay estuarine waters provide one of the best inshore striped bass fisheries of the Northeast. For pure sport and fast action, anglers use light tackle or fly gear and focus on schoolie stripers. Effective methods for taking big fish include freespooling live mackerel, eels, and pogies; drifting chunk bait in the rips; and trolling a tube and worm combination.

Charter and party boats operate out of Rye and Hampton Harbors. Some focus on offshore groundfish species, whereas others work the inshore waters for mackerel, stripers, and bluefish.

NEW JERSEY

Perhaps overlooked by nonresident anglers because of its dense population, industrialized character, proximity to Manhattan, and relatively small size, New Jersey nevertheless has surprisingly diverse angling, as well as wildly enthusiastic anglers. From Greenwood Lake's bass fishing to the Pine Barrens' pickerel and the Delaware River's shad, and from Sandy Hook's stripers to Cape May's drum, not too many important East Coast species escape the hook.

New Jersey has no large lakes, only one major river, and only 130 miles of Atlantic coastline. But this coastline is studded with beaches, inlets, and marinas far beyond what many locations with much longer coastlines can offer, providing access to perennially popular flounder, weakfish, striped bass, and bluefish inshore, and even marlin, tuna, and dolphin offshore. These opportunities have resulted in exceptional catches, which include the largest striped bass ever caught, the second largest known bluefish ever caught, and numerous line-class records for weakfish, flounder, and black drum, as well as bigeye tuna. Inland, numerous small to medium lakes and streams provide opportunities that range from four species of trout to pure-strain muskellunge, landlocked hybrid stripers, walleye, and plenty of largemouth and smallmouth bass, plus what is arguably the best fishery for American shad in North America in the Delaware River.

Freshwater

One of the most covert angling stories in the northeastern United States is the existence and indeed expansion of freshwater fishing opportunities within the confines of the Garden State. Known as the most densely populated state in America, and a heavily industrialized one at that, New Jersey does not bring to mind outstanding freshwater fishing to outsiders. It has no nationally renowned freshwater opportunities, with the possible exception of the Delaware River, and no large bodies of water; yet it offers a diversity—in fact more than is found in a lot of states—it seldom receives credit for.

This diversity exists throughout New Jersey's three distinct inland geographic regions. Indeed, myriad freshwater venues—including lakes, ponds, rivers, impoundments, and a latticework of streams and creeks, all of which support good populations of gamefish and panfish—await the angler. From wild brook trout to pure-strain muskellunge, anglers can find it all in New Jersey.

Northern region. *Greenwood Lake.* Passaic County's 1,920-acre Greenwood Lake shares a border with New York and is recognized as a supreme largemouth bass fishery within the tri-state (including Pennsylvania) area. Smallmouth bass, pure-strain muskies, walleye, and chain pickerel are among the players at Greenwood, and healthy populations of robust yellow perch, sunfish, channel catfish, and bullheads thrive here, too.

The lake is heavily weeded and its complexion fairly turbid. Largemouths get big here, and 7-pounders are not uncommon. Fishing for both largemouth and smallmouth bass begins in mid-April and intensifies into the summer months. Smallmouth average about 2 pounds here, and 4-pounders are caught annually. During the late May to early June spawning period, they are encountered in close to dockside cover; later, they frequent Greenwood's rockier flats and dropoffs.

The muskie is the ultimate prize of Greenwood, one eagerly sought by dedicated fans all season long. Early spring and late autumn are the optimum times to pursue these fish.

Greenwood draws many New York anglers because of its early bass fishing opportunities (the season is still closed in April and May in most New York waters), and because it is one of the larger publicly accessible lakes in the tri-state area. Many tournaments are scheduled here, and the lake is a beehive of activity in summer months. In winter, Greenwood offers excellent ice fishing.

Monksville Reservoir. Also in Passaic County, 505-acre Monksville Reservoir is situated just below Greenwood Lake and provides superb fishing for largemouth and smallmouth bass, walleye, pure-strain muskies, tiger muskies, trout, and panfish. This impoundment boasts a plethora of sunken islands, humps, dropoffs, and flats, as well as stands of drowned timber. It sports a mean depth of nearly 43 feet and a maximum depth of 90 feet, and it is restricted to electric motors.

Stocked trout receive most of the attention in early spring, but come May, walleye usurp the limelight. The bulk of the walleye activity occurs in the south-central and southern sections of the reservoir. Walleye average 3 pounds or thereabouts, but fish up to and exceeding 6 pounds are present.

Both largemouth and smallmouth bass are common throughout Monksville and are caught from April through November. Muskies prowl submerged weedbeds, sunken timber, and breaklines. October to ice-up (usually by mid-January) is the most opportune time to encounter Monksville muskellunge, and the fish also strike baits under the ice.

Lake Hopatcong. New Jersey's largest lake, Hopatcong spans 2,658 acres and is situated in portions of Morris and Sussex Counties.

Undoubtedly the most heavily utilized freshwater resource in the Garden State, Lake Hopatcong offers outstanding fishing. Largemouth and smallmouth bass, chain pickerel, channel catfish, walleye, crappie, yellow perch, rock bass, and sunfish are all present, as are stocked populations of trout (some of which hold over through the winter to attain larger size), hybrid stripers, and both pure-strain and tiger muskies (experimentally). The hybrid striper is the star attraction of Hopatcong, followed in popularity by the largemouth bass, channel catfish, and walleye.

Hybrid striper fishing here is dynamic, with specimens caught in excess of 10 pounds. Stripers begin hitting in earnest in early May and continue into October. The largest fish of the year are taken at night during the latter part of summer. Top areas include Nolan's Point, the River Styx cove, Henderson Bay, Woodport, and the Brady Bridge area.

Largemouths that frequent the many docks and boathouses are particularly susceptible to a flipped or pitched jig, and also assault spinnerbaits and plastic worms. Plenty of submerged weedbeds throughout Hopatcong also hold largemouths, and the lake yields 3- to 5-pound specimens regularly. Fish to 7 pounds are taken every year.

Channel cats are the stunning overachievers on Hopatcong, attaining weights of 20 pounds or more. They are caught throughout the lake from May into October.

Although taken from Hopatcong since the early 1980s, walleye are now just beginning to establish a foothold. Anglers can find walleye to about 5 pounds, and expectations are high for the future of this fishery.

Chain pickerel are also notable on Hopatcong, as they thrive in its weedy environs. Chainsides wax fat on the rich shiner and alewife (also called a sawbelly here) forage base, and larger specimens can exceed 5 pounds.

Hopatcong is New Jersey's most popular ice fishing lake, and crappie, pickerel, yellow perch, and bluegills are the top winter targets.

Round Valley Reservoir. The standard by which all other Jersey waters are judged, 2,350-acre Round Valley Reservoir in Hunterdon County is

 Federal excise taxes on fishing tackle and some marine products are collected by manufacturers and used for fish restoration and access improvement projects.

the Garden State's finest stillwater salmonid fishery. Boasting depths to 160 feet, "The Valley," as it is known to regulars, offers outstanding fishing for brown, rainbow, and lake trout.

This impoundment, which has a 9.9-horsepower outboard motor restriction, is heavily stocked by the Division of Fish, Game and Wildlife, and also receives thousands of rainbows and browns annually from a local association. Trout are taken on a year-round basis, although there is a closed season on lakers that extends from mid-September to the beginning of January, to protect spawning fish.

Round Valley is managed as a trophy trout fishery with minimum size restrictions and very conservative daily limits. The regulations are succeeding; lakers to 24 pounds, browns to 21 pounds, and rainbows to 8 pounds have been pulled from its depths.

Drifting with alewives is the most popular technique, and many people anchor and swim an alewife below a slip bobber. Trolling plugs and spoons also pay handsome dividends. Both the North and South Tower areas are productive, and during the summer months boaters score well after dark. Shoreline anglers have a crack at trout during April and May and again from October through December.

Round Valley also offers excellent largemouth and smallmouth bass fishing along the shorelines and coves, and anglers have a good chance at largemouths over 5 pounds and bronzebacks over 3 pounds.

Spruce Run Reservoir. Located within a 10-minute drive from neighboring Round Valley, Spruce Run Reservoir is a 1,290-acre hotbed for largemouth bass, hybrid stripers, and northern pike. This impoundment, which has a 9.9-horsepower outboard motor restriction, is not as deep as Round Valley, so it has a different angling character.

Spruce Run largemouths hang close to the plentiful submerged weedbeds, creek channels, sunken islands, humps, and dropoffs. The cove to the left of the launch ramp in the state park is a good bet for early-season bass, as is the entire stretch of shoreline extending from the camping area to Black Brook Cove. Hepler's Cove and Black Brook Cove are prime locations for northern pike. This is especially true when using live shiners during April and May and again during October-December.

Hybrids exploded onto the Spruce Run scene and provide thrilling action on drifted alewives and trolled minnow plugs, particularly during May and early June and again during September into October.

Spruce Run is stocked with trout during the spring, although the holdover potential of the habitat is at an absolute minimum. This fishery is, for all intents and purposes, an annual put-and-take proposition. Salmonids are caught into June.

White catfish are also abundant here, as are heavyweight carp. When the lake freezes, northern pike, yellow perch, and crappie spark interest.

Merrill Creek Reservoir. Considered by many to be the state's premier smallmouth bass venue, 600-acre Merrill Creek Reservoir in Warren County also provides good opportunities for rainbow, brown, and lake trout, as well as largemouth bass, yellow perch, and sunfish.

This 210-foot-deep impoundment, which has an electric-motor-only restriction, possesses a variety of structure, including submerged timber, boulder fields, rockpiles, dropoffs, humps, creek channels, and weeds, and is ideally suited to trophy bronzebacks. On an angler-per-hour basis, Merrill Creek provides the best in both sizes and numbers. Smallmouths are found along the entire expanse of the reservoir's shoreline out to depths of 40 feet, but the immediate area surrounding the handicapped access is a place to focus special attention.

Drifting from a boat with alewives and shiners accounts for the majority of salmonid catches, although shore anglers score during April, May, and June.

Big Swartswood Lake. Big Swartswood Lake in Sussex County has been one of the Garden State's most consistent producers of big largemouths for decades. Just 494 acres in size, and 42 feet deep, and with an electric-motor-only restriction, Swartswood has ample and expansive weedbeds, rockpiles, and rocky points to attract largemouths, which are active from mid-April into November. This fishery continues to be first-rate, and largemouths up to 10 pounds have been caught here. Many fish are in the 2- to 4-pound range.

Pickerel, yellow perch, rock bass, and crappie are sure bets year-round and have earned Swartswood a reputation as a first-class ice fishing venue.

Stocked trout contribute to frantic action from April through May on Big Swartswood, and salmonid numbers are augmented by releases from a local club. The holdover potential of the lake is marginal, but every year big browns are wrestled from the depths.

Delaware River. Known outside the region primarily for its run of migratory American shad from April through May, the East's largest free-flowing river also provides exemplary angling for walleye, pure-strain muskies, tiger muskies, smallmouth and largemouth bass, channel catfish, striped bass, carp, a variety of panfish, and, in the state's northernmost stretch from Columbia to Montague, the occasional brown trout.

Top areas on the upper New Jersey portion of the Delaware include Montague, Worthington, Poxono Island, Walpack Bend, and Kittatinny Beach (all in the Delaware Water Gap National Recreation Area), and Columbia, Belvidere, Phillipsburg, Carpentersville, Riegelsville, Bulls Island, Kingwood, and Frenchtown.

On the central stretch of the Delaware, favored areas are Byram, Stockton, Lambertville, Washington's Crossing, and Trenton. Trenton Wharf draws anglers during the spring herring run.

The Green River Shales in Wyoming possess ancient lake deposits that are about 40 million years old and have yielded enormous amounts of fish fossils.

Lower-river hotspots include Bordentown, Florence, Burlington, National Park, Greenwich, Pennsville, Penns Beach, and Salem Cove. Of special interest in the lower Delaware is the Commodore Barry Bridge locale, a prime striped bass spawning ground. Thirty- to 40-pound stripers are caught here each spring.

Tributaries on the lower river provide exceptional angling for striped bass (which spawn in some of them), largemouth bass, and channel catfish. These include Salem Creek, Cohansey River, Oldmans Creek, Rancocas River, Raccoon Creek, Salem River, Big Timber Creek, Crosswicks Creek, and Mantua Creek.

Raritan River. New Jersey's second major river system, the Raritan offers fine fishing for smallmouth bass, channel catfish, largemouth bass, rock bass, white catfish, carp, and sunfish from its genesis at the North Branch/South Branch confluence at Old York Road in Somerset County downriver to New Brunswick in Middlesex County.

Trout are stocked at Dukes Island Park (in Somerset County), and downriver from this location anglers have a fair chance of encountering walleye, muskies, and northern pike. White perch are prolific throughout the lower reaches of the Raritan, especially near New Brunswick. The Johnson Park beat, also in New Brunswick, is one of the Garden State's best-kept largemouth bass secrets.

Millstone River. The 20-mile south-to-north Millstone River, from Princeton (Mercer County) to Manville (Somerset County) is a vastly underrated and ignored venue for largemouth bass, northern pike, channel catfish, chain pickerel, rock bass, sunfish, and carp. Smallmouth bass linger in the lower reaches of the Millstone, particularly where it merges with the Raritan at Manville.

Top spots are in Somerset County at Blackwells Mills in Belle Mead, in the hamlet of Millstone, and at Wilhousky Street in Manville.

Delaware & Raritan Canal. The narrow D&R Canal hosts stocked trout, channel catfish, largemouth bass, crappie, yellow perch, white perch, striped bass, carp, and sunfish. Muskies, walleye, and northern pike, although rare, also frequent the turbid precincts.

Weedbeds, logs, sunken brush, undercut banks, and overhangs typify the D&R Canal habitat. Depths range to 10 feet. Flowing slowly through the counties of Mercer, Hunterdon, Somerset, and Middlesex, the canal provides ample shoreline access via the D&R Canal State Park system and is an ideal venue for the canoe and cartop boat angler.

The D&R Feeder Canal in Hunterdon and Mercer Counties is also heavily stocked with trout and offers good opportunities for largemouth bass, channel catfish, bullhead, sunfish, and crappie.

Other sites. Other northern New Jersey waters worthy of effort are Little Swartswood Lake and Wawayanda Lake in Sussex County, Sheppards Lake in Passaic County, Lake Musconetcong and Budd Lake in Morris County, and White Lake and Mountain Lake in Warren County.

The Newark Watershed reservoirs in Passaic and Sussex Counties offer excellent fishing for a variety of species. Largemouth and smallmouth bass, rainbow trout, and brown trout are notable at Canistear, Oak Ridge, and Clinton; muskies are present in Echo Lake; and they all have pickerel, yellow perch, crappie, and sunfish. These four reservoirs are under the auspices of the city of Newark, however, and access is controlled with a seasonal permit.

The northern region of New Jersey is laced with premium-quality trout streams, brooks, and small rivers. The best include the Big Flat Brook, Wanaque, Ramapo, Rockaway, Paulinskill, Black, Pequest, Musconetcong, Spruce Run Creek, Pequannock, South Branch of the Raritan, and North Branch of the Raritan.

Not to be overlooked are the state's 33 Wild Trout Waters, most of which are in the northern region, where native trout reign and only artificial lures can be used. Many of these are in Sussex, Warren, Morris, Passaic, and Hunterdon Counties; Flanders Brook, India Brook, Parker Brook, Rocky Run, Van Campens Brook, Willhoughby Brook, and Little York Brook really shine.

Central region. *Manasquan Reservoir.* At 740 acres, Monmouth County's Manasquan Reservoir offers a wide range of angling opportunities. Largemouth and smallmouth bass, and stocked trout, are the primary attractions, although numerous crappie and sunfish draw marked interest. During April and May, the put-and-take fishery for brookies and rainbows draws legions of anglers to the impoundment.

The smallmouth bass population at 'Squan has been very good, typically offering fish up to 3 pounds, but this trend may decline as the habitat falls victim to natural progression. Then, it will be better suited to largemouths, which are active from late April through November. Fish over 4 pounds are possible.

This impoundment, which has an electric-motor-only restriction, has been stocked with hybrid striped bass, channel catfish, and tiger muskies. These fisheries are expected to be more prominent in the near future.

Lake Assunpink. Considered the finest largemouth bass venue in central New Jersey, 225-acre Lake Assunpink in Monmouth County is a consistent fish producer, which explains its popularity among statewide bass clubs.

A shallow electric-motor-only impoundment with an average depth of just 5 feet, Assunpink is loaded with road beds, weeds, and brush. It has plenty of bass up to 3 pounds, and some in the 5-pound class. March through June, and September through November, are the most productive periods. Channel catfish also contend for fishing attention on Assunpink, and many

A great deal of freshwater fishing in the Garden State occurs in small waters, such as this south Jersey pond.

anglers frequent this impoundment for a chance at 12-plus-pound specimens.

Two notable small lakes include nearby Stone Tavern Lake and Rising Sun. Both are within a few minutes' drive and offer good largemouth bass, crappie, and catfish angling.

Farrington Lake. Farrington Lake in Middlesex County is rated as one of the Garden State's finest pickerel waters and as a fine largemouth bass site. Chainsides attain very respectable sizes in the 290-acre Farrington, with 30-inch fish present. Thick-bodied largemouths exist throughout the long and narrow length of this electric-motor-only impoundment, hugging the shoreline brush, blowdowns, and weedbeds.

The lake also has panfish, stocked trout, and northern pike. The pike—many of which exceed 15 pounds—hug the weeds like bass and can be found close to the banks or on outside vegetation.

Other sites. Other worthwhile waters in central New Jersey include Carasaijo, Prospertown, and Shenandoah Lakes in Ocean County; Deal Lake in Monmouth County; and Lake Mercer in Mercer County.

Central New Jersey's better trout streams include the Manasquan River and Mingamahone Brook in Monmouth County, plus Toms River and the North Branch of the Metedeconk in Ocean County.

Southern region. *Union Lake.* A particularly productive largemouth bass water, Cumberland County's 898-acre Union Lake has a bountiful forage base of herring, gizzard shad, and shiners; natural structure like weeds, sunken trees, and brush; man-made tire structures; and rockpiles. All of these elements contribute to the lake's optimum largemouth conditions. The average largemouth tips the scales around the 2-pound mark, but 3- to 5-pounders are regularly caught. Smallmouth bass, although rare, show up just enough to provide an occasional surprise.

Union's burgeoning herring population is attributed to the newly constructed fish ladder on the Maurice (pronounced "Morris") River, which permits upstream passage for these fish and provides ample forage so the bass can gain size rapidly. The ladder has also impacted the lake's striper population.

Union's landlocked striper population, once one of New Jersey's shining fisheries, has waned to insignificance, even though the odd 10-pounder might be caught here. However, increasing numbers of 5- to 8-inch estuary-run striped bass from the Maurice River have been using the ladder and entering this impoundment. Because the fish will be entrapped here, there's hope that they will prosper, eat heartily, and grow to tackle-bending proportions in future years.

This lake, incidentally, has a 9.9-horsepower outboard restriction.

Maurice River. The approximately 13-mile stretch of the Maurice (pronounced "Morris") River flowing from the Union Lake dam just above the city of Millville (Cumberland County) southward to Delaware Bay is an amazingly productive stretch of river.

It is one of the hottest striped bass venues in the Garden State, with linesiders up to and exceeding 15 pounds caught here during the spring, summer, and autumn. Swarms of smaller fish inhabit this branch- and brush-infested flowage.

This is prime largemouth habitat as well, with bass up to 5 pounds feasting on herring, shiners, and elvers. Trophy-size channel catfish and white catfish, and jumbo yellow bullhead are here, as are pickerel, white perch, carp, sunfish, crappie, and yellow perch.

Parvin Lake. Ninety-five-acre Parvin Lake in Salem County is newly managed and regulated as a trophy bass fishery, and is expected to be a prime small water for big bass in the future.

With an average depth of just over $3^1/_2$ feet, the slightly stained Parvin is jammed with bass-holding structure, including weeds, stumps, brush, and sunken timber. There's an abundant forage base on this electric-motor-only lake, primarily consisting of shiners and elvers. The ave-rage bass is near 2 pounds, but 5-pounders are not uncommon.

Lake Lenape. Atlantic County's 350-acre Lake Lenape on the Egg Harbor River offers excellent opportunities for largemouth bass, yellow perch, crappie, and chain pickerel. Because of its unlimited outboard access (although park registration is required), Lenape is a popular tournament site for southern New Jersey and southeastern Pennsylvania bass clubs.

The lake has weedbeds, sunken timber, sand flats, and stump fields, and its water is stained brown to black owing to the cedar and pitch pine topography bordering the headwaters. It yields largemouths up to 4 pounds and pickerel up to 24 inches, with an occasional larger specimen.

Malaga Lake. Malaga Lake in Gloucester County packs a lot into just 105 acres of electric-motor-only fishing. Heavy concentrations of lily pads, grassbeds, and other weeds, as well as channel edges, stumps, and brush, make this an optimal site for largemouth bass. The lake produces specimens over 4 pounds each year, especially in spring and fall.

Malaga has a good supply of chain pickerel, which are found throughout the lake and caught year-round. March through June, and September through December, produce the better pickerel.

Other sites. Other noteworthy southern New Jersey waters include Menantico Sand Wash Pond in Cumberland County, Maskells Mill Pond in Salem County, Hammonton and Maple Lakes in Atlantic County, Mirror Lake in Burlington County, Iona Lake in Gloucester County, East Creek and Dennisville Lakes in Cape May County, and Oak Pond in Camden County.

Saltwater

New Jersey has one of the largest saltwater recreational fisheries in the United States due to its long shoreline and the fact that all of its large population is within a two-hour drive of the briny. The northeastern end of the state has the greatest proportion of that population and shares the lower Hudson River with New York. Just below such cities as Newark, Jersey City, and Elizabeth is Raritan Bay, which separates New York's Staten Island and the bay shoreline that stretches to the east.

The 120-mile-long coast starts at the tip of Sandy Hook and is treated as three different areas. The northern portion between Sandy Hook and Barnegat Inlet is referred to as "The Shore," and attracts both vast numbers of anglers and summer visitors, primarily from northern New Jersey. The central coast, from Barnegat Inlet to Atlantic City, is oriented toward Pennsylvania and western New Jersey anglers; the southern coast, from Ocean City to Cape May, is geared toward servicing Pennsylvanians as well as a great many Canadians who summer at Wildwood and Cape May. Al-though the extremes of the northern and southern areas are separated by only 40 miles, these regions might as well be two different states—the interchange of fishing information is so limited and the techniques and even some species are so disparate.

Delaware Bay separates New Jersey from Delaware, and in its upper reaches is vastly different from other parts of the state. The lower end of the Delaware River is shared between New Jersey and Delaware, but an oddity of law from colonial days gives the First State control of the waters up to the shores of the Garden State. New Jersey does have equal rights to the rest of the river, however, where it borders with Pennsylvania and New York. Saltwater fisheries in New Jersey are controlled by the state Division of Fish, Game and Wildlife, which falls within the Department of Environmental Protection.

Many of the marine species taken off New Jersey migrate up the coast in the spring and are generally encountered a week or two earlier within range of Cape May. For instance, mackerel fishing may start there during March as Cape May boats run south off Delaware to locate the first schools. That season generally lasts three to four weeks as schools gradually move north and out of range. The movement tends to speed up along the central coast before those spawning fish sometimes pause for two to four weeks in the New York-New Jersey Bight. In mid-April, northern boats usually begin to seek mackerel, and that fishery can run into May, depending on water temperatures and the proximity of bluefish schools. In general, mackerel move east when water temperatures climb above 50°F, although the presence of even a few bluefish may be an even more important factor.

Bluefish move in from offshore as well as up along the coast from the south. Cape May boats see some on the heels of the mackerel and usually start night chumming trips by the end of April; northern anglers often catch blues moving into warmer inshore waters around the same time, although party and charter boats rarely try to schedule trips before the second week in May. Throughout May and June there's a steady inshore movement of blues, which can be seen finning along the warm surface at first, before gradually moving deeper as the thermocline drops lower.

Sharks also tend to work up the coast and come in from warmer offshore waters. Cape May usually has a good fishery by the first week in June, and northern areas experience similar action a week later. School bluefin tuna move into both areas two to three weeks after the sharks arrive.

The reverse occurs in the fall, as northern areas get the migratory runs first. For instance, migratory striped bass from Chesapeake Bay feed in northern areas before passing by South Jersey from mid- or late-November into December. Cape May often has good bass fishing by October, however, as Delaware River fish start returning through the rips.

Hudson River. Heavily populated areas in northeastern New Jersey have nearby fishing opportunities in the lower and salty portions of the now much cleaner Hudson River. Even though river waters rarely display much clarity, the quality of those waters is far better now than it was for many decades when both industrial and municipal dumping polluted the river. Most of the species that live in the Hudson have shown signs of being pollution-resistant, but they also tend to taste of the river and, in the cases of species with higher oil contents, may contain levels of pollutants that require health warnings. This is especially the case with eels, but PCBs dumped years ago by General Electric accumulated in the tissues of striped bass to such an extent that commercial fishing for that species was prohibited during the 1970s. Ironically, these events ultimately benefited the species, which has since enjoyed many outstanding spawning years and provided a decent fishery in the Metropolitan area—even when the Chesapeake stocks hit rock bottom in the early 1980s.

The abundant Hudson River striped bass population continues to spread out along the coast each spring after providing a good pre-spawning fishery, which occurs a bit farther upriver in New York. Jersey anglers join their counterparts from across the river in catching stripers there from spring through fall. Shore anglers score in March and April from such areas as the Englewood Boat Basin in Bergen County, near the George Washington Bridge, where they cast sea worms for mostly short stripers as well as tomcod and white catfish.

Boaters do best in the lower reaches of the river from May on. Some of the best areas are around the Statue of Liberty and Ellis Island. Anglers can catch bass close to the islands by casting plugs, poppers, and bucktail jigs, but most of the larger stripers fall to bunker chunks fished from anchored boats. The current is very strong and often requires heavy sinkers, but bass in the teens and 20s are abundant. Bluefish also become common in the harbor area of the river by June.

Ironically, although boaters can be observed by literally millions of people in Manhattan and Brooklyn on the New York side, and from the solid line of waterfront communities across the river, anglers can often fish in virtual isolation except for river traffic—and the fishing may be better than anything found outside the river. The Staten Island end of the Verrazano Bridge is a good spot for stripers at times, although with only one support on each side it doesn't provide the fish-holding structure typical of most bridges.

A relative lack of marinas and launching facilities is the biggest problem in accessing the river, although the Liberty State Park development outside Jersey City has made it much easier for anglers seeking marina space and a launching ramp close to some of the river's best fishing. Stripers are caught from the park shores at times, and also from any pier that is accessible along the river. The state is investing some money into providing that access. The Hudson River Fisherman's Association in Cresskill keeps close track of changes in shore access and is the best source of information.

Raritan and Sandy Hook Bays. This may be the most underrated bay system in the country. Although surrounded by densely populated areas with vigorous industry, and subject to water flow from the polluted Kill Van Kull, Raritan Bay has been cleaned up considerably over the years. This bay was once famous for its oysters, but pollution shut down all shellfishing except for relay to clean waters for later harvest or for processing in depuration plants. Although rarely clear, the bay waters are extremely fertile, and bountiful harvests of baitfish and grass shrimp attract droves of such predators as summer flounder (fluke), winter flounder, bluefish, striped bass, and weakfish.

Except for pound nets and the purse seining of menhaden (bunkers), netting isn't allowed in the bay. Even that is prohibited on the New York side of the bay, and efforts are underway, aided by spotter planes, to end the decimation of that most important forage fish each spring and summer by mostly out-of-state bait purse seiners. Unfortunately, a great deal of illegal dragging has been conducted at night by "pirate" trawlers primarily operating out of Belford, although that activity recently has been reduced as law enforcement agencies implemented night scoping technology to nab the well-organized bandits.

A unique fixture on the Jersey side is the Naval Ammunition Pier at Earle, which extends far out in the bay. Fishing is off-limits for boaters inside the buoy line around the pier, but navy personnel enjoy great sport off the pier, especially for striped bass at night. A large party and charter boat fleet sails out of the modern port at Atlantic Highlands, which is near the mouth of Shrewsbury River and also features a large launching ramp. Nearby Leonardo State Marina has a party boat and some charters but caters mostly to private boats and features a good ramp with ample parking. Other party and charter boats sail from Highlands, Keyport, Morgan, and Perth Amboy.

The season starts in March as winter flounder become active; that fishery continues into early May, and the peak usually occurs during April. Although the flounder population along the coast was extremely depressed during the 1990s, Raritan Bay produced excellent angling every spring. Many fish ranged into the 2- to 3-pound class and shorts were few. The clam beds off Staten Island often attract weekend fleets in the hundreds, although many productive flounder grounds are spread throughout Raritan and Sandy Hook Bays. The latter comes alive in April as fish drop out of the Shrewsbury and Navesink Rivers.

The Shrewsbury and Navesink are also noted for their flounder fishing. The Shrewsbury may produce as early as February if the winter is warm and the season is open. March is a sure thing, although the fishery comes and goes with weather conditions. Early flounder turn on when the weather is sunny and mild, leading to warmer and clearer waters. Avoid fishing after rain or snow, which will turn the waters cold and dirty—driving flounder back into the mud. Larger female flounder move

---

A great white shark in Australia was hooked and landed twice in the same day by the same angler—even gaffed in the mouth and photographed—but it escaped both times. Its estimated weight was 3,000 pounds.

out first to spawn and leave the river, so the best fishing usually starts in March and may be over before mid-April, after which small male flounder take over. Most of the early effort occurs between the Sea Bright and Highlands Bridges, whereas the mouth of the Shrewsbury is best in April. The Navesink flows into the Shrewsbury just above the Highlands Bridge and provides excellent flounder catches a bit later than the other river, with small boats doing best during April in shallow waters around the Rumson Bridge.

The last shot at flounder usually occurs from late April into May in the ocean off the Cedars on Sandy Hook, where big flounder may be mixed in with ling (red hake). A Raritan Bay fall run usually develops in November and December, although relatively few anglers seek flounder. More glamorous fish such as striped bass are still available.

Striped bass also start biting in March, when many are hooked on sandworms cast from bay shorelines stretching from South Amboy to Atlantic Highlands. Almost all of these stripers are shorts (sublegal size) caught in waters that are only a few feet deep and warm up faster than deeper waters. As a general rule, this fishing is best from the middle of the flood into the beginning of the ebb both day and night. Flounder anglers catch short stripers from boats starting around late March, but striper enthusiasts rarely make a concentrated effort before April and May, when they begin to drift worms at the usual bay hotspots such as Sandy Hook Rip, Flynn's Knoll, and Romer Shoal, as well as the Highlands and Sea Bright Bridges in the Shrewsbury. Again, the vast majority of these early bass are shorts.

Chunking with cut bunker is a deadly method from June to August in many areas of the bay that have mussel bottoms. Flynn's Knoll and Ambrose Channel draw the largest fleets. Live eels drifted in Sandy Hook and Ambrose Channels and in Flynn's Knoll are the top producers in September and October, unless purse seiners leave enough bunkers in the bay to create an attraction for big bass. If schools of bunkers are available in October and November, there should be good action drifting live bunkers or trolling bunker spoons on wire line. Trolling often produces some bass within the bay into early December.

Bluefish arrive during early May and are usually abundant by midmonth. In some years these are 2- to 3-pounders, although on occasion there may be schools of 10-pounders that not only enter the bay but also go right up into the rivers. Shore casters usually get good shots at blues for a week or two before the fishery becomes primarily a boater's game, and then trolling and jigging are favored. Schools of mostly 1- to 4-pound choppers remain in the bay throughout the summer, and many larger ones are also caught by those chunking for stripers. The fall fishery is primarily outside the bay, however.

Fluking also starts in May, and is normally worthwhile after midmonth. These fish are the predominant bay fishery from June through August. Pursuing fluke throughout the bays is a large party boat fleet at Atlantic Highlands, which is joined by others from such ports as Highlands, Leonardo, Keyport, Morgan, and Perth Amboy. Charter and private boats partake in this fishery as well, and thousands of boats may be involved on weekends. Some fluke tournaments draw well over 200 entries. At times, the best fishing is in the western end of the bay, but sometimes it's preferable to fish closer to the ocean or down the beach at Sandy Hook. Fluking continues through September, when the departing fish tend to pile up in Ambrose Channel, and it often remains viable well into October.

Weakfish arrive early, but very few are caught on hook and line until July. Earlier attempts occur upriver in the Shrewsbury, but volume weakfishing is mainly a bay proposition. Large concentrations of these fish are usually found in Raritan and Chapel Hill Channels. After years of depressed weakfishing, the species bounced back in the mid-1990s and has been improving steadily with ever-larger specimens and relatively few shorts. The best fishing usually occurs in August and September, although schools may remain available into October if there aren't too many early cold northwesters. Whereas jigs work when weaks are feeding actively, the Raritan weakfishery is almost exclusively pursued with sandworms drifted a few feet above bottom on a three-way swivel rig. Although night fishing is effective for weakfish in many areas, those found in the bay almost always stop biting at dark.

Anglers sometimes encounter the full range of bottom fish in the bay. Blackfish (tautog) are caught by fish potters as they come in to spawn during the spring, but anglers take relatively few then. Fall provides the best shot for blacks around rocks supporting navigation aids and on a few shallow wrecks. Some mostly small sea bass are mixed in with the late-summer weakfish, but porgies (scup) are rare except in tiny sizes. Raritan Bay hosted massive runs of large porgies into the middle of the century, before pirate netters from Belford wiped them out.

Northern Shore. Boats that are berthed within Raritan Bay often fish the ocean, but most activity along the Northern Shore comes out of Shark River and Manasquan Inlets, two of the busiest inlets along the East Coast. The large municipal boat basin at Belmar includes a busy party and large-group charter fleet. Boats fishing out of Manasquan Inlet are berthed at Manasquan, Brielle, Point Pleasant Beach, and Point Pleasant. Brielle Yacht Club and Hoffman's Marina on that northern side berth one of the world's largest private offshore sportfishing fleets. Some run from the opposite shore at Southside Marina and upriver at Clark's Landing in Point Pleasant. Still others come out of northern Barnegat Bay via the Point Pleasant Canal.

The only volume of inshore rocky, mussel-covered bottom along the New Jersey coast is located north of Shark River Inlet, primarily from Deal to the famed Shrewsbury Rocks. Not only are those areas noted for bottom fish such as blackfish and sea bass, which prefer a rough seabed, but also for striped bass, bluefish, and large fluke. When doormat fluke were much more common, before intensive trawling sharply reduced the population and prevented most fluke from surviving much beyond their third year, these rugged bottoms attracted many anglers seeking the fluke of their dreams, and they were willing to break off many rigs in the process. Some party boats specialized in that fishing, although most fluke boats today generally opt for smoother bottoms most of the time.

In addition to the rough bottoms, there are many lumps just a few miles offshore all along this coast. The most famous of those is the Klondike, a large area of lumps covered with mussels, which held huge quantities of sea bass and porgies well into the 1900s. That area between the Shark River and Manasquan Inlets was a major attraction when Manasquan Inlet was stabilized in the early 1930s. Unfortunately, extensive dragging has so smoothed the bottom that the Klondike is no longer productive of sea bass and porgies. The lumps do hold sand eels, however, which in turn attract fluke, bluefish, bonito, little tunny, and even stripers at times. Augie's Lump, the Ammo Grounds, and Eagle's Lump are smaller hills close to the Klondike that are particularly noted for bonito chumming during late summer. Manasquan Ridge, about 6 miles from that inlet, offers similar fishing, as does a string of others running to the south, such as Southeast Lump, Tolten Lump, and J. B.'s Lump. Tolten, 17 miles southeast and near the wreck of the same name, is often bathed by blue water late in the summer, which attracts great numbers of little tunny and bonito and an occasional dolphin.

The most prominent structure off the Northern Shore is the Mud Hole, a deep trench that appears to be a geological extension of the Hudson River out to the edge of the continental shelf. Depths range to more than 250 feet in parts of the trench, from the BA Buoy at the northern end to Monster Ledge, which is about 22 miles east of Manasquan Inlet. Beyond that, the Mud Hole acquires different names in the deeper spots farther off. These include Glory Hole (about 35 to 45 miles), which is noted for sharking, and Chicken Canyon (50 miles), which often attracts both bluefin and yellowfin tuna and sharks.

The inshore bluefin tuna fishery focuses on the Mud Hole, especially at Monster Ledge and even closer to shore around the Oil Wreck and the Arundo. This is primarily a late-summer to early-fall fishery. It was depressed during the mid-1990s, but in the past it often produced outstanding action with school, medium, and giant tuna. A small mesh dragger fishery that just about eliminated whiting (silver hake) and greatly reduced the ling (red hake) population is probably to blame for the lack of larger bluefins, because those fish provided the forage that drew the bluefins to the area. Sharking is also popular in the Mud Hole, and little tunny, bonito, skipjack tuna, and chicken dolphin are frequently caught there in late summer by both trollers and chunkers.

Just inside the Mud Hole to the north are some of the most famous fishing grounds worked by northern New Jersey and western Long Island boats. The Mud Buoy, also called the Mud Dump, was the most consistent area for chumming bluefish in August and September during the 1990s, but dumping of dredged muds from New York Harbor was stopped in 1997. The lack of this activity may discourage the bluefish, as happened when the dumping of acids in the stained Acid Waters was stopped three decades earlier.

Just offshore of that huge mound of mud is 17 Fathoms, a rough-bottom area named for its average depth. Bluefish feed there on numerous small bottom fish, and there is very good blackfishing in December and January, as inshore areas get too cold for the tautog. The Farms is a similar area, located nearby just inside the Mud Hole, which is noted for bluefish from May through November. Another rocky area farther inshore and just offshore of Shrewsbury Rocks is the Rattlesnake. This 55- to 60-foot rough bottom produces large quantities of blackfish. Farther north off Sandy Hook is the Scotland Grounds; the wrecks and rough bottom there provide good ling and blackfish catches in spring and fall, and it is the closest such spot for bottom anglers coming out of Raritan Bay.

Due to its proximity to one of the busiest harbors in the world, the Northern Shore has more than its share of wrecks from both collisions and sinkings during two world wars. Those hundreds of wrecks are scattered from just beyond the surf line out to near the canyons. While the inshore pieces harbor blackfish, sea bass, porgies, and ling in season, deeper wrecks often hold cod and pollock even during the summer, although those species were overfished and have been in short supply during the 1990s. Bluefish also commonly gather around wrecks and may even be found over those in 200 to 300 feet in December. The major offshore wreck fishery in recent years has been for jumbo sea bass, in depths over 200 feet and 60 to 80 miles from Brielle. They are caught from late fall through early spring and often run 3 to 5 pounds, although some specimens occasionally range up to 8 pounds.

Among the best-known and hardest fished offshore wrecks during the summer and early fall are the Bacardi and Texas Tower. Both are on the 30-fathom curve, about 65 miles out. They attract a June run of medium and giant bluefin tuna that may be replaced by yellowfins in the summer. In 1989, there were tuna to be caught at the Bacardi every day from June into the fall, and weekend fleets often exceeded 200 boats. These arrived from ports as far apart as Montauk and Barnegat, but that phenomenon has never been repeated. Large school bluefin used to be caught regularly at the Bacardi in October, whereas cod and pollock resided on the bottom, although few have been caught in recent years.

Winter codfishing is conducted mainly on wrecks 30 to 40 miles offshore in depths of 100 to 140 feet or so. The *Virginia* and the many wrecks in the Red Square, plus others to the southeast once produced lots of large cod, although that fishery dropped off to a pick of smaller cod and just a few cows during the 1990s.

Canyon fishing has become a favored attraction for anglers all along the New Jersey coast, and large fleets out of Belmar, Brielle, Manasquan, and Point Pleasant fish 80 to 90 miles off in Hudson Canyon from late June into October for yellowfin, bigeye, and albacore tuna; dolphin; blue and white marlin; and an occasional wahoo. Trolling dominates during early summer, when overnight chunking produces state-record mako and blue sharks but not many tuna. This tends to change around mid-August, when the night bite for yellowfins turns on. A few swordfish are also caught in that fashion, especially around Labor Day. Northern Shore boats also commonly fish a bit farther southeast in the much smaller Toms, Lindenkohl, and Spencer Canyons, but they sometimes have to make longer runs farther south to Wilmington Canyon when cool water moves into northern canyons early in the fall.

Surf fishing is a very important sport along the Northern Shore, especially since the revival of striped bass and weakfish during the late 1990s. Sandy Hook attracts great numbers of anglers to its parking lots, but the best fishing is often at the tip, which requires a walk of more than a mile. On the bay side of Sandy Hook, anglers cast into the mouth of the Shrewsbury River or Spermacetti Cove for weakfish, school stripers, and winter flounder at times. Numerous jetties above Shark River Inlet provide good sport for anglers using cleats to avoid slipping on the rocks. In addition to stripers and bluefish, many fluke and blackfish are caught from the jetties.

Some of the jetties between the Shark River and Manasquan Inlets were filled in by sand during beach replenishment projects, but the area remains very productive for surf casters. The jetties at the Shark River Inlet are short and provide limited fishing, but both Manasquan Inlet jetties are longer and provide extremely popular platforms for anglers seeking stripers, blues, weaks, blacks, and fluke.

The stretch of beaches from there to Barnegat Inlet is almost entirely sand and offers only a few very short jetties in Bay Head and Lavallette. These beaches provide classic surf conditions with fairly deep water nearby and lots of bars, cuts, and sloughs. The "structure" constantly changes, but good-looking water is always available. The roaring northwesters of fall are at the angler's back, and the dunes are high enough in most areas to block the wind somewhat. The surf is sometimes so calm under those circumstances that anglers ply the waters in sneakers in November. After a few days of northwest wind, so much water is pushed offshore that surf casters can wade to the outer bars at low tide.

Beach buggies are permitted after the bathing season from the Brick Township beaches south, although drivers must obtain a permit from each municipality they will pass through. Anglers without buggies can get along fine, however, because end-of-the-street parking is readily available in many spots after Labor Day; it's just a few yards from the parking areas to the surf. Island Beach State Park provides the best access for buggy operators, thousands of whom purchase seasonal permits. Many others pay by the day. An annual Governor's Surf Fishing Tournament is held there in October.

All of the usual species are caught from these sand beaches. The emphasis is on baitfishing during the spring and summer for stripers. Sea worms are the usual choice at first, but from May into December surf clams are the standard, as they are much cheaper and seem to attract larger bass. These clams became particularly popular during the 1990s. The fishery tends to be best right after a hard easterly blow, which tosses clams up on the beach. As the clams die, those not consumed by sea gulls are washed into the surf, where stripers wait for a treat they otherwise can't partake of. As a result, long casts are rarely necessary, and kids often do best with clams because they can't cast far beyond the wash. Mullet have traditionally been prime baits for bluefish, and that's especially the case in September, when the first cold snaps send those small forage fish down the beach in large schools.

Anglers are attracted to jetties and beaches all along the Jersey coast.

Casting lures for bass, blues, and weaks attracts large crowds of anglers in the fall. Popular lures are swimming plugs that are smaller (usually $5/8$ to 1 ounce) than those used to the east, as surf casters here generally opt for light 7- to 8-foot rods and 10- to 14-pound lines with small spinning reels. Jigs from $1/4$ to $5/8$ ounce tipped with soft plastics are very popular for school stripers and weakfish, whereas metal is particularly effective when long casts are required and when bluefish may also be present.

Most surf anglers here fish a teaser a few feet ahead of the lure when bluefish aren't a problem, as the weightless fly or soft plastic often produces more stripers and weaks than the lure. Popping plugs work at times for stripers and blues but aren't a standard. Dawn and dusk are traditionally prime periods for casting, but some of the best catches are made at night. As the season progresses, hot action on lures is possible at any time during the day. Bluefish blitzes are difficult to predict; they appear suddenly to blast baitfish, especially bunkers, and quickly move on.

For jetty jockeys fearless enough to risk their limbs, the north jetty at Barnegat Inlet may be the best spot on the coast for stripers during a northeaster. Fly anglers have done very well casting into the inlet for little tunny (locally called false albacore) during late summer. Anglers land many fluke and small blues in the inlet from the jetty, and there's good weakfishing on jigs cast from bulkheads inside the inlet.

Shore fishing is comparatively limited here. The Long Branch Fishing Pier, the only long public fishing pier along the Northern Shore, burnt down and wasn't replaced. Not only was that a fine summer fishing spot for fluke, but it was also famed for whiting fishing at night during early winter. Anglers often caught bags of whiting there at virtually no expense, but both the pier and the whiting were gone by the 1990s. A short fishing pier still exists at Seaside Heights, as do private piers at Ocean Grove and Belmar. Quite a few docks and sedge banks offer free fishing possibilities on Raritan Bay, and there is a fishing pier at Keansburg.

The Shark River is small, but it offers very good spring and fall winter flounder fishing from both designated piers in Belmar Marina and from rental skiffs, as well as seasonal opportunities for stripers, fluke, kingfish, and blowfish. The Manasquan River also provides only a few miles of tidal waters, although it's heavily fished by small-boat owners for flounder, fluke, weakfish, and school stripers. The walls within the inlet on both sides draw hundreds of anglers. They catch lots of fluke, sea robins, and hickory shad but also get a good shot at bluefish when these species first flood in for a week or so in early May.

The Manasquan River connects with Barnegat Bay through the Point Pleasant Canal, which constitutes the start of the Intracoastal Waterway. The canal is an excellent shore fishing area. Anglers mostly bottom-fish for flounder, blackfish, sea bass, and porgies during the day, but striper and weakfish pros roam the banks at night. Due to roaring currents, the best fishing is usually around slack water. The rough bottom claims lots of sinkers and jigs, and nets are required to get larger fish over the fence that runs along both sides of the canal.

The northern half of Barnegat Bay is ideal for small boats, as this is all shallow water that provides excellent opportunities for flounder, fluke, weakfish and blue claw crabs. The small Metedeconk River, just beyond the canal, is a good spot for weakfish. The somewhat larger Toms River farther south attracts a spring run of white perch, although the wintering stripers that used to reside there were cleaned out by netters long ago. Holes near the Mantoloking Bridge provide an early-spring haven for flounder and are very good for fluke and weakfish later on.

Good-size stripers are caught off sedge banks near Barnegat Inlet during the spring on live herring, and live eels fished at night from summer into fall produce some 30- to 50-pounders in the same areas. A large run of small bluefish usually invades the bay in May and June, producing fine sport over endless shallow eelgrass bottoms. Enthusiasts favor small popping plugs cast on light tackle. The great runs of school stripers that hit bucktail jigs and flies during April and May in the 1960s haven't returned. It was this fishery that sparked establishment of the Salt Water Fly Rodders from Cap Colvin's Tackle Shop in Seaside Park. The ancient practice of chumming with grass shrimp for weakfish in Barnegat Bay has returned, however, because the eelgrass that harbors those tiny baitfish has recovered from a blight that afflicted the entire Northeast Atlantic coast.

Central shore. Barnegat Inlet is much wider than its counterparts to the north, and much more dangerous as well. Shifting sands have been a problem since Henry Hudson first spotted it from sea and gave it a Dutch name—one that roughly translates to Breakers Inlet. A recent project to stabilize the inlet with a new, longer south jetty was only partially successful, but it did provide a great, flat-topped fishing platform. A substantial fleet of private, charter, and party boats is located just around the southern corner of the inlet and within yards of the famous red lighthouse, Barnegat Light. Known as Old Barney, it sits at the northern end of Long Beach Island. Many other boats run a few miles across the bay to the inlet from such ports as Waretown and Forked (pronounced fork-ed) River, which is the site of a state marina. Beach Haven is the major port toward the southern end of the island, but those boaters access the ocean via Little Egg Harbor Inlet.

Stripers and blues of all sizes are commonly caught in Barnegat Inlet, and the north jetty is a favorite for casters who work the broken-down seaward section before it rises up again at the light on the tip. Anglers also troll and jig for plentiful stripers and blues from October into December off Island Beach State Park and at the clam beds just northeast of the inlet and a couple of miles south on Harvey Cedars Lump. Fluking is very good both within and just outside of the inlet. Some of the best sea bass and blackfish wrecks along the coast are located within a short run from Barnegat Inlet. Blackfish specialists regularly catch tautog in the 10- to 15-pound class from those wrecks, especially in April.

Fishing within southern Barnegat Bay is similar to that in the northern section, although Double Creek Channel and Myer's Hole at Barnegat Light provide the deepest holes within the shallow bay and are often the best spots for winter flounder and weakfish. The Forked River Power Plant on the mainland side pushes hot water into the bay and attracts an early run of flounder as well as wintering school stripers.

Offshore fishing centers around Barnegat Ridge, about 16 miles east. The ridge area actually consists of the North, Middle, and South Ridges, which are famed for bluefish but also attract school bluefin tuna, little tunny, bonito, and even dolphin at times during late summer. Barnegat boats also fish lumps to the north, including Ole's Lump, which is a favorite for trolling and chunking school tuna as well as skipjacks and little tunny.

Most northern boats sail toward Barnegat during June to get the first shots at mako sharks along the 20-fathom line near the Resor Wreck, and in such depressions as the Dusky Hole and The Fingers. The sharking area referred to as The Star is at the northern end of The Fingers, where the compass star is located on the nautical chart. Unfortunately, those traditional sharking grounds have been producing mostly blue sharks rather than makos and browns (sandbars) because longlining pressures impacted the latter two species. Therefore, sharkers more frequently run even farther offshore, such as to the Triple Wrecks area, which is about 60 miles to sea but still gives up a few large makos. The Barnegat fleet is closer to Toms, Lindenkohl, and Spencer Canyons but also runs up to the Hudson or south to the Wilmington when necessary.

The Beach Haven charter fleet was much larger earlier in the twentieth century and attracted anglers from all over the East for school bluefin tuna trolling. That fishery has gone downhill over the years, and the Beach Haven fleet now fishes primarily for bluefish, fluke, and sea bass inshore plus canyon tuna and billfish. Little Egg Harbor Inlet produces large stripers on live eels during the fall, and the inshore waters of Great Bay are especially good for fluke and weakfish.

The Mullica River flows into Great Bay and is noted for excellent white perch fishing through the ice during very cold winters. Some stripers also overwinter in the Mullica. Graveling Point, where the river meets the bay, is usually where the first stripers of the season are caught by anglers casting sandworms from the sedge banks in March.

Long Beach Island is also noted for its surf casting, although the light-tackle lure fishing that dominates north of Barnegat Inlet in the fall isn't as common at Long Beach. Baitfishing is standard. Bunkers are most popular for both stripers and blues in the fall, when the chamber of commerce conducts its annual six-week Surf Fishing Tournament for those two species. It usually takes a striper of 40 to 50 pounds or more, and bluefish close to 20 pounds, to win the grand prize for each species, and almost invariably they and the vast majority of other entries are hooked on cut bunker. Clams and worms work here just as they do to the north, but anglers land few really big stripers on those baits.

The entire nature of the coast changes below Beach Haven Inlet, as the shoreline becomes a series of small sandy barrier islands separated by shoals. Brigantine Inlet, at the north end of Absecon Island, is also known as Wreck Inlet and is used only by small boats. At the south end of the island is Absecon Inlet; this wide, stable inlet carries much charter and private boat traffic from Atlantic City, which is on its south side. Fluke and weakfish are the featured species within Absecon Bay; outside fishing includes bluefish at such nearby spots as Atlantic City Ridge, and wreck fishing for sea bass and blackfish. Sharking is popular at the 28 Mile Wreck, which also provides good inshore trolling for school bluefins and dolphin. Canyon anglers from here south tend to run to the Wilmington and Baltimore rather than to the northeast canyons.

Surf casting south of Long Beach Island isn't as good as that to the north due to a more gradual deepening from shore. While stripers and blues aren't as frequently encountered, there is often good baitfishing for kingfish and weakfish. The mouths of inlets are also productive, and it should be noted that the all-tackle world-record $78\frac{1}{2}$-pound striped bass was plugged from an Atlantic City jetty on the stormy night of September 21, 1982.

South Jersey. Great Egg Harbor Inlet is used by boats sailing out of Margate to the north and Ocean City on the south side. No large party and charter boat fleet exists in this area; however, the very lack of pressure on wrecks has made it possible for some party boats to consistently take the largest blackfish in the state. Many trophy blackfish of 10 pounds or more, some to 18 pounds, have been landed. An all-tackle world-record 25-pounder was taken in January 1998.

Boats in this area find good sharking 20 to 30 miles offshore and frequently encounter large quantities of Spanish mackerel while trolling inshore for bluefish both on grounds toward Atlantic City and farther south to such areas as the Stone Beds. They also share areas closer to the inlets directly below them (Corson, Townsend, and Hereford), such as Sea Isle

Rods with shorter sections developed not only out of carrying convenience but also because they could be concealed or camouflaged as walking sticks at a time when angling was considered dishonorable.

Tournament anglers returning from canyon fishing attract a crowd in Cape May.

Lump, Sea Isle Shoal, and Avalon Shoal. The many creeks and channels inside barrier islands provide good action with fluke and weakfish. Striped bass and blackfish are caught at bridges near the ocean.

From Wildwood to Cape May, anglers can experience excellent variety thanks to the mouth of Delaware Bay. Boats here have the unique opportunity to sail through protected waters in either direction to reach the ocean or bay. The navy cut a canal through Cape May that boats can follow from the harbor into Delaware Bay. The ocean is a shorter run through wide Cold Spring Inlet, which is more often simply referred to as Cape May Inlet. Only North Wildwood boats normally run out of Hereford Inlet, which has shoals that limit it to small boats.

Not only is the bay itself cleaner these days, but the legendary oxygen block in the Delaware River near Philadelphia also has been eliminated. This much cleaner river has once again become a major striped bass spawning area. Delaware Bay is an established spawning area for several species, including the weakfish. Although that species is very cyclical, it may well be that the incredible slaughter of them by trawlers, gillnetters, and pound nets, as well as recreational anglers, during periods of abundance is the reason for their sudden disappearance.

The last great cycle, which started in the early 1970s and ran into the mid-1980s, produced tremendous catches of ever-larger weaks during the May to June spawning run. Ultimately, 8- to 10-pounders became routine, and it took weaks in the midteens to win contests. These beautiful fish were coming back again in the late 1990s, but this time the fall and winter slaughter by trawlers in federal waters was prohibited by the Atlantic States Marine Fisheries Commission Management Plan and cooperation from the National Marine Fisheries Service.

Anglers catch most smaller bay weakfish by casting small jigs tipped with shedder crab or on that bait directly. The larger fish taken during the previous cycle, however, were easily attracted to jigs tipped with long plastic worms and other such artificials. Hotspots near the mouth of the bay include Brandywine Shoal in midbay (marked by Brandy-wine Light), Round Shoal, Sixty Foot Slough, Brown Shoal, and the adjacent deep-water anchorage for large vessels coming into the bay on the Delaware side.

Delaware Bay also represents the practical northern range of several species. Black drum follow behind the weakfish each spring, and June is the prime month of the spawning run. Those fish can run up to more than 100 pounds and were almost wiped out for years after tuna purse seiners began to make huge sets on the drum. Bottom fishing at night with clams on the bottom is the usual method for attracting drum. Croaker and spot are frequent summer catches in the bay. Cape May Harbor also produces the northernmost spotted seatrout fishing, as a few anglers wade from the marsh banks in the fall to cast lures for the southern version of the weakfish. There is some fishing throughout the marsh areas for small stripers, as well as for flounder, in the fall.

Shore fishing along the Atlantic here is marginal, as the bay and plentiful nearby structure make this more of a boater's fishery, but jetty and surf anglers connect at times, especially in fall, with striped bass, and occasionally bluefish, from Wildwood to Cape May Point. Accessible jetties with end-of-street parking are available in Wildwood, Cape May, and Cape May Point, but the prime jetties at Cape May Inlet are inaccessible, as they're surrounded by Coast Guard property.

Bluefishing was generally better off the Northern Shore during the 1990s, especially during the summer, than it was in South Jersey, which was spotty at best most of the time. However, a state record 27-pound, 1-ounce blue (which may be the second largest ever weighed) was caught in October 1997 on a Cape May party boat that was chumming at night on Five Fathom Bank.

Because any winter flounder found this far south are usually small and not particularly abundant, fluke are referred to simply as flounder. That fishery is an important one for the Wildwood-Cape May fleet, who get into them as early as April and often continue well into the fall.

The mouth of the bay is protected by dozens of underwater sandbars that create rips. These have become one of the finest places to fish for striped bass in the fall. From October into November and sometimes December there is usually good action in at least some of those rips for anglers drifting live eels. Hundreds of boats pursue the stripers on weekends, but the abundance of rips often makes it possible to get away from the crowd. Strong northwest winds muddy waters at the mouth of the bay, but easterly winds are good if not too strong, as the technique involves drifting through the rough water at the edge of the rip. The bass wait here for prey to be drawn to them. In addition to the private and charter fleets, several party boats also participate in this fishery. A smaller spring run occurs in the rips, but jigs tipped with baits are usually more effective than eels at that time.

The largest stripers caught around Cape May during recent falls haven't come from the rips, where volume is greatest, but from shallow waters near shore where bunker chunking draws big bass to those baits. South Jersey anglers also get into hot diamond jigging for migrating stripers and blues from late November into December, although that sport is primarily pursued on Five Fathom Bank. During the 1990s, it was illegal to retain any size striper from these waters, which are roughly 9 miles offshore and well into federal territory.

Offshore fishing is extremely important to the Cape May fleet, and South Jersey Marina is one of the largest of its kind on the coast. The marina sponsors several offshore tournaments, starting with a shark contest in early June. The king of all East Coast tournaments, however, is held out of The Canyon Club Resort Marina. The Mid-Atlantic $500,000 is actually misnamed, because the official calcuttas bring the pot—in a contest that draws more than 130 boats in mid-August—to well over a million dollars. The target species are blue and white marlin plus yellowfin and bigeye tuna, which are mostly caught in local canyons such as the Wilmington, Poorman's, and Baltimore.

South Jersey boats have a considerable advantage over their northern counterparts in that runs of only 60 miles or so are required to reach the closest spots, although tournament anglers regularly blow past the 100-fathom line to fish 500- to 1,000-fathom areas 100 miles and more from Cape May. The offshore fleet gets into especially good chunking for 50- to 150-pounders during June and July on hills off Delmarva. Yellowfins mix into the same grounds, 40 miles or so from Cape May, during the summer.

Weakfish, fluke, and small blues are featured farther up the bay off the Maurice (pronounced "Morris") River and Fortescue, where a large charter fleet concentrates on these species. Popular areas include Miah Maull Shoal and Egg Island Point. Striped bass have become a more prominent quarry since the art of bunker chunking was introduced to the area, and 60-pound bass have been hooked at the bug light off the Maurice River. Local anglers fish stripers primarily in October and November, although schoolies are present in the Maurice River much of the year. Good bay fishing for private boaters continues up the bay to at least the Cohansy River. Stripers can be caught even during the winter by shore casters around the Rt. 95 Bridge from New Jersey to Delaware. The best Delaware River striper fishing, however, occurs farther upriver.

The Division of Fish, Game and Wildlife has been acquiring parts of the extensive wetlands along Delaware Bay. In cooperation with the federal government and private groups, they plan to eventually have 60 percent under their protection in order to ensure protection for the many juvenile species such as weakfish and fluke that are dependent on those marshes.

NEW MEXICO

Although some perceive New Mexico as a desert state, anglers who frequent the area know better. From its high alpine lakes in wilderness areas to its small streams and rivers that feed large reservoirs, there is ample water to provide varied fishing opportunities. Whether you're a fly fishing purist, a dedicated bass angler, or just enjoy a day on the water or relaxing on the bank, there's plenty of action on the state's 6,000 miles of permanent streams and rivers and 170 lakes and reservoirs—all with good fish populations that are mostly accessible to the public.

The "Land of Enchantment" has seven major watersheds. Among them, they offer almost any kind of fishing. This state is blessed with diverse habitats, ranging from arctic-alpine to mountain forests, prairies, and deserts. These areas are home to various cold- and warmwater species. Of the former, there are rainbow, brown, brook, cutthroat, and lake trout, as well as kokanee salmon; of the latter, largemouth, smallmouth, striped, white, and spotted bass thrive throughout the state, as do good populations of walleye, northern pike, crappie, bluegills, and three species of catfish.

A wealth of public land is another of New Mexico's blessings, giving anglers easy access to recreation statewide. The state's five national forests and 2 million acres of public land are managed by the National Forest Service, the Bureau of Land Management, and other federal agencies. State parks and wildlife areas abound. In addition, many Indian tribes have good fishing waters for which no state license is needed, although tribal permits are required. Excellent fishing opportunities also abound on private land, but permission is required and some landowners charge access fees.

The state Game and Fish Department has regulations and projects aimed at improving fishing for everyone; this is a challenge in a state where drought and demands for irrigation constantly impact the fisheries resource. The state stocks 6.7 million trout each year for a growing number of anglers. Some areas are designated as "special trout waters" and have regulations that promote quality fishing by restricting baits and bag limits. The rules and fees are subject to change, so anglers are advised to check first.

Northwest

Navajo Lake. A 15,000-acre irrigation reservoir, Navajo Lake holds good populations of warm- and coldwater fish. In the spring, there's excellent fishing for large crappie, which are predominantly caught by jigging plastic grubs and spoons around submerged vegetation. Trolling for kokanee salmon is productive throughout the season. In the fall, these fish school to spawn at the spillway and in Francis Canyon. Roe sacks are prime baits for trout in these areas. Navajo also supports smallmouth bass up to 5 pounds, northern pike that approach 20 pounds, and brown trout, some weighing in at more than 10 pounds. Try slow-trolling in the winter months for the big browns.

San Juan River. One of the finest tailwater trout fisheries in the nation was created below Navajo Dam when it was completed in 1962. On this section of the San Juan River, anglers can consistently catch trout from 15 to 19 inches and larger. The well-nourished fish, mostly rainbows, grow 6 inches a year and weigh an average of 3 to 5 pounds. Eight-pounders are not uncommon. Twenty miles of excellent fishing can now be found in what was formerly a muddy catfish river. The cool, clear water flowing from the reservoir's 300-foot depths makes ideal habitat that grows trophy rainbow and brown trout and even a few cutthroats. To enhance and protect this valuable fishery, the state has established special rules. The first quarter-mile below the dam is a catch-and-release section; all fish must be immediately returned to the water. The next $3^1/_2$-mile section is restricted to the use of artificial flies and lures with barbless hooks, and has a bag limit of one trout that must be 20 inches or longer. The river downstream from the "quality" sections does not have special regulations, yet it maintains fine fishing albeit with fewer trout.

The San Juan River flow varies according to yearly snowpack and reservoir storage, but usually runs at 600 to 800 cubic feet per second (cfs) in the winter and summer, and as high at 5,000 cfs in the spring. The current is swift and deep, with intermittent pools, riffles, and flats, some of them 30 to 40 yards wide. Chest waders are recommended, but the big water can be hazardous. There is good fishing in numerous side channels where the wading is easier. Best results come from a modified nymphing technique in which the fly is sunk until it floats just off the bottom. Put a single split shot about 18 inches above the fly and cast upstream, letting it drift back down in a natural manner. Long casts are not necessary.

San Juan trout don't strike like most fish. Instead, they lie on the bottom, rise to take the fly, and slowly float back down with no perceptible hit. A small colored marker, serving as a strike indicator, is placed where the leader and line meet. This is an effective way to determine strikes. Watch the indicator and when it stops or twitches, however slightly, set the hook. This, along with the weighted fly, should guarantee success.

A No. 10 black Woolly Worm and a local fly called the San Juan Worm, along with several lo-cally tied patterns that resemble trout eggs, are good most anytime. Generally, the darker patterns work best, but in one area called the "orange hole," anything seems to work as long as it is orange. Due to stabilized water flows, insect hatches also provide excellent dry-fly fishing using small No. 18 to 20 Renegade and Iron Blue Dun patterns.

The reputation of this river brings anglers from all over the country and beyond. A problem with this is an overabundance of people, particularly on the weekends. Guides who use boats are available and are very successful, and hiring a guide is probably the best option for a first-time angler.

Navajo Indian Reservation/Morgan Lake. At 12,000-acre Morgan Lake, a power plant takes water for cooling purposes, and this keeps the temperature around 60°F in the winter. Thus, Morgan is good for catching 3- to 4-pound largemouth bass from November through March, using slow retrieves with deep-diving crankbaits, jigging spoons, and small plastic worms.

Jicarilla Apache Reservation/Stone Lake. Stone Lake is one of the better trout waters in the state for large rainbows, but it does suffer from occasional winter kills. It is best fished from boats or float tubes because of an abundance of weeds. Anglers are limited to using flies and lures here. Other reservation lakes are La Jara, Mundo, Horse, and Dulce. Some winter ice fishing is available.

Rio Chama. This watershed has three major impoundments. Heron Lake's 8,000 acres is home to the only viable population of lake trout (mackinaw) in the state, with a record 25-pounder in the books. Troll deep via a downrigger or lead-core line, using a heavy jig or some type of swimming lure. Heron also holds good numbers of kokanee salmon, which are best caught by trolling in summer and which gang up to spawn in the late fall. Rainbow trout also show up in creels from this location, where boats are limited to no-wake speeds. Just downstream is El Vado Lake, another reservoir that is best fished from a boat. A state-record 20-pound, 4-ounce brown trout was taken from the river just below the dam. Farther downstream is Abiquiu Reservoir, where there are good populations of trout, crappie, channel catfish, and smallmouth bass. The Chama is fed by numerous smaller tributaries, the most notable being the Rio Brazos, which is mostly on private land.

Jemez Mountain streams. The watersheds of the Jemez Mountains are host to many small trout-filled streams, some of them limited to flies and lures only. Most rainbow and brown trout are in the 8- to 12-inch range, but 20-inch lunkers are not uncommon. Every spring, anglers look forward to the stonefly hatch in the Guadalupe, San Antonio, and East Fork Rivers.

Rio Grande River. The Rio Grande River flows north to south, nearly bisecting the state. As it enters New Mexico it runs through a deep gorge, part of which is designated as a federal Wild and Scenic River. Those who walk into this section

---

Some species of fish can make their own light, and only fish can produce electricity from their bodies.

are rewarded with large rainbow and brown trout, along with northern pike that have migrated downstream from Colorado. The Red River upstream from its confluence with the Rio Grande is particularly inviting in the fall, when brown trout migrate upstream to spawn. Coldwater species predominate in the Rio Grande's northern section and tributaries, where Hopewell Lake is recognized for its brook trout. Cochiti Lake, a U.S. Army Corps of Engineers impoundment, offers coldwater and warmwater species. The lake has some trout and good numbers of crappie, white bass, and channel catfish. The spillway provides good fishing for trout, primarily with baits. Severe drawdowns do have an adverse effect, and the upper end has been silting in. Boats are recommended, but be advised that this is a no-wake lake.

Pueblo Indian waters. The Jemez, Santa Clara, Sandia, Nambe, Zuni, Acoma, and Isleta Pueblos all have lakes, and some have streams that are stocked and open to the public. Permits are required.

Bluewater Lake. At 2,000 acres, Bluewater Lake always produces nice rainbows for those fishing from the bank or through the ice, as well as for lure trollers and bait anglers. Try casting flies in early morning and late evening as well; a spinning rig with a fly and bubble is sometimes a good combination. Water levels in the lake fluctuate significantly.

Northeast

Wilderness trout. In a triangle of the Santa Fe and Carson National Forests bordered by the towns of Santa Fe, Taos, and Las Vegas, are 20 small lakes and 150 miles of streams that can be reached only by foot or on horseback. All have excellent fishing for rainbow and cutthroat trout, but don't expect any lunkers, as the fish grow slowly in the high mountains with their short summer seasons. The 167,000-acre Pecos Wilderness in the Sangre de Cristo Mountains contains the headwaters of the Pecos River, the state's second-largest watershed. Popular secluded lakes include Spirit, Pecos Baldy, Katherine, and Stewart. An ultralight spinning rod and an assortment of small lures, hooks, bubbles, and flies are all that is needed. In the summertime, catch grasshoppers for live bait; this is a killer combination in the high country.

Red River. Small headwater lakes for the Red River include Middle Fork, Goose, Heart, and Lost, all with cutthroat and rainbow trout. Cabresto Lake and stream has brook trout. The main river is stocked with rainbows, and the lower portion below the Red River hatchery is great for brown trout in the fall.

Eagle Nest. Located in the 8,500-foot Moreno Valley, this 3,000-acre Eagle Nest is one of the state's best public trout waters. It provides year-round fishing for all who want a truly quality angling experience. This lake produces 200 pounds of trout per acre. Although 14- to 16-inch rainbows are common, a true trophy is always a possibility. Kokanee salmon are stocked regularly. A former private lake, it is under a long-term lease that provides public access for bank anglers. Boaters do best by trolling. Fishing is most successful in the early morning and late evening, especially casting flies to rising fish. This is also a popular spot for ice anglers.

Cimarron River. A 21-mile stretch of heavily fished water below Eagle Nest Lake, the Cimarron River is stocked throughout the summer, but fishing is mediocre at best. In the fall, this river does a flip-flop, providing exceptional brown trout action, especially for lunkers that become aggressive before spawning. Some portions of the river flow through private land, although most of it is open to the public.

Pecos River. The Pecos is a major river beginning in the Pecos Wilderness and flowing south into Texas. Trout are caught in the upper reaches, and warmwater species in the lower sections. Santa Rosa Lake, a 1,500-acre reservoir, has bass, walleye, crappie, and catfish.

Ute Lake. Located in the broad grasslands, Ute is a large reservoir (8,200 acres) and one of the best warmwater lakes in New Mexico because it is not subject to irrigation drawdowns. Smallmouth bass do well here, and the state record of just over $6^1/_2$ pounds was caught in Ute. White bass, large walleye, largemouth bass, and crappie are also available.

Conchas Lake. A 25-mile impoundment on the Canadian River, Conchas is the top walleye lake in New Mexico. A rocky bottom cut by submerged cliffs makes ideal habitat for this species. Boats equipped with sonar help locate these spots. Conchas is also known for large crappie, which provide best action during April and May.

Southeast

Pecos River. Fishing along the river is good for channel and flathead catfish in isolated holes. Anglers park and walk a 2- to 3-mile stretch using chicken livers, cut baits, and grasshoppers. Much of the river is marginal due to erratic and low water flows. On-stream reservoirs provide good angling for warmwater fish. In addition to Santa Rosa, 4,500-acre Lake Sumner has the usual warmwater species, including white bass. Try fishing here during July and August when the pressure drops off. Use buzzbaits along rocky bluffs and mini-coves. When the water rises after summer showers, fish shallow at the upper end. Brantley Reservoir (3,400 acres) is the last major impoundment with similar species and angling techniques to those at Sumner. Carlsbad Municipal Lake provides urban angling opportunities for trout in the wintertime, as well as warmwater species year-round.

Sacramento and White Mountain streams. These areas have assorted small streams and lakes, plus Ruidoso, Carrizo, and Eagle Rivers. Alto and Grindstone Lakes in the south-central mountains are stocked with rainbows. A natural population of brook trout thrives in Bonito Lake and in the streams. The best fishing is at dawn and dusk.

Mescalero Apache Reservation. A large reservoir at the edge of Ruidoso, plus two other smaller lakes nearby, provide good trout fishing; permits are required.

Southwest
Elephant Butte Lake. This is New Mexico's largest and finest warmwater fishing spot. Its 40-mile length and 40,000 surface acres will satisfy any angler, and it has produced striped bass up to 54 pounds, largemouth bass to 9 pounds, flathead catfish up to 78 pounds, and above-average numbers and sizes of all the other warmwater species. Unsurpassed largemouth opportunities make it home to national bass tournaments. It is one of the first lakes in which spring bass fishing picks up due to its southerly location and shallow, south-facing, protected brushy areas. Better fishing early in the year is in the area above the "narrows" at the upper end of the lake. White bass get active at the same time and in the same area.

Caballo Lake. Located just below Elephant Butte, Caballo is the last reservoir on the Rio Grande River before it leaves the state. It harbors the same fish species, but not the reputation of its neighbor, possibly because of its smaller size and severe drawdowns during irrigation season. It is a good fishery and seldom crowded, best known for its white bass fishing in the summer.

Gila National Forest. The permanent waters offered by Gila National Forest support good populations of smaller trout, but the areas separating them can be very dry. And some of these waters head into the wilderness area, where access is restricted. Others host populations of the Gila trout, an endangered species, and are closed to fishing. Rainbow and brown trout, with a few brookies at higher elevations, are the primary local species. Lakes include Lake Roberts, a 71-acre site with rainbow trout and catfish; Wall Lake, a 10-acre puddle with rainbows; 100-acre Snow Lake, which also has rainbow trout; and 22-acre Bear Canyon, which has rainbow trout, bluegills, catfish, and crappie.

Bill Evans Lake. This 62-acre off-stream reservoir consistently produces big largemouth bass, including a 15-pound, 13-ounce state record. Bluegills, crappie, and catfish are present, and trout are stocked in the winter.

Rio Grande River. The Rio Grande is primarily a warmwater fishery. The only exception is the section between Elephant Butte and Caballo Reservoirs, which runs through the town of Truth or Consequences. There, cool water from the depths of Elephant Butte is home to large rainbow trout, some of which approach 6 pounds. Food is plentiful here. The section is channelized, and access is limited to a few public stretches of bank. Best success here is had by drift fishing with flies or baits from flat-bottomed boats, but launch points are limited.

Gila River. The Gila is a large river flowing from the Gila National Forest into Arizona. Warmwater species include catfish and smallmouth bass. It is stocked with rainbow trout upstream in the national forest.

Best Waters
Although natural circumstances have unpredictable affects on fisheries resources or on anglers' success rates, some waters stand out in New Mexico for particular species. These include the following.

Rainbow trout: San Juan River below Navajo Reservoir, Rio Chama above and below El Vado Lake, Pecos River, Rio de Los Pinos, and the Jemez watershed

Brown trout: Navajo Reservoir, Wild Rivers section of the Rio Grande, San Juan River below Navajo Reservoir, Rio Chama, Cimarron River below Eagle Nest Lake, Mora-Pecos River system, and the Jemez watershed

Brook trout: Hopewell and Cabresto Lakes, and Bonito and Carrizo Creeks

Lake trout: Heron Lake

Kokanee salmon: Heron, El Vado, Navajo, and Eagle Nest Lakes

Largemouth bass: Elephant Butte, Ute, and Conchas Lakes

Smallmouth bass: Ute, Conchas, Elephant Butte, and Abiquiu Lakes

White bass: Elephant Butte, Caballo, Cochiti, and Brantley Lakes

Walleye: Ute, Conchas, Caballo, Santa Rosa, and Sumner Lakes

Catfish: All of the larger waters in the state

Crappie: Conchas, Abiquiu, Ute, Cochiti, Elephant Butte, and Caballo Lakes

Bluegills: Elephant Butte, Sumner, Santa Rosa, Ute, and Conchas Lakes

Green sunfish: Canadian, Pecos, Rio Grande, Gila, and Black Rivers

Yellow perch: Lower Charette, Springer, and Stubblefield Lakes

NEW YORK
To many non–New Yorkers, and even to many people who live in or near New York City, it's a surprise to learn that the Empire State has among the most diverse and abundant fishing resources in North America.

North of Manhattan's skyscrapers and pavement are some 70,000 miles of rivers and streams, 7,500 lakes and ponds, 324 reservoirs, and two Great Lakes that offer angling for most of North America's important freshwater species. To the east, the marine waters of the Atlantic abut more than

1,500 miles of coastline and offer bay, inshore, and offshore opportunities for a broad spectrum of large and small gamefish. The number of species pursued in New York—from yellow perch to yellowfin tuna and brook trout to blue marlin—rivals that found in Fulton Fish Market, the Big Apple's fabled fishmonger's paradise. Accordingly, New York annually ranks in the top 10 in both number of licensed anglers and number of registered boats, despite its large and mostly urban population.

This state discharges water from all of the Great Lakes, the Adirondack Mountains, the Catskill Mountains, and the Delaware Basin, and contains a plethora of warmwater and coldwater environments for the likes of such popular and widely dispersed fish as trout (which once thrived in the waters around Manhattan), bass, salmon, pike, and walleye. The estuary of the Hudson River, a major Atlantic tributary, is the second most important nursery for striped bass on the East Coast. And Montauk, at the eastern end of Long Island, maintains its long and well-deserved reputation as a world-renowned saltwater angling port.

In saltwater, the most prominent inshore and bay species include striped bass, bluefish, flounder, fluke, weakfish, mackerel, black sea bass, blackfish, and porgies. Offshore, various shark species are regularly sought, as are bluefin, yellowfin, and bigeye tuna; albacore; bonito; dolphin; striped marlin; and blue marlin. Among warmwater species in freshwater, largemouth and smallmouth bass are extremely popular. Other prominent fish include northern pike, walleye, chain pickerel, muskellunge, yellow perch, crappie, rock bass, bullhead, and assorted sunfish. Eels, fallfish, suckers, and carp have some following, and migratory American shad are a favored springtime catch. Brown and brook trout top the popularity charts among coldwater species, but the state offers prominent fisheries for rainbow trout, lake trout, and steelhead, as well as chinook, coho, kokanee, and landlocked Atlantic salmon.

New York has the distinction of being the birthplace of fly fishing and fly tying in North America, owing to the efforts of Theodore Gordon, who, around the turn of the twentieth century, applied then exclusively British tactics to trout in the Neversink River and created the first dry-fly patterns appropriate for New World waters. By contrast, New York also has the distinction of producing some of the largest muskellunge ever recorded, among them numerous world records caught by trolling in the St. Lawrence River. It also produced the second-largest striped bass ever taken on rod and reel—a 76-pound former world record from Shagwong Reef off Montauk Point. And it produced one of the most heralded and disputed fish ever landed—a 3,427-pound great white shark taken from a boat captained by a man who the shark-hunting character Quint was patterned after in the book and movie *Jaws*.

From east to west and north to south, from salmon to shark and stream to surf, from farm pond to Finger Lake and rowboat to party boat, New York unquestionably has something to offer any angler.

Hudson Valley

The densely populated and largely suburban southeastern Hudson Valley has surprisingly more fishing opportunities on both sides of the scenic Hudson River than might be expected. These include numerous small rivers and streams, a plethora of ponds and small lakes, and a few publicly accessible motorboat lakes. Warmwater species are the main target in the smaller and shallower waters, but trout—primarily stocked—exist in numerous places.

On the east side of the Hudson River are 15 small to midsize reservoirs that are part of the Croton River watershed and that partly supply New York City with water. These strictly regulated reservoirs are off-limits to everyone except anglers on foot or fishing from rowboats. A prohibition against motors keeps many anglers from venturing onto them, but these bodies of water, as well as their inlet and outlet streams, are home to several trout species as well as bass, and comprise some of the most significant yet underutilized publicly accessible waters in the area. West Branch, Croton, Kensico, and Cross River Reservoirs are among the larger and more notable options, and quality stream fishing for trout can be had on Amawalk Outlet as well as on the East Branch of the Croton River.

Hudson River. From the Tappan Zee Bridge spanning Haverstraw Bay, the widest section of river, to the dam at Troy, the tidal Hudson River offers surprisingly good and diverse fishing. Oft-maligned, oft-abused, but ever-potent, the remarkable Hudson has enjoyed a water-quality comeback and a resurgence in top-rate angling. It is ranked as a top Northeast fishery for largemouth and smallmouth bass, and an awesome spring hotspot for stripers. This reputation perseveres despite marginal shore fishing opportunities and insufficient access for transient boaters.

Fisheries biologists say that between 1 and 2 million stripers migrate into the Hudson each year to spawn. In the process, they traverse 154 miles from Manhattan to Troy, although the greater portion stays in the Hudson Highlands. These fish generally begin moving into and up the river in mid-March. By mid-April they reach Newburgh, and by late April they arrive in the area from Kingston to Catskill and beyond.

Spawning takes place when the water has warmed to the mid- to upper 50s, usually around mid- to late May. By mid-June, the main body of stripers has moved downstream and disperses in New York Harbor and along the coast, a few traveling as far as Cape Cod. Some fish, mostly small schoolies, remain in the river throughout the summer.

On September 2, 1927, O. C. Grinnell caught the first swordfish ever taken on rod and reel off the North Atlantic coast; Grinnell had been trying to catch a swordfish since the middle of June that year.

With the East Coast striper population having rebounded from historic lows, the number and size of fish in the Hudson amazes anglers. Those trolling with downriggers have run into schools so thick that their weights have bounced over the backs of fish and their sonar screens have turned black. In recent times, stripers up to 53 pounds have been caught, but they reportedly can run to 60 pounds and maybe more. Many anglers catch fish in the 20- to 30-pound range.

The prominent spring striper fishing areas in the lower Hudson include Croton Point, Storm King Mountain, Denning Point, Esopus Meadows, and the vicinity of Rondout, Esopus, and Catskill Creeks. Very few anglers cast for these deep spring fish; most drift, anchor, or troll. The tide changes are important, and most activity occurs on a moving tide. In colder weather, more fish are caught on bloodworms, but some are taken on pieces of herring. When the water warms, trolling with large plugs is somewhat effective, usually at depths of between 20 and 25 feet. The largest stripers regularly fall to baits, primarily from early May to early June. Live herring, chunks of herring, and live eels are the mainstays. More people use eels because they are readily available, whereas herring have to be caught and kept lively or fresh. The herring run, which coincides with the striper presence, is also strong, and stripers feed heavily on them.

Overshadowed by the abundance and popularity of stripers in the Hudson are another spring migrant, American shad. Hudson River shad were historically plentiful and among the largest specimens on the East Coast, making them primarily a commercial quarry. Their numbers have fluctuated in recent times, and sportfishing effort for them is marginal even when the population is high.

Shad are bottom-hugging fish that stay in main channels, and the sheer expansiveness of the Hudson daunts would-be shad pursuers. Some anglers have success with flies and darts that are fished behind boats anchored in midriver on the downstream edge of shoals, flats, and islands. The time just before and during low slack tide is good, especially near dawn and dusk; the peak of the run is from late April until early June.

Throughout the year, anglers interested in largemouth and smallmouth bass have plenty to enjoy on the Hudson. All of the major creeks, and portions of the main river from just south of the U.S. Military Reservation at West Point to north of Coxsackie, produce bass. The better creeks get most of the attention, especially from anglers launching smaller boats.

Tidal influences on the Hudson create a unique bass fishery within New York. Cover, current, and tide are interrelated here, and sometimes so is salt content. The Hudson is slightly brackish or completely freshwater somewhere around Cornwall Bay, although the exact location may vary with runoff. Bass do move and become active with tidal changes, as significant water-level fluctuation can occur between tides. Bass fishing is usually best when the water is at peak movement—either rising or falling. A falling tide is prime.

The average size of Hudson bass is fairly good, with 2-pounders common. This is in spite of heavy fishing pressure and is largely due to the release of virtually all bass. Largemouths here have been caught to 7 pounds and smallmouths to 5 pounds, and they are very scrappy fish. Shoals, sandbars, islands, and rockpiles are main river spots. In creeks, the focus is on assorted structure.

The Hudson River offers other species, although none are as highly touted as the aforementioned ones. Crappie and trout are common in many of the creeks, and carp—some large—are plentiful in the main river, as are white catfish and white perch. Sturgeon have historically been present, but there is no sportfishery for them. Bluefish range into the saline parts of the lower river and provide excitement when available.

Catskill Region

West of the Hudson Valley and just a two-hour drive from New York City, the Catskills are renowned for trout fishing, yet the angling is as diverse here as in the rest of the Empire State. In fact, largemouth bass, pickerel, and panfish are virtually as popular as trout. The region is blessed with numerous small lakes and ponds that support these species, particularly in the outlying areas of the Catskill Forest Preserve. Many of these waters are private and provide good angling, yet they seldom attract publicity. Nevertheless, the highlighted focal points for anglers are the New York City reservoirs, the major trout rivers, and the Delaware River. Each system offers something different but is connected to—and to some degree dependent on—the others.

New York City reservoirs. The Catskill watershed and Delaware River Basin are rooted in the rivulets and creeks of the Catskill Mountains, whose waters were dammed long ago to provide water for New York City. The outlet flow of these reservoirs provides cold water for exceptional downstream trout fishing, whereas the reservoirs themselves—Pepacton, Cannonsville, Neversink, Rondout, Schoharie, and Ashokan—are the Rip Van Winkles of New York angling.

These deep but moderate-size (1,145 to 8,300 acres) and undeveloped mountain reservoirs provide the bulk of Gotham's water (the rest coming from Croton watershed reservoirs), yet they are relatively unknown in angling circles. This is due in part to onerous restrictions placed upon their use—no motors, rowboats of a specific size kept at designated sites, mandatory inspections and steam-cleaning, no fishing near the dams, etc.—and rigorous enforcement. Yet in the mid-1990s, nearly 3,000 boating permits were granted for Pepacton, the most popular of the reservoirs.

At all of these waters many boats are chained to trees, and their owners—parking along the roadways—tote oars, cushions, rods, and fishing paraphernalia down steep banks, pull the boats to the shoreline, and row for a chance at brown trout that average between 5 and 8 pounds. Some are in the 10- to 15-pound range. These clear waters, most of which are full of alewives, have also produced 20-pound browns (a 22-pounder caught in the mid-1990s is believed to be the largest). They also contain smallmouth bass and other species. Landlocked salmon, for example, swim in Neversink Reservoir, which drowned some of Theodore Gordon's historic angling grounds; lake trout thrive in Rondout; and Ashokan possesses rainbow trout and walleye.

Some trolling for trout is done in the Catskill reservoirs by anglers using spoons and cowbell attractors on weighted or lead-core line. A fair amount of early-season casting occurs from shore; ice-out varies from late March to mid-April, and open patches of water, usually by creeks, provide some light-tackle near-surface angling. The majority of big trout, however, are taken by anglers who drift or slow-troll with live alewives (locally called sawbellies) fished deep at various levels.

Trout rivers. Possibly no other trout river in North America is known as widely within the continent, and outside it, as New York's Beaverkill. And no other river has been as widely written about or so detailed in contemporary trout and fly fishing literature.

Situated in the southwestern section of the Catskills, the Beaverkill is, in general terms, a relatively modest body of water, flowing some 45 miles to its confluence with the East Branch of the Delaware River. The upper half is almost entirely privately owned. From Roscoe, which is billed as "Trout Town USA," the Beaverkill is joined by the (mostly publicly accessible) Willowemoc Creek at famous Junction Pool. Here, it becomes a larger river with a generous amount of classic water, and the remaining 20-mile length is open to public fishing. This includes a good bit of renowned no-kill water, which produces excellent catch-and-release fishing with artificial lures only all season long, but especially when major hatches occur. The two stretches of water with these special regulations provide the best angling, but these oft-released fish are no dummies.

Brown trout are the primary catch, although anglers take an occasional rainbow. Dry flies are preferred by most anglers, especially because the many well-known pools of the Beaverkill are hallowed dry-fly waters. There's barely a time when the favored pools are bereft of anglers. Many travel from faraway locales to give the Beaverkill a fling.

The Beaverkill receives perhaps disproportionate glory, as numerous Catskill trout rivers and streams are noteworthy in their own right. These cold, clean mountain waters include Esopus Creek, the East and West Branches of the Delaware River, Willowemoc Creek, Schoharie Creek, Catskill Creek, Callicoon Creek, the Neversink River, Rondout Creek, East and West Kill Creeks, and Batavia Kill. Numerous brooks exist as well, and more than 1,500 miles of trout flowage grace the Catskills.

Brown trout, the bulwark of these waters, were imported to the region eons ago. Today, they are found in "native" and stocked forms, primarily in lower and midreaches. The truly native brook trout is widely dispersed as well, especially in headwater streams and spring-fed tributaries. Rainbow trout are the least common species but are scattered about; they occur mainly in larger flowages, especially the stems of the Delaware River, and inhabit some unexpected small waters.

Although Catskill trout fishing starts on the traditional April 1 opening day, better conditions occur after the cold runoff ebbs, the water warms, and the hatches are more pronounced. May and June are terrific months. Insect hatches vary, but a partial and general guide is as follows: quill gordons and hendricksons from mid-April through mid-May; March browns from mid-May through early June; sulfur duns from late May through early July; green drakes from early to mid-June; light cahills and yellow drakes from mid-June through mid-August.

The summer often produces low water conditions, although spring seepages and forested banks help keep small streams cool. Trout anglers focus their attention on Beaverkill River, Willowemoc Creek, and Esopus Creek, as well as the upper Delaware River and its branches. These locations witness many visitors on weekends and summer evenings.

Delaware River. The Delaware River in New York is a multifaceted recreational playground. It is one of the finest wild trout rivers in the Northeastern United States, a prime fishery for American shad, a terrific smallmouth bass river,

A fly hatch is in progress as anglers fish the upper reaches of the Delaware River.

The swim bladder of sturgeon is used as a base for adhesives and waterproof compounds. It was once cleaned, dried, and used as a filtering material for the beer and wine industry.

one of the most popular canoeing and rafting flowages in the East, and part of the National Wild and Scenic Rivers System administered by the National Park Service. Although the degree of superlatives attached to these attributes might be debatable, there is no question that this river, especially the upper reaches, which split the New York and Pennsylvania boundary in the Catskill Mountains and its foothills, is a top angling draw.

The main stem of the river—from Hancock, New York, down to Delaware Bay—has much to recommend it, but 75 miles of the upper reach, which was designated as a National Wild and Scenic River in 1978, is most notable aesthetically and piscatorially, as are the tributaries, which include the East and West Branches of the Delaware, and the Lackawaxen (Pennsylvania), Mongaup, and Neversink Rivers.

Perhaps no species is more abundant in the Delaware or more energetically pursued than the American shad, albeit for a short period of time. The bulk of the fishing activity takes place from late April through mid-June, when the shad migrate all the way upriver and into the upper tributaries to spawn. These fish are frequently caught in 4- to 6-pound sizes, occasionally in great numbers, and they are pursued by both boaters and wading anglers. Enthusiasts focus their attention around Port Jervis, Sparrowbush, Barryville, Lackawaxen, and Narrowsburg. The pools and holes below riffles are the primary spots, and the best action occurs early and late in the day. Most anglers use shad darts, but fly fishing for shad has increased in popularity and is very effective.

Although trout inhabit the main stem of the Delaware, the prime trout water lies in the 27-mile main section from Hancock to Callicoon, and in the two upper stems, which are essentially tailwater fisheries. The stretch of the East Branch of the Delaware between Pepacton Dam in Downsville and Hancock runs for 32 miles, and 18 miles of the West Branch runs from the Cannonsville Dam in Deposit to Hancock. The West Branch is the most intensely fished section, followed by the East Branch. The former has the most consistently cold water and a less diverse fish population.

These waters have abundant brown and rainbow trout. Browns predominate in the East and West Branches; rainbows are abundant in the East Branch from the village of East Branch to the confluence with the main river at Hancock, and southward on the main river. These are primarily wild fish, particularly the rainbows, and anglers have a good chance of landing some in the 16- to 20-inch range—exceptional figures anywhere in the Northeast. Fly fishing is the preferred method, although other artificials and baits are used where regulations permit. Various mayfly hatches are strong from late May on, stonefly hatches occur from June into August, and caddisflies are common in June and July.

The quality of these fisheries, as in all tailwaters where trout are found, depends on continuous releases of water from New York City's reservoirs that is ample in volume and appropriate in temperature. Drought conditions can force a water district to cut back or alter releases, producing thermal stress and potentially seriously impacting coldwater species. Maintaining release levels necessary to the fisheries has been a constant problem here. It is even more problematic in the Neversink River, which enters the Delaware below Port Jervis.

Smallmouth bass are found throughout this river, but good fishing exists in the upper river south of Callicoon, where the water temperatures are more favorable. The smallmouths are not large, although they once were when author Zane Grey cut his angling teeth here. That was before the construction of tributary reservoirs in both New York and Pennsylvania, and prior to a dependence on cool-water discharges to maintain water flow. Few smallmouths over 14 inches long are caught, but plenty of small fish are caught on light spinners, flies, jigs, and small plugs. The bigger fish haunt the deeper pools.

Walleye inhabit the river, too, although they are not intensely pursued. Some large walleye, 8 to 10 pounds, are taken annually. Most angling—largely by locals—occurs in spring and fall.

Access for waders and boaters is limited on the Delaware, and anglers cannot cross private property without permission. Several publicly accessible spots are located on each side of the upper river. Fishing during the day in the summer, especially weekends, is hampered from Callicoon to Port Jervis by heavy canoe and raft traffic.

Central Region

Ample opportunities for all types of angling are at hand in the section of New York that reaches from the capital district westward through the Finger Lakes and that lies between the Catskill and Adirondack Mountains. Bass, walleye, and trout are the mainstays here, and there are numerous large bodies of water to ply.

Finger Lakes. Eleven lakes dot New York's wine country region, just south of the east-west arm of the New York State Thruway connecting Rochester and Syracuse. Some are fairly small, all are relatively narrow, and most have notable fisheries.

The two largest of these lakes, Cayuga and Seneca, are 40 and 36 miles long and have maximum depths of 435 and 632, respectively. The next three largest lakes—Keuka, Canandaigua, and Skaneateles—have water ranging from 187 to 350 feet deep, so you know these are serious trout waters. Some have the potential for monsters. Lakers, browns, and rainbows are prevalent in these locations. Landlocked Atlantic salmon exist in these waters, too, most notably Cayuga. Keuka is often overlooked but once held state records for brown trout and rainbow trout.

Cayuga Lake, which has all of these salmonids, is much like a ravine, with steep sides in many places, no reefs or shoals, and a few bars off points. Here, as is typical of the Finger Lakes, the shallows provide good springtime trout and salmon trolling in the south. As the water warms, angling effort moves northward and deeper. The lake also has a good warmwater fishery—especially in the northern end—for largemouth and smallmouth bass, yellow perch, and crappie.

Seneca Lake, immediately to the west of Cayuga, is similarly long but nearly 3 miles across at its widest point. Seneca is known for plenty of smallmouth bass, large lake trout, large pike, and abundant yellow perch. It has rainbows and browns as well, and fishing for all trout species is hot in the springtime in the warming shallows, especially when smelt and alewives congregate. Seneca has produced northern pike to 20 pounds and is one of the better pike waters in the state. Good fishing exists all along the lake and especially at the northern end near Geneva.

A major tributary of Seneca, Catherine Creek is a famous spawning rainbow trout stream in March and April. Other Finger Lakes tributaries, including Cayuga Inlet, Grout Brook, Keuka Inlet, and Naples Creek, offer spring-run rainbow fisheries. Eggs or egg sacks, worms, and nymphs on light lines or tippets are the primary offerings.

There's fine smallmouth bass fishing in Keuka, Otisco, Owasco, and Canandaigua Lakes. Tiger muskies are present in Otisco, as are walleye. Perch are abundant in most and large in a few. Dipnetting for smelt, which occurs from late March through April, is popular on many Finger Lakes tributaries.

Oneida Lake. Located on the northeastern fringe of Syracuse, Oneida Lake has long been New York's best walleye water. Although Lake Ontario eclipses it in size, the numbers at Oneida make this *the* place. More than 200,000 walleye are caught annually in poor years; in better years, the numbers are several times that. Fish weighing more than 5 pounds are an occasional catch, but 15- to 18-inch walleye are typical. Roughly 100 million walleye fry are stocked in the lake each year, produced by the lake's adults at a nearby state hatchery. Although walleye are the primary target on Oneida, smallmouth bass and yellow perch are also important. Lesser fisheries exist for crappie, carp, catfish, bullhead, largemouth bass, and various panfish.

Oneida is a large but uniformly shallow lake. It is 21 miles long and has a maximum width of $5\frac{1}{2}$ miles, resulting in nearly 52,000 acres of water. The maximum depth is 55 feet, but more than half the lake is less than 30 feet deep. Wide open and with few bays and many bars, reefs, and shoals, the lake can be rough under windy conditions.

Walleye are popular in open water from May into fall, and again in winter through the ice, particularly in the eastern half of the lake. Intense walleye fishing coincides with the opening of walleye season in early May, and continues for several weeks thereafter because the post-spawn fish are shallow and near the shorelines, especially in the vicinity of tributary bays. For most of the summer the fish are in 15 to 35 feet, primarily on the bottom, and are caught by drifting.

Especially popular on Oneida, yellow perch have suffered cyclical swings over the years but are normally abundant. Prime fishing occurs in late summer and early fall and later through the ice. Smallmouth fishing on Oneida is good to excellent, with lots of fish and many of good size. Crayfish are abundant, too, and readily stirred up through wave action. The shallowness of Oneida keeps bass accessible throughout the season.

Other waters. A number of rivers in the central region offer varied fishing, particularly for bass and walleye; these include the Chemung, Chenango, and Susquehanna. Of greatest note, perhaps, is the Mohawk River, a section of the Erie Canal running west to east from Utica to the Hudson River near Troy.

Most of the fishing in the Mohawk takes place in the section from St. Johnsville east. The 9-mile-long portion known as Crescent Lake, between Locks 6 and 7 from Schenectady to Albany, is a premier spot boasting varied species, including some striped bass that pass through from the Hudson.

Smallmouth bass and walleye are the favored attractions in the Mohawk River, which provides ample cover, dropoffs, bridge abutments, islands, vegetation, and other structure. Tiger muskies, many of which are caught coincidentally, as well as many yellow perch and crappie also inhabit this turbid waterway.

Just north of the Mohawk at Gloversville, and just inside the southern boundary of Adirondack Park, is Great Sacandaga Lake, New York's bona fide big pike king. Sacandaga yielded a 46-pound state-record northern in 1940, a fish that stood as the all-tackle world record until dethroned in 1986 by a European pike. A spawned-out 39-pounder was caught in this 29-mile-long lake, also known as Sacandaga Reservoir, in the spring of 1982, and other monsters have been landed over the years, but 20-pounders are a more realistic catch, especially early in the season when suckers are moving in and out of feeder streams.

Western Region

Lake Erie. The whole of Lake Erie appropriately owns the appellation "Walleye Capital of the World," but much of its fame is attributed to the western basin and the majority of its waters in Ohio. The deeper eastern basin between New York and the province of Ontario, and leading to the Niagara River, however, is no slouch, either in number or size of both walleye and smallmouth bass. It is a mixed-bag fishery, as it also holds most of the salmonid opportunities for Erie's lake and tributary anglers. Steelhead and rainbow trout have adapted especially well; in New York, they have been emphasized in salmonid stocking programs. At Dunkirk, a warmwater discharge in the harbor provides open-water fishing for various species in the winter. Charter captains in eastern Lake Erie can provide anglers with an offshore trolling outing that combines lake trout, steelhead, salmon, and walleye.

Walleye are the main interest, however. Due to clear water, walleye on Erie have become sight feeders and often roam near the surface or at suspended depths in vast schools pursuing alewives, perch, shad, and whitefish. The clear water, which looks almost offshore-ocean-blue from high above, has made walleye—a notoriously light-shy fish—wary of bright colors, noise, boats overhead, and any offering presented close to a moving powerboat. As a result, longline fishing is popular now, especially trolling with sideplaners and in-line planer boards. Big fish—8- and 10-pounders—have been common for many years, and some of those in the know deliberately stay away from schools of fish that weigh under 5 pounds; they're simply not large enough to bother with.

It seems that wherever there are rocks on Lake Erie, there's also smallmouth bass. New York shores produce numerous bass, including 3- to 5-pounders, and the potential for 6- to 8-pounders exists; indeed, this area yielded the state-record 8-pound, 4-ounce smallmouth. Jigs, vertical jigging spoons, vibrating lures, and live baits account for most catches. Soft-shelled crabs are a favorite natural, if you can get them. Some of the best bass angling is within sight of downtown Buffalo; Seneca Shoals and Donnelly's Wall are two top spots.

The changes in the lake and fishery are due in large part to zebra mussels, which filter and clarify the water by removing microscopic plants with unbelievable proficiency. Their long-term impact is uncertain, however. Anglers should remember that Lake Erie is a large body of water, one that can get rough in a hurry. When the water is cold and the wind is severe, Erie can be inhospitable.

Niagara River. To most of the world, the word Niagara conjures up visions of thundering falls, tumultuous spray, and a honeymoon haven. But anglers have had a love affair with the Niagara River because it offers excellent and varied angling that is widely famous among the Great Lakes and its tributaries.

Most notable is perhaps the best run of large salmon in the Great Lakes each fall in the Niagara Gorge at Devil's Hole. No boats pass above this spot; it possesses some of the most treacherous whitewater in the East. From the falls to Lewiston, the lower Niagara River is a steep, forbidding gorge. But it yields spectacular fishing to the diligent and careful angler. Drifting with preserved salmon egg clusters is most productive, but flatline trolling with deep-diving plugs is a hot second, especially early in the day. Shore casters fish eggs, plugs, and spoons.

From mid-October through April, steelhead are present in good number in the swift water of the lower Niagara, but the best action is in February and March. Drifting with eggs is the main technique, but other methods are possible, including fly fishing. The river gets a virtually neglected run of lake trout in May, and angling for this species is surprisingly good. At other times, walleye, smallmouth bass, and perch fill the bill. Smallmouth are especially plentiful here, as are walleye that top 10 pounds. These are not caught in the turbulent flow but from Lewiston to the mouth of the river at Lake Ontario. The boat-able section of the lower river is 8 miles long, extending from Devil's Hole to the Niagara Bar.

The upper Niagara River—the section above the falls and extending to Lake Erie—is noted for bass, walleye, perch, pike, and muskies throughout the summer and fall. This outflow water is clear and tricky, and has one of the most unheralded muskie populations in the country, including 40-pound specimens. This is a tricky clear-water trolling fishery, however. Numerous launch sites, piers, and docks exist. If you don't venture north of Grand Island, it's unlikely that you'll be swept over the falls (although great fishing might exist in the pool below the thunder, no one has tried).

Chautaqua Lake. Chautaqua Lake was once long recognized as a formidable muskie fishery and a producer of large fish. The muskies are still there, but they've gone through some hard times. Sizes have dropped, and 20-pounders are less common. The walleye and bass populations have prospered, and although Chautaqua may not bask in the walleye and bass glory of nearby Lake Erie, it has much to offer for these species, and for crappie as well.

The walleye are plentiful; smaller fish are generally heavy in the thick weeds, and larger fish frequent the deeper waters of the north basin. Largemouth bass are found throughout Chautaqua, but smallmouths—some in the 4- to 6-pound

Early morning anglers find salmon success in the turbulent flow of the Niagara River.

range—shine. Crappie, known here as calicos, are a favorite quarry, especially in the south basin.

Lake Ontario

In a state with abundant resources, no fishery has stood out with more distinction in recent decades than Lake Ontario. This lake draws anglers from all over the Northeast for salmon, trout, bass, and walleye fishing that is among the best in the Great Lakes. Although it has shone since the early 1970s, it is also a lake in transition—one that perplexes anglers and fisheries managers and doesn't live up to expectations every year. Variable wind and weather patterns, as well as changing water conditions, contribute significantly to these problems. This should come as no surprise, however, on the 19th largest lake in the world, one that is 193 miles long and 53 miles wide and has an average depth of 283 feet. This voluminous water has an abundance of riches for the savvy angler, in both the lake proper and in its tributaries.

Chinook salmon, lake trout, steelhead, brown trout, walleye, and smallmouth bass have all provided premier fishing opportunities on Lake Ontario. Largemouth bass, northern pike, muskellunge, coho salmon, Atlantic salmon, and yellow perch have also figured significantly. But the main attraction is chinook (king) salmon.

For some time, Lake Ontario has had the best angling and the largest chinooks in all of the Great Lakes. The Oswego and Salmon Rivers in the eastern basin—which are small, narrow, shallow, and generally slow—are magnets for salmon and anglers alike. There has long been shoulder-to-shoulder fishing in these tributaries in September, when dark and soon-to-die chinook and coho migrate upstream. But the western end of Lake Ontario, where the bottom drops off more steeply close to shore and where the incomparable Niagara River enters, has been the best big-water place to consistently catch these nomadic fish from April through September. It is the only section of the lake that has dependable angling for schools of king salmon in the spring and early summer, when the fish are brightest and strongest, primarily because the forceful incoming current piles up baitfish. Most of the big spring kings are caught in the Niagara area.

The western basin can stake a claim for producing the biggest lakers as well. In early 1994, a modern-day Lake Ontario lake trout record was established near the mouth of the Niagara River by a 39-pounder; in November, anglers can jig and release up to 40 fish per day. Although the western end of the lake produces big lake trout and plenty of them, the extreme eastern end of the lake is generally considered the prime laker habitat. Near Henderson Harbor, the rocky reefs and islands make lakers a bread-and-butter fish.

Lake trout are a native Lake Ontario species that were once decimated by lamprey eels and commercial overfishing. The last sport-caught native-strain laker was taken in the 1930s, and the last commercially caught laker by 1950. Restocking efforts began in Lake Ontario in 1973 and have been sustained with federal help. Management regulations have been aimed at making them self-perpetuating, a process that has had modest results. Some anglers feel it is detrimental to more popular nonnative species. Nevertheless, lakers are a reliable catch and a fallback option on tough days throughout most of the lake. Still, their deep-dwelling nature and mediocre fight when taken from deep water lessen their sporting value.

The acrobatic and aggressive steelhead, however, are highly prized. These fish are especially sought by winter and early spring anglers in the tributaries. Steelhead are most reliably found in the established rivers, especially the Salmon, Niagara, Black, and Oswego, throughout the winter. Fresh runs occur at various times and peak when these fish spawn in April. Some early-season near-shore fishing for steelhead exists, and limited offshore fishing is available if and when there is a thermal bar.

Brown trout are the spring mainstays for most of the lake, especially from Rochester to Pulaski. At this time, they're inshore and shallow and make up the majority of the early season catch. In local contests, it usually takes a 15-pound fish to place in the top 10, and a 20-pounder to win; the lake and state record is 30 pounds. Most people troll via flatlines with plugs, graduating to spoons and downriggers as the water warms and fish disperse. But in the early going, pier- and shore-based casters score well, too. Brown trout are widely dispersed along Lake Ontario, but the mideastern section from Mexico Bay to Fairhaven seems to annually outproduce the others for big fish.

These coldwater species, plus coho and Atlantic salmon, are the subject of most interest across the lake. Atlantics have been stocked in greater numbers, especially in the eastern basin and in the Black River. Atlantic salmon were once native to Lake Ontario, the only Great Lake that had these fish. Efforts continue to reestablish this species.

On the warmwater front, walleye and smallmouth bass populations are exceptionally good and, with some localized exceptions, underexploited. Both species are not as widely dispersed as trout and salmon, but along the lake's 712 miles of shoreline there are many places to find them. The far eastern end of the lake, especially from Cape Vincent at the head of the St. Lawrence River to Henderson Harbor, is known for outstanding smallmouth bass fishing, and possesses great numbers of these fish. Bass habitat here is excellent, with plenty of rocky shoals, islands, points, and weed-edged rocks. Walleye are abundant in the same places; the average fish were once so large that 8- to 10-pounders seemed common, although the big fish were heavily exploited. Many good-size fish still exist in this section of the lake, however, and the overall population is relatively lightly tapped.

Good smallmouth action is reliable in the Sodus-to-Oswego sector of the lake, and a nearly unpublicized spring walleye fishery (including fish to 10 pounds) exists at Oswego. Across the lake in Canada's Bay of Quinte is an extraordinary population of walleye that is targeted in spring, fall, and winter; these fish reportedly contribute to walleye numbers across the far eastern end of the lake, as well as in the St. Lawrence River.

Lake Ontario's great fisheries resources have depended heavily on a healthy and prolific population of baitfish, principally alewives and smelt (the record 39-pound laker had 99 smelt and alewives in its stomach). Concerns about these populations will always exist, but Ontario has escaped some of the baitfish-related problems affecting other Great Lakes; many anglers annually see massive numbers of baitfish on their sonar.

Huge baitfish numbers have led to terrific growth rates and a lot of fat fish. Good fishing for many, and large, trout and salmon spoiled many anglers. When the fishing got harder due to adverse weather and increasingly clearer water—thanks to zebra mussels—some thought the lake had gone downhill. Heavy stocking levels and plentiful baitfish, however, essentially means that there are plenty of fish. In this huge and deep lake, finding them is usually the main problem.

St. Lawrence River

It is no secret that the St. Lawrence River is one of the great North American fishing locales. Steeped in history, tradition, and fishing renown, the St. Lawrence has been in the sportfishing limelight ever since there was a limelight. Its natural resources were of tremendous value as long ago as 1535, when French explorer Jacques Cartier discovered it while looking for the Northwest Passage to the Orient.

But it is the 52-mile-long section of the St. Lawrence called the Thousand Islands—known to the Mohawk Indians as the "Garden of the Great Spirit"—that has produced not only a famous salad dressing, but also places it among the continent's foremost bass and muskellunge fishing.

The St. Lawrence is not a typical river featuring pools, eddies, and riffles. It is akin to a mammoth lake, holding a half million surface acres of water. Also known as the St. Lawrence Seaway, the river flows northeasterly from Lake Ontario for 700 miles and serves as a shipping channel for colossal freighters carrying assorted cargoes from Great Lakes ports. It is 200 feet deep in spots, several miles wide at most points, and possesses more than 1,600 islands—the largest of which is 21 miles long—in the Thousand Islands sector.

The St. Lawrence River in New York is bounded on the north by Ontario, Canada, and reaches from Wolfe Island and Cape Vincent at the outflow of Lake Ontario 97 miles to Massena and a boundary with Quebec. That area encompasses 300,000 acres of water, most of which harbors something worth fishing for. Prominent departure points for anglers in this region are at Cape Vincent, Clayton, Alexandria Bay, Ogdensburg, and Massena in New York, and Kingston and Gananoque in Ontario.

The prime angling interests in this great body of water are smallmouth bass, largemouth bass, walleye, northern pike, and muskellunge, although there are ample perch, rock bass, bullhead, carp, and other species, as well as salmonid stragglers from Lake Ontario. The St. Lawrence is a fabled muskie water, and has been renowned for its large muskellunge. The now-dethroned (and disputed) all-tackle world-record muskie (69 pounds, 15 ounces) was caught somewhere in the Thousand Islands stretch in 1957, and several line-class-record 60-pounders were caught in that area during the heyday of the 1950s. No other single locale in North America has been as closely identified with mighty muskellunge as the St. Lawrence.

The huge fish have not been caught here in decades, however, and angling interest has shifted to more abundant and more cooperative species, especially to large salmon in nearby Lake Ontario. Still, dedicated trollers can land 30- to 40-pound muskies here. Much emphasis is still placed on traditional locales, such as Hinckley Shoal off Carleton Island and Forty Acre Shoals off Gananoque. This is almost exclusively a trolling fishery, partaken of from September through early November.

Many more people ply the St. Lawrence for bass. Area chambers of commerce have long billed the local waters as the "Smallmouth Bass Capital of the World," and although some would dispute this claim, there's no arguing that the river has a tremendous population of smallmouths. This is thanks in part to a notable quantity of rocky bars, shoals, bluffs, and island heads near deep water with plenty of current. Largemouths, too, are abundant, in the main river along deep grassbeds and weedlines as well as back in the weedy and lily-pad-filled bays and creeks. The places to find both species are numerous.

Jigs and live baits have historically been the foremost presentations on the St. Lawrence for bass, but the entire gamut of bass tactics and tackle are applicable. Good fishing can be had almost all season long from the opening in mid-June until early November. The last half of June and early July are especially popular. The main section of the St. Lawrence stays cold until summertime. Although the severity of the winter, the timing of ice breakup, and spring weather are factors in river water temperature, the early season usually arrives while the water is cold enough to keep the bass in the shallows; some may still be spawning on shoals and island bars in late June.

Northern pike, although not particularly large here, are abundant and a good spring and winter quarry. They are commonly caught by bass anglers who aren't trying to catch them, and they are a major ice fishing attraction in bays. Walleye were once abundant, then nonexistent, and have now reestablished a substantial population, primarily near Cape Vincent and at the eastern end of Lake Ontario. The 1990s saw a bonanza of walleye over 10 pounds in the confluence with Lake Ontario, making this one of the least-known big walleye fisheries in the country, but the opportunity was overexploited. Walleye are still plentiful, however, and they have become an important fishery once again throughout this section of the river.

No matter what species one pursues, the St. Lawrence is not a place for timid boaters. There are many dangerous places and some swift water, and the river has a propensity for getting riled up by westerly winds, especially in late summer and fall. Traveling from the launch site to various fishing spots one can cover a lot of water; a suitable craft and some boating savvy are required.

Adirondack Region

The northernmost area of New York—bounded by Vermont, Quebec, and the St. Lawrence River—the Adirondack region is an enormous area replete with fishing opportunity and largely devoid of people. Within its borders is Adirondack Park. At more than 6 million acres, it is the largest state park in the contiguous United States and offers 1,300 miles of rivers, many small to medium-size lakes, big waters like Lake George and Lake Champlain, and a surfeit of remote ponds. Although this is considered trout country, it has a great diversity of species, especially some terrific bass fishing, and there is no lack of places to fish afoot or by any type of watercraft.

Trout waters. The region's trout waters flow in every direction from the high peaks of the Adirondacks and have been described as the best trout rivers east of Montana. Adirondack rivers and streams are synonymous with fishing for brook trout, which are still native in many of these waters, and abundant in small flowages, especially feeder streams. Brown trout are very common, however, and rainbows are present as well. Some of the tributaries hold landlocked salmon, and some of the lakes have kokanee salmon, so there's diversity no matter where you turn.

The Ausable River is considered the preeminent Adirondack trout river. Situated in the northeast, it originates in the high peaks and flows northward to Lake Champlain and has two stems. The West Branch of the Ausable is widely favored and has been heavily touted over the years. It is a 30-mile-long, rugged river that flows through the gorges of Wilmington Notch and directly under the chairlift at Whiteface Mountain. This is a cold, steep, and shady river with exceptional aquatic insect forage and copious cover. Upper sections have deep water with undercut banks and some pools; lower reaches have interspersed pocket water and pools below islands. The Ausable is noted for large brown trout, including fish in the 15- to 20-inch range, as well as some in the 7- and 8-pound category, and has a short stretch of specially regulated water offering year-round angling. The East Branch, which originates in the Keene Valley, is a fine trout stream in its own right, although it doesn't possess the size or numbers of fish of its sister flowage.

North of the Ausable, the Saranac River runs for 65 miles from Saranac Lake to Plattsburgh and affords diverse conditions and varied angling for warmwater as well as coldwater species. The river forks at Clayburg, creating a short South Branch that is popular for trout for 5 miles up to Union Falls. Also of special interest for trout—including brookies, browns, and rainbows—is the North Branch. Both are cold, quiet, and in many places thickly wooded. The main stem has several hydroelectric impoundments; fishing below the dams or in the tailwaters is good for brown trout, smallmouth bass, and walleye.

South of the Ausable and on the eastern fringe of the Adirondacks is the Bouquet River, New York's finest landlocked Atlantic salmon river excepting the Lake Ontario tributaries. This is a tributary of Lake Champlain, in fact, and runs for about 40 miles from the headwaters to the big lake. The 12-mile-long lower stretch, from the dam at Wadhams, concentrates salmon, which run from late April through May and from mid-September through October. Salmon up to 10 pounds have been common, and in the lower reaches the action can be mixed with lake trout, bass, and walleye.

Flowing westerly from the Adirondacks eventually to the St. Lawrence River at Ogdensburg is the underrated and often ignored Oswegatchie River. This 102-mile-long flowage is varied in its characteristics. The steep and quick 35-mile-long section above Newton Falls is difficult to access and marked by dams and whitewater rapids. Trout are the main quarry here, and although they may not be as abundant or large as in other Adirondack rivers, they could be found in no lovelier setting nor with more wildlife viewing opportunity. The lower section is generally wider and slower moving, with more diverse angling opportunities, including smallmouth bass, walleye, pike, and panfish.

These are among the more obvious and larger rivers in the Adirondacks, but there are many others, not to mention tributary waters, that also deserve consideration. These include the short but famed section of the Battenkill River in the extreme southeastern corner of this region; the headwater section of the Hudson River, especially above North River and in the Boreas and Cedar tributaries; the North Branch of the Chazy River; Chateaugay River; West Canada Creek; the St. Regis River; Raquette River; and Schroon River. Of the 1,200-plus miles of rivers just within the confines of Adirondack Park, 155 are classified as wild and 511 as scenic, attributes that add immensely to

> The highest large lake in the world is Titicaca in the Peruvian Andes. It is 12,500 feet above sea level and 900 feet at its deepest point.

any angler's fishing experience.

It should be noted that in addition to rivers and streams, hundreds of lakes and ponds abound throughout the Adirondacks, offering good fishing, especially for trout. The Adirondack region in particular is noted for its many brook trout waters, the majority of which are ponds of varying sizes. Some of these exist along roadsides, but most are remote, accessed by foot or portage, and located by reviewing topographic maps.

Lake Champlain. Tourism boosters call 110-mile-long Lake Champlain the "Sixth Great Lake," and they have a point. Twelve miles wide and boasting 585 miles of shoreline and more than 300,000 surface acres, Champlain is a formidable body of water. What to catch here is mostly a matter of what you want and where you are. The bass and walleye fishing is exceptional but rivaled in popularity by lake trout and landlocked salmon. Steelhead, pike, yellow perch, pickerel, and muskies are also prominent, and there are numerous other species as well.

In the New York portion (Champlain borders Vermont), smallmouth bass are the principal quarry along bays, islands, and points. The northern end produces fish up to 5 pounds, and it is not an overstatement to say that you can hardly fail to catch a smallmouth here. Largemouth bass are also present, although less prominent, as they mainly frequent the bays and weeds; they are more evident in the southern section of the lake, where the water is more stained in color due to heavy traffic.

Lake trout and landlocked Atlantic salmon are found in various places around Champlain, but the midlake section, which has depths to 400 feet, garners the most attention. Smelt are the favorite forage of these fish, and deep-water angling is the norm for most of the open-water season, although near-shore and near-tributary fishing coincide with the spring and fall salmon runs. Lakers and salmon from 3 to 8 pounds are frequent catches.

Walleye, perch, and pike are popular with anglers along the lake and are especially sought through the ice. Smelt are another prominent winter catch. Ice fishing for them peaks through mid-February.

Lake George. Considerably smaller than its northern neighbor, Lake George is nonetheless a big body of water. Its 44 square miles of picturesque and fairly narrow water provide good fishing for lake trout, landlocked salmon, smallmouth bass, largemouth bass, and northern pike, as well as various panfish, smelt, and other species.

Angling for lakers and salmon commences with ice out, which occurs around mid-April in the south and later in the north, when the fish are shallow and the smelt are spawning, especially around tributaries. Deep fishing is the game from June on; the lake has a maximum depth of 201 feet, and lakers are usually way down in the summer. Fall provides good opportunity for shallower fish, especially salmon early and late in the day.

Smallmouth bass are found all over Lake George. Hundreds of rocky coves, points, and islands invite smallmouth angling, but anglers land some in very deep water during midsummer. September and October provide splendid opportunity amidst colorful vistas. Largemouths, too, are ample, primarily in bays. This fishery is good from the beginning of the season through fall.

Long Island (Saltwater)

Long Island is shaped like a huge fish whose head and mouth touch Manhattan at the west and whose tail, which is divided into huge flukes called North and South Forks, juts eastward 130 miles into the Atlantic Ocean. The size and location of this landform are unique. It encompasses the Hudson River estuary on the west; is well placed on the continental shelf, which parallels the south side of the island; and within its perimeter are many large, shallow bays that serve as nurseries for numerous species. These physical features have produced one of the greatest marine habitats in the world and contribute to exceptional saltwater angling that is enjoyed by more than 800,000 anglers annually.

Trapped between this island and the continent is Long Island Sound. Extending more than 150 miles, it varies in width to 19 miles near its middle and less than 8 miles at Orient Point on the east. Extending off Long Island's North Fork is a series of islands that end on Wicopisset Passage, which is shared with Rhode Island. The South Fork points into the open Atlantic as Montauk Point, touted as the saltwater fishing capital of the world. The ocean side of Long Island is relatively straight, a great stretch of barrier beaches. Trapped behind this are numerous shallow bays that open into the Atlantic through six inlets. Here, the variety of fishing environments is almost limitless, ranging from back bays and tidal creeks to sounds and the open ocean. Long Island offers anglers 130 miles of ocean surf on the south side and twice that on the North Shore. In between, there's a plethora of docks, bulkheads, floats, bridges, and jetties from which to angle.

Fish variety is particularly abundant, offering a diversity of migratory species, some of which move short distances inshore and offshore while others trek thousands of miles. Because of this, what you catch is determined by when (and sometimes where) you're fishing. During cold months, cod, ling, whiting, and flounder are prime species. From April through November, prominent inshore species include striped bass, bluefish, weakfish, winter flounder, fluke, blackfish, black sea bass, mackerel, and porgies. Offshore, anglers fish for sharks, bluefin, yellowfin, and bigeye tuna, albacore, bonito, and hordes of dolphin, as well as striped and blue marlin.

The size of fish populations is determined by

various factors, including commercial and recreational fishing pressure, natural variations due to climatic occurrences—especially during spawning and nursery periods—and natural cyclic fluctuations occurring within every species. Enlightened state and federal fisheries managers have been attacking overfishing, which has been a problem in New York waters, as it has been along the entire Northeast coast. Today, every species has one or more restrictions as to season, minimum size lengths, and creel limits, all designed to provide enough breeding stock to ensure species survival. Remarkable gains have been made in this direction in relatively few years, but a continuing need for vigilance and proper stewardship is required.

While saltwater fish feed all the time, they do not always feed with the same frenzy and this affects an angler's ability to catch fish. In the waters surrounding Long Island, the best fishing months to catch most species are May, June, September, and October. This doesn't mean that fish cannot be caught at other times. They can, but it takes more skill on the part of the angler to do so.

North Shore (Long Island Sound). *Western Long Island Sound.* Long Island Sound narrows in the west, and anglers from Oyster Bay to City Island and east along Westchester County's shore fish virtually in each others backyards. Little Neck, Manhasset, and Hempstead Bays are spring hotspots for striped bass, flounder, bluefish, and fluke when waters warm. Shoals surrounding City Island, Stepping Stones Reef, and Execution Rocks are well known for flounder and porgy catches. Numerous smaller bays and harbors along the north side of the sound, from Mamaroneck to Rye, harbor the area's biggest bluefish in August and September, as well as numerous striped bass and blackfish.

Lloyd Neck/Cold Spring Harbor/Centre Island. This section offers excellent striped bass fishing. Anglers commonly pursue these fish at night by trolling long, unweighted lines baited with gobs of sandworms. They favor small boats with nearly silent engines and waters from 3 to 10 feet deep, and work along all the beaches of these bays and harbors. The boulder-strewn shores are ideal bass waters. Mixed with bass at night are weakfish and bluefish. In spring and late fall, these beaches produce good blackfish catches. Most fishing in Cold Spring Harbor centers around the northern half. The shallower southern sections produce flounder in April and May, and in August house hordes of snapper bluefish.

Eatons Neck. For numbers, variety, and quality of fish, the shoal north of Eatons Neck Point, known as Eatons Neck Triangle, is exceptional. It is a large extension of shallow water pushing northward into the Sound. The area is filled with sand eels and spearing. Access is easy because of numerous boat ramps in the area. Schools of small bass are abundant here in spring. Eatons Neck also produces weakfish, and big blues are taken for granted. Fluke to 12 pounds have been caught here. The so-called Triangle is derived from three buoys marking the shoal: Can 13 north of Eatons Neck Point, the OB Buoy a mile northwest of Can 13, and Buoy 11B. Waters to the west and north drop from 30 to 100 feet. On the eastern side, the bottom slopes gradually from 22 to 80 feet. Most weakfish and bluefish are taken inside these buoys, whereas striped bass are caught between Can 13 and the lighthouse.

Smithtown Bay/Crane Neck. Smithtown Bay, between Eatons Neck Point and Crane Neck Point, offers 15 miles of good fishing waters. East of Crane Neck is boulder-strewn Oldfield Point, an area with the same characteristics as Crane Neck that is ideal for blackfish. At night, these areas are taken over by striped bass. Three streams flow into Smithtown Bay with varying degrees of salt-, fresh-, and brackish water. Stony Brook Harbor's flow is primarily saline. It offers bass fishing in the channel. Near the SH Buoy, catches of bluefish in August are common. At times, weakfish mix with blues, which are the main summer fishery. A favorite place for striped bass and weakfish is the mouth of the Nissequogue River, a substantial stream that flows into Smithtown Bay. Flounder show here first in the river and are outside by June. Bluefish concentrate off the river's mouth. Short Beach and Sunken Meadow Beach flank the river's mouth and at night offer surf anglers a chance at bass and weakfish.

Mt. Misery Shoal. This is a uniformly flat piece of bottom that extends northeasterly for about a mile under 15 to 25 feet of water off Mt. Misery Point, just east of the entrance to Port Jefferson Harbor. Its outer edge is marked by Buoy C11. In late May and June, it attracts weakfish. At night, surf casters on the beach take weakfish and striped bass. Bluefish are a certainty off the shoal, where anglers head when weakfishing slows. Fluke move into this area during the summer. Closer to the beach, catches are mixed with blackfish. Porgies are on the flat; in late September, jumbo porgies school here. When boat concentrations are dense, the best fishing method is to drift and jig. With light traffic, trolling umbrella rigs produces a potpourri of species.

Mattituck Inlet. One of the most lightly fished areas in all of the marine waters of New York is the north side of Long Island's North Fork, from Mattituck Inlet east 12 miles to Rocky Point. Difficult access is the reason; the few existing ramps in the area are marginal. Striped bass are the prime species, fished off the beaches or along the shore at night, or by drifting or trolling. Daytime anglers usually drift to catch weakfish, fluke, and flounder. The best porgy area is east of Mattituck, from The Firing Range to Duck Point. A shoal north of Horton Point concentrates fluke. Bluefish are along the shore to mid–Long Island Sound. Find feeding birds and fish under them.

 Astacopis gouldi is a crayfish found in the streams of Tasmania, Australia, that has grown to a length of 2 feet and weight of 9 pounds.

East End. *Orient Point.* Long Island's south side offers excellent early season flounder from Long Beach Point to Orient. In late spring, fluke replace flounder, moving into these waters from June through September. They concentrate from Trumans Beach to Orient Shoal. Blackfish dominate catches on the rocks. Plum Gut, between Orient Point and Plum Island, offers great striped bass and bluefish angling. Blackfishing is superb all along the north side of Plum Island. Just north of Plum, in 50 feet of water, the tide rips over a submerged shoal, Pigeon Rip, one of the area's best bluefish grounds in August. This is deep-water fishing, and jigging is the only way to get to the blues. The wide expanse of shallow, rocky bottom between the eastern tip of Plum Island and Great Gull Island is the domain of striped bass.

The Race, Fishers Island. The waters between Little Gull and Fishers Island are no place for small boats. In its depths, throughout summer, are the area's biggest bluefish. Twenty-pounders are not uncommon. Fishing here requires big boats, heavy tackle, and strong-armed anglers. In topography, Fishers Island is more akin to New England than New York. It is rocky and irregular, and ideal for blackfish. During spring and fall migrations of striped bass, drifting eels parallel to the rocky shores on the island's south side has produced great catches.

Gardiners Island. Located between Long Island's North and South Forks, Gardiners Island offers big-bay fishing on its east side, while the more protected west side offers harborlike conditions. The Ruins mark the northern tip of a shoal, both sides of which produce excellent striped bass catches at night with trolled plugs. During the day, these flats produce fluke and flounder. Eastern Point Plains and Tobaccolot Bay, on the east side, are prime snowshoe flounder grounds. Fish to 3 pounds are taken just off the beaches in 25 to 30 feet of water. On the west side, in Bostwick Bay, southwest to Crow Shoals and then southeast to Cherry Harbor, the island offers bluefish anglers excellent inshore fishing in July and August.

Peconic Bays. "The Peconics" include Flanders, Great Peconic, Little Peconic, Hog Neck, and Noyack Bays and Shelter Island Sound, and offer great fishing for porgies and weakfish. Traditional hotspots, which include the hole south of Buoy 16, the cut just west of Buoy 18, the rip south of Buoy 22, and the rip at South Robins Island Race from Buoys 23 to 30, produce most weakfish catches. Porgies prefer deeper waters in the middle of Little Peconic, Great Peconic, and Noyack Bays. There is excellent flounder fishing here in April from Buoy 2, on the western end of Great Peconic Bay, westward through Flanders Bay.

South Shore. *Montauk Point.* In any language, *Montauk* means fishing. This easternmost extension of Long Island juts deeply into the Atlantic and is the focal point for both inshore and offshore activities. There are three fishing locales at

A striped bass is landed near Montauk Point.

Montauk: the north and south shores and off "The Point." It is on the beaches surrounding Montauk that an army of surf casters comes in spring and fall to catch striped bass. The fish migrate close to south-side beaches and The Point when going north or south. Weakfish are also found in the surf and placate striped bass anglers between bass bites. Here, too, bluefish are regular fare.

Inshore fishing at Montauk is world renowned. Water around The Point is moderately deep, between 30 and 50 feet within a mile of shore. Fish are attracted by a great rip formed as the tide from Long Island Sound escapes seaward and boils over a long underwater reef that connects Montauk Point with Block Island, 12 miles away. This confusion of water is known as Pollock Rip. East of The Point is mainly a striped bass fishery, in an area known as The Elbow. However, bluefish often fill the charter boat boxes here. During some years, good catches of weakfish as well as blues are possible in August and September.

Offshore fishing at Montauk rivals the best in the world. From this famous port, angler's boats fan out east and south for such ocean leviathans as giant tuna, mako sharks, blue and white marlin, and swordfish, plus a host of small tuna on the edge of the continental shelf. On the bottom, anglers fish primarily for cod and pollock. The closest offshore areas south of Montauk are the Cartwright Grounds in 90 or 110 feet of water, the CIA grounds just to the east, and Mud Hole East, which is southeast of Block Island. Farther offshore, the well-known blue-water fishing areas include The Fingers, Butterfish Hole, Fish Tales, and others.

Shinnecock Bay. Shinnecock Bay is 8 miles long and 3 miles wide, but it is really two bays constricted in the middle by Ponquogue Point. The eastern part, with the inlet on its southern end and the canal on its northern end, produces the most fish. Three-quarters of its waters are 6 feet deep or less. The main tidal flow is through the western edge of this part of the bay, from Ponquogue Point north along the shore to the canal's entrance. The main navigation channel is located here and is the focal point of the fishery.

The inlet produces good fluking, and at night striped bass are taken on live baits. The rowboat fleet concentrates in the channel just off, and north, of the Coast Guard station, searching for flounder and fluke. An area in the eastern part of the bay known as The Basket yields good flounder catches in April and May. Early fishing for flounder, fluke, and weakfish can be exceptionally good in Shinnecock Canal. The bays here are fine places to start the fishing season because they are better protected from the elements; even more important, the canal concentrates fish.

Moriches Bay. Moriches is a unique body of water but comparatively shallow for a Long Island Bay. It is 12 miles long and less than 3 miles wide, and more than half the bay is less than 3 feet deep. Fishing is restricted to the east-west channel and a large widening west of Moriches Inlet, from Masury Point east to Tuthill Point. The bay is known for excellent fluking and almost year-round flounder catches. This fishery is best from Buoys 15 to 19 in Narrow Bay Reach, around Buoys 27 and 29, and east to 41. Fluke hotspots are around the inlet, or deeper inside, from New Cut to Buoy 29, and the flats from Buoy 36 to the inlet and between Buoys 39 to 41. Waters just inside the inlet have produced large striped bass, usually only at night by anglers drifting live eels or bunkers. Blackfishing can be quite good along the rock jetties. Bluefish are almost always at the 2B Buoy 2 miles outside.

Great South Bay. Long Island's largest enclosed bay, Great South measures roughly 32 miles from east to west and 5 miles at its widest. It is the deepest of South Shore bays, ranging from 7 to 10 feet with some 15-foot spots in dredged channels. A series of channels were cut through it to allow for boat traffic. Most fishing takes place in these channels and where they meet.

On the western edge of Great South Bay is Babylon Cut. There's good fishing for striped bass and weakfish at the cut's southern edge where it meets the State Boat Channel. West Channel, from Buoy 6 on the north to the RB obstruction buoy to the south is one of two prime weakfishing areas in Great South Bay. The other is the main east-west channel on the south side of the bay. Two weakfish hotspots are located off East and West Fire Islands and off Ocean Beach. North Channel is hardly a channel, but a wide area of deep water, 8 to 12 feet between the Fire Island Flats and Nicoll Point in Heckscher State Park. It is the main east-west channel on the northern side of the bay and is well marked with buoys. Heckscher Flats is a wide, level-bottomed part of the bay, south and mostly east of Nicoll Point, and is the outflow of Nicoll Bay and the Connetquot River. The flounder season starts here in Great South Bay in the spring.

Fire Island Inlet. Fire Island Inlet is a complicated piece of turbulent water with traffic and current. If you don't fish from the beaches, you need a stable boat. The area around the remnants of the Sore Thumb is a striped bass hotspot; a barge was sunk there in 1980, and its lee produces good flounder and fluke catches. There's good striper fishing in this area when bass are migrating. Some of Great South Bay's better flounder and fluke fishing takes place in the Oak Beach hole. Another channel, hard against Great South Beach (Fire Island), carries most of the ebb and flow of the tide. The deepest part of this channel runs against the beach, and the cut from the bridge to the inlet is a prime striped bass area. Fish at night while drifting live eels in an area just south of Buoy C13; this spot can really produce bass, especially off the remains of an old construction dock.

Jones Inlet. Waters inside Jones Inlet receive the most intense saltwater fishing pressure off all of Long Island. The area north of the inlet is cluttered with low-lying thatch islands that developed a natural drainage system of guzzles, drains, and creeks to handle the tidal flow. This watershed system has been enhanced and developed by dredging and sand mining to facilitate traffic between the inlet and towns along the south side of Long Island.

The back bays themselves are generally shallow, containing little or no water at low tide. Reynolds Channel is the main east-west waterway just inside Jones Inlet and also the main route taken by migrating fish. Long Creek is the main north-south waterway in the western part of this area, draining a collection of canals and bays. Good, early-season flounder fishing occurs in Baldwin Bay. Several well-known "crossroads" fishing areas have developed, such as where Long Creek and Scow Creek meet and cross Sea Dog Creek. Good flounder and fluke catches are made here. A second major north-south channel is Swift Creek. It produces fluke, flounder, snapper, and weakfish. Swift Creek drains waters as far north as Merrick Bay and yields flounder and some weakfish catches in the summer.

A series of creeks and canals drain into East Bay from Merrick to Wantagh and flow into either Broad Creek Channel, Haunts Creek, or Great Channel. Meadowbrook and Wantagh State Parkways cross over these and other passageways. Some of the South Shore's best blackfishing occurs under their bridges. At night, sharp anglers anchor and dole clam bellies into the current to chum striped bass.

East Rockaway Inlet/Reynolds and Broad Channels. Nine-mile-long Reynolds Channel runs from East Rockaway Inlet to Jones Inlet. Between these points are scores of good fishing areas. Anglers after bluefish and striped bass concentrate between Buoy 5 on the north side of East Rockaway Inlet and a shoal that builds seaward off the Boardwalk in Edgemere. Chummers take bass at night around the base of Atlantic Beach Bridge; worm anglers take flounder and blackfish during the day. A good flounder, and sometimes fluke, spot is the 26-foot hole at the entrance to Banister Creek.

Halfway down the length of Reynolds Channel, Broad Channel from the north drains a series of guzzles and bays. The best fishing is off Duck Point on South Green Sedge, and where Woodsburgh Channel meets Broad Channel at the OB Buoy. South of the buoy is a 20-foot hole that has produced fluke and flounder, and at night some big weakfish and an occasional large striped bass. To the north, in the southern end of Hewlett Bay, flounder are taken in May and June.

New York Harbor, East River, and Hudson River. *Lower New York Harbor/Staten Island.* Efforts to clean up the Hudson River have paid off in fishing dividends as well as clean water. Fishing for striped bass has increased remarkably off piers in the East River; along the waterfront of Queens and Brooklyn; around Ellis, Liberty, and Governors Islands in Upper Bay; around Hoffman and Swineburne Islands in Lower Bay; and on Romer Shoal. Many of these areas are accessed from boats leaving Sheepshead Bay as well as New Jersey. Flounder catches on Romer Shoal, and fluke catches—especially in the cut between Buoys 4S and 5 on the south end of the shoal—have also increased. Bluefish have again returned to the wide expanse of Rockaway Inlet. In fall, stripers up to 40 pounds have been caught by anglers pulling dead bunker baits off the beach into deeper water.

East River. In the late nineteenth century, when someone wanted to fish for striped bass on the East Coast they usually chose one of two places: Cuttyhunk Island in Massachusetts or the East River between Manhattan and Queens. The East River hotspot was, and is still today, Hell Gate, between Wards Island and Astoria. Most fishing now takes place from piers or bulkheads, but anglers are finding it worthwhile to run their boats from distant ramps to the area.

Hudson River. Marine fishes move up and down the Hudson River with the tides; some regular and some unusual species have migrated far upriver, but most go only as far as the George Washington Bridge, which straddles New York and New Jersey in the lower river. When rainfall is lacking, however, the brackish Hudson becomes more saline, and bluefish are taken as far upriver as the Tappan Zee Bridge. The Hudson is an important coastal spawning river for striped bass in the spring, and huge numbers of stripers migrate upriver from March through early June. Many are caught upriver in brackish or freshwater sections. Most leave the river after spawning, but a few hold over, so that some degree of striped bass fishing is always possible in the Hudson. Shad, however, are only a spring visitor, mainly caught farther north near shoals and flats.

Offshore grounds. Fishing the waters among, around, and behind the New York islands is good because they lie over a relatively shallow continental shelf that is from 60 to 80 miles wide. Its outer edge drops off into abysmal depths on the Atlantic's floor. Over this shallow shelf flows the Gulf Stream, a river of warm water that starts in the Caribbean and flows north, then east, to Europe. It carries numerous species of migrating fish.

The shelf is gouged by several canyons, cut by rivers formed from melting glacial ice that 20,000 years ago stood high above Manhattan. These canyons offer great fishing, but comparatively few anglers have the boats to make it to the shelf's edge. Instead, most concentrate their shelf fishing inside the New York Bight, a triangular area from about Cape May on New Jersey's coast to Montauk Point. Inside the bight are dozens of recognized, identifiable offshore fishing grounds that offer a wide variety of species: tuna, albacore, dolphin, bluefish, sharks, and marlins, and, on the bottom, schools of hake, tilefish, cod, pollock, and black sea bass.

Many of the first-accessed fishing areas are close to Rockaway Inlet and Long Beach, and they include such well-fished spots as Iberia Wreck, Black Warrior Wreck, Big Wreck, Nor'west Bass Grounds, Nor'east and Sou'east Grounds, Middle Grounds, The Oil Spot, The Cedars, Flynn's Knoll, Southwest Pit, England Banks, The Elbow, Tin Can Grounds, Subway Rocks, and Scallop Ridge. A bit farther offshore are the Angler Banks, Lightship Ridge, Steel Wreck, COD Wreck, 17 Fathoms, The Farms, and Three Sisters Grounds. Probably the area's most famous fishing ground is the Mud Hole. It is part of the drowned Hudson Canyon and begins south of the BA Buoy. It is not a well-defined hole but the beginning of a trough, 170 feet deep, with banks under 70 to 90 feet of water.

Long Island (Freshwater)

The quality of Long Island's freshwater fishing opportunities suggests that anglers should be standing in line to get their turn. Because of the great variety and quantity of saltwater here, however, the island's freshwater fishery is overlooked and unexploited, except by a small cadre of anglers.

Long Island is a huge terminal moraine, and on its predominantly sandy back are some 40 lakes, ponds, and reservoirs and more than 100 spring creeks, sometimes erroneously called rivers. Because of Long Island's sandy nature, runoff watersheds cannot develop. Instead, all the surface waters are spring fed. About half of the shallower, warmer ponds offer largemouth bass (and pickerel and panfish), whereas the other half offer brook, brown, and rainbow trout.

Thousands of springs and weeps create four predominant streams—the Connetquot, Nissequogue, Carmans, and Peconic Rivers. At 10 miles, the Peconic is the longest, but because it was dammed from colonial times to produce mill power and cranberries, it is too warm for trout but excellent for bass and chain pickerel. The others are idyllic trout streams. The Connetquot, in fact, was the site of one of America's first trout hatcheries and is today a world-class trout stream.

A sea-run fishery has prospered on the Nissequogue and Connetquot Rivers. Early each spring, steelhead to 20 pounds are taken on both rivers, and fall sees brown trout of almost the same proportions. All three streams have developed sea-run brook trout fisheries, and fishing is open throughout the year in their tidal sections.

With all these resources lying so close to the more than 17 million people living in New York's metropolitan area, one would expect the fishery to suffer. To the contrary, fishing in the two state parks—Nissequogue and Connetquot—is conducted with fly fishing and barbless-hook mandates under the English-style beat system. For a modest fee, an angler reserves a beat with its limits marked on the river and gains access to one of three exclusive daily sessions.

NEW ZEALAND

New Zealand is a small nation at the lower end of the South Pacific Ocean, about 3,000 kilometers to the east of Australia. A long, narrow country, it consists of two major islands (the North and South Islands), as well as numerous offshore isles. Several of the latter, including Stewart and Great Barrier Islands, are in excess of 80 kilometers long. As the run of the 2,000-kilometer-long group is roughly north-south, it straddles a wide range of climatic regions, ranging from sub-tropical to sub-temperate.

New Zealand was first occupied by Polynesian voyagers, the Maori, around 1,000 years ago, with European colonization on a large scale over the last 200 years. This nation of $3^1/_2$ million people is today about 25 percent Maori and 70 percent European (Pakeha in the Maori tongue), with English the common language. Approximately 2 million people live in the top half of the North Island, 700,000 in the lower half of the North Island, and only 800,000 in the more sparsely populated South Island.

The geography of New Zealand ensures that no site is more than 170 kilometers from the sea, and nearly all the cities are clustered about large sheltered ports. Away from the coastal plains, rugged mountain ranges trap moist oceanic winds and precipitate rainfall that feeds a multitude of lakes and rivers.

Isolated from other countries by the wide sweep of the Pacific Ocean, with a light population and relatively little heavy industry, New Zealand has few pollution problems compared to other Western Nations. A total ban on nuclear weapons and power plants is enshrined in law in this conservation-minded nation.

It is little wonder, then, that fishing ranks as New Zealand's most popular participatory sport. A survey showed that a staggering one-third of the population tries their hand at some form of fishing each year, with one-seventh of the population classified as regular anglers, and saltwater participation outnumbering freshwater by about five to one.

Freshwater

Isolated from any continental landmass for millions of years, New Zealand developed its own unique native species. Free from predation, this included many flightless birds, including the kiwi, New Zealand's national symbol and the derivation of the nickname "Kiwis" for its residents. Likewise, the many rivers and lakes were populated mostly with small native fish of the galaxid family and several species of freshwater eel.

European settlers brought with them many species of plants, animals, and fish from their home countries. Some of the fish most successful at adapting to their new homes were European brown trout, which were introduced in 1867, and rainbow trout brought from North America in 1883. Both of these species are widespread throughout the waters of much of New Zealand, which can justifiably claim to have the finest wild trout fishery on the planet.

Another successful American import was the chinook salmon, often called "quinnat" salmon in New Zealand. Runs of these great fish were established in many of the rivers on the east coast of the South Island. Also established were restricted populations of sockeye salmon, mackinaw (lake trout), Atlantic salmon (landlocked populations), and brook trout (brook char). Of these three, only the brook trout is available to anglers in any quantity. The prime fishery for brook trout is Lake Emily in the Canterbury region of the South Island, although they are established in a number of other waters.

New Zealand freshwater fishing is split up into a number of regions, each overseen by a Fish and Game council elected by the fishing license holders. A freshwater fishing license bought in any individual region is valid for both trout and salmon over

A trout angler lays out a cast on a crystal clear South Island stream.

nearly the whole country. The single exception is the Taupo region in the center of the North Island. This is run by the Department of Conservation, and a separate license is required to fish here.

Trout fishing regulations vary widely throughout the country, and even from water to water. Any Fish and Game license will have a précis of the rules for that region printed on it, but, while the license is valid in other regions, it will not have those local regulations. Visiting anglers who are not using the services of a local guide are advised to seek advice from the region's Fish and Game office, or a local tackle store, before fishing.

Trout

Most, but not all, of New Zealand's lakes, streams, and rivers contain trout, usually a mix of browns and rainbows. Space considerations do not permit a review of New Zealand's expansive trout fisheries in great detail, but a number of locally published fishing guide books are available, many of them dealing with just one of the main islands, such is the volume of material.

After trout were first introduced into the virgin, food-filled waters of New Zealand, initial growth rates were incredible, with rainbows averaging over 4.5 kilograms and browns close to 9 kilograms. With the introduced trout today striking more of a balance with their environment, average weights have settled to more like 1.5 to 1.8 kilograms. This is still impressive by world standards, and fish over the old magic "double figure" mark of 10 pounds (4.5 kilograms) are still regularly caught.

New Zealand is primarily a fly-fishing-for-trout country. Most fishing laws here were established before spinning tackle was invented or gained popularity, so most of the angling is divided into fly fishing only areas or trolling areas, and, in the latter, non-fly fishing tackle and methods are allowed.

Lakes and tributaries. In a large number of pristine clear water lakes, fish are easily taken by trolling, even by anglers who have never fished before. For the price of a boat and guide, fish are pretty much guaranteed. This is no idle boast; some Lake Taupo accommodation houses offer a free room if their guide cannot hook the guest into a fish.

The most popular fishing lakes include the Rotorua Lakes and Lake Taupo in the North Island, and the Nelson Lakes, Lake Brunner, Lake Hawea, Lake Wanaka, and Lake Wakatipu in the South, in addition to a great many other worthwhile fisheries.

The lake systems of Rotorua and Taupo are in the central region of the North Island, and these two watersheds have been largely responsible for making New Zealand's trout fishing highly respected in international circles. This area has the most prolific rainbow trout fisheries in New Zealand; there are browns here, too, but they're generally outnumbered by rainbows.

The rainbows are of primarily steelhead stock and, though confined to the lakes, are prevented from going to sea by dams. They live in the lakes all summer (December to March), but leave the lakes to run up the streams and spawn. The best fly fishing in streams that flow into the lakes is in April and May, when the big fish move out of the lakes; good fishing also is had in November and December, when the trout return to the lakes. In the summer, most lake fishing is done from boats by longline trolling with lures or flies. However, fly fishing opportunities do exist at the stream mouths, where trout gather for food and also colder water. Streamer flies that imitate smelt are fished on sinking lines when the fish are deep, and on floating lines when the fish are shallow and chasing bait.

There are a number of lakes within a 32-kilometer radius of Rotorua, the most popular being Rotorua, Okataina, and Tarawera. October to June provides good trolling, with May and June offering stream mouth fishing opportunities for fly casters.

Covering 616 square kilometers and stretching for 40 kilometers, Lake Taupo is a huge lake and a recreation and resort showpiece. It is a giant crater-like lake, filled with blue water and reaching a maximum depth of 155 meters. Scores of streams feed into it from all sides, with the major source being the Tongariro River, a major fishery which enters at the southern extremity through a five-fingered delta, and which is filled with spawning rainbows in the winter months. Strong runs of rainbow trout move into the Tongariro (and other tributaries) during June to August and can provide exceptional cold weather fly fishing.

Rainbow trout are the mainstays in the lake, and though the fish may be deep enough in the summer to require weighted lines (lead core) to get down, a lot of trolling is simply done by flatlining a lure or fly (the latter is called harling here). Lake fishing via trolling is essentially effective year-round on this lake, with the western bays being especially favored. Large boats are used to take multiple excursions to

A rainbow trout comes aboard a Lake Taupo charter boat.

areas accessible only by boat, with overnighting done on the boats.

In some locations, trollers can fish within touching distance of rocky cliffs, yet still be over deep water and in rainbow territory. In the summer, the trout tend to be close inshore feeding on smelt, which primarily shoal along shallow sandy beaches, especially where a river or stream enters. Fly fishing at stream mouths is good in November–December and May–June, and often before dawn or after dark on summer days at these stream mouths.

Rivers. New Zealand has dozens of rivers that flow to the sea, some directly from the mountains, others from lakes to the sea. These have populations of resident trout, and an annual migration of sea-run brown and rainbow trout (steelhead). On the North Island, the upper reaches of these provide good dry fly and nymph fishing. On the South Island, South Westland has a fine fishery for silvery spawning sea-run browns in late summer and again in the spring when they follow whitebait into the river.

These provide good fishing, but the major river emphasis is on rivers that are connected to lake systems, and on the high mountain flowages. For the more experienced fly angler, gin-clear mountain rivers and streams on both islands offer the challenge of spotting, stalking, and hooking trophy trout. These fish may range from 2 to 6 kilograms, and are well educated. A cautious approach and flawless presentation is needed to take the large fish regularly. The unspoiled high country waters where they are found are usually flanked by mountainous virgin rain forest or native tussock grasslands.

Most of these high country fisheries are in the mountains of the central North Island, or the alpine region of the South Island. Access is not easy, and may involve backpacking or the use of four-wheel-drive vehicles, inflatable rafts, jet boats, or helicopters.

Lowland rivers of a more pastoral character tend to hold good numbers of smaller, but still substantial, fish which may range in size from 1 to 2.5 kilograms. Access to many waters is free, and, where they run through private land, a friendly approach to the landowner will see access granted in many cases.

Generally, stream and river trouting in New Zealand is a case of quality not quantity, with very few fish on the best waters being caught under 1 kilogram. For good anglers, the average size is more likely to be 2 kilograms or better for rainbows and slightly higher for browns.

The streams are very clear, and it's often necessary to locate and see fish, then stalk them and make pinpoint presentations, often using fine tippets and long (in some cases 12- to 18-foot) leaders. Long casts are seldom necessary, but accuracy often is. Nymphs are used extensively on many waters, dry flies on others, and wet or streamer flies are very popular in rivers that flow into lakes.

Seasons. Although some rivers (including many lakes) are open to fishing year-round, the best time to fish for trout in New Zealand is from November to April, which in this hemisphere is the spring-summer-autumn period. Most waters are open to fishing and the best climatic and river conditions may be expected in this period. The exception to this is the winter rainbow run on the Tongariro River, as previously noted.

In November and December (spring and early summer) the rivers and stream of both islands usually fish well. January and February (midsummer) are considered by some to be the best time for dry fly fishing on the South Island, and a good time for the small streams at Rotorua and Taupo. March and April (late summer) usually still have settled weather, and provide good dry fly and nymph fishing. May and June (autumn) primarily offers stream mouth and big-lake tributary fishing.

Quinnat Salmon

Although there are some small populations of Atlantic and sockeye salmon in New Zealand, it is the chinook, or quinnat, salmon that is the successful species in New Zealand. Introduced from stock captured in the Sacramento River in California around 1900, the kiwi chinook represent the only self-sustaining sea-run salmon fishery established in the Southern Hemisphere.

The bulk of the New Zealand salmon fisheries center on the East Coast rivers of the South Island. The most prolific are the Waimakariri, the Rakaia, the Rangitata, and the Waitaki Rivers. Lesser fisheries are found on the Waiau, Hurunui, Ashburton, Opihi, Orari, and Clutha Rivers.

In addition, there are some salmon runs in rivers on the West Coast of the South Island, with the Hall and Paringa being the most consistent. Both of these drain small lakes only a few kilometers from their mouths, and it is in these lakes that most salmon are caught, mostly by deep trolling from boats.

Other places that chinook salmon may be caught are Otago Harbour, where a stocking program has salmon returning to the harbor each year. Here, fishing a herring under a float or trolling lures from a boat are the common practices. The waters around large salmon ocean-ranching operations in the Marlborough Sounds and Stewart Island also produce salmon, escapees from the cages.

The rivers on the East Coast of the South Island are braided freestone rivers. Fishing is carried out from anchored boats out off the mouth, by shore-based anglers thickly clustered around the river mouths, and in pools upstream as the salmon move up to spawn. Some upriver anglers and those that work off the river mouths use jet boats, a Kiwi invention developed for shallow water work in this region, to access their fish. Fat-wheeled farm bikes or all-terrain vehicles are also a popular means of getting around for shore-based anglers.

The salmon runs start around late November, which is the beginning of the New Zealand summer, and finish around the end of April, as autumn starts to close in.

Fed by snow melt, actively changing their beds much of the time, and carrying glacial-ground rock flour, the salmon rivers are seldom clear running. Local wisdom has it that the best fishing is when the rivers are starting to clear after a flood, or "fresh," has encouraged a run of salmon into the river. Water visibility of about 30 centimeters (approximately 12 inches) is counted as fishable.

Most salmon fishing in New Zealand is done with spinning tackle. In the surf around the river mouths, hex wobblers (a locally made, heavy casting spoon) are the lure of choice, while lighter types of locally made spoons called zed spinners are favorites to use on fish that have entered the river.

Kiwi chinook average 7 to 9 kilograms, with 14 kilograms counted as a trophy and rare specimens of 18 kilograms taken. Salmon fishing is permitted on the same license as is used for trout. The daily bag limit is two fish kept per person, and fishing must stop if the second fish is taken. Any fish foul-hooked must be returned.

Fishing around the mouths of the salmon rivers can be high density when the salmon are prime, as many anglers favor catching fish when they are in the peak of condition. These mirror-scaled beauties fight the best and are prime eating at this time. Anglers preferring a bit more solitude fish further up the river, seeking out fish where they hold in pools, resting after running rapids, or waiting for a rise in river levels to help with their upstream run.

Saltwater

The long island chain of New Zealand is oriented roughly north-south and consequently bridges a wide range of water temperatures and habitats mainly falling into the temperate category.

Although New Zealand does not boast the wide variety of fish species found in tropical waters, the combination of cooler, nutrient-rich waters and a large continental shelf area has resulted in strong populations of a wide range of popular sport and table fish.

New Zealand has long been a gamefishing Mecca. Early Maori colonists considered the capture of the powerful mako shark as a feat equal to killing an enemy in battle. Early European settlers brought a sporting heritage with them, and although early fishing efforts were aimed at filling the cooking pot, they soon discovered the challenges of catching the large yellowtail, or kingfish as it is known in New Zealand. Kingfish grow in excess of 50 kilograms in these waters and were a considerable challenge on the primitive tackle of the day.

Angling for this species led to the 1910 founding of the Bay of Islands Kingfish Club, which eventually became the Bay of Islands Swordfish Club and was one of the world's first gamefish clubs. Kingfish anglers constantly had their tackle broken up by large striped fish with bills, and one of these was finally caught in 1915, a striped marlin of 223 pounds.

Interest then swung to the greatest gamefish of New Zealand waters: striped, black, and blue marlin, and the high-jumping mako shark. The visits of Zane Grey in the late 1920s and early 1930s, and the publication of his book *Tales of the Angler's Eldorado: New Zealand*, put New Zealand gamefishing on the international map.

During the mid 1980s, however, New Zealand's saltwater angling reputation was at risk, as foreign longline fleets plundered New Zealand waters and recreational catch rates plummeted. After considerable pressure by recreational anglers, in 1987, a ban on foreign longline boats and local longline boats taking or selling marlin was secured. The result was a return to the "good old days," with plentiful fish and catch rates exceeding the golden era just after World War II.

Gamefishing for many of the larger species is seasonal in New Zealand, as water temperatures only reach the comfort zone for many species during the summer and autumn (December to May). The positive side of this is the biological fact that the largest members of a population group live on the fringes, in this case because their larger thermal mass copes better with lower water temperatures, and they have the ability to swim further and faster than smaller specimens. Consequently, very large specimens of many species are encountered.

Striped marlin are still the premier catch off New Zealand's coast, and this is arguably the best fishery in the world for that species, having established many world records. Other billfish are also of varying importance here, and various tunas and sharks, especially makos, are major attractions, with record-setting fish possible. Kingfish are still a major sport-caught fish in New Zealand, and the offshore pinnacles here support the world's best fishery for this species. The widely scattered but little-known (outside of New Zealand) kahawai present outstanding inshore light-fishing opportunities. During high summer, mahimahi (dolphin) are occasional visitors to New Zealand waters, and there are incidental catches for some lure-trolling anglers from February through April. A handful of wahoo captures have been made in recent years, and it may be that, due to oceanic warming, these fish are starting to penetrate New Zealand waters.

Striped Marlin

Striped marlin are the mainstay of New Zealand saltwater gamefishing and it is fair to say that the combination of numbers and size would make this the world's premier fishery for the species. The average size of Kiwi striped marlin is about 90 kilograms (200 pounds) and a fish of over 500 pounds was caught in 1995, although disqualified from the record books on a technicality.

A review of IGFA records reveals that New Zealand "owns" nearly all the world striped marlin records, including a 224.10 kilograms (494 pounds) specimen, and a fair percentage of these caught in recent seasons. This is a live fishery, not one living on past glories. In 1997, a charter boat broke all New Zealand records by catching 156 marlin for the summer season. This included a fifteen-fish day, a magnificent effort considering the high average size of these fish.

The first striped marlin of the New Zealand season are usually caught in the month of December, and January through April represents the bulk of the fishing on the mainland. Fish move as far south as the bottom of the North Island in a good year, although the top half of this Island sees most of the action.

Most of the gamefishing charter fleets are based on sheltered East Coast ports in the top half of the North Island, although fishing charters are available in most areas of the country. Houhora, Whangaroa, Mangonui, The Bay of Islands, Tutukaka, Whitianga, Tauranga, and Whakatane are the main charter boat centers.

About 30 kilometers north of the top of the North Island lie the Three Kings Islands. These islands and the associated King and Middlesex Banks support an incredible variety of bottom and pelagic fish, and provide a prime feeding area for a wide range of predatory species. But first and foremost, over the months of March to the end of June, the area has an incredible striped marlin fishery, with "pack attacks" of six or more marlin a regular occurrence.

Recent changes in charter boat regulations have made it easier for boats to fish this area, but there is not a great deal of shelter at either of the anchorages at these islands. These remote pieces of rock are wildlife sanctuaries and landing is prohibited. There are no facilities, so anglers live aboard the charter or private boats. This is a usual thing in many parts of New Zealand, and most boats are set up for this sort of trip.

The Three Kings mostly seems to start producing billfish around mid-February, but they hold large numbers at the end of the season, as fish withdraw from the cooling mainland waters.

Other Billfish

Shortbill spearfish, blue marlin, black marlin, and broadbill swordfish are also found in New Zealand. Spearfish are mostly an incidental catch when fishing for other species, but during some seasons, over 400 of these enigmatic little billfish are caught, mostly in the 20 to 30 kilogram range.

Blue marlin are caught in New Zealand water during the hottest months, usually February and March. Although they are not as common as striped marlin, most blues are between 200 and 300 kilograms. The largest landed weighed 461 kilograms, the only "grander" caught in New Zealand. Most of these fish are captured north of East Cape. Boats targeting blue marlin tend to troll large lures over offshore deep water structures such as canyons.

Black marlin are also caught in much lesser numbers than stripies, but are mostly good-size fish in excess of 150 kilograms. The national record for this species stands at 444 kilograms. Few of these fish venture south of East Cape, and are mainly caught by fishing live or dead baits around inshore reefs and other structures.

Swordfish have been occasional captures in New Zealand waters for many years, but these were mostly incidental, caught by anglers fishing for marlin. The techniques used in the past were not particularly effective on broadbill, so numbers caught were not great, although bycatch from commercial fishermen targeting tuna or deep water grouper (hapuku in New Zealand) indicated a healthy population.

Night fishing with light sticks was first tried by recreational anglers in 1989, and captures have been regular since then. High numbers are not caught (around ten to twelve per season), but this reflects a low effort from anglers rather than a lack of fish. Although commercial longliners are permitted to take broadbill as a bycatch, as of the late 1990s it appears that the fishery is not under stress, and large adults are regular captures. A swordfish of 291.9 kilograms caught on 24-kilogram line in 1998 is an example.

Broadbill are present throughout the country, right through the year, as shown by longline catches, strandings, and sightings. However, nearly all recreational captures have been made off the East Coast of the North Island between East Cape and North Cape, although this represents a concentration of fishing effort in these regions, rather than any pattern of fish distribution.

There have been several sailfish strandings and reported sightings, and although New Zealand waters are a long way south of their usual range, an eventual capture is likely.

Tuna

New Zealand waters are host to eight species of these most migratory fish. Yellowfin are the most common of the large tuna here. They appear in New Zealand waters around December as the water temperatures rise, and leave again around late April. During this period they range south to Taranaki on the West Coast and Hawkes Bay on the East Coast, although occasional stragglers make their way a little further south than this. The average size of sportfishing captures is 20 to 40 kilograms. Fish are caught each year in excess of 70 kilograms, but these are considered to be trophy fish.

The Bay of Plenty, especially the region based near the town of Whakatane, is considered to be New Zealand's tuna capital. Yellowfin in this area are taken by trolling lures, casting jigs, chunking, and live baiting. This last method is most effective when the yellowfin are marauding schools of anchovies and pilchards in the February-March period.

In May 1914, Evinrude and Sears Roebuck both ran advertisements for their "rowboat engines." The Evinrude Magneto cost $80; the Sears Motorgo $49.95.

Bigeye tuna are regularly taken by longliners in New Zealand waters, but only occasionally by anglers, usually on trolled lures over offshore canyons early in the morning. Those fish that are caught are often in excess of 100 kilograms, but there may be only half-a-dozen taken on rod and reel each year. The best areas seem to be the eastern Bay of Plenty, the Gisborne coast, and the North Cape region. Fish are mostly caught in the summer months, although this may be a reflection of fishing effort rather than bigeye concentrations.

Both the southern and northern bluefin tuna are found in New Zealand waters. The bulk of these fish are southern bluefin, with rare northern giants in excess of 300 kilograms occasionally caught by commercial longliners. Southern bluefin were commercially fished to near-extinction in the 1970s and '80s, but a catch limitation agreement between New Zealand, Australia, and Japan has seen a modest increase in the numbers of these fish, despite the depredations of other Asian fleets and a degree of illegal fishing by Japanese boats in the Tasman Sea.

Bluefin migrate into New Zealand waters from Australia, arriving at Fiordland on the southwest corner of the South Island around March. From here, the fish travel up both coasts, mostly sticking to the edge of the continental shelf. The best chance for anglers to intercept these fish is off Fiordland, a rugged, isolated, magnificent, but often storm-beaten region of New Zealand largely protected by national park status. Only a handful of charter boats ply this region, but bluefin can be caught here on trolled lures from March to June. The largest in recent times was a 110-kilogram fish taken in 1997. Fish average between 25 and 50 kilograms.

Skipjack tuna are summer fish in New Zealand, arriving in December and lingering through May. Their distribution is similar to yellowfin tuna. They are popular as a light-tackle sportfish, and much sought after as a cut bait for a wide range of bottom species. The average fish is 3 to 4 kilograms, and the local all-tackle record is 10.26 kilograms. Trolling small lures is the usual method of capture, but casting with spinning gear is successful, as is the use of small live baits and fly fishing when these fish are feeding on a "meatball" of anchovies or pilchards.

Albacore are a common tuna of New Zealand waters and can be captured at any time of year. Most fish are caught over the summer months (partly a reflection of fishing effort), but of note is a midwinter run of large fish in the Bay of Plenty. A popular light tackle sportfish, albacore can be caught the length of the country on both coasts, and are often an incidental catch of anglers seeking larger species. Size is variable, with larger specimens tending to be caught in deeper water. The average fish is 5 to 6 kilograms; 10-kilogram fish are common, and local records are mostly in the 20- to 25-kilogram range. Mostly taken on trolled lures, they are also susceptible to chunking, jigging, small live baits, and fly fishing.

Two less common species are the slender and butterfly tunas. The slender tuna is an elongated fish ranging from 5 to 12 kilograms. Not a good table fish, they are left alone by commercial netters. They do fight well on light tackle, and limited sportfishing is carried out for them off the East Coast of the South Island in April, May, and June, as they move north from Dunedin to Kaikoura. These fish are targeted by casting to surface schools, as trolling results in constantly losing tackle to the razor-toothed New Zealand barracouta (snake mackerel). Slender tuna also put in erratic appearances in the Bay of Plenty in spring months (September–November) where they are sometimes caught on lures set for albacore.

Game Sharks
Sharks listed as "gamefish" by the IGFA and found in New Zealand waters include mako, blue, thresher, white, porbeagle, tiger, hammerhead, and tope.

The most commonly caught game sharks are probably makos, which are usually encountered in the summer months throughout the country in every size from "just-born" to "scary monster" class. A number of specimens over 1,000 pounds have been caught, and very large individuals are encountered each year. They are not heavily pursued by anglers in the northern half of the North Island, but are still commonly caught on lures and baits intended for marlin. They are a popular gamefish with anglers in more southern regions, however.

Blue sharks are also common in New Zealand waters in all sizes from freshly pupped to world record class fish. They, too, are not actively pursued by northern anglers, except for those specializing in light tackle or saltwater fly fishing, but are more popular in the colder waters of the south.

Threshers and hammerheads are less common than the two previously mentioned species, but still regularly encountered. The system that has produced many of the largest fish in years gone by—deep drifting with dead baits—is seldom practiced now, as surface trolling is more popular. But on occasions when it is tried, it can still be effective, as proven by a 312-kilogram thresher caught off Tauranga in 1997. The five heaviest threshers in the IGFA record book, each in excess of 300 kilograms, have all come from northern New Zealand waters.

With recovering seal populations, white sharks seem to be increasing in numbers in New Zealand waters. In recent years there have been several attacks on abalone divers by these creatures. Whites are still far from common, and are seldom actively pursued by New Zealand anglers. The isolated Chatham Islands, or the Manukau Harbour adjacent to Auckland (the country's largest city), are two areas where these sharks are encountered.

Tiger sharks sometimes spread into New Zealand waters from the tropics, but are not often caught. Like whites, they should not be considered a target species by visiting anglers.

The smallest world-record fish is a 1-pound grass pickerel, caught in June 1991 in Indiana. One pound is the minimum weight allowed for record classifications.

The porbeagles is a relative of the mako shark and is sometimes caught by anglers fishing deep water for grouper and bass (wreckfish). In recent years southern sportfishing clubs have given this species some attention, and 'beagles of up to 100 kilograms have been captured.

Tope are medium-size bottom-dwelling sharks, often called school shark in New Zealand. They are common and regularly captured by anglers targeting other bottom species. Although seldom pursued by anglers, they are strong fighters, and New Zealand claims most of the world records on this species, the result of intensive effort by a small group of anglers fishing Northland's Parengarenga Harbour.

In addition to these species, a large inshore shark is the brown New Zealand whaler, called narrowtooth shark by the IGFA. Regarded as a game shark in New Zealand, these fish are common in northern inshore waters during summer, When water temperatures are high, they move into large harbors and estuaries to give birth. They are bottom feeders and relatively harmless to man, but the largest inshore fish likely to be encountered by small boat anglers. They have been captured in excess of 300 kilograms, but average between 100 and 200 kilograms. They occasionally jump when hooked, but are not heavily fished.

Inshore

Although lacking the wide range of sportfish present in tropical waters, New Zealand makes up for this with good populations of what fish are available. Although commercial overfishing has greatly reduced the numbers of many species, angling is still good by world standards.

Kahawai. Kahawai are feisty little fish and one of the most common species caught by coastal and shore-based anglers. The Maori name by which they are known means literally "strong-in-the-water," and these fish freely strike a wide range of lures and baits, fight powerfully, and often jump. If they populated the oceans in the rest of the world, they would probably be one of the foremost light tackle fish in the annals of sportfishing.

In New Zealand, their range is nationwide, and they are found in many coastal areas, frequently penetrating into estuaries and the tidal reaches of large rivers. Schools of surface feeding kahawai are still regularly encountered, and these fish are ideal for light tackle, surf, and fly fishing. They are a reasonable table fish with a strong flavor, and are improved in this area by bleeding soon after capture.

Yellowtail. Southern Yellowtail (called kingfish here) are the kingpins of the inshore fishery. In New Zealand, these fish grow to unprecedented sizes. A glance at the IGFA record book confirms the almost total dominance of the New Zealand branch of the family, including a two-way tie of 52-kilogram fish. Most common in the North Island, yellowtail straggle halfway down the coasts of the South Island in a warm summer. In the northern half of the North Island these fish are available pretty much year-round, although they head out to spawn in deep water around January.

Commercial interests are allowed to take yellowtail only as a bycatch, and recreational anglers are limited to three fish per day with a minimum size of 65 centimeters. In one of the top yellowtail areas around White Island, a voluntary code restricts anglers to one kingfish kept per day each.

These restrictions seemed to have worked well in preserving yellowtail numbers. Top areas for kingfish include the Three Kings Islands, White Island, and the Ranfurly Bank, although fishing for these powerful fish is good in most areas. The average size is around 12 to 15 kilograms, with fish over 24 kilograms not uncommon. A handful of fish in excess of 40 kilograms are caught each year.

Popular fishing methods include drifting with both live and dead baits, chunking, jigging, casting with surface lures ("popper" fishing), casting rigged dead baits, and fly fishing. Some of the largest fish are taken fishing from rocky shores (called "land-based gamefishing" or LBG in New Zealand), as well as from boats of all sizes. New Zealand can confidently claim to have the world's best yellowtail fishery.

Snapper and trevally. In terms of the numbers of anglers that pursue them, snapper are probably the most popular fish in New Zealand. Listed as a gamefish by the IGFA with the locally unheard-of tag "squirefish" attached, these fish are not true snapper, but members of the sea bream family. Excellent table fish, they are handsome, still reasonably common despite heavy commercial and recreational fishing pressure, and a fairly strong fighting fish.

Peak populations are found on both coasts in the northern half of the North Island, but they are reasonably prevalent through to the Marlborough Sounds-Nelson region at the top of the South Island. Available year-round in the north of their range, they are mostly only available in the warmer summer months in the south.

The quality of New Zealand snapper fishing can again be seen by the dominance of the record books, and these are all catches made fairly recently. Average size varies a lot, but any fish over 4.5 kilograms is considered a substantial one, over 9 kilograms is a trophy, and occasional captures of over 13.5 kilograms are made.

Snapper are often caught from rock and sand shores; by small boats fishing unweighted baits in estuaries, harbors and shallow coastal areas; and over deeper reefs. Snappers are usually caught on baits, with strip baits of skipjack tuna or whole pilchards (sardines) popular. Bottom jigging with metal lures is also successful, and snapper can also be caught on flies.

The white or silver trevally is New Zealand's sole representative of this widespread family. Their distribution is similar to that of the snapper. These hard-fighting fish are often found in surface feeding schools around offshore islands, rocks, and reefs in the Bay of Plenty and northern regions of the country. They also feed over deeper reefs and hard on the bottom. Average fish are 2 to 3 kilograms in weight, while 5-kilogram specimens are considered large. Occasional fish exceeding 10 kilograms are captured.

These fish, particularly when surface feeding, are excellent targets for light tackle casters and fly anglers. They are a good table species, although not highly rated by some local anglers.

Bottom fish. Hapuku (grouper) and the closely related bass (wreckfish), in addition to the unrelated bluenose (rudderfish), are keenly sought by both recreational anglers and commercial fishermen using bottom baits in deep water between 100 and 400 feet. The first two species average around 15 to 25 kilograms, but are sometimes taken in excess of 46 kilos. Bluenose are more commonly 10 to 15 kilograms, with large specimens exceeding 25. These excellent table species are found nationwide over moderate to deep coastal reefs and are very popular table species. Previously, fishing for these species was regarded as a food-harvesting exercise; however, the advent of low-stretch braided lines has added a sporting aspect to their capture.

Other popular small- to medium-size species sought for both sport and the table are tarakihi and red gurnard (nationwide); warehou and blue moki (central); and blue cod, red cod, and trumpeter (most prevalent in the south). Several species of flounder and mullet are also common, but are mostly taken by net, and also, in the case of flounder, by spearing in shallow water at night.

NICARAGUA

From a natural resources standpoint, Nicaragua seems to be a paradise. Like its southerly neighbor, Costa Rica, Nicaragua is bounded by the Caribbean on the east and the Pacific Ocean on the west; despite some deforestation, it has the largest rain forest reserves in Central America as well as its two largest lakes, Nicaragua and Managua. Rivers form large sections of its northern and southern borders and are numerous along the eastern lowlands. And, it is the least densely populated country in this part of the world.

Nicaragua was rarely fished through the latter part of the twentieth century due to civil unrest. From a general tourism as well as recreational fishing standpoint, Nicaragua fell off the radar screen. As a result, its fisheries resources have been barely explored with modern equipment and methods; based upon what has been known to exist in the past, plus minor sorties along the southwest coast from Costa Rica, some people are looking at this country's sportfishing opportunities in "new frontier" terms. With changes in the late 1990s occurring in Nicaragua that seem likely to encourage more tourism, sportfishing opportunities may open up, and the country's tarpon, snook, bonefish, permit, marlin, and sailfish resources will be better evaluated. Given the nature of the fisheries in Costa Rica, however, and what is known from the past, there is reason to be optimistic about future angling on both coasts.

It is known that the San Juan River, which forms part of Nicaragua's southern border with Costa Rica, as well as its nearby tributaries and the delta mouth they form, have exceptional numbers of snook and tarpon, as well as machaca, guapote, and mojarra. This area has lately been accessed via a mothership (a 65-foot houseboat towing fishing skiffs), and with permanent facilities planned, it is expected to provide near-virgin fishing in the rivers, lagoons, and near-coast areas.

Anglers will be able to explore hidden lakes and lagoons that don't even appear on maps, including San Juanillo, Silico, La Barca, Ebro Lagoon, Misterioso Lagoon, Fish Creek, the upper waters of Indian River, and Rio Caño Negro (also known as Black Creek). There reportedly is a tarpon nursery in the estuary of Spanish Creek that abounds with 10- to 40-pound tarpon.

These waters have been lightly fished, and there's opportunity to fish the inland lakes for snook, guapote, mojarra, machaca, and other species; in brackish lagoons for the occasional tarpon, as well as snook and snapper; or outside the river mouth for tarpon and occasionally for such species such as jacks, tripletail, barracuda, dorado, snapper, and wahoo when the blue water species move in during certain times of the year.

The vicinity of the river mouth is the most consistent place to find large snook, which run from 15 to 20 pounds. Snook are available all year, but peak from April through June and August through October. Fat snook, which are a smaller species and average 5 pounds, are abundant in the rivers and lakes from November through March. Fall is a good time for the tarpon, too, although they're also available all season. Fifty- to 100-pounders are in the surf, where leadhead jigs do the job. The beaches and surf can be walked, and when conditions are right, a boat can get through the *boca,* or river mouth, to prowl the deeper environs on the oceanside. Reputedly, there are offshore flats that have bonefish and permit.

While this is strictly the activity in the far southwestern corner of Nicaragua, there is reason to believe that the remainder of Nicaragua's Caribbean coast has more, possibly a lot more, of the same. The trouble is that there are few villages along the entire coast (only 5 percent of the country's population is in this area) and extremely poor access. But there's an impressive amount of lagoons, deltas, and small islands here, plus coral reefs scattered offshore. Inland, numerous rivers originate in the highlands and flow through tropical rain forest and the entire lowland area known as the Mosquito Coast.

Fishing up and down this coast from Bluefields to Puerto Cabezas is reputedly excellent, and intrepid adventurers may be able to hire out boats at those two ports from local fishermen. Bluefields is a more popular site, and in the late 1990s, there were regular flights there from the capital, Managua, and continuing on to the Corn Islands. An easterly road from Managua stops far short of Bluefields.

There are two Corn Islands, Big and Little, about 30 miles offshore. Little Corn has a large shallow reef and may provide bonefish and permit; kingfish and dolphin are caught nearby.

Up the coast, northeast and offshore of Puerto Cabezas, is a group of small islands known as Miskito Keys. Flats here contain bonefish and permit; snappers and other species are found in lagoons; and wahoo, mackerel, and barracuda are among species caught in the area. This location has only been lightly fished, and other opportunities are possible.

On the Pacific side, there is some sportfishing out of the southern port city of San Juan del Sur. Sailfish are the main attraction and said to be present all year, with best results from June through October. Blue marlin are caught from November through February. Tuna, bonito, Spanish mackerel, and other species are also found, and more about the Pacific Coast's entire fishery may be learned as tourism develops.

Inland, the freshwater opportunities primarily consist of the aforementioned guapote, machaca, and mojarra species in the middle and upper reaches of rivers. There have been unconfirmed reports of trout in the highlands north of Jinotega. Rivers in the mountainous outback may have gamefish, although the effects of timber harvesting and subsistence fishing are uncertain.

Nicaragua's major rivers run into the Caribbean, with the Rio Grande and its tributaries being the most extensive system. The San Juan River begins in Lake Nicaragua and flows some 110 miles to the salt. Lake Nicaragua is an enormous lake, nearly 100 miles long and containing over 350 islands. With two volcanoes and a national park containing archaeological sites, Lake Nicaragua is a tourist draw and reputed to have plenty of guapote, which are fine light-tackle fish, but unlikely to contend with tarpon and snook along the coast for the attention of traveling anglers. However, it was known to contain a unique species of freshwater shark *(Carcharhinus luecas),* referred to as a bull shark.

NIGHTCRAWLER
The most common earthworm *(see),* usually from 6 to 8 inches long, and a highly popular and effective freshwater bait.
See: Natural Bait.

NIGHT FISHING
In terms of the overall number of people who fish, fishing at night is not nearly as popular as fishing during the day. This is mainly because people are more comfortable fishing during daylight hours than at night. There are many places, and many species of fish, that could provide good night fishing experiences if anglers were more willing to try it. In some cases, less competition from other anglers, chances for larger fish, and sometimes opportunities for a better overall catch are clear incentives to be angling at night.

Some species of fish are very active at night and have physical adaptations that make them more prone than others to night activity. The glossy white, large eyes of walleye, for example, are actually due to a special reflective layer in the retina of the eye known as *tapetum lucidum,* and this same layer is also found in the eyes of cats, raccoons, and deer. It gathers light that enters the eye, making the eye extremely sensitive to bright daylight intensities but well adapted to nocturnal vision.

Species that have an especially well-tuned sense of smell, like catfish and sharks, are more nocturnal than others. And some species that are very reliant on their hearing abilities will use this sense, especially their lateral line, to detect food opportunities even when vision is limited. It is a well-known fact that many fish, especially in midsummer when daylight is greatest, are more active in the low-light hours of dawn and dusk. This may be partly due to the fact that there is less human activity on the water at that time, and the same can be said about fish activity at night. Places such as trout streams that tend to have a lot of human activity in the day may be more productive at night because the fish have found night feeding more advantageous, whether or not they are physiologically attuned to this.

Among the fish that are known to be nocturnally active and that are typically fished for at night are largemouth bass, striped bass, catfish, trout, coho and chinook salmon, and swordfish. Ironically, a good amount of angling is carried out at night under the lights of bridges, roadways, and docks, because the light draws insects, baitfish, and larger predators; a host of species, in both freshwater and saltwater, may be attracted.

The methods used for after-dark fishing vary widely, from casting surface lures in the pitch black for largemouth bass to using glowing lures for deep salmon trolling, and from fishing live eels off a wave-whipped jetty for striped bass to sitting in a lantern-equipped boat while fishing deep bait for catfish or trout. One thing that can be said with certainty about fishing for all species of fish in the inky blackness of night is that you just don't fish like you would in daylight.

Naturally, anglers are accustomed to seeing what they're doing and watching the line or the lure, and this is seldom possible at night, although black lights make it possible to watch fluorescent lines very well. Therefore, intuition and a feel for the line become more important at night than in the

 Modern-day salmon fishing in the Great Lakes started in the early 1960s with Michigan stockings, but coho salmon were planted (unsuccessfully) in the Great Lakes as early as 1873.

Night Fishing

Early evening is a prime time for bass fishing, especially in the summer.

daylight. Obviously, your vision is better on nights with moonlight than on dark or overcast nights (some people also feel that fishing is better before or around the full-moon phase, although this is arguable). Keeping the use of lights to a minimum is a good idea for some types of fishing (like largemouth bass), though it is unnecessary for others. A small headlamp is a dandy accessory for night fishing, since it frees both hands and issues only a small amount of light.

Acclimating yourself to night fishing and to seeing in the blackness takes some adjustment, so you're smart to keep a couple of rods handy with different lures or baits on them in order to minimize the need to use a light and retie. If you're casting with a baitcasting outfit and get a bad backlash, you can put that rod aside and employ a different one. If you're prone to backlashes with baitcasting tackle, consider using spinning gear at night, especially if circumstances don't require accurate lure placement close to cover.

Be attentive to safety when you're fishing in the dark. Landing and unhooking fish caught on lures with multiple hooks is more of a problem in the darkness. Be careful about losing your balance while standing up in a boat at night; in daylight you often brace for a collision with objects, but in the dark you rarely see the objects and are jolted off balance when the boat bumps something. You could wind up in the water, or fall against something inside the boat. Don't leave a lot of things underfoot in a boat, especially hooked lures. When in a boat, keep a high-powered flashlight handy so you can warn an approaching motorboat about your presence. And when you're under power, have bow and stern lights on.

When fishing in pure darkness, you can do several things to enhance your success. Familiarize yourself with the place that you're fishing. It's best to slow down and work an area well rather than hustle all over. And, in many freshwater situations, it helps to concentrate on quiet and stealth. Noise from operating the motor constantly, moving things around in the boat, chucking an anchor overboard, plunking the electric motor into position, etc., can transmit bad vibes to fish, at least for a while. Being silent and stealthy is an attribute at night. When speaking, use a muted tone so that you don't alarm the fish. Smacking the oars against an aluminum boat is bad news. Similarly, when wade fishing, you need to move slowly and walk carefully, since falling and splashing about are seldom conducive to good fishing.

In a boat, you should approach an area silently from afar as opposed to running up on it with motor on. Drifting quietly and working methodically all around a boat is effective in some situations. Ease the anchor into the water if that helps keep you in place or from moving too far too fast.

Finally, have great respect for the water and the forces of nature, especially at night. If you get into some trouble, chances are that there will be few people around to help.

See: Safety.

NIGHT VISION EQUIPMENT

Electronic night scopes and binoculars multiply available light up to about 50,000 times and can almost turn night into day. This equipment can make night anglers safer and more efficient and is being increasingly used by anglers and boaters who spend considerable time on the water after dark. Night vision equipment makes locating buoys, reading channel markers, and spotting other public or personal navigation markers much easier. Hazards, such as floating debris, shoals, poorly marked jetties, partially submerged standing timber, and boats either anchored or running without lights, are made less dangerous. Both binocular and monocular models are available.

Equipment generations. Night vision units are referred to as generation zero, 1, 2, or 3, depending upon their level of technology. Generation zero units represent the oldest technology and require an infrared light source to work. Generation 1 models include improvements that allow them to operate with ambient starlight. Generation 2 models offer better performance with less visual distortion and are usually lighter and more compact. Generation 3 models offer even more performance and can use a broader spectrum of light; their most important internal component, the intensifier tube, should last longer than those in earlier models.

Light enters a night vision unit's objective lens and then is amplified and passed on to the user's eye. Generation 1 units are the most common among imports and offer light amplification from about 2,000 to 30,000 times, depending upon internal enhancements. Generation 2 models boost light about 30,000 times, and generation 3 models multiply light about 50,000 times.

The actual image improvement that your eye sees when switching from one generation to the next depends upon the ambient light on the scene. A major manufacturer did a comparison test to determine how far away a 6-foot-tall man could be seen through generation 2 and 3 models under different light conditions. There was only a 16 percent difference under bright moonlight (.1 lux), but under a dark, overcast sky (.0001 lux), generation 3 performed 50 percent better than generation 2. Generally, the darker the night the more difference a unit's generation and amplification factor makes.

Stepping up to the next higher generation of equipment can mean more than just extra light amplification and a higher cost. Generation 2 and 3 units may have less visual distortion, better resolution, and a wider field of view than generation 1 models. Again, the differences are more apparent under darker conditions. Depending upon conditions, a good night vision unit can provide a view comparable to what the eye sees in normal daylight.

How it works. Light is amplified inside a generation 3 night scope by passing through three components. Each is about the diameter of a quarter, and they are lined up and sandwiched together inside a vacuum tube. The disc closest to the objective lens is called a photocathode. The middle disc is called a microchannel plate and the disc closest to the eyepiece is a phosphor screen.

Light is made up of tiny particles called photons. A photon enters the objective lens and hits the surface of the photocathode. This component is a glass plate with a surface coating of Gallium Arsenide, which converts the photon into an electron. The photon-turned-electron then travels to the microchannel plate to be amplified. This component looks like a wire mesh with more than a million holes passing through it. The holes, called channels, are tilted at a 5-degree angle, and millions of electrons cling to the channels' sides. As the traveling electron enters the closest tube, it can't pass straight through because of the tube's 5-degree tilt. Instead, it ricochets down the sides of the tube, knocking loose more electrons, which join it. The more electrons that join the original one, the higher the tube's amplification factor. The electrons exit the channel and strike the phosphor screen causing it to glow.

Each of the millions of photons entering the front of a scope follow a parallel path through the tube to the phosphor screen. A photon entering at the upper-left edge of the objective lens strikes the upper-left edge of the phosphor screen. Because the particles maintain their orientation as they travel through the tube, the glowing image that meets your eye is an accurate representation of the scene in front of the scope.

Accessories. Accessories include infrared illuminators, head mounts that let you wear a binocular unit like goggles when you need both hands free, lenses that magnify image size, and even adaptors for connecting camcorders or still cameras. Illuminators add light under extremely dark conditions and can help to replace light lost when using a magnifying lens—less light going in means less coming out to your eye. A head mount is helpful when fishing or maneuvering around an unlighted dock or when snaking between hull-threatening obstacles.

Not for high-speed use. Manufacturers warn that boats should be operated at slow speeds while wearing this equipment; it isn't intended for high-speed operation. Military users train for long periods of time before attempting to operate vehicles or vessels at speed, or to fly, using night vision equipment. Although most units have built-in safeguards to keep sudden flares of light from damaging their intensifier tubes, the user can be momentarily blinded by them, perhaps long enough to lose control of his boat.

NIUE

They call Niue "The Rock of Polynesia," and it is just that—the world's largest raised coral atoll, thrust upward by some titanic submarine upheaval. Protruding from abyssal depths, its 260-square-kilometer landmass is fortressed from relentless Pacific swells by rugged hundred-foot-tall limestone cliffs in which the forms of ancient coral heads are still evident.

There are no lagoons or long sandy beaches. Rather, the island is girdled by a narrow, flat, wave-cut coral platform, which drops off rapidly into deep water. The cliffs are broken by intimate coves, canoe landings, and chasms where splits in the bluff open out into ravine-like saltwater swimming pools filled with colorful fish. In some ways Niue is the reverse of a normal island. Instead of the reefs extending out from the shore, many of them extend inland.

Situated in the South Pacific Ocean, Niue (pronounced new-ay) is 2,100 kilometers northeast of New Zealand and 460 kilometers east of Tonga. It has been a New Zealand protectorate, but is now an independent nation in free association with New Zealand, and still dependent on its larger brother in many ways.

The island is around 17 kilometers long by 10 kilometers wide. Because of a lack of job prospects 10,000 Niueans now live in New Zealand and Australia, leaving only 2,000 people on the island. To try boosting tourism there has been much investment in infrastructure, and there's a wide range of good quality accommodation and other amenities.

Niueans are of Polynesian background and amongst the friendliest, peaceful, and honest people that could be encountered anywhere. Crime is virtually unheard of on this island. Many locals have been educated in New Zealand, have worked there, or have relatives there. It is rare to encounter anyone who does not speak English well.

The main town is Alofi, situated near the airport, which is serviced from New Zealand and Tonga. With no sheltered harbor on Niue, it is important that all boats can be pulled out of the water for safe storage in rough weather. This is done with a large crane mounted on Sir Robert's Wharf in downtown Alofi. A 6-meter craft is about the top of the range that can be handled, and most boats are between 3 and 6 meters. A boat ramp and smaller crane facility is available at nearby Avatele.

Launching and retrieving by crane all adds to the experience of fishing out of Niue but does make access to the fishery completely weather-dependent. A series of deep water moorings for visiting boats are available off Alofi, but with little shelter, visiting boats are often forced to cut and run if the weather turns bad.

Charter services, existing only since 1997, are filled by three fishing operators and one dive operator. Safety is of paramount importance, and all charter boats are regularly inspected for safety equipment and required to have a second engine. A VHF radio system is maintained, but the excellent cellular phone system is often used instead. Boats are equipped with basic tackle, but serious anglers might be wise to supplement this with their own equipment.

Seafood is an important part of the Niuean diet, with many people fishing for their own tables, and there's a strong domestic market in pelagic species, particularly tuna and wahoo. There is not much catch-and-release here, although charter operators will usually release billfish at an angler's request. This should be discussed before fishing starts. The rule is that any fish caught belong to the boat, and are usually sold on the local market. This is reflected in reasonable charter rates. Charter operators will usually offer the angler a share of the catch for their own consumption.

For charter trips, early morning starts (5:30) are the norm. This catches the dawn bite and allows a reasonable stretch of fishing before the wind starts to come up around midday. Anglers are back in time for lunch on shore, with the afternoon free to relax and take advantage of the many other activities available.

Local fishermen fish for food from small aluminum boats or one-man outrigger canoes, using heavy monofilament handlines. They are surprisingly sophisticated fishermen in their own way, and familiar with the fine points of chumming, live baiting, chunking, and careful rigging of baits like flying fish.

Baitfish are captured at night by pursuing them with boats equipped with lights and long-handled nets. This nighttime fish netting is an interesting experience in itself, and at least one local operator specializes in taking out guests on these trips.

With basic tackle and small canoes, local fishermen regularly catch wahoo (which many locals claim to be able to smell while they are still in the water) and tuna. Sailfish and larger marlin are also occasionally captured after epic battles. Canoe fishermen often use their legs to brake or slow their handlines and you can tell the most intrepid ones by their line scars!

With a narrow littoral zone, the amount of fish life that can be supported is not great, so the conservation-minded local fishermen tend to pursue pelagic rather than bottom species if possible. During the winter months this is usually wahoo, supplemented with more tuna and some mahimahi in the summer.

Wahoo is the fish of choice. It is the fish that everybody in Niue wants to eat, and so it is also the one everybody wants to catch. Trolling with big bullet-headed lures, or rigged whole flying fish, are popular techniques.

There are strict limitations on the taking of crayfish (lobster) and shellfish. Full protection is accorded to live coral, turtle, moray eel, rays, giant wrasse, and the timid but plentiful Niuean banded sea snake. In this aspect, Niue is well ahead of many Pacific islands.

Along with attempts to stimulate the tourism industry has come the influence of visiting anglers,

---

New Brunswick does not have an officially designated fish, but it does have an official Atlantic salmon fly, "The Picture Province."

mostly New Zealanders. In 1997 the Niue Sport-fishing Club, now affiliated with the IGFA, was formed and it has established a local record chart. Rod and reel fishing is becoming more common than it used to be, compared with the practical, results-oriented method of heavy handlines. Visiting anglers are encouraged to join the local club, which can be contacted through the Niue Tourism Office in Alofi. Fishing is strictly prohibited on Sundays, and this restriction is taken very seriously.

There are two main fishing seasons. The October through February summer period sees a predominance of skipjack tuna, yellowfin tuna, and mahimahi (dolphin), with blue marlin in attendance. It is likely that black and striped marlin are also present in these waters, but as the offshore sportfishery is new, this is yet to be confirmed. Inshore, trevally (giant, bluefin, bigeye and goldspot) hunt the reefs during this period.

During the May through September winter months, wahoo are more common, and sailfish are encountered along with some marlin. Inshore, the trevally seem to depart and the reefs are left to the barracuda and red bass (called *fagamea* locally, pronounced fonga-me-a). The red bass is an aggressive tropical snapper, a smaller relative of the cubera snapper.

In deeper waters off the shoulders of the island there are dogtooth tuna, amberjack, various snappers, black trevally, groupers, sharks (including whalers and tigers), and the usual rash of unidentified fish that can't be stopped. Deep-water fishing with baits fished off low-stretch braided lines can produce some very interesting fishing.

Because of the steep dropoff from the island, much fishing at Niue is done within a few hundred meters of shore. A series of fish aggregation devices (FAD) are only about 400 to 500 meters from the lee coast and are a main focus of fishing effort, as are several underwater ridges extending out off the island. FADs are sometimes set on the latter and provide excellent fishing, but they are not well protected from bad weather and are more prone to loss than those inshore.

Shore casting off the reef at low tide with both lures and baits is good sport, and is at its best in the summer months when trevally are present. Be aware that there are danger spots around the island where unexpected waves can sweep in and endanger shore anglers. The quaint Niuean expression for this disaster is "to lose your hat." Fishing prohibitions also apply to some areas. Seek local advice before going fishing.

NMFS
Acronym for National Marine Fisheries Service *(see)*.

NO KILL
A term applied to a body of water, usually a section of river or stream, that is subject to complete catch-and-release *(see)* fishing regulations. In other words, all fish caught must be released alive and unharmed by anglers. No-kill waters are also often subject to regulations regarding method of fishing or equipment, such as fly fishing only, mandatory use of single or barbless hooks, artificial lures only, etc.
See: Regulations.

NOODLE ROD
A long, limber fishing rod primarily used for light-line river fishing, especially for steelhead, but also employed in open-water trolling. Noodle rods are primarily custom-made, usually about 12 to 14 feet long, manufactured for use with 2- through 8-pound line, and feature a long handle and many guides. The guides are placed so as to curve around the blank, starting near the butt on top of the rod and ending at the tip under the rod; the purpose of this arrangement is to keep the line from contacting the shaft of the rod when it is bent. Being long and limber, these rods get a great bend in them when a stout fish is on, and playing fish requires some adjustment from the normal mode.

When fighting a fish with a noodle rod, the butt should be pointed at the fish; the rod will bend completely over in a large semicircle-like manner. When wading in a river, this can be done with the rod held upright. From a higher vantage point, however, including a boat, it may be necessary with large and strong-fighting fish to play it sideways, with the entire rod held horizontal to the water rather than vertical, although the butt is still pointed at the fish.

NORTH CAROLINA
Although many states claim to have diverse sport-fishing opportunities, North Carolina is one of the few that really do. Tourism interests call the Tar Heel State a "Variety Vacationland," and anglers with eclectic tastes can find that holds true in saltwater, where inshore or offshore this is one of the best places to fish on the Atlantic Seaboard, as well as in freshwater, where mountain stream fishing is complemented by swampland wading.

Inland, the opportunities range from coldwater trout fishing in over a thousand miles of mountain streams to largemouth bass fishing that is virtually within a stone's throw of the fabled surf fishing at Cape Hatteras. Deep mountain lakes are contrasted by shallow, vegetation-filled marsh lakes. Swift-flowing streams and large impoundments are augmented by slow-moving rivers amid swampy floodplains. Popular freshwater sportfish include brown, rainbow, and brook trout; largemouth, spotted, and smallmouth bass; striped bass and their hybrid cousins; crappies, bluegills, and assorted panfish; walleyes; muskellunge; and spawning-run shad in coastal rivers.

In the marine environment there's tidewater fishing, surf fishing, inshore fishing, and offshore fishing, each with highly notable components, whether that be big bluefin tuna in the winter off Hatteras, red drum in the surf on the barrier beaches, or striped bass in the rivers.

About 175 miles of barrier beaches known as the Outer Banks encircle the great Currituck, Albemarle, Pamlico, and Core Sounds, where a variety of popular species also include bluefish, spotted seatrout, cobia, flounder, and croaker, plus the occasional tarpon. Oregon, Hatteras, and Ocracoke Inlets are gateways to marlin, tuna, dolphin, king mackerel, albacore, and many other species.

The North Carolina Wildlife Resources Commission maintains many excellent launch ramps across the state where there are no fees to launch a boat, and there are many privately maintained ramps throughout the state that provide access for a launching fee.

Freshwater
Mountain streams and lakes. North Carolina is home to the largest mountains east of the Mississippi River, and this produces a surprisingly good trout fishery. In fact, some 2,100 miles of high, coldwater streams are recognized as Designated Public Mountain Trout Waters and closely managed by the state's Wildlife Resources Commission for brook, rainbow, and brown trout fishing. The state tries to manage its coldwater streams as mostly wild trout waters, but those with marginal habitat that are incapable of supporting a wild trout fishery receive supplemental stockings of hatchery reared fish.

The federal government manages streams inside the Great Smoky Mountains; many are intensively managed as native trout waters with emphasis on the eastern brook trout, which is the only truly native salmonid found in North Carolina. Some of the streams within the national park are accessible only by crossing Fontana Lake with a boat and hiking into some of the most pristine trout country in the United States. Hazel, Forney, and Eagle Creeks are but a few of the notable trout streams that empty into Fontana, and lack of easy access makes these and other streams lightly fished.

Another outstanding trout fishery exists within the Cherokee Indian Reservation in Jackson County. The reservation's fishery consists almost entirely of stocked fish, but what the fish lack in being truly wild they make up for in sheer numbers and size.

The headwaters of the Nantahala River are high along the border of North Carolina and Georgia and constitute what is probably North Carolina's coldest trout stream. The Nantahala has some of the finest trout of all three species in the state. Small feeder streams, including Big Indian and Kimsey Creeks, hold good populations of small but colorful brookies at their origins. Campgrounds and other facilities are available in the Nantahala National Forest. The lower Nantahala River is heavily used for whitewater rafting, but offers fine fishing for those who get out before the major rafting action takes place.

Some of the best trout streams are small flows that many anglers overlook simply because of their size. They're seldom fished and can hold outstanding populations of surprisingly large, albeit spooky, fish. Stealth plus the ability to make short, accurate casts are important for success.

In contrast, some of North Carolina's larger mountain trout streams are tailwater fisheries. Tailwater rivers such as the Tuckaseigee and Green hold some very large trout. Public access may be a problem at some, however, so anglers need to check into this issue.

Many tourists visit North Carolina's mountains every year and there are numerous pay-to-fish ponds in these areas. For the non-purist, these ponds represent a fine way to collect fresh trout to be cooked at the campfire or cabin.

Trout aren't the only species in the mountain rivers, incidentally. The French Broad River near Black Mountain and the New River are highly regarded for their muskie populations. Local guides have done remarkably well for these fine sportfish.

The mountains also hold some of North Carolina's finest lakes, which are unusual in that they hold coldwater, coolwater, and warmwater fish species. Most notable are Fontana, Hiwassee, Calderwood, Nantahala, Cheoah, Santeetlah, and Chatuge.

Several species of trout are usually present in these, and all contain a good population of smallmouth bass, spotted bass, walleye, and muskie. Panfish, especially bluegill and crappie, are fairly abundant.

Fontana Lake has rainbow, brook, and brown trout, and a remnant population of steelhead, which were introduced there years ago and may migrate up into the feeder streams to spawn in the winter. The winter fishing on these streams is scarcely used and can be quite good; conversely, fishing in the deeper waters of the lakes has produced some very large trout during the warmer months. In spite of its high elevation and relatively cool water, Fontana has produced some very sizable largemouth bass. For years the state record largemouth bass came from this deep lake.

Piedmont region. The larger lakes of North Carolina are east of the mountains in the Piedmont region and have excellent populations of crappie, largemouth bass, catfish, landlocked striped bass, and all varieties of panfish, especially shellcrackers and bluegills. Hybrid striped bass are popular newcomers in these lakes, and are locally called Bodie bass.

Lake Norman near Charlotte is noted for striped bass and largemouth bass fishing. There are numerous campgrounds and marinas located on this lake, and access is easy.

Kerr Lake along the North Carolina-Virginia border is a noted largemouth bass fishery and holds a strong population of striped bass that were trapped in this impoundment when the Roanoke River was dammed. Spring fishing for spawning stripers on the Dan River, a tributary to Kerr, is very popular. Other lakes along this river system, such as Gaston and Roanoke Rapids, also contain large numbers of gamefish.

High Rock Lake near Lexington is acclaimed as one of the state's best largemouth bass lakes, and some prominent fishing tournaments have been held here. It is the second lake in the Yadkin River chain.

Badin Lake was formed when the Yadkin River was dammed near Albemarle. It is bordered on one side by the Uwharrie National Forest, which has excellent campsites and outdoor facilities. Below Badin Lake is the Pee Dee River and Lake Tillery, both of which offer fine warmwater fishing.

The major rivers of the Piedmont—the Haw, Yadkin, Catawba, and Roanoke—offer good float fishing for panfish, catfish, and rock bass. There are numerous impoundments along the rivers that have excellent populations of largemouth and hybrid bass. Some also have a good population of white bass.

Many smaller lakes in North Carolina are owned by the various municipalities or counties. They are usually reservoirs for drinking water. Most allow fishing but are restricted to electric motors only.

These smaller lakes are managed intensively for recreational angling and usually have rental boats available at the site for a nominal fee. Contact the local city or county recreation departments for details on fishing these lakes.

Many small privately owned ponds and lakes are located throughout the state. With proper permission these lakes usually offer fine fishing.

Coastal plain. North Carolina's coastal plain contains some of the most interesting angling that the state has to offer, including saltwater fish in brackish or freshwater environments.

The aforementioned Roanoke River, which is dammed along its upper parts, has a spawning run of striped bass, locally called rockfish, that is one of the strongest and finest on the East Coast. Each spring stripers swarm into the lower river, migrating upstream to the dam at Roanoke Rapids Lake where they spawn.

Thanks to the conservation efforts of many individuals and organizations, stripers are now protected during spawning time, when anglers can catch them but must release virtually all. Single, barbless hooks are required on all waters of the Roanoke River from the Highway 258 bridge at Scotland Neck to the first dam on the river at Roanoke Rapids. Fly anglers flock to the Roanoke Rapids/Weldon area during the spawning run. Some stripers remain in the river on a year-round basis but the truly spectacular fishery is in the early spring.

There are many tributary streams along the lower Roanoke River that have excellent fishing for largemouth bass, crappie, white and yellow perch, and assorted panfish. These streams are bordered by some of the more spectacular scenery in eastern North Carolina, as vast tracts of bottomland hardwoods are still intact there. These tributaries of the Roanoke River wind in and out of huge swamps and it's entirely possible to get lost if you're not very familiar with the waters, making it necessary to have good charts and maps.

Both hickory and American (white) shad also spawn in the Roanoke River, and light tackle anglers have a lot of sport with these gamefish here. Other notable shad rivers include the Cape Fear and the Pamlico/Tar.

The most notable American shad fishery in the state is found below the locks on the Cape Fear River near Fayetteville. This is strictly a springtime fishery when the shad make their spawning run, but angling is quite good for that period of time. Bank fishing is possible but most people prefer to fish from boats, as there is swift current below locks.

In eastern North Carolina, and just across Pamlico Sound from Cape Hatteras, is Lake Mattamuskeet. This is an unusual lake which many people consider to have the finest largemouth bass fishing in the state.

At some 50,000, acres Lake Mattamuskeet is the largest natural lake in the state. It is unique in that it is oblong in shape and extremely shallow. Many other natural lakes in the coastal plain are similar in shape and depth resulting in the theory that the lakes were formed by a meteorite shower at some point in the past. Other lakes such as Phelps, Waccamaw, White, and Pungo are smaller.

Most of this lake is part of the vast Pocosin Lakes National Wildlife Refuge and falls under special rules because of this. The lake is primarily a waterfowl refuge and is closed to fishing for several months of the year.

During the summer months, however, Lake Mattamuskeet is open to boats and fishing and is a light tackle bass angler's dream lake. The best way to fish it is by wading. Anglers use shallow-draft boats to reach their destination on the lake, then anchor the boat and wade in water that's seldom more that waist deep.

While spinning and baitcasting tackle are the most widely used equipment on Lake Mattamuskeet, flycasting tackle is especially useful here, since much of the time the only water clear for fishing is the small pocket of open water between mats of aquatic vegetation. With a fly rod the angler can work small openings and not have to retrieve the entire lure and line through the vegetation.

A European eel held in a Swedish aquarium lived to be 88 years old; it was born in the Sargasso Sea and captured in a river as a 3-year-old elver.

Aquatic vegetation is thick due in part to the enrichment of thousands of tons of waterfowl manure that were deposited in the lake during the winter months. Because of this, weedless or topwater lures are most effective.

Because of its shallow, vegetation-rich nature, Lake Mattamuskeet does not get pressure from the large, high-powered bass boat crowd. Many believe that the majority of fish in the lake have never seen a lure before, which is practically unheard of in this age of high fishing pressure. Other fish found in Lake Mattamuskeet, incidentally, are striped bass, flounder, panfish, and crappie.

Lake Phelps, which is near Mattamuskeet, is quite different in nature. Phelps is deeper, not as rich in vegetation, and much clearer. Most of this lake is best fished by boat but the shallower edges are wonderful for wade fishing. Frequently, largemouth bass can be sighted in the shallows and stalked and sight-fished much the same as bonefish are on saltwater flats. A large state park with campgrounds and full facilities adjoins one side of Lake Phelps, and public boat ramps are available.

One of the most picturesque fishing lakes in North Carolina is found in Merchant's Millpond State Park near Gatesville. This is a large millpond full of standing, live timber. Gasoline motors are not allowed on this lake, canoes are available for rental, and camp sites exist. Largemouth bass, assorted panfish, and catfish are abundant.

Lake Waccamaw, located in the southern coastal plain, is also a popular largemouth bass lake. It is deeper than many of the other lakes that dot the eastern part of the state, and, since it is easier to maneuver bass boats here than in many of the more shallow bodies of water, it receives more fishing pressure.

Coastal plain rivers such as the Alligator, Chowan, Pungo, Pasquotank, Tar (which becomes the Pamlico River at Washington, NC), Neuse, Trent, New, Cape Fear, Northeast Cape Fear, and Waccamaw are widely known as fine largemouth bass rivers. They also produce good catches of redbreast sunfish, various catfish, and the primitive bowfin or blackfish. Many of these rivers also produce striped bass seasonally.

There are many brackish water coastal streams where an angler may catch both saltwater and freshwater fish on the same lures or bait in the same water. Largemouth bass populations are good in these mildly saline rivers, but also present are red drum, bluefish, speckled trout, striped bass, white and yellow perch, and flounder. Any of these might be caught on the same fishing trip to these coastal rivers.

Don't discount the possibility of catching the larger saltwater fishes in these coastal streams. Even trophy tarpon or large red drum (redfish) are found well into the "fresh" waters of some of these rivers.

Many coastal streams are classified as "commercial" waters below a certain, arbitrary, point, and no fishing license is necessary there, although a proposed universal fishing license might change that. Be sure to check local fishing regulations.

Perhaps the most widely recognized bass fishing in the coastal plain is found in Currituck Sound in the northeastern part of the state. Like Lake Mattamuskeet, this is an extremely shallow body of water that is filled with aquatic vegetation during the warmer months. Like other shallow bodies of water that have large amounts of weeds, lures must be worked through brush and submerged vegetation in order to be effective, and shallow draft boats are the best transportation.

The most unusual freshwater fishing in North Carolina is found in several small ponds located a few hundred yards behind Cape Point at Hatteras. Surf anglers can literally go a small distance behind the famed point and fish for largemouth bass and bluegills.

Saltwater

Atlantic Inlets. Saltwater fishing in North Carolina is divided by Diamond Shoals. This 12-mile-long sandbar marks the meeting place of the cold Labrador Current from the north and the warm Gulf Stream from the south. The merger of these produces excellent fishing, but also treacherous conditions that cause it to be referred to as the "Graveyard of the Atlantic." The shoals that extend seaward from Capes Hatteras, Lookout, and Fear, are littered with broken, rusted skeletons of ships wrecked by storms or sunk by enemy torpedoes, and they also possess artificial reefs.

Waters to the north of Diamond Shoals tend to be colder and harbor fish more common to the north Atlantic, while waters to the south are warmer and hold fish more common to the south Atlantic. Fish such as yellowfin tuna, dolphin, blue marlin, and white marlin are found along the edge of the Gulf Stream on both sides of Diamond Shoals.

Proximity to the Gulf Stream means that the offshore waters harbor lots of white marlin and record-size blue marlin. In fact, the waters off North Carolina can lay claim to having the best potential in the coastal U.S. for catching a grander, if not an all-tackle record.

Oregon Inlet has been the port of record for several Atlantic blue marlin granders. Others have been registered at Hatteras and Morehead City. A 1,142-pounder taken in August of 1989 at the 80-fathom mark northeast of Cape Lookout is a former all-tackle world record holder, and a 1,128-pounder caught in June of 1975 held the 80-pound line class world record until replaced in 1993 with a fish from the Azores.

While there is opportunity for large blue marlin out of any of the major coastal ports, the area to the northeast of Oregon Inlet has been especially productive in modern times. In the late 1980s, there were four blue marlin caught in a three-day span off Oregon Inlet that each weighed over 800 pounds.

The marlin season off North Carolina generally begins earlier than it does further north, thanks to the warm Gulf Stream influence, and this brings northern boats down for the June and July action. Hatteras often produces well in the beginning of the summer, and then the attention in August and September shifts more to the Oregon Inlet waters.

As for white marlin, the offshore waters have plenty in season. It has been called the best white marlin fishery in North America, and in a productive year the action can border on the unbelievable at times. Locals still talk about the phenomenal catch and release of 108 white marlin made in a single day in 1983 by one sportfishing boat, and that during a tournament.

Certainly that was a blitz, but in a good day a boat here might see upwards of 15 fish. Pods of white marlin are a frequent sighting, especially when they're chasing bait in the fall. These fish aren't large, with 45 to 60 pounds being average size. There are no record-makers here, but they provide good light-tackle action, as well as opportunities for casting a fly or using spinning tackle. The problem, however, with white marlin fishing here is that it occurs offshore where the big blue marlin roam as well, meaning that there are many times when the bigger blues hit a small bait meant for whites and a great tackle mismatch can occur.

Of course, coastal North Carolina is also noted for other species, particularly channel bass and bluefish. Most of the biggest, and record-setting, bluefish caught in North America have come from coastal North Carolina, including the 50-pound line-class and all-tackle record of 31 pounds 12 ounces. That particular trophy was garnered in 1972, when bluefish reappeared here in great numbers. They had been missing for several decades prior to that.

Virtually all of the monster fish have been taken between November and January in their respective years, which is fitting. The bluefish blitzkrieg in the fall on the Outer Banks is renowned, and as long as the bluefish population—thought by some to be cyclical—remains at a high level, the fall action will be excellent.

Nevertheless, small blues are available here all season long. Bluefish provide surf casters and inshore boaters with a good level of action in the fall, so good, in fact, that using light tackle, including a fly rod, is feasible. However, the bigger blues do not always migrate into the surf for the shore fishermen, nor do they necessarily stay long when they come in, so sometimes there will be light action off the beach while a good mass of fish is offshore.

Outer Banks blues average about 12 pounds in the spring prior to their northward migration, and 15 in the fall. They winter off the various capes and generally provide the best fishing in the months of May and November. The Nag's Head–Oregon Inlet area is one of the better locales, as is Cape Hatteras.

A cobia is boated off the North Carolina coast.

When the blues aren't the quarry, big red drum (also called channel bass) can fill the void. As with bluefish, North Carolina waters have produced a lot of record fish, at one point filling 15 of a possible 20 categories, including the all-tackle and 50 pound line-class record with a 94-pound 2-ounce monster. The hottest fishing is in November, with action all along the banks, but great activity in the surf at Cape Hatteras.

Oregon Inlet is the first opening to the sea south of the North Carolina/Virginia boundary. There are large charter fleets on Manteo Island, plus an excellent launch ramp and varied accommodations. The charter fleet here works the offshore waters on a year-round schedule. Yellowfin tuna are taken all year, with best fishing in the spring and fall. White marlin provide great action during the summer, with the occasional big blue marlin moving into the trolling spread for added excitement.

About 30 miles from Oregon Inlet, the Point is the center of all fishing activity. A very steep drop from 28 to 224 fathoms and another from 200 to 600 fathoms a few miles to the east draw bait and gamefish. The fleet may work north and south of the Point but this is the place where they are likely to begin the day.

Trolling with ballyhoo, mackerel, mullet, and squid is about the only technique used by the Oregon Inlet offshore fleet. A few lures find their way into the spread and chunking has found a few followers, but trolling some type of dead bait is the standard operating procedure.

Not every boat out of Oregon Inlet runs offshore. King mackerel and amberjack are caught over inshore wrecks and around the Navy Towers on live bait, plugs, and spoons. Spanish mackerel, big bluefish, and striped bass are taken on trolled plugs, spoons, and bucktails just beyond the surf line and over the shoals at the mouth of the inlet. Mackerel and amberjack are common in the summer, with the best bluefish and striper action in the spring and fall.

The next outlet to the sea is in the shadow of Diamond Shoals at Hatteras Inlet. Several marinas in the town of Hatteras Village offer charter boats, slips, and a launch ramp.

Hatteras is the nearest point—about 12 miles—to the Gulf Stream north of mid-Florida. Working along the edge of the Gulf Stream out of Hatteras Inlet produces yellowfin, blackfin, and bluefin tuna, as well as marlin, dolphin, and wahoo. The appearance of giant bluefin tuna during the winter has drawn anglers from all over the world and been the subject of a lot of publicity. Fish approaching 1,000 pounds are taken on dead bunker tossed out a few feet behind the boat. When the fishing is hot, and it often is, catches of 25 or more giants per boat per day are recorded. Due to federal regulations, most of these fish are released and many tagged; tagging data from released and recaptured tuna have been valuable to marine biologists.

In the fall, a run of big king mackerel develops over inshore wrecks and shoals. Slow-trolled live menhaden account for most of these big fish. Under favorable conditions the king mackerel run will carry into the winter, adding to the great fishing for giant bluefin.

The inshore grounds out of Hatteras Inlet produce Spanish mackerel, bluefish, red drum, and amberjack. Bottom fishing shows the influence of warmer southern waters, as grouper and snapper replace sea bass and tautog.

It's a long way from Hatteras Inlet to Beaufort Inlet, which is the next major outlet heading down the Tar Heel coast. Barden Inlet behind Cape Lookout Lighthouse serves Harkers Island, but Beaufort Inlet carries the larger charter, private, and head boat fleet out of Morehead City and Atlantic Beach.

King mackerel are major players of the inshore fishery here. Trolling with live menhaden or with dead cigar minnows and ribbonfish has been raised to an art form along this stretch of the North Carolina coast. Small treble hooks and light wire leaders are hidden in the bait in an effort to fool the keen eyes of the mackerel. The big mackerel are played with a light drag to prevent pulling the small hooks out.

Offshore action centers on the Big Rock, an upwelling close to the 100-fathom drop that produces tuna, dolphin, wahoo, and marlin. Big blue marlin show up in late spring to get the offshore season off to a fast start. Several head boats fish the waters near the Gulf Stream for grouper, snapper, triggerfish, amberjack, and African pompano. The boats run all year and most schedule 18- or 24-hour trips at least once a month.

Masonboro Inlet serves the charter and private boat fleet running out of Wrightsville Beach. New Topsail Inlet to the north serves a smaller fleet at Topsail Beach. Both inlets are serviced by several launch ramps and marinas.

King mackerel provide most of the inshore fishing excitement, with yellowfin tuna the major focus on the offshore grounds. Live bait is used for the kings, and trolled rigged ballyhoo for the yellowfins. Bottom fishing for grouper, snapper, triggerfish, and other deep water species is done from both head boats and charter boats. Natural rocks and artificial reefs attract bottom fish and king mackerel.

The Cape Fear River empties into the ocean at Bald Head Island creating shoals that attract numerous species. Anglers troll or drift live baits along the edge of the shoals or at the color change where the turbid water from the river meets the cleaner water of the ocean. This is a good area to find big king mackerel and cobia. There's a marina on the south side of the Cape Fear River at Southport, and a boat ramp on the Intercoastal Waterway at Dutchman Creek.

There are several more inlets between the Cape Fear River and the South Carolina line at Little River Inlet. Lochwoods Folly, Shallotte, Tubbs, and Mad Inlets provide passage to the ocean, but all are a bit dangerous due to shifting sandbars that can change the channel overnight. Boat ramps and marinas are located behind the barrier islands on the Intercoastal Waterway.

The Sounds. The famous Outer Banks of North Carolina is a sandy strip 175 miles long that runs from the Virginia line south to Cape Lookout and then curves back to the mainland. This open-beach barrier reef encompasses 2,000 square miles of sounds or shallow bays that hold great fishing potential, and which offer a potpourri of freshwater, saltwater, and brackish water angling. This is the ideal situation for light-tackle anglers. Even though the bigger sounds can get rough, they have an abundance of sheltered water that can be fished from a small boat or by wading.

In North Carolina, enormous volumes of freshwater daily enter the upper sounds. This water piles up and, depending on volume, creates a lot of brackish water that supports some freshwater species, especially largemouth bass. Currituck Sound, an upper sound that begins at the Virginia line, was once one of the greatest bass factories and shallow-water fisheries in the nation, but the salinity of Currituck has increased greatly since the mid 1980s due to lower freshwater inflows. Bass cannot tolerate it when the salinity becomes too high, and such species as speckled trout, flounder, croaker, and white perch become more prevalent. A good deal of the fishing for these species takes place in the Currituck before it meets up with Albemarle Sound at the Wright Memorial Bridge in Kitty Hawk. This is a very shallow body of water that will not accommodate large boats. Most of the fishing is done from prams or skiffs, or from shore. Albemarle Sound is deeper and larger than Currituck with a greater variety of fish. Striped bass are a primary catch here and found throughout the year, but strict regulations keep the season short and the bag limit low.

Croatan Sound and Roanoke Sound surround Roanoke Island before emptying into Pamlico Sound. Speckled trout are taken from the shallow edges of both waterways on live bait, jigs, and plugs. Striped bass are common at the Mann's Harbor Bridge over Croatan Sound, where plugs, jigs, and bucktails take fish all year. Weakfish, flounder, blues, croaker, and spot keep bottom bouncers happy.

Pamlico Sound is a huge inland sea stretching from Roanoke Island in the north to Cedar Island in the south. It is wide but shallow, seldom reaching over 20 feet in depth. Weedbeds are common along the shoreline, and speckled trout find this a suitable home. The water is 3 to 5 feet deep and usually clear, requiring a careful approach to avoid spooking fish. Live shrimp or mullet will fool even the biggest fish, but many anglers prefer to use jigs, plugs, and flies.

In recent years more anglers have taken up wading in Pamlico Sound, using spinning, baitcasting, and flycasting tackle. Speckled trout are the primary target, but bluefish, channel bass, flounder, croaker, and spot are also caught. It takes experience or an experienced guide to consistently find productive weedbeds or deep holes in the sound, but the action can be fast and exciting with lures or bait.

Tarpon range as far north as Hatteras, and the best action for them in North Carolina is in Pamlico Sound during the summer. They can be difficult to find, however. Most are caught on dead or live bait fished on the bottom in sloughs and holes known to be tarpon hangouts. Local guides have the best idea of where the tarpon hotspots are. Tarpon in the 100-pound class are usually taken each year.

Core Sound runs behind Core Banks from Cedar Island to Cape Lookout, and Bogue Sound begins at Cape Lookout and runs behind the Bogue Banks to Bogue Inlet at Swansboro. Core Sound doesn't see the fishing pressure that Bogue Sound gets because Cape Lookout National Seashore has protected the barrier islands of Core Banks. This is a very shallow sound, but trout, flounder, blues, croaker, and spot are caught in the deeper holes and sloughs.

Bogue Sound lies between the well-developed Bogue Banks barrier island and the equally populated mainland. Morehead City and Atlantic Beach anchor the east end with Cape Carteret and Swansboro at the western end. In spite of the heavy boat traffic, good fishing is found throughout the sound. Speckled trout take refuge in the shadow of bridges crossing the sound. Gray trout are caught in the turning basin at Morehead City, with croaker, spot, and flounder taken in the channels.

From Bogue Inlet south, the narrow Intercoastal Waterway separates the mainland from the barrier islands. Speckled trout, flounder, croaker, and spot are caught here but boat traffic is always a problem. There are boat ramps located on both sides of the sounds and along the Intercoastal Waterway. Few charter boats work these shallow waters but guides with skiffs are found in most waterside communities.

The Surf. North Carolina offers the surf caster more fishing opportunities than most are able to use. Most of the North Carolina beach between Virginia and South Carolina is open to surf fishing, and a good deal of that is accessible by beach buggies. The fishing is so good that even a beach with poor structure can produce good action.

Corolla provides the northernmost access point for beach buggies. Anglers can drive north from here to the Virginia line where access is denied at False Cape State Park. The beach is natural, with no bulkheads or other manmade structures, and fishing can be good for drum, bluefish, speckled trout, and croaker. The beach south of Corolla is developed and vehicular access is restricted.

Development really becomes a problem from Duck to Nags Head. Walk-on fishing is possible but beach buggies are restricted to fall and spring. Special permits to drive on the beach are required in each town, but the fall run of big blues and striped bass can be worth the cost and trouble of obtaining a permit.

Oregon Inlet has a variety of surf fishing possibilities. The beach north of the inlet has good structure with deep holes and sloughs where drum, trout, bluefish, and mullet are caught. At the mouth of the inlet, an old trawler went aground and its bones attract big blues and striped bass in the fall.

Pea Island from Oregon Inlet to Rodanthe is closed to vehicles due to beach erosion. Walk-on access is allowed but parking alongside Route 12 can be a problem. This is a great stretch of beach for big blues in the fall, especially around an old boiler left over from one of the many shipwrecks along this dangerous coastline.

Beach buggies can be used from Rodanthe all the way to Buxton, and from the Hatteras Lighthouse south to Hatteras Inlet. A small section of beach behind the motels in Buxton is set aside for walk-on fishing. Those who stay in one of the motels and walk to the beach often do as well if not better than their motorized brethren.

The Point at Cape Hatteras is the greatest surf fishing location in the world. The Labrador current hits it on the north side and the Gulf Stream hits it on the south, resulting in a mix of bait and gamefish found nowhere else.

Big red drum drop by in the spring and fall, and are often joined by big blues and stripers. Most are caught on chunks of cut bait fished on rods designed to handle big fish in rough water. Known as Hatteras Heavers, the rods have pool cue-size tips and enough backbone to tip over large boulders. Matched to a big conventional reel filled with 30-pound line, the combination can throw 8 ounces of lead and a big hunk of bait into a gale.

Ocracoke Island across Hatteras Inlet has a wide beach that is open to vehicles. This is a quiet outpost that can only be reached by ferry, and the fishing is as good as found anywhere along the coast.

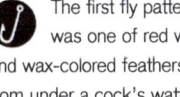

The first fly pattern was one of red wool and wax-colored feathers from under a cock's wattles; it was reportedly used by the Macedonians in the third century A.D.

Portsmouth Island was once a busy seaport but is now part of the Cape Lookout National Seashore. It, too, may only be reached by ferry. Known for a good run of red drum in the spring and fall, the island still attracts a hardy band of surf casters.

Cape Lookout National Seashore also protects all of the Core Banks. Surf fishing is allowed here but access is difficult. Small boats can travel across Core Sound to the barrier island, where anglers can walk over the sand to the surf. This is too much work for most people, but those who make the effort are pleased with the quality fishing experience.

A private ferry from Harker's Island will carry anglers and their vehicles over to the beach above Cape Lookout Lighthouse. Primitive camping is allowed, so anglers may enjoy an extended stay.

Bogue Banks is highly developed but most of the beach remains open to vehicles. Speckled trout, bluefish, flounder, and croaker are the most common species here, with an occasional puppy drum and Spanish mackerel caught from the beach.

Though black marlin have been intensively pursued in recent decades, no one has bested the world-record 1,560-pounder caught at Cabo Blanco, Peru, in August 1953.

Bear Island at Bogue Inlet can only be reached by boat, but red drum are taken here on a regular basis in the spring and fall. Fresh cut bait is the best choice, but the heavy tackle required at Cape Hatteras is not needed here.

The federal government controls the beach from Bogue Inlet to New River and they do not let surf anglers on the property. The rest of the coast from New River to the South Carolina line is open to fishing. Vehicle use may be restricted in some locations by local ordinances, but the walk to the surf is usually short.

Big fish are rare here but spot, croaker, flounder, speckled trout, weakfish, and Spanish mackerel provide good action. The best fishing for trout and flounder is in the fall and winter when they stage in the deeper sloughs and around inlets.

Piers. North Carolina has an abundance of fishing piers extending into the ocean, some reaching more than 1,000 feet out. They begin in Kitty Hawk and continue down to Sunset Beach. Pier fishing is a great way for the whole family to enjoy the sport at a reasonable cost. Most piers have some type of entertainment center, a restaurant or snack bar, and a tackle shop. The cost is less than a movie and you get to take your catch home.

A few serious pier jockeys will spend hours fishing live baits in hopes of hooking a big king mackerel, tarpon, cobia, or bluefish. This takes patience, skill, and a serious investment in tackle. It is easier and more productive to soak a bait on the bottom and catch a mixed bag of blues, trout, sea mullet, croaker, spot, and anything else that happens to swim by. Blues and Spanish mackerel often stage feeding frenzies at the end of the pier early in the morning or late in the afternoon. Lures cast into this melee will bring instant strikes and exciting action.

In the spring and fall, big red drum and striped bass are caught from piers north of Cape Hatteras. Chunks of cut bait fished on the bottom at night collect most of these trophies.

NORTH DAKOTA

In North Dakota, the water meets the prairie and fishing season never actually closes. North Dakota is open to angling activity throughout the spring, summer, winter, and fall seasons, each of which offers a unique freshwater experience for a variety of gamefish, including northern pike, walleye, sauger, saugeye, chinook salmon, rainbow trout, brown trout, muskellunge, smallmouth bass, largemouth bass, and a wide variety of panfish. The most popular year-round species is the walleye, closely followed by a relative and favorite winter quarry, yellow perch.

The diversity of species in North Dakota is largely a result of stocking programs by the state game and fish department and a combination of natural reproduction in some waters. To add to existing fisheries, chinook salmon were introduced to the Missouri River system. A growing population of these fish represents one of the most successful inland populations of disease-free salmonids in the country. Though void of blue-ribbon trout streams, North Dakota's lakes and farm ponds are becoming popular inland trout fisheries also, a direct result of stocking programs and the catch and release ethic of anglers.

However, most angling effort in the state centers on warmwater and coolwater species, and the three large bodies of water that comprise the state's most popular fisheries are the Missouri River System, which includes two reservoirs (Lake Sakakawea and Lake Oahe), Devils Lake, and the Red River of the North.

The Missouri River System

A main character in the prairie landscape, the Missouri River runs from the North Dakota border in the northwest through the central part of the state and along the capital city of Bismarck. From its headwaters at the confluence of the Yellowstone River, the Missouri is broken into four sections: the upper Missouri River, Lake Sakakawea, the Missouri River Tailrace, and Lake Oahe. Anglers know these sections of water for their excellent populations of walleye, northern pike, chinook salmon, and world class sauger and saugeye fishing.

There are more than 60 recreational access points along the Missouri River system, making it a favorite destination for both the casual and trophy angler. For the heavily favored walleyes, pre-spawn early spring angling, and late fall angling, typically produce trophy fish from 8 to 13 pounds. Average weights depend on the life cycle of the river section and can vary from 2 to 5 pounds.

The Upper Missouri. Originating from Montana, the Missouri River enters North Dakota's northwest border near Williston. Here, the confluence of the Missouri and Yellowstone Rivers form the upper section of a 180-mile-long reservoir called Lake Sakakawea. This area holds the largest remnant population of naturally reproducing paddlefish in the United States. Both fish and angler congregate in this area each spring. The largest paddlefish landed on rod and reel was a 120-pound specimen caught in 1993, and the oldest fish on record was 45 years old.

Lake Sakakawea. The Garrison Dam that contains giant Lake Sakakawea was built for hydroelectric power and flood control and completed in 1953. It is the third largest rolled-earth dam in the world. The United States Army Corps of Engineers manages the lake project. As a result, Sakakawea, named after a legendary American-Indian woman who helped guide the early 1800s explorers Lewis and Clark up the Missouri, is largely void of private development and is unpopulated along its shoreline.

Lake Sakakawea's fishing opportunities heat up at ice out, which usually occurs in early to late April. Twenty-pound northern pike can be found cruising the shallow bays at this time. Shore anglers fishing with floats and quick-strike rigs tipped with dead bait often produce lunkers. Noted hotspots for pike, which incidentally is the official state fish, include Parshall and Steinke Bays. Jigging and live bait rigging in 12 to 20 feet of water produces many nice catches.

Walleyes are usually found in the upper third of the reservoir in late April and early May as they haunt the traditional spawning grounds of White Earth Bay and the Van Hook Arm. Meanwhile, rainbow and brown trout offer anglers on the lower end of the reservoir plenty of rod-bending opportunity near the Garrison Dam and the Riverdale Bluffs.

By midsummer, fishing action heats up throughout the reservoir. The lake's midsection holds many traditional hotspots for walleye, including Nishu and Beulah Bays, as well as points and bays near Indian Hills. Crankbaits and spinner rigs pulled in 8 to 25 feet of water are top producers.

The Missouri River Tailrace. The Missouri River begins again immediately below the Garrison Dam and stretches downstream for 70 miles until it reaches the headwaters of Lake Oahe.

Fishing action on the river begins below Garrison Dam at the Missouri River Tailrace, where Lake Sakakawea's water is generated into hydroelectric power. The fast current and generators create a constant buffet of churned-up baitfish, which provides a smorgasbord to both fish and angler. The Tailrace chute produces catfish, chinook salmon, rainbow trout, sauger, walleye, and burbot, plus a variety of non-gamefish species. This area is a favorite year-round open water fishery.

From the Tailrace, the Missouri River winds downstream through heavily wooded timber bottoms and sparsely populated areas to the riverside city of Washburn and the metropolitan areas of Bismarck-Mandan. The fast current changes the river's flow constantly, challenging even the best anglers' navigational ability. The walleye fishery within this section is good, but primarily a resident secret. The stretch from the dam to around Stanton has good-size rainbows, and with riffles and holes is a rather surprising trout river.

Lake Oahe. Lake Oahe's headwaters begin in south-central North Dakota, below the capital city of Bismarck. Identifying where the Missouri River ends and where Lake Oahe begins is often disputed. The Fort Rice boat landing, a fishing hotspot, marks the headwaters of Lake Oahe, which, at full pool, contains 90,000 acres of water in North Dakota, although vastly more in neighboring South Dakota.

Famous for spring and fall runs of northern pike and walleye, North Dakota's section of Lake Oahe has gained notoriety for its wintertime production of lunker pike, and it gets heavy angling pressure during peak periods.

Devils Lake

As North Dakota's largest natural prairie lake, and one of the United States' only closed basin lakes, Devils Lake is unique by nature's design. With no direct tributary inlet or outlet, the emerald waters of this lake are difficult to predict. Since the mid-1990s, this prairie lake has been on the rise, surpassing a 500-year high-water mark and offering more than 35 square miles of new fishable water.

The prairie waters of Devils Lake originally consisted of 70,000 acres of spring-fed waters and runoff. The lake's maximum depth is 35 feet, with an average depth of 15 to 18 feet. The basin structure is edged with rocky points, sand, weedbeds, and hardwood timber. Since the lake is a prairie basin in a valleylike floor, the water spreads out instead of climbing to higher elevations.

Devils Lake is a top producer throughout the seasons, with a special emphasis on the winter fishery. Local promoters use snow removal equipment to keep and provide good access onto the lake's traditional winter fishing areas, which wind miles around the lake. Winter anglers move a lot here, looking for jumbo yellow perch, some 2 pounds or better. Wax worms tipped on small jigs are the main offering for these fish. Walleyes are also a winter favorite here.

Spring and summer activity heats up an abundant population of white bass, the so-called piranha of the prairie. These feisty schooling fish turn on in numbers at Devils Lake. Shore anglers do exceptionally well for white bass along bridge abutments and roadbeds in the spring. The vicinity of the Highway 19 bridge and Graham's Island State Park are both white bass hotspots.

Suspended walleyes are caught in the summer on Devils Lake by those using big-water trolling tactics. A growing population of walleye has proven that Devils Lake is a "sleeper" for this species.

The Red River of the North

The great Red River of the North is unique for its northbound flow toward Manitoba, Canada. Serving as a natural border between North Dakota and Minnesota, and aptly named for the color of its runoff from nutrient-rich soil found in surrounding agricultural lands, the Red River is known as one of the most volatile rivers in the country, and is prone to both drought and floods.

The mighty Red's claim to fishing fame is the annual production of lunker channel catfish, some weighing 20 pounds or more. The northern portion of the Red is considered one of the premier catfish spots in the nation, producing up to 30-pound specimens. The Drayton Dam area north of Grand Forks has been a traditional catfish hotspot for years, but the entire river system offers good opportunities.

From its headwaters in Wahpeton, where a tribute to the catfish was built as a tourist attraction, through the cities of Fargo and Grand Forks, anglers find plentiful access to good-old-fashioned riverbank fishing. Heavy-duty rods and reels are employed here for the behemoths, with dead baits and stink baits being the preferred bottom offerings. Night fishing is very common here. Although catfish reigns as king on the Red, the river also supports sauger and walleye fishing.

Other Waters

Because of the notoriety of the larger bodies of water, anglers often overlook North Dakota's smaller lakes. There are 53 counties in North Dakota that host more than 170 fishable waters that are listed by the game and fish department as publicly accessible. Notable major lakes include Audubon, Ashtabula, Darling, Pipestem, Sweet Briar, and Nelson.

A sister to Lake Sakakawea, Lake Audubon has summer and winter popularity for walleye, northern pike, and yellow perch. Located in central North Dakota, next to Lake Sakakawea, it is the headwaters of a chain of irrigation lakes known as the McClusky Canal System, where the state's highest density of largemouth bass and muskellunge are found.

Nelson Lake, in the west-central region of the state, is unusual here because it receives the warm-water discharge from a nearby power plant. Good populations of panfish exist in Nelson, with bluegills a favorite, and some believe that this lake has the potential for a new state record largemouth bass.

The state record walleye, which weighed in at 15 pounds 12 ounces, was taken on Wood Lake in 1959. Though Wood is a small natural lake, that older catch nevertheless underscores the fact that some good fishing, and indeed big fish, can be had in the smaller and lesser known waters of North Dakota. Furthermore, some small lakes have limited success rates as summer fisheries but become extremely popular as through-the-ice winter fisheries.

NORTHWEST TERRITORIES

The newly reconfigured Northwest Territories is the vast western Arctic region of Canada's far north. The eastern Arctic region, now known as Nunavut Territory *(see)*, was separated from the former configuration of the Northwest Territories (NWT) in 1999, leaving a huge region that encompasses 1.5 million square kilometers of land—equal in size to Alaska and comprising 15 percent of the entire country of Canada. It includes two of the largest lakes in the world, Great Bear and Great Slave, one of the most formidable rivers in North America, the Mackenzie, and is populated by more caribou than people.

Arguably the best lake trout fishing region in the world, but indisputably home to the biggest lakers on the planet, the NWT has some of the finest and least pressured fishing waters anywhere, with Arctic char, northern pike, and grayling being premier attractions besides lake trout, and with opportunities for less-noticed species like walleye, Dolly Varden, bull trout, whitefish, and inconnu.

Nearly all fishing in the NWT is done on wild rivers and lonely lakes. The big waters dominate the angling scene but are contrasted by diminutive spring creeks in the Mackenzie Mountains and secluded small Canadian Shield lakes. East of the Mackenzie drainage, waters flow to the polar sea via barren land rivers. The Anderson, Horton, and Hornaday Rivers drain the tundra north of Great Bear Lake. Further east, the famous Coppermine, Thelon, Dubawnt, and Kazan Rivers all rise along the treeline before flowing into Nunavut.

Often referred to as the western Arctic, the Northwest Territories extends north from its boundary on the 60th parallel with the Canadian provinces of British Columbia, Alberta, and Saskatchewan to the islands of the western Arctic archipelago. To the west, the mainland portion of the NWT bounds the Yukon Territory along the continental divide. The new eastern boundary with Nunavut skirts the barren lands east of the tree line.

Settlements of three land claims in the northern part of the territory have created a vast amount of private land. Generally, casual passage along waterways is provided in the claims, but fishing parties traveling on their own need to determine if they will be crossing land where they need permission. Optional stamps are now required to validate NWT fishing licenses for the Inuvialuit claim area and within the Great Bear Lake special management zone. Land claims in the southern part of the NWT are not finalized, but may have an impact on sportfishing for the adventure traveler. The angler who visits a lodge will be largely unaware of the changes that have occurred, as nothing will have altered the vast, wild, open spaces of the north.

Most visitors to the NWT arrive by commercial air carrier, and many lodge visitors arrive via chartered flights that go direct to the lodge from the south, often from Winnipeg or Edmonton.

Highway access from the south (through Alberta) exists on the Mackenzie Highway system, which reaches the communities south of Great Slave Lake, the capital city of Yellowknife on the north shore of Great Slave Lake, and the small Dene community of Wrigley midway down the Mackenzie River. Inuvik in the Mackenzie River Delta is serviced by the Dempster Highway through the Yukon Territory. The roads lead to jumping off points, but fishing along the highways in the NWT is not good by Arctic standards. The famous waters of the NWT are only accessible by air and long boat trips.

Typically, the Arctic angling season is compressed into the short period of open water from Late May to mid-September. The lakes are ice covered for the remainder of the time, although this varies from north to south, with some being open only briefly (or in cold years not at all) and others (usually smaller and more southerly ones) being open for up to 120 days in warm years. Even when open, most NWT waters are cool or cold, meaning that fish are seldom very deep in the lakes. While this means that fish are more accessible to anglers than they would be in warmer climes, it also means that midsummer days here can be inhospitable. The air temperature ranges from the 70s to 30s, occasionally on the same day, so visitors must be appropriately attired. Wading anglers are advised to wear neoprene chest waders, and since there is much use of float planes, it is necessary to pack judiciously.

Fishing has traditionally been limited to the open-water season; however, recently outfitters from Fort Resolution, Yellowknife, and Inuvik have begun to offer ice fishing packages. These winter expeditions are often coupled with snowmobile treks to isolated waters, like the Anderson River, which are hard to reach in the summer. In late March, when longer periods of daylight return to the north and the hard bite of winter is past, it is a wonderful time to travel and fish.

As anyone who has flown over this region can attest, the NWT is chock full of lakes of all sizes, as well as rivers, many of which drain from one lake to another and another. Not every body of water contains sportfish, although most do. Not every one has huge specimens, and some have lots of fish that are generally small. There is a lot of area in the NWT that is lightly if at all touched by anglers, since most sportfishing is clustered at lakes that can be serviced by outfitters and where there are established camps.

Although adventure travelers can have extraordinary experiences by undertaking wilderness canoe-camping excursions, due to the ruggedness of the land and wildness of many waterways, this activity is only advisable for experienced adventurers. While it is possible to enjoy bountiful fishing on these expeditions, the largest fish, especially lake trout, are usually found in the biggest bodies of water and seldom caught by those who run the rivers and have to cover a lot of territory from put-in to take-out locations.

Just as there is a great breadth of waters in the NWT, so, too, is there diversity in fishing methods and tackle. Trolling, though a staple for lake trout fishing in the lakes, is by no means the only method of fishing. Casting and jigging in lakes, and casting in rivers, are very productive, and the range of tackle choices for different methods runs the gamut from ultralight spinning gear for river grayling to heavy-action rods with large levelwind reels for trolling 2-ounce spoons. Light- to medium-weight fly fishing outfits, light to medium spinning outfits, and light to medium-heavy baitcasting tackle all have a place as well, depending on the location, the size of fish likely, and the means necessary for achieving success. This may seem wide open, but it underscores the fact that the abundant resources of the NWT truly provide a diversity of angling opportunities.

Species

The NWT is the "land of charr," the foremost native species of the Arctic. In this region, that includes lake trout (which, despite their name, are actually a species of charr), arctic charr, Dolly Varden, and bull trout. Populations of these distinctive native charr have spread across the territory since the last Ice Age. The wild charr of the NWT are an extraordinary treasure when contrasted with the diminished ranges of wild salmon and trout in North America.

That these extraordinary fish are generally little known has both protected them by keeping them out of sight and out of mind, and has left them exposed because they lack strong champions. The consequence is that, other than lake trout, which grow largest of these fish, northern charr have historically been undervalued to all but the native peoples. Most visiting anglers pursue lake trout in the NWT, and occasionally take a side trip to a famous arctic charr river in Nunavut. A journey to fish for all of the northern charr found in the NWT, would take an angler from the high country of the Mackenzie Mountains to lakes on the edge of the barrens and along the Arctic coast.

Lake trout. The long-lived and large-growing lake trout is king of NWT charr. Great Bear and Great Slave Lakes have produced a string of angling records for this species dating back to 1938, when pioneering outfitter Warren Plumber first fished Taltheilie Narrows on Great Slave Lake. He opened the first fishing lodge on that lake in 1950, and ever since, lake trout have been the staple of 60-odd lodges and guiding services in the NWT.

Great Bear and Great Slave are likely the two most prominent waters for lake trout fishing, although these monstrous lakes are only fished by a few thousand people in total annually. But they have produced a disproportionate number of North America's giant lakers, including numerous all-tackle and line-class world records. Leviathans from 60 to 72 pounds have been registered, some of these in the 1990s, and bigger fish have been hooked, especially in Great Bear.

> The New York City Common Council passed a law on May 28, 1734, to regulate the method of taking brook trout in Fresh Pond to "angling, with angle-rod, hook and line only." No nets allowed.

A big laker is netted from the deep water of Christie Bay at Great Slave Lake.

Big waters notwithstanding, spectacular lake trout fishing is found in many smaller lakes, like Coville, Providence, and Mackay, and they have also been known to yield some monster lakers; a 54-pound lake trout, for instance, was caught at Point Lake on the Coppermine River.

As a general rule, small lakes produce smaller fish, and most bodies of water that contain lake trout can offer ample numbers of fish daily. Lake trout are also caught in flowing water here, and scores of large and small rivers have terrific light-tackle angling opportunities for these fish.

One great river angling adventure for lake trout is during the so-called "river run" at Lac la Martre, which offers great action on light spinning and fly tackle. This occurs in late August when the fish start their spawning run. Five- to 12-pounders are common and bigger ones are regularly taken. An unusual situation occurs near the coast in the Eskimo Lakes, which is part of a native settlement area in the northwestern part of the territory. Lake trout there haunt the area where the lakes join Liverpool Bay on the Beaufort Sea, and this is likely as close as lake trout in North America come to having a "sea run."

Lake trout records, as well as the majority of large specimens (over 20 pounds) are usually taken by trolling. Flatline trolling is the norm, primarily in shallow water. As the value of the native stocks of lake trout has become better understood, outfitters have discouraged the use of downriggers and weighted lines, which were never very prominent in a lot of places here, as a means of getting very deep, since there is so much action to be had from shallower stocks of fish.

Many outfitters now encourage their clients to replace treble hooks with single barbless ones to facilitate the easy release and minimal handling of the fish. Single, barbless hooks, though not mandated, are much more prevalent, and may be a policy at better lodges and camps. Likewise, catch-and-release has become much more prevalent; the excessive removal of many trophy lake trout from NWT waters in past decades was felt for many years with reduced numbers of big fish. The longevity of these fish and their slow growth have mandated that a new conservation ethic be practiced, and this has been evolving throughout the NWT among anglers.

Ice out on the lakes in the NWT generally occurs between mid-May and early July depending on the water and location. This late breakup and brief summer help maintain very cold water temperatures throughout the open-water season. Cool waters encourage lake trout to stay shallower for most of the fishing season. This allows anglers to use lighter tackle for much of the season.

Immediately after the ice goes out, it's common to catch lake trout at creek and river mouths on the lakes, and some of the fastest fishing can be had then. If there are baitfish available at the sites, large lakers may be present. The fish are more scattered when the ice is fully gone. Late season fishing can produce some heavyweights and is an overlooked time, partly because of the possibility of poor weather (wind, cold, and occasionally snow). Lake trout spawn in late "summer" here, primarily on shallow reefs.

Arctic charr/Dolly Varden/bull trout. The NWT lies at the western boundary of the eastern subspecies of arctic charr that are so famous in the Nunavut Territory. These venerable fish are only found on the Horton and Hornaday Rivers in the northeast corner of the mainland, and on Banks Island and western Victoria Island *(see: Nunavut Territory)* in the archipelago. West of the Tuktoyatuk Peninsula in northwesternmost NWT, there is a change in subspecies. The landlocked arctic charr found in lakes along the north slope of the Yukon and Alaska is related to Siberian strains.

There is a small population of landlocked eastern arctic charr in the Keith Arm of Great Bear Lake, and anglers occasionally pick up one of these when fishing for lake trout near the Great Bear River. According to lodge owners, they are not found anywhere else on the lake.

The charr in rivers west of the Mackenzie River is the northern subspecies of Dolly Varden. Their range extends west from the Mackenzie River in the NWT to the Alaskan Peninsula in southwestern Alaska. (Lakes west of the Mackenzie in the Yukon Territory have the landlocked form of arctic charr.) Anglers can differentiate the northern Dolly Varden from the arctic charr based on its red spots, which are generally smaller than the eyes of the fish and have a blue halo around them. The spots on anadromous eastern arctic charr are splotchier, typically larger than the eye of the fish, and lack the bluish halo. However, to confuse things somewhat, landlocked lake-dwelling arctic charr tend to have small, pupil-size red or white spots. There are anomalies and variations as well.

Anglers familiar with arctic charr will notice that the Dolly Varden has a more compressed, or flatter, profile and a less rounded tail fin. The tail in Dolly Varden is large and is not forked, as it is in char. These differences reflect the Dolly Varden's adaptation to flowing water, and the arctic charr's preference for flat water. Arctic charr generally spawn and overwinter in lakes. Dolly Varden spawn in moving water, and overwinter in deep runs and river spring holes.

Anadromous northern Dolly Varden run into four rivers along the west side of the Mackenzie River Delta and the north slope of the Yukon Territory. These are the Rat, Big Fish, Babbage, and Firth Rivers, and they also have nonmigratory populations of smaller grilselike male fish. The highly aggressive nonmigratory males sneak in behind the redds of bigger, mating sea-run fish and may fertilize up to half of the eggs. The Big Fish and Babbage Rivers have landlocked populations above their barrier falls.

The headwater lakes and rivers of the Mackenzie Mountains are home to Dolly Varden and their cousin the bull trout, which are difficult for most people to tell apart. Locals lump them together as "river trout." They are vigorous feeders and enjoyed by both lure and fly casters. The North Nahanni, Redstone, Keele, Carcajou, Godlin, and Mountain Rivers all have fine populations.

Dall sheep hunters taking a rest from the saddle have found some fine fish under the overhanging banks of the Godlin River. Further south, a healthy run of Dolly Varden hit the Drum Lake outlet around Labor Day. The Dolly are on the go at the same time that lake trout move into the Cabin Creek tributary of Drum Lake. Between the two charr runs and frisky Arctic grayling, Drum Lake is worth the trip.

Landlocked arctic charr, Dolly Varden, and bull trout feed readily and can be voracious. While small charr concentrate on insects, bigger specimens feed on fish and opportunistically on mice, baby ducks, and even small muskrats. The number of large carnivorous charr in a lake is very small compared to the total population. In small Arctic lakes, it is easy for anglers to remove the few really big cannibals from the food chain. Maintaining large fish in the population of lakes is one of the reasons many guides and outfitters now advocate catch-and-release.

Anadromous arctic charr and Dolly Varden go to sea for 2 or 3 months a year to feed on a diet of invertebrates, capelin, cisco, herring, and sculpin. After they return to freshwater to spawn, they hang out under the ice for the next 10 months. They will continue to feed throughout the winter but the edge is off their appetite.

The feeding habits of arctic charr, Dolly Varden and bull trout make them ideal for spinning tackle users. Anglers use light- to medium-weight spinning rods with 6- to 10-pound lines. A variety of small to medium spoons, especially with orange and pink inserts and in the hallowed five of diamonds pattern, are a must. Silver-bladed spinners are also effective. Generally, fly anglers use sinking lines and streamers. Successful fly patterns include the red-and-yellow Seaducer, Mickey Finn, and large sculpin imitations.

Northern pike. Though northern pike aren't the first fish that nonresident anglers associate with the Northwest Territories, their popularity has been steadily increasing. These shallow and near-surface fish are widely distributed throughout the drainage systems of the mainland from the southern boundary of the NWT to saltwater in the Mackenzie River Delta, with big lakes usually producing the better specimens.

Northern pike here generally average from 18 to 30 inches in length. The slow growth of a northern pike in Arctic drainages with little fishing pressure makes it possible to frequently break 30 inches. A 10-pound, 32-inch Great Bear Lake northern pike is a fifteen-year-old fish. Forty-inch fish from near

Trout Rock in the north arm of Great Slave Lake average around 20 pounds.

It is reasonable to expect that in a week of fishing at a hot pike spot, an angler will take some fish that verge on 20 pounds. One reliable pike location is Beaver Lake on the upper Mackenzie River; it produces pike up to 27 pounds on a fairly regular basis, and a few every season break 30 pounds.

The unexpected happens frequently enough that anglers take considerably larger northern pike. Rare fish are found that exceed 50 inches. The largest known pike from Great Slave Lake is a reputed $60^{3}/_{4}$-inch fish taken through the ice near Trout Rock; the fish was not weighed or officially recorded.

Action for northern pike commences with ice out in the spring. Pike are abundant in the shallows and often pounce on lures or flies. On the big waters, large pike stay in shallow water most of the summer. When the water warms in the shallower lakes, pike go deep.

Grayling. The Arctic grayling is the signature species of the NWT. A resident of clean and cold water, this colorful fish is found across the region. The average mature grayling is a $1^{1}/_{2}$- to 2-pound fish. Three-pounders are 12 years old and have reached the average life expectancy for this species in far northern waters. Fish over 3 pounds are trophies.

Great Slave and Great Bear Lakes and their tributaries have some of the best Arctic grayling fishing in the world. Great Bear's tributaries have produced most of the line class and world records, including some over 5 pounds, and have superb grayling fishing. The tributaries to Great Bear River, which flows to the Mackenzie, are also excellent. Northeast of the lake, Colville Lake provides access to grayling for anglers who really want to get away.

The outlet of Great Slave in the Mackenzie River is an especially productive grayling habitat. The fishery there took a hit in 1989 when high water temperatures nurtured a deadly gill infection. Since that time, a combination of undisturbed habitat and restrictive angling regulations have helped grayling bounce back.

In the same region, the well-known Brabant and Kakisa River runs are recovering. Some years, the Kakisa is the only river on the east side of the mountains from the Arkansas River to the Mackenzie River that is clear and full of fish in late May and early June.

On the East Arm of Great Slave Lake, the mouth of the Lockhart River, Taltheilie Narrows, and the Stark River are famous for grayling. Both the lower Lockhart and Stark Rivers have rapids that stay open throughout the winter. Open rapids that force oxygenated water under the ice are characteristic of the best grayling haunts.

Arctic grayling are generally caught on flies or light spinners, the latter in gold or silver in sizes from 0 to 2. On the surface, they rise for a range of caddisflies, mayflies, stoneflies, and terrestrials, including grasshoppers. A good selection of dry fly patterns in sizes 12 to 18 is advisable, although in many places almost any small dark offering will do. Grayling often respond better to a fly in the meniscus than one floating on the surface, so soft-hackle flies can be effective. When grayling are not rising, they are normally on the bottom nymphing. A broad selection of nymphs in sizes 2 to 16 is then necessary.

Walleye. Walleye are among the three most popularly sought fish in the NWT. Consistent walleye fishing is found in parts of the Talston River system, Great Slave Lake, the Hay River, the upper Mackenzie River, and small lakes northeast of Yellowknife. The spring fishing at Trout Lake in the southwest corner of the NWT is locally famous.

The most productive time to fish for walleye in the NWT has been in the late May and early June spawning period when the fish are congregated. In the summer, with coldwater temperatures, walleyes can often be found shallower than in more southerly climates. For example, walleye are taken in 4 or 5 feet of water in the Hay River in early July, and in 8 to 10 feet of water in midsummer on the upper Mackenzie River. As a result, they offer an opportunity not only to successfully use plugs and jigs, but also flies. Fly anglers work a full sinking line, a short tippet, and a weighted yellow or tan minnow imitation along the bottom. A soft plastic worm on a sinking fly line is also deadly.

On the upper Mackenzie River, walleye average 2 to 4 pounds, with a few each year reaching about 6 or 7 pounds. Nine to 10 pounds is the top end of the walleye weight scale in the NWT.

Whitefish. Lake whitefish are available in most lakes and many rivers in the NWT. Broad whitefish are found along the western Arctic Coast and up the Mackenzie River to the Camsell Bend below Fort Simpson. Few lodges advertise them and relatively few visiting anglers deliberately pursue whitefish, but these are a commendable fish, and

Major flows, like the Stark River here, course throughout the Northwest Territories.

an increasing number of Arctic fly anglers claim them as their favorite. Whitefish are one of the best table fish in the north. Fried whitefish makes a great shore lunch, and smoked whitefish (some lodges have smokehouses) is a real treat.

Like grayling, whitefish are almost never caught on the hardware and tackle used for pike and trout, and angling for them is more specialized, requiring light or ultralight spinning and fly gear. They can be taken on light jigs, and to a lesser degree small spinners, but are best caught on flies, including soft-hackle and emerger patterns, and they are a delightful fish to catch.

Whitefish are sometimes seen dimpling the surface in the evening, and can be available to anglers then. Rising whitefish on a midsummer's eve are not actually rising to flies on the surface; they are nymphing for caddis and mayflies swimming up to hatch. The slight downturn of the whitefish's small mouth does not allow it to easily snip dry flies from the surface. If you watch their rises carefully, you'll see that it is the back of the fish which breaks the surface as it positions itself to come down on the rising insect. Ideally, an emerger should be fished several inches under the surface for whitefish. Small spinners fished in the top of the water column will often take them, too. When whitefish aren't feeding on the surface, they're often munching on scuds further down; count your offering down to locate the depth where they are feeding.

Other species. The waters of the Mackenzie River drainage and the Anderson River are home to the elusive inconnu, a species that few people are acquainted with. Known as sheefish in Alaska and the Yukon, they are commonly called "conni" in the NWT. Averaging 18 to 30 inches long, this member of the whitefish clan is a strong fighter that deserves more attention.

Good early spring inconnu fishing is found near the community of Fort Resolution, in the Slave River Delta. Many are also caught to the west in the Hay River in May or early June. Anglers fish shallow bays with bright spoons as the ice goes out. Later in the summer and in early fall, strong runs are found in the Big Buffalo and Talston Rivers, below the Slave River Rapids at Fort Smith, and in the small creeks of the Mackenzie River Delta. A local guide is needed to successfully fish for inconnu. They average from 9 to 20 pounds, but some specimens weighing up to 70 pounds have been reported by commercial fishermen.

The ugliest, but perhaps best-tasting, fish in the NWT is the burbot. A freshwater cod, and also known as ling cod and eelpout, it is found in most of the lakes and larger rivers of the Northwest Territories. They are commonly caught to 24 inches in length, and some up to 30 inches and 8 or 9 pounds have been reported.

Burbot, which live in deep water and prey on smaller fish, are rarely caught by anglers fishing for the more prominent species. Local guides from Aklavik take people out to jig for burbot in the Mackenzie Delta byways, and some still use traditional jigs made of sheep, muskox, or caribou antler. It's common for an angler jigging for burbot near Aklavik to pick up an inconnu. The Dene and Inuit prize the burbot's liver, incidentally, which is a good source of vitamin B. The fillets of a burbot make delicious fish and chips.

On the outer northwest edge of the Northwest Territories, the Mackenzie River has the only run of dog or chum salmon east of the continental divide. Chum salmon are the least predictable of the NWT's gamefish, but are taken annually in gill nets by Dene harvesters on the Mackenzie River, Liard River, and below the Slave River Rapids. On rare occasions, one is picked up in Great Bear Lake near the Great Bear River, where they are referred to as "the strangers."

Fresh chum salmon enter the Mackenzie River from the Beaufort Sea in July. There are unconfirmed reports that fish have been taken by anglers in some of the small rivers that flow into the Mackenzie Delta. Local guides in Aklavik or Inuvik might know where to find this elusive fish, and it is conceivable that salmon might be encountered on a trip for sea-run Dolly Varden.

Locations

Fishing destinations in the NWT can be broken down into six angling regions: south of Great Slave Lake, the western barren lands, Great Slave Lake and the upper Mackenzie River, Great Bear Lake, the Mackenzie Mountains, and the Mackenzie River Delta.

There are numerous fly-in lodges on Canadian Shield lakes east of Fort Smith. These operations specialize in northern pike, lake trout, walleye, and whitefish, with plentiful and large lake trout and pike the foremost attractions. Some of the better sites are along or close to the Saskatchewan *(see)* border, and include Selwyn, Snowbird, Scott, Kasba, and Wignes Lakes.

The western barren lands contain the headwaters of the Kazan, Dubawnt, Thelon, Lockhart, and Coppermine Rivers. Notable lakes include Mackay Lake on the Lockhart River, and Providence and Point Lakes on the Coppermine River. Treeline lodges here offer lake trout, northern pike, whitefish, and trophy grayling.

Great Slave Lake. The 11th largest lake in the world, Great Slave is 298 miles long and in some places over 2,000 feet deep. Containing over 11,000 square miles of water, it can hardly be missed on almost any map, and its fishing has to be viewed by four areas: the East Arm, the North Arm, the Slave River region, and the Mackenzie River outlet.

This lake has long been renowned for its lake trout. The laker fishing was especially prime in the mid-1960s, when 20- to 25-pounders were caught (and kept, unfortunately) regularly. Then it slumped in terms of producing large fish, and is still rebounding, helped by conservation practices. Now, rare is the large fish that gets kept at the fishing lodges here.

The prospect of catching giant lake trout, however, remains the lake's prime lure. A 74-pounder is reputed to have been netted at Great Slave some years ago, and anglers have caught them to $58\frac{1}{2}$ pounds. This mammoth body of water does contain some monsters. It also contains plenty of trout that have never seen a lure, and you don't have to be a veteran angler to catch fish. Trolling near shore around points, reefs, and islands has long been the predominant tactic for lakers here. The water is always cold, and most trout are caught only 10 to 20 feet deep.

The East Arm is blessed with islands and peninsulas, which make it geologically distinct from the wide-open remainder of the lake. It has been made famous by Talteilei Narrows and the Stark and Lockhart Rivers, which are known for big lake trout, grayling, pike, and whitefish. Some lodges feature side trips to inland lakes for walleye.

Talteilei Narrows acts as a river or channel between McLeod and Christie Bays. Wind-driven currents on the big bays push the water back and forth through the narrows creating wonderful eddies and backwaters, and the Talteilei area continues to produce spectacular trophies. If the East Arm of Great Slave Lake is gold medal water, Talteilei is in a class by itself.

Remarkably good angling takes place at the shallow, cold, and swift Stark River, using light spinning or fly gear for grayling up to 3 pounds, small pike, and the occasional whitefish. At the best of times it is a virtual bonanza, and there is good reason to understand why some have called the Stark the greatest grayling river in the world. The possibility of catching 3- to 4-pound grayling is very good.

The North Arm is a maze of granite reefs that shelter some of the best northern pike fishing in the NWT. Not only do the low islands and submerged structures provide great habitat, but they protect the spectacular pike waters around Trout Rock from casual boaters. Visitors to the North Arm are only a few air minutes from jet service to southern Canada at the Yellowknife airport.

Fort Resolution is the jump-off point for fishing the Slave River Delta and the lower Taltson River. Local outfitters take clients out for northern pike, inconnu, walleye, and whitefish. Road access allows Mackenzie Highway travelers to drive in and meet their guides.

Perhaps the best-kept angling secret in the NWT is the outlet of Great Slave Lake into the Mackenzie River. The waters around Brabant and Lobstick Islands have superb grayling, pike, whitefish, and walleye angling. The Mackenzie Highway spur to the community of Hay River on the south shore of Great Slave Lake is a short bush flight from the lodge at Brabant Island.

Great Bear Lake. There is no locale that is known more widely for lake trout than this one, and considering its stature as the eighth largest freshwater lake in the world, Great Bear Lake perhaps might be more appropriately called the Great Bear Sea, or, better yet, Great Trout Sea.

Great Bear is actually the fourth largest lake in North America, ranking behind Lakes Superior, Huron, and Michigan in size. When you consider that it has an infinitesimally small percentage of the boat traffic and fishing pressure of those other large North American lakes, and that it is so remote as to straddle the Arctic Circle, you can comprehend the allure it has as a distant fishing locale, especially for lake trout aficionados.

Great Bear has been known as the world's best fishery for record-size lake trout and Arctic grayling since it was first sportfished in the early 1960s. For over 20 years it held the all-tackle laker record with a 65-pounder, which it bested with a $66\frac{1}{2}$-pounder in 1991 and then a 72-pound 4-ounce fish in August of 1995. The current IGFA all-tackle world record for Arctic grayling, 5 pounds 15 ounces, was also established here, and more than a score of line-class world records have been certified from Great Bear or its tributaries.

Each year, fewer than 600 anglers have the opportunity to experience the waters of Great Bear. The lake remains frozen until the early part of July, and fall winds and freezing temperatures put an end to angling at the beginning of September. The closest road to Great Bear is over 100 miles to the south, so the only way in is by plane.

A prominent aspect of Great Bear's legendary fishing is the relative shallowness of its lake trout fishing throughout five major arms. With 12,000 square miles of surface area, depths of up to 1,400 feet, and only three months of ice out, the waters of Great Bear never warm to the same extent as smaller lakes in the area. The middle of the lake will not go above 35°F all summer. Due to the frigid waters, lake trout move to shallow bays and reefs to find the baitfish in warmer waters. Lake trout are caught all summer in depths of 4 to 35 feet. They are never caught in the 60- to 100-foot range synonymous with lake trout fishing in smaller bodies of water.

Lake trout at Great Bear average 6 to 15 pounds. Every year more than a thousand in the 20-pound range will be caught, with many reaching 30 to 50 pounds, and some in the 50- to 70-pound range. Experts believe that the lake trout in Great Bear grow at a rate of just $\frac{1}{4}$- to $\frac{1}{2}$- a pound per year. That dates some trout between 100 and 150 years old. Current lodge policies ensure the survival of these fish. No lake trout over 28 inches (10 pounds) is allowed to be harvested.

The tried-and-true method of lake trout fishing here, trolling with the biggest spoons and plugs, is

---

The Amazon River annually produces one-fifth of all the freshwater that drains into the oceans of the world; the salt content and color of the Atlantic Ocean is altered for about 200 miles from the mouth of the river.

the technique that works day after day, week after week, and season after season.

Great Bear anglers also get in some mighty fine arctic charr fishing on the Tree and Coppermine Rivers, via fly-outs from main lodges. These rivers have been known to produce really big charr, from 15 to 22 pounds, plus the all-tackle world record, a 32-pound 9-ounce fish taken in 1981.

Mackenzie Mountains and Delta. The Mackenzie Mountains, with feisty Dolly Varden, bull trout, grayling, lake trout, and whitefish, is the most underrated and poorly known angling destination in the NWT. Difficult access makes the mountains a dream destination for adventurous anglers who have advanced wilderness canoeing and expedition skills.

A trip to the Mackenzie River Delta or the Eskimo Lakes offers lake trout, Dolly Varden, northern pike, grayling, whitefish, inconnu, and burbot. Whether you arrive by road or air, it's a good idea to utilize a local guide, and it may be necessary to obtain a separate sportfishing license (in addition to the NWT license) from the Inuvialuit and/or Gwich'in Settlement Regions as well. The lands within these regions are privately owned by natives, and a permit to cross private lands may also be required and obtained in local villages.

To the east of the Delta are the Horton and Hornaday Rivers, which have arctic charr but no sportfishing facilities or outpost camps. The small community of Paulatuk, located near the mouth of the Hornaday, is a possible source of local guides, but there's no organized angling service.

Arrangements for local charr guides can also be made in the community of Holman Island on Victoria Island to fish the Kuuk and/or Quunnguq Rivers on the western end of Victoria Island. The western portion of Victoria and other westerly islands in the Arctic Ocean are within the NWT, but most anglers access it via Nunavit through Cambridge Bay and an established charr and lake trout camp on Merkley Lake.

NORWAY

With magnificent waterfalls, tens of thousands of lakes and tarns (mountain lakes and ponds), deep fjords, spectacular mountains, large forests, rich wildlife, and a long beautiful coast, Norway is a dream destination of world-traveled anglers. To most visitors, sportfishing in Norway is synonymous with big powerful rivers and equally big and powerful Atlantic salmon. However, few visitors realize that this country also has a wealth of trout and sea fishing opportunities.

Situated in the heart of Scandinavia northwest of Denmark and west of Sweden, Norway runs from the 58th parallel in the south to the 71st parallel north of the Arctic Circle. It covers an area of 301,585 square kilometers, a third of which is more than 300 meters above sea level. Norway has a 2,542-kilometer border in the east with Sweden, Finland, and Russia, and its coastline is 21,347 kilometers long (including bays and fjords), which, in proportion to the country's area, is longer than that of any major country in the world. That coastline faces the North Sea in the south, the Norwegian Sea (Atlantic Ocean) in the west, and the Barents Sea in the north, all of which is dotted with over 85,000 islands. And the whole country only has a population of 4.5 million people!

Amongst all these bounties, Norway has over 700 registered salmon and sea trout rivers. It is believed that 16,000 years ago Norwegian waters were populated only with such salmonids as sea charr, salmon, and brown trout, but after the last Ice Age, such white-fleshed species as pike, perch, grayling, and carp slowly made their way here from the Baltic in the east, and spread into Norwegian water systems.

With so many natural resources, fishing and hunting in Norway have long provided—and still do for many families—not only recreation but a substantial supplement to the larder. Angling for salmon in particular has a long rich history that goes back to the beginnings of European gamefishing, and was dominated and cultivated by the English fly fishing gentry. Wealthy Englishmen at the turn of the twentieth century, in their constant pursuit for bigger and better sport, leased large stretches of all the best Norwegian rivers from local landowners and farmers. These fishermen built fine and extravagant fishing lodges, most of which still exist today, to accommodate their guests and staff. They remained close by the river the whole summer in order to pursue their Victorian dream of landing not only the biggest but also the greatest volume of salmon.

Trout Fishing

The most common and probably the most popular gamefish in Norway is the native brown trout, which is found here in thousands of small forest lakes, tarns, rivers, and streams. Many of the remote mountain lakes and especially the tarns are surrounded by floating mats of living boggy peat, which drift around according to the wind direction. For the first-time angler these are a little unnerving, as traveling over this is similar to walking on a giant grass-covered waterbed, which moves underfoot with every step. They are generally safe enough, although due caution should be taken. These floating mats can also have small holes or pockets of water, which should not be forgotten when fishing, and should be approached carefully. In hot weather conditions, as exists in late summer, the trout use these large insulating mats to keep cool and shaded from the brightness of the midday sun, and these holes are used as feeding windows.

The average weight of a wild trout in Norway varies from place to place, but fish of 0.5 to 1 kilogram are common. Hip waders or rubber boots are adequate for most lake fishing but chest waders are

a must in rivers. For trout fly fishing a 9-foot No. 5 or 6 rod with a floating line is a normal outfit, and will cover most conditions.

The main insect staples for trout are mayflies, midges, caddisflies, damselflies, and dragonflies. The only terrestrials of any importance are ants and craneflies. The most productive fly patterns are deer-hair caddis imitations, but muddler minnows and large nymphs also work well. Spinners and small spoons designed for trout fishing constantly produce good fish. Trolling with large spoons and wobblers (minnow plugs) on big lakes can produce very large brown trout up to and over 15 kilograms, but smaller fish are normal, with individuals between 5 and 10 kilograms possible. Lake fishing for trout is sometimes done with a set of five or six hookless attractor spoons or blades that are all attached to a leader ahead of a worm-baited hook. This is trolled deep and slow, normally from the back of a rowboat.

Southern Region

Southern Norway has quite large areas of wilderness that are dominated mostly by coniferous spruce and pine forests, with birch also present in smaller numbers. Fish populations and fishing in the south were devastated in the 1960s by acid rain from Great Britain and eastern Europe, but in recent decades the cultivation of waters through a restocking and liming policy has re-introduced indigenous fish into all but a few waters. Although brown trout is the most common species, pike, perch, and charr are very widespread. Brook trout can also be found in some areas instead of brown trout; due to their greater tolerance of acidic water, brown trout were formerly stocked in lakes that had a low pH.

Norway's largest lake, Mjøsa, which covers 368 square kilometers, is in the southeast, as is its longest river, the 598-kilometer-long Glåma (Glomma), which, with its tributaries, drains about one-eighth of the country's area. Both are rich in fishing possibilities. Mjøsa is 60 miles long and 10 miles wile at its greatest point. On the banks of Mjøsa lies the town of Gjøvik, home and museum of the Mustad fish hook company. The lake is famous for it's trolling for huge trout and pike, and has produced many double-digit specimens of both, some over 15 kilograms.

Glomma has a reputation as Norway's best and most diverse sportfishing river with over 25 fish species, and just about every type of river condition from almost still to fast rapids. Although coarse fishing is very new in Norway, most of it is done here, along with grayling fishing.

East of Glomma is the Femundsmarka National Park. Dominated by the effects of the Ice Age, this is a typical glaciated landscape, with boulder fields, spruce forests, and bare mountain. Also found here is an abundance of some of Norway's best trout lakes and streams, which make it a Mecca for fly and spin anglers alike. The rich natural pH level in the lakes here makes them high in insect life, which includes the largest mayflies. The trout here are also very special, dressed in a butter-yellow color and with large thumb-size spots of red and black along the sides. These are some of the best and most beautiful brown trout that exist.

Norway has 18 national parks, the southernmost and largest being Hadangarvidda, which encompasses 3,422 square kilometers and lies to the west of the capital, Oslo, and is northern Europe's largest high mountain plateau. Famous for large herds of wild reindeer, mountains, and glaciers, Hadangervidda National Park provides wild brown trout sport in spectacular surroundings.

There are also landlocked charr in many lakes in southern Norway, but these are not really of interest to the visiting angler, as they spend the warmer months of the year in the deepest colder water, only coming shallower and being caught when the water is covered with a thick layer of winter ice.

Winter ice fishing is very popular in southern Norway, not only for charr, but also for trout, pike, perch, and sea fish such as cod. The tackle for this sport consists of a small rod that is 30 to 40 centimeters long, special "anti freeze" monofilament line, and small weighted and baited hooks and spoons that are jigged through a hole in the ice.

Trout, pike, and perch fishing locations are readily accessible in southern Norway. There are normally local fishing clubs and organizations that sell licenses, but many private farms and landowners also supplement their income by selling day tickets on private lakes, but this can be a little hit-and-miss regarding quality. Pike and perch can also give excellent sport, after spawning is over in the spring. Fishing with plugs, spoons, wobblers, and even flies can be very effective.

Salmon and sea trout. Common belief has it that all of Norway's finest salmon rivers are situated in the north. However, as with the rest of the country, the southern region has many salmon and sea trout rivers. Fishing on most is reasonably priced and well organized. Rivers such as Mandalselva, Otra, and Drammenselva, have had good runs in the late 1990s. Perhaps the foremost attraction in this region is the Numedalslågen River, which, with stable yearly catches of about 20 metric tons, is rated as one of Norway's top five most productive salmon rivers every year.

With its source in Haddangervidda National Park, the Numedalslågen runs 325 kilometers downstream to Larvik, where it enters the sea into the Oslofjord. Like many other large rivers in Norway, this is regulated for power production but still has a fairly stable water flow. The upper stretches that have no salmon can also provide good fishing for brown trout, pike, and ide throughout the summer.

There are two "best" times for salmon fishing here. The first is in mid-June. There are fewer fish in this first run but they are big, with an average weight of around 7.5 kilograms. The second major run of fish occurs about late August or early September. These are smaller (3 kilogram average) but are normally in great numbers.

The archipelago coastline of the southern region is excellent for sea trout fishing with both fly and spinning tackle from shore. During winter and spring, sea trout often swim within a few meters of land, occurring in or near sandy beaches with weed growth, boulders, and small rocky bays that have patches of kelp. Areas with lots of small peninsulas and bays are also ideal fishing sites.

The best time for sea trout is normally at high tide. But in southern Norway there is no real "high tide" because tidal fluctuations only differ from 50 centimeters to 1 meter most of the year. The sea trout come in with higher water to hunt in the shallows for ragworms, prawns, baitfish, and sand eels, all of which come out of their hiding places to feed on what the tide brings in. The optimum opportunity is presented when high water occurs in the evening just after dark, or in the morning just before daylight. If you're lucky enough to be in the right place with a warm southerly wind (which experienced Norwegian sea trout anglers call "happy hour") the sport can be tremendous. Salt-water sea trout here normally weigh up to 1 kilogram, but fish of 10 kilograms have been taken on a single-handed fly rod or lightweight spinning tackle.

With it's lengthy coastline and greatly varying sea depths, southern Norway is an el dorado for the sea fishing angler. The small village of Langesund in Telemark has gained an international reputation with deep sea anglers, breaking many European and world records for such species as ling, tusk, and mackerel. Although you can enjoy traditional sea fishing here, the bay of Langesund offers deep sea fishing for some species weighing over 150 kilograms, such as halibut and Greenland shark. Fishing at a depth of 300 to 400 meters is not uncommon here. This is an extremely physically tough and demanding sport and only for the experienced angler.

Sea fishing in general is very well organized and reasonably priced, with many charter boats of varying size, accommodation, and tackle available for hire in most coastal towns throughout Norway. The best seasons vary from species to species, but fishing in general is available year-round. A medium-weight spinning rod is suitable when fishing from land, but deep bottom fishing requires specialized tackle, such as a minimum 50-pound-class boat rod with roller eyes fitted with a heavy conventional reel that has enormous line capacity, and a line of at least 50-pound strength. Leader material should be 2-millimeter monofilament, and Swedish pilks (heavy jigging spoons) or lead weights of 1 kilogram are the norm.

Middle and Northern Norway

The middle and northern regions of Norway are

A Norwegian salmon angler lays out a long cast.

well known for their big salmon rivers, and the latter has what is arguably the best salmon rivers in the world.

Along the west coast are such famous rivers as Gaula, Orkla, Stordalselva, and Namsen, the latter of which alone produced 21.1 metric tons of salmon and sea trout as recently as 1997.

Although there has been a clear downfall in recorded catches of salmon in Norwegian rivers over the last few years, in 1997 the Tana and Altaelva together still produced a fantastic 62.3 metric tons of salmon and sea trout, and both yielded fish over 20 kilograms, but these are special rivers and fishing on them is sometimes difficult to arrange. Fishing on Altaelva in the month of June is for local residents only, and in July and August licenses are obtained by a lottery method. All applicants who apply in January have their names placed in a box and the first to be drawn get to fish. There are some special beats available but these command a very high price. But there are other rivers. The Neiden, Repparfjordelva, Vefsen, and Lakselv all have delivered steady numbers of fish in the late 1990s.

These are all big rivers with named pools and beats, but it's still advisable to book a gillie *(kleppe)*, as this will definitely increase the chance of success. Powerful rivers and fish mean big, powerful, two-handed rods and deep wading; a recent trend with Norwegians is to fish with a single-handed trout rod, although many look upon this as madness. The most popular methods for salmon fishing here are with fly, worm, and spoon.

All of these rivers have world-famous fly patterns named after them, but most successful fly anglers use their own simple-dressed hairwing patterns, normally tied on a double hook.

Sea fishing on the coast in this region also has a reputation for giant cod, and the angling record stands at over 40 kilograms. Excellent sea fishing in spectacular scenery can be had at the Lofoten archipelago. This is a group of 80 islands off the coast of Nordland that are dominated by high snow-clad mountains that rise steeply out of the sea. The best season here for big fish is from January to April.

Arctic Region
For most would-be visitors, Arctic Norway conjures up visions of constant snow and ice, though nothing could be further from the truth. Northern Norway is also the "land of the midnight sun," and can often produce Mediterranean-like summers. The explanation for this is simple: when the sun doesn't go down, it's bound to get warm. Thus, it's possible to fish around the clock.

Finnmark is Norway's largest, least populated, northernmost county, and borders Finland and Russia. Øvre Anarjåkka National Park is a remote and wild part of Finnmarksvidda and adjoins Lemmenjoki National Park in Finland. Together they form a large area of undisturbed wilderness that is characterized by an ancient rolling land-scape with birch forests, extensive bogs, and numerous lakes. This region contains some of the largest glaciers in Europe. Here, there is first-rate fishing for charr, grayling, and trout. All are common in sizes up to 2 kilograms. East of Finnmarksvidda, the waters are heavily populated with perch and pike, and guides are necessary to help one find the trout and charr spots. There are several tour operators and fishing camps here that have helicopter fly-in service for those who don't have the time or interest to walk and find their own way around. This is highly recommended for the first-time visitor.

This region is also a popular destination during the late winter months, when there is a combination of sun, snow, and ice fishing for big charr and pike.

Regulations and Seasons
Rod-and-reel fishing in the sea from land or a boat can be done year-round without charge, but some special rules apply to salmon, sea trout, and sea charr.

To fish in freshwater, anglers need to purchase a state (national) license, which is available from any post office, has weekly and yearly terms, and can be for an individual or family. Anglers under the age of 16 don't need a state license except for water systems where there are salmon, sea trout, and sea charr. Licenses for private waters are issued by their owners or by clubs.

Salmon fishing in general is from May 15 through September 30. Trout fishing, other inland fishing, and sea fishing can be done year-round. Local regulations vary from county to county. There is no "catch limit" in Norway, except on rivers with salmon, sea trout, and sea charr, or where stated in the local regulations. Live bait fishing is not allowed. The use of float tubes is forbidden in most fishing club waters. Rules and regulations will also vary with different fishing clubs, so there may be a minimum size limit, boat restrictions, maximum hook size, etc., that is imposed by them; fishing should not commence until one has purchased the appropriate area license, and checked the local fishing seasons and regulations.

Norway also has a "right of access law." Access to woods, fields, mountains, rivers, lakes, etc., regardless of who owns them, is an ancient right in Norway. When using a boat or canoe, you can go where you like in the sea, rivers, and lakes. With the exception of some canals and locks, this is totally free of charge. But you are not allowed to fish unless you have gained the owner's permission or purchased the appropriate local license.

NOVA SCOTIA
While salmon and trout are both synonymous with angling in Nova Scotia, the province should be known for its diversity in both species and angling opportunities.

The mainland portion of this Maritime province is connected to New Brunswick via an isthmus; to the north, separated by the Strait of Canso, is the island of Cape Breton. Between these two, Nova Scotia has a total area of 55,491 square kilometers (21,425 square miles) and is shaped somewhat like an old boot sticking out into the Atlantic Ocean. This boot runs nearly north and south, with the southern tip located below the 49th parallel, meaning that some parts of the United States are north of some parts of Nova Scotia.

If unraveled, the shoreline would stretch 7,500 kilometers (4,625 miles) across North America. Since the province is bordered on the east by the Atlantic Ocean and on the west by the Bay of Fundy and the Gulf of the St. Lawrence, it offers abundant opportunities for saltwater sportfishing, which is lightly utilized, although saltwater species were of great historical importance to colonists, and the province harbors a large commercial fishing fleet.

Inland, Nova Scotia has 6,674 lakes that are over a hectare (2.4 acres) in size, and over 1,200 watersheds fed by 5,000 rivers and streams, offering a profusion of diverse freshwater angling opportunities.

No place in Nova Scotia is any farther than 60 kilometers (37 miles) from saltwater, so the rivers are fed by moderate watersheds and tend to be small and intimate. With a population of approximately one million people, finding open water for fishing is rarely a problem.

Freshwater
With the exception of American shad, Nova Scotia does not offer a world-class fishery for any single species, but it is an exceptional area for species diversity, and it has a plethora of angling opportunities. Different species, in distinctive types of terrain, makes for interesting fishing in Nova Scotia. The pastoral rivers of the Annapolis Valley, the rolling hills of Cape Breton, the tumbling streams along the South Shore, and the wilderness lakes, are all only a few hours apart, making Nova Scotia a

unique destination for the versatile angler.

Most angling regulations in the province are similar to those elsewhere; however, when angling for Atlantic salmon, only fly fishing is permitted, and that with only single or double hooks. Additionally, some streams are posted for fly fishing only, regardless of the species present or sought by the angler. Although it is not mandated, catch-and-release for smallmouth bass is the rule of thumb for anglers. This is particularly true during the spawning season in May and early June.

Freshwater management can be divided into six geographic areas, and the species fall in different climatic, terrain, and water-quality regions. Although Nova Scotia is known for Atlantic salmon and trout, few people have taken advantage of the abundance of such warmwater species as smallmouth bass, chain pickerel, white perch, and yellow perch. It is also home to lightly fished but magnificent spring runs of American shad in numerous rivers. Introduced brown and rainbow trout have also found an appropriate niche in many parts of the province.

Cape Breton

The four counties in Cape Breton offer some of the most magnificent and unique salmon rivers in Nova Scotia, as well as some fine trout fishing.

The Margaree River in Inverness County is a beautiful river that has the distinct characteristic of a spring, summer, and fall run of salmon. The fall run is the most popular, not only because water levels are at their highest, but because of the high percentage of large multi-sea winter fish. The Middle River has a good fall run of salmon, while the Cheticamp River offers a spring-summer run. As an added bonus, all these rivers are surrounded by spectacular scenery.

The Baddeck River in Victoria County is a fall river with a large run of salmon, and the North River features an excellent run of spring-summer Atlantics.

In Richmond County, the Grand River is fished mainly along the lower stretches during the spring-summer run of salmon. There are also minor tributaries that, if timed right, will offer smaller runs of Atlantic salmon.

Speckled trout (brook trout) inhabit hundreds of small streams throughout Cape Breton. Their size is modest, but their abundance can make up for this in action. The Cape Breton National Park has a number of streams in a wilderness setting that provide excellent trout fishing. The Baddeck, Middle, Margaree, and River Inhabitants all offer a sea run of speckled trout in June. If timed right, the fishing can be excellent.

Lake Ainslie in Inverness County is one of the largest lakes in the province and has a unique speckled trout population, which moves into Trout River in late summer. It is restricted to fly fishing only, and at times the bottom is literally covered by large schools of trout.

An Atlantic salmon angler casts on the Margaree River.

Rainbow trout have become established in Bras' d'Or Lake, with the western side of the lake a preferred fishing area. But, the best angling is when these trout move up the Baddeck, Skye, and Middle Rivers to spawn.

White perch are found in a large number of lakes in Nova Scotia. Generally, they are not a target species but are simply an incidental catch when angling for other fish. The spring spawning run, which is on the south side of Lake Ainslie, is very impressive.

Northern Mainland

The northern end of the mainland adjoins Cape Breton and covers the counties of Antigonish, Guysborough, and Pictou.

River John in Pictou County features a favorable run of sea-run brown trout each spring. There are also smaller rivers here with respectable runs, but much depends on water levels.

The St. Mary's River has a spring-summer run of Atlantic salmon. Excellent dry-fly fishing can be found in the many pools on this river, but changes in water levels and water temperature make fishing difficult as summer advances.

The best area for speckled trout is on the eastern shore of Guysborough County; the area around the Liscomb Game Sanctuary is probably the most productive, and the most popular.

The rivers in Guysborough also have sea-run trout in late spring and early summer. Some of the most popular rivers are the Musquodoboit, Sheet Harbour, and Ecum Secum. The headwaters of these rivers are remote and can produce a good wilderness fishing experience. Sea-run brown trout are also found in the estuary of the Salmon River and are angled mainly in the tidal pools.

Southcentral Region

This is a large area encompassing the county of Lunenburg and the Regional Municipality of Halifax (RMH). There are a number of Atlantic salmon rivers in this zone and they all have spring-summer runs. The main rivers are the Medway and La Have in Lunenburg County, and the Moser in RMH. All have large pools that are excellent for dry-fly fishing. Although crowded during the mid-June peak run, both the number of available pools, and the practice of anglers rotating through the pools, provides everyone with an equal opportunity. The exception to this are the boat pools, with a few on the La Have, and for the majority of the Medway. The runs of Atlantic salmon vary from year to year and are very water-dependent. As the season advances, temperatures rise and water levels decline, and fishing becomes much more difficult.

Halifax is the capital city of Nova Scotia, and the regional municipality of Halifax also includes the city of Dartmouth. This metropolitan region has innumerable lakes containing smallmouth bass. Dart-mouth is known as the City of Lakes for good reason. The majority of these lakes, all of varying size, are classified as urban fisheries. Of the 20 or more lakes in this area, the two largest, Porter's and Grand, are the most popular and the most productive.

Along with smallmouth bass, Grand Lake also features a sizable population of landlocked salmon and striped bass. The big lake is subject to sudden changes in wave and wind action, so boaters should exercise caution. The salmon and striped bass are usually fished by trolling with downriggers, while smallmouths are pursued by casting to limited structure and using deep tactics.

Southern Region

This area covers the southern tip of Nova Scotia and the counties of Yarmouth, Digby, Shelburne, and Queens. The latter two have particularly felt the effects of acid rain, and subsequent damage to habitat has reduced the number of salmonids in many rivers. Trout and salmon can still be caught, however.

There is a spring-summer run of Atlantic salmon on both the Medway and Tusket Rivers. Brook trout can be found in a number of streams, but their numbers are reduced through competition with smallmouth bass and chain pickerel.

Smallmouths are becoming the most popular species in this region, with a 20-inch specimen always a possibility. While Nova Scotian smallmouths typically inhabit lakes, the Mersey is the one river in the province where these bass can be found. Good bass fishing can be had in Killams, Ogden, and Parr Lakes (Yarmouth County); Spectacle, Lac d'en Bas, and Salmon River Lakes (Digby County); and Ten Mile Lake (Queens County).

It is believed that chain pickerel were first established in Digby County in 1924. From this introduction, the species has spread throughout the area. The most popular pickerel sites include June, Spectacle, Henriette, and Amero's Lakes (Digby County); and Utley, Annis, and Long Lakes and Western Duck Pond (Yarmouth County).

As smallmouth bass and chain pickerel expand their range, the opportunities to fish for both these species continues to grow.

Northcentral Region

This area comprises Annapolis, Kings, and Hants Counties, all presenting great angling opportunities. The topography of the northcentral region encompasses everything from rolling agricultural land to wilderness retreats, with fast running brooks, slower rivers, and very productive lakes. All this flows to the floor of the Annapolis Valley, which is bounded on each side by the North and South Mountains.

The valley floor has three main rivers, the Annapolis, Gaspereau, and Cornwallis. All three ultimately flow into the Bay of Fundy, so the waters are tidal in their lower reaches. The Cornwallis is a unique limestone river, which accounts for its alkaline water. The upper part meanders slowly through a tranquil pastoral setting, and although the lower parts have limited shore access, the tall grass and low gradient make this a beautiful float trip. The river has a large population of both resident and sea-run trout. The sea-run fish arrive from mid-May through mid-June, with a later run in September. Although both rivers share the same headwater, the Annapolis flows in a westerly direction while the Cornwallis flows eastward.

The paramount feature of the Annapolis River is the major run of American shad late in May. The run is mainly fished at the confluence of the Annapolis and Nictaux Rivers in the town of Middleton. Angling is primarily from the bank, but there is excellent flycasting opportunity. Neither river is very large, and once a school is located, it is quite possible to hook and land over 20 shad. Some tributaries can provide interesting brook trout fishing, but the numbers and size of the fish are not great.

The Bay of Fundy has the highest tides in the world (commonly 20 to 40 feet), which accounts for the largest tidal generating station in North America at the estuary of the Annapolis. This creates a headpond with a good population of striped bass, which travel upriver to spawn and provide freshwater angling.

Also within this region is the smaller Gaspereau Valley. The Gaspereau River is a hydroelectric generating system with its headwaters as a series of lakes. George, Gaspereau, Aylesford, Little River, and Black River Lakes all provide some of the best smallmouth bass fishing in the province, both in sheer numbers and size. These impoundments have great structure for bass and rarely experience anything more than low to medium fishing pressure. The lakes also feed the lower river, which has spring-run salmon in May, June, and July, with the main pool located below the White Rock power plant. Another lake in the valley, Lumsden, is heavily stocked with trout. White perch are said to be abundant in all of these lakes.

Isthmus

This area connecting mainland Nova Scotia to New Brunswick is comprised of Cumberland and Colchester Counties.

Cumberland borders the neighboring province with Northumberland Strait to the north and the Bay of Fundy to the south. It has few lakes of any size but many small streams and rivers. The rivers feeding Northumberland Strait have good runs of sea-run brown trout in the spring, with the best being at River Phillip and Wallace River. A number of smaller rivers have good runs, but this is very dependent on water levels that are heavily influenced by short length of flow and a limited watershed.

There are also good runs of Atlantic salmon in Cumberland County, with the best time being October when the water levels should be higher. While there were some salmon rivers on the Minas Basin side, the runs there have disappeared despite ongoing restoration efforts.

Colchester County has several good rivers, with the main river system being the Shubenacadie. This is fed by a series of lakes and rivers, with the Stewiacke being the principal tributary. The Stewiacke once had one of the largest runs of Atlantic salmon in the province, but this has also disappeared in recent years, although there is hope for return of these fish. In the meantime, spring runs of American shad, and resident brown trout throughout the season, are the major fisheries. The Waugh River also produces good angling for sea-run brown trout in the spring.

Saltwater

With so much coastline, one would expect Nova Scotia to be a saltwater fishing Mecca. It is, to a degree. But, it is largely underutilized by recreational anglers. As more people are introduced to this marine activity, mainly promoted through saltwater sportfishing tournaments around the province, interest is slowly increasing.

Historically, big game fishing here centered around giant bluefin tuna, but now blue-water fishing includes mako and blue shark. Inshore fishing features striped bass, mackerel, bluefish, cod, flounder, halibut, and haddock.

Nova Scotia was historically *the* place to be for catching giant bluefin tuna. A major fishery years ago made the province a favorite haunt of Ernest Hemingway and top big-game anglers. But bluefin tuna numbers worldwide have declined, and the number of fish that can be caught is federally regulated.

Nevertheless, the bluefin tuna is one of the most sought-after fish in Nova Scotian waters, Tuna boats depart from Halifax and along the eastern shore up to the Canso Causeway. The fishing peaks in the last week of August through October in the area of Port Hood and Mabou on Cape Breton Island. The size can be impressive; a 1,000-pounder is not uncommon, and in 1979, the all-tackle world record specimen, a 1,496-pounder, was caught out of Aulds Cove.

There are charters available through the commercial sector, principally out of Aulds Cove at the Canso Causeway. In Nova Scotia, tuna must be fished on rod and reel on a registered commercial fishing vessel to which a bluefin tuna license is attached.

Shark fishing is growing in popularity here each year, with the blue shark being the main species. Blues weighing from 200 to 300 pounds and being from 10 to 12 feet long are not uncommon, with the average running approximately 100 pounds. Larger mako and porbeagle sharks are occasionally taken. Recreational shark fishing is on a catch-and-release basis except for tournaments, where the catch is weighed and sold with all proceeds going to a provincial charity. Shark are fished here by chumming to a floating bait. The best season is in August and September, with a number of charter boats operating out of the Halifax area.

Fishing for groundfish (cod, haddock, pollock, and others) is widely available via charter boats around the coast. The best time is from July through September.

In August, people fishing from wharves, shore, and small boats set their sights on mackerel, a migratory species that runs in the millions along the coastline of Nova Scotia. The hotspot for mackerel is either Mahone Bay or St. Margaret's Bay along the south shore.

Bluefish hit Nova Scotia in August as well, but the runs are unpredictable and of short duration. Basically, this fish is only found on the southwestern end of Nova Scotia, through the numerous islands in and around the mouth of the Tusket River. When you do catch the run, its an unforgettable experience, as these voracious predators attack baitfish (mainly mackerel) with such ferocity that slicks of fish oil calm the waters and overpower the salty scent of the sea.

There was a time when large striped bass (up to 70 pounds) sought out the estuaries of many rivers around the province, but overfishing adversely impacted the population. More recently, a resurgence of this fish has re-invigorated its popularity. The sizes have been smaller than they were years ago as it takes a number of years for the fish to reach maturity, but that may change. Because of the reduced populations, this fish is highly controlled and regulations should be carefully checked before you go fishing. The May spawning run in the Annapolis River can produce good results, but the best time is during July and August. The Tusket, Annis, Bear, and Annapolis Rivers in the southern part of the province are best for stripers, although Porter's Lake near Halifax also produces good runs.

Perhaps the most primitive of the commonly known fish is the sturgeon, which dates back 350 million years and whose flesh was considered a delicacy even in Roman times.

In fact, any river on the mainland can produce a reasonable run. There are no runs, however, on Cape Breton.

NUMBERS
The latitude and longitude coordinates for a given position. Someone who is navigating by the numbers has called up specific lat/lon coordinates from the memory of an electronic navigational device such as GPS or Loran to determine the direction to steer a boat in order to arrive at a specific destination.

See: GPS; Loran; Navigation.

NUNAVUT TERRITORY
Officially existing only since April 1, 1999, Nunavit Territory is the vast eastern Arctic region of Canada's far north that was separated from the former configuration of the Northwest Territories *(see)*. Nunavut means "our land" in the native language, and was formed for Canada's Inuit (Eskimo) people after a plebiscite in 1992. The country's newest territory, Nunavut is an enormous region that encompasses 1.9 million square kilometers of land—about one-fifth of the entire country of Canada. It includes the geographic and magnetic North Poles as well as the geographic center of Canada (30 kilometers northeast of Baker Lake), and is populated by less than 25,000 people. The Inuit have direct ownership of 350,000 square kilometers of this new territory, and now own some of the best fishing waters in the world.

Despite the change in land ownership, the right of innocent passage along waterways is guaranteed to non-beneficiaries in the Inuit land claim settlement. For those who angle the Arctic by canoeing its many splendid rivers, there will be little or no change. The shift in land ownership may see some lodges change hands, and it may see the names of some of its lakes, rivers, and towns change. Gradually, there is likely to be improved access to many previously uncelebrated and lightly visited angling "hotspots," such as Chantrey Inlet on the far northern mainland, as the Inuit selectively develop sportfishing in one of the last great wildernesses on earth.

It's not as if this region hasn't seen any anglers. Some of Canada's most famous and heralded angling waters are within this region, and they have been fished to varying degrees for decades. But due to remoteness, expense, and short seasons, and given the number and size of its waters, the region has hosted comparatively few anglers, and there are many lakes and rivers that rarely see a sport angler. In essence, the adventurous people who have ventured into Canada's remote eastern Arctic have had the arctic charr, lake trout, northern pike, and Arctic grayling virtually to themselves.

Visiting the far north to angle is an experience that goes beyond the act of catching frisky fish. This is a land of stark contrasts that ranges from the edge of the trees on the western barren lands to the towering barren cliffs of north Baffin Island's fjords. The Nunavut Territory is huge, stretching from it's southern boundary with the Province of Manitoba to the North Pole and from the tundra of the barren lands to the icebergs in Davis Strait off Greenland. It is equal in landmass to the entire country of Mexico, larger than Alaska, and could fit the entire states of Texas, California, Michigan, and Minnesota combined within its borders. And the amazing thing, as anyone who has flown over it in a plane can attest, is that there is water everywhere.

Typically, the Arctic angling season is compressed into the short period of open water from late June to mid-September. The lakes in Nunavut are ice covered from 240 days a year near the tree line, to 300-plus days a year in the northern islands of the Arctic archipelago. Recently, Inuit outfitters on Baffin Island have stretched the old open-water fishing season by offering adventurous anglers the opportunity to travel by dog team and jig for arctic charr and tomcod through cracks in the sea ice. Traveling by sled on a bright Arctic spring day to a distant bay, where you will jig with traditional Inuit caribou bone lures, provides a new and unique dimension to ice fishing.

Species
Arctic charr. The arctic charr is the storied fish of Nunavut. Anglers who know them well consider arctic charr a fish worth the same passionate pursuit which many accord steelhead and Atlantic salmon. They are spirited fighters on both spinning and fly tackle, capable of solid drag-burning runs when at their peak and newly arrived back in their home rivers from the salt.

Feeding in the ocean on small silvery herring and capelin, arctic charr are particularly good sportfish. They can be very aggressive and frequently fall victim to bright silver spinners and wobbling spoons. Although arctic charr can be taken on dry flies, fly anglers are generally more successful with bright steelhead patterns and large weighted sculpins fished near the bottom.

The eastern arctic charr found in Nunavut is broadly considered one of two distinct subspecies of arctic charr found in North America (the other being western arctic charr). It is a fish that challenges taxonomists and geneticists, who have split and re-lumped the various subspecies and relatives over the years as they have sought to understand the relationship between the broadly dispersed circumpolar populations. Anglers who have fished widely in Nunavut know that there are even some visible differences between populations within the eastern Arctic stock.

The connection between arctic charr and Dolly Varden is strong, since they are closely related.

The Tree River arctic charr live on the western boundary of the eastern arctic charr. They are well east of the known range of Dolly Varden. Despite this, they exhibit some characteristics reminiscent of the northern Dolly Varden, found west of the Mackenzie River in the Northwest Territories.

Tree River charr have small reddish spots with blue halos around them that are typically smaller than the eye of the fish; their bodies exhibit a compressed or flattened profile. Arctic charr generally have splotchy spots that are larger than the eye of the fish, they lack the blue halos, and they have a rounder body profile. If you compare a Tree River arctic charr with one from Victoria Island a few miles north across Coronation Gulf, the differences are visible, even though the scientific certainty of the lineage of the Tree River fish is undecided. Taxonomic subtleties aside, the Tree River contains one of the Arctic's great charr stocks, and it is where the biggest fish run.

Arctic charr in Nunavut occur in anadromous, nonanadromous, and lacustrine or landlocked forms. Anadromous males and females go to sea yearly to feed after spending five to eight nursery years in freshwater. They return to freshwater lakes in the autumn to spawn. The nonanadromous arctic charr are smaller males that stay in freshwater rivers that have access to the sea. Landlocked arctic charr are found in many isolated interior lakes that no longer have free passage to the sea. They are generally smaller than the sea-run form, but they are still an impressive gamefish on light tackle. Historical accounts by early missionaries from the Bathurst Inlet region refer to lakes fished by the Inuit with large populations of landlocked arctic charr.

Today, the arctic charr is found in many isolated interior lakes, and most of the coastal rivers and streams that rise from lakes that can support spawning. The majority of charr are caught in rivers; however, the larger specimens are primarily caught in the lower stretches closer to the salt. Arctic charr rivers flow into the Arctic Ocean, Hudson Bay, and the Atlantic coastlines of Nunavut. The well-known charr of Lake Hazen on northern Ellesmere Island are, at 82 degrees north, among the most northerly known populations. Lake Hazen has two distinctive stocks of arctic charr, incidentally; one is larger and has longer fin rays than the other; these charr, sometimes referred to as landlocked, do have access to the sea but apparently do not go to sea. Technically, the most northerly known populations are found in lakes near Alert and on the northern end of Greenland (about 84 to 85 degrees north).

Charr do not run huge distances inland like Pacific salmon, and it is usually small specimens that are in the lakes. The charr that are caught early in the season are very bright fish, looking in coloration like a steelhead or fresh-run salmon, but they develop remarkable colors, and the later-season fish can possess beautiful shades of red and orange, plus spots. Non-spawning fish, especially the sea-run forms, tend to be silver. Many lacustrine populations have individuals which haven't sexually matured and which retain a pale color even at non-spawning times.

The most lasting image of the arctic charr is that of a spawning fish's brilliant orange belly set against a dark-green back, highlighted with orange spots and white-edged fins. However, non-spawning fish range from the dull-silver coloration of landlocked specimens to the blue silver flash of the returning sea-run specimen. Arctic charr average 15 to 18 inches in length in Nunavut; specimens longer than 30 inches are rare but possible in some runs. Sea-run fish average 2 to 10 pounds.

The largest known arctic charr taken by anglers have come from the Tree River. The Tree River stock and related runs from the Coppermine and others rivers that flow along the Northwest Passage have consistently produced big fish. This is where the great pictures of huge, brightly colored charr draped across anglers' arms comes from. The IGFA all-tackle world record for arctic charr is a 32-pound 9-ounce Tree River fish caught in 1981.

Practically speaking, to trophy-seeking anglers a large charr is one that is over 15 pounds, and Nunavut has several locations known to produce such fish, in addition to the Tree and Coppermine Rivers. Chantrey Inlet is one, although it has a very small window of opportunity at the time of ice out. More reliable are various rivers on Victoria Island (shared with the Northwest Territories), which have produced 18- to 24-pound arctic charr and assorted line-class world records over the years. Although there are plenty of charr in the various rivers of Baffin Island, these waters have not been known for large specimens, and fish over 15 pounds have not been common there.

Size aside, most of the Inuit maintain that the best-tasting arctic charr comes from around Pelly Bay on the central Arctic coast's Boothia Peninsula, although any visiting angler who has eaten freshly caught charr, especially small and midsize specimens, has enjoyed a gastronomic delight.

Lake trout. Lake trout, of course, which are actually in the charr family, are perhaps Nunavut's greatest claim to the angler's affection. Lakers are found in the greatest numbers in the rivers and lakes of the barren lands on the Arctic mainland. These rivers flow north to the Arctic Coast's Coronation Gulf and Queen Maud Gulf, and east into the west side of Hudson Bay.

Lake trout are also found on the southern half of Victoria Island on the western end of Nunavut. On many rivers, lake trout inhabit and dominate the upper reaches, while arctic charr inhabit the lower and share it with smaller-size lakers. Unlike their cousins, lake trout are generally intolerant of the saltwater in coastal estuaries.

The extremely cold water of the lakes and rivers of the barren lands allow lake trout to remain at shallower depths in the lakes and to thrive in the

 Creation of the first glass fishing rod is credited to Dr. Glen Havens, who experimented with fiberglass and resins starting in the mid-1930s.

oxygen-rich water of brawling rivers. This characteristic of Nunavut lake trout allows the angler to pursue them with varied tackle, including lighter spinning gear and fly tackle. On those rare occasions when big caddis hatch in early July, it is not uncommon to pick up 6- or 7-pound fish on a bushy Goddard caddis.

In lakes, the abundance of trout at shallow depths, including the availability of good-size fish, makes it generally unnecessary to use the deep trolling tactics and equipment that are common for catching lakers in the southern parts of their range, especially after ice out and in late summer. Almost no lodges provide downriggers, for example, and it is rarely necessary to get down more than 35 or 40 feet in most Nunavut lakes, even in the middle of the (short) summer. Not all of the fish are caught by trolling, although the majority are; jigging and casting are possible, especially at inlets and along shorelines. The cold water also contributes to distinctively marked and hard-fighting fish.

There are few places outside of Nunavut where it is common to catch lake trout in rivers. The largest lakers are not likely to be in swift-flowing water; however, they are very likely to be in the vicinity of a tributary, especially where it enters a big lake, since this will also attract a lot of forage fish, including suckers, whitefish, and small trout. However, smaller fish, in the 5- to 10-pound range, are often caught in the rivers of this region, and they are a terrific prize for the light-tackle angler.

The largest lake trout of the Nunavut Territory are generally found in the biggest lakes. Although there are some huge lakers on Victoria Island, mainly in Merkley Lake, the northernmost waters don't seem to produce the monster fish, probably because of the short open-water seasons. The big lakes of the more southerly region of the territory, from Baker Lake south to the Manitoba border, most reliably produce huge trout. Nueltin Lake, which is a 125-mile-long body of boundary water, two-thirds or more of which is in Nunavut, is the most renowned lake trout water in the territory. Huge in this region means over 30 pounds, as there are great populations of small trout in nearly all of the places that hold this species, and most lakes can produce fish in the 15- to 20-pound range. Some lakes, however, have been subject to netting by native people, and these are less likely to have a good supply of large lake trout.

Northern pike. Northern pike are distributed across the barren lands from the tree line to Hudson Bay and north to the southern edge of the Arctic coastal plain. The upper Thelon, Dubant, Kazan, and Thlewiaza Rivers have good pike fishing. Nueltin Lake is the most renowned pike water in the region and has produced numerous 50-inch fish.

The popularity of barren-land pike fishing has increased over the years, either as an adjunct to people seeking lake trout, or as a sole quarry unto itself. Shallow-water casting, which appeals to many anglers, dovetails nicely with northern pike in Nunavut waters, as these fish are accessible and aggressive throughout the limited season. A greater interest in fly fishing for these fish has been evident, and flies sometimes succeed at moving fish when other offerings do not. Nevertheless, as is true elsewhere in Canada, the great majority of Nunavut's pike are caught on spoons, and there is virtually no trolling done for this species. The greatest action for shallow fish is usually had early in the season, especially in the backs of bays, which lose their ice early and warm up.

Grayling. The Arctic grayling is a favorite fish of the far north for light-tackle devotees. Like charr, it's a species that is primarily found in the remote north, with a similar range to that of northern pike. Though caught in some lakes, it is mainly found in rivers here. Light spinning and fly tackle is more than adequate for these fish, which typically run about $1^1/_2$ pounds but may be much larger. A 3-pounder is a fairly large grayling, but fish of this size are caught in various Nunavut locations, and are common in a few. Record-size grayling have been caught in various locales here, including the Kazan River.

This frisky and flashy blue fish lives off insects and very small fish fry. Its keen interest in flies makes it a natural for the fly caster. However, the grayling is a fragile fish—one that never stops squirming when caught—making it susceptible to harm through handling and requiring careful release.

Some of the largest grayling can be found in lakes, but they are generally overlooked in still-waters here. It is possible in some places to spot cruising fish in the shallows nearshore, taking insects off the surface, and to cast to them. This is often an evening affair, and most lake anglers are resting then, having spent all day casting or trolling for the pike and lake trout in these waters. Evenings in summer, however, seem to never end in Nunavut, as this is the fabled Land of the Midnight Sun, and it presents delightful opportunities.

Grayling are rarely the sole, or even primary, quest for far-north anglers. They are usually caught as an adjunct, or side excursion. A suitable light rod must be brought for these fish, however, as the small-mouthed grayling almost never succumb to the larger offerings made for lake trout and pike. Focusing exclusively on grayling requires having a guide or outfitter who is well acquainted with the white water on the rivers, and the small streams that feed the lakes.

Whitefish. Lake whitefish are found in the lakes and rivers of the barren lands and in the littoral zone along the Arctic Coast and Hudson Bay. No lodges advertise them and relatively few anglers seek them out, but when the opportunity presents itself the lake whitefish is a prize worth pursuing.

Like grayling, whitefish are almost never caught on the hardware and tackle used for pike and trout, and angling for them is more specialized, requiring

Piled rocks are a traditional Inuit marker for an important fishing site; this one overlooks Bloody Falls on the Coppermine River.

light or ultralight spinning and fly gear. They can be taken on light jigs, and to a lesser degree small spinners, but they are best caught on flies, including soft hackle and emerger patterns, and they are a delightful fish to catch.

Whitefish are sometimes seen dimpling the surface in the evening, and can be available to anglers then. Rising whitefish on a midsummer's eve are not actually rising to flies on the surface; they are nymphing for caddis and mayflies swimming up to hatch. The slight downturn of the whitefish's small mouth does not allow it to easily snip dry flies from the surface. If you watch their rises carefully, it is the back of the fish which breaks the surface as it positions itself to come down on the rising insect.

Whitefish is one of the best table fish in the north. Fried whitefish makes a great shore lunch, and smoked whitefish (some lodges have smokehouses) is a real treat.

Locations

There are several ways to approach a fishing trip to Nunavut, but each depends on the type of experience and the species the angler is interested in. It is important to remember that Nunavut is still a remote (and often harsh) land that has no roads, limited scheduled air service, and a tourist industry that is still evolving and developing. The options for the angler include well-established lodges (which are not as numerous as one might think in this vast region), community-based guiding services, guided canoe trips, and self-managed canoe expeditions. Self-managed canoe expeditions are only for accomplished wilderness travelers and often do not provide the type of angling, or amount of fishing time, that dedicated anglers want, although they can provide access to rarely visited locations. For anglers going to Nunavut with a limited amount of time and a desire to get in a lot of fishing, visiting an established lodge is the best option, and it is the one most frequently taken.

The most varied angling opportunities are available at the lodges on the barren lands. There are well-established facilities at Nueltin Lake, Kasba Lake, and Ferguson Lake/Yathkyed Lake, which can provide excellent lake trout, Arctic grayling, and northern pike fishing. There are also community-based guides in the Inuit community of Baker Lake on the barren lands, and some outfitters provide tent camping expeditions to locations that are not serviced by established lodges. There is also good arctic charr fishing along the north shore of Baker Lake and along the lower Thelon River.

There are established arctic charr lodges on the Tree River along the central Arctic Coast, and at Merkley Lake on Victoria Island, with an outpost on Hadley Bay. The latter is in close proximity to the most northerly lake trout in North America. More adventurous anglers will find community-based angling services for arctic charr available in Kugluktuk on the Coppermine River, at Rankin Inlet on the west coast of Hudson Bay, at Coral Harbour on South Hampton Island in northern Hudson Bay, at Iqaluit on Frobisher Bay on southern Baffin Island, at Pangnirtung on Cumberland Sound in the central section of Baffin Island, at Pond Inlet on north Baffin Island, and near Resolute Bay on Cornwallis Island along Barrow Strait in the High Arctic. Bloody Falls on the lower Coppermine River has fine charr fishing in late August or early September. Close proximity to the community of Kugluktuk means that Bloody Falls is not a wilderness experience, but it can be very good fishing.

Fishing gear is almost never available at Nunavut locations, or extremely expensive, so anglers must bring a good supply of whatever they will need. Since most access is by float plane in this country, it is necessary to pack gear compactly so that it will fit with others in a small aircraft. It is often said that summer lasts one day, or one week, in this country, and while that is an exaggeration, a beautiful, warm 75°F day can be followed by a dark cloudy day with blustery winds, which, when blowing across cold water, can make it seem like fishing in the winter. Therefore, good rain gear, boat boots, sweaters, and wind breakers are imperative *(see: travel)*.

Nueltin Lake

Although most of this huge lake is located in Nunavut, it is generally viewed as a Manitoba lake. Greater details about this lake are noted in that entry *(see: Manitoba)*. There is one lodge on the lake, located at the southern end in Manitoba, although there are several outpost camps for this lodge, two of them situated in Nunavut. This outflow of Nueltin, which is above the tree line and flows to western Hudson Bay, is one of the more interesting and least visited sites of the far north, primarily hosting lake trout and, further along, grayling. Sealhole Lake at the outflow of Nueltin has prodigious water flow and terrific lake trout fishing, and it is probably visited by only a handful of people each season.

Ferguson Lake and Vicinity

By far north standards, Ferguson Lake is a small body of water south of the community of Baker Lake and west of Rankin Inlet in south-central Nunavut. However, in addition to good July and August fishing on its own waters, Ferguson provides access to excellent angling in the nearby waters of 35-mile-long Yathkyed and 125-mile-long Kaminuriak Lakes. Although there are some grayling in this area, this area is almost entirely a lake trout experience.

There is one base camp lodge in this area, on Ferguson; a few outpost facilities in the region, including several at Kaminuriak and one at the north end of Yathkyed (where the Kazan River enters); and some daytrip fly-in access to other areas. Undisturbed by commercial fishing, domestic netters, and few other anglers, these huge lakes have become places for multi-faceted lake trout fishing, where trollers and casters each enjoy success.

Light-tackle angling is especially feasible in these waters, since the trout are usually shallow, ice out normally doesn't occur until about July 4, and there are many feeder rivers and outlet tributaries that stack the fish up. Smaller lake trout are available in the various rivers, some of which provide adventurous hike-to whitewater fishing, and bigger specimens are available in the lakes and at tributaries where heavy flows exit, creating back eddies that are magnets for lake trout.

Ferguson Lake, being relatively shallow, and the other lakes here, are conducive to thin-water fishing through the entire open-water season, and most of the fish that are caught here are taken in under 12 feet of water. Catching a 20-pounder is a distinct possibility in these waters, and fish to 30 are likely. There are big lakers here, too, and specimens up to 50 pounds and more were caught in the 1990s.

Some of the largest far-north herds of caribou traverse the tundra in this region, and anglers are quite likely to see varied numbers of these in this area, as well as, perhaps, musk ox.

Chantrey Inlet

Located in the Arctic tundra on the mainland Nunavut Territory, Chantrey Inlet is the place where the mighty Back River courses through Franklin Lake. It attracts a prodigious run of big charr (10 to 20 pounds) in early July as the ice leaves, and it hosts scores of lake trout, including specimens that have reputedly topped the 60-pound mark, the rest of the season till mid-August. Most of the trout are in the 10- to 20-pound range, but there's a good chance of getting one from 30 to 40 pounds here. Grayling, too, exist along the shoreline in less tumultuous water and in two nearby small lakes.

Swift water and back eddies provide challenging moments for shore or boat anglers hooked to charr or lakers, with most anglers using heavy spoons to troll or jigs for casting and drifting. This is not the place to try light tackle, fly fishing, or gear of questionable endurance. Deep, rapid water, a boulder strewn bottom, and extremely hard-fighting fish combine to provide some of the most demanding freshwater fishing and boating.

This remarkable place has had varied accessibility over the years. In the past, some operators have brought groups of anglers in for a few weeks, but the stability of these operations has varied. The problem with Chantrey is that everything is dependent on ice out, which varies from year to year. The big charr run through so fast that even in the best case, the hottest charr angling, and the big fish, lasts less than two weeks at the mouth of the mighty Back. No established operation was being run here as of the late 1990s; however, this is an area—including the upriver lakes—that bears watching.

Victoria Island

The moment that you step off the commercial airliner at Cambridge Bay you realize that Victoria Island is a special place. Across from the airport is a Distant Early Warning (DEW) radar site. In the bay is the wreck of the Maud, the round-hulled vessel used by Norwegian explorer Roald Amundsen to make the first east-west crossing of the Canadian Arctic at the turn of this century. A few yards from that is the site of the first church here, a Roman Catholic building made of double stone walls, with caribou hides for insulation. Perhaps a visit will coincide with the biggest event of the season, the arrival of the supply barge that is laden with goods ordered a year earlier, and whose passage is cleared by icebreakers. In Cambridge Bay, drying charr and animal skins hang outside houses. Dog sleds lie next to ATVs and snowmobiles.

Above the mainland Northwest Territories, 270 miles north of the Arctic Circle, in the lower reaches of the Arctic Ocean, Victoria Island is a long way from anywhere. It's a particularly long way to go to stand waist-deep in a river that never gets warmer than 40 degrees, under a gray, sometimes drizzly or snowy sky, and cast for a fish that may not be there. Much of the time there is only the whistling of wind for company, or an occasional caribou a half mile away on the horizon. Other than caribou, musk oxen, and rocks, there is nothing here that rises more than a few inches off the ground. The nearest tree is 400 miles to the south, across a spongy, moss-covered, nearly level plain that hides an always frozen substrata.

But in this apparently desolate spot are treasures that only several dozen anglers are able to enjoy each summer. In some of Victoria Island's rivers, which flow north to the Viscount Melville Sound and south to the Coronation and Queen Maud Gulfs, not far from the permanent polar icecap, the lucky ones will intercept the elusive, brilliantly colored arctic charr on the way to its spawning grounds. This is one of the premier spots in North America for a chance at catching trophy charr.

Although most visitors fish the western and northern rivers for this species, arctic charr run along the south coast of Victoria Island near the community of Cambridge Bay in early July. Locals search for them by driving along the coast on ATVs watching for flocks of seabirds and seals swarming after capelin. The charr will be found feeding in the middle of the scrum. Casting bright spoons, spinners, and wet flies from shore often brings explosive action. Surf casting for charr is good fun.

Cold Victoria Island rivers produce colorful spawning-run charr.

Certainly arctic charr are found all across the North American Arctic. The largest charr appear to come regularly from Victoria Island and the Tree River on the mainland Northwest Territories. Geographically, these places are not that far apart, yet their charr are distinctly different. Tree River charr in their spawning colors have a dark back and are not fully swathed in red or orange. They have a humped back, too, and often a more pronounced kype. Many taxidermists, more familiar with these trophies, have painted this pattern on Victoria Island trophies.

The biggest charr caught at Victoria Island was a line-class world record 24-pounder taken in 1982. Several other line class world records have been established here as well. Summer charr here typically run from 12 to 20 pounds, a weight well above that found in most other regions.

Charr spawn approximately every three years, and it is the spawning fish that change color and are largest and most prized. Silver charr, those descending lakes and rivers and running out to the ocean for the summer, are smaller and bright, though a lot of fun to catch. Fishing is done for silver charr in July and holdover (spawning) charr in August. The season, which is just six weeks long, begins in mid-July and runs through August, by which time the weather is already starting to get worrisome.

In addition to having tremendous charr fishing, Victoria Island has some exceptional lake trout angling. Lakers up to 44 pounds have been caught in relatively shallow 15-mile-long Merkley Lake. The larger lakers are usually taken right after ice out during the first two or three weeks of fishing. Casting and fly fishing opportunities are best then for both trout and silver charr. Throughout the season, small lake trout can be taken on ultralight spinning tackle and fly rod in shallow water by sight casting to feeding/cruising pods.

Victoria Island has various fishing locales that

have seldom, if ever, seen a lure in years. This is partly due to the fact that some waters here open up only every few years, usually after a mild winter.

NUN BUOY
A cylindrical buoy, tapered at the top and usually red, used as an aid to navigation.
See: Buoys.

NURSERY
The part of a fish's or animal's habitat where the young grow up.

NYLON LINE
See: Line

NYMPH
The immature form of some aquatic insects in freshwater; also an artificial fly that imitates or suggests the natural insect.
See: Fly.

OCEANIA
The combined island areas of the western, central, and southern portions of the tropical Pacific Ocean. The area is subdivided into Micronesia, Melanesia, and Polynesia.

OCEANIC
Pertaining to or living in the open ocean.

OCEANOGRAPHER
A person who studies the environment of the oceans, including currents, wind, tides, sea-air interactions, geology of the sea floor, and the living organisms.

OFFSHORE
Although this term practically signifies the direction away from land, in fishing parlance it generally means that portion of the water from which land is not visible, and to most saltwater anglers it pertains to deep-water areas, on the edge of ocean currents or shelves, where big-game species, particularly billfish and tuna, are pursued.
See: Inshore; Offshore Fishing; Sportfishing Boat.

OFFSHORE BOAT
See: Sportfishing Boat.

OFFSHORE FISHING
The term "offshore" is largely a generic one used by saltwater anglers to refer to deep-water areas on the edges of ocean currents or to shelves commonly called blue water. Although there's no strict definition as to where offshore begins and inshore (see) ends, in general offshore applies to the pursuit of big-game species, particularly billfish and tuna, and inshore refers to angling for resident and migratory species in estuaries, rivers, bays, and near-shore ocean waters.

Because of the expanse of water and the nature of the pelagic species there, offshore environs are primarily fished by trolling and by chumming while the boat is drifting or at anchor. Trollers use both lures and rigged natural baits, but some live bait fishing occurs. Although offshore fishing is done at great distances from some mainland coasts, it can be done fairly close to other coasts if hydrographic contours and currents provide appropriate conditions suitable to the presence of big-game species. Thus, offshore fishing may be enjoyed by anglers fishing from private sportfishing boats of various sizes, from charter boats, and, less commonly, from long-range party boats.

Generally, offshore fishing is done with medium- to heavy-duty conventional tackle or big-game tackle (see), even though some of these species, or smaller specimens, may be caught with other equipment where circumstances permit.

The various elements of offshore fishing—from setting and using drag to lures and baits and tactics for specific species—are covered in more detail in separate entries.
See: Bait Rigs; Billfish; Billfish on Fly Tackle; Conventional Tackle; Kite Fishing; Sharks; Sportfishing Boat; Stand Up Fishing; Trolling; Trolling Lures, Saltwater; Tuna.

OFFSHORE LURES
See: Offshore Fishing; Trolling Lures, Saltwater.

OHIO
With an army of anglers and a meager sprinkling of small reservoirs, Ohio certainly depends on a large share of Lake Erie to satisfy its residents. The most fertile and productive of all the Great Lakes, Erie and its sprawling waters and plentiful fish schools can easily accommodate a crowd.

Lake Erie's shallow Western Basin is a world premier freshwater spawning ground, a bonanza that has earned it its reputation as the "Walleye Capital of the World." The walleye fishing is great, and the often ignored smallmouth bass fishing is even better. The wide range of gamefish inhabiting Lake Erie will test any angler's interests and abilities.

Although anglers flock to northern Ohio to feast on Lake Erie's bounty, if they ignore the Buckeye State's inland lakes and the Ohio River, they're missing out on a smorgasbord of treats. Ohio's collection of small reservoirs features fine angling for panfish, catfish, bass, and walleye, as well as surprisingly good muskies. The darling of the modern fisheries programs is the saugeye, a walleye-sauger hybrid generously stocked in many of the state's reservoirs.

Most visiting anglers fail to realize that although Lake Erie and the Ohio River have a long history of pleasing recreational anglers, natural inland lakes are few and far between. The largest natural lake in Ohio is little Chippewa, a 300-acre private patch of water about 40 miles southwest of Cleveland. The 31 inland lakes that boast 1,000 acres of water or more are all reservoirs. Most have been created over the past 50 years, and some are considerably younger.

Lake Erie

Western Basin. Ohio shares western Lake Erie with Michigan and Ontario, but Buckeye anglers have the largest slice of the big lake and the best of the fish-attracting reefs. Since the removal of Ohio's commercial gillnet fishery, bought out by the Ohio Division of Wildlife on behalf of anglers many years ago, the walleye angling on Lake Erie has flourished. There have been changes, however.

A parade of exotic species of fish and organisms have found their way to the Great Lakes over the years, most from European waters. The pace accelerated in the 1980s, with clouds of spiny water fleas and even Chinese mitten crabs making an appearance. The most notable critters hitchhiking in the bellies of ocean freighters have been the zebra mussel, a small mollusk; and the round goby and ruffe, two small but aggressive and prolific species of fish. The zebra mussel has significantly impacted the fishery, and although their initial appearance prompted a forecast of doom and gloom, the effects haven't all been bad.

Billions of the filter-feeding mollusks now live in Lake Erie, covering every available piece of rock and rubble, and the once dingy Western Basin has become a place of clear water. That clarity has liberated the walleye, allowing them to do what they do best, which is to use their large, opaque eyes to feed primarily after the sun goes down. This is, of course, a frustrating change in behavior for daytime anglers.

At the same time, the clear waters have broadened the spawning grounds for fish, allowing light to penetrate and letting some species, especially smallmouth bass, find success in deeper waters. As a result, hordes of smallmouth bass have been a delight for anglers.

Western Lake Erie is at its very best in the spring. The average depth of the Western Basin, from the Bass Islands to the Michigan shoreline, is just 30 feet, a reason why walleye swim here from all over Lake Erie and beyond to spawn each March and April.

If the winter is chilly enough to provide safe ice along the mainland and around the Bass Islands, ice anglers often get the first taste of walleye. When Lake Erie warms in spring, and walleye swarm over and around the limestone reefs to spawn, the fishing season begins in earnest. Although roughly 70 percent of the walleye spawn on Lake Erie's reefs, the remainder that head up the Maumee, Portage, and Sandusky Rivers give wading anglers a spring walleye fling in late March and early April, followed by some hot white bass fishing.

In May, western Lake Erie's smallmouth bass move to the shallows as post-spawn walleye head for open water. Many walleye will roam the big lake, some even heading up the Detroit River to Lake St. Clair and beyond. Large schools of walleye will remain, however, and June through August are excellent months for western Lake Erie anglers.

During the spawning season, walleye anglers rely on jigs and jigging spoons tipped with minnows. When the spawn is winding down, anglers begin casting traditional weight-forward spinners tipped with nightcrawlers, and pull out diving plugs to troll for trophy fish. The clear waters of Lake Erie and the scattered schools of walleye now make trolling the most consistent technique, whereas drifting was favored in the days before the zebra mussel.

The smallmouth bass fishing is especially impressive along the western Lake Erie shoreline and around the western lake islands, and it's also very consistent. The bass are vulnerable during their April and May spawning seasons, which can extend into June in deeper, cooler Canadian waters. When the spawn is over, though, smallmouths simply move to deeper waters and begin to feed on crayfish and emerald shiner minnows.

Almost all of Ohio's bass tournament trails have set their records on Lake Erie because of the plentiful smallmouth bass and the faithful fishing. At times, the arsenal of bass baits, from jerkbaits and deep-diving plugs to spinners, will catch big bass. From spring through fall, the Lake Erie favorites are tube jigs, jig-grub combinations, live crayfish, and sparkling live emerald shiner minnows.

Anglers looking for smallmouth bass can narrow their focus to two critical ingredients. Successful anglers must find the depths the bass prefer, which can vary from day to day and throughout the day, and the rockpiles that are magnets for this species.

Western Lake Erie yellow perch are popular, but they are generally slightly smaller than their deep-water cousins in central Lake Erie. They make up for that by being more plentiful and easier to find. Yellow perch prefer deep-water dropoffs along the

Put-in-Bay on South Bass Island is a major departure point for Lake Erie walleye and smallmouth bass fishing.

mainland and around the islands. Local anglers keep tabs on their whereabouts, hoping to learn where they can find a supply of perch fillets for dinner.

Central Basin. The spring and fall yellow perch fishing attracts legions of boat anglers to Lake Erie, and for good reason. The large schools of perch can provide nonstop action, and they're not hard to catch. Using weighted crappie rigs or wire spreaders with long-shanked hooks tipped with lively shiner minnows, anglers can easily find success.

Yellow perch populations have fluctuated over the years, but the bar sided fish are still the second most popular for Lake Erie anglers. When the perch gather in near-shore schools in spring and fall, it's easy to spot the small flotillas of perch boats that have pinned down the largest concentrations of the flavorful fish, a staple of northern Ohio fish fries. These flotillas will be stationed off ports like Lorain, Cleveland, Fairport Harbor, Conneaut, and Ashtabula.

Although some walleye spawn in Central Basin rivers and streams, most spend the spring spawning season on western Lake Erie reefs and up western Ohio rivers. When the spawning season has ended, they head for the deeper, cooler waters of central Lake Erie; there, large schools of walleye thrill anglers from Huron to Conneaut.

Deep-water schools of walleye often suspend along the thermocline in summer, heading to the surface to feed on schools of shiner minnows after dark. Although the schools are often surprisingly large, trolling techniques designed to catch scattered walleye work best. Planer boards, diving planers, and a range of one-line weighting systems are used to take lures to the walleye. Veteran walleye anglers know that techniques must take into account that walleye are exceptionally shy of the sight and sound of fishing boats.

Crankbaits and spoons dominate the choice of trolling lures, although spinner rigs tipped with nightcrawlers and even heavy weight-forward spinners and nightcrawlers will catch many walleye. A good sonar unit is a must, and electronics that measure trolling speed and water temperature can help to fine-tune lure presentation.

As a bonus, walleye anglers can also catch Lake Erie's steelhead. Not as plentiful as the walleye, these trout are often caught on walleye lures, and at the same depths as walleye.

The secret of the Central Basin is its superb smallmouth bass fishery. Generally neglected by anglers more eager for perch or walleye, the near-shore bass fishing can range from good to spectacular, and trophy bass are always a possibility. Lake Erie's Central Basin has a featureless sand, sediment, and clay bottom, offering bass little deep-water structure. Bass flock to the harbor areas, where breakwalls provide bass habitat. Artificial reefs in the Lorain and Cleveland areas are gold mines for bass anglers, as are even the smallest rock humps.

As in the Western Basin, bass are generally easiest to find around structure, but temperature and water clarity dictate the preferred depth. When schools of minnows are suspended, the bass will rise to the occasion.

Northeastern Streams

Steelhead are the glamour fish of Lake Erie tributaries ranging from the Rocky River in Cleveland to Conneaut Creek near the Pennsylvania border. The young trout are stocked each year in the Rocky, Grand, and Chagrin Rivers, and in Conneaut Creek, and head to Lake Erie to feed and grow much larger than stream rainbow trout. In early winter, they head back to the streams where they were stocked, and can be caught there by wading anglers through April.

Both fly and bait anglers target the big trout, which favor the deeper pools and will run many miles up the rivers in a mostly futile effort to spawn. Fly anglers cast with 7- and 8-weight fly rods, and the choice of flies ranges from traditional egg patterns to small nymph imitations, Woolly Buggers, and sucker spawn. The top bait choices are spawn bags, jig-maggot combinations, and minnows worked near the bottom of the deep pools under a float, as well as nightcrawlers weighted to bounce along the rocky stream bottom.

High water conditions after rain and snowmelt lure trout into the rivers. Prime fishing conditions arrive when the water levels decline and the stream flow is lightly stained but not clear.

Ohio River

The Ohio River can be the Buckeye State's most frustrating of bass fishing holes, but it's a grand, old river for channel and flathead catfish and for walleye, sauger, and saugeye, as well as white bass, striped bass, and hybrid stripers. Anglers can also expect to find carp, crappie, bluegills, and smallmouth bass, with a few spotted bass and even muskies tossed in to the fisheries mix of the muddy river.

The distribution of Ohio River fish is curtailed by 19 dams designed to accommodate barge traffic, not populations of fish. The dams have slowed the flow of the Ohio River, creating a series of smaller "pools," much like lakes, and each is a bit different.

The best Ohio River fishing is in the dam tailraces, where gamefish are attracted by large numbers of baitfish in the highly oxygenated water. That's where many of the walleye, sauger, and saugeye are caught, as well as the big hybrid bass, white bass, and stripers.

Anglers commonly cast jigs tipped with plastic tails or minnows, or jigging spoons or blade baits, to the tailrace current. The catch is often surprising; instead of a walleye, a rough and rugged striped bass may test their tackle.

The best largemouth bass fishing occurs in the backwaters of the Ohio River; the creek channels provide suitable spawning habitat, and the snags, stumps, and weedbeds offer the cover fancied by largemouth bass. Bass fishing in the main river usu-

ally begins to warm up in May and June, and can be good throughout the summer if main-channel weedbeds are abundant.

Smallmouth bass prefer to hang around the rock and rubble in the river current. The smallmouth and spotted bass are especially abundant in areas downstream of tailwater areas, and around the heads and tails of the many main-channel islands. Warmwater discharges are bass magnets during the cold weather. Once plentiful in the Ohio River, spotted bass ("Kentuckies") have lost a territorial battle to the hybrid stripers, as well as the smallmouth and largemouth bass.

Reservoirs

Dozens of bass clubs are sprinkled around Ohio, and bass tournaments are held on many of the reservoirs each weekend from spring through fall, although sometimes one wonders why there's such a big effort. The bass fishery on inland lakes isn't much to brag about, as trophy fish are difficult to find.

Not surprisingly, the best bass lakes are those with motor restrictions and those closed to high-powered bass boats. Clendening, Piedmont, Leesville, and Pymatuning all have 10-horsepower motor limits and boast the best bass fishing in Ohio. Bass anglers have discovered that small lures work best in Ohio; tiny 3- and 4-inch plastic worms and small jigs are the mainstays. Summer pleasure boaters crowd the lakes, and bass anglers—while dodging aggravating personal watercraft—have learned to move away from wave- and wake-washed shorelines to probe the deeper waters with crankbaits and Carolina rigged worms.

Ohio has surprisingly good muskie fishing, and trophy muskies are caught each year at Piedmont, Leesville, Clear Fork, Alum Creek, West Branch, and Milton, and at sprawling Pymatuning Lake when it's at its peak. Trolling a big lure is the best way to hook a trophy muskie.

Just as the walleye is king on Lake Erie, so is it on many inland lakes. The best inland walleye waters are Pymatuning, Mosquito, and C. J. Brown Reservoir. Most anglers resort to jig-minnow rigs early in the year, and either drift spinner-crawler combos or minnow-style plugs once summer arrives.

The walleye certainly isn't Ohio's fish of the future, at least not on the state's inland waters. Ohio fisheries experts have turned to the saugeye, a walleye-sauger hybrid, to provide the best fishing. Saugeye will thrive better in dingier, warmer water than will walleye. They'll hit the same lures as walleye and are more likely to bite during the waning days of summer, when walleye prefer deeper waters and are hardest to catch.

Saugeye have become a welcome addition on Ohio fishing waters, from the Ohio River to such inland reservoirs as Alum Creek, Atwood, Beach City, Burr Oak, Caesar Creek, Charles Mill, Clendening, Deer Creek, Dillon, Hoover, Indian Lake, O'Shaughnessy, Paint Creek, Piedmont, Tappan, and Turkeyfoot. Whereas hybrid fish such as saugeye won't spawn, walleye have experienced little spawning success on Ohio's inland lakes.

Central region. Alum Creek Lake is busy with summertime boaters, but this 3,387-acre impoundment has good largemouth bass, crappie, and bluegill fishing. Muskies are making a splash, and saugeye stockings have been a success. Some saugeye are caught in the tailwaters during the cold weather months.

Buckeye Lake is a 3,300-acre lake whose shoreline is crowded with homes and whose waters can be filled with summer skiers. Big hybrid stripers and channel catfish are plentiful. Anglers also catch largemouth bass, bluegills, crappie, and saugeye, and a few focus on the plentiful carp.

Deer Creek Lake spotlights white bass, saugeye, and channel catfish among its 1,277 acres. Its tailwater fishing for saugeye is famous for producing state-record fish.

Delaware Lake covers 1,330 acres and is managed for big crappie. It is also a favorite of weekend recreational boaters from nearby Columbus, and has good fishing for largemouth bass and saugeye.

Hoover Reservoir's 10-horsepower motor limit helps trim the crowds. Fish production at this 3,843-acre Columbus-area lake is hampered by fluctuating water levels. Anglers focus on largemouth bass, crappie, white bass, and saugeye.

Indian Lake, covering 5,800 acres and built in 1852, is large, shallow, and weedy. Largemouth bass are a traditional favorite, and saugeye and channel catfish are plentiful.

Southwestern region. At 2,210-acre C. J. Brown Reservoir, walleye are the top fish. The main lake is at its best in spring, and the tailwaters lure anglers in winter. Channel catfish and crappie are good bets in spring and summer.

Caesar Creek Lake's largemouth bass fishery attracts large numbers of fair weather boaters, and shallow water anglers find fulfillment by dunking small baits for bluegills. Schools of late-summer white bass are an annual attraction at this 2,830-acre lake, and saugeye are fairly plentiful.

Grand Lake St. Marys draws crappie anglers from afar. This sprawling 13,500-acre reservoir is shallow, and channel catfish are easy to find throughout the summer. Ohio's oldest reservoir, built in 1845, it also offers bullhead, yellow perch, and some largemouth bass.

Paint Creek and Rocky Fork Lakes are a stone's throw from one another. Respectively 1,190 and 2,080 acres, they have slightly different complexions. Paint Creek is noted for its saugeye, largemouth bass, crappie, and channel and flathead catfish. Rocky Fork features muskie and channel catfish, with a taste of walleye, largemouth bass, and crappie.

Northwest region. Charles Mill Lake draws springtime anglers for its crappie and saugeye. This shallow, marshy 1,359-acre lake also provides channel and flathead catfish in the summer.

Clear Fork Lake is an excellent muskie reservoir and provides muskie eggs for Ohio stocking programs. The 1,000-acre lake also has good largemouth bass and crappie fishing.

Pleasant Hill Lake's spring crappie and summer saugeye fishing are high points; the tailwaters are a saugeye hotspot winter. Weekend boaters fill the 850-acre lake, which also has good crappie, largemouth and smallmouth bass, and channel catfish populations.

Northeast region. Atwood Lake's saugeye have slowly become the fish of choice. This 1,540-acre lake was once known only for its sailboat races. The good largemouth bass fishing is usually overlooked, and spring anglers can score on crappie.

Berlin Lake's smallmouth bass, crappie, and white bass have long been favorites, making spring a prime time to visit its 3,590 acres. Walleye are caught in good numbers, as are a few muskies.

Clendening Lake is a rural 1,800-acre lake with little shoreline development and numerous largemouth bass. Rated Ohio's best little lake for bass, perhaps due to its 10-horsepower motor limit, Clendening also has good fishing for saugeye.

A stone's throw from Cleveland, LaDue Lake covers 1,500 acres and allows only electric motors. This restriction makes it tougher to cruise the ample shorelines for the big bass that live here. Big channel catfish, some walleye, and little perch are also caught.

Leesville Lake's muskies thrive along its long and narrow 1,000 acres, and catch rates are high. With a 10-horsepower motor limit, the lake is conducive to trolling the extensive weedbeds. The bass fishing is also top-notch, and crappie are a spring treat.

After Milton Lake's dam was renovated, the 1,685-acre lake became known once again for its trophy muskies. This time around, crappie and largemouth bass numbers have improved, and walleye are also present.

Lake Mogadore has fast-growing redear sunfish among its 1,000 acres, where only electric motors can be used. The best fishing is actually for bullhead, but some nice largemouth bass are caught each summer.

Mosquito Lake walleye anglers can get bit by the Mosquito walleye bug, with huge stockings of walleye fry helping to maintain bountiful schools of fish in the face of heavy fishing pressure. Largemouth bass and crappie are also favored, and some northern pike are caught each year.

Pymatuning Lake is Ohio's largest inland lake, if you count Pennsylvania's share of this 14,650-acre border reservoir. With outstanding walleye fishing and lots of crappie, smallmouth bass, and largemouth bass, Pymatuning is protected by a 10-horsepower motor limit. It was once Ohio's best lake for trophy muskies.

Tappan Lake's 2,350-acres experience light fishing pressure, although excellent numbers of channel catfish and good fishing for saugeye and largemouth bass are available.

West Branch Lake's muskie fishing has peaks and valleys, but when it peaks, the muskie catches are spectacular. A few large striped bass are caught here every summer along the dam, and some largemouth bass inhabit the bays and coves and linger along main-lake weedbeds.

Southeastern region. Dillon Lake is a rural 1,330-acre lake that has surprising numbers of channel catfish, largemouth bass, and saugeye.

Piedmont Lake is a clear, 2,270-acre lake with a 10-horsepower motor limit. It has some of Ohio's biggest muskies and owns the state mark for that species. Walleye schools are thinning, whereas saugeye are on the upswing. The good largemouth and smallmouth bass fishing is one of the lake's big secrets. In summer, plenty of channel catfish are caught after the sun goes down.

Salt Fork Lake was known for largemouth and smallmouth bass, but the spotlight has turned to muskies. Walleye and channel catfish are available in good to outstanding numbers.

Seneca Lake has been a mainstay for channel catfish and largemouth bass, and anglers often hook a few walleye on this 3,550-acre lake. Striped bass are a rare treat.

Small Lakes

For big largemouth bass, Knox Lake's 495 acres and 12 miles of shoreline in central Ohio can't be beat, thanks to length limits and a 10-horsepower motor limit. Just north of Lancaster, Rush Lake also features largemouth bass and 10-horsepower motors.

In northeastern Ohio, Highlandtown Lake is managed for trophy bluegills and allows only electric motors. The Portage Lakes around Akron get lots of pressure, with Nimisila Lake's largemouth bass fishing a bonus. Punderson Lake, east of Cleveland, is stocked with trout and plenty of bluegills. Spencer Lake, south of Lorain, has 78 acres of bluegills, bass, and catfish.

Southwestern Ohio's East Fork Lake has 2,160 acres of water and numerous hybrid bass, crappie, channel catfish, and largemouth and spotted bass.

Jackson Lake in southeastern Ohio is a narrow, winding largemouth bass haven, where anglers with electric motors can hook a trophy fish. Nearby Jackson City Reservoir also has lots of largemouth bass, some redear sunfish, and stockings of trout and saugeye. Southeastern Ohio channel catfish waters include small Lake Logan, smaller Monroe Lake, and Lake Rupert, which is also a 325-acre sleeper for bass, bluegills, walleye, and saugeye. Tycoon Lake allows only electric motors and has plenty of bass and catfish.

Kiser Lake, north of Dayton, prohibits all motors on its 396 acres, but anglers catch many bluegills there. The top bluegill fishing hole in Ohio is the Lake La Su An Wildlife Area in northwestern Ohio, near Toledo; permits are needed to fish this series of lakes and ponds, where bluegills grow to surprising size.

One out of five Americans age 16 and older fish and/or hunt in the United States and create a total nationwide economic impact of $106.1 billion.

OKLAHOMA

To those unfamiliar with the Sooner State, Oklahoma is often stereotyped as a dry, desolate landscape of oil wells and flat grassland. The real Oklahoma, though, offers anglers more surface acres of freshwater to fish in than every state in the nation—except its southerly neighbor, Texas—and more miles of shoreline than the Gulf of Mexico and Atlantic coast combined.

Almost 5,000 lakes and a quarter-million farm ponds beckon anglers in this state. All together, Oklahoma offers more than a million acres of fishable water in lakes and ponds. Largemouth bass, reservoir-strain smallmouth bass, and spotted bass all inhabit Oklahoma's many lakes, as do walleye, saugeye, striped bass, hybrid striped bass, channel catfish, blue catfish, flathead catfish, black crappie, white crappie, white bass, and a variety of sunfish species.

Stream fishing opportunities also abound; some 25,000 miles of streams and rivers cross Oklahoma's diverse landscape. Although stream and river fishing are available throughout the state, the eastern half of Oklahoma contains the most popular clear-water streams. These cool flows offer excellent smallmouth bass angling, and two even provide year-round fishing for brown and rainbow trout.

Lake Texoma

Undoubtedly Oklahoma's most productive fishery, Lake Texoma sprawls along the Oklahoma-Texas border, creating an 88,000-acre angling paradise, one that boasts some 300 fishing guides. Nationally recognized as a top inland striped bass location, Texoma's clear waters have supported a self-sustaining striper population that has numbered in the millions for more than 20 years.

Although the lake was built in the early 1940s, it remains particularly productive and fertile, primarily due to naturally occurring salt deposits that flow from the western reaches of the Red River into the lake. The salt binds with clay particles, thereby taking the clay out of suspension and leaving the lake's water clear.

Striped bass get top billing at Lake Texoma. The hottest striper fishing takes place during fall and winter, when large schools of fish actively chase shad. Locating stripers at this time of year is fairly easy; just look for large schools of sea gulls diving into the water. The birds feast on injured shad driven to the surface by voraciously feeding stripers.

Once the fish have been located, catching them usually isn't hard. Slab spoons—1- to 3-ounce chunks of lead with a hook attached—are lowered into the depths and pulled in an upward motion. Crankbaits and soft-bodied paddle-tailed jigs are also effective.

The most reliable fishing occurs during the summer months, when stripers are taken in most parts of the lake using a vast array of tactics. Trolling is a common technique, and flatline trolling with crankbaits and plugs regularly takes large numbers of fish holding in 10 to 30 feet of water. Downriggers are used to catch stripers that suspend in deep water off points and creek channels.

A striped bass is landed on Lake Texoma.

Summer also offers the most exciting topwater action of the year, when stripers often break the surface, particularly on calm days. Popping plugs are local favorites, but anything that splashes on the surface is apt to draw a bone-jarring strike.

Live shad are particularly effective baits, regardless of season. Many anglers use a cast net to catch shad for baits, but it can be difficult to locate shad at times. Special holding tanks are required to keep these baitfish lively.

Texoma stripers typically run between 12 and 22 inches, although fish up to 15 pounds are not uncommon. Trophy fishing opportunities are available in the Red River, immediately below the dam. During periods of heavy water releases, stripers up to 40 pounds move up below the dam to feed on stunned baitfish that have gone through the dam's turbines. Free-lining live baits is an effective tactic, but many large fish are caught on jigs and topwater plugs.

While Texoma's great striper fishing draws the most attention from anglers, excellent smallmouth bass fishing is also available. The lake produced three straight state-record smallmouths, and fish in the 5- to 7-pound class are not out of the question.

February through March are prime months for catching big smallmouths, although good action also can be had from late spring through early summer. Smallmouths congregate on the lake's many rocky points, and the top fishing locations offer deep water close to shore.

Jigs tipped with either soft-bodied crayfish or pork chunks are excellent smallmouth producers. Spinnerbaits and crankbaits are also good bait choices. Because of the lake's relatively clear water, light line (4- to 8-pound test) is recommended.

Catfish anglers also call Texoma one of the state's best. Blue and channel catfish are numerous here, and anglers employ diverse tactics to land them. Drifting with live or cut shad, a method favored by striper anglers, is dynamite for catching both channels and blues. Drift anglers usually concentrate on flats—the mid-depth areas between the shoreline and deeper creek channels. Platter Flats, Willafa Wood, and Willow Springs are favorite areas to drift for catfish.

For those who prefer a more relaxed style of fishing, Texoma offers excellent jug fishing and trotlining. A state-record 116-pound blue catfish was taken at Texoma by a jug angler, and trotliners usually report heavy catches for both channel and blue catfish. Cut or whole shad are standard bait choices for channels, whereas anglers concentrating on blue catfish favor live shad or live sunfish.

Texoma is also known for good crappie and largemouth bass fishing. Crappie enter shallow water to spawn in late March and early April. Anglers who dabble small jigs or soak live minnows in and around shoreline cover do well then. Largemouth anglers do well fishing in and around flooded cover in spring. Spinnerbaits, jigs, and plastic worms are productive lures.

Lake Eufaula

Often called Oklahoma's gentle giant, Lake Eufaula covers more than 105,000 acres of the state's east-central landscape. A relatively shallow, murky water lake, Eufaula offers a little of everything in the way of fishing opportunities.

Known throughout the state for its excellent springtime crappie fishing, Eufaula each year produces hundreds of catches of slab-size crappie weighing between 2 and 3 pounds each. Crappie action usually heats up first on the southern portion of the lake, and the fishing peaks in April. As the lake warms, fishing in the northern half of the lake improves, usually a few weeks after it turns on in the southern half.

Wading and fishing from float tubes or belly boats are two of the most common tactics at Eufaula. Although much of the lake's standing timber has disappeared, enough woody cover remains to provide constant targets for spring crappie anglers. Cane pole fishing with either live minnows or crappie jigs is a local tradition, one that's hard to beat. Regardless what equipment is used, anglers who concentrate on timber in 2 to 5 feet of water consistently report the best catches.

Eufaula is also a top catfishing destination. Trotline users and jug anglers do well from spring through fall, and drifting is a popular technique during the winter months. Those using trotlines usually concentrate on coves, whereas jug users usually target flats in 10 to 20 feet of water and main-lake points. Whole or cut shad are popular bait choices for both trotlines and juglines.

Drift fishing with live or cut shad is particularly productive during the dead of winter. Deeper water in the main body of the lake yields the best wintertime catches. Old creek channels and flats near creek channels are top midlake areas.

Another popular catfishing technique involves probing nooks and crannies along riprap during the early-summer spawning period. Catfish are cavity nesters that make spawning nests in rocks in shallow water. Big cats are extremely territorial, so dropping a bait in front of them is sure to draw a voracious strike. Shrimp, shad, live sunfish, and nightcrawlers are standard baits for catching spawning catfish.

In summer, Eufaula produces good white bass action. Large schools of sand bass, or sandies as they are called locally, can be seen surfacing from July through September. The fish are actually chasing shad, and any lure thrown in the middle of the slashing, splashing melee will usually result in an immediate strike. In-line spinners, slab spoons, topwater plugs, and crankbaits are all productive for catching sand bass from surfacing schools. Once the fish retreat to deeper water, surface activity decreases, and then trolling with crankbaits becomes productive.

The lake is also home to a rapidly developing smallmouth bass fishery. First stocked in the early 1990s, smallmouth bass took hold in the lake's rocky, clear-water areas, and natural spawning has been documented. Porum Landing and the Number Nine area are the best spots for smallmouth fishing, and plastic crayfish, jig-and-pork combos, and crankbaits are favored offerings.

Eufaula also has good largemouth bass fishing, and the lake holds some walleye. Largemouth bass anglers often concentrate on woody cover and flooded bushes, particularly in the spring and early summer. Main-lake points and dropoffs are good areas for largemouth later in the year. Walleye hold in some of the same places as smallmouth bass. Live worms and minnows fished on jigs are good walleye fare, as is an assortment of crankbaits.

Northeast

Grand Lake O' the Cherokees. One of Oklahoma's crown jewels, Grand Lake offers 46,500 acres of diverse fishing opportunities. More than 10,000 square miles of Ozark Mountain foothills drains into Grand Lake, and the Neosho and Spring Rivers provide significant inflows at the lake's north end. Largemouth bass, spotted bass, crappie, and white bass are abundant at Grand Lake, which is known not only for producing large numbers of fish, but also for yielding many trophy bass and crappie each year.

Spring (April through June) finds both bass and crappie in shallower water. Bass anglers do well fishing with spinnerbaits, jigs, and topwater lures at this time. Flooded willow bushes, grass, and timber are top springtime bass-holding locations, and these areas also attract spawning crappie.

The lake is widely known for excellent nighttime bass fishing during the heat of summer. July

and August are top months for night fishing. Plastic worms, spinnerbaits, and surface lures are top local offerings. Boat docks, which are plentiful on the big lake, provide excellent structure during the summer.

Live minnows and small jigs are tops for springtime crappie fishing. Specimens up to 3 pounds are reported each spring, but fish in the 10- to 14-inch range are most common. Winter angling for crappie is also popular at Grand Lake, where heated fishing docks draw many anglers from December through February.

The Neosho River above Grand Lake is home to a nationally famous paddlefish run each April. Fish up to 140 pounds have been taken during the spawning season. Grand Lake also contains good populations of catfish, walleye, and white bass.

Sooner Lake. This unique lake is home to a power-generating station that keeps the lake's waters relatively warm year-round. During winter, warmwater discharges concentrate baitfish, and large numbers of largemouth bass and hybrid striped bass enter the discharge canal to feed heavily. Trophy hybrids in the 12- to 15-pound range are a real possibility at Sooner Lake, especially during December and January.

Live minnows, topwater plugs, and large jigs catch both largemouth bass and hybrid striped bass here. In addition to fishing the discharge area, local experts ply deep-water areas near the dam, and underwater islands in the main lake.

Sooner also produces good action for crappie, white bass, and catfish, although these species are not as popular as largemouths and hybrid stripers.

Lake Tenkiller. A deep, clear-water impoundment, Lake Tenkiller offers fishing for all three types of black bass species: largemouth, smallmouth, and spotted bass. Largemouth and spotted bass are far more common than smallmouth bass, and nighttime fishing is often necessary during the summer months due to the lake's extremely clear water. Boat docks, deep-water points, and rocky structure are key black bass locations.

Although not widely known, Tenkiller offers good sunfishing, particularly for bluegills. May and June are top months for catching spawning panfish, with live worms, crickets, and small jigs among the top bait choices. White bass are also abundant at Tenkiller. Trolling small crankbaits and casting small spinners to surfacing schools are two popular techniques.

Below the lake's dam, the lower Illinois River offers year-round rainbow and trophy brown trout fishing. Almost eight miles of trout stream are found below Tenkiller, and wintertime and early spring are most productive for trout anglers. Artificial and prepared trout baits like salmon eggs are popular with anglers, as are small spinners and spoons. Light line (2- through 6-pound test) is recommended for these finicky fish.

The section of the lower Illinois that contains trout, and the 2 miles of river below the trout area, is widely regarded as the state's number one trophy striped bass resource. Anglers have landed stripers nearing the 50-pound mark, and numerous 20- and 30-pounders are taken from this coldwater fishery each year.

Summer is the best time to pursue these tackle-busting monsters. The cold water of the lower Illinois River is a refuge for big stripers, drawing fish from the Arkansas River and Robert S. Kerr Lake. Both live bait fishing and casting artificials are productive, but drifting, trolling, or anchoring and then fishing with live shad or trout is by far the best technique. Standard bass tackle can be used, but strong line in the 15- to 25-pound class is a must.

Northwest
Canton Lake. One of Oklahoma's premier fishing destinations, Canton is a walleye mecca, both in total numbers of fish caught and numbers of trophy fish (6 to 10 pounds) taken. Spring and summer find Canton's walleye most cooperative; April through June are excellent months, and anglers employ a variety of fishing methods.

Trolling is a popular technique for covering large expanses of water to locate active fish. Mid-diving crankbaits are good lure choices. Drifting with bottom rigs, weight-forward spinners, and live bait also yields good results. Weedy bays provide good cover and forage for walleye, but fish also congregate on midlake underwater islands and creek channels.

Although walleye are Canton's claim to fame, the lake also hosts incredibly hard-fighting hybrid striped bass. Anglers can catch hybrids by using the same techniques as those employed to catch walleye, and hybrids are even found in many of the same locations as walleye. In addition, hybrid striped bass tend to school around the many small islands along the lake's northwestern shore. Drifting and trolling live sunfish, crayfish, or large minnows are good tactics for catching big hybrids in the 5- to 15-pound range.

White bass and crappie are frequently taken incidentally when anglers troll crankbaits or drift live minnows. Both species are quite common at Canton, but angling pressure is focused on walleye and hybrid striped bass.

Lake Carl Etling. Located in Black Mesa State Park in Cimarron County in the Oklahoma panhandle, Lake Carl Etling offers incredible angling diversity in its 160 acres. Walleye, hybrid striped bass, and white bass are key species of interest. Rainbow trout fishing is available in the winter months (November through April).

Both bank and boat fishing opportunities are available, and excellent primitive camping facilities are located within the state park. Live minnows and worms are good choices for trout, walleye, and hybrid striped bass. Crankbaits and stickbaits are effective for walleye and hybrids, and they will also produce white bass.

It has been calculated that a stream trout can swim up to 102 inches per second, but you shouldn't try to fish a lure or fly at anything approaching that speed.

Great Salt Plains Lake. Characterized as a shallow, windswept lake, Great Salt Plains offers good fishing for saugeye and channel catfish. Saugeye anglers mainly rely on shallow-running crankbaits and jigs tipped with minnows or nightcrawlers. The spillway, located below the dam, is a great spot for these tasty fish.

Top catfishing techniques include jug fishing and trotlining. Whole, cut, or fresh shad are top baits for these activities. For those who prefer drifting, dragging nightcrawlers or stinkbait on the bottom is a popular technique.

In addition to catfish and saugeye, the lake also offers fishing for hybrid striped bass and white bass. Jigs, crankbaits, and spinners are recommended for catching these species.

Southwest

Altus Lugert Reservoir. At 6,200 acres, Altus Lugert is one of southwest Oklahoma's bigger lakes. Walleye, hybrid striped bass, white bass, and largemouth bass are all abundant at Altus Lugert.

Anglers regularly have excellent success fishing the east side of the lake when the wind has been blowing from the west, and their results speak loudly. State-record hybrid striped bass and walleye both were taken by anglers fishing from the bank at Altus Lugert.

Midlake humps and underwater islands are key locations for those fishing from boats. Trolling is an excellent method for locating these structures. Once identified, vertical jigging and live bait fishing can be employed to fish these areas.

Summer action for white bass and hybrid striped bass is good, whereas walleye bite best from fall through spring. The top seasons for catfish are spring and fall. Jug fishing and trotlining opportunities are good, but catfish are also taken from the bank with live baits or stinkbaits.

The North Fork of the Red River, located below the dam, offers rainbow trout fishing during the winter months (November through March). Prepared baits, small jigs, and in-line spinners are standard trout fare.

Ft. Cobb Reservoir. Known as an excellent lake for bowfishing, Ft. Cobb also offers good opportunities for white bass, largemouth bass, walleye, catfish, and hybrid striped bass. Running primarily north and south, Ft. Cobb offers white bass, walleye, and hybrid anglers a wide variety of potential hotspots from late April through June. Trolling around points is a popular approach to catching fish, as is casting or drifting live baits around the large island on the lake's west side.

A common method for catching various species at Ft. Cobb is to cast from the dam, located on the lake's south end. After successive days with a north wind, baitfish will be pushed toward the dam, with hungry white bass, walleye, and hybrid striped bass following closely along behind. Soft-bodied fish-imitating jigs are extremely effective, but heavier jigs are usually necessary for long casts out from the dam.

Catfish anglers find that a variety of tactics work at Ft. Cobb, including bank fishing, trotlining, and jug fishing. For largemouth bass, May and June are good months, and plastic worms, topwater lures, and spinnerbaits usually produce good results.

Southeast

Konawa Lake. Known for its high fertility and productivity, Konawa is a premier trophy largemouth bass lake that is affected by a power plant. Due to warmwater discharges, December, January, and February are the best months to fish here. Plastic worms and lizards, crankbaits, jigs, and live minnows are effective baits on Konawa.

Hybrid striped bass and white bass also thrive in good numbers on this lake. Trolling and casting crankbaits or spoons are effective approaches to catching these species. Riprap along the dam, the discharge canal, and main-lake submerged roadbeds are prime fishing locations.

McGee Creek Reservoir. Situated in the scenic mountains of southeast Oklahoma, McGee Creek is an excellent bass lake, although naturally high levels of mercury have caused consumption advisories to be placed on larger bass. Bigger fish are generally taken in March and April, but summer produces the fastest action from surfacing schools of bass in the 1- to 3-pound class.

McGee Creek also contains good populations of spotted bass, and smallmouths have been introduced. The lake offers good channel catfishing, and crappie cause excitement during the spring spawning season (April and May).

Murray Lake. A deeper, clear-water lake, Murray is an exceptional smallmouth bass fishery. It contains good populations of largemouth bass as well, offering fish weighing up to $13^1/_2$ pounds. April through June is prime for black bass action. Rocky shorelines and submerged timber attract bass during spring. Soft-plastic baits, spinnerbaits, and jigs are standard bass catchers.

Murray offers good catfishing, too. Because of its clear water, drifting live bait is a good way to catch channel cats at Murray; live minnows, cut baits, and nightcrawlers work well for this.

White bass and crappie are in abundance at Murray, although bass and catfish are the primary angling targets.

Oklahoma City—Metro Area

Thunderbird. A murky water lake close to the Oklahoma City metropolitan area, Thunderbird happens to be one of the most productive reservoirs in Oklahoma. It hosts an outstanding saugeye fishery, with good numbers of large saugeye (3 to 6 pounds) taken each year. Live minnows, jigs tipped with minnows or nightcrawlers, and crankbaits are good saugeye medicine.

Winter is the best time to fish for this species, and fall and early spring also offer good angling.

Main-lake points, sunken brush rows, and dropoffs are ideal places to prospect for saugeye.

Excellent channel and flathead catfish are another mainstay at Thunderbird. The lake favors trotlines and juglines, but many catfish are caught each year by bank anglers.

Crappie populations are high, with late April through early June being most conducive to catching large numbers of shallow-water crappie. Flooded brush, sunken brushpiles, and shallow coves usually contain spawning crappie during these times. Small tube jigs and live minnows are local favorites for these panfish.

Rivers

Arkansas River. From Kaw Lake to Webbers Falls Reservoir, the Arkansas River offers multiple angling opportunities ranging from striped bass fishing to limblining for catfish. The river is subject to varying flows depending on rainfall and lake releases. Anglers achieve the best success by searching for deeper pools filled with submerged rocks and timber.

Live minnows will take a variety of species, including flathead catfish, striped bass, white bass, and largemouth bass. Live worms and cut shad are good choices for channel catfish.

Because access to the river is mostly over private land, anglers must gain permission to fish from the banks. Boat anglers can travel the river by putting in at boat ramps scattered along the river.

Lower Mountain Fork River. Towering pines and submerged bald cypress trees mix along the lower Mountain Fork River to form spectacular scenery. Running from Broken Bow Lake to the Little River, the lower Mountain Fork is most noted for year-round rainbow and brown trout fishing.

Opportunities exist for both fast action and trophy specimens. Catfish and largemouth bass inhabit some stretches of the river, and white bass are available during the spring spawning season.

OLIGOTROPHIC

Low nutrient levels; an absence of nutrients. An oligotrophic lake is one that is young and deep-sided, with clear waters and a rocky or sandy bottom. It is usually located in areas where the surrounding substrate is rocky and where soils are limited and generally infertile. Both planktonic and rooted plant growth are sparse; thermal stratification is usually pronounced in the summer, and there is abundant oxygen at deeper levels. Oligotrophic lakes support such coldwater fisheries as trout, salmon, charr, and cisco.

See: Eutrophic; Mesotrophic.

ONSHORE

Waters abutting a coastline. This word is also used synonymously with ashore, meaning physically on the land adjacent to water, but is even more specific than nearshore (see). It is not the opposite of offshore (see) in common angling usage.

ONTARIO

Few localities in the world can match Ontario, Canada's second largest province, in diversity and quality of freshwater fisheries. About one-sixth of Ontario's 413,000 square miles is water, including 34,000 square miles alone in its share of four of the Great Lakes. In a typical year, Ontario caters to roughly 2.5 million anglers of all ages, including residents and nonresidents, and its angling opportunities are unlimited.

Ontario has 250,000 lakes and countless waterways spread over distances of 1,050 miles from east to west, and 1,075 miles from south to north—an area almost the size of Texas and California combined. Fishing destinations vary in size from 350-mile-long Lake Superior, which demands the sturdiest of boats; to peaceful cottage lakes that can be fished by canoe; to powerful rivers such as the Niagara, St. Lawrence, and Ottawa, which challenge even the most experienced anglers; to small trout streams that can be crossed in chest waders.

Ontario's fishing country is as varied as the many species found within its boundaries. Southern areas bordering the Great Lakes are characterized by extensive agricultural lands and urban development. The heavily forested, rocky terrain of the Canadian Shield spans the middle of the province, an area that has become prime cottage country and a scenic fishing haven. To the north, the flat bogs, small spruce, aspen, poplar, birch, and balsam fir trees, and complex river systems of the Hudson Bay Lowlands beckon anglers seeking true wilderness adventure.

Of the 158 species of fish found in the province, about two dozen are of special interest to anglers. Walleye (known as pickerel here), yellow perch, lake trout, brook trout, steelhead, rainbow trout, brown trout, smallmouth bass, northern pike, muskellunge, largemouth bass, coho salmon, and chinook salmon are the predominant fish, although trout, pike, perch, and walleye probably draw the most attention province-wide.

Southwest Ontario

Lake Erie. Lake Erie, once proclaimed a virtually dead fishery because of pollution, has made a remarkable comeback. Although it is the shallowest of the Great Lakes with an average depth of 62 feet, Lake Erie supports a variety of both warm- and coldwater species.

In a typical year, data from the Ministry of Natural Resources (MNR) show that more than a half million sportfish are caught in Ontario's 4,783 square miles of the lake (the equivalent of 48 percent of the lake's total area). Walleye, smallmouth bass, yellow perch, and freshwater drum make up 70 percent of the catch. Unlike anglers from bordering states, Ontario anglers share the fisheries resource with commercial interests, which account for an additional 20 to 40 million pounds of various species, nearly half of which are rainbow smelt.

The prime sportfishing target is walleye, which average 5 to 7 pounds, but 9- to 12-pounders are not uncommon. In western Lake Erie—from Holiday Beach, near the mouth of the Detroit River, eastward to Leamington—in May and early June, walleye are taken by anglers trolling, drift fishing, or casting weight-forward spinners armed with a minnow or worm. As summer progresses, the fish move toward the deeper middle and eastern sections of the lake.

Pelee Island, 14 miles off Kingsville, is an early season walleye favorite. It is also a prime spot for smallmouth bass, some up to 4 pounds, which hang out over rock, rubble, and gravel bottoms. The best smallmouth opportunities are in late June, September, and October; in midsummer they often suspend in deeper waters. Anglers in large boats can make the run across the open lake to the island; those with smaller craft cross on the ferry.

Walleye and yellow perch are favorite catches from piers and near shore in the central and western parts of Lake Erie in May and June. As the water warms in July and August, anglers may have to venture out 10 miles or more to 100-foot depths to find walleye that suspend while feeding on baitfish; departure points for this trip include Port Burwell, Port Dover, Port Maintland, and Port Colbourne.

Zebra mussels have made the pursuit of walleye throughout Lake Erie somewhat more difficult by dramatically increasing the water clarity. Anglers have been forced to travel farther and farther offshore as the walleye move deeper to find their preferred light levels. The long-term impact of these exotic bivalves on fish populations and on fish size is uncertain.

Steelhead, Pacific salmon, and lake trout are also popular in Lake Erie. In the spring, steelhead ascend the creeks and small streams that notch the clay bluffs so predominant along Ontario's Lake Erie shoreline, but receive less attention from anglers than they do in Lake Ontario or Lake Huron because of the primary interest in walleye and yellow perch. The most significant runs are in the eastern portion of the lake on Big Otter Creek at Port Burwell, Big Creek at Long Point, and Young Creek near Simcoe. In the summer, these fish roam the deeper portions of the lake and return to near-shore waters in the fall for pre-spawn staging.

Angling for salmon and trout in July and August calls for locating fish and trolling minnow-imitating plugs and spoons via downriggers, sideplaners, and flatlines. From late August into the fall, salmon move closer to shore off the mouths of the numerous larger creeks found along the central and western portions of the lake from Erie to the Niagara River.

The inner bay at Long Point, bordered by the Big Creek and Turkey Point marshes, provides the best inshore fishery along the lake. The shallow, weedy waters are a haven for walleye, smallmouth bass, largemouth bass, northern pike, sheepshead, and a variety of panfish (yellow perch, crappie, and catfish). Within sight to the east is the Nanticoke Generating Station, which attracts the largest spring run of white bass along Erie's north shore.

The fast currents at the mouth of the Niagara River at Fort Erie hold ample feed for a mixed bag of sportfish and keep the water ice free so keen anglers can fish most of the year. Depending on the season, catches from shore or from small boats in the vicinity of the Peace Bridge can include walleye, smallmouth bass, yellow perch, rainbow trout, brown trout, chinook salmon, and coho salmon.

Grand River. The Grand River at Port Maintland is the only significant river on Lake Erie's north coast. The 175-mile-long Grand flows through southern Ontario's heartland of farms, cities, marshes, Carolinian forest, deep valleys, and cliffs. It is the first nonwilderness river to be designated as a Canadian Heritage River and has an excellent fishery to match.

Walleye, rainbow trout, and white bass run as far as 20 miles upstream to the Caledonia Dam during spring spawning. Largemouth and smallmouth bass, northern pike, and panfish are also found throughout the river below Kitchener. There are 15 miles of classic brown trout water on the Grand's upper reaches between Inverhaugh and Belwood Lake. Browns here, which average 15 to 22 inches but can reach 30 inches, are a delight for fly anglers, and special regulations have been adopted to promote catch-and-release.

Lake St. Clair. Ontario possesses two-thirds of heart-shaped Lake St. Clair, which measures 35 miles by 26 miles and has an average depth of 11 feet. It remains a productive and important recreational fishery despite significant ecological changes over recent decades. These were caused by such things as chemical pollution, population explosions of white perch and gobies, and the appearance of zebra mussels.

The clearer water caused by the filtering action of the zebras has resulted in expansive areas of new weed growth that have befuddled walleye anglers using traditional methods. But sight feeders, such as smallmouth bass, yellow perch, and muskellunge, seem to have benefited from the improved visibility.

In May, anglers intercept post-spawn walleye moving away from the Thames and Ruscom Rivers along the southern shore. As the water warms, anglers have to adapt to fishing in the weeds or go 3 or 4 miles offshore to find clear bottoms for trolling crankbaits or drifting live baits.

Mitchell's Bay is a top panfish and smallmouth bass area, with plentiful largemouth bass in and around the 63 square miles of the Walpole Island marshes. A special license is available from the

 Placoderms, which were primitive jawed fishes existing 420–355 million years ago, were generally torpedo shaped with bony plates that formed head and trunk shields.

native community to fish the island's maze of channels and backwaters.

Lake St. Clair has a strong muskellunge population, which benefits from abundant forage found in the vast shallows and from a relatively long growing season. Trolling spoons and large plugs in 12 to 15 feet of water from late September to November is the best tactic for boating fish that average 15 to 20 pounds but could reach 30 pounds. Muskies inhabit the southern shore from the Thames River westward to Belle Island at the mouth of the Detroit River, and range to the northeast in Mitchell's Bay and St. Luke's Bay.

The seasonal walleye patterns in the nearby Detroit and St. Clair Rivers are somewhat similar. This includes a spring run of migrating mature fish returning to Lake Erie or Lake Huron after spawning in the Thames River, and a resident summer population of smaller fish. Clear water and heavy boat traffic call for trolling near bottom with minnow-imitating plugs at night.

Steelhead, brown trout, and chinook and coho salmon are also in the St. Clair River in the spring, from the warmwater discharge at the Port Lambton Power Plant north to Sarnia.

Lower Lake Huron. In spring and early summer, steelhead and chinook salmon are the predominant fish along the sandy shores of lower Lake Huron, from Sarnia north to Southampton. Steelhead have been in Lake Huron since 1904, having been introduced by the U.S. Fish Commission in Lake Superior in 1895. Annual stocking supplements natural reproduction in such rivers as the Maintland, Bayfield, Lucknow, Sauble, and Saugeen. Chinook, first planted in Lake Huron by Michigan in the late 1960s and later by the MNR and volunteer fishing clubs, have been the catalyst for popular salmon derbies along lower Lake Huron and southern Georgian Bay.

The Saugeen River at Southampton is one of Ontario's best-known steelhead waters. Here, anglers can wade and drift spawn bags in the fast water below the Denny's Dam lamprey control barrier, or troll from small boats downstream for 3 miles to Lake Huron. Steelhead enter the river in April and May and again in October and November. In summer, walleye, channel catfish, and stray Skamania-strain steelies from Michigan plantings attract anglers who don't have the boats or equipment to pursue salmon and trout in the deep offshore waters. In the fall, chinook and brown trout add variety to river fishing.

Above Denny's Dam, rainbow and chinook move upstream as far as 30 miles to Paisley and Walkerton in the spring and fall, respectively. The Upper Saugeen, as it twists and bends through farmland, also holds resident smallmouth bass, northern pike, and muskellunge.

Bruce Peninsula and Southern Georgian Bay. Virtually all of the agricultural watersheds along the southern shore of Georgian Bay support migratory steelhead populations. Heavy stocking has created opportunities for chinook, brown trout, lake trout, and splake offshore.

The city of Owen Sound is a focal point for fishing the nearby Georgian Bay waters of Owen Sound, Colpoys Bay to the north, and the numerous nearby rivers that flow into Georgian Bay to the east. These include such legendary steelhead waters as the Pottawatomi and Sydenham Rivers at Owen Sound, the Bighead River at Meaford (with 80 miles of fishing), the Beaver at Thornbury, and the Nottawasaga at Wasaga Beach.

The Nottawasaga—along with such tributaries as the Pine, Boyle, and Mad—is the largest river system flowing into Georgian Bay and has more than 400 miles of pools and riffles open to steelhead. A 29-pound, 2-ounce Ontario record steelhead was caught off its mouth. Although best known for rainbow and walleye, the Nottawasaga also harbors browns, chinook, northern pike, smallmouth and largemouth bass, and a variety of coarse fish.

Although whitefish are often thought of as a commercial species, Colpoys Bay near Wiarton has produced some whoppers for recreational anglers over the years. In 1996, the Ontario record of 14 pounds, 12 ounces was caught in the bay through the ice.

An angler fishes the shoreline of a Georgian Bay fjord for smallmouth bass.

South-Central Ontario

Niagara River. The mighty 27-mile-long Niagara

River is best known as the site of the famous Niagara Falls and as a place for honeymooners and daredevils, but with all of Lake Erie's water—with the exception of what flows through the Welland Canal, exiting here and entering Lake Ontario—there is much to attract a smorgasbord of species.

The Upper Niagara River from Fort Erie to Grand Island has smallmouth bass and walleye throughout the summer, and the channels in and around the smaller islands offer good trolling opportunities for muskellunge. The muskellunge fishery is unheralded but highly commendable. This is a clear-water trolling fishery that produces 25- to 40-pound fish for dedicated anglers.

Steelhead and brown trout, and the occasional salmon, move into the upper river from Lake Erie in the fall. Ontario's long-standing and somewhat controversial 22-pound, 4-ounce record walleye came from the Fort Erie end of the Niagara River in 1943.

The Lower Niagara River (that section below Niagara Falls) is not for the faint-hearted or ill-prepared. It can be dangerous water, with daily fluctuations in levels caused by upstream power-generating stations. Fishing by boat is possible from Niagara-on-the-Lake up about 8 miles to the Devil's Hole pool near Queenston, although the upper reaches are turbulent and demand sturdy craft and capable boat handling.

Anglers on foot have access to the swirling water in the river's pools from the Niagara River Parkway. Above Queenston, this means a long hike down steep man-made trails carved into the rugged Niagara Gorge.

In winter and throughout spring, steelhead move into the Lower Niagara from Lake Ontario and are found as far upstream as the Niagara Whirlpool. Anglers land lake trout at the mouth of the river in early spring. In summer, yellow perch, silver bass, walleye, and smallmouth bass are the predominant catches for both boat and shore anglers from Niagara-on-the-Lake to the vicinity of Queenston. Walleye are plentiful here, including some in the 6- to 8-pound class, as are smallmouth bass. From August through October, chinook salmon are the main attraction, but coho, lake trout, and browns are available as well.

Western and central Lake Ontario. The recreational and economic spinoffs of massive plantings of salmon and trout have benefited the heavily populated northern side of 193-mile-long Lake Ontario more than any of the province's other waters on the Great Lakes. Although stocking levels have fluctuated, especially through the 1990s, and the species mix has varied, salmon and trout continue to be important and prominent in this region. Introduced species of chinook salmon, coho salmon, and steelhead are especially popular; and the native lake trout are not only popular, they are also being revitalized. Biologists have planted Atlantic salmon, once native to Lake Ontario, in an effort to reestablish this species with a self-sustaining population, but they are so far largely incidental to the other fish. Nevertheless, specimens to 24 pounds have been recorded.

The earliest salmonid angling action occurs in the western end of Lake Ontario in late April and May from the mouth of the Niagara River west to St. Catharines and Burlington primarily from downrigger- and sideplaner-equipped boats out of such places as Niagara-on-the-Lake, Port Weller, Port Dalhousie, and Grimsby. Coho, chinook, steelhead, brown trout, and lake trout are likely catches.

As the water warms, salmon move deeper, swinging eastward and south into New York waters. Later in the summer they migrate back to the central and eastern portions of the north shore, where trollers intercept them at such places as Bowmanville, Brighton, and Wellington.

From September into November, chinook and coho school off the mouths of most Lake Ontario rivers, especially in the western end, where they are within reach of small-craft trollers and casters on piers and breakwalls. Ontario's 45-pound, 6-ounce record chinook was caught from the Credit River at Oakville in 1980, and the 26-pound, 10-ounce coho record came from nearby Lake Ontario off Bronte in 1987. Lake Ontario also produced the provincial brown trout record in 1994, a 34-pound colossus. Huge browns, some in the 15- to 20-pound class, are a possibility for shallow trollers in the spring, and for deep anglers in the summer. Cohos are normally caught in the 4- to 8-pound range, whereas chinook run the gamut, with most heavyweights taken in late summer and fall.

In 1994, a 39-pound lake trout was caught off the mouth of the Niagara River. Lakers are abundant here but are not as popular in this part of the lake as salmon and steelhead. In contrast, lake trout are the bread-and-butter fish for anglers at the Kingston end of Lake Ontario, especially around Main Duck Island, because migrating salmon are outside the reach of all but the largest boats.

In summer, shallow-cruising steelhead are often caught in offshore Lake Ontario waters as a bonus for salmon anglers, but the spring and fall fisheries off the mouths of rivers and streams are more popular.

The Credit River is the best steelhead water west of Toronto, with lesser runs in Bronte Creek and the Humber River. The best-known steelhead hotspot to the east is the Ganaraska River at Port Hope. Other area creeks noted for substantial spring and fall steelhead are Duffins, Sopers, Wilmot, and Shelter Valley.

Lake Simcoe. An hour's drive north of Toronto, Lake Simcoe is the fourth largest inland lake in the province and one of Ontario's most important year-round recreational fisheries, providing a million hours of angling throughout an average year. A surprisingly rich and diverse fishery has been maintained in this 287-square-mile lake, despite heavy development and angling pressures.

Simcoe made its reputation from lake trout and whitefish, but native strains have seriously declined since the 1970s; populations are now maintained by heavy annual stockings. Typical lake trout range from 3 to 6 pounds, but fish up to 20 pounds are always a possibility. Whitefish in the 10-pound category are now rare, but hatchery-raised specimens average a respectable 2 to 4 pounds. Smelt appeared in Lake Simcoe in 1962 and are thought to be an additional detriment to both trout and whitefish.

Lake Simcoe's present water quality favors yellow perch, smallmouth bass, and other warm- or coolwater species. Anglers target perch, especially in April and May, at the Atherley Narrows between Lakes Simcoe and Couchiching, at Cook's Bay, and from public wharves and private docks around the lake. Perch up to 2 pounds have come from Simcoe; this is large by Ontario standards, but the average is under 10 inches. Black crappie appeared in significant numbers in Lake Simcoe and adjacent Lake Couchiching in the mid-1990s.

During the summer months, smallmouth bass move to the shoals, reefs, and weedbeds along the eastern side at Brechin, Beaverton, and Big Bay Points, and around such islands as Thorah, Georgina, and Snake.

Lake Simcoe has walleye over 10 pounds, but the fish are difficult to locate in summer. The best opportunities are in mid-May, when post-spawn fish drop back into the lake from the mouth of the Talbot River, a major spawning area, and head out to Thorah and Georgian Islands. Other opportunities exist in the south end in Cook's Bay off the Holland and Jersey Rivers. The shallow waters of Cook's Bay, however, primarily favor largemouth bass, northern pike, muskies, and panfish.

Lake Simcoe has been dubbed the "Ice Fishing Capital of the World." It supports more than 4,000 registered huts—both commercial rentals and privately owned structures—and hosts 6,000 to 10,000 anglers on a good February weekend. Yellow perch are the most common catch, followed by lake trout, whitefish, and herring. Popular jumping-off spots for winter fishing include Georgina, Big Bay Point, Jackson's Point, and Beaverton.

Trent-Severn System and the Kawarthas. The Trent-Severn Waterway, which winds for 230 miles through the heart of central southern Ontario, linking Lake Ontario to Lake Huron's Georgian Bay, is one of Ontario's busiest recreational playgrounds for boaters and anglers alike. Its 15 major natural and man-made lakes, connected by an intricate network of canals and locks, provide excellent shallow-water habitat for walleye, bass, muskies, yellow perch, rock bass, bluegills, crappie, and bullhead.

Anglers land walleye around many of the dams and locks throughout the system in the spring and fall, and in the interconnecting rivers and lakes in the summer. Pigeon is considered the best lake for walleye, followed by Rice, Clear, Stony, Lovesick, Buckhorn, Chemung, Sturgeon, and Balsam Lakes. A typical walleye weighs 2 pounds, but trophies up to 10 pounds are not unheard of.

Largemouth and smallmouth bass range throughout the system in varying abundance. Buckhorn is a top lake for both varieties, Pigeon and Stony are noted for largemouths, and 10-mile-long Balsam hosts smallmouths.

The Kawartha lakes in the Trent-Severn system provide the best opportunity in Ontario to catch that first muskellunge. This situation is unique in that muskies aren't in competition with northern pike as they are elsewhere in the province. Among the better muskie lakes are Rice, Stony, Buckhorn, Chemung, Pigeon, and Balsam. The fish are mainly 6- to 10-pounders but are relatively abundant; the occasional lunker is in the 20- to 30-pound range. Nearby Lake Scugog, connected to the Trent-Severn through the Scugog River, also offers good muskie fishing in early June and from mid-September until the end of October. With an average depth of only 5 feet, the lake's massive weedbeds are a haven for largemouth and smallmouth bass, and myriad panfish, including black crappie and pumpkinseeds.

Haliburton/Muskoka. North in the Haliburton Highlands, muskellunge are found only in Elephant Lake northwest of Bancroft. Adjoining Baptiste Lake also has muskies but achieved some notoriety when a 37-pound lake trout was landed in 1980. Both lakes have populations of walleye, smallmouth bass, and largemouth bass.

To the west, in the heavily cottaged Muskoka country, smallmouth bass have been the predominant sportfish for generations in Lake of Bays, Lake Muskoka, Lake Joseph, Lake Rosseau, and Skeleton and Three Mile Lakes.

From Bancroft to Dover, numerous small lakes deep enough for trout are stocked with lakers, brook trout, rainbow trout, and splake. Among these waters, the ones with road access are most sought after. Liberal regulations are in place for rainbow trout and splake lakes, to ease the fishing pressure on lakes with native populations of lake trout and brook trout (called speckled trout here).

For a small daily fee, anglers have a choice of 21 lakes in the privately owned Haliburton Forest and Wildlife Reserve, 15 miles north of the town of Haliburton. The 78-square-mile forest has easily accessible lakes varying in size from 12 to 450 acres, and these have lake trout, rainbows, splake, speckled trout, and smallmouth bass, which are maintained by regular stocking.

Algonquin Park. Algonquin Park, which boasts 325 lakes and rivers within its 2,900 square miles, has a reputation for both quality fishing and wilderness canoeing. It's still possible to catch a 5-pound speckled trout within 150 miles of downtown Toronto if you're prepared to work at it.

The 55-mile-long corridor along Highway 60, which cuts across the southern end of the park, provides road access to Lake Opeongo, the largest lake in Algonquin and the major jumping-off point for the backwaters. No motors are allowed in the interior lakes, and special regulations are in effect to protect native speckled and lake trout.

Specks, or brookies, are the most widespread species in Algonquin, occurring in 230 lakes and typically weighing from 1 to 4 pounds. Coveted wild brookies are found in lakes requiring one or more portages; hatchery trout predominate in the eight smaller lakes along the highway. The best fishing is in May, and three-quarters of the season's harvest from the park is taken then.

Eleven park lakes are noted for lake trout, notably Smoke, Canoe, Cache, and Opeongo along the Highway 60 corridor. The average lakers weigh 2 to 4 pounds, but a 20-pounder can always come along in remote interior waters. Splake have been introduced in 10 area lakes.

Smallmouth bass inhabit 15 of the park's lakes, many along Highway 60 and within easy reach of campgrounds. Popular smallmouth lakes are Opeongo, Canoe, Cache, and Smoke. Late June and early fall are best.

Eastern Ontario

Bay of Quinte and Eastern Lake Ontario. After a hefty pollution cleanup, curtailment of commercial fishing, and a string of ideal spawning years, Bay of Quinte and its adjoining Long Reach and Hay Bay have become one of North America's top sites for walleye over 10 pounds and have plenty of them. The larger fish, which can reach 18 pounds, move into the bay from Lake Ontario in the late fall, positioning for spawning in the Napanee, Salmon, Moira, and Trent Rivers in April. Walleye that remain in the bay over the summer average 1 to 4 pounds.

The MNR has counted close to 4,000 boats along the 50 miles of bay waters from Trenton to Picton at the opening of the walleye season in early May. Many anglers find success bouncing bottom with a jig-and-minnow from an anchored or drifting boat. Trolling with a crankbait that resembles an alewife, the primary food for Quinte walleye, has also been effective. In 1997, the MNR estimated that anglers caught 80,063 walleye during the open-water season and an additional 22,631 through the ice. The average weight, including released fish, was more than 2 pounds.

In the quest for walleye, other Quinte gamefish are often overlooked. Smallmouth bass averaging $1^{1}/_{2}$ pounds inhabit the channel edges near Belleville, largemouth bass are in the back bays between Rossmore and North Port, and northern pike haunt Muscote Bay and the mouths of the Trent and Salmon Rivers. Hay Bay has produced numerous muskellunge over 20 pounds in past years. Both yellow and white perch, along with other panfish, are also common in Quinte waters.

In waters offshore from the bay are lake trout and salmon. The eastern end of the big lake is noted for smallmouth bass and walleye. Offshore, the Main Duck Islands are a long run but produce good fishing for various species. Muskies are caught at the far eastern end, off the head of Wolfe Island at the entrance to the St. Lawrence River, and closer to Kingston.

St. Lawrence River. The scenic Thousand Islands is without a doubt the most famous fishing region along the Ontario portion of the vast St. Lawrence River and the stretch least affected by the massive seaway construction of the 1950s.

It's a structure angler's dream, with countless points, rocky shorelines, shoals, sharp dropoffs, and brisk current all concentrated in a 30-mile stretch from Wolfe Island, at the mouth of the river, eastward past Gananoque to Brockville. A traditional fishing technique here, and one still employed successfully by charter captains, is stillfishing with a shiner minnow on the bottom from an anchored boat around Howe, Tar, and Grenadier Islands, and around hundreds of smaller islands and reefs. More mobile and well-equipped anglers, however, cast around the countless reefs, bays, islands, weedbeds, and docks for fish, particularly largemouth and smallmouth bass.

Northern pike, yellow perch, and bullhead are popular catches in May and June. Smallmouth bass are numerous and are found throughout the islands in summer; they are caught shallow early in the season, as the water is still cool, then move to deeper haunts. Largemouths are not as abundant as their smallmouth cousins but are still available in ample quantities, especially in creeks, bays, and shallow, weedy environs. Roaming walleye are intercepted at the west end of Howe Island and around the Ivy Lea Bridge. Muskellunge are most active in September and October.

This section of the St. Lawrence was once internationally known for huge muskies, especially 50- and 60-pound fish, and produced the disputed world-record 69-pound, 15-ounce muskie in 1957. Although believed to have been caught downriver near Ogdensburg, New York, the record fish was also claimed by Gananoque, Ontario; it was purged from the world-record books in the mid-1990s, although it is still honored by New York.

In recent decades, trophy muskies have become scarce in the river, and especially at renowned Forty Acre Shoals, a patch of river bordered by Howe, Wolfe, and Grindstone Islands and historically the most famous fishing reef in the Thousand Islands. Overharvesting and ecological changes appear to have been at fault. Although the glory days are gone, fall trolling around the islands can still produce muskies in the 15- to 17-pound range, and 25-pounders are caught every season. Occasionally, someone lands a 40-pounder or better. Northerns up to 20 pounds are also attracted to baits intended for muskies, especially in the Bateau Channel along Howe Island. Ice fishing for pike is especially popular in the bays.

The Henshall Van Antwerp Black Bass Reel, patented in 1887, was a forerunner of the baitcasting reels used through the first half of the twentieth century.

Carp are available throughout Ontario waters, but nowhere are they more abundant than in Lake St. Lawrence between Morrisburg and Cornwall. Conventional sportfishing pressure is minimal for these fish; a small number of anglers have focused on these species and experience good and virtually uncontested angling. There is significant interest in bowfishing for these lumbering giants during June, when they come into the marshes to spawn. Area derbies take place then, and a fish weighing between 40 and 45 pounds is generally needed to win.

Lake St. Francis, as the St. Lawrence River east of Cornwall is known, is a productive section of the Ontario portion of the St. Lawrence River because of its large weedy areas interspersed with numerous channels and holes. The walleye and perch runs in May at the mouth of the Raisin River at South Lancaster attract anglers from across eastern Ontario and from as far as Montreal. The yellow perch, known here as "Lancaster perch," are a local favorite because they feed heavily on small river snails, which gives the flesh an exceptional flavor.

In summer, anglers pursue walleye, which average 4 pounds, with spinners and nightcrawlers in the cooler currents of the shipping lanes while dodging oceangoing freighters. The lake has an abundant population of northern pike up to 15 pounds, smallmouth bass up to 4 pounds, and muskellunge in the 15- to 25-pound class, all of which are largely ignored except by a small core of serious anglers.

Rideau Lakes and Canal. The Rideau Canal and its 120 miles of lakes, rivers, and cuts has been renowned for fishing since colonial times. The system, opened in 1832 for possible military use, runs from Kingston on Lake Ontario north to Ottawa, Canada's capital city.

At the shallower southern end, the Cataraqui River and Cranberry, Whitefish, Opinicon, and Newboro Lakes are prime habitat for largemouth bass that can reach 7 pounds, which is roughly the largest found in Ontario. Splake have been stocked in deeper Indian Lake with mixed success.

Big Rideau Lake, the jewel of the Rideaus with depths exceeding 200 feet, is a popular trolling water for lake trout in the 2- to 10-pound class. The islands near Portland hold good populations of small- and largemouth bass and panfish.

In the north, the Rideau River from Burritts Rapids near Kemptville to downtown Ottawa holds good numbers of muskellunge in the 10- to 20-pound range, walleye that can exceed 10 pounds, and smallmouth and largemouth bass to 5 pounds for anglers who have the skills and patience to fish heavy weeds. Black crappie are a popular target in April and May along the creek mouths and numerous canal locks.

Most of the other Rideau lakes have a variety of bass, pike, walleye, bluegills, crappie, and other panfish. Loughborough, Bob's Lake, Crosby, Christie, Otty, and Wolfe Lake (which produced a 9-pound, 4-ounce smallmouth in the 1980s) are known as consistent producers.

Ottawa River and Ottawa Valley. Shared with Quebec over much of its 350-mile length, the Ottawa River is eastern Ontario's second major river after the St. Lawrence. Power-generating stations have created numerous vast reservoir systems that harbor a variety of warmwater gamefish.

The 50 miles of the lower river from Ottawa downstream to Hawkesbury is the most productive section. Walleye in the 2- to 3-pound range are actively sought by anglers throughout the seasons, but the largest fish, some over 10 pounds, are taken through the ice in late December and January. Smallmouth and largemouth bass, northern pike, and a variety of panfish are abundant.

Interest in the muskellunge fishery has grown in recent years, and fish up to 50 inches are being caught in the fall by dedicated and knowledgeable muskie enthusiasts. A 62-inch muskie was caught and released in 1997 in the Ottawa-Hull area.

Upstream, the shallower bays of Lac Deschenes, from Ottawa to the dam at Fitzroy Harbour, are noted for walleye, smallmouth bass, northern pike, and the occasional muskie. The Lac des Chats portion at Arnprior holds walleye, smallmouth bass, and muskies in the 35-pound class. The upper reaches past Pembroke, Deep River, Mattawa, and New Liskeard on to Lake Timiskaming are vast waters primarily holding walleye, northern pike, and smallmouth bass. It's worthwhile for visiting anglers to contact outfitters located along the river for guidance about the best fishing areas.

The foremost draw here is walleye. Most of these fish are in the 2- to 3-pound range, and some are in the 8-pound class. Pike are plentiful, as are smallmouths, some of which weigh up to 4 pounds; there are no muskies up here, but there's an overlooked supply of largemouth bass in backwater locales.

Smallmouth and largemouth bass are found in nearly all of the cottage lakes within a few hours' drive of Ottawa, such as Mississippi, Bennett, Christie, Clayton, Dalhousie, and White. But north and west of Ottawa, throughout the Pembroke and Bancroft regions, trout fishing is a tradition, and bass are generally underexploited. Healthy bass populations also inhabit such lakes as Constance, Golden, Round, Dore, and Muskrat.

Madawaska River. The Madawaska River, which flows southeast from Algonquin Park to the Ottawa River, is another significant fishing water in eastern Ontario. Power dams have created a series of reservoir lakes that include Centennial, Black Donald, Calabogie, and Lake Madawaska.

In these flooded waters, jigging for walleye in depths up to 60 feet may be necessary for success. Smallmouth bass exist throughout the river, and largemouth frequent the weedy bays of Lake Calabogie. There is a chance of catching a muskellunge just about anywhere, but most angling effort is concentrated on Lake Madawaska at Arnprior.

The father of modern taxonomy—the biological ordering system—was Swedish naturalist Carl von Linné, known as Linnaeus; many fish were first identified and named by him in 1758.

Eastern Ontario trout waters. Eastern Ontario lake trout have declined in recent decades, but they remain an important recreational catch in 46 Canadian Shield lakes, of which 29 have some natural reproduction. A higher fertility compared with lakes farther north helps maintain natural populations, which are augmented with stocking programs, despite easy road access and high angling interest.

Popular trout lakes south of Highway 7 are the Big Rideau, Charleston, Devil, Big Salmon, and Sharbot. North of the highway they include Lucky, Mair, Mazinaw, Palmerston, Mosque, and Weslemkoon Lakes.

In the mid-1980s, large stocking programs of splake were begun on a put-grow-take basis in 26 lakes that were no longer suitable for lake trout. The splake have done well in some of these waters; the better ones include Little Salmon and Little Clear in Frontenac Provincial Park, and in Indian, Draper, and Upper Rock Lakes.

The Near North

Lake Nipissing. Covering 350 square miles and extending 40 miles in length and 15 miles in width, huge Nipissing is a lake of contrast and marks the transition into northern Ontario. The east end is shallow and possesses the sand, mud, and rock shoals suited to walleye and yellow perch, whereas the west end is a melange of rocky islands and bays, reefs, and sheltered waters best known for northern pike and muskellunge.

Nipissing is a very productive lake by northern Ontario standards, but not by southern standards. Fishing, especially for walleye, gradually slid downhill in recent times but has shown signs of bouncing back in the late 1990s, thanks to restocking programs and tighter angling regulations.

In May and early June, walleye are found close to shore off the sandy bottoms at North Bay, and the mouths of the Sturgeon, Veuve, Wasi, and South Rivers. The Manitou Islands in the center of the east end of the lake are a year-round favorite location. Fish in the 1- to 2-pound range are abundant, and prospects of hooking into an old-timer up to 12 pounds still exist.

The lake has good populations of smallmouth bass, which are often ignored. The best areas are Callender Bay and the south shore, the islands near the mouth of the French River, and the West Arm.

Catching a 40-pound muskellunge from Lake Nipissing is still possible, but its reputation, along with that of nearby Nosbonsing and Restoule Lakes, of the 1950s and 1960s for numbers of big muskies has diminished from too much fishing pressure. The best opportunities today are in South Bay, West Bay, and Cache Bay. Ling, sheepshead, and sturgeon are also well established in the lake. White bass run the Sturgeon River on the north shore in May.

There is as much fishing on Nipissing in winter as there is during the summer. An average of 1,700 ice shacks pop up in January, and walleye are the prime target, followed by yellow perch, northern pike, whitefish, and herring. In 1996, MNR surveys indicated that 165,118 walleye, pike, and perch were caught during the open-water periods, and 213,639 were hauled in by ice anglers.

French River. Mention the French River and people immediately think of fishing amidst glacier-scoured bedrock of pink and gray granite. This scenic and historic river is a 68-mile-long series of island-dotted lakes connected by rapids and falls between Lake Nipissing and the isolated eastern shoreline of Georgian Bay.

Most fishing effort is devoted to walleye that migrate from Georgian Bay in search of alewives in the maze of channels and outlets of the French River delta, which include the Bad and Pickerel Rivers. May until August are the best times for trolling deep-diving plugs or stillfishing with live baits in the fast waters. In July, night fishing is best for walleye that could weigh 10 pounds, but they are usually half that. As fall progresses, the walleye move farther upriver.

Northerns up to 15 pounds and smallmouth bass up to 4 pounds permeate the French River system. October is the best time for trolling for trophy muskellunge, especially in Hartley Bay. Many muskies fall in the 25- to 40-pound class, but a 59-pound, 7-ounce leviathan was boated here in 1989.

Ahmic and Cecebe Lakes. Two of the lakes in the Magnetawan River chain, Ahmic and adjoining Cecebe, are among the largest lakes in the Parry Sound District and are prolific walleye, northern pike, and smallmouth bass waters. In summer, night trolling with minnow plugs, and stillfishing in the evening with a leech suspended under a float, are locally proven ways to catch elusive Ahmic Lake walleye, which average 4 pounds and gorge themselves on smelt.

Moon River. The Moon River, flowing into Georgian Bay farther south, has remained a top-notch fishing location but with an emphasis on quality rather than quantity. The river gained fame for huge walleye in the 8- to 14-pound range, with the occasional eye-popper hitting near the 20-pound mark. The size of walleye now is more modest, in the 5-pound class. Popular places in the basin for walleye that move in for the winter are Woods Bay, Captain Allan Straits, and Moon River Bay.

Abundant populations of smallmouths and largemouths are there but are often overlooked in the quest for walleye. Pike up to 25 pounds thrive throughout the river. Muskies are present, too, including some monsters; the Moon River produced a Canadian-record 65-pound, 58-inch muskellunge in Blackstone Harbour in 1988.

Manitoulin Island and the North Channel. Rural Manitoulin Island, the largest

freshwater island in the world at 100 miles long and up to 60 miles wide, dominates the northern shore of Georgian Bay and is a focal point for Ontario anglers.

Smallmouth bass, northern pike, and yellow perch are abundant in most of the island's 19 inland lakes and surrounding waters. Small walleye, 2 pounds or under, are found in Mindemoya and Windfall Lakes. The May run of jumbo perch at Lake Wolsey draws a lot of attention. Sixteen-mile-long Lake Manitou, the largest of the island's lakes, has a lake trout population that is critically important to the province, not only for sportfishing, but also as a source of trout eggs for a nearby government hatchery. The lakers have been known to reach 30 pounds, but the average catch weighs closer to 5 pounds.

Some island creeks have resident speckled trout, but better known is the migrant steelhead fishery in the spring and fall near the mouths of the small rivers. The most prominent of these are along the south shore and include Blue Jay Creek and the Manitou River on Michael's Bay, and the Mindemoya River at Providence Bay.

Manitoulin's 250 miles of rocky shoreline, with its sheltered bays and nearby island waters, also host Pacific salmon, steelhead, brown trout, and lake trout, which have been stocked by the millions over the years or wandered in from the massive plantings in Lake Huron waters by Michigan. Salmon fishing is centered at Meldrum Bay, followed by Providence Bay and Gore Bay, from mid-July through October.

Manitoulin Island was the site of a greatly influential fisheries research program aimed at restoring Georgian Bay's lake trout fishery, which collapsed in the 1950s due to lamprey eels and overfishing. The program involved planting millions of first-generation splake in the 1970s, followed by millions of the second generation of these hybrids in the 1980s. Although these fish filled a gap in the spring fishery, they failed to reproduce or to live long; the MNR then switched to annual plantings of pure-strain lake trout in the 1990s.

In the shadows of the nearby La Cloche Mountains, McGregor Bay has one of the few remaining populations of native Georgian Bay lake trout. Northern pike, muskellunge, and smallmouth bass are also found throughout the rocky islands and small bays.

To the west, northern pike, smallmouth bass, and yellow perch are the most common species throughout the North Channel waters, which extend 100 miles from Little Current to Thessalon. In May and June, opportunities for walleye exist at the mouth of the Spanish River.

In the fall, stray chinook show up at the mouths of such rivers as the Thessalon, Mississagi, and St. Mary's, but pink salmon—accidentally released into Lake Superior in 1956—are a curiosity. The pinks, which typically weigh 2 pounds but have been known to exceed 10 pounds, show up every odd year when they can be caught from shore by anglers using flies, spinners, and other small lures.

Ontario's North

Lake Temagami region. Walleye populate the lakes north of Lake Nipissing, but their size diminishes with the shorter growing season. The Marten River system and nearby smaller lakes are noted for eating-size "pickerel" under 2 pounds; anything over 5 pounds is trophy class. Walleye up to 7 pounds inhabit Lake Temagami and its four sprawling arms, but this 78-square-mile site is better known for lake trout and whitefish in both the open-water and ice fishing seasons.

Highway 17 to Highway 11 Belt. Walleye, northern pike, and smallmouth bass are common in hundreds of lakes in the huge belt of rock and forest terrain between Highways 17 and 11 from Sudbury to Lake Superior—Obabika, Gowganda, Wanapitei, Onaping, Biscotasi, Missinakwa, Mattagami, Panache, Chiblow, Wakomata, Horwood, Missinaibi, Dog, and Remi, to name a few.

This rough, lightly populated region is also the heart of Ontario's trout country. Of the 2,000 Ontario inland lakes holding lake trout, the districts of Sudbury and Algoma have a significant share. Northwest of Espanola, former logging roads provide access to numerous trout lakes. Mozhabong, Sindaminda, Savage, and Whiskey are among the better-known waters. The greatest concentration of trout lakes, however, is in the Elliot Lake– Blind River area, where Rawhide, Kirkpatrick, Semiwhite, Flack, Matinenda, and Bark Lakes are among the most consistent producers of large lakers.

As a bonus, countless difficult-to-reach and not-easy-to-find smaller lakes in the Sault Ste. Marie–Chapleau area have healthy native populations of speckled trout. It's said that woods-wise locals may take the locations of the best brookie waters—where a 6-pound speck is still a possibility—with them to the grave.

Lake Superior. The rocky cliffs, deep crystal water, rushing rivers, and limited access along Lake Superior, which is the largest of the Great Lakes, make the northern shore one of Ontario's most awesome fishing destinations. Lake trout, steelhead, coho salmon, chinook salmon, and pink salmon are the primary coldwater attractions. In the shallower bays and rivers, northern pike, yellow perch, and remnant walleye are the dominant warmwater species.

Pacific salmon have given a boost to a declining lake trout fishery, especially in the east end of the lake. Summer and fall trolling are popular in Goulais Bay, Batchawana Bay, Montreal River, and Michipicoten Bay. This latter bay, located at Wawa, is the best spot on Superior for spring and fall chinook, boasting salmon to 30 pounds. In the west, salmon and lake trout linger offshore around the lake reefs at Marathon, Terrace Bay, Rossport, and Thunder Bay.

Lake Superior's north shore is the preserve of Ontario's finest classic steelhead waters, although getting there can be a challenge. Steelhead runs can be short because the rivers are quickly blocked by falls. Among the dozens of unpolluted rivers that can be fished from Highway 17 (the Trans-Canada Highway), the better-known ones are the Batchawana, Montreal, Michipicoten, Steel, and Nipigon. In Pukaskwa National Park, steelhead run the Dore, University, and Pukaskwa Rivers, but there is no road access. Anglers must boat in from Lake Superior.

North in the Lake Superior drainage are hundreds of coldwater lakes, rivers, and streams scattered throughout an exceptionally rugged terrain with few good roads. These waters are low in productivity but suited for brook and lake trout and provide a wilderness trout experience for those willing to make the effort.

Lake Nipigon/Nipigon River. The speckled trout is king in the huge undeveloped waters of Lake Nipigon, which, at 1,740 square miles, is the largest lake entirely within Ontario's borders.

The best time for a trophy, which can weigh up to 7 pounds, is from ice out in late April through early June. Proven techniques include trolling a spinner-and-worm rig around the lake's profusion of rocky points and islands. Lake trout are found throughout the lake, and walleye and northern pike inhabit the mouths of such rivers as the Ombabika, Gull, and Poshkokogan.

The 20-mile-long Nipigon River spilling into Lake Superior is one of the most famous speckled trout rivers in the world, still reveling in the past glory of a 14$\frac{1}{2}$-pound world record caught in 1916. Although such a catch is unlikely today, specks of half this size are still possible from the fast current around various dams and narrows, especially in May and September.

Jesse Lake, a widening of the river about halfway between Lake Nipigon and Lake Superior, has walleye, northern pike, yellow perch, and whitefish for midsummer action.

Northwest

Northwest Ontario, the region west and north of Thunder Bay, has more fishing camps than any other part of the province, with countless Canadian Shield lakes and rivers flowing either easterly to Lake Superior or northerly to Hudson Bay.

Quetico region. The 1,750 square miles of Quetico Provincial Park, south of Atikokan and north of the Ontario-Minnesota border with a labyrinth of interconnected waters, is a popular destination for canoeists and anglers seeking the solitude and beauty of the wilderness. Smallmouth bass, northern pike, walleye, lake trout, and whitefish range throughout the park. Beaverhouse, Quetico, Sturgeon, and Lac la Croix are among the better lakes.

To the west, 30-mile-long Rainy Lake, with Fort Francis at its center, has good to excellent populations of walleye, smallmouth bass, and northern pike, especially in Ash, Alexander, and Seine Bays in the north arm. A 51-pound, 8-ounce muskie came from nearby Pipestone Lake in 1975.

Dryden District. To the north, the Dryden District contains among Ontario's most famous muskellunge waters: Lac Seul, Eagle Lake, Wabigoon, and Big Vermilion Lake. Here, dreams of a 50-pound muskie could come true. In particular, 60-mile-long Eagle Lake claims more trophies than any other water in Ontario, yielding fish in the 30- to 40-pound class every year. Special catch-and-release regulations are in place on some lakes, to protect a world-class fishery.

Lake trout, walleye, and northern pike are abundant in many Dryden District lakes. Stocked decades ago, smallmouth bass are found in lakes accessible by road, but not in remote waters.

This is the home of the floatplane, and anglers have a choice of hundreds of waters to fly into for unpressured walleye, northern pike, and lake trout. Planes depart from such locations as Sioux Lookout, Red Lake, and Pickle Lake.

Lake of the Woods. Ontario shares the 1,485-square-mile area of Lake of the Woods with Minnesota and Manitoba. The Ontario waters are sheltered by most of the 14,000 rocky islands found in the lake. Those islands contribute to an estimated 3,800 miles of shoreline, which gives anglers plenty to focus on. The lake has a reputation for its variety of sportfish—especially pike, lakers, and muskies—to match its vast size.

Walleye are the primary target of both resident and nonresident anglers out of such places as Rainy River, Nestor Falls, Sioux Narrows, and Kenora. Anglers will find walleye throughout the lake, although they're less common in deep Clearwater and Whitefish Bays. Walleye here are typically in the 1- to 3-pound range, and older fish weigh near 10 pounds; although good and above the average size for Canadian Shield waters, these fish are not in a league with the lunkers found in Lake Erie or the Bay of Quinte.

Smallmouth bass of 2 to 3 pounds are abundant, especially in the waters around Nestor Falls and Sioux Narrows, but they are often overlooked by anglers in their pursuit of walleye. Largemouth bass, which are less abundant, are found in the back bays and weedbeds in these areas.

Northern pike exist throughout the lake and are often called "jackfish" in this part of the province. Pike are typical in the 5- to 8-pound range but can reach 25 pounds. As big as they are, it seems unlikely that Lake of the Woods northerns will break the long-standing Ontario record of 42 pounds, 2 ounces, caught from nearby Delaney Lake in 1946.

Lake trout are a particularly important species in Lake of the Woods and can reach 30 to 35 pounds. Prominent areas for them are Whitefish

Lake Superior, which covers 31,800 square miles, has the largest surface area of any lake in the world.

Bay at Sioux Narrows, and Clearwater and Echo Bays near Kenora.

Lake of the Woods is among Ontario's top producers of large muskellunge, and numerous fish in the 55- to 58-pound class have been taken over the years. Today, however, there's a greater likelihood of encountering a fish in the 30-pound range, and enough of these are hooked every year to make this one of the most likely places in North America to have a good chance at such a fish. Mid-August to early October is the peak time in proven spots such as the Nestor Falls-Sabaskong Bay area and Labyrinth Bay.

Among other species in the lake, yellow perch is the most common. Black crappie are targeted in Sabaskong Bay in the spring and through the ice. Other established species include sauger, bullhead, cisco, lake whitefish, and sturgeon.

To the north of Lake of the Woods, the sprawling Winnipeg and English River systems have good populations of walleye, northern pike, smallmouth bass, muskellunge, lake trout, and whitefish. The Winnipeg River near Minaki has a reputation for muskies in the 10- to 30-pound category, and legendary past catches have exceeded 50 pounds.

Far North (James/Hudson Bay Watersheds)
Rivers. The pristine and remote large river systems that drain north into James Bay and Hudson Bay, accessible mainly by air, are the answer for the true angling adventurer. This area of northern Ontario, its gateway to the Arctic, is rich in North American and Canadian history. Here, near the southern shore of James Bay at Moosonee, the Hudson Bay Company originated, amassing a fortune and helping to forge a country through the trapping and trading of beavers. This is where the Moose River and such tributaries as the Missinaibi, Kwataboahegan, Kapuskasing, Mattagami, Onakwahegan, and Abitibi Rivers now beckon wilderness adventurers and explorers. These are rough, rugged rivers, however, and fishing on them is seldom the main focus of visitors.

Moosonee is the only locale in this region that is accessible by ground, via train from Cochrane. This train, the Little Bear, provides dropoff and pickup service to those making multiweek canoe expeditions. A village of 3,500, Moosonee sits along the mile-wide Moose River in a large deltalike area that experiences 6- to 7-foot tides and is still a 20-minute boat ride from James Bay. Fishing opportunities are limited, mostly for small pike and walleye and an occasional whitefish. Three- to 6-pound charr come into the bay from mid- to late May, and again in September. This is not an angling hotspot, but it is one worth taking a day to see when headed into or coming from the interior.

The interior portions of rivers such as the Ogoki, Attawapiskat, and Albany, however, are less accessible and have more angling attraction. They are virtually untapped waters for northern pike up to 15 pounds and walleye to 7 pounds, with the occasional larger specimen. Speckled trout averaging 2 to 3 pounds are found at the mouths of tributaries of many of these rivers in early summer and move farther up the tributaries into the cooler water of deep holes and whitewater rapids as the main rivers warm. The brookies return as the temperature falls in late August and September.

Farther north, resident speckled trout in the lower reaches of the Sutton, Winisk, and Severn Rivers are augmented by sea-run trout that spend most of their time in saltwater and enter freshwater in preparation for fall spawning. These far-north brookies, although respectable in size, seldom reach the weights of those found in Northern Quebec and Labrador. The Sutton River has the province's most northerly established lake trout population.

Outfitters from jumping-off points such as Nakina, Jellicoe, and Armstrong provide fly-in services for anglers to outpost camps and dropoffs for canoeing/fishing expeditions to these remote watersheds.

Kesagami Lake. One of the finest and most unique pike and walleye lakes in northern Ontario, Kesagami is a little-known gem in the northeast corner of the province, about 60 miles south of James Bay and accessed via floatplane from Cochrane or Moosonee. An isolated water without road access, Kesagami Lake makes up most of Kesagami Provincial Park in a flat and poorly drained region of peat bog and muskeg. It's an unusually shallow lake, with an average depth of 7 feet and a maximum depth of 29 feet, and offers 180 miles of shoreline, many bays, and seven islands.

Being shallow, Kesagami warms early, contributing to a growth rate well above normal for the region. This, combined with a baitfish population of cisco, suckers, and whitefish, produces prodigious walleye and many unusually plump northern pike. Many Kesagami pike weigh 15 pounds or more, and some are in the 25- to 35-pound range.

An evening walleye fishing scene at Kesagami Lake.

The only lodge here has instituted conservation policies, including catch-and-release for pike, and the use of only barbless hooks and fish cradles for landing pike.

OPALEYE *Girella nigricans.*
Other names—green perch, black perch, blue-eyed perch, bluefish, Jack Benny, button-back; Japanese: *mejina*; Spanish: *chopa verde*.

A member of the nibblers in the Kyphosidae family of sea chub *(see: chub, sea)*, the opaleye is a tough species to catch but a determined fighter on rod and reel.

Identification. The body of the opaleye is oval and compressed, the snout is thick and has an evenly rounded profile, and the mouth is small. Its coloring is dark olive green, and most individuals have one or two white spots on each side of the back under the middle of the dorsal fin. Bright-blue eyes and a heavy perchlike body distinguish it from related species.

Size. They are reported to attain a maximum weight of $25\frac{1}{2}$ inches and weight of $13\frac{1}{2}$ pounds.

Distribution. Opaleye occur from San Francisco, California, to Cabo San Lucas, Baja California.

Habitat. This species inhabits rocky shorelines and kelp beds. Concentrations of adults are found off California in 65 or so feet of water.

Life history/Behavior. Opaleye form dense schools in shallow water when spawning, which occurs from April through June. Eggs and larvae are free floating and may be found miles from shore. Juveniles form schools of up to two dozen individuals. At about 1 inch in length, they enter tide pools, gradually moving deeper as they grow. Opaleye mature and spawn when they are roughly 8 or 9 inches long and between two and three years old.

Food and feeding habits. Opaleye primarily eat marine algae with or without encrustations of organisms. Other food sources include feather boa kelp, giant kelp, sea lettuce, coralline algae, small tube-dwelling worms, and red crabs.

Angling. Although extremely difficult to catch due to their largely vegetarian diet and nibbling nature, opaleye are strong battlers. They are not the subject of intensive angling effort but may take mussels, sand crabs, and cut baits. Some anglers use hooked plant matter.

OPEN-FACE REEL
A spinning reel.
See: Spinning Tackle.

OPEN WATER
(1) A term used to distinguish a lake or pond that is not frozen from a frozen one. In locations

Opaleye

where lakes are subject to freezing in the winter, the "open-water season" begins when the lake is free of ice.

(2) A loosely used reference by freshwater anglers to indicate that area of a large body of water, usually a reservoir or lake, that is away from the shore, with no visible structure or cover. "Open water" is used by some anglers to differentiate between fishing along or close to the shoreline, and fishing the broader expanse (as in "We caught them out in open water"). In a sense, it is analogous to the primarily saltwater term "offshore" *(see)*.

OPERCULUM
The largest and uppermost bone that forms the gill cover of a fish.
See: Anatomy.

OPTIMUM YIELD
The recreational and/or commercial harvest level for a species that achieves the greatest overall benefits, including economic, social, and biological considerations. Optimum yield is different from maximum sustainable yield, which considers only the biology of the species.
See: Fisheries Management.

OREGON
Oregon spent much of the waning part of the twentieth century trying to beat back the warm ocean conditions of El Niño and save several of its salmon and steelhead populations. Unfortunately, headlines surrounding these matters overshadowed the presence of Oregon's truly diverse sportfisheries, most of which are alive and well.

Fishing for fall chinook salmon on the Oregon coast, for example, is the better than it is in either of the neighboring states, and the chinook in some Oregon estuaries are, fish for fish, larger than those in most Alaskan rivers.

The nation's largest sturgeon fishery, a million fish strong, lies within a few minute's to an hour's drive from Portland. Sturgeon coming and going from the lower Columbia River reenter river estuaries from Washington to northern California.

Some anglers believe that the next world-record walleye will be caught in the Columbia River, where these fish were introduced in the 1940s. State records in the river's border states of Oregon and Washington are nearing 20 pounds, and 12- to 16-pounders are no longer rare. Big walleye are so numerous that many salmon managers consider walleye unwelcome predators on baby salmon and steelhead and would just as soon see them all caught.

And although the salmon are imperiled in the Columbia, more shad (several million) enter this river every spring than most East Coast rivers, where the species originated. So many shad make it to spawning grounds 200 miles upriver that biologists worry about shad plugging fish ladders designed for salmon.

Additionally, two Oregon rivers routinely produce catches of more than a hundred smallmouth bass a day; 3-pounders there are hardly worth noting. And Oregon's fine trout fishing remains intact, if changing.

Offshore fishing for bottom fish and rockfish is excellent and improving as federal regulators tighten controls on commercial fishermen. And you don't even need a license for the state's most popular fishery, Dungeness crabs.

Saltwater
Oregon has more than 350 miles of coastline to take the brunt of Pacific storms, and U.S. Highway 101, which runs within a few feet to a few miles of the beach for its entire length, offers a path to the West Coast's most accessible and diverse saltwater fishing.

Coastal bays. A diversity of sportfishing opportunity is the hallmark of Oregon's bays, and many also have excellent crabbing.

Columbia. The end of Lewis and Clark's journey is now a long jetty with good fishing from large rocks for most species of rockfish, sturgeon, and salmon (in season). Large Columbia Bay has long reaches that can get choppy with afternoon winds, yet there's excellent crabbing here—the largest Dungeness crabs, sometimes 8 or 9 inches across, on the coast. The estuary up to freshwater (about 20 miles) usually has good sturgeon fishing. There's a nasty bar here that should always be crossed on an incoming tide; watch for shipping traffic and don't anchor in the channel.

Nehalem. Pleasant, scenic little Nehalem Bay is popular for crabbing and has good chinook salmon fishing on the bar during incoming tides from July through September. The south jetty is accessible, but fishing is not as good as at Tillamook, a short distance south. A bonus for sightseers occurs when elk herds on the Nehalem Spit come to the water's edge; playful calves often chase harbor seals into the water.

Tillamook. Extremely diverse, Tillamook Bay is fed by five tributaries and has good winter crabbing if it hasn't rained enough to force the crabs out into the ocean. Sturgeon anglers welcome the rain because the same freshwater that pushes crabs out draws sturgeon inside when there are no pesky crabs to rob the bait. Jetty fishing is good for greenling and sea bass, and some crabbing occurs off the jetty instead of from boats. There's a long public fishing pier, and bay tidal flats are good for clamming. Tillamook's biggest draw is large fall chinook salmon; a few 50- to 60-pounders are caught each year from September through Thanksgiving. The bar is tricky and narrow, and shouldn't be crossed during a strong ebbing tide.

Netarts. When freshwater runoff stops crabbing on Tillamook Bay, locals head just a few miles east of Tillamook to Netarts, a bay without tributaries and thus always salty enough for crabbing. It also offers an unusual shore fishery for surfperch from a highway shoulder that hugs the bay's northeast shoreline. Boat launches are available, but no jetties or channel. This is not an ocean-access bay.

Nestucca. Limited crabbing occurs in Nestucca Bay, but the bay entrance is several miles from boat ramps and there's no ocean access. Two tributaries provide good fishing for spring chinook from May through June, and fall chinook from August through November. Fall chinook fishing is best from the bank, with spinners, or slip-stop bobbers over clusters of salmon eggs. Pacific City, on the ocean side of the upper bay, is home to Oregon's famous beach dory fleet. Dories launch directly into the surf at all times of the year to gain access to bottom fish, halibut, salmon, and albacore.

Depoe Bay. Tiny Depoe Bay has a good public launch and is home to an active charter-fishing and whale-watching fleet. Offshore reefs harbor lingcod, sea bass, cabezon, red snapper, and other species. The ocean floor drops sharply, allowing easier access to deep-water fishing. The bay erupts abruptly from a hole in the rocky coastline, over which U.S. 101 passes on a bridge. There is no jetty, but the bay is so small it has no runoff problems. Turn two corners and you're immediately into sea swells that are easily read before launching.

Siletz. Although there's little boat access or angling opportunity at Siletz, it is a pleasant and scenic bay with a good run of fall chinook into the estuary and an unusual beach fishery for salmon and steelhead crossing the bar in a narrow channel. It's best to fish toward the top of an incoming tide.

Yaquina. A premier Oregon coastal estuary, Yaquina has a generally forgiving bar and plenty of crabbing, perch fishing, jetty angling, and seasonal salmon fishing. A marina and public launch are on the south shoreline, between the Oregon State University Hatfield Marine Science Center and the Oregon Aquarium, and there's also a public crabbing and fishing pier. Crabbers should use caution with their bait because the bay houses

Oregon's most aggressive, trap smashing sea lion population. Locals avoid trouble by baiting crabs with mink carcasses, chicken and turkey wings, and watermelon rinds. Killer whales sometimes enter the bay specifically to hunt and eat seals and sea lions. Bay flats east of the Marine Center offer good clamming plus sand shrimp for use as baitfish on the jetty, for perch fishing in the bay, or steelhead fishing in several nearby rivers. Surfperch give live birth to young fish in the bay from late March through early May. This is also the coast's only reliable jigging fishery for herring, which spawn from February through early May. Some winter and spring sturgeon fishing exists upriver to Toledo.

Alsea. A good crabbing bay, Alsea has a solid fall chinook run in September and October. Do not cross the bar.

Siuslaw. One of Oregon's longest estuaries, Siuslaw has good fall chinook fishing in September and October. Crabbing is seasonally fair in the lower bay from November until May. As in all bays, crabs molt and get soft during the summer. Unlike blue crabs of the East Coast, soft-shelled Dungeness crabs are not good to eat. Jetty fishing can be good, but access is a hike. Be cautious about crossing the bar.

Winchester. The outlet of the Umpqua River, Winchester is a good winter and spring sturgeon fishery and has Oregon's best striped bass fishing. Stripers live in a tributary, the lower Smith River, and the long, wide Umpqua estuary. Sturgeon are found from Winchester upriver past Reedsport to deep holes just below Scottsburg. Crabbing is good, and the bar can be treacherous.

Coos. The Coos is a large, relatively calm bay that also serves as southern Oregon's seaport. Crabbing is almost always good out of Charleston, at the bay's entrance, and charters offer access to bottom fish and tuna in season. Surfperch and sturgeon use the bay, and striped bass are found in three large sloughs. Jetty fishing is good for lingcod, but getting to the jetty is a bit tricky, requiring a drive across sandy tidal reaches. North and south shorelines outside the entrance offer a unique surf fishery for stripers. The bar here is more forgiving than others and can be good for chinook salmon fishing on incoming tides in the fall.

Coquille. Coquille Bay is a small scenic bay that has good crabbing and seasonal jigging for smelt. The entrance is narrow. Use caution when crossing the bar.

Port Orford. Although there is no bay or river at Port Orford, it instead has a protected harbor and a unique system of lowering boats into the harbor with a lift. This provides almost instant access to numerous offshore reefs and bottom fish.

Rogue. The Rogue is a small bay with an outlet to the ocean that is relatively safe because there is little or no tidal runoff. Crabbing is available but limited, and some smelt jigging occurs in the spring. The bay's primary attraction is Oregon's longest trolling season for chinook salmon, which extends from March through October.

Chetco/Brookings. Even smaller than Rogue Bay, Chetco/Brookings has good, instant ocean access to offshore reefs for bottom fishing and a productive late season for chinook salmon in October.

Coastal salmon and steelhead. Coho salmon seasons have been limited since the late 1970s. Chinook salmon, however, are available offshore most months of the year, and the fishing season runs from April through October. Most anglers troll deep off harbor entrances from August through October.

The best fishing occurs in estuaries in the late summer and fall, when trollers pull cut-plug herring across the bottom in or near bay entrances, and spinners in the midbay zones, or cast bobbers and baits (egg roe or sand shrimp) in tidewater sloughs.

Most rivers have runs of both native or hatchery steelhead or a combination. Wild steelhead must be released unharmed in most rivers, but hatchery steelhead with clipped adipose fins may be kept. There is little fishing for steelhead in estuaries.

Crabbing and clamming. Dungeness crabs are prevalent in most coastal bays and offer plenty of excitement. The best baits are salmon parts or bits of bottom fish, but many shad anglers freeze their catches for use in crabbing.

Don't pass up clamming and mussel gathering. Like crabbing, a license is not required, but there are daily limits. The best beach for digging razor clams is at Seaside and Gearhart, in about the first 20 miles south of the Columbia River entrance. Look for low tides and a calm ocean, as pounding surf tends to drive clams deep into the sand.

Jetties. Jetties always require caution, often being awash in large waves. Huge rocks require tennis shoes or rubber boots. The rewards for jetty fishing are perch, greenling (a small member of the lingcod family with brilliant blue-green flesh), and other bottom fish.

Sand shrimp, clam necks, and herring pieces are good baits. Don't cast too far from the rocks, as fish often bite within a few feet of rocks showing at the surface. The best time for jetty fishing is the last two hours of an incoming tide through the first 30 minutes of the ebb.

Albacore. Albacore tuna have rebounded since the high seas driftnet fleet was forced off the Pacific Ocean. From July through September, schools of albacore work north off the Pacific Northwest coast to Vancouver Island. They usually pass within striking range, no more than 100 miles for overnight charter boats, of Oregon ports. In the late 1990s, the same warm ocean currents that wreaked havoc on coldwater-loving salmon drew tuna to within 10 to 15 miles of some ports, and even the small private boat fleet reaped the rewards within sight of coastal mountains.

Tuna are slashing, diving fighters that don't give

A big female largemouth bass can lay up to 30,000 eggs in a nest, but she never stays to watch over them; males guard the eggs and fan the nest to keep silt away.

up and fight far harder, pound for pound, than any other coastal Oregon fish. Oregonians aren't equipped for live bait fishing like California boats, opting instead for pulling feathered and rubber-skirted jigs at high trolling speeds.

Freshwater
Coastal region. Oregon stocks rainbow and cutthroat trout into most of the lakes in the strip of land between the ocean and the Coast Mountain Range. Trout fishing in streams is a catch-and-release effort, to protect sea-run cutthroat trout and juvenile steelhead.

Many lakes also contain good populations of largemouth bass, and Tenmile Lakes between Coos Bay and Reedsport is such a good bass fishery that it supports year-round angling and several tournaments in the spring and summer.

Columbia River. For more than 200 miles from its mouth upriver, the Columbia is both the boundary between Oregon and Washington and a jointly managed fishery that provides the most and largest fish in both states. To prevent confusion, angling regulations along the Columbia are the same in both Oregon and Washington, despite different rules in other parts of both states. The following is a condensed review of angling opportunities starting from the mouth upriver.

Buoy 10. This channel marker near the entrance of the Columbia River has become synonymous with Oregon's best-known coho salmon fishery. Actually, both chinook and coho are caught in the lower river from Buoy 10 upriver to Tongue Point, east of Astoria.

Astoria to Bonneville Dam. The lower Columbia's estimated 1 million white sturgeon come and go at will from their birthplace in this stretch of river to numerous other coastal bays. Sturgeon fishing is good most of the year out of Astoria but concentrates from Longview to Portland in February and March, as sturgeon follow the smelt run to the mouth of Washington's Cowlitz River. After March, they move upriver to below Bonneville, where large fish spawn in the heavy spring runoff current below the dam. Anglers catch and release 7- to 10-footers, and some specimens are even larger. When the shad are in, whole shad make good sturgeon bait; at other times, sand shrimp, smelt, and herring are popular.

Shad enter the Columbia in May, when fish move well into Washington's reaches of the upper Columbia and through Portland up to Willamette Falls near Oregon City. Shad strike small bright spinners and shad darts, both trailed from the sterns of anchored boats or fished from shore.

Bonneville Dam upriver. Four major hydroelectric dams are barriers to salmon and steelhead runs, but they also provide rich reservoir pools for smallmouth bass, walleye, channel catfish, and other species. Smallmouths love the rocky shorelines and are plentiful. The best fishing is from The Dalles to Umatilla, and plugs and jigs are especially preferred.

Large walleye are caught well below Bonneville Dam, even in and around Portland, but the best fishing is below John Day Dam from April through September and from Arlington to McNary Dam at Umatilla year-round.

Willamette River/northwest region. Portland is Oregon's largest city and also has one of the state's largest spring chinook salmon runs; the fish pass between skyscrapers from March through June. The Willamette River here sometimes has a thousand or more boats during the run's peak, and businessmen often fish during lunch hour.

The lower Willamette from the falls at Oregon City to where it enters the Columbia also holds good numbers of sturgeon, small- and largemouth bass, crappie, walleye, and yellow perch. On state-owned lands of Sauvie Island, within half an hour's drive of most of Portland, crappie, bullhead catfish, and carp attract year-round attention. Upriver from the falls, the Willamette and its sloughs are good for large- and smallmouth bass.

The Clackamas River, which drains the southwest flank of Mount Hood and enters the Willamette at Oregon City, gets spring chinook and summer and winter steelhead. So does the Sandy River, which drains the northwest flank of Mount Hood and enters the Columbia directly at Troutdale, east of Portland.

Tributaries with salmon and steelhead runs are the Molalla, South and North Santiam, and McKenzie Rivers. The Santiam, McKenzie, and upper Willamette systems are dammed, and reservoirs here teem with stocked trout, kokanee salmon, and landlocked chinook salmon.

Trout fishing in valley streams is limited by rules requiring the release of wild fish to help protect juvenile steelhead, which closely resemble small trout. Ponds and borrow pits (where gravel has been extracted for construction and the depressions filled with water) in Albany, Canby, Willamina, Junction City, Salem, and Eugene are routinely stocked with trout in late winter and spring, before they become too warm.

Southwest region. The Umpqua River originates in the Cascades and flows through Roseburg. From Roseburg to Scottsburg, above tidewater, this is a trophy smallmouth bass fishery. Daily catches in some stretches exceed a hundred fish a day. A strong run of shad inhabit the lower river, and there are good spring chinook and winter and summer steelhead runs. The summer steelhead run into the fly fishing–only waters of the North Umpqua is legendary.

The Rogue River is consistently Oregon's best steelhead and salmon producer, offering long stretches of scenic water and plentiful fish almost year-round. Portions of the river are accessible by boat only, and this has spawned an entire industry devoted to building the famous Rogue River drift boat. The river is also large enough to accommo-

Drift boat anglers prepare to float an Oregon river for steelhead.

date jet powered boats, but rapids inhibit powerboat navigation in places. The Rogue also harbors an unusual run of "half-pounder" steelhead. These are young fish that go to sea and return the same fall as 12- to 16-inchers, then return to the sea again to come back the following year as adult steelhead. Half-pounders travel all the way upriver to Medford.

Lakes and reservoirs throughout southwest Oregon are routinely stocked. Applegate and Selmac Reservoirs hold some of the state's biggest largemouth bass.

Central region. The Deschutes River is often called the queen of trout rivers because of its rich population of native redside trout that stuff themselves on the rich aquatic insect life of this desert tributary. By far the best time of year on the Deschutes is May and June for the salmonfly hatch, but October and its huge caddis hatch is terrific, as is the March brown hatch. The Deschutes, which empties into the Columbia 100 miles east of Portland, also shortstops much of the Inland Empire's run of summer steelhead. Steelhead get to the mouth of the Deschutes and choose its cool, mountain-fed water instead of continuing on through the reservoir-warmed Columbia. This makes the lower 25 or so miles of the Deschutes a steelhead haven. Baits are not allowed and aren't necessary.

Upriver from impassable Pelton Dam, the Deschutes creates Lake Billy Chinook, which offers a good population of bull trout that feed on the lake's abundant kokanee. Kokanee are so numerous in Billy Chinook that the state allows anglers to keep 25 fish per day.

South of Bend, the Deschutes is born in subterranean rivers that erupt from lava cliffs and create several natural and man-made lakes in the famous 120-mile-long Century Loop, a collection of trout waters with trophy lake trout, rainbows, kokanee salmon, brown trout, and brook trout.

Located southeast of Bend, natural East and Paulina Lakes in Newberry Crater have huge brook trout and kokanee big enough to sometimes look much like their seagoing sockeye salmon brethren.

Odell and Crescent Lakes southwest of Bend are premier kokanee and lake trout waters, and they offer good services at several resorts. Both lakes are often snowbound and ice covered well into April and May.

Diamond Lake is at the headwaters of the North Umpqua River and in the shadow of Crater Lake National Park. Diamond was once only a fish-barren puddle of snowmelt runoff inaccessible to trout because of impassable falls. Voracious Klamath basin rainbow trout are stocked annually and grow to huge proportions.

The Klamath system flowing to the sea through Northern California is born in legendary streams like the Williamson and Sprague Rivers north of Klamath Falls. Klamath Lake itself has several cold-water spring inlets where native rainbow trout seek protection from warm summer temperatures.

Central Oregon also has several private ponds where anglers can pay a fee to fish for various stocked trout and warmwater species. These are more than mere fish ponds but can be extremely expensive.

Northeast region. The John Day River enters the Columbia a short distance east of the Deschutes but is neither a product of glaciers nor cool mountain streams. Instead, it flows through desert country and warms quickly as sunlight bakes its canyon walls. This makes it the second of Oregon's premier smallmouth bass streams. Fish aren't quite as large as those in the lower Umpqua but are nearly as big and just as numerous. The water is best run in kayaks, canoes, and rafts in spring. Water levels get very low in the summer. It also has good runs of spring chinook and steelhead, which get through the lower sections well before the water warms.

Grande Ronde, Imnaha, and Wallowa Rivers are heavily stocked with summer steelhead. Some of these fish fail to head for the ocean and remain in freshwater, which makes the rivers excellent summer trout fisheries in a pristine, nearly alpine setting beneath the flanks of the Wallowa Mountain range and Eagle Cap Wilderness.

The Snake River forms the border between Idaho and Oregon, and dams along its length create an ideal habitat for more smallmouth bass and the state's best channel catfish populations. Brownlee Reservoir and its Powder River Arm create a crappie fishery so good that fish grow up to 12 inches long and are frequently taken illegally for the black market in Portland.

Numerous alpine and high desert lakes are good trout fisheries; Phillips and Thief Valley Reservoirs near Baker City are the best.

Southeast region. Oregon's largest fishing region is almost totally owned by the federal government and is thus public land. The Bureaus of Land Management and Reclamation provide fish habitat and offer numerous ponds, small reservoirs, and large impoundments. The state stocks these with fingerling trout every spring. The alkaline-base waters are insect rich, and trout grow up to an inch a month. By the following spring, the holdover fish are large and hungry.

Owyhee Reservoir is a 54-mile-long impoundment on the Owyhee River that was built to irrigate desert farms along the Snake River. It holds healthy crappie and largemouth bass populations, a few trout, and even some sturgeon. The river flowing into the reservoir is tough to reach but rewards the hardy with a good smallmouth bass and channel catfish experience.

Mann Lake, southeast of Burns, is a small, windswept natural lake at the base of Steens Mountain, an escarpment several thousand feet high. Only fly fishing is allowed for Lahontan cutthroat trout, and this is one of only a few Lahontan fisheries north of Pyramid Lake in Nevada.

Oregon protects many of its desert redband trout streams by closing them, but it stocks some of the same fish in lakes. The state has stocked hybrid striped bass in Ana and Thompson Valley Reservoirs to control scrap fish populations, and these battlers are best fished in early spring.

Crayfish. Nearly all of Oregon's freshwater holds populations of crayfish. The meat in the tails of these crustaceans is delicious, although some anglers prefer to use them as baitfish.

"Crawdads," as they are called here, are usually caught in mesh traps, baited with a variety of fish and animal parts to lure them inside. Chicken wings, fish heads and carcasses, and tuna liver catfood tins are favorites. Some Oregon lakes, like Timothy and Lake Billy Chinook among others, are so rich in crawdads that they support commercial fisheries for the Portland restaurant market.

Crawdads are prepared just like crabs; pop them into water heated to a roiling boil and leave them there for 12 to 15 minutes. The tail breaks off from the body, and you can pull or work out the flesh as you would with a miniature lobster.

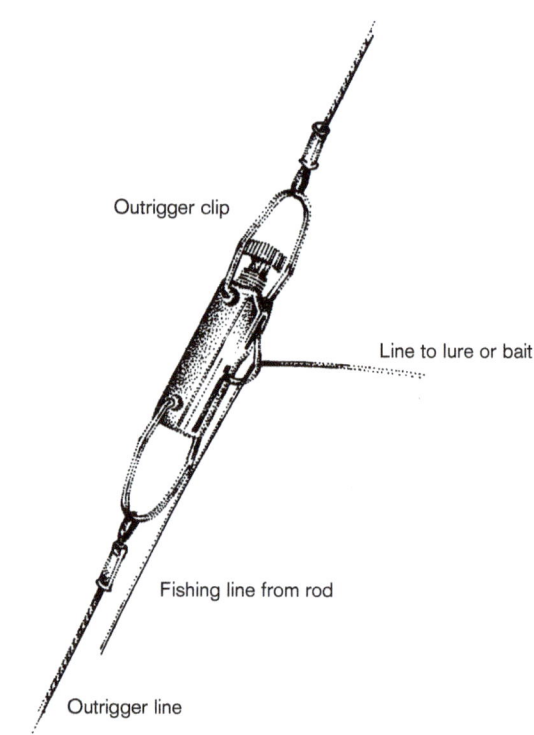

OUTBOARD BOAT
A boat powered by a transom-mounted outboard motor.
See: Bass Boat; Boat; Flats Boat; Jonboat; Sportfishing Boat; Walleye Boat.

OUTRIGGER
Indispensable tools for offshore trolling, outriggers consist of long poles mounted on the top or sides of offshore sportfishing boats. Once made of bamboo, outriggers are now almost exclusively aluminum.

Outriggers are designed so that they can be

raised or lowered. They are kept in the raised position when running and not trolling. They are fished in the lowered position, with some type of cord running in a loop to the outrigger's tip. This lanyard contains a release clip, to which the fishing line is attached. The clip is then run up the outrigger pole so that the fishing line leaves the rod tip, goes up to where the release clip is situated on the outrigger line, and then back to the bait behind the boat.

Outriggers are used for several purposes, depending on the kind of fishing being done, and the bait or lures being trolled. The most common use is when trolling either bait or offshore lures for pelagic species. Here, using an outrigger causes the bait or lure to be pulled from an elevated point, making it skip across the surface (on a fairly short line), thereby imitating the action of many important bait species.

In big-game fishing, and also when used in freshwater trolling (on large lakes and primarily for trout and salmon species), outriggers allow for a greater horizontal spread of lures or bait, permitting increased spacing of these objects and sometimes less likelihood of tangling trolled lines. Increased spacing is often a benefit in freshwater angling to reach fish that are outside of the boat's path of travel, although there are also other means of doing this *(see: sideplaner)*.

When fishing bait in big-game trolling, using an outrigger creates an automatic dropback when a fish strikes the bait, and the line releases from the clip and comes tight. This gives the fish a moment to mouth the bait and results in a better hookup.

Outriggers vary in length according to the size of boat. A 40- to 45-foot boat might have 33-foot outriggers; a 28-foot cabin boat might have 24-foot outriggers. Smaller versions are mounted on the gunwales or T-Tops *(see)* of shorter cabin and center console boats, with the latter seldom having outriggers over 15 feet in length due to the stress they exert on the top itself. The longer outriggers used on large boats employ spreaders to eliminate flex and stiffen the poles. Extra strong models are advisable for towing heavy objects when trolling, and when setting the release clip tension heavy, because a hard strike can put a lot of stress on the outrigger. Trolling with large baits and lures puts a lot of drag tension on the outriggers, as does getting whipped about in rough water.

See: Sportfishing Boat.

OVERFISHING

Harvesting fish at a rate that does not generate a desirable, sustainable, or "safe" population or stock level. This term is especially applied to saltwater, where many fish stocks have been depressed owing to overfishing, primarily, but not entirely, as a result of national and foreign commercial efforts. It is ordinarily used with respect to the harvesting of fish and the landings *(see)* reported, although it can be generally applied to fishing effort, with or without harvest; excessive fishing effort in freshwater, which may not reduce populations but which may result in more difficult angling and a lower success rate, is a form of overfishing, and is usually referenced as fishing pressure *(see)*.

See: Fisheries Management.

OVERHEAD CAST

A basic cast when using all forms of tackle.

See: Casting; Flycasting Tackle.

OVERRUN

A backlash *(see)* in a revolving spool reel, caused when the spool turns faster than the line is carried off that spool, resulting in a snarl of line that must be untangled to continue fishing.

OXBOW

A small lake or channel to the side of a river, formed when the main river meanders and cuts through a point of land and then rejoins itself downstream, creating an island that separates the two sections of water. Generally, the upstream opening of oxbows becomes silted and the meandering side channel is abandoned except in high water periods, thus creating a small lake in the abandoned channel. Oxbows may harbor some species of fish that do not acclimate to the large or swift flow of the river.

See: Backwater.

OXYGEN

The presence or absence of oxygen in various levels of a water body determines where such organisms as fish and zooplankton, which require oxygen, are found. Some waters—especially lakes, ponds, and still backwaters of rivers, or some sections of estuaries—are especially prone to oxygen depletion.

In most water bodies, oxygen concentration is chiefly caused by the infusion of molecular oxygen at the surface and by photosynthesis. In the ocean, there is usually sufficient oxygen throughout all but the most extreme depths, although coastal waters and estuaries may receive such an amount of nutrients and inactive organic matter (including the dumping of waste materials) that areas with slow circulation may be subject to excessive oxygen demand and possibly oxygen depletion. This situation has been known to cause fishkills *(see)*.

The same can happen in freshwater, but lakes and ponds have a different situation, since they are more often prone to poor water circulation, especially in the heat of summer, and they have clear thermal stratification *(see)*.

In the spring, when water in a lake is well mixed, oxygen is usually present at all depths and organisms may be distributed throughout the lake. In the summer, under layering conditions, little or no oxygen is produced in the lowest layer, or hypolimnion *(see)*. As oxygen is consumed through decomposition, levels may become too low for fish and zooplankton, which then must occupy the upper waters. If these low levels are prolonged and the upper waters become very warm, species that require cooler temperatures may die or be forced to move to places that have both suitable temperatures and sufficient oxygen (a tributary spring, for example). With the onset of cooler temperatures and wind activity in the fall, the lake layers break down and the turnover *(see)* replenishes oxygen to the bottom waters.

Formation of ice in winter severs the atmospheric supply of oxygen to the lake. If sunlight can penetrate through the snow and ice, algae and weeds will continue to produce oxygen. If the snow cover is too great, this process will be inhibited. Since respiration and decomposition continue, the amount of oxygen consumed may exceed the amount produced. This is quite common in lakes that have large amounts of weeds, leaves, and other organic debris available for decomposition in the sediment. If oxygen levels fall too low, fish and other aquatic life may die.

Monitoring oxygen would seem to be a strategy that anglers would employ under the theory that an area with insufficient oxygen will not contain sportfish. Although oxygen monitoring devices (meters) have been developed for testing this aspect of water, they have not been popular because the most popular sportfish species seldom inhabit the more stagnant waters that are likely to have low oxygen levels. Nevertheless, factors that cause oxygen depletion should be of concern to anglers, at least from the standpoint of environmental awareness.

OXYGEN METER

A portable electronic device used by a relatively small number of anglers, primarily freshwater bass anglers, to measure the oxygen content of prospective fishing water. If the oxygen level is unsuitable to the fish they seek to catch, they reason that those fish are unlikely to be in that location, and they move elsewhere.

Fish, like people, must have oxygen to survive. Most of the oxygen in our fishing waters comes from photosynthetic algae, bacteria, and plankton. A lesser amount comes from rooted plants and the interaction of wind and waves. The oxygen level in water is often directly connected to the amount of available light and water pH. Photosynthesis, for instance, has a localized effect on both pH and available oxygen. Whether due to rooted plants in shallower water or from plankton in open water, photosynthesis tends to raise pH as it removes carbon dioxide and generates oxygen. When dead plants decay, however, an almost opposite situation occurs: The process of decay removes oxygen from the water, generates carbon dioxide, and lowers the local pH.

Most research with regard to the effect of oxygen levels on fish has been done with freshwater bass. Oxygen dissolved in water is measured in parts per million (ppm), and 8 to 9 ppm is considered ideal for bass. In research, investigators report that bass were seldom found where oxygen levels dropped below 5 ppm.

An oxycline, or a layer of water containing enough oxygen to support fish, may form in freshwater lakes although the water stratified beneath it may not contain a survivable amount. Naturally, this varies with species because some can survive in less oxygenated water than others, and it varies by time of year. In some lakes and reservoirs that have trout, the oxygen content at the depth that contains their preferred temperature may be inadequate in the midst of the summer; this may cause the fish to die, or send them to cool shallow tributaries with springs, where both temperature and oxygen needs can be met.

The use of an oxygen meter may be helpful in determining where to fish for selected species in stillwater environments, but it has not been demonstrated to be a necessity for anglers.

PACK ROD

A multi-piece fishing rod whose sections (usually three or more) are of small enough length to be packed inside a protective tube and carried within or outside of various luggage, especially a daypack or backpack used by hikers and campers. Pack rods are usually either of fly or spinning configuration (a few are convertible) and may also be called travel rods *(see)*.
See: Rod, Fishing.

PADDLEFISH *Polyodon spathula.*

Other names—spoonbill, spoonbill catfish, spoonbill cat, American paddlefish, Mississippi paddlefish, shovel-billed cat, duck-billed cat, spadefish, shovelfish.

Members of the primitive Polyodontidae family of bony fish, paddlefish are distant relatives of sturgeon *(see)*, whose closest living relatives are gar *(see)* and bowfin *(see)*. They are large, slow-maturing, and long-lived freshwater fish of large inland rivers. They have a distinctive appearance and a prehistoric lineage that dates back hundreds of millions of years. They are not related to catfish.

There are only two known species of paddlefish. The American species *(P. spathula)*, which is profiled here, is commonly referred to simply as paddlefish, lives only in the United States in the Mississippi River system, and is a threatened species, although it is pursued in some areas by both commercial fishermen and recreational anglers. The other species is the Chinese paddlefish *(Psephurus gladius)*, which is native to the Lower Yangtze River in China; also known as the Chinese swordfish, it is believed to be near extinction due to dams and overfishing, and, according to one report, attained a maximum weight exceeding 1,000 pounds.

Paddlefish have been steadily declining in numbers due to overexploitation in the late nineteenth and early twentieth centuries, habitat degradation (e.g., construction of dams, locks, and other migratory obstructions), and pollution. The life history of this species, and its slow-maturing and intermittent spawning, have contributed to its vulnerability to these activities. Paddlefish are protected in some states, and restricted fisheries exist in others. Populations of North American paddlefish that can sustain fishing pressure exist in only a few localities, and poaching is a continued threat. Poaching occurs for the purpose of securing eggs, which are substituted for sturgeon eggs and valuable when made into caviar.

Paddlefish became commercially important for their flesh in the late 1800s and early 1900s after the collapse of sturgeon fisheries. Some states established regulations in the early 1900s in hopes of protecting paddlefish from similar overexploitation.

The roe carried in large, gravid female paddlefish was not recognized as valuable until the 1970s, when diplomatic relations between Iraq, Iran, and the U.S. deteriorated and a ban was enacted to stop all imports from Iraq and Iran into the U.S. This fueled a demand for caviar, with an associated price increase for roe to $26 to $33 per kilogram by 1979 (which more than doubled 10 years later). Although caviar has traditionally been made from sturgeon, the caviar made from paddlefish is said to be equal in quality to that of sturgeon.

The paddlefish caviar market was strong in 1980, when 340 kilograms of roe were taken from Tennessee and Cumberland River impoundments, the major source of paddlefish in the U.S. By the mid-1980s the Tennessee River populations had been overexploited, and commercial fishermen turned to less exploited stocks. They went to other areas, such as Louisiana, where emergency closures were necessary to study the population dynamics before the species collapsed. There is still a demand for paddlefish caviar because sturgeon, especially in Asia, continue to be imperiled. In addition some recreational fisheries for the species still exist, although they represent a fraction of the interest experienced in the late nineteenth and early twentieth centuries.

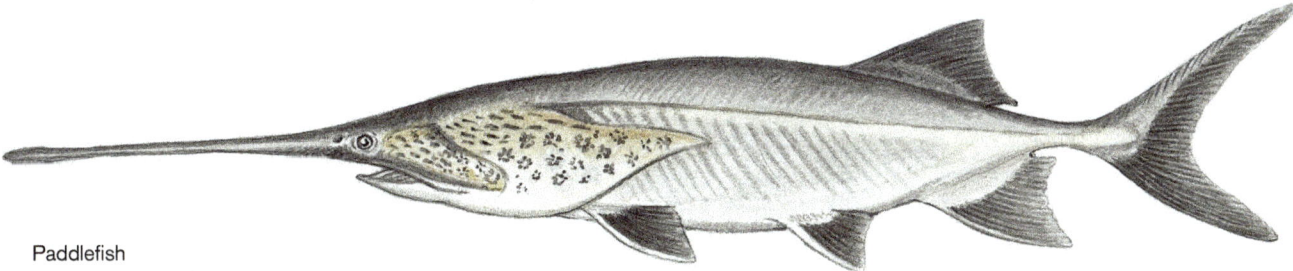
Paddlefish

Identification. The paddlefish is almost shark-like in appearance, and if its long paddle extension were cut off, it would look even more like a shark. Unlike sharks or other fish, paddlefish have a unique, long, paddle- or spoonlike snout. The function of the snout has not been completely determined, although it is highly enervated. Paddlefish are suspected of using their snout to locate prey, perhaps to stir sediments on the bottom. There are two small barbels on the snout, and the underside is dotted with sensory pits.

Paddlefish also have a greatly elongated operculum flap, an extremely large basketlike mouth, long gill rakers, and a deeply forked tail with a high dorsal fin that resembles a shark fin. Adult paddlefish are toothless, but juveniles have teeth on their jaws. The color is slate gray to purplish above. They have an almost white belly, and the skin is smooth, like that of a catfish, with the only scales being on the caudal peduncle.

Size/Age. Paddlefish may live to be 25 to 30 years old. They often grow to 100 pounds, although the average fish is much smaller. Literature from the past contains reports of paddlefish that grew to more than 200 pounds. World records are not kept for this species by the International Game Fish Association (IGFA) because they are not hooked in the mouth, but snagged. Nevertheless, state records show that Montana produced a 142-pound, 8-ounce fish in 1973 in the Missouri River; Missouri produced a 134-pound, 12-ounce fish in Lake of the Ozarks in 1998 and a 130-pounder in 1992; North Dakota produced a 120-pounder in the Missouri River in 1993; and Oklahoma produced a 112-pounder in the Grand River in 1992. The 130-pound fish from the state of Missouri was determined to be 20 years old. The 134-pounder from Missouri was more than 20 years old, 76 inches in overall length, 52 inches from eye to tail fork, and 44 inches in girth.

Distribution. The American paddlefish ranges throughout the Mississippi River drainage, from the Missouri River in Montana southward. Some populations are self-sustaining, whereas others are maintained with stocking. American paddlefish have been sent to Russia (50,000 paddlefish eggs were shipped from Missouri in the mid-1970s) in an attempt to establish the species there and augment caviar production, which has suffered due to dwindling sturgeon populations.

Habitat. Paddlefish prefer low-gradient rivers, pools, backwaters, and oxbows; they also exist in flood-plain reservoirs as a result of dam building. When not spawning, they are pelagic and are found in open water.

Life history/Behavior. Adults migrate upstream to gravel bars in the spring, spawning in high currents with temperatures between 50°F and 60°F. They are commonly found in tailwaters below dams, which impede their upstream migration. In rivers where they are able to travel unimpeded, sturgeon may migrate significant distances; in 1996, Iowa biologists tracked a radio-equipped 32-pound female paddlefish more than 100 miles from its suspected spawning site in the Cedar River, through the Iowa River and into the Mississippi River.

Spawning occurs in midstream, and the adhesive eggs attach to the gravel on the bottom. When hatched, the fry are moved downstream by swift currents into deep pools with lower water velocities. Where oxbows occur, they may serve as alternate spawning sites and important nursery areas for young paddlefish, whose early growth is rapid. Males mature at 7 years of age and females at 9 to 10 years, sometimes longer. Females are very fecund, with 10,000 eggs per kilogram, but they are intermittent spawners, breeding approximately every 2 years. Several males spawn with each female. Growth and fecundity of paddlefish vary with latitude; higher growth and lower fecundity occur in the more southerly portions of its range; the inverse is true for more northerly populations.

Food and feeding habits. Paddlefish eat zooplankton, microscopic plants and animals that live in open water. They swim through the water with their large mouth open and strain out the zooplankton with numerous (hundreds) gill rakers. Contrary to popular belief, they are not bottom feeders and move about in shallow water or near the surface of slow-moving currents with favorable foraging conditions.

Angling. Because they eat only plankton, conventional angling methods using lures, flies, and baits are not applicable for paddlefish. For this reason, and also because they are usually encountered only in spring when spawning, these fish are taken by snagging *(see)*, a practice that cannot be considered sportfishing or angling, and one that disqualifies any fish from world-record consideration.

Snagging seasons exist in some states, and casting or trolling with snag hooks takes place in tailwater pools, where paddlefish are most likely to be found. Snagging fisheries exist for paddlefish in Montana, North Dakota, South Dakota, Missouri, Arkansas, Oklahoma, and Iowa, primarily in the Mississippi, Arkansas, and Missouri Rivers, but also in some inland waters. This species is still part of legal commercial fisheries in some states and may be part of indigenous fisheries, which often entails netting.

Due to the generally low numbers and feeding habits of paddlefish, it is extremely rare for anglers to legitimately catch one, or even to inadvertently snag one while fishing legitimately for other species. Anglers should check regulations regarding fishing for, or catching, paddlefish. Although they are fairly hardy, to help preserve their existence, paddlefish should be handled carefully and returned to the water quickly.

See: Sturgeon.

PAKISTAN

As with other southwest Asian and also Middle East countries, little has been reported in the Western world about sportfishing opportunity in Pakistan, and it is not a hotbed of international angling travel. Situated in the northernmost part of the Arabian Sea in the western Indian Ocean, Pakistan's coast is the recipient of warm ocean currents moving up from East Africa and also up along the coast of western India. In addition, the main port and largest city of Kar chi is in close proximity to the deep Indus Canyon and its neighboring shelf.

As a result, a wide variety of pelagic species remains close to Pakistan's shores throughout the year, among them Pacific sailfish, striped marlin, yellowfin tuna, bigeye tuna, wahoo, bonito, and dolphin. Other available fish include various sharks, barred mackerel, cobia, barracuda, amberjack, giant trevally, queenfish, rainbow runners, and barramundi, as well as an assortment of grouper, snapper, and coral reef species.

The Arabian Sea is rough in summer, making September through late April the locally preferred angling period. Cape Montze, Churna Island, and Kaio Island are the favored nearshore fishing spots; offshore trolling occurs in the shelf waters beyond Churna Island. Some boats available for charter may be found in Kar chi.

PALATINE TEETH

Teeth located on the palatine bones inside the upper jaw bone, usually behind the vomerine tooth patch.
See: Anatomy.

PALM

To apply variable pressure with the palm of the hand or, more often, with several fingers, to the revolving or turning spool of a reel when fighting a fish that is taking line. This technique is used with smaller reels, primarily fly, spinning, and baitcasting versions, and may be practiced with concurrent tension on the reel from its own drag (see) mechanism. If a fish surges, the hand or palm can be immediately removed from the reel, lessening drag tension and returning it to the tension previously set. Palming a reel spool is often done when the preset drag tension setting on the reel is insufficient to help tire or control the fish, or when a large fish is close to being landed.
See: Playing Fish.

PALMING RIM

The overlapping rim flange on the spool of a fly reel, manually used as an auxiliary spool brake.
See: Flycasting Tackle.

PALOMAR KNOT

A fishing knot for terminal connections.
See: Knots, Fishing.

PALOMETA *Trachinotus goodei.*
Other names—gafftopsail pompano, joefish, longfin pompano, sand mackerel; French: *carangue quatre*; Portuguese: *galhudo*; Spanish: *palometa, pampano.*

This small species is a member of the Carangidae family of jacks and pompano.

Identification. A bright silvery fish with a deep body, the palometa may be grayish green and blue above and yellowish on the breast. It has dark, elongated dorsal and anal fins that are bordered in a bluish shade, and a black-edged tail. It also has four narrow bars that vary from black to white and are located high on the sides. Traces of a fifth bar appear near the tail.

It is similar to the Florida pompano *(see: pompano, Florida)*, but the front lobes of the dorsal and anal fins are blackish and very elongate (the tips reach back to the middle of the caudal fin).

Size. The palometa rarely reaches 1 pound in weight and is usually 7 to 14 inches long; 18 inches is its maximum length. The all-tackle world record is a 1-pound, 3-ounce Bahamian fish.

Distribution. In the western Atlantic, palometa extend from Massachusetts to Argentina as well as throughout the Caribbean Sea, the Gulf of Mexico, and Bermuda. They are common in the eastern and southern Caribbean, occasional in the Bahamas and Florida, and uncommon to rare in the northwest Caribbean.

Habitat. Inhabiting waters up to 35 feet deep, palometa generally form large schools in clear-water areas of the surf zone, along sandy beaches and bays, occasionally around reefs, and in rocky areas.

Spawning behavior. This species is thought to spawn offshore in spring, summer, and fall.

Food. Palometa feed on crustaceans, marine worms, mollusks, and small fish.

Angling. The palometa readily strikes small artificial lures but is seldom a deliberate quarry of anglers owing to its small size.
See: Inshore Fishing; Jacks.

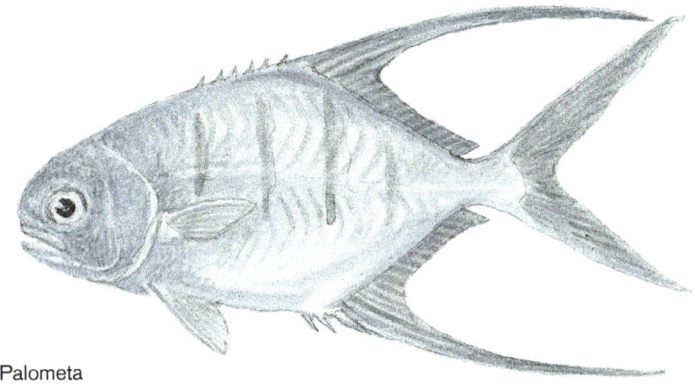

Palometa

PAN DRESSING

A method of cleaning small fish that may not be suitable for filleting or that are to be cooked whole. See: **Fish Preparation—Cleaning/Dressing.**

PANAMA

One legend concerning the derivation of the word *Panama* says that when Cuna Indians were asked where to find gold by Spanish soldiers hundreds of years ago, they responded in their language with the words *panna mai,* which means "far away." Panama is neither far from nor near to most of the North American anglers who are likely to visit it. Linking Central and South America and hosting the famous east-west canal passage, however, it is well situated to receive anglers, and well positioned to host popular gamefish, which are found in abundance both near and far from its Pacific shores.

Ironically, the second explanation for the derivation of this country's name is that it came from an Indian word meaning "land of many fish." Among the various species common to Panama are black, striped, and blue marlin; sailfish; wahoo; dolphin; yellowfin tuna; sharks; roosterfish; cubera snapper; skipjacks; jack crevalle; bigeye and bluefin trevally; mullet and Colorado snapper; houndfish; rainbow runners; snook; tarpon; and corvina. You know the quantity and variety of fish must be substantial when you see just how many specimens caught in Panamanian waters currently fill, or previously filled, the International Game Fish Association (IGFA) record book, especially in the fly-rod categories.

These include wahoo fly-rod records for dolphin, roosterfish, Pacific sailfish, and wahoo, and line-class world records for swordfish (now rare), Pacific sailfish, black marlin, and dolphin. Most of these and others are light-line/light-tackle catches of considerable accomplishment, further underscoring the evidence of great abundance. Many attempts and many lost opportunities must typically occur before an angler connects with a record-setting fish on fly or light tackle.

The freshwater angler, incidentally, will also find angling opportunities in Panama and can catch peacock bass in Gatún Lake, an impoundment along the Río Chagresito, which flows into the Panama Canal. Although not known for large peacocks, these waters offer them in abundance.

Caribbean

Panama is washed by the Caribbean Sea to the north and the Pacific Ocean to the south. The Caribbean winter is often windy and rough, whereas winter on the Pacific is the dry season and features generally sunny, warm, and calm days. Saltwater sportfishing was virtually undeveloped along Panama's Caribbean coast until the late 1990s. It is best fished from May through December. Isla Grande, 35 miles east of Colon (the beginning of the canal), features excellent wahoo trolling, plus yellowfin and blackfin tuna and a shot at sailfish or blue marlin. Bottom fishing and jigging for grouper and cubera snapper are also productive. The San Blas Islands to the east are the home of the Cuna Indians and remain very primitive. The offshore opportunities are complemented by inshore angling for tarpon and snook. The latter are also found around some mainland rivers draining into the Caribbean, but many have been ruined by agricultural pesticides.

Tarpon and snook live in the Panama Canal, too. Tarpon by nature are strictly an Atlantic species, and it was long assumed that the colder water on the Pacific side kept them from adopting a new home. During the 1990s, however, tarpon were caught in many areas along the Pacific coast.

Pacific

For most of the latter part of the twentieth century, the Pacific side of Panama has provided the most notable angling. Many anglers equate Panamanian fishing with live baiting for large black marlin over Hannibal Bank, a seamount off the nation's southwest Pacific coast. Others think of both billfishing and light-tackle angling near Piñas Bay on Panama's southernmost Pacific coast on the South American mainland near the border with Colombia. To still others it means fabulous light-tackle action for inshore species off that same coast or around the island of Coiba.

The Hannibal Bank area sees large numbers of black marlin, and occasionally Pacific blues, from January through March each year. Pacific sailfish and wahoo pass through in great numbers in the summer months. Pelagic species are attracted to Hannibal Bank, a hump that rises from 1,000 fathoms to merely 20 fathoms, and when the proper mix of currents washes by here, the marlin fishing is excellent. This bank is also fished for bottom fish and other nonbillfish species.

At Piñas, the big blacks run from December through March and are soon followed by sailfish throughout the summer. Light-tackle inshore fishing is excellent year-round at Piñas. Inshore anglers generally seek roosterfish and cubera snapper on plugs, baits, or jigs close to beaches or rocky outcrops near shore. Various jacks, plus grouper and offshore targets such as rainbow runners, yellowfin tuna, and dorado, also keep the light-tackle angler busy at Piñas Bay and around Coiba Island. Piñas Bay has long been serviced by the only camp in the area, Tropic Star Lodge, noted for first-class accommodations and food. Anglers are flown in to a nearby airstrip and then driven partway before boarding small boats to complete the trip to the camp.

The 100,000-acre island of Coiba, at the edge of the Gulf of Chiriqui, has long been a prison camp. Club Pacifico de Panama was established there in the early 1970s but stopped operating after 1987 and is now the National Park Headquarters, as Panama's government encourages ecological tourism even while maintaining the prison. It is possible to run to Hannibal Bank from Coiba, but an abundance of all varieties of fish inshore makes this unnecessary. Access to Coiba is provided by the mother ship *Coiba Express*. Anglers are flown into the prison landing strip on Coiba and transferred to the mother ship by the smaller fishing boats.

Some billfishing and a full range of inshore fishing are also available in the Contadora Islands between Panama City and Piñas. Those islands are mostly a tourist destination, however.

The excitement of black marlin fishing in Panama is heightened by a popular and effective technique: catching and rigging live skipjacks for bait, then power-drifting them behind the boat. The hapless baits (small yellowfins are also used but rarely available) are first to sense the predators approaching, signaling their panic by swimming frantically to the side of the fishing boat in an attempt to flee. When this happens, the angler experiences a great sense of anticipation, an adrenaline rush exceeded only by the fight that follows. The 2- to 3-pound skipjacks are trolled alive and rigged with a hook in front of their snout via a loop of line sewn through their eye sockets, a method that takes practiced anglers just a few seconds, keeping the baitfish alive and frisky.

Although Hannibal Bank is known for black marlin, billfishing enthusiasts have focused more attention in recent times on the Piñas Bay area, and this trend is responsible for many of the aforementioned records. Piñas is situated close to deep water and the influence of currents that lure clusters of baitfish.

At Piñas, a great deal of the billfish trolling occurs out in the Gulf of Panama, about 10 miles from the mainland at Zane Grey Reef, named after the pioneering author/angler but evidently not because of local exploits. Seamounts there feature dropoffs from 130 to 600 feet, and these are the main attractions for marlin. In fact, many species favor this area, sometimes so many that preventing nontargeted fish, such as dolphin, from nabbing baits becomes difficult.

Although billfish are caught off the Panamanian coast year-round, the hot marlin action generally runs from December through April. Blue marlin, which are the least prominent of the three marlin species found here, show up first in December in a normal year, followed closely by blacks. Blues are more prominent to the east than they are near Coiba, and blacks are the mainstay of the fishery in both locales. Both fish average in the 300-pound range, although fish in excess of 500 pounds are taken, as are some blacks in the 700-pound category. The biggest black marlin taken from Piñas waters weighed nearly 900 pounds.

Striped marlin become available in March at Piñas but are rare around Coiba; they are a less-frequent catch than black marlin at any time. March also brings the heaviest concentration of sailfish; although sails are present throughout the year, April and May are prime times. On the most extraordinary days, boats have reported landing between 15 and 30 sailfish, but an average good day takes in roughly 20 billfish. Sailfish are also present all year off Coiba, but never in such large quantities. The best sailfishing there is during the May to December rainy season, which features mostly late-afternoon and nighttime rain, except during September and October, when it can be persistent.

Piñas Bay is a focal point for excellent light-tackle and big-game fishing.

The billfishing slows from late September through early December. That, however, is also when the wahoo fishing is at its peak, and reports indicate that several dozen of these fish have been caught in a single day, although this is not the norm. Wahoo are noted as rainy-season fish and can be trolled in great quantities at times during that period. Most range from 15 to 30 pounds, with some larger specimens mixed in. Throughout the rest of the season, they are an occasional catch.

With an abundance of fish, opportunities are plentiful to use light big-game tackle for marlin, spinning tackle for sailfish, and fly tackle for sails, striped marlin, and small blacks. These waters are one of the foremost locations for light-tackle (and big-game fly) angling precisely because so many fish are raised. The boats favored here are predominantly small because the water is often calm, and the ability to fight and land such attractive species from smaller craft does enhance the fishery. The boats used at Coiba are generally diesel-powered 23- to 28-foot open boats that operate from the mother ship. At Piñas, 31-foot Bertrams have been used since the early days. When fishing is at its peak, anglers in Panamanian waters actually switch to lighter tackle to increase the challenge. Surely that speaks reams about the angling.

Trolling and billfishing are not the only pursuits here. As mentioned, many opportunities are present inshore for casting and jigging for hard-hitting, strong-pulling creatures. This is especially true off Coiba Island, where casting popping plugs, plug trolling, jigging, and making deep drops with live or dead baits can yield cubera snapper, jack crevalle, bigeye trevally, bluefin trevally, mullet snapper, and roosterfish, plus assorted other species. It is not uncommon to ring up a catch of 20 fish species over several days.

The bottom drops off significantly around Coiba, so anglers needn't go far to reach productive territory. And, with plenty of baitfish schools around, anglers are virtually guaranteed opportunities to cast to various species marauding baits during a normal day.

Tarpon and snook are also present in Panama's Pacific waters. Tarpon have migrated to new grounds in the Pacific via the Panama Canal, and they have been caught at Coiba. Some rivers near Panama City seem to be developing regular runs of tarpon. Among them is the Bayano, about 35 miles to the west. Fish of 100 pounds are common here, and there are reports of commercially netted specimens weighing between 200 and 250 pounds. The activity is seasonal, concentrating in January and February. Snook are also present in that river, primarily from December through May, and have been caught to 47 pounds.

PANFISH

This term is used widely by anglers and fisheries managers to collectively describe a variety of small fish of several species. There is no individual species called a panfish. The term is used almost universally in freshwater, seldom in saltwater; although common to anglers, it may be unfamiliar or even confusing to nonanglers.

The term "panfish" often refers to fish that, when fried whole, can fit into a pan, but it is also often understood to mean species that are not technically classified as gamefish (see) and that are usually abundant and as valued for their tasty flesh as for the enjoyment of catching them.

As explained elsewhere, the classification of species as gamefish, and the public view of their sporting value or virtue, are variable issues. Therefore, in some quarters, panfish are viewed as gamefish, whereas in others they are not. "Gamefish" or not, small species that are susceptible to angling are valued highly for the recreation they afford, and for the delicious table fare they become.

Although panfish are commonly linked by these factors, the species that fit under this umbrella are not all linked biologically. Many "panfish" are members of the sunfish (see) family, the perch family, the bass (see: black bass) family, the catfish (see) family, and the sucker (see suckers) family. These include, but are not limited to, such sunfish as the green, longear, orange spotted, spotted, and redear varieties; plus bluegill, Sacramento perch, rock bass, warmouth bass, black crappie, white crappie, yellow bass, white bass, yellow perch, and white perch. In some areas, people include suckers, bullhead, pickerel, and even carp in this category. The primary, and most widely distributed, panfish are discussed separately here.

Whether panfish fit into a pan or are classified as gamefish is immaterial to most people who fish for them. Although black bass, trout, and walleye garner higher accolades for sport, and thus greater media attention, it is an indisputable fact that more time is devoted to angling for the collective group of panfish than for any other freshwater species. They are not only a strong component of spring and summer open-water fishing, but in many places they are also the prime quarry for ice anglers.

Furthermore, panfish are especially significant for peaking children's interest in angling, and for providing family fishing opportunities.

The fun in catching panfish is a significant factor in their popularity, as most are very scrappy when hooked on light tackle. Sunfish, rock bass, perch, crappie, and other panfish dart and dive, run and turn, and offer a fine short-term fight on light fishing equipment, even if they are only 6 or 7 inches long and a half pound in size. Compared on an ounce-for-ounce basis, panfish are among the most determined and vigorous fish caught by anglers.

As mentioned, the popularity of panfish—crappie, perch, white bass, and bullhead in particular—rests equally in their appeal as table fare. They are among the most favored freshwater food fish, in part because of their size, and they are delicious when prepared in a variety of ways. A feast of fresh panfish is one of the finest—and usually simplest—meals that a fish lover can have.

Feasts, in fact, are usually possible because panfish are relatively abundant in most places where they are found. Fisheries managers generally encourage harvesting panfish and apply a fairly liberal creel limit (see) to facilitate this. Although panfish provide a good forage base for larger gamefish, they can quickly overpopulate a lake or pond. Most panfish are generally prolific spawners, and harvest-

Yellow perch are a popular panfish for ice fishing.

ing them is helpful in keeping fish populations in balance. When populations get out of balance, a body of water can be populated by stunted sunfish, crappie, or other species, and removing significant numbers is necessary to help with this problem. Fortunately, delectable flesh makes this a task that many anglers are willing to take on.

There would be a lot more eating and catching, however, if more anglers would take more time to learn about panfish and to pursue them more carefully. The following information is condensed, somewhat generalized, and focused on the bluegill, crappie, yellow bass, white bass, and white perch, although much of what is contained here applies to species with more limited or similar ranges. Yellow perch *(see: perch, yellow)*, bullhead *(see)*, and pickerel *(see: pickerel, chain)* are covered under their respective headings.

Most people think panfish are caught strictly on live baits, and much of the time this is true. At times, however, lures or flies will take more panfish than will live baits. So don't become a one-bait or one-tactic panfish angler. The more versatile your approach, the more panfish you'll get on your line.

Panfishing isn't difficult, but it can be frustrating, and catching the larger specimens with some consistency often involves more than being on the right body of water. If you are a beginner, consider seeking out an experienced angler for the species you're after; offer to furnish the lunch and soft drinks in appreciation for the coaching. Lacking that, hire a good guide for a day; guides who take clients panfishing are hard to find in many northern states but are more common in Southern waters, especially on big lakes and impoundments.

Bluegill

Bluegills are a schooling fish; where you find one, there are others nearby. They are aggressive and will eat most anything you offer them when hungry, but they can be mighty picky on occasion. So it pays to take along both live baits and artificial lures when you're specifically seeking these fish. When bluegills are on a feeding spree you can often see them churning the water, voraciously attacking a larvae hatch, mosquitoes, or the eggs of nesting bass or crappie.

Where to fish. The cliché that "fish are where you find them" is old but so true with bluegills. And, except for springtime, when bluegills are bedding against shallow-water shores, you just have to shop around from one cover type to another until you meet up with a school.

Spring is when the fishing is easiest. Be out early in the day, when the water usually is calmest. Move quietly around the shoreline and look for two things: gravel, rock, or sandy bottom areas; and shallow water off points or around weeds and lily pads. All of these are typical spawning spots.

As you move, keep your eyes ahead to watch for the sudden darting movement of bluegills spooked by other fish, fish-eating birds, or your approach. Have a cold drink, wait until things quiet down, then quietly approach and fish the spot.

After spring gives way to summer, finding bluegills can be tougher because they hie to deeper hangouts. Now is the time to pay attention to cover, including logs, bushes, and brush, and to places like grassy flats, channels, lily-pad clusters, and away-from-shore humps.

When midsummer weeds become denser, try this old trick: Take along a sickle and run your boat into the weed mass. Usually the weeds are no more than a foot deep. Cut a bushel-basket-size hole on each side of the boat, then leave for about an hour. While you're gone, the minute zooplankton and algae you have shaken loose may have attracted nearby bluegills. When you return, approach quietly and fish your handmade hotspots.

During fall and early winter, food is scarcer, forcing bluegills to roam in search of food supplies. Keeping this in mind, anglers should investigate both shallow and deep dropoff areas, remaining alert for any school movement. Try a bait at different depths until the float nods its head to signal not only a strike, but also the location of a school of fish.

Once you locate seasonal hangouts, you're set for the year. Keep notes on these spots, and be aware of feeding times. You'll discover that habit patterns are dependable from one year to the next. However, these times and places will differ from one lake to another. Much of this is due to variances in cover types, lake temperatures, and hangouts in deep and shallow lakes.

Tactics. A cricket comes as near to being infallible for bluegills as any live bait. Never take along just a few dozen. Feeding crickets to bluegills is like feeding popcorn to a hungry youngster. It disappears in a hurry, so be sure to bring plenty. Many old-timers never venture out without a couple hundred. Keep the crickets cool and feed them oatmeal between trips, and they won't go to waste.

A commercial cricket box makes them easy to grab in a hurry. You can make a cricket container out of a large oats box. Near the top edge, cut a quarter-size hole and staple it over with a half-dollar-size flexible rubber cover. When you want a cricket, just raise the flap, shake out a cricket, and the flap will automatically close the hole.

Use a No. 8 long-shanked Aberdeen hook with crickets; this is easy to grasp and remove when the fish is deeply hooked. Impale the cricket through the tougher shoulder area and let it wiggle loosely on the bend. Bluegills will swipe a bunch without getting hooked, but the catch is worth it.

One way to reduce fish pilferage and increase your catching average is to learn to read a sensitive float *(see)* or bobber. Use one shaped like a slim pencil, and paint the very tip bright red. Watch this for the slightest movement. If it tilts to the left, it means a bluegill has sucked in the cricket from the right side. If it rises the slightest bit, a bluegill has slurped the cricket from above. Set the hook at any of these indications and you'll not only catch more but also bigger bluegill.

The best artificial lure is a green, sponge-rubber spider with white legs on a No. 10 hook. This can be used on a fly rod, below a float on a casting rig, or dunked at the end of a line on a cane or graphite pole.

As it absorbs water and sinks naturally, the rubber legs make a minute movement that seems to trigger a bluegill's feeding instincts. Cast near cover, let it sink very slowly, and if the line stops sinking, set the hook—a bluegill has inhaled the spider. At times, a tiny bit of red worm on the hook barb adds a touch of magic.

When using the spider with a spinning or spincasting outfit, try attaching a small spinner to it. If it is too light to cast, add a couple of split shot in front of the spinner to give needed weight. Keep the retrieve very slow; the blade should barely turn over. If you get followers but no takers, try adding a dab of marshmallow on the hook.

Bluegill are caught on other items, of course. Pieces of worms and small grubs impaled on small hooks and fished under a float are commonly used when crickets aren't available. You need to use a small hook and fully thread the bait onto it to keep the bluegill (and other sunfish) from nibbling it away. Small spinners sometimes catch bluegill, although seldom in quantity to compare with natural baits. Small flies (wet flies, nymphs, and dry flies on No. 12 and 14 hooks) and tiny cork-bodied popping bugs catch shallow-water bluegill, especially during the nesting season, and getting these fish to take on the surface is great fun.

Crappie

There actually are two species of crappie, the black and white varieties *(see: crappie, black; crappie, white),* but there's so little difference between the two that they can be treated as one when it comes to finding and catching them.

Also a sunfish family member, the crappie is considered by many to be the most desirable for table fare because of its tender, succulent flesh. Commonly called specks, crappie in the South are considered better tasting than those up North; however, northern waters are likely to hold yellow perch, which are as good to the palate as any crappie.

Where to fish. When you set out on a strange lake in search of crappie, think brush, brush, or the nearest thing resembling brush. The reason is simple. Crappie are mostly minnow eaters, and minnows hide around any kind of brush, or weeds, to avoid being eaten. So crappie go where minnows hide. Other hideouts are fallen trees, bushes, old piers, flooded weeds, or shoals covered with coontail or sphagnum moss, plus wrecked boats, docks, building blocks or brushpiles *(see)* that have been planted to attract minnows, and undercut banks.

When these don't pay off, try drifting with the wind or slow-trolling across a lake, plying a minnow at different depths until you cross paths with a school of roving crappie.

Big yellow perch, sunfish, and crappie add up to a memorable day of panfishing.

Tactics. Get a long cane pole, or a telescoping graphite one for handiness, and attach an equal length of No. 6 nylon monofilament line. A popular crappie hook is a No. 2 Model Perfect or Carlisle fine wire. Either will make a small hole in a minnow's carcass and have a bend wide enough not to injure a minnow as you insert the hook.

For drift fishing, hook the minnow in the lips and be careful not to go deep enough to enter the brain area. For dunking the minnow into brush, hook it through the dorsal fin base, being careful not to penetrate the spine.

Keep moving from brush to brush, easing in close so you can dunk the minnow right against the cover—the closer the better. Be sure to keep minnows lively to catch the bigger crappie, called "slabs." An aerated minnow bucket helps. Drifting is also a standard tactic because crappie roam around in schools, and it sometimes takes a roaming angler to find them.

When you catch your first crappie, remember this: Let it splash around a bit on the surface, then toss in a live minnow right beside it. Crappie are like chickens; each chicken wants a piece of what the eating chicken has. So it is with avid crappie. The minnow helps keep other crappie looking for food.

As a last resort, when crappies seem to be in Nowheresville, try this old cracker trick. Anchor your boat near a patch of weeds, brush, or lily pads.

Spend about a minute slapping the surface with the tip of your crappie pole. Wait five minutes, then repeat.

Other anglers will think you're a bit daffy until you begin hauling in crappie. This commotion sounds like a school of feeding crappie. Again, like chickens, a roving school will come to the sound believing minnows are there for the gorging.

Although crappie are caught from time to time on various lures (occasionally on a surface lure or a diving plug), the one artificial that pays off regularly is a small leadhead jig with a soft-plastic body resembling a minnow. The trick is to fish this so s-l-o-w-l-y you yawn. Jigs weighing from $1/64$ to $1/16$ ounce are often better than heavier ones, and obviously this technique requires light line. It also reveals how crazy crappie can be— they want minnows lively but prefer artificial lures as near dead as possible.

White Bass

The white bass is the largest and most sporting of all the panfish. In fact, some are so big that one specimen can more than fill a skillet. Few fish in freshwater hit harder, pound for pound, or fight longer, than an energetic white bass. Maybe that's because it's a member of the saltwater striped bass family. Many a fishless day has been saved by a school of white bass showing up when all other species are void. At many impoundments today, an abundant population of white bass is a saving grace when other popular species fall off.

Where to fish. Much of the time you needn't worry about where to fish for white bass. They tell you either by sight or sound. You'll see anglers cruising around open water, or in backwater bays, standing up, looking in all directions. They're scouting for white bass.

The silvery bodies of these fish can be seen flashing at a distance; you'll spot them much sooner than you hear them. Other times, you'll be fishing for other species and suddenly hear a terrific commotion as a school of white bass erupts nearby and slashes into shad minnows just under the surface.

When you see, or hear, a feeding school, approach as quietly as possible, using the wind to drift you toward them if possible. Once within casting distance, cast your lure ahead of, not into, the moving school. If you spook them, they dive deeply and appear elsewhere, usually out of casting range. Stay with a school until it sounds from sight, then scout for another.

At times, such as in early spring, finding white bass can be extremely difficult. Just remember that these fish are a gravel spawner, so look for long shorelines showing white stones, rocks, or riprap.

Catching tactics. White bass are easier to catch on artificial lures than on live baits for one salient reason: They spook easily, and an angler must normally get closer to use live baits than artificials. A good caster can power an artificial lure a long distance and catch a number of white bass before the school gets jittery.

Among live baits, of course, the threadfin shad is tops because it's the favorite food of white bass. Most seasoned anglers use a baitcasting, spinning, or spincasting outfit with just enough sinker to cast the minnow. Two split shots placed about 2 inches apart above the minnow will tangle less than one sinker. No float is used because this would impede the cast. A free-running minnow looks more natural to a white bass and rarely has time to move before a white bass nabs it.

Artificial lures must meet certain requirements to be effective. They must be compact, close to the size and look of shad, and cast well into a breeze. The most popular is a weighted tailspinner, with a lead body, a treble hook on the belly, and a spinner on the tail. Also effective is a minnow-type surface lure that will dart and sashay when twitched, and a shiny slab spoon with a treble hook.

Each of these lures will cast well into a wind, and will enable long casts that don't alarm the school. Stay parallel with a working school and cast ahead of it to avoid spooking the leaders. To take bigger bass, try this trick: Cast over and beyond the working school, then let the lure sink for a 10-count before retrieving. This lets it get down below the school where the bigger, smarter white bass cruise along to slurp up the wounded shad drifting down from the slaughter going on above.

In early spring, when white bass are scarce, look for gravelly or rocky shores. Put on the tailspinner, cast into shallows, and let the lure sink until slack line tells you it is on bottom. Lower your rod tip, reel in slack line, and, with a sharp upward sweep of the rod tip, jump the lure off bottom. Keep it coming, fast, until something almost jerks the rod from your hands. At this moment, you will know how hard a white bass can sock a lure!

Remember these spots and return next year about the same time. White bass cruise here following urges for the spawning season. Even though they may not be hungry, the super-fast lure causes impulse strikes.

Yellow Bass

Yellow bass are somewhat similar to white bass in behavior; although smaller on average, they'll amaze you with the impact of their strikes and vigorous fight. Yellow bass are more bottom dwelling than are white bass and rarely give away their presence. When they do, they are typically feeding on a bottom hatch, especially during the early, warm days of summer.

Here's a sign to watch for. As you fish, keep examining surface waters close to you and look for large patches of tiny bubbles. These are caused by a school of yellow bass grubbing on the bottom. Ease a small spoon vertically down from the tip of your rod until it touches bottom. Jig it in a small circle. The action will be fast and superb.

White Perch

No relation to the yellow perch, this fish is a member of the true bass family, white and yellow. Why they hung the name "perch" on it is anyone's guess, but the misnomer is here to stay. Like many panfish, however, the white perch is a schooling species and a fine sportfish; it is similar in many respects to the white bass, which it somewhat resembles.

Where to fish. Look for tributary streams and long points in moving water, which are favored hangouts of roaming schools of white perch. They also inhabit sandy and gravelly bottom estuaries and shallow bays. Finding them is a matter of moving about, and being alert to school movements.

White perch are creatures of habit. If you find them in an area one day, return there the next day. They usually run the same daily courses, as long as the food supply continues.

Catching tactics. The majority of white perch are caught on live bait, including crabs, minnows, and worms. But canny anglers take an appreciable number on artificial lures that require less fuss.

Some anglers use the first-caught white perch for bait, cutting it in small pieces and impaling these on light leadhead jigs. Fly anglers use tiny nymphs and larvae flies inched slowly over bottom on a sinking line and leader. Miniature crankbaits, spinners, and spoons are good.

Spring is the best time for the biggest catches. In any season, it is important to keep artificial lures as weedless as possible for fishing right on bottom in varied cover.

Simple Care and Cooking

The following brief advice will help you get the most out of a fresh batch of panfish. A comprehensive review of caring for fish, cleaning, and cookery issues is contained elsewhere *(see: fish preparation—care; fish preparation—cleaning/dressing)*.

Proper keeping. The sooner you eat panfish after catching them, the better the flavor. Here is a condensed review of ways to keep them as fresh as possible.

If the water is cold, panfish can be kept on a stringer. In hot weather, keep them in a big plastic bag laid on ice. Because these fish are small, laying them directly on ice can turn their flesh soft, which will deteriorate the flavor.

If your catch is big enough for freezing a batch of fillets, you need to avoid freezer burn, which turns flesh white and robs it of both juices and natural flavor. The best thing is to freeze the fillets in water for long-term storage. For short-term freezing, place the fillets flat on a sheet of plastic wrap, fold the four flaps over, and squeeze out all possible air. Enfold this packet in a sheet of aluminum foil or freezer wrap. Lay the packets side by side, not atop each other, and freeze as fast as possible.

Tasty cooking. What constitutes a "fine kettle of fish" to some is a mess to others, but it's hard to go wrong with the small fillets or whole bodies of panfish unless you overcook them.

To deep-fry, wipe off excess moisture, dip small whole panfish or fillets in buttermilk, dredge in flour seasoned to your taste, and deep-fry until they are done as crispy as you like them. Drain on folded paper toweling and cover with foil to hold the heat until the entire batch is ready.

To broil, place whole panfish on a broiling pan, baste with Italian salad dressing, broil five minutes on one side, turn, baste, and broil three more minutes. The oil in the dressing melts and drains into the pan. The seasoning remains, and the result is surprisingly tasty.

To bake, try this simple and delightful Swedish recipe. Place each serving in foil; add a quarter stick of butter, a squeeze of lemon juice, a shake of salt and pepper, and a few small potatoes and carrots, then garnish with a sprig of fresh dill. Fold the foil lengthwise and pucker up the ends. Broil in an oven or over charcoal for about 30 minutes, or until done to suit.

See: Sunfish; and individual species.

PAPUA NEW GUINEA

This nation in the southwestern Pacific consists of the eastern half of New Guinea, the second largest island in the world, and an assemblage of more than 600 islands of varying sizes. With its mainland separated from Australia's Cape York Peninsula by just 150 kilometers across the Torres Strait linking the Arafura and Coral Seas, and bordering the Irian Jaya territory of Indonesia, Papua New Guinea is diverse in cultures, wildlife, natural resources, and fisheries.

Volcanic islands, coral atolls, low-lying mangrove swamps, plunging valleys, fog-shrouded mountains, dense rain forests, numerous jungle rivers, and tropical seas characterize this country, which contains lightly explored fisheries along the coasts and in the lush interior. That interior, although marked by many rivers and some lakes, is not known so much for its variety of fish but for two of the meanest and hardest-battling species—Niugini bass and spottail bass—caught in freshwater. The abundant low-lying swampy regions along the coast are known for equally compelling species, including barramundi, saratoga, and threadfin salmon; offshore, the reefs and blue water contain marlin, sailfish, various tuna, mahimahi, trevally, and a host of gamefish.

Regarded as one of the last sportfishing frontiers, Papua New Guinea has had little infrastructure for freshwater and saltwater angling, and relatively few angling-oriented operations have been established here, mainly due to the remoteness of opportunities (in freshwater) and to the difficulty in attracting people from afar for saltwater fishing (when there are other more well-developed and easily accessed locations, like Australia's Great Barrier Reef). Some

Fish have been in existence for approximately 470 million years, making them the oldest vertebrates.

mobile operations have existed for coastal and interior fishing expeditions, however, and a few island or coastal camps do provide inshore and offshore fishing.

Just south of the equator, Papua New Guinea has a tropically humid climate. Daily temperatures range from the mid-20s to the mid-30s Celsius, and the humidity is between 70 and 90 percent. There are two seasons, or "monsoons." The southeasterly monsoon, or dry season, runs from April through October. It is hot and humid during this time, but rains are infrequent (although rain in the interior at this time can still bring several inches). Near coastal areas, a constant sea breeze makes the climate very balmy. The westerly monsoon, or wet season, runs from late November through March. This period tends to be oppressively humid, bringing frequent tropical downpours and associated brief heavy winds. From late September into November, oppressive days leading up to the rainy season can be good for fishing, but April through June is also prime. Although many saltwater species are caught year-round, fishing is generally best just before and just after the rainy season.

Saltwater

Papua New Guinea is bordered by the Bismarck Sea on the north, the Solomon Sea on the east, and the Coral Sea and Gulf of Papua on the south. The northerly coast faces deep water with steep dropoffs close to shore and is especially productive for a range of pelagic and reef species. The southern coast, particularly in the western sector, is shallower and deeply indented with bays, estuaries, and extensive mangrove swamps along the low-lying coast.

The major center for inshore and brackish-water species is at Daru in the Western Province. The entire southwestern coastline from the Irian Jaya border east to the city of Kerema is lowland swamp and sparsely populated, most prominently containing the expansive Fly River Delta north of Daru. Navigable in its lower reaches, the Fly is one of the country's major rivers and drains much of the western interior. Barramundi are the principal catch here, followed by saratoga and threadfin salmon.

Farther east, some sportfishing along the southeastern coast originates out of the capital city of Port Moresby, and on the eastern coast near Huon Peninsula out of Lae in Morobe Province.

Off the northwest coast of Papua New Guinea, anglers have experienced extraordinary light-tackle fishing for a host of offshore species, without going far offshore. Blue marlin, black marlin, Pacific sailfish, yellowfin tuna, dogtooth tuna, bigeye tuna, kingfish, wahoo, giant trevally, barracuda, mahimahi, and various sharks are among the area's plentiful species, caught close to the mainland as well as at several islands nearby, including Karkar and Bagabag, respectively about 18 and 43 kilometers from the mainland.

Marlin and sailfish are available here year-round. The best season for blue marlin is from September through November, for sailfish from December through March, and for black marlin from April through June. Blue and black marlin between 200 and 500 pounds have been caught, although larger fish have reportedly been lost. During periods of greatest abundance, sailfish hunt in packs and run to good sizes. Reefs offer fishing for dogtooth tuna, Spanish mackerel, giant trevally, sailfish, and other species. Dogtooth tuna are especially plentiful, large, and powerful.

Freshwater

The inland region of Papua New Guinea features tropical rain forest, jungle vegetation, and grassland, as well as rugged mountains running through the center of the mainland. Jungle highlands have clear, fast-flowing streams coursing from either slope to larger flows and the sea. In some areas, especially along the southern coast, the rivers wind through plains and swamps infested with mosquitoes (malaria is a concern).

The jungle rivers are known for Niugini bass and spottail bass, freshwater relatives of cubera snapper with deep muscular bodies; these fish grow large and are truly ferocious. They are seldom caught in great numbers, owing to their demeanor and to their proclivity for thick cover, which demands accurate casting. They number among the most demanding river fish to catch. They have a well-honed knack for striking a lure as they turn and swiftly head back to cover; so strong are they that a high percentage are never landed.

Niugini bass (locally called black bass or Papuan black bass) and spot-tail bass are commonly caught from 15 to 20 pounds; 30- to 40-pounders are considered large. Some have reportedly been caught to 60 pounds, and Australian anglers with experience in angling for this species use stout 6-foot rods, wide-spool baitcasting reels, and 40-pound line, and that often doesn't do the job. Large, heavy diving plugs and surface plugs are used to entice the fish from bank-side log and tree cover. Known for busting up tackle, demolishing lures, and making blistering initial runs, these fish do not have great stamina for long fights, but the first-moment encounter is usually so explosive that, in snag-infested jungle rivers, they win their freedom in a short but furious tussle.

Barramundi are caught in some of the rivers as well, and the lower tidal reaches provide action for a variety of species. Numerous rivers have Niugini bass and spot-tail bass fishing potential, although opportunities to fish these are scarce and have not been continuously reliable. The Kikori River of the Southern Highlands has been fished by a mothership houseboat operation with fishing skiffs in tow; it empties into a large deltaic region of Bevan Sound at Saumao Peninsula but is flanked by such large systems as the Purari, Turama, and Guavi Rivers, not to mention the many tributaries to all of these—all with angling potential. On the northwest coast, the Sepik River flows more than 1,200 kilometers, beginning high in the central mountains near the Irian Jaya border. It is navigable for almost its entire length, and floods numerous lakes, including the vast, shallow expanse of Chambri Lake, although the fisheries here are unknown.

Niugini bass and spot-tail bass also thrive in the rain forest rivers of New Britain, Papua New Guinea's largest offshore island. Dogtooth tuna, trevally, and other species are found near shore around this and other easterly islands and reefs.

Sections of interior Papua New Guinea's pristine wilderness have been compromised in recent years through timber harvesting, including clearcutting along rivers, and the watersheds have been impacted. The effect on rivers and their fisheries, as well as on the deltas and possibly beyond, is already being felt, according to some accounts.

PARAGUAY

Nestled in the middle of South America and surrounded by Brazil, Argentina, and Bolivia, the country of Paraguay is true to the meaning of its name—"land of rivers." These rivers contain a host of warmwater fish species—some 250 in fact—not unlike those of the Amazonian region of Brazil. An exception is the greater prominence in Paraguay of dorado, a species of great sportfishing interest. The dorado is the one species with which this country is most identified by anglers.

All rivers and watersheds in Paraguay belongs to the Plata (Plate) Basin, which is formed by the Paraná River—the most important river in the basin and one of the world's largest rivers—and the Paraguay River. Both originate in Brazil, where the Paraguay is formed from various tributaries in southwestern Brazil's Pantanal, a large swamp or a huge marsh that is the only river here not affected by dams.

Successful dorado anglers pose with their trophy along the banks of the Paraná River.

The Paraguay River divides the country into diverse regions: the Gran Chaco alluvial plain in the west, and Paraguay Proper, which is the southerly portion of the Paraná Plateau. The latter has elevations up to 2,000 feet and gives rise to numerous tributaries of the Paraguay River on its west and the Paraná River on its east.

The mighty and beautiful Paraná forms part of the border with Brazil until it is joined by the Iguaçu River downstream of famous Iguaçu Falls, and then forms the border with Argentina until it is joined by the Paraguay River near Corrientes and leaves the country. The character and fisheries of the Paraná River have been affected by several huge hydroelectric constructions, including one of the world's largest, the Itapúa Dam, and the Yacyreta Dam. Unfortunately, fish ladders were not constructed to allow upstream passage of migratory fish, including dorado, to their spawning grounds, and because fish congregate in the spillway below the long dams, poaching has been common and resulted in adverse impacts.

The Uruguay River, incidentally, is the third of these important flows that are part of the Plata Basin, although it is not in Paraguay. It, too, has been seriously affected by dams. The Uruguay River borders Brazil and Argentina, then Argentina and Uruguay, before emptying into the Plata estuary at the Atlantic Ocean near the mouth of the Paraná River.

The Paraná is the most significant river for sportfishing, although the dams have changed habitats and gamefish behavior. Nevertheless, there is still good fishing along its length, and the best season is spring. In this hemisphere, spring occurs from September through early December.

Along the southern Paraguay River, there is notable fishing in its tributary, the Tebicuary River, which flows westerly and is easily reached by road 100 miles south of the capital city of Asunción. Sportfishing here is particularly attractive, especially for dorado, although the river is affected by rains; angling success is therefore dependent on the river level. The Tebicuary is best in spring, summer, and fall; the winter months of May and June provide slow action due to colder water temperatures.

Other important tributaries that also flow into the Paraguay River are the Manduvira—located 35 miles north of Asunción—the Negro, the Ypane, the Aquidaban, and the Apa. The Apa is Paraguay's northernmost tributary and forms the border with Brazil. All are excellent rivers when water conditions are good. These tributaries and the upper Paraguay River are fishable year-round but are best in spring.

There are several species of the golden fish, dorado, in Paraguay, but the most important of them is *Salminus maxillosus (see: dorado)*; the hard-fighting glamour species, it runs strong, jumps in the air like a tarpon, and fights to the last moment. This fish may reach 40 pounds in Paraguayan waters (though larger fish were known in the past), is the object of considerable local attention, and is highly sought by international anglers.

Sportfishing for these aggressive predators is approached in many ways. Trolling with lures is the most common activity; anglers frequently drift from a boat with live baits, depending on water clarity and the type of river. Casting from a drifting boat or from the shoreline is possible at some times and places, and is great sport with light tackle.

In northern Paraguay, some pristine jungle rivers like the Apa provide exciting light tackle and flycasting for dorado in the dry season from September through November, when fish are moving upstream and can uniquely be caught in the rapids. The occurrence of rains, however, floods the rivers and ends low clear-water sport.

Some of the better dorado fishing occurs along the Paraná's southernmost border with Argentina, on the Paraná above its merger with the Paraguay River to south of Posadas, and across into Argentina *(see)* in a large swampy backwater region known as Esteros del Ibera, where consistently clean water provides good action, including casting with lures and flies.

The equipment normally used for dorado is 16- to 25-pound line on appropriate spinning and baitcasting tackle. Steel leaders are mandatory, and lures and terminal gear must be of premium quality, as the power of the dorado's jaws can destroy equipment. Eight- and 9-weight flycasting tackle with large streamers are also used, and line types vary with the circumstances.

Other prominent sportfishing targets in Paraguay are the spotted catfish, *Pseudoplatistoma coruscans,* and striped catfish *Pseudoplatistoma fasciatum,* locally and regionally called *surubi*. The striped catfish appears in both the Plata and Amazon Basins, whereas the spotted catfish occurs only in the Plata. These species can be caught with artificial baits and even by fly fishing. The spotted catfish easily reaches 120 pounds and is a good fighter that does not jump, but makes strong, sometimes tackle-busting runs, looking for stumps or rocks to snag the line. It is found in large rivers and tributaries, feeds mainly on other live fish, and prefers strong currents.

Both species are night feeders, roaming shallow banks and sandbars, but both are easily spooked. Anglers approach them quietly from shore or anchored boats, and they are usually caught on a single-hooked live bait attached to a sliding sinker. During the day they linger in deep channels or in deep eddies, near the mouths of tributaries to a large river. Trolling for catfish with deep-diving lures in the channels is a common practice in the Paraná River, as is drifting with live baits.

Surubi are highly prized for their flesh in South America, and considered top gourmet fare. They are widely offered in restaurants as a special menu item. Dorado are also good tasting, and are preferred when grilled.

Another important gamefish is the pacu, *Colossoma mitrei,* a mainly herbivorous fish that is not considered a predator. It is, however, great to hook on light tackle and provides a powerful, deep fight. Pacu occur in all rivers and lagoons in the Plata Basin and reach 30 pounds or more. Pacu are pursued with natural baits from shore or from a drifting boat. Hooks are baited with fruits, snails, freshwater crabs, parts of fish, or processed corn baits.

Sportfishing season in Paraguay is generally good almost year-round; however, the peak angling season for most species is from September through early December. Some waters still do not receive much fishing pressure, although others are subjected to excessive fishing, including killing fish, and also to poaching problems.

PARASITES
See: Diseases and Parasites.

PARR
Small, young anadromous fish, particularly salmon and trout, living in freshwater prior to migrating out to sea. During this life stage, parr develop large vertical or oval rounded spots (sometimes called bars) on the sides. Called parr marks, these help camouflage the fish and also identify it; they will gradually disappear as the fish becomes silvery, regardless of whether the fish goes to sea (some do not). In the silvery phase, the fish is known as a smolt *(see)*. Migration to sea occurs between 2 and 8 years.
See: Salmon, Atlantic.

PARTY BOAT
The term party boat encompasses a variety of sportfishing vessels that are known by various local names, including drift boats, long range boats, head boats, and day boats. A party boat is usually a large vessel that accommodates individual anglers, mostly on a nonreserved basis and with daily fares applied per head, generally paid upon boarding. This is different from a charter boat *(see),* which charges a boat rate and is generally reserved by a small group of people in advance. Party boats offer an economical way for people of any skill level to spend a day fishing on a large body of water, sometimes for a diversity of species.

Party boats range in size from vessels carrying as few as a half dozen anglers to huge vessels a hundred feet or more in length, complete with bunks, galleys, and accommodations for trips of a week or more. They are primarily a saltwater angling possibility, found in most every coastal port on the Atlantic, Pacific, and Gulf Coasts, and depending on the season, offering angling for a range of fish species. In freshwater, midsize party boats are found on a few large bodies of water, such as Lakes Michigan and Erie, and their species options are much narrower. Party boats are usually easy to find in major ports, and in popular sportfishing areas there are often many options as to what you can fish for, the time of day that party boats sail, and the duration of the trip.

In the United States, the Coast Guard licenses the captains of these vessels, and the owners must adhere to strict regulations designed to ensure the safety of passengers. Each vessel must undergo a meticulous inspection to be certified as safe, ensuring that the fishing public's best interests are foremost. Captains of these vessels (as well as captains of charter boats) must pass a comprehensive written exam before receiving their license to carry passengers for hire.

Party boat anglers catch everything from giant bluefin tuna and marlin to bottom feeders weighing but a pound, with most fish being small- to medium-sized inshore specimens. They catch fish by trolling, drifting, chumming, bottom fishing, jigging, and occasionally casting, and employ a wide variety of tactics within these disciplines. Mastering all of this aboard the fun-filled party boats that head daily to the fishing grounds is an exciting challenge.

Benefits of Party Boats

Good for beginners. Party boat fishing is a great way to get started in sportfishing. Newcomers are usually welcomed aboard by veteran anglers, who are quick to share techniques and to help in any way they can. The captain and mates also go to great pains with the beginner, realizing that they may gain a regular customer as a result. Among the regular customers aboard party boats, this type of fishing becomes almost an addiction, with anglers often sailing on a specific day each week the year-round, taking advantage of the changing seasons and changing species and types of fishing.

Open to the public, party boats depart daily during the season from major ports.

Camaraderie and diversity. Many people feel that fishing aboard a party boat is among the most enjoyable of angling experiences. The camaraderie of those who board these vessels, in addition to the actual fishing, adds to the excitement of the trip.

On a party boat a group of people is brought together with the common interest of going fishing and catching fish. They are young and old, male and female, from all ethnic and religious backgrounds. Most have never met before, but during the course of the trip relationships develop, fishing stories are exchanged, and a bond develops. Some people enjoy this fishing so much that people have been married on party boats, and it's not unusual for just-married couples to spend part of their honeymoon onboard, enjoying the fresh air, sunshine, good fishing, and, importantly, the affordability.

The duration of the fishing day aboard a party boat varies, depending on the location, time of year, and species availability. The normal day trip usually leaves dockside at seven or eight in the morning and returns at three or four in the afternoon. There are, however, half-day, three-quarter day, and twilight-fishing party boats. In many areas a second shift takes over the craft on its return for the night schedule. There may be half-, three-quarter, and all-night trips.

Along sections of some coasts, there are trips of several days' duration. Examples include weeklong excursions off Mexico's Baja Peninsula, two- and three-day trips to the Dry Tortugas off Florida, deep-water wreck fishing off Massachusetts' Nantucket Island for two days or more, and multi-day trips to the underwater canyons along the edge of the Continental Shelf off New York and New Jersey. Depending upon the boat, some include a bunk as part of the regular fare, while on others a bunk is optional for a limited fee.

Wide variety of species. Anglers may elect to board a particular party boat to seek a certain species of fish via a specific method of fishing. Almost all party boats have signs prominently displayed at the docks identifying the species that will be sought and the method of fishing.

Bottom fishing is the hallmark of party boat angling. This may be with the boat either anchored over wrecks, reefs, or irregular broken bottom, or while drifting over smooth bottom. Some boats specialize in chumming, and this may be done at anchor or while drifting. Trolling is often done, too, but this limits the number of anglers who can stream their lines from the stern. Trolling is often used to locate schools of fish, after which chum is used to hold the school close to the boat and attract the fish to hooked baits. Jigging is still another popular party boat activity, also done either at anchor or while drifting.

There are many variations to the above. In the Great Lakes, downriggers may be used while trolling, and an angler is assigned a specific station. On the Pacific Coast, when deep-water trolling with breakaway sinkers to get baits deep, anglers often rotate positions with their tackle, to ensure that each has a chance of his baits working in a productive area as the grounds are covered.

Because sea conditions change frequently and the habits of fish change just as quickly, the party boat captain and his mates or deckhands quickly adapt. So, although you may anticipate bottom fishing all day, if the skipper locates a school of surface-feeding fish, he may ask anglers to switch techniques to take advantage of the developing opportunity.

General Issues

Selection. Whether you're a veteran or a newcomer to party boat fishing, it's wise to do some homework before boarding a boat. As a first step, you might watch the local fishing reports in coastal newspapers. Fishing reporters talk with captains regularly and usually relay reliable fishing information, from which you can make a determination as to the length of the trip, species sought, and costs.

Perhaps the best approach, especially if you're new to this fishing or visiting an area for the first time, is to go to the docks and visit as the boats come in after a trip. Find out what time they usually return so you can be available when they first arrive. Talk with the people who are disembarking. Ask how the fishing and weather was, and whether or not they were satisfied with the attention of their captain and crew, and their diligence on the fishing grounds. Toward this end you have good and bad in every profession. You want to board a boat where the captain and mates work together as a team and will move from spot to spot until they score. If a disembarking passenger tells you the captain anchored on a reef and spent the day in one spot, asleep in the pilothouse, while the mate handled the decks, you may be best served looking elsewhere.

It's fair to say that you'll find party boats that are dirty, but you'll find charter boats and guide boats that are dirty, too. Appearance may or may not be an indication of whether they are worth fishing on, but conscientious captains try to keep their boats reasonably clean and in good shape. When you're at the docks taking stock of things before paying to fish on a party boat, don't hesitate to ask the captain if you can board, and then discreetly inspect the boat. In this way you'll know what's in store for you before you sail. Look at the restrooms. They should be as clean as your bathroom at home. If the toilets are grimy it's generally a reflection on the crew. Likewise in the galley. If it's a greasy grill or dirty microwave that doesn't appear to have been cleaned in ages, perhaps you should move on to another boat.

Tackle is another consideration. Look at the tackle in the event you'll be renting an outfit. Is it what you'll enjoy using? If the reel only has half a spool of line, or a guide is missing on a rod, or the metal parts of the reel are corroded, it shows lack of concern on the part of the crew, and using this kind of gear will diminish your enjoyment. Find a boat that's right for you before you enlist, by walking the docks, talking to people, and just plain observing.

Costs. It's difficult to identify the exact cost to be encountered aboard a party boat. The general rule is, the closer to shore that you fish, and the shorter the duration, the lower the cost. Many of the half-day boats that bottom fish close to port charge $30, or $35 if chum is used, when targeting bluefish and bonito. The three-quarter day boats are around $40, while all-day fishing fares are usually $45 to $50 for close-in runs. For night trips, the same applies, depending on duration and distance to the grounds.

As you move into specialized fishing, such as twenty-four hour trips to far offshore wrecks and reefs, and trips to the Bahamas and Dry Tortugas, fares move into the $100 to $125 range. For two-day trips, such as those targeting tuna and other pelagic species in the Northeast canyons, the fares move up to $225 per angler. In some cases bunks are included, but it's best to check this out before boarding. Ask about tackle rental too, as the charge is often $20 for the heavier gear required for big game.

On really long range trips, such as those bound for Mexican water from San Diego, Newport Beach, and other California ports, it's all a matter of the boat and its accommodations, whether or not meals and bunks are included, and the length of the stay. Figure in the range of $100 to $150 per day. While this may seem costly, it's really quite economical when you consider that the same trip on a charter boat would cost several times that per person daily. Considering the camaraderie of those aboard, the excellent sport for truly great gamefish, and the prospects of bringing home great table fare, these long range trips are certainly worthy of consideration.

Regulations and Limits. Each state has jurisdiction over fishing in its coastal waters, while the Federal government presides over offshore ocean fishing. It's wise to check with the party boat captain to determine whether or not you need a state license (issued by the state of the port from which you sail). In some jurisdictions you do not need a separate license while onboard a party boat, as the boat is licensed. However, some jurisdictions require an individual license, and these may be obtained for varying time periods, usually at a tackle shop in the area of the docks.

There are state and, in some cases, federal regulations *(see: regulations)* in effect in most jurisdictions with respect to specific seasons in which fish may be caught, minimum and sometimes maximum size that may be kept, and the quantity, or daily bag limit. Some jurisdictions have possession limits, too. It is generally prudent to be guided by the instructions of the captain or mate in this regard. They are usually very knowledgeable, and the mates carefully measure regulated fish, ensuring that undersize specimens, or those in excess of the limit, are carefully returned to the water. However, you are ultimately responsible for your own fish and for knowing current regulations, so it's wise to obtain a booklet of regulations (usually available at bait and tackle shops) and keep it with you.

Because of numerous regulations governing size and bag limits, many fish caught on party boats must be released. Fish are carefully measured so as to comply and then promptly released. It's important that fish be handled carefully and released quickly to ensure survival. Many captains and mates take this very seriously because they realize the future of the sport rests with the released fish surviving. However, aboard some boats the opposite is true, particularly with part-time mates, who are employed during the summer months at the peak of the party boat tourist season. They sometimes do not realize that the fish will not survive careless handling and ripping hooks from their mouths or gills. Anglers and mates should be encouraged to release fish carefully and properly (see: catch-and-release; handling fish).

As with any other type of fishing, when you do keep fish on party boats, you should keep only what you can use, even when there are very liberal (or no) bag limits. Before size and bag limits were established for many coastal species, there was often a horrible practice by some irresponsible anglers who killed everything they caught, failed to properly care for the catch, and later dumped much of the fish in the trash. Thanks to regulations, this practice has for the most part disappeared from the coastal scene, but not all fish are covered by regulations. There are still instances where excessive killing continues, especially in fishing for Atlantic mackerel, scup, sea bass, croakers, spot, and other species. This excessiveness and greed is unnecessary, and certainly does not mark the participant as a sportsman. All species, big or small, popular or unpopular, are resources that should be treasured; releasing fish you can't or won't use ensures a viable fishery in the future.

Equipment and Fishing

Renting. Of particular interest to the beginning party boat angler is the fact that you're not required to supply anything. Rental rods and reels are available with a nominal fee in addition to the regular fare. The rental outfit is equipped with the basic rig to be used that day, including a bottom rig, drift rig, or artificial lure for jigging or trolling. If you should lose the rig, you may purchase another from a mate, whose job it is to assist you in any way possible. They are always circulating around the rail, rigging tackle, baiting hooks, gaffing or netting fish, or otherwise being helpful.

In the Florida Keys, party boats generally charge a fixed fare, and if you lose a hook or bottom rig while fishing the reef, the mate simply replaces it as a part of the basic fare. The additional nominal amount that the fare is increased as a result of not charging for hooks, lines, or sinkers is a welcome convenience to passengers and results in less work for the mates.

Using your own. Anglers who regularly fish on party boats have their own tackle and bring it with them, usually needing to be supplied only with bait. After you have made a few excursions on party boats and seen what veteran anglers have and what the boats provide, you'll probably want to outfit yourself and bring your own equipment.

Much can be learned from veteran party boat anglers, as they have this type of fishing down to a science. Because time on the fishing grounds is often limited, the veteran is extremely well organized with his tackle, so not a moment is wasted. Many of the pros develop a personal party boat checklist to ensure that they have everything with them necessary for a successful day. This includes:

- Proper clothing, including rain gear and hat
- Ice chest with ice for fish, and a compartment for food and beverages
- Plastic bags in which to place cleaned fish on ice
- Deck shoes or slip-on boots to keep dry
- Pills for seasickness, headache, or pain relief
- Polarized sunglasses
- Folding toothbrush and toothpaste
- Sunscreen of 25 SPF or higher
- Sleeping bag for overnighters

These items ensure that you'll have an enjoyable trip, regardless of duration. Little things like a toothbrush to freshen your mouth after a night in a bunk, or an antacid tablet for indigestion, or especially sunscreen to prevent a burn, often make the difference in a trip's enjoyment. Regulars carry all of this gear with them and at least one completely rigged rod and reel. Since there is plenty of room on the bigger party boats, they also bring a spare outfit as insurance, and a tackle box loaded with essentials.

A party boat tackle box should be roomy, plastic, and waterproof, with all items easily accessible. It should contain:

- Sharp filleting knife
- Serrated knife for steaking, cutting bone
- Diamond knife sharpener
- Stainless steel dehooker
- Vise-grip cutting pliers in sheath
- Eight-inch broomstick for wrapping line around to pull free from bottom snags
- Sinkers for the type of fishing expected
- Terminal rigs for the type of fishing expected
- Jigs, spoons, feathers, and other lures and rigged leaders

Getting started. Having boarded with this array of equipment and tackle, most veterans discuss with the mates the exact method to be used on

---

French spinners were introduced to America after World War II by Mepps, which was known as the manufacturer of precision equipment for sportfishing.

arrival at the fishing grounds, and the techniques that have proven most effective. They rig accordingly as the boat travels to the fishing grounds and wear their cutting pliers and bait knife in a sheath on their belt. Time on the fishing grounds is limited, so it's smart to be totally prepared.

Many party boat anglers wear a carpenter's tool apron in which they place a couple of extra sinkers and complete terminal rigs so they can quickly retie and get back in the water should they lose a rig. This saves time from rummaging through a tackle box, or having to make up a rig or purchase one from a busy mate.

Included in the tool apron is the 8-inch piece of broomstick; this is a godsend when it's necessary to break off a snagged bottom rig. It prevents breaking costly tackle as you try to break off, but, more importantly, it keeps the line from cutting your hands.

Once the fishing grounds are reached, the captain either announces over the boat's loudspeaker that fishing will begin, or signals this by sounding

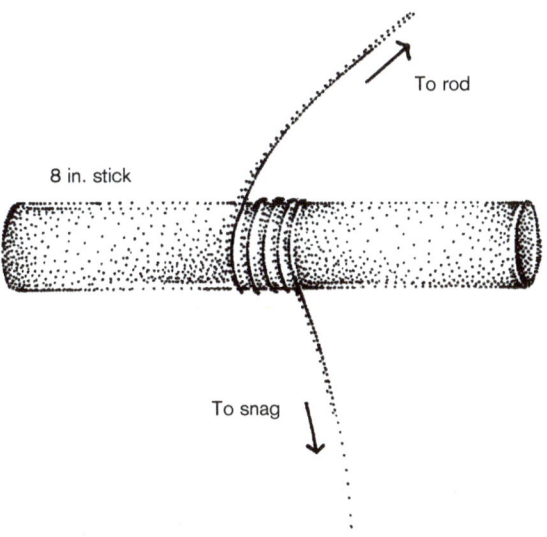

To free a bottom-snagged rig when fishing on a party boat, wrap the line several times around an 8-inch piece of broomstick, hold it with both hands, and pull to free the rig or break it off. This is especially useful when fishing with strong and low-stretch lines.

the horn. At each fishing location along the rail, the mates will have placed a container of bait; if live bait is used, it is readily available at the circulating tanks. After you are baited up and fishing, it's a good practice to be aware of the actions of other anglers. Watch the first people to score, and don't hesitate to mimic their technique.

Rail position. Although initially it may sound unimportant, rail position in certain types of party boat fishing can often put you at a decided advantage. In many types of reef and wreck fishing, the boat is anchored over sand bottom and the current holds the boat in position either close to or over the choice bottom. In this kind of situation, the people who occupy the stern have the choice spots; as the fish are chummed, the first baited hooks they respond to are those of anglers positioned at the stern.

As a rule of thumb, it's difficult to beat the stern position for any kind of party boat fishing, and it's not unusual to see party boat regulars arrive extra early, even hours before boarding time, so they can place their outfit in a choice stern location.

When drift fishing, the captain usually positions the boat so the lines of anglers on one side will stream away from the boat, and the lines of those on the other side will drift under the boat. Every half hour or so the skipper will make a move over new bottom, and alternate the position of the boat, so the anglers whose lines drifted under the boat will stream away from it and vice versa for the other side. It is usually best to have your lines drift away from, rather than under, the boat.

The best position on boats that drift is the bow, where only two or three anglers can fish. In this way they can take advantage of their lines streaming away on either drift, and it enables them to cast out and away from the bow, which results in more bottom being covered.

When party boats are crowded, each angler has a spot at the rail, usually marked by a painted stripe on the rail, or where there is a piece of cord tied, to which you can attach your outfit. Some boats have rod holders at each position.

When the boat isn't crowded, it's much more comfortable and you can move about more readily. At such times, it's often wise to move away from where the anglers tend to cluster near the stern, and to situate yourself alone, which often results in more strikes and less chance of a tangle.

Bring two outfits. As anglers become proficient on party boats, some expand their horizon from the species normally targeted to seek bigger game. As a case in point, many boats chum for yellowtail snapper throughout their southern range. These average 2 to 4 pounds and are pursued with small hooks and light tackle. Frequenting the same grounds as yellowtails are big grouper and snapper, some weighing 50 pounds or more, which are targeted by anglers who bring heavy tackle and use big baits to catch these Goliaths of the deep. Many anglers bring a pair of outfits aboard, one heavy and one light; they first make a catch of the smaller gamesters and then switch over to target the heavyweights, making for a fun-filled and well-rounded day.

Along the mid-Atlantic Coast, the catch of species such as summer flounder is limited with respect to size and bag limits, and once anglers have filled their limit, they'll often switch over to diamond jigging or squidding for species such as bluefish, striped bass, Atlantic bonito, and Spanish mackerel, which often frequent the same grounds and result in a bonus catch.

Pacific Coast anglers fishing off kelp beds often experience mixed-bag action, with Pacific bonito, white sea bass, and kelp bass being the target of baits drifted near the surface, while bottom rigs down on the sand bring strikes from Pacific halibut, rockfish, and other bottom feeders. The key on all three coasts is to be prepared, and to quickly respond as situations develop.

Patience with big fish. In some types of party boat fishing, such as when working the Pacific kelp beds, chumming around shrimp boats in the Gulf, or seeking bluefish when chumming in the Atlantic, the fish that are hooked are so large and strong that you just can't stand at the rail and bring the fish directly to you. At such times, it's necessary to follow the fish up and down the rail. Most party boat anglers are extremely courteous and when they hear the time-honored call, "fish on, coming through," they'll clear the rail, and raise or lower their line to permit you to follow your fish. With a big fish, the mate frequently accompanies the angler making certain no tangles occur en route.

As a big fish is brought alongside, it's especially important to be alert to any last-minute runs. The mates are at the ready with a long-handled net or gaff (sometimes two gaffs are necessary, as with large yellowfin tuna) and as soon as the fish is within range, they either net or gaff it. At this time, it's critical that the angler just reel the fish close enough for the mates to handle. Sometimes, in the excitement, anglers try to lift the fish, and with a big fish thrashing at boatside, this can often result in a line break. Stay calm, reel the fish within range, and let the mates show their skill. It's much easier for a fish to be gaffed or netted when it is a foot or so beneath the surface, and not thrashing on the surface or with its head lifted from the water. As the fish is brought aboard, place your reel in freespool or open the bail on a spinning reel, so the mate can move away from the rail and other anglers can move freely as he unhooks your fish.

The road to success. It's worth noting that party boat regulars often become extremely proficient, and their skills are on a par with the best of guides, mates, and charter skippers. This doesn't just happen. It's a result of dedication, learning fundamentals, and honing techniques to perfection. It's not at all unusual to see veteran anglers aboard party boats consistently catching more and bigger fish than other anglers. This should never be construed as luck, although occasionally it may be, but more as an understanding of the species sought, its feeding habits, the weather conditions, speed of drift, current, water clarity, and a host of other factors.

It's often the little things that count. On a sum-

mer morning with a lazy drift, all of the anglers onboard may be catching summer flounders while using a 4-ounce sinker to hold bottom. As afternoon winds develop velocity, the boat's speed of drift accelerates, and at times it may take a full 16 ounces of sinker weight to keep a rig on the bottom. Those anglers who respond by changing weights continue to score, while those who maintain their 4-ounce sinkers actually have their baits drifting at midlevel, well above the bottom-feeding fish.

Always having a fresh bait on your hook, keeping the hooks sharp, using lightweight or fluorocarbon leaders less visible to fish, tying the correct knots, and, above all, being alert, are just a few of the many small things that collectively make a big difference in success.

Other Matters

Fish care. When bottom fishing or drift fishing, where the species sought are small in size, it's customary for anglers to reel their catch to boatside, lower their rod tip, and gently swing the fish aboard. The mate will quickly unhook your fish, rebait, and place your fish on ice or in your bag. On some boats, the mate places the catch on a stringer and then puts the fish on ice in a community box. On long-range boats or party boats whose excursions last several days, when the target is big species such as tuna, wahoo, and dolphin, the fish are often identified by a tail tag, then placed either on ice or refrigerated until you return to dockside.

In some areas, particularly in Florida and along the Gulf Coast, where the weather is often hot and fish can easily spoil, the mates place fish in a community box filled with crushed ice. Each fish is scored with a specific marking that is assigned to each angler onboard. As an example, the first angler to catch a fish is assigned "one cut on the bottom," which means the mate makes a single knife cut on the bottom of the fish near the head. The next angler to score is assigned "two cuts on the bottom." After four cuts are assigned, the next spot is the top of the head, with one to four cuts assigned. Next, the top of the tail is cut, then the bottom, and a single X on the left side of the head, then the right, then a double X, and so on.

The system works extremely well. The angler doesn't have to handle the fish, as it is unhooked, marked, and placed on ice immediately by the mate, who is often assisted by the captain when the fishing is hectic. Upon returning to dockside, the anglers disembark and form a semicircle with their opened ice chests. The mate removes each fish from the community box, calls out "top tail," and places the fish in the ice chest belonging to the angler assigned the top tail cut. "Two cuts on the bottom," "bottom tail," "double X on the left," and the chant goes on. In just a few minutes, hundreds of fish from the community box can be distributed. The fish are in excellent condition with this system.

Immediately after distributing the fish to the people who caught them, the mate goes to the cleaning table, where he will fillet and package your fish if you wish. For his efforts, he is rewarded with a tip based on the size and number of fish cleaned.

In tourist areas, many mates have Styrofoam coolers available and will clean your fish, pack them in double plastic bags, and then bury them in bagged ice in the cooler, sealing it with duct tape so that the fish may easily be transported home by air or car. Double-bagging fillets keeps them from becoming soaked with water, and double-bagging ice prevents water from leaking as it melts. Packed in this way, the fish easily keep for several days, arriving home in prime condition.

In many tourist locales, restaurants encourage you to bring your catch in, and they'll use their local recipes to prepare it, which is a great way to conclude a pleasant day's fishing on a party boat.

Selling fish. As a general rule, the fish you catch aboard a party boat are yours to keep. However, some mates on party boats will agree to clean your catch for you at no charge, providing you share some of the catch with them. They subsequently sell the fish they accumulate this way, which supplements their regular income.

Some boats permit experienced anglers to sail at a reduced fare or, in some cases, no fare at all, providing the angler agrees that the fish he catches become the property of the boat, which sells them at market. This is most likely to be an option when the action is exceptional and the fish price high. Often, just one or two fish are worth more on the commercial market than the boat's fare; this is especially so in the case of bigeye tuna, yellowfin tuna, and albacore. This works to the advantage of both boat and angler when the fishing is good, and good anglers are onboard. But if fishing is poor, the angler financially benefits while the captain suffers.

In those few places in freshwater where party boats operate, this is not an option, since freshwater sportfish are also designated as gamefish and cannot be sold. In saltwater, this is often different; sportfish may not be designated as gamefish in certain places, and may legally be sold, although there's an ethical question *(see: ethics)* as to whether it is right for an angler to sell fish and whether the selling of sport-caught fish in fact makes an angler a commercial fisherman.

Certainly party boat patrons may give their catch to the mate, captain, or other customers if they don't want them (although there is another ethical question: If you couldn't use the fish, why not release them when they were caught?). But certain saltwater fish have a lot of market value, and in some places they may be sold with or without a special permit or commercial license. Because it is normal for customers to assume that whatever they catch is theirs, they should be advised up front if that is not the case; if the option to sell fish exists, they should consider whether this is a practice they wish to engage in.

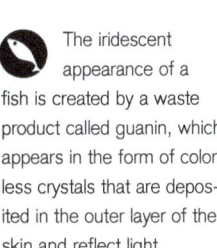

The iridescent appearance of a fish is created by a waste product called guanin, which appears in the form of colorless crystals that are deposited in the outer layer of the skin and reflect light.

Rail positions are often important on party boats; the stern, which produced a bluefish for this angler, is one of the preferred locations.

Big fish pools. Almost all party boats have a pool, to which anglers contribute a nominal amount, ranging from a couple of dollars to ten or more. The pool money ultimately goes to the angler catching the largest fish of the day. Rules identify which species of fish are eligible for the pool money, and it's great fun if momentum swings from one angler to the other as the size of the biggest fish increases throughout the day. Often the pool money is divided into two or three places, especially if the boat is crowded. It's not unusual to be rewarded with several hundred dollars for the biggest fish of the day, a double-barreled bonus considering that you've got a big one for the dinner table.

There are, however, those rare occasions when not a single fish is caught during the trip. Then the pool money is awarded via a drawing, so even on the poorest fishing day some lucky angler disembarks with a bonus. It's customary that the pool winners share a portion of the pool with the mate(s). These deckhands work hard, and it's their deft gaffing or netting that brings the winning catch aboard, so they deserve the consideration.

Gratuities. The crew members aboard many party boats are paid on a per diem basis. Their wages are fair, and they depend in part on gratuities from passengers for services rendered. Use the same tipping judgment you might render when at a restaurant, with a 10 to 15 percent tip in order for good service.

If, however, you board a boat in the morning and the mate is sitting there reading a newspaper instead of helping you with your gear, and throughout the day he's not helpful in removing the hook from a deeply hooked fish, or isn't interested in cleaning your catch, then it's certainly appropriate not to tip. Be leery of the mate who is more interested in catching fish for the market, instead of being concerned with your welfare.

If, on the other hand, he greets you with a smile, gets you set at a spot, keeps your bait container filled, is immediately at hand to net or gaff your fish, and gets them into the cooler or on ice, and back at dockside does a professional job of cleaning your catch, then certainly some extra consideration is in order.

No GPS. With increased fishing pressure on all coasts, party boat skippers must continually work hard to find fish for their patrons. Often this means finding spots not fished by others. Historically, party boat captains have taken pride in their own "spots." During periods of slow fishing, many party boat owners sail far from shore with their sonar probing the depths as they look for new places that could provide good fishing. Frequently, these spots, such as wrecks, reefs, rocks, and ridges, are reported from commercial men who get their nets fouled in bottom obstructions. Party boat skippers reward finders of such locations with sizable cash payments because it expands their fishing opportunities and results in more enjoyment for their anglers.

The captains are very secretive about some of their spots, as they are indeed investments.

On the inshore grounds, private boaters could easily follow the party boats and record the Loran or GPS locations. With the passage of time, party boats have had to go great distances offshore, as is the case off New England, the New Jersey and North Carolina Coasts, the Florida Keys, and Gulf Coast ports, in order to find spots never before fished. When they find a wreck, ridge, or reef they're often able to provide exciting fishing for their patrons for a short period of time. But because of sophisticated electronics and the fact that private boaters have fast, long-range boats, the spots aren't "secret" for long. This is a sad dilemma for the party boat owners whose livelihood depends upon providing a relaxing trip and good fishing on a daily basis. The world has gotten smaller as a result of electronics, and this has certainly had a negative impact on the exclusivity that party boat captains and their patrons have enjoyed for years with respect to their spots.

In recent years, there has even been piracy of some spots from aboard party boats. Individuals have brought electronic equipment, especially handheld navigation devices like GPS units *(see)*, and recorded the locations when they were on the fishing grounds, much to the consternation of the captains. As a result, some captains will not permit portable GPS units, or similar electronic position-monitoring gear, to be carried aboard by passengers.

The following is language from a notice to patrons that one may find upon boarding a coastal party boat:

"Party and open boat fishing is one of the few businesses where you still find a spirit of friendly competition. The captains on these boats compete to find the most productive fishing grounds. This is a long-time tradition, and part of what makes fishing fun. Finding these spots is also time-consuming and a lot of hard work. New technology is wonderful, but greedy unscrupulous people can always find a way to use it for ill purposes. In this case it is being used to steal the location of fishing grounds. This information is then sold. Everyone should understand that it is policy aboard this boat to not tolerate this form of stealing, nor will the boat's owners participate in this scheme by purchasing information stolen from other boats and their captains. Be aware that a diligent effort will be made to prevent GPS and other devices from being brought aboard. If such devices are found after departure, they will be confiscated by the captain and destroyed."

While no captain lays claim to any spot, as the oceans are available to anyone, they feel very strongly when people try to take advantage of them. This is particularly true of captains who use their off-season time or slow days to run many miles seaward as they methodically monitor their electronics to search for bottom conformations and wrecks that may hold a bonanza catch.

See: Bottom Fishing; Charter Boat; Chumming; Fishing Regulations; Inshore Fishing.

PATTERN

The particular appearance of an artificial fly, comprised of the parts that make up its likeness, the way they are incorporated onto the fly hook, and the colors.
See: Fly.

PAVÓN

The Spanish word for peacock bass (see: bass, peacock).

PAYARA *Hydrolycus scomberoides.*

Other names—dogfish, saber-toothed dogfish; Portuguese: *cachorra, peixe-cachorra, pirandirá*; Spanish: *payara, chambra.*

The payara is an excellent South American gamefish and a fearsome-looking characin that is noted for its saberlike teeth. A member of the Cinodontidae family and a relative of tigerfish and piranha, it is only known to a small number of anglers, and little has been reported about it in the scientific literature. The total number of species in this family is unknown, and there are three genera.

Identification. The payara is distinctive because of its unusual head and mouth. It has two long canine teeth on the tip of its upturned lower jaw, which slip into a sheath inside the tip of the upper jaw when the mouth is fully closed. These slightly backward-curved saberlike teeth can be between 2 and 3 inches long in a 20-pound fish. On some large individuals, these two long lower jaw teeth may be broken. The snout of the upper jaw is also equipped with two shorter forward-curved canine teeth, and the rest of the mouth has shorter but sharp-pointed teeth, more of which are on the lower jaw.

The body of the payara is compressed and elongate. The dorsal fin is high, originates at midbody, and is squared off. There is an adipose fin just ahead of the caudal peduncle, and the tail is squared in some specimens and rounded in others. Both tail and adipose fins darken on their posterior, and may have a small whitish fringe. The body coloring is a steely gray with blue gray to olive tones, darker on the back and lighter on the belly. The lateral line runs the length of the body and is slightly decurved toward the head.

Size. The maximum size that *H. scomberoides* can attain is uncertain. It was reported as 33 pounds until a 39-pound, 4-ounce all-tackle world-record specimen was caught at Uraima Falls, Venezuela, in 1996. It can evidently attain 4 feet in length.

Distribution. *H. scomberoides* occurs in the Orinoco and Amazon River basins. A species that is believed to be smaller (up to 20 inches) is reported to exist in southern Brazil in the upper watershed of the River Plate. This fish is called biara *(Raphiodon vulpinus)* and is also known as *cachorra* in Portuguese, and *chafolete* and *machete* in Spanish.

Habitat. Payara are primarily a river fish and prefer swift-flowing areas. They also exist in flooded backwaters and in the shallows and depths of lagoons and impoundments. They are said to be a schooling species, but it is unclear whether they

A payara from the São Francisco River, Brazil.

Payara

are actually schooling fish or happen to be concentrated at certain locations.

Food. The complete diet of payara is unreported, but their dentition and aggressive nature make them clearly a formidable predator of other fish.

Angling. Payara strike hard and usually leap out of the water upon being hooked. Although good fighters, they tire fairly easily (at least in comparison to species like dorado). They are not difficult to land, although in slower flows big payara can be challenging if they turn their considerable broadside mass against the current, and in thickly timbered waters they may be initially hard to coax away from obstructions.

A variety of plugs are effective on payara, particularly noisy, flashy lures. Shallow-running crankbaits, lipless crankbaits, and large minnow-shaped swimming plugs are productive; big spoons and jigs may also be effective. In lakes and flooded backwaters, payara are usually caught incidentally by anglers pursuing peacock bass. In some rivers—especially the clearer, swifter flows of tributaries and headwaters—they can be deliberately targeted, particularly in the pools and eddies below falls and in the head of pools below a rapids.

In rivers, payara often prefer the swiftest water and areas near the largest boulders. In reservoirs, they are a less predictable catch and are sometimes landed by deep jigging. A specimen exceeding 20 pounds will make several runs and spectacular jumps. Their sharp teeth frequently puncture plastic and wooden lures. A strong steel leader and snap swivel are necessary, and lures must be durable and the hooks and attachments extra-strong. Heavy-action rods, with baitcasting reels capable of holding 100 yards of 17- to 30-pound-test line, are commonly used in locations where bigger fish may be present.

Payara caught in swift waters may be difficult to revive and release, especially if taken on light tackle. As the distribution of these fish is somewhat limited, especially the large specimens, it is important for anglers to handle and release them carefully. The flesh of payara is edible but not notable; they are regularly consumed by local peoples.

Venezuela and Brazil are known for payara, although mainly in certain types of waters. The upper tributaries of the Orinoco and Amazon Rivers, with blue- and black-water characteristics (see: Brazil; Venezuela), are best. Venezuela's interior waters produce among the biggest payara; Brazil has payara in certain waters from the upper to lower regions of the country; and Colombia has good payara waters.

PECTORAL FIN
The fin usually found on each side of the body directly behind the gill opening.
See: Fish.

PELAGIC FISH
Free-swimming fish that inhabit the open sea and are independent of the seabed or water bottom.

PELVIC FIN
The pair of adjoining fins ventrally located beneath the belly and in front of the anus; also called ventral fins.
See: Fish.

PENCIL FLOAT
Also known as a pencil bobber, this is a term for a long and slender-profile float (see), usually one made of plastic.

PENDULUM CAST
A long-distance cast used by surf anglers.
See: Casting; Surf Fishing.

PENNSYLVANIA
Called the Keystone State because it was the link binding the original 13 northern and southern states, Pennsylvania is also a "keystone state" for sportfishing, serving as a link between northern and southern fisheries, and between the Atlantic Ocean and the Great Lakes. Although Pennsylvania has no saltwater fishing to speak of—other than for tidal-river species—fishing opportunities are diverse and surprisingly good here; Pennsylvania annually ranks among the leading states in fishing license sales, and this is reflected in angler enthusiasm.

Except for narrow strips along the southeastern and northwestern corners of the state, the terrain is hilly to mountainous. Trout streams, larger creeks, or rivers flow through most valleys. Several small lakes and ponds dot the glaciated northeast and northwest corners. There are four substantial man-made reservoirs—Pymatuning, Allegheny, Raystown, and Wallenpaupack—and numerous smaller reservoirs and lakes. Important watersheds are the Ohio/Allegheny Rivers, the Susquehanna River, and the Delaware River.

The favorite gamefish in Pennsylvania are brook trout, brown trout, rainbow trout, smallmouth bass, largemouth bass, walleye, muskellunge, northern pike, chain pickerel, and channel catfish. American shad and striped bass migrate into the Delaware River, and steelhead are plentiful in Lake Erie and several tributaries.

The most popular or widespread panfish are white crappie, black crappie, yellow perch, bluegills, pumpkinseeds, rock bass, and brown, yellow, and black bullhead. Additionally, white bass, white catfish, white perch, warmouth, green sunfish, and redbreast sunfish are common in some waters.

Carp are prevalent throughout the state, as are several sucker species. Freshwater drum are abundant in Lake Erie. Through stocking, lake trout are common at Lake Erie and a few inland lakes. Flathead catfish are especially common in the Allegheny River. Sauger and spotted bass are available in the lower Allegheny and Monongahela Rivers and in the Ohio River. Some chinook salmon are still stocked in Lake Erie, which also has a small population of pink salmon.

Trout Streams/Small Lakes
Trout have traditionally been the most popular fish among Pennsylvania anglers. The state stocks trout in nearly 5,000 miles of streams and has more than 400 miles of Class A Wild Trout Water. Roughly 10,000 miles of streams and rivers provide suitable trout habitat, and there's good trout fishing in every part of the state. Many streams, or sections of streams, are subject to special regulations that restrict fishing methods and/or the harvest.

The Pennsylvania Fish and Boat Commission stocks brook, brown, and rainbow trout in streams. Brookies are the only native species, but browns and rainbows have established self-sustaining populations in several flows.

Trout anglers can go wild in the Allegheny Highlands, a rugged, hilly, forested, sparsely populated region covering most of north-central Pennsylvania. The Allegheny National Forest and several enormous state forests provide public access to hundreds of miles of fine trout streams. Many small flows are populated by wild brook trout and are rarely visited by anglers, as numerous stocked streams experience most of the pressure. Famous area creeks include the Kettle, Pine, Tionesta, Kinzua, and First Fork of the Sinnemahoning.

There may be snow on the ground when trout season opens in mid-April. Fly fishing is best during the great hatches of May and June. During summer, stream flows are normally very low, making fishing difficult; then, early morning is best for those who are extremely cautious and use fine tippets.

Pine Creek forms in Tioga County and eastern McKean County, then turns southward at Ansonia through the Pine Creek Gorge. The first 17 miles through the "Grand Canyon of Pennsylvania" to Blackwell are accessible only by foot, bicycle, or water. A float trip through the canyon is one of the finest trout fishing adventures in the East. Camping is permitted along the creek.

Kettle Creek is the next major drainage west of Pine Creek, flowing southward from Oleona to the West Branch of the Susquehanna River at Westport. Its deep, narrow valley is about as far off the beaten path as you can get in a car. Most businesses survive here only because of trout anglers. Cross Fork, an important tributary, is a favorite of fly anglers.

Tionesta Creek flows through the Allegheny National Forest from Barnes, where its east, west, and south branches join, to the Allegheny River at the village of Tionesta. It can be canoed from Barnes to Tionesta Reservoir during April and May. The better fishing is in the main branches. As with most Allegheny Highlands creeks, wild brook trout are abundant in many tributaries.

Pennsylvania limestone streams are part of America's fishing heritage and are frequently cited in classic angling literature. These streams are characterized by a stable pH of 7.5 to 8.0, low gradient, large numbers of aquatic plants, and abundant aquatic insects, particularly mayflies, midges, and freshwater shrimp. These streams tend to emerge from springs at nearly full flow, preferring stable flow and virtually constant temperature year-around. Trout grow quickly in this environment.

The limestone streams are located generally in the south-central and southeastern portions of the state, in the Appalachian Mountains and Piedmont. Penns Creek in Union County is considered by many people as the finest trout stream in the state. Access is much better here than along most limestone streams, and much of it is floatable during April and May.

Limestone creeks include Ottown Run (Bedford County); Moselem Run, Peters Creek, Spring Creek, Willow Creek, and Wyomissing Creek (Berks County); Boiling Spring Run (Blair County); Cooks Creek (Bucks County); Buffalo Run, Cedar Run, Elk Creek, Lick Run, Little Fishing Creek, Logan Branch, Penns Creek, Pine Creek, Sinking Creek, Slab Cabin Run, and Spring Creek (Centre County); Little Valley Creek and Valley Creek (Chester County); Bald Eagle Creek, Cedar Run, and Fishing Creek (Clinton County); and Big Spring Creek, Cedar Run, Green Spring Creek, Hogestown Run, Letort Spring Run, and Trindle Spring Run (Cumberland County).

Deep-dwelling halibut are prolific fish; a female halibut weighing 150 pounds is capable of producing as many as 2 million eggs.

Also Buck Run and Falling Spring Branch (Franklin County); Spring Run (Fulton County); Donegal Creek, Eshleman Run, Indian Run, Londonland Run, and Swarr Run (Lancaster County); East Branch Mill Creek and Mill Creek (Lebanon County); Catasauqua Creek, Cedar Creek, Coplay Creek, Little Lehigh Creek, South Branch Saucon Creek, Spring Creek, and Trout Creek (Lehigh County); Antes Creek, the source of which is the largest limestone spring in Pennsylvania (Lycoming County); and Allegheny Creek, Bushkill Creek, East Branch Monocacy Creek, Jacoby Creek, Monocacy Creek, Nancy Run, Saucon Creek, and Shoeneck Creek (Northampton County).

Roughly 100 small lakes covering more than 5,000 surface acres are heavily stocked with trout. Stocking is spread out through the year to provide recreation in every season. Because these lakes are stocked by formula, one is about as good as another, although fishing pressure varies. Lists of stocked lakes are widely published, and any tackle shop should be able to assist. Many of these lakes are in state parks, and many have special boating regulations, predominately permitting only electric motors.

Ice fishing is particularly popular at some lakes stocked with trout. Those along the northern tier typically freeze over by Christmas. Lakes along the southern border do not have any safe ice during many winters.

Most lakes are stocked with brook, brown, and rainbow trout. Marginal fisheries do exist, however, at a few inland lakes that have been stocked with lake trout. The best opportunities may be at East Branch Lake in Elk County, and Raystown Lake in Huntingdon County.

Delaware River

The Delaware River is Pennsylvania's link to the Atlantic Ocean. Forming the eastern border with New York and New Jersey, it enters the state in Wayne County, flowing southward about 200 miles past Philadelphia and into Delaware Bay. Tides reach upriver as far as the Route 1 bridge at Trenton Falls.

The Pennsylvania portion of this river contains a diverse and high-quality fishery. Many American shad and some striped bass migrate in from Delaware Bay; trout fishing is superb in the headwaters; and in between there's smallmouth bass, largemouth bass, walleye, muskellunge, white and channel catfish, and a variety of panfish.

The Delaware is a popular floating river, but it has several treacherous rapids. Among the worst are Skinners Falls, 5 miles above Narrowsburg in Wayne County; another about 2 miles above the Zane Gray House access site in Pike County; Sambo Riff just below the mouth of Flat Brook in Monroe County; Foul Riff just above the PP&L access site in Northampton County; and wing dams in Bucks County. In the tidal portion, boaters must beware of the wakes of seagoing vessels and tidal rips.

The upper Delaware from Hancock, New York, down to the Delaware Water Gap adjoining New Jersey is a designated National Wild and Scenic River. Scenery is spectacular, with hills rising 800 feet above the river. This is all Class I water, a series of short riffles and long pools, perfect for relaxed float fishing. Float fishing for brown and rainbow trout is popular along Wayne County from Hancock to Callicoon, New York, a distance of about 31 miles. Excellent insect hatches occur from late May through September.

The Delaware has especially fine shad fishing. Shad move into Pennsylvania water during early to mid-April. They'll reach the Delaware Water Gap by late April, and Wayne County by mid- to late May. Action continues through June in the upper river. Shad darts are the traditional lures, but small spoons, sometimes fished behind downriggers in the deeper midriver sections, are also effective. Fly fishing has gained popularity in the upper reaches. The best fishing is generally in the main channel.

Striped bass migrate up the Delaware into Bucks, Philadelphia, and Delaware Counties from May through July, and a few stragglers go much farther upriver. In the lower section, look for them where tidal currents are heaviest. Bloodworms are the top natural baits, but these fish are also caught on white jigs and silver or white crankbaits.

Largemouth bass inhabit tidal water near tributary mouths and in weedy coves. Smallmouth bass

A shad comes into the boat on the Delaware River.

are more abundant from Trenton Falls upriver to Damascus in Wayne County. Anglers also encounter walleye and muskellunge through this stretch, although very few muskies are caught above Delaware Water Gap. The deep Narrowsburg Pool is a favorite spot among walleye anglers, especially during spring and fall.

Larger tributaries generally have fair to good warmwater fisheries in the lower areas, and coldwater fisheries toward the headwaters. The Schuylkill River, which meets the Delaware at Philadelphia, has both smallmouth and largemouth bass, channel catfish, walleye, and muskies. The Lehigh River, entering at Easton, has good smallmouth bass fishing and some largemouth bass, muskellunge, channel catfish, and panfish. The Lackawaxen River in Pike County is fine trout water. Big browns migrate from the Delaware into the Lackawaxen seeking cooler water during summer. The area near the Delaware is a favored shad spot in May.

Susquehanna River

The Susquehanna River is a nationally renowned smallmouth bass fishery. Walleye, muskies, catfish, and panfish are also fairly abundant in some areas. Before dams were built and water quality declined, large numbers of American shad, eels, herring, and other anadromous fish migrated into the river from the Chesapeake Bay. The restoration of shad runs was one main reason for the establishment of the Pennsylvania Fish Commission (now the Fish and Boat Commission) in 1866. The same act that established the commission directed dam owners to provide fish passage facilities, but it was not until the last three decades of the twentieth century before any real progress was made in this regard.

The Susquehanna River forms in the northeast corner of Pennsylvania, flowing northward into New York. It re-enters Pennsylvania in Bradford County, near Sayre, flowing southward. Its largest tributary, the West Branch, enters at Northumberland, where an inflatable dam creates Lake Augusta. The Juniata River joins at Clarks Ferry. At Harrisburg, the Susquehanna is a mile wide. Its watershed is the second largest in the eastern United States and includes more than half of Pennsylvania. Four hydroelectric dams between Harrisburg and Maryland create large lakes.

Except for the dams, the Susquehanna is all floatable. Typical low-water conditions in summer, however, make floating difficult in many areas, particularly above Laceyville and from Halifax to Harrisburg. Below Harrisburg, a low-head dam and three larger dams make long floats burdensome. The more rugged rapids of the river are in this area.

The Susquehanna is ideal smallmouth habitat all through Pennsylvania; it is rocky and, except above the hydroelectric dams, shallow. Through Bradford and Wyoming Counties, the bottom is a mix of gravel and rubble. Smallmouth anglers here often drift hellgrammites in the current. This is a delightful stretch for float fishing. Pools are short but can also produce walleye and muskies.

Farther downstream, the Susquehanna flows through the Appalachian Mountains. The river offers long pools, lengthy stretches where it flows swiftly over exposed bedrock, and numerous islands. Smallmouth fishing is spectacular. For a change of pace, channel catfish are also quite abundant.

Lake Clark, Lake Aldred, and the Conowingo Pool, created by three large hydroelectric dams, offer excellent fishing for smallmouth bass and channel catfish, along with some walleye, muskellunge, crappie, and yellow perch. Largemouth bass are common in the Conowingo Pool. Striped bass have been stocked as well. All three lakes are deep enough for powerboats. There are many rocks just beneath the surface, however, primarily toward the heads of the lakes.

The West Branch Susquehanna River drains most of the Allegheny Highlands, a sparsely populated forest. Despite its beautiful scenery and clear water, the West Branch is virtually without fish until it reaches Lock Haven, primarily due to acidic coal mine runoff, and does not become a good fishery until the Williamsport area. From that point, fishing for smallmouths, walleye, muskies, and panfish gets progressively better.

The Juniata River is smallmouth bass heaven. Along its headwaters, smallmouths are incredibly abundant, if somewhat on the small side. Farther downstream, larger smallmouths become more common, as do walleye and muskellunge. Stonecats (madtoms) are the favorite live baits here, and natural-colored jigs work during summer when the water is low and clear.

Walleye and muskellunge are fairly plentiful in the Juniata, although not nearly as widespread as smallmouths. Look for muskies in the calmer pools, especially in the lower half of the river. Walleye fishing is usually best during winter in the deeper pools up to Huntingdon. Rock bass, locally called redeyes, are the most popular panfish.

The Little Juniata River and the Frankstown Branch, which meet to form the Juniata River, are both loaded with smallmouth bass and trout. The smallmouths tend to be quite small. The trout, mostly browns, tend to be larger, however.

Ohio/Allegheny Rivers

West of the Appalachian Mountain divide, most waters flow into the Ohio/Allegheny River system. The Ohio River begins at Pittsburgh, where the Allegheny and Monongahela Rivers meet. These are all large rivers at this point, made navigable to heavy barges by a system of navigation dams and locks that provide a water transportation link to the Mississippi River. Upriver, the Allegheny and Monongahela flow over rocky beds in a series of riffles and pools. Fair to excellent fishing is available throughout most of this watershed.

The Allegheny River seeps from the ground on a farm near Coudersport, in Potter County. Within a few miles it becomes a fine trout stream and gains volume quickly. Only a few miles below Coudersport, pools are deep enough to hold a few muskellunge.

By Port Allegheny, the river has become a warmwater fishery that can be floated, although only with light boats or canoes. The valley is broad, and the river is surrounded by either farms, swamps, or dense bottomland forest. Floating is the only practical way to reach most of this stretch, although it gets very shallow during summer, when it is often necessary to get out of the boat to pull. Much of the water between Port Allegheny and the New York border experiences minimal fishing pressure. Smallmouth bass are scattered throughout most of this area. Walleye and channel catfish lurk in the deeper water, and muskies lay by abundant wood cover.

After making a swing through New York, the Allegheny re-enters Pennsylvania as the Allegheny Reservoir, which is created by the Kinzua Dam. The middle Allegheny, from the Kinzua Dam 107 miles downstream to the head of the navigation pools near Emlenton, provides exceptionally fine multispecies fishing. Most of this stretch, except for the areas around Warren and from Oil City to Franklin, has been designated the Allegheny National Wild and Scenic River. Shore access is good, especially from the dam to Tionesta, where the river either borders or is surrounded by the Allegheny National Forest.

Suitable for canoes and light boats, the middle Allegheny is perfect float fishing water. Riffles are mild, although shallow, during normal summer flow. Seven islands between Irvine and Tionesta, 30 miles by river, have been designated the Allegheny Wilderness Islands. Primitive camping is allowed on these and on several other islands.

From the Kinzua Dam to the mouth of Conewango Creek at Warren, and to a lesser extent for another 15 miles or so downstream, is among the best big trout water in the state. The typical trout is 15 to 18 inches long, and a few in the 6- to 8-pound class are taken. Small spoons or shallow-running minnow-shaped plugs provide action in the riffles around the many islands, but the biggest browns fall to large minnow lures in the pools. The best fly fishing is during May and June, preferably when outflow from the dam is no more than 1,200 cubic feet per second.

Muskie fishing is good throughout the middle Allegheny, and particularly from the dam to Oil City. Look for muskies in the calmer pools. The best fishing occurs in October, November, and June.

The middle Allegheny might be the best trophy walleye fishery in the East. The trophy standard is 10 pounds, but a few weighing more than 15 pounds have been caught. Favorite areas during fall and winter are the Kinzua Dam tailwaters and the dredged pools at Warren, Starbrick, and Tionesta. During summer, look for walleye in deeper troughs, more than 4 feet deep, in the riffles. Live minnows are the best winter baits. Use either nightcrawlers or minnows in summer.

The rock-bottomed Allegheny is perfect smallmouth bass habitat. Fishing for smallmouths is only fair for the first few miles below the Kinzua Dam, but it improves considerably below the mouth of Conewango Creek, peaking between Irvine and Kennerdell. Soft-shelled crayfish are the best summer baits, but you'll have to catch your own. The best fishing occurs during June and October, and most of the larger smallmouths are caught then.

Less known but enthusiastically sought by a few anglers are channel and flathead catfish. Channel cats to 20 pounds, and some larger, are found in most of the deeper pools throughout the river. Flatheads are not abundant above Tidioute. Commonly weighing 6 to 10 pounds, and with a few more than 40 pounds, they primarily inhabit pools that are at least 15 feet deep and filled with boulders. Above Tidioute few pools are deep enough.

Several of the larger tributaries also provide good fisheries. Conewango Creek has fine smallmouth bass and pike fishing, and a few walleye in the deeper pools. Brokenstraw Creek, which meets the river at Irvine, has some smallmouths and walleye in its lower half, good stocked trout fishing in its midportion, and pike where it drains swamps near the headwaters along the New York border. French Creek, which flows into the river at Franklin, has spotty but good fishing for smallmouth bass, walleye, and muskellunge.

The Clarion River, which meets the Allegheny between Emlenton and Parker, has fair smallmouth bass fishing and excellent scenery. A 36-mile float fishing trip from Ridgeway to Clarington is a relaxing experience. In Armstrong County, the lower portions of Red Bank, Mahoning, Cowanshannock, Crooked, and Buffalo Creeks offer good smallmouth bass action, along with walleye, pike, and muskies.

The Monongahela River flows northward into Pennsylvania from West Virginia. Fishing is fair for smallmouth bass, walleye, muskies, and channel catfish. Its major tributary, the Youghiogheny River, drains the highest land in Pennsylvania. Best known for whitewater rafting, it has fair to good smallmouth bass, and trout fishing from the Youghiogheny Dam to Connellsville.

Fishing is surprisingly good even within the urban and heavily industrialized region along the navigable portions of the lower Allegheny and Monongahela Rivers, and the Ohio River. The biggest challenge lies in evaluating the surface; almost everything looks the same from above. Good places to fish are around the many bridge piers, which can hold walleye, sauger, smallmouth bass, spotted bass, white bass, and crappie.

Below the navigation dams is another likely place to find bass, walleye, sauger, hybrid stripers, channel catfish, and flathead catfish. Look for walleye near the mouths of tributaries, especially during fall, winter, and spring.

Lake Erie

Though only a small portion of Lake Erie lies within Pennsylvania, Erie is still the biggest fishing hole in the state, covering 640,000 surface acres and 42 miles of shoreline. Here is excellent fishing for walleye, smallmouth bass, lake trout, and steelhead. Several of the 14 permanent tributaries are visited annually by steelhead. The only natural bay, Presque Isle, and its connecting lagoons, hold good numbers of both largemouth and smallmouth bass, northern pike, muskellunge, and panfish.

Erie was declared dead in the national news media during the 1960s, although it never was; water quality has improved considerably since, as has the fishery. Unfortunately, some species were lost. Most notable was the blue pike, a close relative of the walleye, which was a mainstay of both sport and commercial fisheries. It is now presumed extinct. Gone also are the native lake trout, although strong efforts are being made through stocking to re-establish a self-sustaining population.

Exotic species have also had an enormous impact on the native fish, sea lampreys being most notorious. This species may have done more to wipe out the native lake trout than anything else. Other exotic intruders include alewives, white perch, zebra mussels, and spiny water fleas. Pacific salmon were heavily stocked in Lake Erie and flourished for a while, but they are now only a minor part of the Erie's sportfishery.

Lake Erie is a notoriously treacherous body of water, one that requires big-water boats. Anglers unfamiliar with it need to be cautious. The popular access areas in Pennsylvania are at Walnut Creek, the City of Erie, Presque Isle State Park, and Safe Harbor Marina near Northeast.

Smallmouth bass fishing is exceptional at Lake Erie. Five-pound smallmouths are common, and 6-pounders are caught frequently enough. Skilled anglers expect their daily catches to number in the dozens. The best smallmouth action is during May and June, before and following the spawn, when these fish are in relatively shallow water.

Water clarity, wave action, and sunlight play significant roles in determining where the smallmouths are. As a general rule, the larger bass will be beyond the depth where bottom disappears (on calm, sunny days when the water is clear, you can see bottom in under 35 feet). Smallmouths congregate near irregular, rocky structure and over rocky rubble; dropoffs and humps are best located with sonar, and vertical jigging is effective when there's a concentration of smallmouths.

This is the only place in Pennsylvania where guiding is big business. The guiding or charter boat

Lake Erie provides Pennsylvania's most significant big-water fishing.

business was first built on salmon, but now walleye are the primary goal, and guided anglers, as well as many good private boaters, have no trouble catching 6- to 8-pound walleye. During July and August, anglers troll using various methods for walleye that are suspended over deep water (90 to 130 feet).

There are two distinct types of walleye behavior in Lake Erie. One group spawns in the western basin, in Ohio, then migrates throughout the lake in summer and provides deep-water suspended fishing. Another group spawns in Pennsylvania and inhabits nearshore water generally less than 75 feet deep. These walleye tend to hug bottom. Although not as widely known as the deep-water fishery, anglers land them by trolling, drifting, or jigging at night in water as shallow as 15 feet. Probably the best shore-fishing pattern for these walleye occurs as they feed on young steelhead entering the lake from tributary creeks during spring.

Steelhead management was intensified, and salmon management reduced, after it was determined that the return rate (from the lake to tributaries) was much better for steelhead. An aggressive stocking program has built an excellent steelhead fishery, although in the lake steelhead are caught incidentally. The best steelhead fishing, however, occurs when they migrate into tributaries from late September through the following May, and the best action is usually when creek flow is rising.

The significant Lake Erie tributaries in Pennsylvania are, from east to west: Twentymile Creek, Sixteenmile Creek, Twelvemile Creek,

Walnut Creek, and Elk Creek. Because most of the Lake Erie shore is privately owned, fishing access is limited. The Fish and Boat Commission maintains access along Elk and Walnut Creeks.

Although it is adjacent to the third largest city in the state (Erie), Presque Isle Bay and connecting lagoons in Presque Isle State Park offer good fishing for smallmouth bass, largemouth bass, northern pike, muskies, panfish, and steelhead. Ice fishing is very popular.

Inland Lakes/Reservoirs
Aside from Lake Erie, Pennsylvania's natural lakes are small. The largest is 928-acre Conneaut Lake, in Crawford County. It has good numbers of muskellunge, smallmouth bass, largemouth bass, northern pike, crappie, sunfish, and some large white bass. Boating pressure is heavy during summer, and anglers prefer October or November.

Conneaut is one of several glacial lakes in the northwest corner of the state. Others are Edinboro, LeBoeuf, Canadohta, and Sugar Lakes. All have native muskie populations, as well as bass and panfish.

Pymatuning Reservoir straddles the Ohio border in Crawford County. Covering 13,920 acres, it is a relatively shallow lake with a maximum depth of 35 feet. Best known for its walleye and muskies, it also provides good fishing for smallmouth and largemouth bass, crappie, and channel catfish. A favorite walleye fishing pattern occurs during spring, when they move onto shallow bars and shoals at night. During summer, walleye anglers troll or drift in the central and lower parts of the lake, concentrating their efforts close to humps and dropoffs.

Few waters can match Allegheny Reservoir for producing trophy fish. Located in northeastern Warren County and reaching across the New York border, the reservoir has 99 miles of shoreline and roughly 12,000 surface acres. Maximum depth near the dam is about 135 feet. Shoreline access is limited because there are no roads along most of the lake. Allegheny Reservoir has given up walleye over 17 pounds, pike over 33 pounds, and several muskies over 40 pounds. Smallmouth bass are abundant. Although not a major part of the angling catch, brown trout are highly prized. The prevalent panfish are yellow perch, white bass, rock bass, and crappie. The white bass fishery is overlooked by most anglers, but fish over 15 inches long are common. Some of the largest walleye, pike, and brown trout are taken through the ice. During summer, local anglers favor fallen trees and artificial structures. Vertical jigging with spoons around major points is an effective method for walleye.

A number of notable but smaller man-made lakes are in the northwest corner of the state. These include Tionesta Lake in Forest County, which has excellent smallmouth bass and muskie fishing; Woodcock Creek Lake and Tamarack Lake in Crawford County, which have an abundance of bass, muskies, and panfish; 1,860-acre Lake Wilhelm in Mercer County, which offers good crappie fishing along with walleye, largemouth bass, and pike; and 3,560-acre Shenango Lake in Mercer County, which has a good supply of largemouth bass, smallmouth bass, walleye, muskellunge, pike, catfish, and crappie.

Lake Arthur, a 3,225-acre impoundment in Butler County, is the premier lake in the west-central part of the state. Although fishing pressure is particularly heavy, wise management practices have led to a quality fishery—the best trophy largemouth lake in the state. Many largemouths over 5 pounds have been caught through the ice. Fishing is also good at Arthur for muskies, crappie, hybrid stripers, channel catfish, walleye, and pike.

In the southwestern region, Glendale Lake—a 1,600-acre impoundment in Cambria County—is among the state's better pike waters. It also has fine largemouth bass, along with muskellunge, channel catfish, chain pickerel, crappie, and other panfish. This is one of the few Pennsylvania waters where anglers stand a reasonable chance of catching a bowfin.

In Armstrong County, smallmouth bass, muskies, walleye, pike, and crappie are abundant at Mahoning Creek Lake; Crooked Creek Lake provides good largemouth bass fishing. In Somerset County, smallmouth bass and walleye are the main attractions at Youghiogheny River Reservoir, which is shared with Maryland; Lake Somerset has fair to good pike fishing, and High Point Lake, which is near the top of the highest mountain in Pennsylvania, is a sleeper for walleye.

Anglers usually think trout when they look at the north-central region. A few small man-made lakes provide good warmwater fishing, however. Cowanesque Lake in Tioga County is one of the best, providing smallmouth and largemouth bass, muskies, walleye, channel catfish, and crappie. Others include Hammond Lake, which offers bass, pike, muskies, walleye, and channel catfish; and Hills Creek Lake, which occasionally yields exceptionally big muskellunge and largemouth bass.

In Centre County, Blanchard Lake has plenty of largemouth bass, smallmouth bass, and crappie. Black Moshannon Lake is a good largemouth bass fishery. Kettle Creek Lake, a deep but small impoundment in Clinton County, supports a fair smallmouth bass fishery in addition to stocked trout. In Elk County, 1,240-acre East Branch Lake had produced a few exceptionally large muskellunge and brown trout to go along with fair smallmouth bass, yellow perch, and lake trout. In Cameron County, George B. Stevenson Lake has a little-known fishery for largemouth bass and crappie to accompany stocked trout.

Raystown Lake steals the show among south-central Pennsylvania lakes. Winding 30 miles in a serpentine manner through the Appalachian

---

About 1860, Robert Barnwell Roosevelt, uncle of Theodore Roosevelt, complained that "streams in New York [City] that were formerly alive with trout are now totally deserted . . . ."

Mountains, it has a surface area of 8,300 acres and, except for a few areas that have been developed for recreation, is surrounded by forested mountains. Fishing pressure is heavy, yet with the help of stocking it sustains a lively sportfishery.

Stripers bring hordes of anglers to Raystown Lake. These fish have been taken to 50 pounds here, including state-record specimens, but the big brawlers are elusive. Visiting anglers might consider hiring a guide. Largemouth and smallmouth bass, lake trout, muskies, and crappie are plentiful. Some very large brown trout are caught occasionally. Because of its rich forage base, this lake has the potential to grow extremely large trout. Walleye have been stocked, but so far anglers have been able to make good catches only during spring when walleye are in shallow water.

Lake Marburg, a 1,295-acre York County impoundment, has the best pike fishing in the area, along with smallmouth bass, walleye, channel catfish, muskies, and better-than-average yellow perch, bluegills, and crappie. In Blair County, much smaller Canoe Lake is best known for largemouth bass and panfish, but some anglers also find large walleye.

Lake Wallenpaupack, with a surface area of 5,700 acres, is the largest body of water in the northeastern corner of the state. Although heavy pleasure boat traffic makes fishing difficult during the tourist season, a rich forage base sustains a quality fishery. Get on the water before sunrise during summer and cast surface lures along rocky banks. The better fishing is generally during May, October, and November, when most boats belong to anglers. Smallmouth bass fishing is very good at Wallenpaupack, and the lake also offers largemouth bass, muskies, walleye, and stripers.

Numerous small natural lakes and reservoirs dot the northeast, especially in the Pocono Mountains region. Some are private. Most have a mix of bass, chain pickerel, panfish, and trout. The state's best native pickerel fishing is found here. Pike and muskellunge, although they have been stocked into some northeast lakes, are not natives.

Among the better lakes in the Poconos are Lake Idlewild, Sterns Lake, Stillwater Reservoir, and Tuscarora Lake in Susquehanna County; Prompton Dam in Wayne County; Shohola Falls Dam in Pike County; and Lackawanna and Newton Lakes in Lackawanna County.

South of the Poconos in Carbon County, walleye and muskellunge highlight a fishery that includes largemouth bass, smallmouth bass, channel catfish, and panfish at Beltzville Lake. Mauch Chunk Lake has fine largemouth bass fishing along with smallmouth bass, walleye, channel catfish, muskies, and panfish.

Largemouth bass action is good at Harveys Lake in Luzerne County, at Lake Chillisquaque in Montour County, and at Stevens Lake in Wyoming County.

Several small reservoirs support quality fishing in the heavily populated southeast. Most have a good mix of fish, including largemouth bass, walleye, channel catfish, and panfish. Largemouth bass and muskies provide the best fishing at Blue Marsh Lake in Berks County and at Chester-Octoraro Lake in Lancaster County. Crappie fishing is better than average at Ontelaunee Reservoir in Berks County. Largemouth bass and walleye are mainstays at Lake Galena. In Delaware County, largemouth and smallmouth bass are the primary sportfish at Springton Reservoir, and Marsh Creek Lake in Chester County has good crappie fishing.

PERCH

The Percidae family of freshwater fish consists of hundreds of species, some of which are unarguably among the best-tasting species available and among the most important sportfish in North America and Europe. By far the largest number of species in this family are much too small to be eaten by humans, although they are important and presumably tasty forage for a host of larger predators. Among the smaller species are some 160 species of darters, which represent 20 percent of all fish in the United States.

All members of the perch family share basic features, however. The body is typically long and slender, and the two dorsal fins are distinctly separate. The anal fin has one or two spines, and the pelvic fins are located far forward, near the throat. The gill covers end in sharp, spinelike points. The scales are heavy and toothed along their exposed margins.
See: Darters; Perch, European; Perch, Yellow; Sauger; Saugeye; Walleye; Zander.

PERCH, EUROPEAN *Perca fluviatilis*.

Other names—perch, English perch, English river perch, Eurasian perch, redfin (Australia), redfin perch, reddie; Dutch: *baars*; Finnish: *ahven*; French: *perche europeénne, perche fluviatile;* German: *barsch, berse, flubbarsch*; Hungarian: *süger*; Italian, Portuguese, and Spanish: *perca*; Norwegian: *abbor*; Russian: *okun*; Swedish: *abborre*; Turkish: *tatlisu levregi*.

A member of the Percidae family, the European perch is popular with many anglers for its table fare and light-tackle virtues, and it is a common target of anglers throughout Europe. In places where it was introduced, especially those where trout exist, it is viewed less favorably, as it competes with trout for food and feeds on small trout. In some areas, anglers are asked not to return caught fish to the water.

Identification. A deep-bodied fish with a large mouth, the European perch is olive on the back, which grades to green on the sides and merges into white on the belly. The two dorsal fins are distinctly separated, the first being spinous with a black spot

European Perch

or blotch at the rear. There are five to six vertical bars across the back and sides, and these are more prominent among younger fish. The pelvic fins, anal fin, and the lower margin of the caudal fin are bright orange or red, hence the name.

Size. Although this species has been reported to grow to 500 millimeters in length and 10 kilograms in weight, most specimens are far smaller; 6.5 kilograms is reported to be the maximum for Eurasian specimens.

Distribution. European perch are native throughout Europe (except in Spain, Italy, and Greece) and to Siberia's Kolyma River. They have been widely introduced elsewhere, including Australia (Tasmania) in 1862, where they are now found in many streams and impoundments across the bottom half of the continent.

Habitat. This fish prefers slow-moving or stillwaters, and favors those areas where weed growth and underwater structures offer shelter and food. In streams they prefer slow-flowing pools and backwaters. In large farm dams and impoundments, they choose to roam in schools.

Life history/Behavior. This species is capable of breeding in both streams and dams, and females can produce more than 100,000 eggs, each about 2 millimeters in diameter. Spawning takes place in late winter and spring (August through October) at night in quiet waters away from strong current flow and among aquatic plants or underwater structures. The egg mass can be up to 3 meters long, and the eggs hatch out in seven to eight days. Growth in impoundments can be rapid, and overpopulation often results. High fecundity leads to a lot of small fish and few large ones, so overfishing is never a problem. Regular fishing and harvesting reduces numbers and the demand on food stocks, and the quantities of larger fish increase as a result.

Food. The carnivorous perch feeds on other fish, crayfish, mollusks, shrimp, worms, and insect larvae.

Angling. Fishing methods in general are similar to those for the North American yellow perch *(see: perch, yellow)*. Bait anglers use a variety of natural baits, including pieces from fillets of fish (especially saltwater mullet). Lure anglers choose among plugs, spinners, or soft plastics, either casting or trolling. Fly anglers use streamer patterns worked deep. European perch in lakes and impoundments tend to school more readily than in streams, and jigging for them is often popular among boat anglers, as well as for those fishing through the ice.

PERCH, GOLDEN *Macquaria ambigua*.

Other names—yellowbelly, callop, Murray perch, white perch, Murray bream, tarki.

A member of the Percichthyidae family of temperate bass and native to Australia, the golden perch is one of that country's most important inland fish. At one time, it supported a commercial fishery in the Murray-Darling system in the West of New South Wales. The impact of farming, irrigation schemes, drought, and pollution has reduced numbers considerably, but increased culture and stocking of small and large impoundments has secured their future. A placid fish that can be handled quite easily, it is, nonetheless, a fine sportfish and provides excellent table fare.

Identification. The golden perch is a deep-bodied, laterally compressed fish that has a conspicuous shape, especially in the adult: a concave forehead profile, a tapered snout, a protruding lower jaw, and a humped back that accentuates the small head and is more prominent in large females. A small eye sits above and behind the corner of the mouth. Although there is some variation in color due to water clarity, the back coloration can vary from dark brown to olive green, shading to yellow and white on the lower sides and belly. The soft dorsal and rounded caudal fins are muddy black, and the other fins are yellowish.

Size. This species is known to grow to 23 kilograms and a length of 760 millimeters; the Australian angling record stands at 9.52 kilograms. Captures of specimens up to 5 kilograms are not uncommon and are usually taken by anglers in large impoundments.

Distribution. The golden perch appears naturally in the rivers and tributaries of the Murray-Darling system in central and southern Queensland, western New South Wales, Victoria, and South Australia, and in some coastal streams in northern New South Wales. They have also been introduced to many large impoundments in these states, as well as in northern Queensland and the Northern Territory.

Habitat. Most of the waterways in which golden perch live are slow moving, turbid, and warm. They are also found in clear-water environments to a lesser degree, as well as in backwaters and billabongs that form after floods. They swim at all depths, and generally live among weedbeds; in and around underwater structures such as submerged trees, logs, and rocks; and under overhanging banks.

Life history/Behavior. Golden perch migrate upstream to spawn at night during spring and summer. This movement, which can exceed 1,000 kilometers, ensures that the eggs and larvae are not washed downstream into the sea. The spawning urge appears to be triggered by a rise in water level, runoff from flooding, water temperature, and water chemical content. Their fecundity is high; a female can produce more than 500,000 eggs. The floating eggs are nonadhesive and are carried away by the current. Hatching occurs within 24 to 30 hours at a water temperature between 20° and 31°C, and the fish mature within 20 to 25 days. Growth rates in water impoundments where food is plentiful and little effort is required for swimming (as opposed to stream effort) are usually high.

Food and feeding habits. The carnivorous golden perch feeds chiefly on yabbies, shrimp, small fish, mollusks, and aquatic insect life. They also take worms and moth larvae.

Angling. Trolling, lure casting, and baitfishing are all favored for golden perch. Light to medium weight spinning and baitcasting outfits with lines to 7 kilograms are favored, and 15-kilogram handlines are used where underwater obstructions are a hazard. Plug casting from a streambank or from a canoe, particularly in the clearer headwaters of a stream, is frequently successful.

Slow trolling with deep-diving plugs while also casting plugs or spinners to likely spots is another successful technique. If fishing is slow, some boat anglers circle a pool at high speed to disturb the bottom conditions, a tactic that can uncover mollusks and crustaceans and other aquatic life. This ruse will often evince interest from golden perch and, if live baits are suspended under a float, it will cause the fish to home in on their prey. A deep-diving, rattling lure cast into the roiled water is also productive.

Anglers should exercise care when handling golden perch. The spines on both dorsal and anal fins can puncture a wayward hand, and the wound can become inflamed if not treated. The gill covers also have a sharp cutting edge that must be avoided, and it is preferable either to grasp the fish by the lower jaw in much the same manner as that used to grasp a bass, or swim it into a net.

The golden perch is a highly regarded table fish with white, firm flesh. Unfortunately, however, it sometimes carries a muddy flavor if the perch has been taken from muddy water.

Golden Perch

PERCH, JUNGLE *Kuhlia rupestris*.
Other names—rock flagtail; Japanese: *okuchi-yugoi*; Tagalog (Philippines): *damagan*.

A member of the Kuhliidae family of aholeholes, the jungle perch was once a celebrated freshwater sportfish in Australia. Its numbers have declined, however, and today in Australia it is viewed as a species to be released upon capture. It is a fine food fish.

Identification. A strong, sturdy species, the jungle perch has a compressed body that is colored brown over the back and becomes paler on the sides, fading to silver or white on the belly. Its large mouth extends back to below a large eye. The majority of its scales have a central black spot, and the tail is emarginate with rounded lobes. The dorsal fin is deeply notched and almost forms two separate fins. A white bar on the upper lobe, and a cream bar on the lower lobe, serve also as identifying characteristics.

Size. This species grows to 500 millimeters and 3 kilograms, but such specimens are rare. Most Australian anglers are lucky to catch one larger than 1 kilogram.

Distribution. Jungle perch have been recorded from Fiji, Papua New Guinea, and from Durban, South Africa, north to the Red Sea and most islands of the Indian Ocean. In Australia they range from Fraser Island in southern Queensland to the eastern streams of Cape York.

Habitat. Jungle perch live in the crystal clear waters of rock pools in rain forest streams. They are capable of surviving in brackish water and are thought to move downstream to brackish waters to spawn.

Food and feeding habits. The jungle perch is primarily carnivorous and lives on crustaceans, insects, and small frogs and fish.

Angling. Considered a challenge by anglers using plugs and lures, the jungle perch is a clean, strong fighter that responds well to casting with baitcasting and spinning tackle. Lines to 4 kilogram-strength, and rods up to 2 meters long, are the

Jungle Perch

norm; shallow- to mid-diving plugs, surface poppers, and small plastic jigs are favored. The fish will take an artificial fly, but the difficult terrain and the overhanging nature of streamside vegetation make this technique less popular. Although it will readily attack a lure, it can be easily spooked if the angler carelessly approaches the crystal clear rock pools of its home stream. It can be found in greater numbers in streams accessible only to the dedicated and adventurous angler.

PERCH, NILE *Lates niloticus.*

Other names—giant perch, Niger perch; Arabic: *Am'kal, Am'kaltyâya;* Swahili: *mkombozi, sangala.*

A member of the Centropomidae family and a relative of snook and barramundi, the Nile perch is one of the world's largest freshwater fish and one of the most highly valued food and angling species of the African continent. It was cultivated by Egyptians in fish ponds at least 4,000 years ago (along with tilapia) and has been widely introduced to other areas, sometimes with disastrous results for native species.

Identification. The Nile perch looks very much like a large version of the barramundi *(see).* Juveniles are mottled brown and silver. By age 1, they measure 8 inches in length and are completely silver. Adults are generally brown to greenish brown above and silvery below. The top of the head is strongly depressed, and the tail is rounded (convex). The first dorsal fin consists of seven or eight strong spines, and the second dorsal fin, which immediately follows the first without a complete break, has one or two spines and 12 to 13 soft, branched rays. Large Nile perch have deep, distended bellies, and pack a lot of girth.

Size. In some parts of their range, Nile perch up to $6^1/_2$ feet long and weighing 176 pounds have been caught and recorded by native fishermen and were once common. Much larger ones, up to 500 pounds, are said to have been taken in nets but have gone unrecorded. An all-tackle world record was a $191^1/_2$-pound fish landed in Lake Victoria, Kenya, in 1991. A 213-pounder was caught on rod and reel in Lake Nasser, Egypt, in 1997.

Distribution. The Nile perch is endemic to the African continent and exists naturally or via introduction in various river systems and lakes in Egypt, Ethiopia, Uganda, Kenya, Zambia, and Zaire. It is present in the Blue and White Niles, and the Niger, Benue, Chad, Senegal, Volta, and Zaire Rivers, and in Lakes Rudolph, Albert, Tanganyika, Turkana, Victoria, Kyoga, Nasser, Fayoum, and Menzaleh. Good Nile perch fishing is well known below the Aswan Dam and at the junction of the Blue and White Niles. Nile perch were introduced to Lakes Kyoga and Victoria in the 1950s and 1960s, and were extremely successful, to the detriment of native cichlids and other smaller fish.

In many if not most of these sites, Nile perch are valued more for commercial and subsistence fishing (their white meat is tasty, especially in smaller fish) than for angling, and various pressures have made the largest specimens less common.

Life history. Nile perch grow about 9 or 10 inches a year during their first two or three years, then growth slows. They reach maturity at a length of about 20 to 24 inches, the females being larger at maturity.

Food. Nile perch are voracious predators, as well they have to be to reach their enormous sizes. Any abundant small fish are targeted, and tilapia are believed to be a primary food source, although they will eat other perch.

Angling. Fishing for Nile perch is done primarily by drifting or stillfishing with live baits, and trolling with large plugs or spoons. Some casting

Nile Perch

may occur, especially in smaller portions of rivers where the fish are likely to be in pools or eddies. Casters may use plugs, spoons, and large streamer flies. Baits may include any common fish up to a pound, such as tigerfish but especially tilapia. In lakes, anglers concentrate on rocky bays and inlets.

Nile perch are good fighters in small and medium sizes, and sheer brutes in the heavyweight class. They make several sustained runs and may take considerable line if large enough. Anglers fishing with large natural baits and lures for giant specimens often use extremely heavy tackle. River perch are much more challenging to land than those in lakes, especially by anglers who must fish from shore, do not have the assistance of boats to chase after running fish, and have to accommodate swift currents and eddies. Behemoths can take hundreds of yards of line from a reel. Heavy concentrations of water hyacinths increase the level of difficulty of catching large fish in some rivers and lakes.

See: Kenya; Uganda.

PERCH, SILVER *Bairdiella chrysoura*.
Other names—sand perch.

The silver perch is a member of the Sciaenidae family (drum and croaker). It is one of the most common and abundant Atlantic drum, harvested by commercial netters but seldom prominent in the angler's catch. This small panfishlike species is good to eat, but it is more likely to be used by anglers as live bait for larger predators.

The closely related bairdiella, or gulf croaker *(Bairdiella icistius)*, is one of a number of marine species introduced successfully to the Salton Sea from the Gulf of California. It grows to 12 inches there and is an important forage fish.

Identification. The body of the silver perch is high and compressed. As with others in the drum family, its dorsal fins are separated by a deep notch. There are five to six pores on the chin and no barbels. Its mouth is terminal and has finely serrated teeth. Its coloring is silvery, with yellowish fins and a whitish belly. It commonly has no spots.

The silver perch can be distinguished from the unrelated white perch *(see: perch, white)* by the dark stripes that line the sides. It can also be distinguished from the sand seatrout *(see: seatrout, sand)* by its lack of prominent canine teeth, and by its chin pores.

Size/Age. The average fish is less than 12 inches long and weighs $1/2$ pound or less; it never weighs more than a pound. The silver perch can live up to six years.

Distribution. Silver perch occur from New York southward along the Atlantic coast and also in the Gulf of Mexico.

Habitat. The silver perch is an inshore fish, most common in bays, seagrass beds, tidal creeks, small rivers, and quiet lagoons near estuaries. It is sometimes found in brackish marshes and also occasionally in freshwater.

Silver Perch

Life history/Behavior. The silver perch migrates offshore in winter and returns inshore to breed in spring. Spawning occurs inshore between May and September in shallow, saline areas. Silver perch reach maturity by their second or third year, when 6 inches long.

Food. Adults consume crustaceans, worms, and small fish.

Angling. The silver perch is easily caught on shrimp and cut baits.

PERCH, WHITE *Morone americana*
Other names—silver bass, silver perch, sea perch, bass, narrow-mouthed bass, bass perch, gray perch, bluenose perch, humpy; French: *bar blanc d'Amerique*.

White perch are something of a mystery to many anglers. They are abundant in some places, rare in others, similar enough to other species to be misidentified, and underappreciated as table fare. Many anglers catch white perch incidentally while pursuing other species, except in places where they are numerous. In all, there is not much of a constituency for the white perch, but it is a robust fish that provides excellent sport on light tackle.

In some places, white perch are disdained because they compete with favored gamefish for food. In other places, a lack of harvesting—either by anglers or other species of fish—can lead to large populations of stunted, small white perch. Nevertheless, where there is a population with larger than average size, white perch could rival crappie as a desirable quarry.

There is a limited commercial fishery for them in coastal areas, especially in the Chesapeake Bay and in the Great Lakes. Many restaurants that offer "lake perch" are serving white perch in lieu of the more traditional yellow perch. This usually happens when the latter are less available. White perch taken from coolwater lakes have a firm, white flaky flesh and are of excellent eating quality.

Identification. The white perch is not a true perch but a member of the temperate bass family and a relative of white bass and striped bass. It is similar in shape to the striped bass, but it has a deeper, less-rounded body and lacks the horizontal lines found on striped bass. Although shorter, stockier, and smaller in weight than a striper, it is very similar in appearance to a white bass *(see:*

White Perch

bass, white), except that it has no stripes. A more appropriate name for this species would probably be silver bass, and it is called by that name in some areas.

The white perch has a deep, thin body that slopes up steeply from the eye to the beginning of the dorsal fin and which is deepest under the first dorsal fin. On large, older specimens, it can be nearly hump-backed at that spot. Its colors can be olive, gray green, silvery gray, dark brown, or black on the back, becoming a lighter silvery green on the sides and silvery white on the belly. The pelvic and anal fins (both on the belly) are sometimes rosy colored. Like all members of the temperate bass family, it has two dorsal fins on the back, and the pelvic fins sit forward on the body below the pectoral fins. The first dorsal fin has nine spines, but the second one is soft rayed. There are three spines at the front of the anal fin, and a single spine precedes the second dorsal fin and each pelvic fin. The white perch has no teeth on its tongue, its scales are relatively large, and the lateral line is complete.

Size/Age. White perch are generally small and slow-growing after attaining juvenile size. The average white perch caught by anglers weighs under a pound and is probably close to three-quarters of a pound and 9 inches in length. These figures can obviously vary among regions and populations. In some places, the average white perch is just 6 inches long.

These fish have a normal life span of between 5 and 7 years, but some specimens may live for 14 to 17 years. They are said to be able to grow to 19 inches and 6 pounds, but these dimensions are extremely rare; the largest white perch in angling records is a 4-pound, 12-ounce Maine fish that was caught in 1949.

Distribution. White perch are found along the Atlantic coast from the southern Gulf of St. Lawrence to South Carolina and inland along the upper St. Lawrence River to the lower Great Lakes. They are present in all three Maritime Provinces, common in Lake Ontario, and especially abundant in the Hudson River and Chesapeake Bay areas. The white perch is far more coastal in occurrence than is the white bass, and most of the overlap in their distributions occurs in the area of the Great Lakes and upper St. Lawrence River.

Habitat. Like its striped bass cousin, the adaptable white perch is at home in saltwater, brackish water, and freshwater. In marine waters, they are primarily found in brackish water, estuaries, and coastal rivers and streams, and some of the latter have sea-run populations. Some white perch remain resident in brackish bays and estuaries, whereas others roam widely in search of food.

White perch inhabit scattered freshwater lakes and ponds throughout their range, but in varied abundance. A prolific fish, they have overpopulated some ponds and small lakes and have been deemed a nuisance, especially when crowding out black bass, trout, and other species. For marine purposes, white perch are considered demersal (bottom dwelling), and in general they do tend to stay deep in their home waters, on or close to the bottom.

Life history/Behavior. White perch are spring spawners, usually accomplishing this act when water temperatures are between 14°C to 24°C, and in shallow water over many kinds of bottom. Males and females each spawn several times in random fashion, and females may produce from 15,000 to more than 200,000 eggs. The tiny eggs become sticky after fertilization and attach to vegetation and bottom materials. The length of time for hatching depends on the water temperature. When the water is cooler, hatching takes longer (four days at 15°C versus about 30 hours at 20°C). Newly hatched white perch are 2.3 millimeters long and feed on plankton. For unknown reasons, white perch in some bodies of freshwater are extremely successful at reproduction, whereas in others they are virtually unsuccessful.

These fish are a schooling species that group even while young, and continue to stay in loose open-water schools through adulthood. They do not orient to cover and structure, and tend to be deeper than yellow perch, with whom they occupy the same lakes and ponds in parts of their range.

Food and feeding habits. White perch in lakes are known to feed both during the day and night but are generally more active in low light and nocturnally. Freshwater and saltwater populations move to surface (or inshore) waters at night, retreating to deeper water during the day.

Perch eat mostly aquatic insect larvae when they are small. As they grow, they eat many kinds of small fish, such as smelt, yellow perch, killifish, and other white perch, as well as the young of other species, particularly those that spawn after them. They also reportedly consume crabs, shrimp, and small alewives and herring.

Angling. In those freshwaters where white bass are not numerous, white perch are usually caught at random and accidentally, although it is possible to catch more than one if not many in the same location. Where white perch are abundant, creel limits are generous, and fish are caught with rapidity at times. In saltwater and in brackish environs, an angler who locates a white perch has typically come upon a school and may catch a few dozen fish.

Despite the sometimes relative abundance and schooling nature of white perch, the biggest problem many anglers face is finding these fish, or finding them when they are active. Tides, current, and water movement may affect their activity in estuaries, but in lakes and ponds the stimulant may more likely be low morning light or nightfall. In some places it is possible to find schools of white perch behaving a lot like white bass and chasing small baitfish to the surface. If the water's surface is fairly calm, you may observe this behavior, and if you carefully and quietly approach the school, you can experience steady casting action. More often than not, however, you have to search for schools of fish that are not visible to the eye, using sonar in open water, casting in estuary creeks and current-funneling pools, and otherwise prospecting.

Some anglers troll in freshwater, primarily with small spinners and spinner-bait combinations, but casting with jigs, small jigging spoons, diving plugs, and minnow-shaped plugs is more common, as is drift fishing or slow-trolling with worms or minnows under a float. Small spoons and jigs equipped with grub tails or small eel-like plastic tails are effective in the shallow backwaters of estuaries. Getting any of these offerings near the bottom is usually important, except when surface schools are present. Whatever you use, when you catch a white perch, stop and work the area thoroughly for more fish.

And don't overlook ice fishing with small jigs and baits either. There is some constituency for this in freshwater, and especially in coastal rivers that have enough ice for safe travel. It may be necessary to move to keep up with active schools.

Although small on average, and not prone to acrobatic maneuvers, white perch are extremely robust fighters, and a highly enjoyable catch on light spinning or flycasting tackle.

PERCH, YELLOW *Perca flavescens*.
Other names—ringed perch, striped perch, coon perch, jack perch, lake perch, American perch; French: *perchaude*.

The most widely distributed member of the Percidae family, the yellow perch is one of the best loved and most pursued of all freshwater fish, particularly in northerly states and provinces in North America. This is due to its availability over a wide range, the general ease with which it is caught, and its delicious taste. Yellow perch do not attain large sizes and are not known for superior fighting characteristics, so they receive much less press than some freshwater species, including such equally popular panfish as crappie and bluegill. Nevertheless, the yellow perch is a favorite in large and small lakes alike, and it has some commercial importance, particularly in the Great Lakes. This role is limited by the small size of the fish and by its varying abundance. It is particularly popular for ice fishing; typically generous bag limits allow anglers to provide a family's worth of meals on a given outing.

Identification. Unlike the white perch, which is actually a temperate bass, the yellow perch is a true perch. Although it resembles true bass in many ways, it is more closely related to fellow Percidae family members, the walleye and sauger. Its most striking characteristic is a colorful golden yellow body, tinged with orangy fins.

Yellow perch are colored a green to yellow gold and have six to eight dark, broad vertical bars that extend from the back to below the lateral line, a whitish belly, and orange lower fins during breeding season. Their bodies are oblong and appear humpbacked; this is the result of the deepest part of the body beginning at the first dorsal fin, then tapering slightly to the beginning of the second dorsal fin. This trait is somewhat similar in white perch *(see: perch, white)*, to which the yellow perch is unrelated, although both fish may inhabit the same waters.

Yellow perch are distinguished from trout and salmon by their lack of an adipose fin, which is ordinarily located between the dorsal and tail fins, and from sunfish by their separate dorsal fins (connected in sunfish) and two or fewer anal fin spines (sunfish have three or more). They are distinguished from walleye and sauger by their lack of canine teeth and by a generally deeper body form.

Size/Age. The average yellow perch caught by anglers weighs between $1/4$ to $3/4$ pound and mea-

Yellow Perch

sures 6 to 10 inches in length. In lakes with stunted populations, the fish are on the lower end of this range, and a 10-inch fish is usually considered fairly large. Some lakes produce perch in the 1-pound and larger class, although fish greater than $1^{1}/_{2}$ pounds are infrequent. The all-tackle world-record yellow perch, taken in 1865, weighed 4 pounds, 3 ounces and is the oldest freshwater sportfish record in the books. Yellow perch can grow to 16 inches in length and can live up to 12 years. In general, northern populations grow more slowly but live longer, and females grow faster than males.

Distribution. Yellow perch are widespread in the northern United States and Canada. They range east from Nova Scotia to the Santee River drainage in South Carolina and west throughout the Great Lakes states to the edge of British Columbia and into Washington. A small number extend north through Great Slave Lake almost to Great Bear Lake in Canada's Northwest Territories. Although they appear in nearly every state due to stocking, they are sparsely distributed in the South, most of the West, and parts of the Midwest; they are also sparse in British Columbia and northern Canada. Although the yellow perch is a freshwater fish, Nova Scotia fisheries personnel report that it is occasionally found in brackish water along the Atlantic coast.

Habitat. Yellow perch are found in a wide variety of warm and cool habitats over a vast range of territory, although they are primarily lake fish. They are occasionally found in ponds and rivers. These fish are most abundant in clear, weedy lakes that have a muck, sand, or gravel bottom. Smaller lakes and ponds usually produce smaller fish, although in very fertile lakes with moderate angling pressure, yellow perch can grow large. They inhabit open areas of most lakes and prefer temperatures between the mid-60s and the low 70s.

Life history/Behavior. Yellow perch usually spawn in early spring when the water temperature is between 45°F and 50°F. Eggs are spawned in the shallow areas of lakes or up in tributary streams in gelatinous ribbons by an adult female and are fertilized by as many as a dozen males in weedy areas several feet deep. The ribbons, which may be up to 7 feet long and several inches wide, attach to vegetation until one-quarter to one-half of the 10,000 to 48,000 eggs hatch into fry in 10 days to three weeks after spawning. Without protection from parents, slow-swimming and slow-growing yellow perch travel in schools and are avidly preyed upon, especially by walleye, during the first year of life. Their odds of survival are perhaps 1 in 5,000 in the first year, yet yellow perch manage to produce in abundance in favorable habitat.

Yellow perch travel in schools composed fish that are similar in size and age, and there is some evidence of the sexes dividing into separate schools. In large lakes, adults move in schools farther offshore than the young. They move between deeper and shallow water in response to changing food supplies, seasons, and temperatures.

Because of their predaceous nature and swift breeding, overpopulation is a problem in many lakes where yellow perch have been introduced; the fish may become stunted, and other species may be adversely impacted as a result. The introduction, through natural or artificial means, of yellow perch into ponds containing trout usually results in a collapse of the trout population, and this may be true for other species of fish that were dominant before yellow perch entered.

Food and feeding habits. Young yellow perch feed on zooplankton until they have grown to several inches in length and then feed on larger zooplankton, insects, young crayfish, snails, aquatic insects, fish eggs, and small fish, including the young of their own species. Yellow perch are commonly believed to feed in shallows at dawn and dusk, remaining inactive at night, but the conditions under which they feed and under which they can be caught vary widely with their environment and the skill of the angler.

Angling. Yellow perch are very popular for food and sport. They are not strong fighters, but in cold water and on light spinning or spincasting gear they engage the angler in a feisty battle. Their inclination to avoid turbid and muddy environs and to reside in clean and cool habitat no doubt accounts for their firm white flesh, which has a flavor equal to that of its cousin, the highly touted walleye.

Anglers land yellow perch in open water throughout the season, and these fish are especially popular among ice anglers. They are also caught during their spring spawning runs, in which they ascend tributaries and seek warm shoreline areas in bays and back eddies. Primarily, yellow perch like cool water and will school deep wherever surface temperatures are warm, although they will move shallower to feed.

Yellow perch are a schooling fish, so when you catch one, there will be more in the vicinity. It pays to scour an area thoroughly. The best locations are often the weedbeds in shallow lakes, where it is advisable to fish on or close to the bottom. Fishing deep, vertically with jigs or baits, is also important in larger bodies of water.

Yellow perch are caught on a variety of baits and lures, with live worms, live minnows, small minnow-imitating plugs, jigs, spoons, and spinners being among the best attractors. Small jigs with hair or curl-tail grub bodies are productive. The range of acceptable colors varies but includes white, yellow, shad-imitation, and gray or silver, especially if imbedded with flakes. Baits are very effective, but these fish are adept at nibbling and stealing baits. Floats and bobbers are frequently employed with live baits; nightcrawler rigs, sporting a No. 2 hook and a No. 2 spinner, are also effective. Chumming has its devotees as well, including those who use mealworms and more fragrant ground concoctions.

Light spinning or spincasting outfits, equipped with 2- through 8-pound-test line, are more than adequate for perch. Fly fishing, although less popular, is also effective, particularly when yellow perch are in shallow water in the spring.

Seldom are yellow perch caught on larger lures that are meant for other gamefish, and rarely do they come to the surface or travel far in pursuit of a lure. It is usually important to work slowly and deep, with smaller lures.

In the winter through the ice, minnows, worms, waxworm larvae, small jigging spoons, and small jigs are the top producers.

PERIGEE

The point in the moon's orbit closest to the earth, producing a greater tidal range.
See: Tides.

Float-fished bait lured this yellow perch from a New York pond.

PERMIT *Trachinotus falcatus.*

Other names—French: *carangue plume;* Portuguese: *sernambiguara;* Spanish: *palometa, pampano, pampano erizero, pámpano palometa.*

An important gamefish and a particularly prized member of the Carangidae family of jacks and pompano, the permit is a tough fighter and a handful on light tackle. This is especially true for sight casting on shallow flats. The permit is also an excellent food fish, although it is much less importantly commercially than the Florida pompano. The greatest concentrations of permit are off southern Florida, and this is also where the biggest fish are taken.

Identification. In overall appearance, the permit is a brilliantly silver fish with dark fins and a dark or iridescent blue to greenish or grayish back. The belly is often yellowish, and sometimes the pelvic fins and the front lobe of the anal fin have an orange tint. Many individuals have a dark, circular black area on the side behind the base of the pectoral fin, and some have a dusky midbody blotch. The body is laterally compressed, and the fish has a high back profile; young fish appear roundish, adults more oblong. Small permit have teeth on the tongue. The permit has 16 to 19 soft anal rays, and the second dorsal fin has one spine and 17 to 21 soft rays, compared with 22 to 27 in the similar Florida pompano. It is further distinguished by its deeper body and a generally larger body size. Also, the second and third ribs in the permit are prominent in fish weighing more than 10 pounds, and these ribs can be felt through the sides of the

Permit

fish to help in differentiating it from the Florida pompano.

Size. Permit commonly weigh up to 25 pounds and are 1 to 3 feet long, but they can exceed 50 pounds and reach 45 inches in length. The all-tackle world record is a 53-pound, 4-ounce Florida fish caught in 1994.

Distribution. This species occurs in the western Atlantic, ranging from Massachusetts to southeastern Brazil, including the Bahamas and much of the West Indies. They are most common in Florida, the Bahamas, and the Caribbean and are rarely encountered in the northern part of their range.

Habitat. Permit inhabit shallow, warm waters in depths of up to 100 feet, and young fish prefer clearer and shallower waters than do adults. Able to adapt to a wide range of salinity, they occur in channels or holes over sandy flats and around reefs, and sometimes over mud bottoms. They are primarily a schooling fish when younger, traveling in schools of 10 or more, although they are occasionally seen in great numbers, and they tend to become solitary with age. They are sometimes attracted to areas where the bottom is stirred up.

Food and feeding habits. Over sandy bottoms, permit feed mainly on mollusks, and over reefs they feed mostly on crustaceans such as crabs, shrimp, and sea urchins. Like bonefish, they feed by rooting in the sand on shallow flats.

Angling. An elusive, coveted, and heralded saltwater fish, permit are renowned for being difficult to approach, difficult to entice to strike, difficult to set a hook in, and difficult to land. As a warmwater fish pursued mostly in South Florida, the Florida Keys, and the Bahamas, permit are unavailable to most North American anglers, and these conditions only enhance their mystique.

Although some anglers favor bait fishing or jigging in intermediate depths over reefs, wrecks, and the like, the vastly preferred practice is to sight-fish for permit while stalking the same shallow flats inhabited by bonefish and casting a jig, fly, or live crab or shrimp. Permit venture onto sandy flats on a rising tide to scour the bottom for food and are often seen cruising or tailing while feeding on the bottom. They feed much like bonefish do, rooting in the sand for shrimp or crabs. As mentioned, these fish travel in schools, which are occasionally large, but the big fish are usually solitary.

On the flats they are skittish creatures, and anglers stalk them carefully in a boat or by wading. Although it is often critical to make a precise presentation, this is made easier and less critical when a school is encountered, as the competitive instinct may prevail. Nonetheless, it should be noted that relatively few fish are hooked, and fewer still landed, in comparison to the number of fish seen, so the importance of stalking and presentation should not be underestimated. Furthermore, the nature of their feeding behavior—rooting down on the bottom—reduces their field of vision, making it important to position the offering where the fish can see it, and then to move it just enough to interest them.

Most permit are caught on live crabs; some respond to live shrimp. Medium-size blue crabs about 2 inches across are best, and many anglers clip the claws off before impaling them on a 2/0 or 3/0 hook. Small jigs produce a fair number of fish. Weighted flies are a more challenging offering, and therefore less effective, but a select few patterns produce consistently. Overcoming the difficulty of maneuvering into an optimal casting position while countering the effects of wind and other factors, and simultaneously making an accurate presentation with an enticing crab-imitating fly, are among the top challenges and achievements in sportfishing.

No matter what the offering, the hook must be sharp, and it is advisable to set the hook forcefully several or more times to effect penetration, as a permit's mouth is extremely leathery. Similarly, if slack develops during the fight, the hook will likely drop out; it is essential to keep a constant tight line.

To provoke a strike, it is important to work the bait or lure into position, but not by casting right on top of the fish, or by casting beyond the fish, letting the offering sink, and then retrieving it across the bottom (where it may snag). The angler should cast the offering a few feet in front of the fish, keeping the rod tip high and working the bait, lure, or fly on the surface toward the permit, then letting it swim or fall down to the fish. A moving object presented in this way is likely to get the fish's attention.

When the hook is set, permit bolt off like a streak of lightning, zooming over the flats on a long, sustained run toward deep water. They might try to cut the line on an obstacle or try to dislodge the hook, so the angler must keep the rod high and use a reel with ample line capacity and an excellent drag. Permit have superior stamina and will fight for a long time (a 40-minute or longer fight for a 20-pound fish is likely). They are often caught on light- to medium-action 7-foot spinning rods and 8-pound line. Fly rodders use a 9- or 10-weight fly rod and floating sink-tip line.

Although the fishing method is similar to that for bonefish, most permit are caught in slightly deeper water—2 to 4 feet; bonefish prefer only a few inches or so. Sighting permit, and knowing when and where to find them, are key elements of the game.

A rising tide, as noted, brings permit onto shallow flats, but they also congregate around channel edges, where a falling tide will wash food off the flats. Early mornings on warm days are good for bringing these fish into the shallows. If the water is calm, however, the fish are so spooky that maneuvering within casting range is nearly impossible. A breeze improves the odds greatly.

Although spring is a highly desirable time for permit angling in South Florida, these fish are on the flats from spring through fall there. Only when the water temperature turns cooler (mid-70s or less) do they head for deeper water and the reefs.
See: Jacks.

PERSONAL FLOTATION DEVICE

Commonly referred to as a PFD, this is a lifesaving device that is meant to float a person in the water and to hold their head above water so they

A large permit landed near Marathon, Florida.

can breathe. In an emergency, it could be the most important item that you have.

PFDs are primarily used by people in boats, but they may also be worn by anglers who wade in swift water, by anglers who fish out of float tubes and kick boats, and by young and old people when they are on a dock, pier, or other location where it is possible that they might fall into the water. In the latter instances, it may be prudent, although not mandatory, that a PFD be either worn or available. However, Federal and state laws require that every vessel have a U.S. Coast Guard–approved personal flotation device of correct size for each person onboard. It is not required that they be worn in some places, but it is required that they be available. Regulations vary between states, provinces, and countries, and may depend on what agency has jurisdiction over a particular body of water; in some locations, children under a certain age, as well nonswimmers, must wear a PFD.

Most anglers do not wear a PFD in their boat, or wear it only in adverse conditions or when operating a boat at high speed. Look at most of the photos that appear in this book, as well as current outdoor periodicals, and you'll see few anglers, especially adults, wearing a PFD. People who are good swimmers, who are in stable boats, who fish in shallow water, who fish in warm water, and those out on fair weather days in moderate or calm water conditions usually are in no danger. However, accidents happen; even a good swimmer can slip and fall out of a boat, knocking himself unconscious

PFD Types

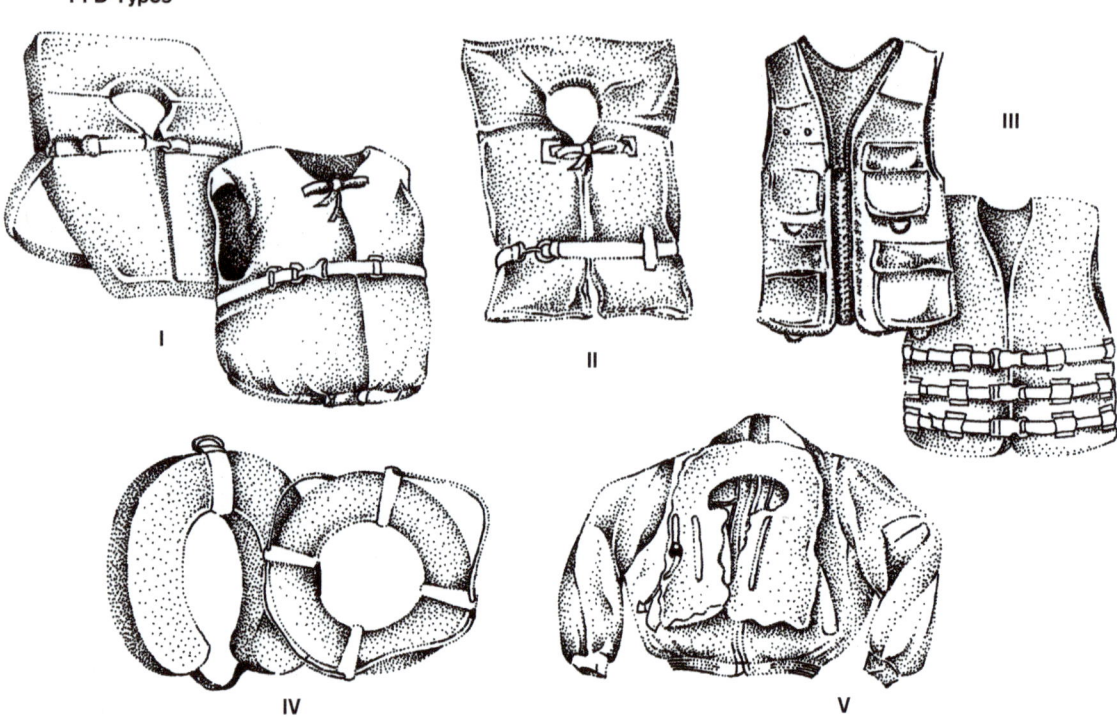

on the gunwale. Novice anglers and novice boaters typically underestimate the consequence of changing wind and wave conditions or current, and fail to realize that they can be very vulnerable, especially in a small boat, even on a day that looks harmless or in a location with warm or placid water.

Few people expect to end up in the water when they go fishing from a boat. But it happens, and not just in the extreme case of a boat sinking or capsizing. Small boats and canoes do get swamped, and people do fall out of boats. It is one of the leading causes of boating-related fatalities. Falling into the water without a PFD increases the chance of drowning, especially if the water is cold and/or a person is injured. In cold weather and when boating on cold water, it is smart to wear a PFD all the time because the degree of danger is heightened due to quick onset of hypothermia.

Of course, it does little good to have a PFD in the boat, but not on or at least available when you need it. People who suddenly find themselves in the water may not be able to locate their PFD, or may be too panicked or numb from cold water and shock to put it on even if they do find it. In most fatal boating accidents, PFDs are onboard but not worn; 80 percent of boating-related drowning victims were not wearing PFDs.

Types. There are five categories of PFDs:

Type I Also known as an offshore life jacket, this is designed to turn most unconscious wearers to a vertical or slightly backward position. Adult sizes provide a minimum of 22 pounds of buoyancy and child sizes a minimum of 11 pounds. This is the best PFD to keep a person afloat in large and rough waters where rescue may be slow in coming; it is commonly found aboard commercial craft, and is regarded as the easiest to put on in a sudden emergency. There are bib and jacket versions, the latter generally favored for warmth and comfort.

Type II Also known as a nearshore buoyant vest, this is designed to turn some unconscious wearers to a vertical or slightly backward position, but does not do so as effectively as a Type I. Adult sizes provide a minimum of 15.5 pounds of buoyancy and child sizes a minimum of 11 pounds. This PFD is more like a bib design than a vest, and is intended for calm inland water where there is a chance of a fast rescue. It is a commonly used PFD, although not one that is preferred by anglers and rarely worn continuously by anglers.

Type III Also known as a flotation aid, this is generally considered the most comfortable PFD, available in many different styles for different activities; vest styles are frequently referred to as a life vest or life preserver and coat styles as a life jacket. They will not turn an unconscious person face up, but are designed to make it easy for a conscious wearer to

	place themselves in a face-up position. They have the same minimum buoyancy as Type II devices and are intended for calm and moderate nearshore waters where there is a chance of a quick rescue. Some of these devices provide warmth for a bit of hypothermia protection, and some are available also as fishing vests. Some versions have collars that help keep a wearer's head up. Type III PFDs are a favorite of many freshwater anglers, but few people actually find them comfortable enough for all-day use.
Type IV	Also known as a throwable device, this is not intended to be worn in a boat, but to be tossed to someone in the water. Buoyant boat cushions, ring buoys, and horseshoe buoys are the main devices, that are grasped by the person in need of help and should be kept at hand for sudden use. They are intended for calm inland water, especially where there is heavy boat traffic, for a quick rescue.
Type V	Also known as a special use device, this is any PFD approved for restricted use, including wet suits, so-called survival or anti-exposure suits, boardsailing vests, and whitewater vests. Most Type V PFDs must be worn to be acceptable to law-enforcement authorities, and they must be used for the type of activity for which they are approved as a flotation device. In other words, if you are alone in a boat and your sole PFD is a Type V device that is stowed in storage, it will not meet legal requirements.

Some inflatable vests and jackets had been listed as Type V garments, but newer (and Coast Guard approved) versions have been reclassified as Type III. The label of Type V garments indicates the approved use and limitations. Coverall-style Type V PFDs, such as survival and anti-exposure suits, offer excellent hypothermia protection in cold water, and also provide wind and cold air temperature protection for fishing in extreme conditions.

Practicalities. All PFDs that are approved by the U.S. Coast Guard bear labeling certification and type designation. In order for these devices to be useful, they must be worn or closely available, they must be in serviceable condition, and they must fit the wearer. Such fitting is based upon the weight of an individual, keeping in mind that sometimes anglers wear bulky clothes. They must also provide enough buoyancy. Not all flotation is the same in PFDs. A PFD with $15^{1}/_{2}$ pounds of flotation will not keep the head of many people out of the water; one manufacturer claims that at least one in every four persons will float under the water surface when wearing a PFD with this amount of flotation. Not all PFDs of the same classification (Type III, for example) have the same amount of buoyancy; some may have $15^{1}/_{2}$ pounds, some 22 pounds.

The amount of buoyancy that you need depends on such factors as height, weight, and body fat, since body weight on the water is not the same as on land, evidenced by the fact that heavy or husky persons do not necessarily need more flotation support than lighter individuals. Nevertheless, the greater the amount of buoyancy, the more its influence on flotation for a given person.

Another factor that affects the usefulness of any PFD is its condition (see the following information on maintenance), and it is possible that a PFD, despite its labeling, might no longer be capable of providing flotation support. You should check your PFD occasionally in a controlled setting to see how it performs and to verify that it is still serviceable.

Still another factor that one should consider in a PFD is the amount of hypothermia protection it provides. Type I PFDs have virtually no protection against hypothermia while Type V anti-exposure suits have the most you can get. In between, there are varying levels of protection. Body heat is primarily lost from the head, the sides, and the groin. PFDs that trap cold water and mix it with the ambient heat of the body provide more protection than others. Although many people think of hypothermia in regard to cold weather and cold water, serious body temperature cooling can develop if you are exposed for a sufficient time in water that is 70 degrees Fahrenheit, a temperature that is much different when you are in the water than when you are exposed to it in the air.

The main reason why people do not wear PFDs is that they aren't comfortable enough, especially when worn over a moderate amount of clothing. So you should make sure that your own PFD fits you properly, with or without heavy clothes. To get some confidence in it, you should try it out in the water (a pool is a good place). Make sure that it doesn't ride up on your body, which makes swimming difficult. Remember that you could be in the water some time, so you want enough buoyancy to keep your head out of the water. Also remember that you might need to swim a considerable distance to safety, so your PFD should accommodate that.

In recent years, the U.S. Coast Guard has approved some manually inflated PFDs as Type III life vests (and was evaluating automatic-inflating PFDs as Type II vests. Inflatable PFDs will probably become more popular in years to come because they are mainly suspender-like devices that are very comfortable to wear even over bulky clothing, and they do not inhibit arm movement for casting or normal fishing activities. Some inflatable PFDs

Australia's Great Barrier Reef, which stretches 1,260 miles and holds the world's finest black marlin fishing, comprises thousands of small reefs.

(using a CO_2 cartridge) inflate upon impact, while others have to be activated by the wearer or can also be blown up orally; automatic-inflating PFDs are best for people who do not swim, since they might be prone to panic and unable to activate a manual model if suddenly thrust into the water. Approved inflatable PFDs (manufactured after 1996 and bearing a Coast Guard–approval certification on their label) will be of special interest to freshwater anglers who use small boats, to those who use canoes and inflatable boats and float tubes, and also to those who wade in cold rivers. Inflatable PFDs are the kind of item that is meant to be worn all the time, so they are available when needed and activated by a replaceable CO_2 cartridge (get a rearming pack so you have a spare cartridge on hand).

Anglers who travel to distant or exotic locations often find that only boat cushions are provided as PFDs (which may be acceptable there but is certainly not safe), or that the PFDs available are inadequate because of their poor condition or improper size. If your fishing activity will take you into potentially dangerous situations (long hauls over rough cold water), you should find replacements or plan accordingly. This is a situation where carrying an inflatable PFD makes a lot of sense; it is light, takes up little space, and provides top security (but it will have almost no anti-hypothermia protection).

Maintenance. PFDs are usually used more often as seat cushions, boat fenders, and kneeling pads than they are worn, and this compression and fabric tension can adversely affect their primary function. If the fabric is torn or if it is faded and worn, consider replacement. If the fabric tears when you pull on it, get rid of the PFD. A Kapok-material PFD will lose its buoyancy due to splitting or compression, so check this carefully as it may actually sink.

Whether they have been used or not, it's a good idea to check the serviceability of your PFDs every summer in shallow warm water or in a pool. They should float the wearer for an extended period and should not restrict breathing. After you've tested them, dry them in a well-ventilated area and make sure that no mildew or rotting develops. Clean PFDs with a mild soap and warm water, and replace any worn or broken parts, like buckles or straps. Store PFDs in a dry well-ventilated place away from heat, moisture, and frequent sunlight. Keep them away from oil, grease, and gas, which could deteriorate some PFDs and cause them to lose buoyancy. For inflatable PFDs, make sure to replace a used CO cartridge, and keep a spare cartridge or rearming packet on hand for each device. You should also inspect the inflatable material periodically.

Know the law. As mentioned, Federal and state laws require that every vessel have a U.S. Coast Guard–approved PFD of correct size and in good serviceable condition for each person onboard. Boats less than 16 feet in length, and canoes and kayaks of any length, must have one approved Type I, II, III, or V device for each person, and boats over 16 feet must have one approved Type I, II, III, or V device for each person plus one throwable Type IV device. Type I, II, and III devices must be readily accessible; a Type IV device must be immediately available or on hand; and Type V devices must be worn to qualify. These are minimum requirements.

Check local regulations for requirements regarding who is legally required to continuously wear a PFD, or under what circumstances (some competitive events require that a PFD be worn whenever the main engine is operated). Remember that a PFD could be the best insurance you'll ever have, and a lifesaver.

See: Boat; First Aid.

PERSONAL WATERCRAFT

An ambiguous term that through aggressive marketing has primarily come to mean small one- or two-person jet-drive vessels. Since the late 1980s, personal watercraft have been the fastest growing segment of the boating market, and the vessels responsible for a high percentage of boating-related accidents, usually due to reckless operation. Personal watercraft are seldom used for fishing, although a few operators have employed them on occasion for this purpose. They are more likely to be a source of annoyance for anglers, even more so than water-skiers and accompanying tow boats, due to their noise, the fast speeds at which they are operated, the shallow waters that they can navigate, and the tendency of some careless operators to interfere with others on the water. As a result of problems with the operation of personal watercraft, their use has been banned in some places (such as sections of the Florida Keys) where they threaten habitat. The term personal watercraft is sometimes also applied to float tubes (see).

PERU

The third largest country in South America, with 2,700 kilometers of Pacific coastline, as well as mountain rivers, jungle waters, some of the highest peaks in the world, and the continent's largest lake, Peru is something of an enigma to anglers. It has been of minor sportfishing interest for traveling anglers since at least the early 1980s.

Saltwater

Although most general accounts of the natural resources of Peru indicate that its coast is rich in fish life, these statements mostly reference commercial catches of anchovies, smelt, pilchards, mackerel, and flatfish; they usually don't indicate that Peru's marine resources have been hard hit by national and international commercial fishing operations.

Peru's greatest piscatorial claim to fame was northern coast big-game fisheries that diminished

Only 1 percent of the freshwater on Earth is contained in surface reservoirs, lakes, and streams; of that, 20 percent is located in the Great Lakes of North America.

long ago. Cabo Blanco was a hotspot for huge black marlin, and it drew many top anglers, personalities, and skippers to the sardine-rich waters nearby, where the (Peru) Humboldt Current helped make it the first place in the world where anglers had a good chance of encountering "granders," or marlin weighing more than 1,000 pounds. In August of 1953, Alfred Glassell caught the still-standing all-tackle 1,560-pound world-record black marlin, and in April of the following year Mrs. Charles Hughes caught a women's 130-pound world-record 1,525-pound black. These are two of the Babe Ruth–like records of sportfishing. Even in its heyday, however, Peru did not produce large numbers of black marlin; striped marlin were more common, as were swordfish. Yellowfin and bigeye tuna rounded out the big-game menu.

During the best times, however, fish were caught within sight of land, and sometimes within sight of the historical Cabo Blanco Fishing Club, which ceased operations in 1965. Whether due to current changes, overfishing of baitfish, or other factors, the glory days are ancient history, and big-game species have since been evidently far from shore in an area with few or no appropriate vessels capable of distant voyages.

Peru's coast was also home to other species, including snook, corvina, and various flatfish. Surf fishing was once popular and productive in accessible sites. Numerous tributaries entering the Pacific from the coastal plains would seem to still invite fishing opportunity, but current information about these, or about sportfishing operators, is lacking.

Freshwater
The Peruvian freshwater fishing scene—its current fisheries status, operators, and accessibility—is likewise largely unknown, with the exception of some rain forest opportunities in the northeastern region.

In the southeastern Andes, Lake Titicaca was once not only reputed to be the world's highest trout lake, but, between 1940 and 1960, also one of the world's best producers of trophy rainbow trout. Titicaca had yielded a 34-pound specimen and was a source of numerous fish weighing between 12 and 20 pounds. Situated in the Andes at around 12,500 feet, and the largest freshwater lake in South America, Titicaca is 110 miles long and has an average width of 35 miles; its gamefisheries were heavily exploited, and nothing has been heard of its angling significance in decades. The region remains noted for its ancient civilization and is a tourist draw. Titicaca drains into Lake Poopó in Bolivia via the Desaguadero River, and it has several northerly tributaries that once held trout.

Perhaps because it is a large and generally undeveloped and unpopulated area, the eastern and northeastern tropical forest region of Peru (the *montaña*) bordering Brazil and Colombia has the most viable currently known sportfishing opportunity in this country. In the northeast, the fishery is accessed from the city of Iquitos. It is in this large region that Peru's tributaries of the Amazon River originate, abound, and gain size and character, and where peacock bass and other warmwater species predominate. The many rivers and fishing opportunities here are described in the Amazon review under Brazil *(see)*.

PFD
Acronym for Personal Flotation Device *(see)*.

PFIESTERIA
A harmful algal bloom, resulting from a toxic single-celled dinoflaggellate, *Pfiesteria piscicida*. The Latin name means "fish killer," and it has been dubbed "cell from hell" by some, since it has been responsible for huge fish kills and also illness among humans.

This algal bloom has attracted great media attention in the 1990s, particularly in Chesapeake Bay and in North Carolina, because of the fish kills that it caused. Between 1992 and 1995 in North Carolina, it reportedly killed billions of fish in estuaries.

What stimulates these organisms to bloom and become toxic is unknown. However, when it happens, the toxins eat into the skin of fish, and ugly lesions the size of a quarter are common. The fish die when their bodies become wracked with the infection.

See: Algae Bloom; Dinoflaggellate.

pH
A measure of the acidity or alkalinity of water on a logarithmic scale from 1 to 14. A pH of 7.0 is neutral; the lower the reading below 7.0 the more acidic the water, and the higher the reading above 7.0 the more alkaline the water. Normal rainfall is slightly acidic, with a pH ranging from 5.6 to 5.7.

The majority of freshwater fish require pH levels from 6.0 to 8.5. Changes to either end of the spectrum can have adverse impacts on fish, as well as other organisms, with some more susceptible than others. Brook and brown trout numbers are severely reduced at a pH value of 6.5, and rainbow trout eggs have a much reduced hatching rate. Smallmouth and largemouth bass are unable to survive at a pH value of 5.5. Most species are absent at levels below 5.0, and even if they are able to survive, their food sources may not be able to do so. Some waters have become so acidified that no life can survive.

PHARYNGEAL
Bones in the throat of certain fish that are used like teeth to crush food. These bones are hard and strong and will crush such objects as clams, mussels,

and snails. Carp *(see)* have pharyngeal teeth, which play an important role in their forage habits.

PHILIPPINES

The Philippine Islands are not a prime destination for globe-trotting anglers, and very little is heard in most quarters about sportfishing opportunities, facilities, or services there. The waters of the western Pacific in and around the Philippines, however, have produced at least five line-class saltwater world records, and big Pacific sailfish and great barracuda are known to frequent its tropical waters. Numerous yellowfin tuna, dolphin, wahoo, and assorted jacks are here as well. To the surprise of many anglers, largemouth bass have been introduced in the country's freshwater resources.

Any country that covers roughly 115,830 square miles is bound to offer some angling opportunities. Sandwiched by Taiwan to the north and Indonesia to the south, and bordered by the South China Sea on the west, the Celebes Sea on the south, and the Philippine Sea on the east, the Philippines comprises more than 7,100 islands, only 460 of which are more than 1 square mile in area. The largest of these is Luzon in the northern Philippines, bounded by the Babuyan Channel on the north. Along Luzon's irregular western coastline is the well-known harbor of Manila Bay.

The northeastern region of Luzon is locally known as sailfish country, and in the months of May and June it hosts national and international billfish competitions. Sailfish are the main quarry here, but this species is found in many areas throughout the islands. A 93.75-kilogram 30-pound line-class record Pacific sailfish was caught far to the south of Luzon at the Tubbataha Reefs in the Sulu Sea in May 1990.

Dolphin, wahoo, and yellowfin tuna are among the offshore catch as well. Philippine anglers are fond of drift fishing for yellowfins at night. Tuna in the 60- to 90-kilogram range are commonly caught, and anglers use 30- and 50-pound outfits, which occasionally also bring in a swordfish.

Two spots in particular are favored for this fishing. One is off the island of Palawan, where sportfishing is based out of the city of Puerto Princesta. The ecologically compelling Palawan is reached via a 1-hour plane trip or a 20-hour ride on a modern air-conditioned ferry. The other is off Surigao on the northern part of Mindanao, the second largest of the islands. There, fishing is often done from local outrigger boats called *bancas*. Powered by reconditioned diesel truck engines or 16-horsepower inboard engines, the *bancas* are an adventurous way of pursuing tuna, as well as sailfish and marlin, although they are cramped.

The *bancas* are used for nearshore lighter tackle angling, too, and various species are enjoyed along the irregular shorelines throughout the islands. Barracuda are prominent in the Philippines, and some are huge; Scarborough Shoals produced a line-class world-record 38.5-kilogram specimen in March of 1991. Jacks from 1 to 10 kilograms provide the majority of inshore interest, however. They are especially prominent and popular near the resort area of Matabongay, a three-hour drive from Manila, where locals hire out their *bancas* for anglers who cast with live shrimp.

Inland, the bigger islands are mountainous, some with navigable rivers. On Luzon the larger rivers include the Cagayan, Chico, Abra, Pampanga, and Bicol. The longest river of the Philippines, the Cagayan flows northerly for about 354 kilometers. The Río Grande de Mindanao (also called the Pulangi in its upper reaches) and the Agusan are the principal rivers of Mindanao. On Luzon, south of Manila, Caliraya Lake hosts largemouth bass that were brought to this island as bass fry evidently from the U.S. The two largest lakes on Luzon are Laguna de Bay and Taal, but it is unknown if they contain bass.

The Philippines possesses some modern sportfishing vessels, but most angling for the visiting tourist is rather adventurous and unorganized. The Philippines are within the Tropics and experience a lot of rain. In most of the region the rainy season lasts from May through November—the summer monsoon. Typhoons sometimes occur from June through October.

pH METER

A portable electronic device used by a relatively small number of anglers, primarily freshwater bass anglers, to measure the acidity or alkalinity of prospective fishing water to determine its pH level. If the pH level is unsuitable to the fish they seek to catch, they reason that those fish are unlikely to be in that location, and they move elsewhere.

The common pH scale ranges from 0.0 (highly acid) to 14.0 (highly alkaline). A reading of 7.0 is considered neutral, having equal parts of acidity and alkalinity. Most of the research done to determine the effect of water pH on fish has involved largemouth bass. In freshwater, some biologists feel that pH is critical because it affects the ability of fish to use oxygen, to feed in a wide range of temperatures, to reproduce, combat disease, handle stress, and even to survive pollution. Fish can survive in a pH range of from 4 to 10, but researchers say they are least stressed and hypothetically most catchable in a range between 7 and 9.

Manufacturers of pH meters advise looking for a surface pH between 7.5 and 8.5. If all of the water seems to be below 7, find the highest pH you can. If all of the water seems to be above 9, fish where you find the lowest pH. The level of pH usually drops as you go deeper, so check below the surface for a pH cline; this is where there is a pH change of two tenths or more per foot of depth. If there is a pH cline, they advise that the most catchable fish will probably be at or above it. A pH cline is generally tied to water clarity. If the water is clear, the pH cline will probably be deeper. If the water is murky, it will be shallower. Its depth can change from one part of a lake to another.

The use of a pH meter may be helpful in determining where, or where not, to fish for selected species in some environments, but it has not been demonstrated to be a necessity for anglers.

PHYTOPLANKTON
Microscopic suspended algae *(see)* in the surface waters of seas and lakes where there is enough light for photosynthesis to occur.

PICKEREL, CHAIN *Esox niger.*
Other names—jack, pike, eastern pickerel, eastern chain pickerel, lake pickerel, reticulated pickerel, federation pickerel, mud pickerel, green pike, grass pike, black chain pike, duck-billed pike, river pike, picquerelle, water wolf.

This member of the Esocidae family of pike is a lean, sporting, evil-eyed bandit, yet it is virtually neglected by most nonwinter anglers, rarely specifically pursued by open-water anglers, and often downgraded by those who catch it unintentionally while seeking more popular fish. Respectable battlers on appropriate tackle, these aggressive, available fish also offer a good chance of angling success.

Long, slimy, toothy, camouflaged in green brown and bearing chainlike markings, the chain pickerel has cold-blooded eyes and is a smaller but equally fearsome-looking version of its northern pike and muskellunge cousins. It has an unusual arrangement of bones, but the flesh is generally white, flaky, and sweet. At some times and from some places, however, the flavor is not as good. This deficit may be remedied by removing the skin before cooking. Many chain pickerel are caught through the ice.

This fish is sometimes confused with the walleye, particularly in southern Canada where walleye are called "pickerel," but the walleye is a member of the perch family and is unlike the true chain pickerel in all respects save one: It too has many teeth. Chain pickerel are abundant where pike and muskies are not found or are not particularly abundant.

Identification. With its long, slender body, the chain pickerel is very similar in appearance to the northern pike *(see: pike, northern)* and the muskellunge *(see)*, especially when young. It gets its name from its markings, which appear in a reticulated, or chainlike, pattern of black lines that cover the golden to yellowish or greenish sides. The small, light-colored oval spots on the sides of the northern pike resemble the very large, light oval areas on the chain pickerel but may be distinguished by the dark background behind the pattern on the northern pike; also, the northern pike's spots never appear large in relation to the background, whereas in the chain pickerel the lighter areas are more prevalent. The chain pickerel has fully scaled cheeks and gill covers. These further distinguish it from the northern pike, which usually has no scales on the bottom half of the gill cover, and from the muskellunge, which usually has no scales on the bottom half of either the gill cover or the cheek. It has only one dorsal fin, which is located very far back on the body near the caudal peduncle. There is a dark vertical bar under the eye, and the snout is shaped like a duck's bill. The lower jaw has a row of four sensory pores on each side, and the mouth is full of needlelike teeth.

Size/Age. The chain pickerel can exceed 30 inches in length and 9 pounds in weight, although the average fish is under 2 feet long and weighs less than 2 pounds. In some waters it may be even smaller. The all-tackle world record is a 9-pound, 6-ounce fish caught in Georgia in 1961. The maximum age is roughly 10, although the average is around 4. Females grow larger and live longer than males.

Distribution. This species extends along the Atlantic slope of North America from Nova Scotia to southern Florida, as well as along the Gulf Coast west to the Sabine Lake drainage in Louisiana and from the Mississippi River basin north to southwestern Kentucky and southeastern Missouri. Chain pickerel have been introduced to Lakes Ontario and Erie drainages and elsewhere. Their primary abundance is from the mid-Atlantic states north and in Florida and Georgia.

Habitat. Chain pickerel inhabit the shallow, vegetated waters of lakes, swamps, streams, ponds, bogs, tidal and nontidal rivers, and backwaters, and the quiet pools of creeks and small to medium riv-

Chain Pickerel

Pickerel, Chain

Two big chain pickerel caught on a large minnow plug.

ers, as well as the bays and coves of larger lakes and reservoirs. Solitary fish, they prefer water temperatures between 75°F and 80°F and are occasionally found in low-salinity estuaries, although they can tolerate a wide range of salinity. They move into deeper water during the winter and continue to feed actively.

The environs preferred by chain pickerel are somewhat similar to those of largemouth bass, particularly in regard to vegetation and abundant cover. Their primary hangouts are among lily pads and various types of weeds, and they sometimes hold near such objects as stumps, docks, and fallen trees. Invariably, the waters with the best chain pickerel populations are those with abundant vegetation, much of which is found near shore.

Life history/Behavior. This fish reaches sexual maturity when three to four years old, perhaps earlier in more southerly climates. They spawn in the swampy or marshy backwater areas of lakes and rivers, from late winter to early spring (March through May) just after ice out in 46°F to 51°F water. Parents do not build nests or guard the eggs, and the 5,000 to 50,000 eggs are dropped in long glutinous strands over the bottom, where they stick to vegetation and brush. The eggs hatch in 7 to 10 days or in a couple of weeks, and the young fish stay among the weeds and close to shore throughout their first summer.

Food and feeding habits. Capable of eating fish almost as long as they are, chain pickerel feed primarily on other fish, as well as the occasional insect, crayfish, frog, or mouse. Small minnows and fry are among their favorite prey, but they are fond of midsize fish like yellow perch and other pickerel in the 4- to 6-inch range. They will often eat larger fish, and it is not uncommon to catch a large chain pickerel that is still trying to digest another pickerel half its own length. Mainly sight feeders, they lie motionless in patches of vegetation, waiting to snatch small fish, but they can sometimes be lured from a distance to prey that appears vulnerable.

Angling. Not many other sportfish will follow a lure right to the boat with impunity as chain pickerel will, and it is common for them to strike viciously just as a lure is about to be lifted from the water. They often make a V-shaped wake in shallow water when dashing out from cover to intercept a lure, and they may hit a lure three, four, or five times in a row while chasing it.

Chain pickerel are primarily attracted to movement and flash. Nearly any lure with a spinning blade or sparkling appearance will catch at least one chain pickerel in its lifetime. Standard spinners and small spoons are traditionally effective lures, but they are prone to hanging up in thick cover. Spinnerbaits, weedless in-line spinners, and weedless spoons are a better option. Worms and jigs are also taken by chain pickerel, but the result is often a line severed by the fish's teeth. Fly fishing is also worthwhile for pickerel, with streamers being especially ravished. Tandem-bladed spinnerbaits with a white or chartreuse skirt are probably the single most popular pickerel lure, fished with a trailer hook and equipped with silver, copper, chartreuse, white, or yellow blades. A variety of colors works in other lures, but silver and shad are among the favorites.

Live baits may be the top chain pickerel catchers for most anglers, certainly in the winter. Minnows or shiners up to 6 inches long are popular. Chain pickerel often strike their prey to stun or cripple it so they can reattack and consume it headfirst. Therefore they usually take a bait sideways in their mouth and run off with it a bit, maneuver it around, then swallow it headfirst.

In typical chain pickerel water, the best fishing occurs in spring. Chain pickerel spawn in shallow bays and marshy areas after ice out in the north, and in the mid- to late winter in the south. Warmer water temperature and the development of cover are usually two indicators of progressing activity. Chain pickerel feed all year and can be caught in modest numbers in the cold water of early spring. When the water temperature exceeds 50°F, they become more active; 55° to 70°F temperatures offer excellent conditions. At this time, weed growth is developing, providing more cover in which the chain pickerel can lie motionless in anticipation of the inevitable baitfish ambush. When vegetation becomes thick in late spring or early summer, there is usually more forage available, which lessens fishing productivity. From this time through midfall, it is important to fish heavy cover effectively. In the coldwater conditions of early spring and fall, fish slowly for chain pickerel, as you would for bass. Shallow-running crankbaits and minnow-imitation plugs are best.

Many anglers unfortunately pursue and land chain pickerel on tackle that is too heavy to allow these fish to make a good showing. The best gear for chain pickerel is a spinning outfit with 4- or 6-pound line, as the average chain pickerel weighs

no more than 1½ pounds. On light tackle or a fly rod, chain pickerel will run, jump, and cavort in a pleasing manner. Only large chain pickerel put up a really good fight on medium to heavy tackle. Where cover is extremely thick, and where largemouth bass are also being pursued, you'll have to temper this go-light advice with practicality.
See: Pike.

PICKEREL, GRASS AND REDFIN
Grass pickerel *Esox americanus vermiculatus.*

Redfin Pickerel *Esox americanus americanus.*

Other names—banded pickerel, little pickerel, mud pickerel.

The grass pickerel and the redfin pickerel are two nearly identical subspecies of *Esox americanus*, differing only slightly in range. Because they occur only in small populations and are of small size, they have little importance as sportfish, although they are significant predators in many waters of more prominent small sportfish. Although the white, sweet flesh of these members of the Esocidae family is bony, it has an excellent flavor.

Identification. Slender and cylindrical, grass and redfin pickerel look much like the chain pickerel *(see: pickerel, chain)*, with the same fully scaled cheeks and gill covers. They are dark olive to brown or black above, amber to brassy white below, with 20 or more dark green to brown wavy bars along the sides. On the grass pickerel, there are pale areas between the bars that are wider than the bars. The grass pickerel is lighter in color than the redfin pickerel and has a pronounced pale midlateral stripe. The grass pickerel also has yellow green to dusky lower fins and a long narrow snout (although shorter than the chain pickerel's) with a concave profile, whereas the redfin pickerel appropriately has red lower and caudal fins as well as a shorter, broader snout with a convex profile. Both have large mouths with sharp canine teeth and several sensory pores on the lower jaw. A dark vertical bar extends down from the eye, which is more vertical in the grass pickerel than in the redfin. An easy way to distinguish the redfin from the grass pickerel is to examine the scales on the sides of the redfin, of which there are more notched or heart-shaped ones, specifically six in the area between the pelvic fins. There are up to three on the grass pickerel. Also, the redfin has more than seven of these scales between the dorsal and anal fins, whereas the grass pickerel has four or fewer.

Size/Age. Both species seldom exceed 10 inches in length (the redfin pickerel can reach 14 inches) and three-quarters of a pound in weight; the redfin pickerel generally grows faster and slightly longer than the grass pickerel. The all-tackle world record for the grass pickerel is a 1-pound Indiana fish; for the redfin pickerel, the record is a 1-pound,

Grass Pickerel

15-ounce New York fish. They can live up to eight years, although they usually live five years or less. Females live longer and grow larger than males.

Distribution. In North America, grass pickerel range from the Great Lakes basin north to southern Ontario in Canada, and to Michigan, Wisconsin, and Nebraska; they also occur in the Mississippi River and gulf slope drainages west of Pascagoula River in Mississippi to the Brazos River in Texas. Redfin pickerel are found in Atlantic slope drainages, from the St. Lawrence River drainage in Quebec to southern Georgia; they also occur in gulf slope drainages from the Pascagoula River in Mississippi to Florida. Populations for both species are generally small on a local level.

Habitat. Grass and redfin pickerel inhabit quiet or small lakes and swamps, bays and backwaters, and sluggish pools of streams. Both prefer heavy vegetation in clear waters, but the grass pickerel favors waters with neutral to basic acidity, and the redfin inhabits comparatively acidic waters.

Life history/Behavior. Reaching sexual maturity when they are roughly 2 years old and at least 5 inches long, grass and redfin pickerel spawn in late fall, early winter, or spring; grass pickerel require water temperatures between 36° and 54°F, and redfin favor waters approaching 50°F. Spawning takes place in heavily vegetated, shallow areas, and the backs of the fish appear at the surface as they scatter eggs in small batches over the vegetation. Grass pickerel may produce twice as many eggs as do redfin pickerel. They do not build nests. The grass pickerel's eggs hatch in 11 to 15 days, the redfin pickerel's in 12 to 14 days, without the protection of the parents.

Food and feeding habits. Grass and redfin pickerel are largely piscivorous, feeding mainly on other fish such as minnows, although they occasionally eat aquatic insects, small crayfish, and frogs. They will remain virtually motionless among the vegetation for hours at a time, waiting to dart out and seize a potential meal.
See: Pike.

Redfin Pickerel

PIER

A structure raised on piles that extends perpendicular from shore out into a body of water. Most often found in coastal areas, piers are usually made of wood but may be made of masonry or metal. Many piers are important fishing locations for land-based anglers.

See: Pier Fishing.

PIER FISHING
Fishing Coastal Piers, Bridges, Docks, and Bulkheads

Fishing from the shore varies from freshwater to saltwater and from one species to the next in either environment. Most land-based freshwater anglers fish from open shore or bank, or from a small dock although in huge bodies of water, such as the Great Lakes and its connected rivers, they may fish from larger docks that are used to accommodate yachts and ships, or from long piers that are usually part of a wharf or harbor jetty.

In coastal areas, these include fishing from the beach *(see: surf fishing)*; from a jetty, groin, rockpile, or breakwater *(see: jetty fishing)*; and fishing from or around a pier, bridge, dock, or bulkhead. Structures such as piers, bridges, docks, and bulkheads exist in tidal rivers, harbors, inlets, waterways, and marinas; and, in some cases, they are also found in open bays or along otherwise unobstructed oceanfront. The diversity and the productivity of the fishing opportunity offered by these structures will vary with location, and are influenced by many factors, including water depth, water salinity, tides, current, season, size and location of the structure, amount of cover present, and, of course, species of fish.

Most of the following information is directed at coastal structures. However, it is also applicable to fishing such structures in tidal estuaries and rivers, in brackish water, and in some entirely freshwater environs (primarily large lakes, rivers, and canals that provide navigation for large vessels), even though the species differ and even though tides may not be an influence, or a minimal one.

Before general points about what to use and how to work these structures can be given, it is necessary to explain what they are, especially because different terms are often used to describe the same things. "Dock," "wharf," and "pier" are examples of such words.

Technically a pier is a structure, usually wood but sometimes masonry or metal, that is raised on piles and extends in a perpendicular manner from shore out into a body of water. It is usually meant for pedestrian access but may be large enough to accommodate vehicles. Some piers are not accessible to boats and do not provide a landing place, usually because of location. For example, a pier that extends from a beach would be exposed to the elements, and a boat fastened to such a pier might be subject to the full force of wave and current action, a situation that would often make the loading or unloading of passengers unsafe and subject the boat to damage during docking.

Many of the coastal piers that are used strictly for fishing are too far above the water, even at high tide, to be a suitable boat landing; these are seldom confused with docks or wharves, and they are often quite long. Some fishing piers extend hundreds of yards into the ocean or an inlet; South Carolina's Paradise Pier, for example, reaches 1,120 feet into Fripp Inlet.

In a more-protected environment, however, a pier is typically used for docking and landing, often for temporary (short-term) dockage or for loading and unloading passengers and gear.

Although a pier might serve purposes similar to a jetty *(see)* or breakwall it is neither. A pier may be referred to as a wharf, although a wharf is a structure that is parallel to the shore and used for the docking, loading, and unloading of large vessels.

Both piers and wharves are commonly called docks by many people, and the word "dock" is often used to refer to any site where a boat of any size might be berthed, as well as to the entire area where wharves and piers are located ("I'm going down to the docks"). Technically a dock is an enclosed or nearly enclosed water area that is relatively small and is used for mooring a boat. However, in today's usage, the small wooden structure alongside a waterfront home is known as a dock, as is the large area alongside a pier or wharf. The former, however, will almost always be close above the water surface, regardless of tide, whereas the latter will usually be high above the water and at a level that will fluctuate with tidal changes.

Although the upper structure of a pier or a dock will offer shade, it is the support pilings that are especially important (this applies to the old freestanding pilings of dilapidated docks as well). The pilings break the force of the current and attract

Piers that are washed by current or have other features that either attract or hold fish provide the best angling.

small fish that feed on the organisms encrusted on the pilings.

A bulkhead is simply an embankment or retaining wall along the waterfront. Also known as a seawall, it might be metal or masonry but is often wood, positioned parallel to the water. It is used to buffer boats, but its chief purpose is to keep the water from eroding the shore behind. The water is usually moderately deep alongside a bulkhead, although the depth obviously varies with tidal extremes.

Bridges don't need explanation, although they do vary from small road bridges over streams, rivers, marsh creeks, and canals, to long expanses over open water, usually bays. Bridges have varying numbers of piles or pilings, and sometimes bulkheads. Bridges that expand over large water bodies are fished from boats; smaller bridges, and the ends of larger bridges, can be fished from land. Such smaller bridges that are fished from land are the focus of review here.

At first glance, fishing at or around these structures may not seem challenging, but there is exciting angling to be had for a wide variety of species, which may be sought with diverse tackle, using both natural baits and lures. Methods, in fact, can become a matter of choice.

The species available at these structures range from large to tiny, from major gamefish to major table fish. Huge tarpon are regularly taken from bridges in the Florida Keys; snook and redfish are also common southern bridge catches. In South Carolina, which is known for its fishing piers, anglers may catch such larger game as cobia and king mackerel, and possibly sharks. Anglers casting from New Jersey piers often encounter big striped bass, bluefish, and weakfish, all of which strike a variety of lures and natural baits. In San Diego, it might be fast-moving Pacific bonito and barracuda, and in the Northwest it might be king salmon.

Although the gamefish in these structures are the attraction for many anglers, bottom feeders are the bread and butter quarry. In New York, miles of structures located along the north shore of Long Island attract both summer and winter flounder, plus tautog. In Maine, dock anglers tussle with harbor pollock and small cod. Structure anglers in the DelMarVa Peninsula can often catch spot, croakers, and seatrout until their arms are weary. The broad expanse of Pacific offers many species of surf perch, rockfish, sand bass, and halibut that are within reach of bridge, bulkhead, and pier casters. (Whiting and ling once provided pier and bridge casters with a great winter fishery along the mid-Atlantic Coast, but foreign factory trawlers decimated these species. If these fish ever return to plentiful numbers, they might provide pier and bridge casters with the great sport and fine eating enjoyed in an earlier era.) All of these species are excellent table fare and provide some of the finest and freshest seafood available for the dinner table.

Perhaps the most leisurely type of fishing available to coastal anglers is fishing from the piers, bridges, docks, and bulkheads that are readily accessible and are located almost everywhere along the seacoast. In certain places, some of the best publicly accessible non-boat angling is at these structures and may be nearly unknown to casual or unobservant anglers. Small bridges, road causeways, and old docks or piers or bulkheads, for example, are less obvious than piers but can provide some good results, often to anglers who fish at night on the right tide, especially in estuaries and canals. These structures can be enjoyed at nominal cost compared with other types of fishing; in fact, although there is usually a fee to access piers built expressly for fishing, for the most part there is no cost associated with using structures and enjoying the relaxed atmosphere and camaraderie associated with this type of fishing.

Fishing these structures can develop into a lifelong activity for some anglers. This kind of fishing is rather easy to master and is especially suited to those who are prone to seasickness when boating. Because it is not very physically demanding (especially in the case of piers and large docks), it is accessible and enjoyable for those with physical limitations. Not to be overlooked either, especially when bottom-feeding species are available, is that these structures provide an excellent opportunity for family fishing and offer an inexpensive means of introducing children to angling.

Tackle

Conventional, baitcasting, and spinning tackle may all be effectively employed when fishing from most piers, bridges, docks, and bulkheads. Choice is generally a matter of personal preference or suitability to the species, water conditions, and necessary means of fishing. There is no perfect all-around outfit, since you need heavier gear for big fish like tarpon, redfish, striped bass, and bluefish than for bottom feeders like flatfish, seatrout, sand perch, and rockfish.

All of the species sought around these structures are mostly attracted to them because they provide foraging opportunity. Forage species take up residence in and around these structures, and predators move in and out of them when tides and current make that forage more abundant or more vulnerable. As a result, the predominant activity is fishing with bait rigs; casting, though frequently practiced, is often less of a consideration than it is when fishing from jetties or the surf.

Rods and reels. For heavier gamefish, a rod measuring $6^1/_2$ to 8 feet long is ideal. Because you'll often use big baits and heavy lures for tarpon, stripers, bluefish, and redfish, a rod with a stiff action is preferable, since it handles baits and lures with ease and has the muscle to pressure a big fish. Graphite and graphite composite rods are preferred. Reels are usually conventional models for heavier fish-

A variety of species are caught from piers, both by fishing with bait and by casting lures.

ing, and baitcasting or spinning versions for lighter duty, such as casting small plugs and jigs.

Since snags or other obstructions are seldom found around these structures (with the exception of barnacle-encrusted pilings), you can usually get by with lighter lines than in many types of coastal fishing. A reel holding 150 to 200 yards of 12- to 15-pound-test line is usually more than adequate. However, big tarpon and striped bass have been known to spool a reel, especially when hooked from a bridge where the current is swift and the angler is unable to follow the fish. Obviously, such situations dictate stout tackle.

For the bottom fishing enthusiast, a spinning outfit with a 6-foot rod, or a baitcasting outfit that includes a $5\frac{1}{2}$- to 6-foot rod with a long handle for two-handed casting, is fine for fishing from piers, docks, and bulkheads. Because the bottom feeders usually range from half a pound to 5 or so pounds, there's no need to use big reels. Indeed, the reels used by many people for this type of fishing are too heavy and cumbersome. A spinning or baitcasting reel capable of holding 100 yards of 8- to 12-pound-test monofilament line is more than adequate.

Bottom bait rig. When fishing from most piers, bridges, and other structures, anglers are elevated from the water by levels that will vary from just a few feet to 50 feet or more. Although occasionally the line may be cast out, most often the fishing line will be nearly perpendicular to the bottom. This differs from surf and jetty fishing, where the line and rig lay parallel with the bottom once they've been cast out.

Dozens of different bottom rigs can be used for fishing from these structures, and naturally there are regional favorites. However, a few time-proven favorites always bring good results no matter where they are used.

The fish-finder bottom rig is a popular rig that may be used to present a natural bait to anything from a half-pound spot to a 100-pound tarpon. It's built around an egg-shaped sinker that has a hole through the middle. Slip a sinker of sufficient weight to hold bottom—usually $\frac{1}{2}$ ounce to 4 ounces or more—onto your line. Next tie in a tiny barrel swivel, which will prevent the sinker from slipping off the line yet permit it to slide on the line ahead of the swivel. To the barrel swivel, tie a 12- to 36-inch-long piece of monofilament or fluorocarbon leader material, of a size balanced to the hook and bait you're using. When pursuing winter flounder, spot, or croakers, use a No. 6 Claw or Beak style hook and 12 inches of 8-pound-test leader. If the target is channel bass or snook, use a 5/0 or 7/0 Claw or Beak style hook and 36 inches of 30-pound-test leader material.

When this rig is adorned with bait and lowered from a structure, it rests on the bottom, and a feeding gamefish is able to pick up the bait and move off with it without feeling the weight of the sinker. This gives the fish an opportunity to get the bait well into its mouth before you set the hook, and the result is more hooked fish. Several variations of this rig are commercially available; some have a plastic sleeve that you slip onto the line, with a sinker snap attached to the sleeve, whereas others have a metal ring through which the line is slipped, with a sinker snap attached to the ring. All three methods are very effective.

Another popular bottom rig is the single hook version, which is built around a three-way swivel. Tie the three-way swivel directly to the end of your line. Attach a snelled hook to one eye of the swivel; the hook should be appropriately sized for the targeted species and should be snelled to a length of leader. Finally, to the remaining eye of the swivel, either tie-in your sinker or use a small duo-lock snap to attach it. Bait the hook and lower the rig into the water.

A high-low rig is a third type of bottom rig favored by many who fish from these structures. With the line perpendicular to the bottom, the high-low rig enables you to fish one bait directly on the bottom and a second (or high hook) bait 24 to 30 inches off the bottom. Many tackle shops have ready-made high-low rigs available, but with a little effort you can tie up your own right on the fishing grounds.

To make this rig, begin by using a Double Surgeon's Knot to tie a loop in the end of your line and attach the sinker to this loop. Tie in a dropper loop just a few inches up from the loop; when the loop is completed, it should extend approximately 10 to 12 inches from the standing part of the line, meaning in effect that you've used 20 to 24 inches of line in preparing the dropper loop. Next slip a Claw or Beak style hook (with a turned-down eye) onto the loop, looping the hook through the loop twice. If you loop it only once, it will slip and slide free, but putting it through twice will firm it up tight and, in effect, will result in a double leader leading to the hook. Repeat the same procedure where you want to place your high hook, which should be anywhere from 12 to 36 inches up from the low hook.

These three rigs will work effectively in most situations where you want to present a bait to a bottom-feeding fish. They work effectively either when cast away from the structure or when just dropped to the bottom from it.

Lures. Most of the same lures employed in the surf and on jetties may be used effectively from bridges, piers, docks, and bulkheads. However, an important difference is that at the latter structures you usually fish from a greater height above the water. Although you may be fairly close to the water when fishing from bulkheads and docks, you're likely to be fully 30 feet or higher off the water when casting lures from bridges and piers. As a result, the techniques used from the surf or jetty simply don't apply when fishing from these structures. In fact, these structures present new challenges and really exciting fishing once you master the variables.

The most popular items in the arsenal of lure casters are plugs, bucktail or plastic-tailed leadheaded jigs, and metal squids and jigs. Lures ranging in weight from $1/2$ ounce to $1 1/2$ ounces, which are sufficiently heavy to be easily cast from these structures, are among the most popular. Since they are relatively light, they don't require heavy tackle to make a good cast and presentation.

Other gear. Unlike other kinds of fishing, pier fishing doesn't require a lot of gear beyond the basics. You will need a tackle box/satchel and bait container; for nighttime bridge casters, a miner's headlamp, worn loosely around the neck, may come in handy.

Many of the species caught from these structures are of a size that can readily be reeled in with little difficulty. But if you have the good fortune of hooking a big striper, bluefish, or tarpon, landing it can present a problem. Sometimes you can walk it to shore and beach it with little difficulty, or bring it close enough for a companion with a long-handled net to capture. Other times, bridge tender facilities, light poles, bulkhead features, and other obstructions make this impossible.

To help in the landing of heavy fish, many public piers have landing nets fabricated from a heavy round metal rod to which is attached a net bag and a length of $1/8$-inch cord. The net is lowered into the water, and the fish maneuvered above it; an assisting angler lifts the net, capturing the fish, and then lifts net and fish to the top of the structure. Large treble hooks, with lead molded around their shanks (elsewhere known as snag hooks), can be lowered to the water with nylon cord and used as a gaff to snatch the fish when it is brought within range, although the use of this method has decreased in recent years because of various size limit restrictions in coastal states (to avoid misjudging the fish and gaffing an undersized fish).

Anglers fishing for snook and tarpon, which are often released, regularly crimp the barbs of the hooks on their lures. Once a fish is brought within what would be landing range, they give it slack line; usually the fish then either jumps or rolls, ridding itself of the hook and gaining its freedom. Thus, the angler is not obliged to handle a fish that would have been released anyway.

General Tactics

Casting bait away from structure. In some instances it is good to cast a bait rig away from the structure. For certain species, a cast and retrieve approach is best; this is especially true when seeking summer flounder and weakfish, since they like to work shell beds that are located in the vicinity of structures. To cast effectively away from structure, cast as far as you can from the structure, let the rig settle to the bottom, and then lift your rod tip. This causes the rig to slide along the bottom, hesitate, and then slide forward again when retrieved. The fish spots the bait, which is usually a live minnow, sees it move and falter, and is often on it in a flash.

With some species, a motionless bait placed away from a structure gets the most strikes. This is particularly true with spot, croaker, rockfish, surf perch, and other species that move about searching for seaworms, shrimp, clams, and other forage on the bottom. Keep in mind that the stage of the tide may have a bearing on whether you should fish away from a structure or close to it. When the current is strong, some fish, flounder in particular, are more likely to be away from the structure; when it is very slow or nonexistent, they may be under the structure or within a few feet.

Fishing bait close to structure. Some species, such as tautog and sheepshead, often feed extremely close to the pilings that support piers, bridges, and bulkheads. They search for crabs, shrimp, and other forage that cling to these structures, and they'll also use their teeth to rip mussels from the piles. To score, you've got to present your bait just inches from the pilings or concrete. It's not unusual to see veteran pier and bridge anglers moving from piling to piling, carefully lowering their high-low rig and permitting it to rest motionless for a few minutes; if no hits are received, they move to the next piling and then the next until they receive a strike. Both sheepshead and tautog are extremely fast, and you've got to strike immediately or else they'll strip your bait from the hook.

Fishing live bait. Fishing from piers, bridges, docks, and bulkheads proves extremely effective when using a wide variety of live baits, which can easily be presented in a natural manner to many species of gamefish. There are many ways of fishing a live bait, though unquestionably the simplest technique is to tie a hook directly to the end of the line, bait it, and lower the bait into the water. As simple as this rig is to make and use, it is among the most effective of live bait rigs.

Wherever striped bass are found, anglers use this setup with excellent results. They employ a size 1/0 or 2/0 Claw or Beak bait-holder hook and place a single large sandworm on the hook by inserting the hook into the sandworm's mouth, exiting about an inch down on the worm. This enables the angler to lower the worm into the water and drift it out with whatever current moves about the structure, where it swims enticingly and draws strikes.

This same rig is also effective for striped bass and weakfish when used with live eels, which are hooked through the lips and fished in the same manner. Live spot account for many big weakfish when used in this manner, and both grunts and pinfish are very effective baits when live-lined for snook and redfish; these baits are hooked either through the lips or eyes, or just forward of the dorsal fin, which permits them to swim about freely.

Because many live baits are small and will invariably stay close to the structure you're fishing from, you might add a float to the line anywhere from a foot to several feet above the hook. Favored floats are those that can be easily snapped anywhere on the line to hold the bait at the desired depth. The float rig is particularly effective for weakfish.

Many bridge and pier anglers chum *(see)* for weakfish and seatrout by using tiny grass shrimp, which they sparingly dribble into the water, to be carried by the current and attract the fish to the baited hook. A favored float of those seeking weakfish and seatrout is one with a scooped-out head; when you pull on the fishing line, it causes the float to pop and gurgle, often arousing the attention of the fish, which then sees the bait suspended just beneath it.

Buoy rig for live bait. Live baits such as herring, mackerel, mullet, menhaden, and pinfish will often stay very close to the structure you're fishing from, seeking what little sanctuary it offers. Because big baits are difficult to cast and are easily ripped from the hook when the angler casts with force, many pier and bulkhead anglers employ a unique buoy rig approach to get the bait far from the structure from which they're fishing.

To prepare this rig, tie a 2- to 4-ounce pyramid sinker directly to the end of the line. Next tie a 36-inch-long piece of 20- or 30-pound-test leader material to a barrel swivel with a coastlock snap on it. Tie a Claw or Beak style live bait hook, or a treble hook, to the end of the leader material.

Cast the pyramid sinker to the general area where you want your bait to be. Once the sinker is firmly secured into the sand or mud bottom, slip the coastlock snap over the line and close it so that it can slide on the line. A live baitfish, usually impaled through the back, is then placed on the hook and is permitted to slide down the line and into the water. Once the bait enters the water, it can swim only from its entry point down to the sinker; often it will move back and forth, perhaps excitedly fluttering on the surface and attracting striped bass, bluefish, snook, tarpon, redfish, king mackerel, barracuda, and other large gamefish. If sharp-toothed species, such as king

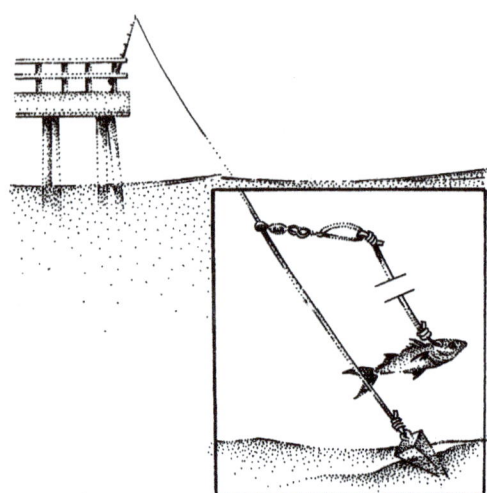

Shown here is a live bait rig fished at a good distance from a pier. Setup begins by casting a pyramid sinker without bait and lodging it securely in the mud or sand; then, live bait, which has been attached to a leader and snap swivel (inset), is placed on the fishing line. The bait slides down into the water and achieves a free-swimming position. This method allows the angler to make a distant presentation of live bait without having to actually cast the bait.

mackerel, barracuda, and bluefish, are in an area, it's often wise to use a 6-inch-long piece of No. 8 or 9 stainless steel leader material between the hook and the monofilament leader, employing a tiny barrel swivel to join the two.

This method of fishing a live bait from piers and bulkheads often brings exciting strikes because the baitfish moves to the surface when being stalked by the quarry. Once the bait is taken, the hook is usually set as the fish mouths it, so you quickly reel up the sinker until it comes taut with the coastlock snap and then you lift back to ensure that the hook is set.

Chumming. Used in concert with the techniques just discussed, chumming *(see)* often enhances your fishing opportunities from these structures by attracting fish within range of your natural baits. Many operators of commercial fishing piers regularly chum from their structures. Ground menhaden is often used to attract baitfish and keep them in the vicinity of the pier, which in turn attracts a variety of species.

The time-proven technique of using a weighted chum pot, filled with ground menhaden, herring, mackerel, mussels, clams, or crabs, is regularly used to bring fish within range. Almost all bottom feeders will move toward the source of chum when it is carried along by the current.

Chumming with live grass shrimp readily attracts weakfish and seatrout to dock areas. Pacific bonito and rock bass will respond to small pieces of fish dispersed from structures. The same is true for bluefish, striped bass, snappers, and groupers. When an easily obtained meal is available, most bottom feeders and gamefish will take advantage of it, much to the advantage of the angler who employs any of the wide variety of chums.

Casting from Bridges and Piers

Both bridges and piers position you high off the water. Currents moving through beneath these structures are most often caused by tidal flow but are affected by wind as well. As these currents reach the pilings, towers, or other structure that support the pier, they cause what are popularly called "dead spots" just before the structure, or behind it as the current passes swiftly through. At both dead spots, the current separates and fish can take up station in quiet water, waiting for food to be swept along. Freshwater anglers have long known that trout often take up station ahead of, or behind, a large rock in a stream, as do smallmouth bass where a deadfall breaks the current in a river. A similar situation occurs at coastal bridges and piers. Knowing this, the bridge and pier caster can target placement so that lures can be worked to these areas, much like a baitfish being swept along by the current.

Many gamefish, especially weakfish, striped bass, tarpon, and snook, take up a feeding station in the quiet water facing the current. If the structure permits, position yourself so that you can make your cast to position the lure 20 or 30 feet up from where you expect the fish to be feeding. This enables you to work the lure and to swim it with the current to within range of the fish. Often this requires a faster rate of retrieve than you would employ elsewhere, since the current is pushing the lure. You've got to speed up the retrieve to give the plug a swimming action or to make the jig appear to be darting downcurrent and faltering as it moves along.

If you don't receive strikes casting directly upcurrent, move to the left or right of where you think the fish are holding. Cast up and across at a 45-degree angle, with the lure dropping in a spot past where the fish may be feeding. Work it across and downcurrent, within view of the fish. Sometimes you can work a swimming plug or leadheaded bucktail or plastic-tailed jig so that it comes within the sight line of the feeding fish, which will often dart out to engulf it, right within view from your vantage on the bridge or pier.

Situations such as described often occur during the swiftest of tides with boiling currents that the fish prefer to avoid. Often, as the tide or current moderates, the fish will expand their range, moving up and down along the structure looking for a meal, and you should adjust accordingly. Don't hesitate to move about. Most veterans look for spots devoid of anglers, so that they can work their lures through new territory, often receiving strikes on their first presentation.

By crossing to the other side of the bridge—watch out for bridge traffic—you experience an entirely different set of circumstances. The current is running beneath the structure, often forming rips and eddies, with the same dead spots of minimal current where the fish like to hold and feed when the current is heavy. In this situation, you can often cast out a swimming plug and "swim" it in the current. If the current is sufficiently swift, only a very slow retrieve, or a twitching of the rod tip, is necessary to keep the plug working. Many anglers just walk the plug, moving it back and forth along the bridge or pier rail, permitting the lure to move in and out of the spots holding fish, much as a struggling baitfish would do in order to stem the current.

Leadhead jigs work effectively in this situation, too. The lighter jigs will work near the surface, and the current will do tricks with them, permitting them to settle, be shifted to the side, and then swept toward the surface as they ease into the fast current. In this kind of situation, the addition of a strip of pork rind or a soft tail does wonders to enhance the action in the current. Twitch your rod tip, and move it back and forth, ensuring that the lure resembles a struggling baitfish.

Don't hesitate to switch to a heavy jig that will get down in the current. The old adage that "if there's a fish feeding on the surface, there's a dozen down on the bottom" holds true with fishing these structures. A heavy jig, perhaps in the $1^{1}/_{2}$-ounce range, can be worked deep while fishing either upcurrent or downcurrent. The key is using the current to your advantage and always maintaining control of the jig's movement. A heavy jig bouncing on the bottom is often observed as it's swept along; and just as the current, or the angler, works it off the bottom, it's taken by a hungry snook, striper, weakfish, or tarpon.

Fish it all. On all piers and bridges, it's important to thoroughly fish all the water surrounding the structure. Anglers tend to bunch up at the end of a pier or the middle of a bridge. Veteran anglers avoid the crowds and work the perimeter. This is especially true where a pier extends out from the beach. Often there are eelgrass beds, marsh grass, or

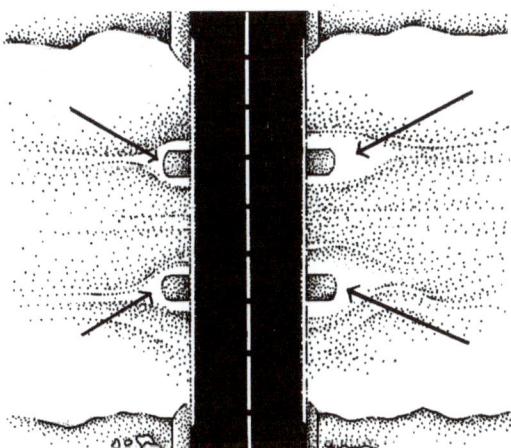

Bridge pilings deflect current, and the dead area (arrows) in front of upstream pilings and below downstream pilings may hold fish.

 Fishing with a fly for Atlantic salmon is either mandatory or de rigueur today; the first record of an Atlantic salmon on a fly in North America was in 1787 on the Saranac River in New York.

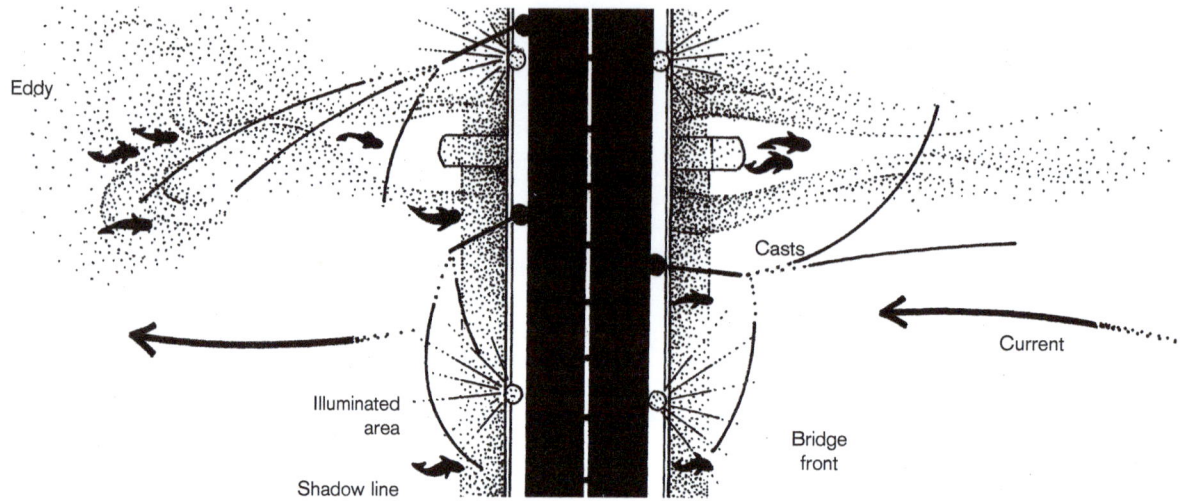

Depicted is a typical major bridge with walkways and with lights that illuminate the water beyond a shadow line at night. Feeding fish will locate in the shadow line on the bridge front and outside of the shadow line on the back (downstream side) of the bridge, as well as in dead water ahead of and below bridge pilings and where the water eddies. Anglers fishing from the bridge should position themselves to make casts to these areas.

reeds extending out from the beach that hold baitfish, and the fish know this and move in close. An ocean pier —along the surf line where the tumbling waves harbor baitfish or expose crabs, shrimp, and seaworms—is another spot often devoid of anglers, yet one certainly warranting several casts.

Work shadow lines. Although daytime sport is enjoyable, there is excitement on the night tides because many coastal species are more active nocturnal feeders and the success ratio is often far superior at night. A unique situation develops after dark on many structures. Illumination from bridge or pier lights, and even a bright moon, develops a shadow line, with the water close to the structure in total darkness and the water beyond the shadow line brightly illuminated.

With the water flowing toward the bridge or pier, which is popularly called the "front of the bridge," gamefish often take up station facing into the current in the darkness, with their noses tight to the shadow line. On the opposite side, or the "back of the bridge," the opposite occurs, with the fish in the brightly lit area, but still with their noses tight to the shadow line, facing into the current or darkness. It's not unusual to see 100-pound tarpon lined up side by side in the shadow line of the bridges in the Keys or to see striped bass doing the same in the waters of many bridges.

Use the same techniques described earlier: Either cast up into the current and retrieve your lure within the vision window of the fish, or cast at an angle and work the lure across and toward the shadow line where the fish are holding. The key with either plugs or leadhead jigs is to fish the lure parallel with the surface, whether working it near the surface or in the depths. Strikes often come as deep-running lures lift off the bottom at the conclusion of a retrieve.

Cast under bridge. If you observe fish holding on the backside of the bridge, waiting for forage such as crabs, shrimp, and small fish to be carried under the bridge toward them, you have to work extra hard to properly present a lure. Often the shadow line is tight to the bridge, and if you permit a lure to work in the rips and eddies, it is many yards behind the line of vision of the feeding fish. At such times, by pointing your rod tip downward and properly timing your cast by rocking the rod and flipping the lure up into the current beneath the bridge, you can then quickly take up the slack as the lure is swept along by the current and to the shadow line and waiting fish. At first this may seem awkward to do, but once you master the motion you'll find it rewards you with many strikes.

Work the corners. Not to be overlooked are the corners where the structure meets land. Often you can fish from rock riprap that is adjacent to the bridge foundation. Sometimes this is a beach or shore, and sometimes it is a bulkhead. Frequently

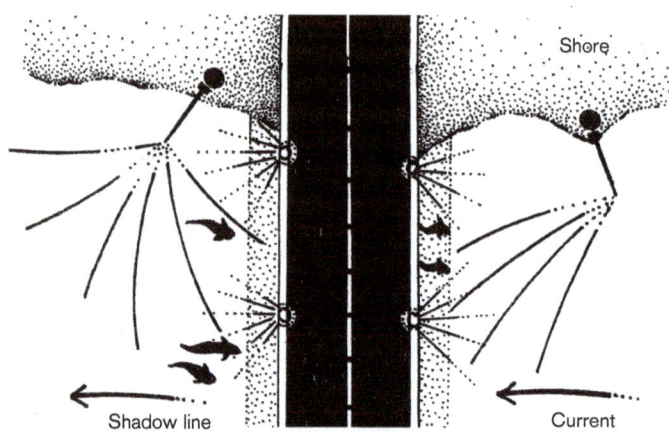

Anglers fishing from shore at night should cast out and across the current to properly scour the area around a bridge. It is especially important to work the shadow lines above and below the bridge. Note the positions of fish near the bridge relative to overhead lights.

the bridge is located at a narrow point of a bay or river, so there is an open expanse of water funneling through beneath the bridge structure. This can cause back eddies, tidal rip lines, and currents of varying speed, which, when combined, sometimes cause miniature whirlpools that trap forage species and attract gamefish.

By positioning yourself in the corner, using a bracket approach to present your lures, and using the tidal flow to your advantage, you can cover a lot of water and catch some beautiful fish. Corner spots often provide exciting tarpon, redfish, and snook angling in southern waters, and striped bass, bluefish, weakfish, and summer flounder in northern waters. All of these bunch up in corners where food is swept their way on a moving tide.

Casting from Docks and Bulkheads

Somewhat different techniques are brought into play when you're positioned fairly low to the water while fishing from docks and bulkheads. Both structures provide good fishing because they offer sanctuary for forage. Shrimp tend to cling to bulkheads and dock pilings, and hungry fish regularly cruise along these structures. Crabs often cling to the pilings, too, or can be observed at night in the area swimming beneath the dock lights. When there is a seaworm hatch, it's not unusual to observe literally millions of inch-long squirmers swimming just beneath the surface. At such times the water often boils as practically every species in residence gorges on the tiny, yet plentiful, food. Where there is abundant food around docks and bulkheads, there will be predators to catch.

Natural drift. Under natural drift conditions, a single sandworm or bloodworm, impaled on a hook and drifted along with the current, quickly brings strikes. A plastic worm may also bring strikes. The key is presentation, with the most successful approach being to drift these items with the current as unimpeded as possible. Veteran bulkhead casters often "walk the worm," permitting the current to carry it along just inches from the bulkhead.

Work tight to bulkhead. Plastic-tailed leadhead jigs also produce excellent results when worked tight to the bulkhead; often snook, redfish, striped bass, bluefish, seatrout, tarpon, ladyfish, snapper, and other species feed just inches from where you may be standing. Tight to the bulkhead means just that, casting out and permitting the current to carry your jig as you walk along the bulkhead or dock, working your rod tip so that the jig darts ahead into the current, then falters and is swept along again, much like a struggling shrimp or tiny baitfish. Work the jig just 6 to 12 inches from the bulkhead or pilings, and you'll be surprised by exciting strikes. Do not overlook the corners of these structures either.

Know the tides. Depending on location, many dock and bulkhead areas come alive at or near slack tide. With swift currents, many gamefish take up station anywhere they can get out of the quick flow, which may be in the middle of a bay or river. As the current slows, they move about, searching for food; they know that the dock and bulkhead areas often have an abundance of forage.

To capitalize on this situation, try to time your visits to key locations an hour before to an hour after either the flood or the ebb tide. By timing your movements, you can often cover three or four spots in different areas, capitalizing on the slow-moving water in each location. As you gain experience, you'll no longer be surprised to see a spot having a 4-knot current and no fish life whatsoever suddenly erupt in a maelstrom of surface-crashing, feeding gamefish. Then, as the current begins to boil, the bonanza shuts off as quickly as it began.

This phenomenon proves that gamefish typically move several miles per day. Anglers often observe huge schools of fish before, during, and after the slack tide. As the current begins to boil, their sonars go blank, indicating that the fish promptly vacated that area rather than fight the energy-sapping current. This happens at docks and bulkheads, too.

Dead spots and shadow lines. Some of the techniques employed by bridge casters have application for fishing from docks. As current flows to the pilings or supports of the dock, there is a dead spot in the current, as is the case on the downcurrent side of the dock. Work these spots diligently with swimming plugs and leadhead jigs.

The same can be said for a shadow line from the dock lights. The difference is that you're usually close to the water. Keep your rod tip low so that the plug or jig works parallel with the surface, and work the lure right up close to the pilings.

See: Tides.

PIGFISH *Orthopristis chrysoptera*.

Other names—Spanish: *corocoro burro*.

Anglers catch this species in large numbers on hook and line and also in nets in warm temperate waters. It is used mainly as a bait for larger predators.

Identification. Pigfish have long anal fins, matching the soft dorsal fin in shape and in size. The head is sloped and pointed, the snout almost piglike, and the lips thin. A background color of bluish gray is marked with brassy spots in indistinct lines that are horizontal below the lateral line but extend obliquely upward and backward above the lateral line. These oblique markings are also found on the cheeks. The fins are yellow bronze with dusky margins.

Age/Size. The maximum length and weight is 18 inches and 2 pounds, but pigfish are commonly 7 to 9 inches long and weigh no more than a half pound. Pigfish normally live for three years.

Distribution. The pigfish exists in the western Atlantic, from Massachusetts and Bermuda to the Gulf of Mexico. They are most abundant from the Chesapeake Bay south and do not inhabit tropical waters.

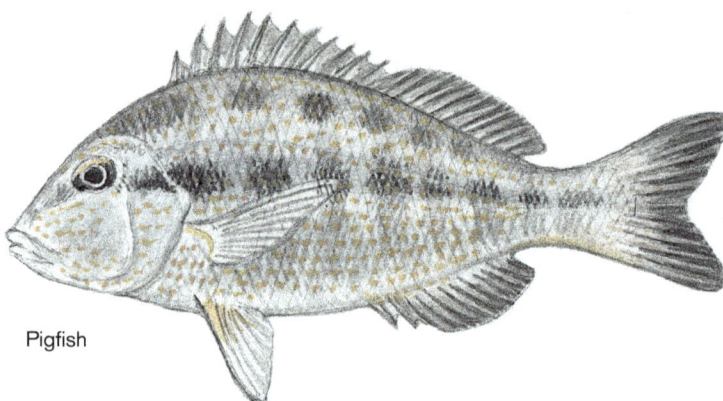

Pigfish

Habitat. Pigfish are found in coastal waters over sand and mud bottoms.

Life history/Behavior. These schooling fish are mostly nocturnal. Spawning occurs inshore in spring and early summer, prior to when the fish move into estuaries.

Food. Pigfish are bottom feeders that forage on crustaceans, worms, and small fish.

Angling. A common catch in late summer and fall, pigfish are taken by bottom anglers offering various natural baits.

See: Grunt.

PIKE

The Esocidae family of fish, categorically known as pike, numbers some of the most popular, aggressive, and important sportfish of cold and cool waters in the Northern Hemisphere. Six species constitute one genera in this circumpolar group, and they are categorized as pike, pickerel, and muskellunge. The three pickerel and one muskellunge occur naturally only in North America. The pike include two species, *Esox lucius* (northern pike) and *E. reicherti* (Amur pike); the latter is found only in Eurasia, and the former is widely distributed in North America and Eurasia.

All species have slim, elongated bodies with dorsal and anal fins located far to the rear, just in front of the forked caudal fin. The front of the head is flattened, and the long, depressed jaws and snout, when viewed from overhead, appear shaped like a duck's bill. The overall bodily appearance is very much arrowlike. The rays in the fins are soft, the large mouth contains numerous sharp canine teeth, and the coloration is usually greenish or brassy. Pike are distantly related to salmonids, although they lack an adipose fin and do not look or behave like salmonids.

Pike, pickerel, and the muskellunge are solitary, aggressive predators. They do not build nests. In spring, the female scatters or broadcasts her eggs in shallow water where the males fertilize them. The young are given no parental attention, and the species, where they overlap, readily prey upon and compete with each other. Where their ranges overlap, some species hybridize, making the identification of certain individuals extremely difficult. This is compounded by variations in color due to water characteristics and habitat, and some fish having extremely distinctive body markings. Some northern pike have a genetic color variance that results in a markedly silver or bluish appearance, causing them to be called silver pike *(see: pike, silver)*.

Pickerel are the smallest of the group, and only the chain pickerel is capable of growing to more than 5 pounds and no more than 8 pounds. The muskellunge is the largest, once capable of attaining at least 70 pounds if not more. The northern pike routinely exceeds 20 pounds in some waters and is capable of growing to more than twice that weight. The latter two are among the most prized freshwater sportfish.

See: Muskellunge; Pickerel, Chain; Pickerel, Grass and Redfin; Pike, Northern.

PIKE, BLUE
(1) *Stizostedion vitreum glaucum.*

Not a pike, but a subspecies of the walleye *(see)* and a member of the Percidae family, the blue pike is believed extinct. It was a deep-water species endemic to Lake Erie and of great commercial significance in the 1920s, possibly more so than the native lake trout. The blue pike was distinguished from the larger walleye (walleye were called walleyed pike or yellow pike at one time) by virtue of its larger glassy eyes, lack of yellow pigmentation, and narrower distance between the eyes. This bluish or blue gray walleye was said to be present in Lake Erie into the early 1970s, and may have occurred in limited numbers in Lake Ontario, Lake Huron, and

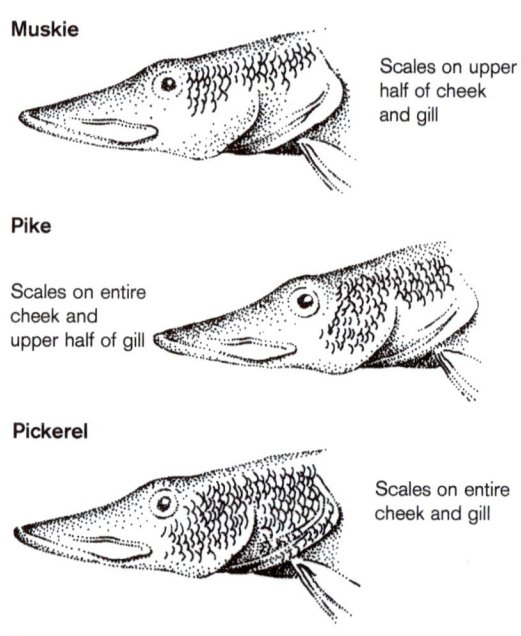

The scale pattern on cheeks and gills helps differentiate the pike species.

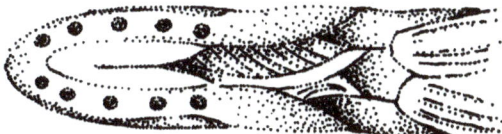

There are six or more pores on each side under the jaw of muskellunge, and five or fewer pores on the northern pike.

some other connected Great Lakes waters, although this has never been confirmed. Commercial overfishing, interbreeding with walleye, and the introduction and spread of lamprey eels are among the factors that may have led to the demise of this species.

(2) A term for the so-called silver pike (see: pike, silver).

PIKE, NORTHERN *Esox lucius.*
Other names—pike, northern, jack, jackfish, snake, great northern pike, great northern pickerel, American pike, common pike, Great Lakes pike; Danish: *gedde;* Dutch: *snoek;* Finnish: *hauki;* French: *brochet;* German: *hecht;* Hungarian: *csuka;* Italian: *luccio;* Norwegian: *gjedde;* Portuguese: *lcio;* Russian: *shtschuka;* Spanish: *lucio;* Swedish: *gäddo.*

Malevolent-looking and spear shaped, the northern pike might well have been named "water wolf." Often likened to the notoriously vicious barracuda of saltwater, it is the namesake member of the Esocidae family of pike. Although disparaged by a few people who catch it while seeking other species of fish, the pike is a worthy angling quarry, one that grows fairly large, fights well, and accommodates anglers frequently enough to be of substantial interest in the areas where it is found.

The majority of northern pike are released by anglers, but a minor amount of commercial fishing for them exists in North America and also in Eurasia. This species is not usually thought of as a good food fish, but it is actually excellent, especially those specimens that come from cool, clean waters. Although bony, the flesh is sweet, white, and flaky, and cooking preparations are best with the skin removed to avoid flavors that may accompany its mucus-coated skin.

Identification. The northern pike has an elongated body and head. The snout is broad and flat, shaped somewhat like a duck bill. The jaws, roof of the mouth, tongue, and gill rakers are armed with numerous sharp teeth that are constantly being replaced. A single soft-rayed dorsal fin is located far back on the body.

Male and female pike are similar in appearance, and both are variable in color. A fish from a clear stream or lake will usually be light green, whereas one from a dark slough or river will be considerably darker. The underparts are whitish or yellowish. The markings on the sides form irregular rows of yellow or gold spots. Pike with a silvery or blue color variation are occasionally encountered and are known as silver pike (see: pike, silver).

The northern pike can be distinguished from its relatives by three main features. Most noticeably, the greenish or yellowish sides of these fish are covered with lighter-colored kidney-shaped horizontal spots or streaks, whereas all other species have markings (spots, bars, stripes, or reticulations) that are darker than the background color. Its markings are most likely to be confused with those of the chain pickerel (see: pickerel, chain). The second distinction is the scale pattern on the gill cover and cheek. In the northern pike the cheek is fully scaled, but the bottom half of the gill cover is scaleless. In the larger muskellunge, both the bottom half of the gill cover and the bottom half of the cheek are scaleless. In the smaller pickerel, the gill cover and the cheek are both fully scaled. The third distinctive feature is the number of pores under each side of the lower jaw; there are usually 5 in the northern pike (rarely 3, 4, or 6 on one side), 6 to 9 in the muskellunge (rarely 5 or 10 on one side), and 4 in smaller pickerel (occasionally 3 or 5 on one side only).

Size/Age. Pike are normally 16 to 30 inches long and weigh between 2 and 7 pounds. Females live longer and attain greater size than males. Pike up to 20 pounds are common in some Canadian and Alaskan rivers, lakes, and sloughs, and fish weighing up to 30 pounds and measuring 4 feet in length are possible. Fish exceeding 25 pounds are quite rare, and the North American record is a 46-pound, 2-ounce New York fish caught in 1940. Larger northern pike have been recorded from various European countries, and the all-tackle world record is a 55-pound, 1-ounce German fish captured in 1986. The average life span of northern pike is 7 to 10 years, but in slow-growing populations they may live up to 26 years.

Distribution. The northern pike occurs around the world in northern or arctic waters, extending from northwestern Europe across northern Asia to northern North America. It is densely distributed throughout Alaska with the exception of the offshore islands, and widespread throughout Canada and the arctic islands above Hudson Bay, being conspicuously absent from the coastal plains (most of British Columbia and the Canadian Atlantic coast east of the St. Lawrence River). In the United States, it is found south of Maine in New Hampshire, Vermont, and Massachusetts (except along the coast), and in all the Great Lakes states

Northern Pike

(although it is largely absent from lower Michigan and Indiana), as well as west of the Great Lakes in Minnesota, Wisconsin, Iowa, Illinois, Missouri, Nebraska, and Montana. It is restricted primarily to the extreme eastern portions of North and South Dakota. It has been widely introduced outside this native range, even into southern and western states.

In Europe and Asia, this fish is primarily known as pike, not northern pike, and is accompanied in northeastern Asia by the Amur pike *(E. reicherti)*, which is native to the Amur River system. Also known as the blackspotted pike, this fish can grow to more than 3 feet in length and weigh up to 35 pounds; it is of some commercial interest, and has been introduced to a few waters in the U.S.

Habitat. Although classified by biologists as a coolwater species, the northern pike exists in diverse habitats, somewhat like largemouth bass but without a tolerance for extreme warm conditions. It is especially known to inhabit the weedy parts of rivers, ponds, and lakes, but it may be found in deeper, open environs in waters without vegetation, or when the temperature gets too high in warm shallower areas. Warm shallow ponds and cold deep lakes both support pike, but large individuals have a preference for water that is in the mid-50°F range. Smaller fish are more likely to be in warm shallow water.

Life history/Behavior. Northern pike spawn in spring, moving into the heavily vegetated areas of lakes and rivers either just after ice out or in some cases prior to ice out. In many places they spawn in wetlands or marshes that will have little or no water later in the season. They are broadcast spawners, and the scattered eggs that fall to the bottom are adhesive. They usually hatch in 12 to 14 days, but do so later in much colder waters. In waters that also contain muskellunge *(see)*, the two species may crossbreed naturally; this occurs rarely and is more likely to be achieved deliberately in a hatchery, but it has occurred naturally, as muskies spawn in the same or similar environs, although usually after pike.

Young pike grow rapidly and in much of their range are capable of attaining 6 inches by the end of their first summer. Females mature at age 3 or 4, and males at age 2 or 3, although they may do so later in more northerly waters.

Food and feeding habits. Pike are voracious and opportunistic predators from the time they are mere inches long. They are solitary, lurking near weeds or other cover to ambush prey. Their diet is composed almost entirely of fish, but it may occasionally include shorebirds, small ducks, muskrats, mice, frogs, and the like. Other pike—as well as whitefish, walleye, yellow perch, and suckers—are common food items in waters where these species are abundant. The northern pike is highly specialized for feeding individually on large food items, and it may attack and eat forage that is one-third its own length; in pike waters, it is common to find scarred fish that were grabbed by but escaped the large toothy maw of a pike. Pike feed most actively during the day and are heavily sight-oriented. They are less affected by cold fronts than are other gamefish.

Angling. Born in weedy waters, pike spend much of their life in similar habitat, holding motionless in the vegetation, camouflaged to strike suddenly at passersby. Key locations in lakes include weedy bays, river inlets where weeds are plentiful, shoreline points with beds of cabbage weeds on their open-water sides, reefs with coontail weeds, marshy shorelines, lily pads, and reedy pockets along sandy and rocky shorelines. Many other areas may hold pike, but some form of vegetative structure obviously hosts a significant portion of the pike population. Some pike, especially large ones, inhabit open waters where they forage on schools of baitfish, so it is not necessarily the case that every pike in a given environment will be in the weeds.

Pike remain fairly shallow in the early part of the year, and some (mostly smaller ones) stay in shallow water throughout the season. Bigger pike, however, usually gravitate to deeper, heavy-cover haunts as the water warms. During early summer, they move to cabbage weeds (also called pike weeds), for example, in water that exceeds 6 to 7 feet and drops off to 15 feet or so. Look to the outer edge of these weeds for trophy fish, and especially in pockets or indentations.

In rivers, pike are a lazy fish and usually try to establish an easy ambush position. Look for them where small rivers and streams merge with the main flow, in the small eddy beneath a beaver hut, downstream from islands, in shallow backwaters, under docks, on shorelines just below riprap or wing dams, on the inside of large eddies, and where brush and slow water meet.

Even relatively small pike may attack a big lure, so the big lure/big fish theory doesn't necessarily hold with these game creatures. Smaller pike are often more eager and more vulnerable to angling, and they out-hustle larger fish to a lure of any size. This is especially true where pike are very abundant. Using fairly large lures is nonetheless advantageous, not only because they discourage some smaller fish from attacking, but also because they represent more of a meal to a larger pike than would a diminutive lure, which makes them more worthy of pursuit.

Pike lures include the traditional red-and-white spoon, plus a fluorescent orange-bladed spinnerbait or bucktail spinner; an orange-and-yellow-backed minnow-imitation plug; a yellow, Five-O-Diamonds pattern spoon; a black bucktail with a single fluorescent spinner; and various shallow- and deep-diving plugs in gaudy and metallic colors. Good pike lures often tend to be brightly colored and to work with a broad, wide-wobbling action. Lethargic fish may be more inclined to hit large hair- or rubber-bodied jigs, as well as soft-plastic jerkbaits and weightless plastic worms.

Pike are attracted not only to a lure's size and shape, but also to its swimming action, flash and visibility, and noise. They are one of the more curious freshwater fish, and getting their attention is often a key to catching them. That would seem true of most fish, but many other freshwater species are keenly aware of the presence of certain lures in their domain yet remain otherwise disinterested.

Lure types and the techniques used to present them vary greatly for northern pike, although many would-be pike catchers stick to the simplicity of casting spoons in and around weeds. Although casting weedless spoons directly into a mass of shoreline vegetation and retrieving outward can have merit, it is a fairly standard tactic that suffers in heavily fished waters.

All types of plugs can be useful in catching pike—surface plugs, shallow-running plugs, and medium to deep divers—but shallow runners are especially popular, as are long and slender plugs that imitate small fish. Most anglers think only of shallow-running minnow-style plugs for pike; these are useful, of course, and are perennial pike catchers, but anglers should broaden their arsenal. Many of the larger minnow-shaped plugs used for striper and muskie trolling, for example, are effective pike catchers, both in casting and trolling applications.

An overlooked hot pike plug is a super-shallow-running (1 foot deep and less) bulbous crankbait that rattles noisily. This plug not only calls pike up out of deep weeds in the summer, but it can also be worked in back-bay shallows in the spring. In lieu of this particular lure, you could try a surface plug, such as a walking-type stickbait or a propellered plug (perhaps even a popper), to get a pike's attention and bring it up for a strike. Another option is a medium- or deep-diving crankbait that possesses rattles; these are worked stop-go fashion over and through the weeds. Still another option is a non-rattling deep-diving plug; this type should first be worked around the edges of the vegetation to entice

A northern pike from Scott Lake, Saskatchewan.

the pike to move out of the weeds, and then worked through the weeds in a slow, twitching style.

The diving minnow is ideal for parallel casting to banks and weedlines, and also for shallow pull-pause retrieves; it's helpful to use the same lure—which has good flash and looks like a small fish—for deep edges as well as for relatively shallow work. Barbless hooks, incidentally, are the only way to go when using multihook lures, especially plugs, for pike. Some plugs can be switched to single barbless hooks, which diminishes the chances of inflicting damage (on you and the fish) and facilitates unhooking.

A spinnerbait is another effective northern pike lure, fished through weedbeds, around timber, up against stumps, in and about brush, and across rocky points. Their weedless nature is especially beneficial, and they work especially well in the spring, when pike stage in extremely shallow water during spawning and post-spawning periods.

Jigs work well for these fish, although when used without a wire leader, many jigs are lost to a pike's razor-sharp teeth. Good pike jigs include plastic eel-like versions, or those formed of natural hair, in bright colors. Some anglers slow-troll these along the deep edge of weedbeds, slowly lifting and lowering the rod tip. Casting along the edges is also productive.

Fly fishing for pike has gained a following in recent times, simply because these fish are aggressive and are often available in shallow water, which makes presentation less difficult. In the northern parts of their range, where pike stay shallow in cool water well into the season, pike can be stalked and sight-fished. This method allows flycasters fishing from boats to make presentations akin to those used on tropical saltwater flats.

Fishing with live or dead baits is a small overall component of the pike angling scene, although in some areas a dead bait stillfished on the bottom in spring takes the larger pike.

Baitcasting, spincasting, and spinning gear are all suitable for pike fishing, although baitcasting is most preferable for large lures or baits or when the opportunity exists to catch large fish. The generally stiffer baitcasting rod has an advantage over other types of tackle in hook setting, which is not always accomplished well in the big toothy maws of a pike. Line capacity is not a big factor in pike fishing. Rods should be $5^1/_2$ to 7 feet long, with a stiff butt and midsection, and a rather fast tip. Most pike anglers prefer heavy line; 12- to 17-pound test is favored, but many opt for 6- to 10-pound-test line where the cover is not thick.

Steel leaders are used by many pike anglers, but avoided by others. A large pike may take a lure deep or get some of the line in its mouth, and certainly many lure-hooked pike get free when they cut leader-less line. Yet many fish are caught without the use of leaders, although this is sometimes pure luck. Small, 6-inch, 20-pound-test leaders do not hamper casting but afford some protection.

Pike aren't hard to subdue. They do a lot of thrashing and short-distance darting, and some don't really fight until they eyeball the boat or angler. Reel drag is significant when playing larger fish, but only briefly. The heavy weeds these fish prefer can cause a problem with light lines; big pike tend to make long, steady runs through thick vegetation. A leader can be beneficial in these instances.

The greatest difficulty in landing pike is facilitating a smooth release that doesn't injure the fish or the fish handler. Netting pike is inadvisable, as they often thrash wildly when captured, and multihook plugs can be dangerous and harmful. Unhooking and releasing fish in the water, by the boat, is the best tactic. Leading them into fish cradles is also useful.
See: Pike.

PIKE, SILVER

Taxonomically there is no species of fish, or subspecies of northern pike (see: pike, northern), that is identified by the name "silver pike." This term is occasionally used to describe pikelike fish that have a silvery or blue gray coloration but otherwise look like northern pike. Most scientists classify this fish as a color variation of the northern pike, the result of genetic mutation. This determination has not been scientifically proven. Some North Americans refer to it as "silver muskellunge," although it is a pike; many call it a blue pike, and some call it a deep-water pike.

Smaller than the northern pike (it has been reported up to 20 pounds) and distinctly uncommon, the silver pike has occurred across most of the range inhabited by northern pike in North America and Eurasia. Its body coloration is light and predominantly silver, although it may be bluish; it is darker on top and lighter on the belly, and has no spots. Silver pike that have mated with "true" northern pike have produced offspring with black mottled markings on a silver base, similar to crappie and leading to the term "black pike."
See: Pike.

PIKE-PERCH

Also written as pikeperch and pike perch, "pike-perch" is a European term for zander (see).

PILCHARD

(1) An angling term for various small members of the Clupeidae family of herring (see) that inhabit the western Atlantic. These include three members of the *Harengula* genus: false pilchard (*H. clupeola*); redear sardine (*H. humeralis*); and scaled sardine (*H. jaguana*). It may also include the Atlantic thread herring (*Opisthonema oglinum*).

These species occur from Florida and the Gulf of Mexico southward to Brazil, and some range farther north. They are commonly 5 to 7 inches in length and are caught on small multihook bait rigs and with cast nets for use as inshore and offshore live baits. Pilchards may also be known as white baits in parts of Florida.

(2) A term for Pacific sardines (see: sardine, Pacific).

PILE CAST

An in-air technique for presenting a fly or mending a fly line.
See: Mending.

A silver pike from Wollaston Lake, Saskatchewan.

PILOTFISH *Naucrates ductor.*

Pilotfish are a unique and circumtropical species widely found in the Atlantic, Pacific, and Indian Oceans. They are renowned for accompanying large sharks on their oceanic wanderings, as well as whales, ray, schools of various other fish, and ships. A pilotfish is said to have followed a sailing ship for 80 days.

This species has no angling value but is often observed by offshore anglers. It feeds on scraps of the host's leftovers, as well as on parasites, small fish, and invertebrates. Minor commercial interest exists for this species, which is of the jack family and looks somewhat like an amberjack.

Pilotfish have five to seven dark vertical bars on their elongated body, and a low spinous first dorsal fin with four spines. They can grow to a maximum of 27 inches.

PINFISH

Other names—bream, saltwater bream, sailor's choice, Canadian bream; Spanish: *sargo salema.*

This abundant, small member of the Sparidae family is important as forage for predatory species of fish and is widely used by anglers as bait. There was once a fairly good commercial fishery for pinfish, but it is now a minor one; the flesh is oily and has a strong flavor.

Identification. Pinfish have a compressed panfishlike body with a head that is high through the area just in front of the dorsal fin. It has a small mouth and incisor-like teeth with deeply notched

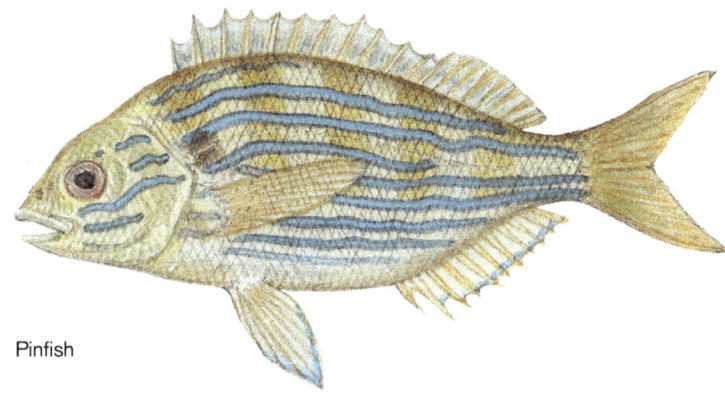
Pinfish

Pilotfish

edges. Its coloration is silvery overall, with yellow and blue horizontal stripes. A round black spot at the upper rear margin of each gill cover is distinctive. The name of the species comes from the needle-sharp spines on the first dorsal fin. All fins are yellowish.

A similar small porgy, the spottail pinfish (*Diplodus holbrooki*) averages less than 10 inches in length, but occasional larger individuals do exist. It is identified by the large black band across the base of the caudal peduncle and by the black margin on the gill covers. Otherwise, the body is silvery, with only faint black bars. The spottail pinfish is common over rocky bottoms and around docks and piers. In the Caribbean it is replaced by the almost identical silver porgy (*D. argenteus*).

Size. Pinfish are capable of growing to 15 inches, but they rarely reach 10 inches in length and are common at about 7 inches. They live at least seven years, and probably longer.

Distribution. The pinfish occurs in the western Atlantic, from Massachusetts to the northern Gulf of Mexico, including Bermuda, to the Yucatán Peninsula in Mexico. The spottail pinfish is found in the Gulf of Mexico and in Florida.

Habitat/Spawning behavior. Pinfish are coastal and inshore species that travel in schools, sometimes in great numbers, over vegetated and sometimes rocky bottoms and around docks and pilings; they also frequent mangrove areas and may enter brackish water or freshwater. Pinfish move out of coastal waters in winter, and spawning occurs in winter in offshore waters.

Food and feeding habits. Pinfish consume crustaceans, mollusks, worms, and occasionally small fish associated with grassy habitat. They nibble at most foods, a habit that makes them a nuisance for anglers fishing baits for other bottom-dwelling species.

Angling. To catch pinfish, anglers use small pieces of bait on small hooks and bottom rigs around docks and piers, and in shallow nearshore water. They are captured with cast nets for live (and cut) bait use and for chumming.
See: Inshore Fishing.

PINTADO

A shovelnose catfish of South America, also known as spotted sorubim.
See: Catfish.

PIRAÍBA

The largest South American catfish and one of the largest freshwater fish in the world.
See: Catfish.

PIRANHA

Piranhas (pronounced pee-ron-yahs) are the best known and most storied members of the Characidae family, most of which are minnowlike but possess teeth and an adipose fin. There are reportedly some 800 characins, and piranhas make up a large group that are related to such gamefish species as payara, dorado, and tigerfish.

Also known as *caribe* in Spanish, piranhas and some closely related species belong to the subfamily Serrasalminae, which has two different groupings. One includes seven genera and some 60 species that are primarily plant-eating fish. The tambaqui *(Colossoma macropomum)* of the Amazon is the most prominent member of this group; it is an important food fish, eats fruit, grows to 66 pounds, and is occasionally caught incidentally by anglers.

The other group has six genera and includes silver dollar fish, which belong to the genus *Metynnis* and are well known to aquarium hobbyists. It also includes four genera of piranhas—*Pygopristis, Pygocentrus, Pristobrycon,* and *Serrasalmus*—which include approximately 50 species. Some of these piranhas have yet to be described by scientists, and a good deal remains unknown about many of them, especially the extent of their range.

It is known that piranhas, like most characins, are schooling species. Most are fairly small, under 10 inches in maximum size. They are also good sportfish on appropriate tackle, and their firm, white meat is excellent table fare.

The fearsome flesh-eating image of piranhas is exaggerated on the whole, as many piranhas are herbivorous and eat seeds, although many also eat other fish. Many species of piranhas are termed harmless to humans; however, some species can be extremely dangerous. The questions, of course, are which ones are harmless, are they always harmless, are the dangerous ones always dangerous, and what gets them excited?

Native South Americans are known to swim in waters that contain dangerous piranhas; in some Brazilians waters, it is not unknown for an angler to catch a large black piranha, a dangerous species, from a particular section of water, only to have the native guide slip over the side of the boat a short while later to retrieve a snagged lure.

The presence of blood is generally thought to be a stimulant to a feeding frenzy of flesh-eating piranhas. However, there is ample evidence to indicate that schools of these fish are triggered into attacking

A black piranha from the Trombetas River, Brazil.

behavior by the frenzied and panicked activity of victims, and many if not all piranhas have a highly developed auditory ability. Many gamefish hooked by anglers, particularly peacock bass, are literally attacked by piranhas while they are in the midst of a wild struggle against a fishing rod. They may suffer minor or major mutilation in the process, perhaps being consumed from the tail to belly in such a manner that the angler lands little more than a still-breathing head. This action is not unlike the frenzied behavior of sharks. It is true that people and animals have been killed by piranhas, and that some animals have been reduced to a carcass within a few minutes.

Piranhas can be such effective eating machines because they have numerous upper and lower teeth that are short, triangular, and sharp. The teeth interlock and the jaws are extremely powerful, allowing these fish to chew continuously and to remove flesh in clean bites. There is some belief that the larger the school of piranhas, the greater the propensity for an attack.

Piranhas are confined to the Orinoco, Amazon, Paraguay, and São Francisco River basins of South America, but few species apparently occur across this entire range. They are primarily river species but can adapt to stillwaters, and are commonly found in rivers, lakes, and lagoons in most watersheds within their range.

Species of note. Piranhas are deep-bodied and generally slender fish. Although they vary in size,

Red Piranha

color, and pattern, all have an adipose fin and a broad tail, and most have a rather blunt snout with a slightly upturned lower jaw. Many piranhas are hard for nonscientists to distinguish from each other. Species of prominence are given below.

Red-bellied piranha *(Pygocentrus nattereri)*. This species is also known as red piranha and red pirai; and in Portuguese as *piranha caju* and *piranha-quexicuda*; and in Spanish as *paña, paraña, caribe boca de la locha, palometa,* and *palometa de rio*. Perhaps the most wide-ranging of these fish, the red-bellied piranha occurs from Venezuela to Argentina's Paraná River system, as well as in the tributaries of the Amazon River in Peru. It is classified as dangerous; shows hierarchies in schools; feeds on insects, worms, and fish; and is reported to be active mainly at dusk and dawn. This species is relatively small; a 3-pound, 7-ounce specimen holds the world angling record.

White piranha *(Serrasalmus rhombeus)*. The white piranha occurs in the Orinoco and Amazon basins; in Brazil it is known as *piranha-preta*, and it may also be called redeye piranha and yellow piranha. A potentially dangerous fish, it is a small species that grows to a maximum of 13 inches.

Black piranha *(Pygocentrus piraya)*. This species is also known as blacktail piranha and São Francisco piranha, and in Portuguese as *chupita*. It is endemic to and widely spread in Brazil, including the São Francisco River basin, and may occur elsewhere. The dangerous black piranha is the largest of all piranhas and is also a commercial species. It is reported to grow to 13 pounds; the all-tackle world record is a 6-pound, 15-ounce Venezuelan fish, and 2- to 4-pounders are common in some waters.

The black spot piranha *(Pygocentrus caribe)*. A small and harmless species from Venezuela, this fish is also called blackspot piranha and, in Spanish, *caribe pinche*. It is listed among record species, with a 1-pound, 4-ounce fish being the largest caught.

The pirambeba *(Serrasalmus humeralis)*. This is a Brazilian piranha that established a breeding population in Dade County, Florida. It is believed to be the only escaped piranha species to have accomplished this, and it was eradicated in 1981.

Angling. Piranhas are great sport on light tackle. Large specimens are especially good fighters. Most piranhas are caught incidentally by anglers fishing for other species, primarily peacock bass, and are seldom the deliberate target of angling. Because of this, they are usually caught on heavy tackle that mitigates their fight. Anglers can take advantage of the schooling behavior of piranhas, however, by having on hand lighter tackle and smaller lures. Small spoons, jigs, and lipless crankbaits are very effective for these species. A steel leader is advisable.

PIRARARA
A South American catfish.
See: Catfish.

White Piranha

PIRARUÇU
See: Arapaima.

PISCIVOROUS
Fish eating. Most predatory fish, and most of those considered sportfish, are piscivorous.

PISTOL GRIP
A type of handle, especially common on short baitcasting rods.
See: Baitcasting Tackle.

PITCHING
Pitching is a technique for casting under obstructions by using a low-trajectory approach to the targeted area. It is a cast that does not develop a lot of rod tip speed and isn't used for great distances, yet one that provides accuracy and soft presentations for lures dispatched to hard-to-reach places.

Pitching is often confused with flipping *(see)*, perhaps because of its use by bass anglers and because it primarily involves baitcasting reels and long rods. Although both techniques have similar purposes and achieve similar results, they accomplish them differently, and in pitching, unlike flipping, the reel is used to cast.

Pitching works best where there is heavy cover and where the clarity of water prevents you from getting close enough to make a short flip cast without spooking fish. In many places where pitching is used, there are overhanging obstructions, especially tree cover. In such situations, a conventional overhead cast will cause the lure to get hung up. Pitching lets you keep the lure down close to the surface all the way from your position (usually in a boat) to the target. If you make a pitching cast properly, you can get your bait under most kinds of overhanging cover.

Rods that are best for pitching are often $6\frac{1}{2}$ feet long, shorter than a standard flipping rod, and are designed for lines ranging from 8 to 17 pounds. This is a versatile tool that can be used for many other activities. It should be matched with a

Pitching

A two-handed pitch cast is made by holding the lure (be wary of hooks) in your left hand and pulling on the line to bring your rod tip down so that it has a slight bend (top). Bring the rod up as you let go of the weight, and take your thumb off the reel spool (bottom) to send the lure toward its target on a low trajectory.

good-quality baitcasting reel, preferably one with a flipping feature for versatility, since you might get a strike as soon as your lure enters the water, in which case it's good to have a reel that engages the moment you release pressure on the freespool device.

The pitch cast is made with either a two-handed, low-trajectory cast or with a one-handed pendulum motion. Both work well but serve slightly different purposes. Practice is the key to learning either one.

To execute the pendulum cast with a practice casting weight, let out line so that the weight hangs down to just above your reel. Put the reel into freespool, and keep your thumb on the spool. Raise the rod tip to swing the lure forward, and then permit it to swing back toward your body. Swing it forward again, and release thumb pressure on the reel's spool as the lure comes forward. If your timing is right, the lure will fly out in low, level flight to its intended target. When practicing on land, the weight should stay down close to the ground so that in actual fishing the lure stays down close to the surface of the water. The key to making this cast properly is getting enough movement in the practice weight to pull line off the spool as you release thumb pressure.

Be sure to use a $5/8$-ounce weight in practice sessions. This weight may be heavier than the lure you'll use for fishing, but the beginning objective is to learn how to execute the cast and polish your timing, and such a weight makes it much easier to do this.

An educated thumb and a low spool-tension setting on the reel are critical to successful pitching. You won't be able to develop the power in pitching that you get with a conventional cast. Unless you've got your reel set so that the spool operates fast and easy, you might as well forget about pitching. Having the tension set lightly means you have to control things with your thumb. The only way to do that is through practice.

The pendulum method for pitching is best when using fairly heavy lures and where most of the targets are close in. Most pitching is done with a jig and pork frog or perhaps a jig and grub combination. The pendulum method works best with a leadhead jig weighing $3/8$ ounce and up.

Like the pendulum cast, the two-handed pitch technique permits you to keep a lure down so that it can be made under an overhanging obstruction. The main advantage is greater distance without sacrificing accuracy or soft presentation.

To make a two-handed pitch cast, put the reel into freespool and let out enough line that the practice weight drops down even with your reel. Hold the practice weight in your left hand, and pull on the line to bring your rod tip down until it has a slight bend. Bring the rod up as you let go of the weight, and take your thumb off the reel spool at the same time. If you do it right, the lure will speed away to its target with a low trajectory.

Make sure you don't overload the rod on the two-handed pitch. If you pull the tip of your rod down hard to get more distance, the reel will start with a quick jerk that even an experienced thumb can't control; you don't have to pull hard on the line to bring the rod tip down. It is essential that your pitching rod have a fast enough tip to send the lure to its target with just one smooth movement. Practice lifting your rod arm at the exact instant you release the casting weight. This is the key to good pitching. If your timing is just right, the practice weight or lure will shoot out easily and give you adequate distance.

Some may question the wisdom of holding a lure with a sharp hook in the left hand to execute this two-handed pitch cast. It's not a problem if you handle the lure carefully. Practically all of the lures used for pitching while bass fishing have some kind of weedguard or have the hook buried inside them. With reasonable care you can hold them without hooking yourself. Of course, when practicing, you'll be using a dummy plug that doesn't have hooks.

Timing and coordination are critical in mastering both of these pitching casts. Practice is the way to develop your timing and coordination. Don't be frustrated if you fail to get things together in the first 10 minutes of practice, since few do. But stick with it, and you'll become a better angler.

Make certain that you become adept at keeping the lure down close to the surface of the water. This is accomplished by having the proper timing when you release the lure with your left hand. If you

release the lure too late, it will go right up. If this happens, learn to let go of it sooner. If you're right-handed, hold the lure in your left hand and bring it back so that your hand is alongside and slightly to the rear of your left leg. Try releasing the lure (or practice weight) when your hand is about even with your left leg. If you do it right, this should bring the lure down where you want it.
See: Casting.

PITHING
A method of killing fish.
See: Fish Preparation—Care.

PLAICE, AMERICAN *Hippoglossoides platessoides*.
Other names—dab, long rough dab, plaice, Canadian plaice; Dutch: *lange schar*; French: *balaide de l'Atlantique*; Icelandic: *skrápflura*; Norwegian: *gapeflyndre*; Spanish: *platija americana*; Swedish: *glipskädda, ler flundra*.

The American plaice is a large-mouthed, right-eyed member of the Pleuronectidae family of flatfish *(see)* that is currently an insignificant catch by anglers, but has been an important component of commercial fishing, mainly caught by otter trawl. The commercial catch of American plaice has seriously declined over recent decades, and this species is greatly overexploited. Like other flatfish, it undergoes a unique maturation from egg to adult in which the one eye migrates to the opposite side of the head.

Identification. The mouth of the American plaice is large and reaches below the rear edge of the eye. The lateral line is nearly straight, but the front part is slightly higher. The color on the eyed side is uniformly reddish to grayish brown, the edge of the dorsal and anal fins is whitish, and the blind side is white. It has a rounded rather than a forked tail, which helps distinguish it from the immature Atlantic halibut.

Size. The American plaice can grow to 32 inches and 14 pounds. Growth is rather slow; three-year-old fish are normally between 9 and 11 inches long and weigh less than one-third of a pound. After age 4, females grow faster than males.

Distribution. This species occurs along the northwest Atlantic continental shelf, from southern Labrador and western Greenland to Rhode Island, in relatively deep waters. It is now less abundant off Georges Bank, and greater commercial landings occur in the Gulf of Maine. In the eastern Atlantic, it occurs off eastern Greenland and from the English Channel to the coast of Murmansk.

Habitat. American plaice are commonly found between 300 and 600 feet over a soft bottom.

Spawning behavior. Sexual maturity begins between ages 2 and 3, but most individuals do not reach maturity until age 4. Spawning occurs in spring, generally from March through May.

Food. Invertebrates and small fish make up the plaice's diet.
See: Drift Fishing; Inshore Fishing; Plaice, European.

PLAICE, EUROPEAN *Pleuronectes platessa*.
Other names—plaice, fluke, hen fish; Dutch: *schol*; French: *carrelet, plie, plie d'Europe*; Icelandic: *scholle*; Italian: *passera, solla*; Norwegian: *gullflyndre, rødspette*; Spanish: *solla europa*; Swedish: *rödspätta, schol*.

The European plaice is a right-eyed member of the Pleuronectidae family of flatfish *(see)*, which has long been prominent in commercial and recreational fishing in the eastern Atlantic but has seriously declined over recent decades. Mainly caught by commercial trawlers, it has been an important market fish, and the most important flatfish in Europe. Like other flatfish, it undergoes a unique maturation from egg to adult in which one eye migrates to the opposite side of the head.

Identification. The lateral line is nearly straight, curving only near the pectoral fin. The color on the eyed side is uniformly reddish to grayish brown, with red spots on the body, and on the dorsal, anal, and caudal fins. The edge of the dorsal and anal fins is whitish, and the blind side is white. It is distinguished from the similar-appearing and larger-growing American plaice by its red spotting.

Size. The European plaice can grow to 30 inches and 10 pounds, although fish weighing 15 pounds have been reported.

Distribution. This species occurs in the northeast Atlantic, from Greenland and Norway south to Morocco; in Spain and France in the Mediterranean; and in the White Sea.

Habitat. European plaice range from tidal shallows out to depths of 650 feet over mixed bottoms. They move into shallower water in summer and into deeper water in winter. Small plaice are occasionally observed along beaches; older individuals seek deeper environs. Their preferred water

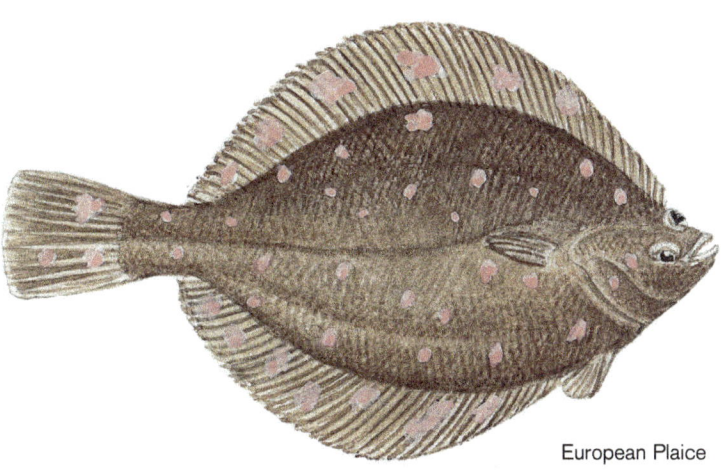

European Plaice

temperature is between 2° and 15°C.

Food. Their primary diet is mollusks, but plaice also consume worms.

Spawning behavior. Sexual maturity occurs between ages 2 and 3, but most individuals do not reach maturity until age 4. Spawning occurs in offshore environs from February through May.

Angling. *See: Drift Fishing; Inshore Fishing.*

PLANER BOARDS

Planer boards are devices that aid flatlining substantially and increase the versatility of trolling presentations. Planer boards can be used for all kinds of fish but are primarily used in freshwater for trout and salmon. Planer boards increase presentation capabilities by allowing lures to pass near fish that may be spooked by your boat or that are in areas where you can't, or don't want to, take your boat.

There are two versions of planer boards, sideplaners and in-line planers. A sideplaner is a plastic or wooden surface swimming board that evolved on the Great Lakes for trout and salmon trolling and works something like a downrigger on the surface. A nonfishing line or cable tethers the board to the boat and allows it to run at varied distances off to the side (there are port and starboard models that sport two or three runners). One or more fishing lines, using almost any type of tackle, attaches to the planer or tow line via release *(see)* clips; you fight a fish unencumbered when it strikes your lure and the release frees the fishing line.

There are commercially made sideplaner boards and retrieval devices, but many people make their own. Most sideplaners are about 30 inches long with double runners, but some homemade models are longer, up to 4 feet in length for some charter boat captains who deal with rough water.

An in-line planer is smaller but similar to a sideplaner. As the name suggests, an in-line planer attaches directly to your fishing line; a lure is set out the desired distance; then the fishing line is run through a snap at the rear of the board and also into a release clip at the towing point. The in-line planer is set out at whatever distance off the side of the boat you desire. When a fish strikes, the line pulls out of the release and the board slides down the line. The board can be rigged to stop ahead of the hooked fish by using a barrel swivel, bead, and leader. It can also be rigged to fall completely away from the fishing line, but then it will have to be retrieved from the water; few anglers use it this way. Because of the heavy towing strains, a stout rod and fairly strong line are necessary for in-line planer fishing.

Several types of in-line planers are commercially made. In-line planers should have a large snap at the back—on some the snap is positioned on the side at the rear, which may cause the planer to run awry. Many anglers change the connecting release on their in-line planers and wrap (or tape) their favorite release into place. If a release fails to let the line go when a fish strikes, you'll have to reel the planer up to your rod tip and then unfasten it, which is not a good move when you're trying to keep pressure on a fish. If it doesn't release, you can tell that a fish is on because the board will fail to pull out to the side, and the tow will be more toward the stern.

How far you set out the boards depends on how close to shore you want to be, how far apart you want to spread your lures, how much room you have to fish, and how much boat traffic there is; 80 to 100 feet out is standard when boat traffic is moderate. They can be run out as much as 200 feet if you have a high anchor point in your boat for the tow line. Some anglers use a 6- to 8-foot pole. In-line boards are run 30 to 100 feet out.

You can run a lure behind a planer board any length that seems feasible. Because lures are trolled well to the side of the boat behind a relatively unobtrusive planer, they often don't have to be run as far back as when a flatline alone is used. You still need a lot of line on your reel, though, because the fishing line extends first to the release clip on the planer board, then to the lure.

Lines fished off boards don't have to be run shallow, and they needn't be fished with only shallow running plugs or spoons. You can use whatever lures are appropriate for the conditions; moreover, by adjusting the tension of the line release, you can troll a hard pulling, deep diving plug or a line with weights on it. The keys to success are knowing how deep those lures run at the length of line you have them set behind the planer board tow line, and having the tension on the release set properly. The tension must be tight enough to withstand the force of the lure or the weight being trolled, but not so

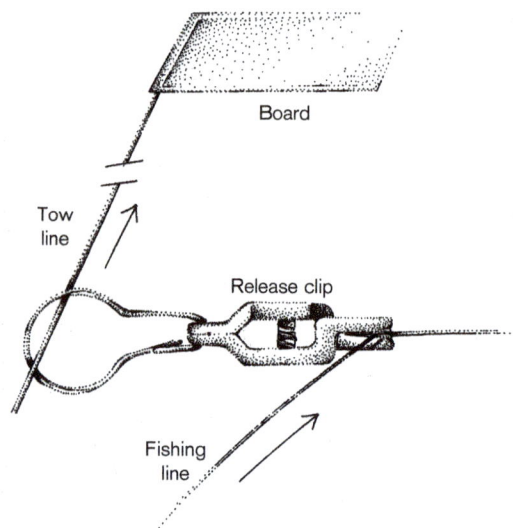

A release clip, which is attached to both the tow line and fishing line, is critical to using a planer board; fishing line can be placed deeper within the clip to increase tension.

tight that it is hard to pull out on a strike or free from the boat.

There are a number of releases suitable for sideplaner-board trolling, and they work much the same as downrigger releases, except that their position on the tow line is not fixed—it is determined by the length of fishing line let off the reel. Many anglers use spring tension, rubber-pad releases with large clips that fasten to the tow line easily and run down it smoothly.

One of the advantages of sideplaner-board fishing is that if you have multiple lines on one side of the boat and the outermost release pops, you can slide the inner lines out, then put the released line back out as the inside line. This is all accomplished without having to pull in fishing lines or the board. If you want to replace one lure without bringing the board and other lures in, you can pick up your fishing rod, reel up the stack, pop the fishing line out of the release, reel in the lure to be changed, reposition the other lines and releases on the tow rope, and set the new lure out in the inside position.

There are a few drawbacks to using sideplaners, though. They require a little more equipment and cash outlay than flatlining (though some trollers make their own sideplaners); it takes some practice to get used to them and to drive the boat properly; it can be tough to work everything if you're alone; and sometimes they pose logistical problems in heavy traffic. Planer-board fishing is most efficient with two or three people, all of whom are capable of setting lines and maneuvering the boat effectively as a team.

Retrievers. You must have a method of tethering sideplaners to your boat and retrieving them. Several companies make sideplaner retrievers with one or two reels mounted on a pole, and some people fashion their own, spooling it with 150- to 200-pound-test line and attaching it to a pole with a swiveling pulley at the top. Most sideplaner tow line is made of braided, low-stretch, highly visible green Dacron.

Ideally, the sideplaner retriever should be mounted as far forward in the boat as possible to get a high line angle to the board and to keep the boards relatively abreast, instead of behind, the boat. On small boats, mount the poles as close to the bow as you can. On large boats, such as those with cuddy cabins that don't allow you to get up to the bow quickly, it's best to mount sideplaner retrievers on the gunwales amidships, or flush to the cabin wall. Some big-boat trollers mount a retrieval pole on the bow, despite the difficulty of getting to it. They have plenty of releases, so they seldom have to pull in the boards, and they use a loose tether (wrap a line around a cleat, connect a snap to the line, and snap it onto the tow line) to reach the tow line to clip a new release and line onto it.

Fishing with planer boards. Sideplaners exert a lot of pull. They act much like a rudder, especially on small, lightweight boats—the pull of the board

Trolling tools include a planer-board retriever, large planer boards, and small in-line planers.

turns the boat toward the board. When using one double-runner board in a small boat, you'll constantly fight the steering to compensate for the drag. If you want to fish off only one board (when you're alone or want to get lures close to only one side, near shore, for example), it may be necessary to put a board out on the other side of the boat, without a fishing line, in order to offset the drag of the board being fished. With big boats, the effect of using one sideplaner isn't much of a problem. Some planers, incidentally, are available as triple-runner models; that is, three boards spaced about 10 or 12 inches apart but bolted together as one unit. Triple runners exert much more pull and are principally for use in rough water.

There will be times when you won't want to run either sideplaners or in-line planer boards because of the water conditions. In extremely rough water with high waves, boards do a lot of bouncing, which can knock the line out of the release if the tension isn't set tight enough, or they can flip over, which could cause a big problem by tangling lines and sending the board off in the opposite direction. In rough water, the releases also may foul by flopping over behind the tow line; when that happens, you can't pop the line out of the release properly, especially if light line is being used.

Under windy conditions, boards don't run as far off to the side of the boat as you might like; sideplaner releases may be hard to run down the tow line. When this happens, jiggle the fishing line or the tow line to bounce the release along, or turn the boat so that the angle of pull of the trailing line forces the release down to the proper spot. Strong wind also causes boat maneuvering problems when a good-sized fish is hooked.

If you catch a fish while heading downwind, you can, if you like, leave the motor in neutral and play the fish in. When heading upwind, however, you cannot stop the boat because of the possibility of tangling lines, tow ropes, and the like if the boat drifts backward. If the fish is really big or fights particularly well, or if you're using very light line, you should play it while a companion retrieves the other lines and the boards and maneuvers the boat for landing. If it's a small fish, you may be able to keep the boat headed into the wind, with the other tackle out, moving slowly with several stop-and-go actions executed by a partner. If you're alone, you must manage as best you can. Because they are attached to the fishing line, in-line planers don't pose this problem.

When using either type of board, a host of fishing combinations is possible. In nearshore areas, you can run two or three strategically spaced lines off the shoreward sideplaner. On the open water side of the boat, you have the option of running a surface or diving lure on a long flatline, running a lure deep via a downrigger, or running one or more lures off another sideplaner. Moreover, the range of water that can be covered is vastly increased. If you run two sideplaners, each 60 feet off the sides of the boat, and have two anglers in the boat, you could run four lines over a 40-yard span of water. If the bottom drops off sharply near shore, as it does in many inland lakes, you could work water a few feet deep on the nearshore side of the boat and over 40-foot depths on the opposite side, presenting lures to fish that would not ordinarily see them—and they won't be frightened by the passage of your boat.

When you're using sideplaners and fishing several shallow lines, you can experiment with their distance from the boat and with the distance the lures are set behind the tow line. Sometimes, when running two or three similar lures off one sideplaner, you may run them at approximately the same distance behind the tow rope to imitate a small school of baitfish. Be careful not to put short lines on the outside. If a fish strikes a short outside line, there's a chance it would cross over one or more of the longer inside lines after the hookup. Take this into account when setting lines out, and try to arrange them so that a fish caught on the outside line will drop back, clear of the inside lines, and can be played up the unfished center alley. Perhaps it's coincidence, but a high percentage of fish fall to the outside line.

Trolling strategies and boat maneuvering techniques when using boards are similar to those used for flatlining. When you turn, however, the outside board increases its speed and the inside one slows (or stalls). But because the fishing lines are well separated, there is less chance of tangling when you turn, particularly if all the lines are nearly the same distance behind the boat, or if the inside lines are not as far back as the outside lines. Be careful though not to turn so sharply that the inside board stops dead in the water and the lures attached to it don't move; if you're in shallow water and using a sinking plug or a spoon, the motionless lure can settle to the bottom and hang up. The release on the tow line can also get tangled when the board picks up speed. Furthermore, many fish strike a lure on a turn. If your lure is floating upward or fluttering down and a fish strikes it, there will be no tension on either the fishing line or tow rope line; the release cannot be snapped or the hook set, and you could potentially lose a fish. If you must make a sharp turn, make sure you keep the inside board moving slightly, which keeps tension on the line.

Boat maneuvering in heavy traffic when boards are being fished is a little more complicated than usual. That's why many big-boat trollers run flatlines off outriggers, and small-boaters shorten the distance they run their boards away from the boat. If your sideplaner hasn't yet collided with someone else's sideplaner, you've missed one of trolling's most embarrassing, aggravating, and mayhem-causing experiences. If a collision seems imminent, the worst thing you can do is turn the boat away because that causes the outside planer to speed up and arc outward, making a collision all the more probable. You might turn inward, but then you'll have to sit still until the other boat passes. The best tactic is to reel the board in toward your boat as quickly as you can.

Not all fish swim horizontally. A catfish indigenous to the Nile and other African rivers swims in the vertical posture. Many mid-water deep-sea fish swim or rest vertically.

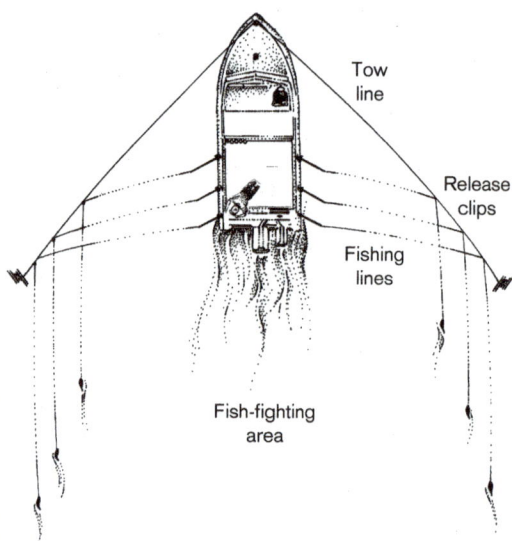

You may not fish this many lines, but this is how they would be arranged with sideplaners. Note that the setback distance is staggered on both sides. When a fish takes any lure, it is played in the middle ground behind the boat, and the other lines are moved outward along the tow line.

Those who find sideplaner boards too much trouble simply run flatlines. But when it is necessary to get your lures away from the boat, when you want to cover a wide spread of water with each passage of your boat, or when you troll some hard-to-reach places, boards will put your trolling lures over a lot of fish that you couldn't reach otherwise. **See: Flatlining.**

PLANER, DIVING

A diving planer is a trolling accessory that attaches to fishing line a few feet ahead of a lure and dives deeply. No weights are used with this device; the design of the planer and the forward motion of the boat make it dive. When a fish strikes, the back-pulling tension trips a release that causes the diver to flatten and offer minimal water resistance as the fish is played. Diving planers are an alternative to using downriggers, wire or lead-core lines, or weighted lines to troll deep.

There are two versions: nondirectional, which only run straight down, and directional, which can be run straight down as well as down and off to the left or the right of a straight path. Directional divers are more versatile and more popular.

Diving planers offer several benefits in addition to taking lures deep. Their size, color, and swimming motion make them attractive to trout and salmon. They offer an action that can't be attained by lures set behind downriggers: Because the lures are set a short distance behind the boat, they are less responsive than divers to boat movement (turns and wave effects, for example).

Because directional divers can take lures down and to the side of a boat, many anglers use them in conjunction with downrigger-set lines. Some fish in the path of the boat are spooked by downrigger weights and move down or away from them. Directional diving planers direct lures off to the side of other presentations. They help to cover more deep territory and, as a result, offer further presentation opportunities to shores, piers, and the like.

To determine the depth that a diver will run, consult the chart supplied by the manufacturer. Because divers run deep, you cannot estimate the amount of line let out; you must use the pull or pass method of line length determination *(see: flatlining)*. You have to let out a certain length of line to get to a specific depth. This varies with different diving planers and with the diameter of line being used.

Many diving planers have an adjustable tension screw release, and you need to set this just right for the strength of line you're using and the depth you'll fish. Diving planers pull awfully hard. If you want to retrieve one and the release won't trip (or, worse, if a small fish is on and the release won't trip), it's hard work bringing it in. There are a few planers that can be reset without retrieving the planer, although you still need to watch line length in order to get it to the desired depth.

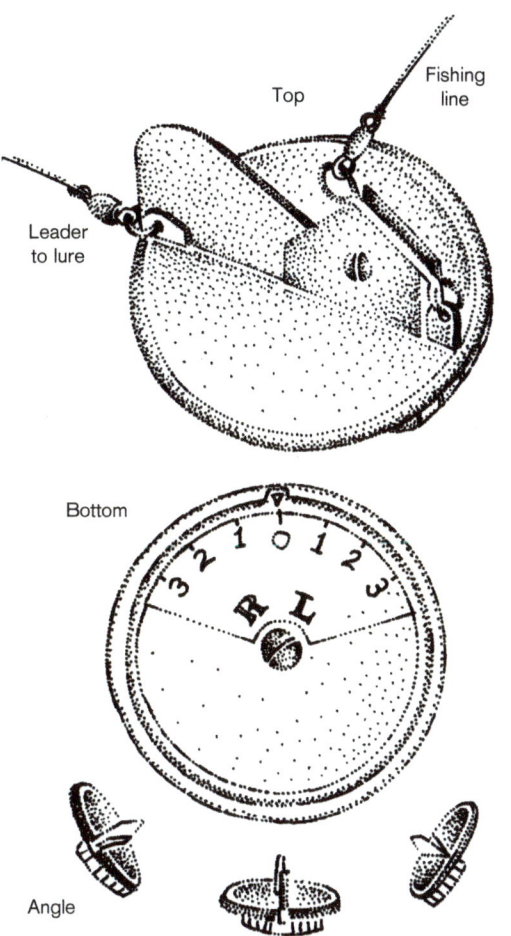

This representation of a directional diving planer shows how the line is attached to the device via a release pin, and how the keel on the bottom can be moved from right to left to affect swimming angle; the greater the adjustment, the more the planer swims to either side.

A variety of lures can be fished successfully behind a diving planer. Spoons and cut plugs are especially favored because these devices are used primarily for trout and salmon trolling. Minnow plugs of various sizes also get the nod, as do dodger-fly or dodger-squid combinations. Diving plugs aren't usually worked unless they are very shallow-runners and can withstand sometimes erratic planer action. It's best to use a short setback because of the difficulty of netting a fish that is 5 or so feet behind a diving planer; 3 to 5 feet is a common setback length. Leader strength should be as strong or stronger than the main fishing line, preferably 17 to 20 pounds if big fish are likely to be encountered, and perhaps 25 to 30 if a dodger is trolled.

The main fishing line should be strong, at least 14 pounds; most anglers use 20. High-tech braided lines can be very effective, but beware of pulling the hooks out of fish since these lines have no stretch and many strikes with diving planers are very sharp. Also, a 20-pound braided line with the same diameter as 8-pound monofilament slices through the water so easily you have to completely reevaluate diving depth attainment.

Long, stout rods are necessary for diving planer use. On big boats, beefy 9- to 10-footers are used, and on smaller ones, beefy 7- or 8-footers are worked. Because diving planers pull so hard, a good rod holder is necessary, preferably an adjustable one that can take a lot of handle torque and that is easy to get the rod out of. It's better to place diving planer rods on the gunwale, several feet ahead of the transom, and at a low angle.

One drawback to diving planer use is occasional uncertainty about the depth the planer (hence your lure) is running. Therefore, it's important to judge accurately how much line you've let out, especially if you catch fish and want to reset the rig at the same level.

Another criticism is that planers inhibit the fight of some fish. But the extent to which this is true depends on the fish. Large fish pull very hard, and some, including cohos and steelhead, jump. When fighting a fish, you'll know that the planer, even though it has tripped, is there; the fight is not quite as satisfactory as on an unencumbered line. A way to get around this is to use a diving planer like a downrigger—that is, attach a release clip to the diving planer, attach a handline or separate rod to the diving planer, and attach the fishing rod and line to the release clip. (Just about no one does this, but it is a way to fight a fish on a free line.)

In any event, diving planers can account for an extra fish or two during the course of a day's trolling when used as an adjunct to downrigger fishing. They merit consideration to round out your trolling repertoire, or for use in places where other systems are unavailable.
See: Trolling.

PLANER, IN-LINE
See: Planer Boards.

PLANING HULL
One of two broad categories of boat hulls that are noted for speed and quick steering response; speed is largely a function of engine power, but is enhanced by planing hulls because most of the hull, usually in some form of V shape, is raised out of the water while running.
See: Boat.

PLANKTON
Passively floating or weakly swimming organisms in a body of water. Planktonic organisms may drift and float freely, range widely in size, and include the larval stages of many fishes. Some are invisible without magnification and others are visible to the unaided eye.

PLASTIC WORM
A highly popular soft plastic lure that primarily imitates a worm, but may also imitate a snake, leech, or salamander.
See: Soft Worm.

PLATFORM
A raised section on a small boat used for increasing visibility when shallow-water fishing. A transom platform is most common, and some boats are equipped with smaller bow casting platforms; a few shallow-water guide boats possess a tall midship console platform that is more like a mini tower.

Transom platforms are a signature characteristic of flats boats, and are used for poling as well as sighting and/or fishing in inshore waters. They are raised several feet high, enough to cover an outboard motor when fully tilted, are usually 36 to 48 inches wide and 20 to 30 inches deep, and are bolted to the deck and transom. This platform is also useful for sitting and casting, and can be used in conjunction with a remote-controlled transom-mount electric motor. Some flats boats feature a bow casting platform that elevates the angler a shorter distance than the transom platform, and which can also double as a seat while playing a fish. It may be bolted to the deck or removable, like a wide stool.
See: Flats Boat; Tower.

PLAYING FISH
Once a fish has been attracted to your lure, bait, or fly, and before you can either release it or toss it on ice, you have to hook it, play it, and land it. For many species of gamefish, these activities are significant enough to warrant thorough separate discussions (see: hooksetting; landing fish).

When it comes to playing a fish, which is also commonly referred to as fighting it, the degree of work that is involved obviously varies from a second or two for the smallest species jerked out of shallow water, to many hours of muscle-aching, perspiration-inducing, and tackle-straining exertion for offshore leviathans. There is not much out of the ordinary involved in the playing of small or less powerful species, but those that strain fishing equipment—and that includes small but very strong fish caught on light tackle—require more than just holding the rod and winding the reel handle to catch.

This is an elementary part of angling, one taken for granted by many anglers in part because they rarely (especially in freshwater) experience difficult fish-playing situations and are unfortunately ill-prepared to handle them when such situations do occur. That partially explains why many large fish are lost after being hooked. Guides and charter boat mates and captains constantly have to teach their clients how to deal with large and strong fish.

There are certain techniques for manipulating the rod that help land fish without adversely affecting the tackle (such as causing twist in the line). These techniques help you to apply maximum pressure to a fish throughout the entire period of playing, keep the fish away from obstacles that might cut the line or tear out the hook, and land the fish as quickly as possible.

Why would you want to apply maximum pressure constantly and land a fish quickly? For a number of very important reasons other than the obvious one of simply wanting to catch the fish. First, there is no glory in having a hooked fish cut or break the line on obstacles and then be left swimming freely with a hook or hooks in its mouth. For some species of fish and in some circumstances, it is critical immediately after hooking them, or later during the fight, to use pressure and angle position to keep the fish away from any objects—reef, piling, vegetation, the bottom of the boat, etc.

In addition, a prolonged period of fish playing may result in losing the fish because the hook has worn a large hole in its mouth and then pulled out. Furthermore, in some saltwater environs, long battles attract large predators, primarily sharks, that will attack and kill a hooked fish. This may happen even during shorter fights, but it is more likely the longer the fight plays out.

Also, and sometimes most important, prolonged fish playing can exhaust a fish to the point that it cannot recover its strength and be released alive and well, whether you are releasing it by law or by choice. Lactic acid buildup *(see: catch-and-release)* can be fatal to fish, and this is increased during a long fight.

It should be noted that in some instances landing fish as quickly as possible is not advantageous to releasing the fish. This occurs for some very deep and generally bottom-dwelling fish in both freshwater and saltwater, which need a slower playing time so that they depressurize.

Methods. Fish-playing activities generally take place in a short period of time, and the action is often fast. Your reactions must be swift and instinctive, and your tackle, particularly line and reel drag, must be capable and of good quality. Many fish are lost as a result of the way in which the angler plays the fish, usually by allowing the fish to do things that it could be prevented from doing. Within the capabilities of your tackle, take the fight to the fish; don't sit back and be casual. Confidence in playing fish well and hard is derived from experience and also from knowing what your tackle can do.

Line breakage is often the reason for losing large fish, and much of this boils down to inferior-quality line, line that is damaged, or bad knots *(see: line)*.

In this sequence of a guide and angler landing a 9-pound bass in a Mexican lake, note how the angler strains to direct the active fish toward the netter and into the outstretched net; he keeps a tight line even as the fish nearly escapes while the guide is trying to get both hands on the handle.

Playing Fish

Another reason for losing fish is an improper reel drag setting. When the drag is set too tightly, line won't freely come off the spool under the surges of a strong fish *(see: drag)*. Granted, the drag is meant to put pressure on a fish that is streaming off, making it exert itself rather than swimming without impedance; but when the drag is too tight, it's a problem because tension increases as the diameter of the spool decreases and as the amount of line in the water increases.

Playing a fish begins with hooking it well and staying with its antics from the moment that the hooks gets stuck in its mouth. The position of the rod is very important. Right from the start, the rod butt should be jammed into the stomach or midchest area, and the full arc and power of the rod should be utilized. You cannot play and land a fish well if your rod is held up over your head or extended out and away from your body. These are not power, or control, positions. You do have to keep the tip up, however, throughout a normal fight and constantly maintain pressure on the fish. Slack line must always be avoided.

In a boat, you generally don't need to move once a fish is on the hook; but if the fish is a very large one, you will need to move to one corner of the stern so that the captain has a clear view of the line and the action in case it's necessary to move the boat quickly. If you are wading in a lake or river and hook a good fish, you should immediately and carefully step backward until you're in ankle-deep water or on the bank, where you can move quickly up or down a river if necessary. Do not be afraid to move, but do it carefully, not in a panic. Keep an eye on obstacles in the river so that you can work the fish in advance away from any obstruction (like a fallen tree along the bank), or be prepared to move swiftly to get your line safely beyond the obstacle.

"Pumping" is a technique that is used for playing all but the smallest fish, and it is critical when fighting a large or strong fish and/or when using light line. It is employed whenever a fish is deep and often when the fish is straight away and shallow but not budging or swimming to one side or the other. To pump, keep the rod butt in the stomach, lower the rod tip and reel in line simultaneously, and then pressure the fish as you bring the rod back up. Once the rod is up, lower it and reel. Continue doing this. Some fish and some tackle require constant short pumping motions, often called short stroking; this is more common when using stand-up tackle *(see)* for tuna and billfish. To best really tough bruisers, the pumping must continue unabated because on some fish, like tuna, if you stop to rest, the fish does too, and it can regain strength and prolong the battle when it rests.

Often when a fish is fairly close to you, it is still energetic. Continue to keep the rod tip high or fully taut when held to the side. This is a time to be directing the fish. If you're in a boat and the fish streaks toward it (perhaps to swim under it), you could be put at a disadvantage, particularly when using light tackle. You must reel as fast as possible to keep out slack. If the fish gets under the boat, stick the rod tip well into the water to keep the line away from objects.

You should anticipate that a fish will rush the boat and should be prepared to head it around the stern or bow (easier done in an uncluttered boat). Sometimes a companion can manipulate the boat to help swing the stern or bow away from a fish; this is a smart maneuver that can aid the playing of a large fish. If possible, go toward the bow or stern to better follow or control the fish. Walk around the whole boat if you have to (several times if necessary). Don't hang back in a tug-of-war with a large, strong fish; use finesse rather than muscle.

When a fish swims around your boat, keep the rod up (sometimes out, too) and apply pressure to force its head up and to steer it clear of the outboard or electric motor and the propellers. (Sometimes it's best to tilt motors out of the water.)

At times you need to change the angle of pull on a strong and stubborn fish, perhaps to help steer it in a particular direction or make it fight a little differently. For example, when a strong fish continues to bulldog straight away from you, slow it down and change its direction by applying side pressure. Bring the rod down and hold it parallel to the water while turning your body partially or entirely sideways to the fish. Fight the fish as you would if the rod were perpendicular to the water. Instead of the rod tip being high and bent, it is sideways and bent. You can pump fish while in this position. Switch sides as necessary when the fish moves far enough in any direction.

To deal with stubborn fish, change the angle of pull. When a fish is running straight away, change the rod from an overhead to a side position (1) and continue with this method until the fish changes attitude (2). To dissuade it from streaking to the side, switch rod position and apply pressure from the opposite direction (3).

The killing of a white man fishing on Attawompset Pond in Massachusetts by Indians led to King Philip's War in 1675 and helped advance European colonization in southern New England.

With very large fish that get near the boat but are still energetic, or with big fish that stay very deep below the boat and can't be budged, you may have to quickly move the boat a fair distance away, letting line peel off the drag. This changes the angle of pull on the fish and usually helps bring it up from the depths. This situation does not happen very much in freshwater but is more likely in saltwater.

Using a boat to play a very big fish is a standard practice in large bodies of water. Under some circumstances, it may be questionable from an ethical standpoint, though not from a practical one. Chasing a fish is sometimes necessary to prevent the reel from being de-spooled, or to avoid obstacles (lobster or crab pots, buoys, anchor lines, etc.), or to help a struggling and inexperienced angler. Many big fish in offshore waters are caught as much by the boat-handling and boat-maneuvering actions of the captain than by the angler. In some cases this includes backing down in reverse toward the fish, and in others it involves circling to redirect the angle of tension or head a fish away from a certain direction.

In current, a big fish that gets downriver and through rapids where an angler is unable to follow, may return upriver if the angler releases line from the reel and allows slack line to drift below the fish. The line below the fish acts as a pulling force from downstream (instead of ahead) and may cause the

Keeping the rod too high is not an effective way to control a strong fish when it is very close to the boat. To keep it clear of the boat and motors, reel down, dip the tip of the rod in the water if necessary, and steer the line clear of objects.

fish to head upstream again. If this strategy does not work, your chances of pulling the fish to you are slim, and you'll have to figure out a way to get below it or break it off. On the other hand, if you get below a fish before it gets to the end of a pool and into the rapids, and pull from the downstream angle, it is likely to want to head away from you and upriver, which is a better scenario.

With some species of jumping fish (Atlantic salmon and tarpon, for example), and when using flycasting tackle, you need to slacken the tension when the fish jumps by bowing the rod toward it so that the jumper cannot use taut line as leverage for pulling free of the hook. Sometimes you can stop a fish from jumping by putting your rod tip in the water and keeping a tight line, which changes the angle of pull and may stop a fish from clearing the surface.

A momentary slack line also may prevent a fish from jumping, although slack is an invitation for the hook to fall out. The only good reason to prevent a fish from jumping—and jumping is one of the thrills that anglers live for—is that you know the fish is poorly hooked and you fear that a jump will cause the fish to throw the hook. Otherwise, you should enjoy the jumps, because leaping out of the water takes considerable energy and helps tire the fish.

Final moments. Eventually the fish is next to you and may be ready for landing. If it still has a last burst of energy, however, this will be a crucial moment. Because of the short distance between you and the fish, there will be a lot of stress on your tackle. You must act swiftly when the fish makes its last bolt for freedom.

As it surges away, don't pressure it. This is no time for a standoff. Let it go. Point the rod at the fish at the critical moment so that there is no rod pressure, just pressure from the drag on the reel.

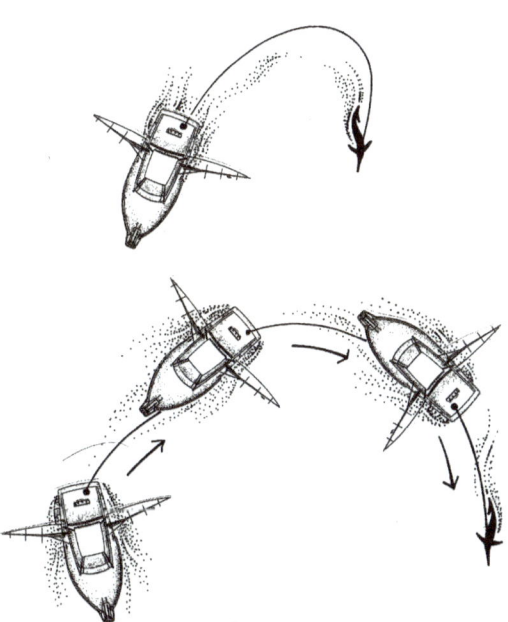

In this exaggerated view of a big-game fishing scene, hundreds of yards of line separate the angler and a turning fish, forming a belly in the line (top) that causes a great amount of drag tension, which in turn can lead to line breakage. When this belly forms, the boat needs to move in the direction of the line (bottom), not directly toward the fish, to remove the belly; this action also lets the angler quickly regain line on the reel and puts the line in a straight position with the fish.

A large fish will peel line off the drag, which if set properly (and not sticking), will keep tension on the fish within the tolerance of the line's strength and provide the least amount of pressure possible. As the surge tapers, lift up the rod and work the fish.

If a companion is landing the fish for you—by netting, gaffing, hand-landing, etc.—guide the fish toward that person, and try to get its head or snout out of the water, or partially so. If you and the lander work as a team and are proactive, your chances of a successful landing are much better than if you stand like a statue and wait for your companion to snare the fish.

Do not reel the fish right up to the rod tip; stop reeling at the point where the line is equal to the length of your rod, or slightly less in the case of a long rod (offshore fishing may differ, since you need only get the wire leader to the rod tip or within reaching distance of a crew member). In some instances, it is better to walk backward (on shore or in a boat) to bring the fish within landing range rather than to reel down and heft up more; however, in some large boats, this takes you away from the action, keeping you from seeing where the fish and the terminal end of the line are and preventing you from reacting appropriately if necessary. Even when the fish is initially captured, anticipate a landing miscue (it slips out of hand, falls out of the net, etc.); be prepared for the fish to bolt away by making sure that no line has been wrapped around your rod tip and that you're in position to give it line or to point the rod at it the instant it flees. This sudden dash happens from time to time with big strong fish and can spell disaster, since the fish is making a furious last sprint for freedom. To prepare for such an emergency, with baitcasting or conventional tackle, put the reel in freespool but keep your thumb on the spool; with spinning tackle, open the reel bail but keep your index finger on the spool; and with a lever drag reel, move the preset drag lever back from the running or full drag position to a lesser drag position, and keep your thumb on the spool. If the fish gets free, exert just enough contact on the spool with your thumb or finger to prevent an overrun when the fish stops; as soon as the fish stops or slows sufficiently, re-engage the drag or gears. Don't set the hook; just keep steady pressure on the fish and pump it back to the boat, whereupon it is often much more docile.

More information about the actual landing of fish is contained in that entry *(see: landing fish)*.
See: Hooksetting.

The deepest lake in the world is Lake Baikal in Siberia at 5,371 feet. The deepest in the United States is Crater Lake in Oregon at 1,932 feet.

PLIERS

Pliers are nearly indispensable tools for a host of applications in fishing and boating. A wide variety of pliers is used for such common and important purposes as cutting fishing line, heavy leaders, and wire; unhooking fish; pulling on knots; pinching lead weights or sinkers; crimping connector sleeves; and tightening bolts.

For the most part, the tool needs of freshwater anglers are different from those of saltwater anglers; the former predominantly use light nylon monofilament lines, and the latter are likely to cut heavier material, crimp hard objects, and grasp and unhook large and thick hooks. Freshwater anglers generally are well served with standard needle nose pliers, for example, which are very popular for unhooking fish and used in conjunction with nail clippers for cutting line and trimming fishing knots. Pliers with side cutters are also useful, and multipurpose utility pliers—those with knife blades, screwdriver blades, awl, and so on—are also favored by many people for general use, although they are generally not as well suited for heavy-duty uses, especially in saltwater applications, as specialty pliers.

From a fishing perspective, the major concerns with pliers are durability, ability to stay sharp, performance at cutting fishing line and wire, and ability to crimp objects such as sleeves and sinkers. Pliers with side-cutting blades are generally preferred for wire and most monofilaments except the lighter strengths; models with spring-loaded jaws, which keep them open when at rest, are favored by many users. Some pliers have replaceable cutting blades so that the worn-out cutting surface on an otherwise serviceable tool can be replaced. Anglers who regularly make up wire or nylon monofilament leaders and fishing rigs must have a top-quality pair of crimping pliers to do the proper job because crimping the retaining sleeves, not simply crushing them, is essential.

Most pliers come with sheaths that are worn on a belt so they are immediately handy; sheaths should keep pliers snug but be open for fast access. Taking care of pliers by cleaning them, rinsing with freshwater, and coating with a corrosion-inhibiting lubricant, is important to proper performance.
See: Leader.

PLUG

A plug is a relatively buoyant wooden or molded hard plastic lure with built-in swimming action, although due to diverse materials with different properties and a plethora of lure designs, there are many plugs that do not exactly fit this umbrella-like description. Most plugs float, but some sink and others combine floating and sinking characteristics. Most imitate or suggest some type of fish, although they may also imitate or suggest many other types of aquatic food. Though the vast majority are constructed from wood or hard plastic, many are fashioned from other materials, such as soft plastic or urethane foam, or a combination of materials.

Plugs exist in all sizes, shapes, colors, and performance functions, in straight as well as in jointed versions. There is some type of plug for virtually every freshwater gamefish of importance to anglers (although it is usually out of character for carp, sturgeon, whitefish, and catfish to strike a plug). There are also plugs that will catch many species of saltwater fish, although the usage of plugs in freshwater far outweighs that of saltwater.

The derivation of plugs dates to the late nineteenth century and the rising popularity of baitcasting tackle *(see)*. Lore has it that while waiting for a fishing friend, Michiganite James Heddon whittled a chunk, or plug, of wood into the shape of a fish and tossed it into the water. A bass struck the object, and the idea for "fishing plugs" was born *(see: antique fishing tackle)*.

Of course, Heddon did not create the first artificial fishing lure. Artificial flies had been in use since at least the fifteenth century, and metal lures had developed during the nineteenth century as fishing reels progressed. However, flies were too light to be cast with non-flycasting tackle, and metal lures were heavy and always sank, which was not desirable in many circumstances (like when the line on the reel backlashed). So the plug represented the first buoyant artificial lure that could be used with non-flycasting tackle, and which had its own built-in action. It has since become one of the foremost lure types, with certain types of plugs widely used in casting and trolling applications.

There are three categories of plugs: floating/diving, sinking, and surface. The first two are primarily fished under the water's surface, at various depths, with sinking plugs much less prominent than floating/diving plugs, which exist in countless forms. Both are reviewed in greater detail here. Surface plugs are perhaps the most popular category of plug in terms of preference, but generally the least regularly useful; they are detailed in a separate entry along with other types of lures that are exclusively fished on the water's surface *(see: surface lure)*.

Floating/Diving and Sinking Plugs

Characteristics. Floating/diving plugs sit on the surface of the water at rest and dive to various depths when retrieved or trolled. The extent to which they dive usually depends primarily upon the size and shape of their lip, and the location of the line-tie on the nose or lip of the plug; the lip and overall body shape determine the inherent swimming action.

Perhaps most popular among floating/diving plugs are minnow- or baitfish-shaped versions with small lips, which are designed to be fished very shallow, and which may double as surface lures. Other floating/diving plugs of intermediate size are more bulbous or elongated (referred to as crankbaits by many freshwater anglers). These are strictly meant for below-surface retrieving or trolling duties. Some of these models have small round weights, or BBs, inside that allow them to rattle when being retrieved and thus have a greater noise-making value. Their running depth may vary from 1 to 25 feet, and accordingly, they are classified as shallow, medium, or deep divers. The larger bodied plugs, which may be 6 to 9 inches long, are used for large species in freshwater and saltwater. These lures generally reach greater depths when trolled than when cast and are usually fished close to the bottom.

An exception to these basic types is a popular trolling plug for salmon in the Great Lakes and West Coast waters known as a cut-plug lure that weaves wildly and is predominantly used in conjunction with a downrigger. This is a floating/diving lure, but one that attains very little depth on its own.

Sinking plugs are simply plugs that do not float but are weighted to sink when they enter the water and will sink as far as the angler allows. These are

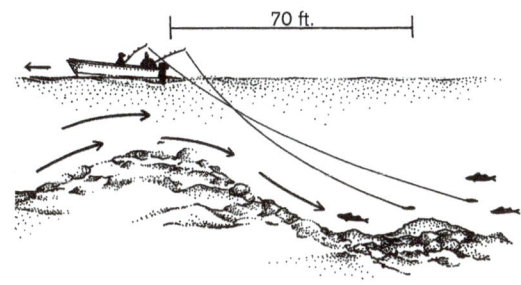

Backtrolling in rivers, as depicted here, is a good way to get plugs into deep holes and to control their exact placement.

often allowed to sink to a specific depth by counting roughly a foot of depth per second of descent (or whatever rate equals one second), and then are retrieved. These are primarily used in freshwater bass fishing and are also referred to as sonic vibrators. There are metal, plastic, and wood-bodied models. Some of these, as well as some floating/diving plugs, are specially balanced to have a neutral buoyancy, so they will not sink or float upward once they have achieved a running depth. This makes them appear to maintain a certain depth and be retrieved in a swim-stop motion like a natural baitfish. Pure sinking plugs are greatly outnumbered by floating/diving models, and are primarily fished in a similar manner once they are allowed to sink to the desired depth.

Regardless of whether they float at rest or sink, plugs that swim under the surface can be typecast as shallow, intermediate, or deep divers. Though most are between $2\frac{1}{2}$ and 5 inches long, their bodies range from under 1 inch to over 10 inches long. Weights are typically from $\frac{1}{4}$- to $\frac{1}{2}$-ounce, but some weigh several ounces and a few are under $\frac{1}{8}$-ounce. Longer and heavier versions are typically used in saltwater and for certain large freshwater species. Nearly all of these plugs are equipped with treble rather than single hooks, although some are equipped with single hooks by the manufacturer or can be changed by the user; the number of hooks varies, generally depending on the length and swimming action of the lure. Smaller models normally have two treble hooks; others have either two or three, usually the latter.

Most plugs are one-piece lures, but some have segmented bodies; the latter are called jointed plugs, which are more expensive to produce but

Assorted diving plugs fill the drawers of a tackle box.

have an appealing action. The most notable aspect of jointed lures is that they wiggle and shimmy wildly because they move with two or three segments rather than as a straight, one-piece body. The stimulating action of jointed plugs has not been lost on anglers since the early days of lure making. Apparently the first "jointed animated minnow" lure was made by the K&K Manufacturing Company of Toledo, Ohio, which received a patent for a double-jointed "artificial minnow fishing bait" in June 1907. Jointed plugs were very popular in the 1920s and 1930s, and were responsible for some significant world-record catches, including the all-tackle world-record largemouth bass in 1932, and an all-tackle world-record muskellunge in 1957.

The old jointed plugs were made of wood, often cedar. To some anglers, wooden jointed lures simply "work" better than modern plastic ones, but there are some jointed plastic plugs that are able fish catchers, including models used in muskie, salmon, steelhead, pike, and bass fishing. Some excellent jointed wooden lures, of course, are commercially manufactured today as well, in a variety of sizes. Whatever the material, in addition to having great swimming action, most jointed plugs dive as deep as, or deeper than, their nonjointed counterparts.

As previously mentioned, many of the small and midsize plugs are referred to as crankbaits, a term derived from the throw-it-and-reel-it-in nature of these lures. These more bulbous-shaped plugs are especially associated with bass fishing and widely used in walleye fishing, but are useful for a wide range of angling activity, particularly in freshwater. Most are easy to cast. A novice angler who has mastered the very basic casting motions will have no difficulty tossing out most intermediate-sized plugs, even under windy conditions, provided that the lure is not too light or too heavy for the rod, reel, and line being used. Because of their streamlined shape, crankbaits do not meet the air resistance that some other types of lures and other styles of plugs do, so they do not have a tendency to tumble in the air and will fly well even if a cast is poorly executed.

Fishing with plugs. As a group, floating/diving and sinking plugs have a fair degree of versatility. They can be trolled and cast depending on species or circumstances, but in general, they are used more for casting than trolling. Most are relatively easy to use, and fish often hook themselves on these lures, although it is still important for the angler to set the hook. These factors add up to an excellent hooking potential and arguably more fish caught per strike than with many other lures, as well as the likelihood (with the average plug) of catching good-sized fish (more fish of intermediate or large size than small fish).

Most plugs have clear plastic lips, which are presumably less visible to fish than metal or colored plastic ones. Many people have found little difference in fish catching ability among these different lipped baits, although there is an action difference between rectangularly fronted lures and ovally fronted lures.

It is the lip, of course, that generally controls the standard running depth of the lure and contributes greatly to its action. The larger the lip, the greater the running depth. The exception to this are lures that are not designed to float and that sink immediately to the bottom. These, too, may have smallish lips, but it is their weight, the amount of line out, and the method and speed of retrieval that determine their working depth.

Depending upon lip size, all floating/diving and sinking plugs can be classified as shallow, intermediate, or deep divers, and the style to use depends on the depth that you need to reach when casting or trolling.

When casting, it is not enough to just cast a plug anywhere, of course. Keeping in mind the depth of water you want to work, it is generally a good idea to retrieve fast in warm water and slow in cold water, and fast in clear water and slow in muddy water. Regardless of water color, it is a good technique to work sharp shoreline dropoffs by casting in close to shore and retrieving a deep-diving plug fast. Rocky shorelines are particularly good for this, especially in fishing for largemouth and smallmouth bass; often the strike comes after a few feet of retrieval.

If you're working the shoreline without results, you may be scratching only a short section of the bottom. Depending upon how sharp the dropoff is and whether you're casting into shore from your boat, the lure may not be reaching all of the bottom that it should and therefore not getting to the depth of water where the fish are holding. Try casting parallel instead of perpendicular to the shore and make sure that your plug is working the right depths.

Bottom scratching is critical in most fishing situations when casting with plugs. Try to keep your plug rooting along the bottom, over objects, and along impediments. This is no problem with

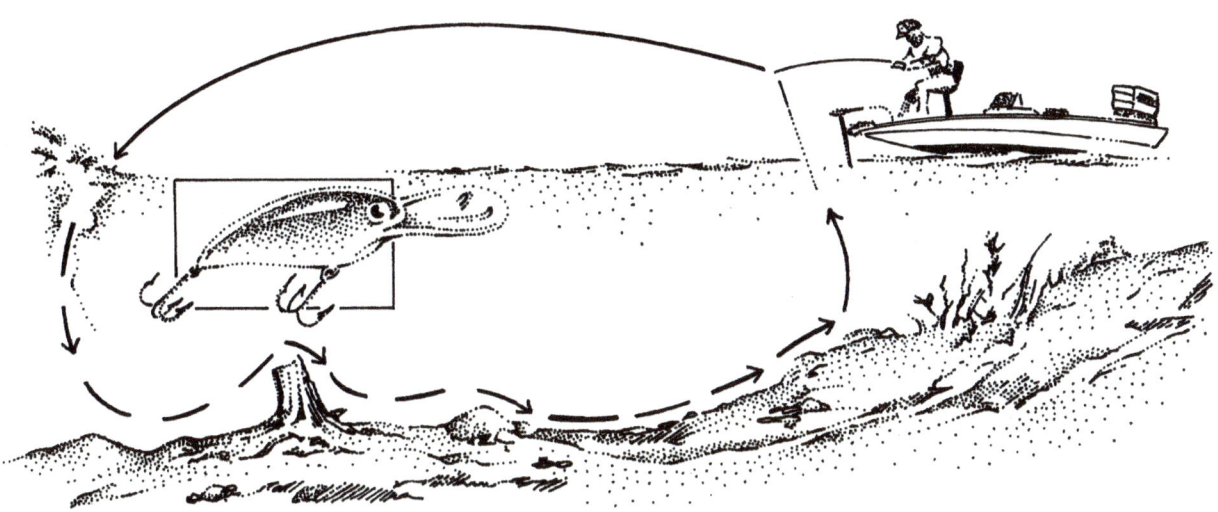

Although most plugs, especially diving versions, are fished along the shoreline, it can be worthwhile to cast deeper running versions (inset) away from shore. A bottom-scouring stop-and-go retrieve is often best.

the right floating/diving crankbait. For sinkers, let it settle to the bottom (or count it down to a particular level) and make your retrieve at a rate slow enough to keep the plug on or as close to the bottom as possible.

Many floating/diving plugs are exceedingly buoyant, a feature that adds a different dimension to their retrieval than to other lures. If you stop the retrieve, such plugs bob toward the surface like a cork. You can take advantage of this feature. A pull/pause action is easily accomplished by retrieving in the standard fashion and stopping momentarily, then repeating the procedure. In its most exaggerated form, this can be extended to stopping the retrieve long enough for the lure to float to the surface, and then resuming the retrieve. When fishing for bass, try making the lure hesitate by objects that might hold gamefish. This technique can be used repeatedly throughout the entire retrieve and might be the tactic to stir up otherwise unexcited fish.

The buoyancy of plugs varies from one product to another. Obviously, sinking models sink and floaters rise. How fast they rise or fall depends on their density in relation to the density of the water. Some plugs that rise quickly are not as beneficial to anglers as those that rise more slowly. At times, fish strike a plug only when a retrieve that produces a steady swimming action is interrupted momentarily, which lifts the lure up slightly.

A few plugs (usually smaller sizes) have little buoyancy or are neutral in buoyancy. These lures remain stationary in the water when stopped. Suspension has a lot of validity in fishing plugs, especially smaller crankbaits, which essentially represent small baitfish. Baitfish rarely rise or sink to a significant extent in their natural environment. When they stop, they stay at the same level, using their fins as stabilizers and relying on their internal organs to maintain their level. Making a lure stop and suspend at its running level has the most usefulness when fishing over some type of cover. A good example would be when working a crankbait over a submerged grassbed, which likely holds bass buried in the holes in the vegetation. These bass might hit a crankbait swimming briskly by. They probably won't be induced to strike a lure that is stopped but floats quickly back up to the surface. But a lure that is stopped and that hovers over the grass could be the most attractive offering of all. The same can be true when fishing over treetops or dropoffs. You can make plugs suspend or rise slowly by adding adhesive lead strips or dots to them.

Certain places are particularly well worked with plugs. In freshwater this includes rock walls and roadways, underwater islands, and other irregular features that the lures can reach. Sunken or exposed bridge abutments are worth working and so is flooded timber; in all cases fish to, from, over, and around these objects, and don't be concerned about bumping the lures against them.

The best way to fish a particular object with a plug is to cast beyond it so that when you retrieve, the lure will be able to get down to its running depth before it reaches the object. This is only possible, of course, when there is enough area behind the object to permit this. When casting to a long fallen log, for instance, cast beyond the target but position yourself to be able to retrieve your plug down the length of the log as closely as possible.

It is possible to work plugs around heavy cover, a tactic that can be successful if you can keep from getting hung up or enmeshed in weeds. Six or more wiggling, vibrating, exposed hook points do not make much of a weedless bait; however, for fallen trees, heavy weed growth, thick lily pads, etc., a specifically weedless lure can be used with more effect and less chance of being alarming. Occasionally a plug that gets hung up can be freed by giving slack to the line, allowing the lure to float free. Plugs will work well for the shore-based angler, too, if near-shore weed growth is not too great.

One critically important aspect of plug fishing

that is overlooked by many anglers, particularly beginners, is the diving ability of the lure. If bass, for example, are holding at 12 feet on a rocky bank and you're using a plug that you think dives that deep but in reality only reaches 8 feet, you can cast till your arms fall off and be unsuccessful. You must know how deep any diving plug runs to be effective with it. Diving abilities depend on the lure, the size of your line, and the speed of retrieve. Use the information supplied by the manufacturer with its product as a guideline, but don't rely on it. Find out for yourself how deep your lures run.

When retrieving, it is not necessary to crank the handles as fast as possible to achieve maximum depth. In fact, some lures lose depth when worked too fast. Crank the lure fast for a moment to get the plug down, then effect a moderate pace of retrieve; this keeps the lure as deep as it will go depending on your line. High-diameter lines offer more resistance and inhibit lure diving. The thinner the line, the deeper a diving plug will go. If you are flinging

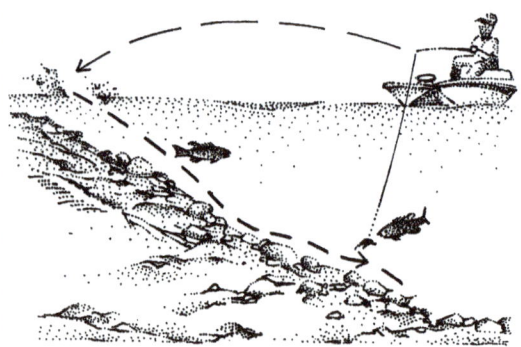

To fish a crankbait deep, you have to use the right plug, make a fairly long cast, keep your rod tip down, and reel at a moderate, steady pace.

long casts, this makes a difference. If you are trolling, with relatively long lines out, this is especially significant. Also, remember that current, if it is present, affects diving ability. Lures retrieved with the current, or sideways to it, do not run as deep as those worked into it.

Determining the diving depth of a plug can be simple if you fish it over known bottom terrain or around objects of a known depth. For example, find a flat that is 7 feet deep. Try a medium- or deep-diving plug; if it touches bottom you know it will go that deep. Move out a little deeper until you lose contact with the bottom to determine running depth at its maximum. If you're not hitting bottom, go shallower until you make contact.

There are, incidentally, lipless plugs that are not used as divers so much as swimming plugs. Many of these sink; some float. They are primarily used in bass fishing (sometimes for northern pike and redfish) and are excellent for catching schooling fish, for casting over submerged vegetation, and even for deep running using a count-down method to get sinking models near the bottom. In cooler water, these are often fished in a stop-and-go manner, retrieving a few feet and then pausing momentarily before retrieving again.

When fishing any kind of plug, it is usually a benefit to keep the rod tip down. This not only assists in hook setting and reacting to a strike but also allows the lure to run deeper. If the rod tip is close to the water, you'll gain an extra foot or two of depth over someone in the same boat with the same lure whose rod is angled toward the sky. Those extra few feet could make the difference in getting down where the fish are holding, which is especially relevant in dingy water. To attain the most depth possible when casting, you can kneel or sit down in the boat and lean over and stick the rod tip into the water. The longer your rod is and the farther you stick the tip into the water, the deeper the lure will go. It makes no sense to do this, however, if you can achieve the same thing by using a similar plug that dives deeper. On the other hand, you may find a situation where one particular size and color of plug is working and you have just one of these; then you may need to do whatever you can to get the lure down to the proper level.

Another key pointer for successful plug usage is how to present your lure and position your boat when working the shoreline or a weedline. The best way to cast to such areas is by working parallel, rather than perpendicular, to it. When two anglers are in the boat, it is a good tactic for both of them to fish from the front (as when casting from a bass boat), with each one's cast overlapping the other as the boat is maneuvered close and parallel to the area.

The vibration and noise of some plugs is another aspect worth considering. The best plugs have an enticing side-to-side action that does more than look good. It produces vibrations that are detectable to fish and that may signal not only the presence of potential forage, but a wounded, erratically swimming prey. Fish like bass strike some plugs they cannot see, such as in murky water or at night, because they've been able to detect them due to the water they displaced and the vibrations produced. The better the lure, the better its action and vibration qualities.

Some plugs also possess rattle chambers within their bodies. These lures feature one or more BB-like spheres, which are free to move back and forth in the chamber, creating a rattling sound. These can be especially effective near a riprap bank or rocky cliff shore.

Of course, the food eaten by predatory fish doesn't rattle; however, fish do produce vibrations, and some prey, such as crayfish, may very well produce audible noise as they crawl over rocks. Most important is that the rattle can draw the attention of a fish and make the lure more detectable under low light and turbid water conditions. Sometimes rattling plugs are more effective than nonrattlers, but many times there's no difference. However, it pays to realize what the advantages of rattling plugs are and when they can be useful.

The last major element of good plug usage is color. The color choice of a plug should relate to that of the major forage where you're fishing as well as to the color of the water and its visibility. Although many colors are available, the bestsellers for most manufacturers year in and year out are the silver, shad, and crayfish versions. These best resemble the predominant natural forage of most fish, especially bass. A full palette of lure colors is available, however, and there are good reasons for using some of the ones that do not conform to the norm. Chartreuse and neon red plugs, for example, are top colors for trout and salmon in some waters, purple has worked well as a plug color for many walleye anglers, and so forth. The issue of color in lures is addressed in more detail elsewhere *(see: lure)*. It pays to have a varied selection of plugs in your tackle box, not only in terms of color, but also body shapes and diving abilities, so you can handle whatever conditions you may encounter.

Two remaining aspects of crankbaits should be mentioned in this section. The first is that crankbaits must run true to be effective. They must run straight on the retrieve, not lie on their side or run off at an angle. Some lures do this fresh out of the box, and some don't. There are ways to "tune" your crankbaits and ways to make them run true. The fine-tuning of these and other lures is reviewed separately *(see: tuning lures)*. The second is the issue of when and how to replace treble hooks with single hooks, which sometimes has distinct fishing advantages.

Replacing Treble Hooks with Singles

Spoons are commonly used with single hooks, especially lightweight trolling versions. In the Great Lakes, many anglers replace the manufacturer supplied treble hook on a trolling spoon with a single hook, with no apparent loss in catch rate, in order to make the lure work better. Spinners can accommodate a single hook quite well, and all spinnerbaits, which are favored for bass and pike, are single-hooked. So are virtually all flies and nearly all jigs.

But these lures have different actions and are used in different ways than plugs. So, do anglers use treble hooks on plugs or other lures on the theory that more hooks equal more chances to catch a fish, or because treble hooks make lures work better by providing stability, affecting buoyancy, and enhancing swimming action? Both. Most anglers take out-of-the-box plug action for granted. The fact that plugs can accommodate two, three, or more treble hooks means to most anglers that they have extra chances to stick a fish, and a lot of them want, or feel they need, every chance they can get.

Yet there is good reason to use single instead of treble hooks on plugs with some species and in certain situations. Many plugs swim nearly or just as well with single hooks as they do with ordinary trebles. A few actually have enhanced swimming action and even enhanced hooking effectiveness. Some do not swim properly when modified—usually those that are more delicately balanced by design and which have poor tolerance for alteration. In general, diving plugs and swimming plugs that pull hard and show a lot of action are especially good lures for single-hook modification, and these are lure types that are especially prone to causing damage to fish.

Getting the right action, however, is largely determined by which size and style of single hook you use. You can replace manufacturer supplied trebles with out-of-the-box singles, but some lures (especially saltwater plugs) don't swim well enough that way, so you can cut two points off the existing treble (making a "cut-down single"). Cutting two hooks away from each treble at a point slightly past the middle of the bend, and therefore a tad closer to the shank, leaves enough of the treble's dynamic configuration to keep the plug swimming convincingly. The small part of each hook bend remaining perhaps acts as a micro "keel."

However, hook-cutting also slightly reduces the overall weight of the lure, which is sometimes critical and which affects action. So, while cutting two hooks off each manufacturer supplied treble is a quick way to produce a single-hooked plug in the field, using a treble two sizes larger than the original, with two hooks similarly removed, may be better. This obviously requires advance preparation,

A troller displays an assortment of plugs for catching walleye and lake trout.

but it eliminates the weight loss problem, and the larger gap of the remaining hook misses less strikes.

The alternative to using cut-down singles is a conventional single hook that is many sizes larger to get good action and also hooking efficiency. As a replacement, the Siwash, or so-called salmon hook, is an excellent choice. Siwash hooks have a short strong round bend with a long point. Most manufacturers make them with an open eye, so putting them on the split ring of a plug is easy, provided you have a pair of sturdy pliers to crimp the eye closed.

On a smaller lure in which two trebles are replaced by two singles, it may be necessary to place the hooks so they face in opposite directions to get the best action; for some lures, the direction makes no difference. But that raises the question: Do you replace all the trebles with singles?

Even without any other hook modification, some anglers remove the center treble hook from some plugs that come with three sets. When doing this, if the two remaining trebles are also replaced with hooks two sizes larger, the action of the lure is essentially unaffected. The hookup rate is higher, and hook tangling is far less of a problem.

Taking that one step further, you could remove all three trebles and replace the front and back sets with cut-down singles that are three sizes larger than the original trebles, or with the appropriate single hooks. You might be able to get good action and hooking effectiveness out of a plug with just one cut-down single (at the tail), but if not, try two cut-down singles, one at the tail and the other at the forward part of the lure.

Reducing a plug's multiple treble armament all the way down to one hook, a cut-down single or an out-of-the-box single, isn't always cut-and-dried. One clever way to do this is to remove both treble hooks from a deep diving plug and attach a single large short-shanked Siwash hook to the front hook eye via a split ring, with a small barrel swivel located between the split ring and the eye of the single hook. This creates a lure that, for some types of fishing, is more active than the original and even more effective.

This replacement approach seems to work best with shorter plugs, since the single on floater/divers and swimming plugs must usually be attached to the forward hook hanger. If the plug body extends much farther back than the bend of the single belly hook, the odds of missing strikes increase with that distance. One way to reduce that threat is to attach the single to the tail of the plug, and on the forward hanger use a treble three sizes larger than the original with all three hooks cut off at their bends.

Another advantage for using single-hooked plugs is that it increases their snagless and weedless abilities. Floating grass is always a great frustration when it comes to using surface plugs. For example, summertime fishing on the shallow flats for redfish is a great time for using a slowly slurping surface plug, but only if it's not loaded with vegetation. Getting the fish's attention is almost a guaranteed thing if you can keep the hooks from fouling on the overabundant turtle grass.

Going to one or two single hooks, either cut-down singles or out-of-the-box versions as appropriate for the specific plug, may solve the weed problem by using light wire or heavy monofilament line to make weedguards for them. As long as the attachment point for the line is placed so it doesn't create a sideways V to catch grass (right on the end of the "nose" is ideal), a plug with weedless single hooks swims and crawls through a hayfield without catching anything except fish.

Fishing surface, shallow-running, and diving plugs around and among brush and flooded timber is also very effective, but when it is important to cast accurately, and when the dirty water impedes your ability to see obstructions, treble-hooked plugs hang up frequently, and are difficult to reach by boat to unsnag. By using single hooks, with or without a guard, and by fishing with a deft touch to stop a lure when it strikes a limb and let it float up, you can effectively fish a plug in thick stuff.

This prompts the question: just as a single-hooked plug hooks less grass and brush, might it also hook less fish? Often the answer is no, although admittedly this is a subjective issue that is hard to quantify. Some hard-mouthed fish, such as tarpon and snook, are especially difficult to hook with plugs sporting single hooks. Some fiercely aggressive fish, like northern pike, are no problem at all.

Generally, as long as you can get the right action out of a plug with single hooks, you can catch fish well. As well as the same plug with treble hooks? Overall, probably not, but close enough. Obviously, you will not be able to catch fish that swipe at a lure and get foul-hooked by one out of six or nine hook points. On the other hand, you can fish single-hooked plugs in places that others with treble-hooked plugs can't, and you can release fish without injury to them and with far less chance of problems to yourself. Who is to say what those benefits are worth?

Not everyone wants to use single-hooked plugs. Tournament anglers, including many bass and walleye devotees, probably don't want to do so except in isolated instances, especially if they fish in open, unobstructed waters, and/or seldom use a net. Comparatively few other people fish for money, but that doesn't mean they aren't serious about *catching*. Nevertheless, anglers who've had very little problem with releasing fish that are caught on treble-hooked lures and are not hurt or bleeding, are likely reluctant to take a chance on losing fish, especially a trophy. Also, many people have gotten along well by unhooking treble-hooked fish with pliers and don't feel compelled to use single hooks, even for personal safety reasons.

Because replacing the treble hooks on plugs

The greatest distance for a cast ratified under International Casting Federation rules is 574 feet 2 inches in the Bait Distance Double-Handed 30-gram event.

with single hooks is not a common tactic yet and because you may need a specific type of hook, you'll probably have to do some searching to find the type and size of single hook or treble (to cut down) that you'll need. If you have a lot of lures, especially older ones that aren't in use, you may find suitable replacements among your supplies. Some well-stocked tackle shops may have the hooks that you need, especially in areas where trout and salmon are caught (for the Siwash hooks), and you should check mail-order tackle suppliers as well.

See: Antique Fishing Tackle; Catch-and-Release; Lure; Surface Lure.

PLUG CASTING

A term for casting and fishing with baitcasting tackle *(see)*, derived from its early-day use, which was primarily with plugs *(see)*.

PLUMBING

Determining the depth, usually with a plummet *(see)*, of the water when using a float *(see)*.

PLUMMET

A small weight clipped onto the fishing fine and lowered to the bottom to determine depth when fishing bait on a float *(see)*.

POCKET WATER

A boulder-strewn or large rock-studded section of river or stream composed of fast and slow current, in which the commotion downstream of one rock meets another rock and so on, creating small pools or eddies downstream of the rocks. The creases or edges of the currents along these places hold trout.
See: Finding Fish.

POD

A small, tight group of fish swimming together.
See: School.

POINT

A place where the land juts out in the water away from the shore and where the bottom terrain that is underwater continues to taper down and off. Some points are very obvious, some are subtle; some taper gradually and extend (almost like a bar) a long distance into the water body, although others end abruptly and drop off quickly.

Points are important features in lakes and reservoirs, in large tidal and nontidal rivers, and in saltwater along the shorelines of bays and along the coast. They are much more numerous in freshwater, especially in lakes and reservoirs, where bass, walleye, pike, muskellunge, and trout in the spring are reliably caught on or near points.

For certain species of fish, points are natural obstacles for travel and good places to eat. Baitfish congregate at points, a fact that means consistent and reliable feeding opportunity for other fish. In many places they are washed by current, which also presents feeding opportunities.

Not all points are the same. There are main points, secondary points in back bays, points with long gradual tapers, points with sudden dropoffs, points with little cover, points with plenty of cover, brushy points, rocky points, woody points, grassy points, sand-and-clay points, and long underwater points not obvious to the eye when scanning the shoreline.

No one place has every type of point, but at various times some are more attractive than others. In freshwater, points with some cover, for example, are usually better than those without cover. Yet some points that yield good fish have scant cover; many reservoir points, for example, are nearly bare unless someone has planted brushpiles. Proximity to cover or to deep water are factors that make some points stand out.

Fishing a point properly means knowing which parts to work, and how. Using sonar *(see)* is an important element of fishing a point from a boat because you need to define the underwater contour of the point and the depth variations so you can identify them properly. You also need to locate any submerged objects, such as stumps, boulders, stone walls, and the like, which are not obvious and which may be on or slightly off the point, since these can be particularly important objects on which to concentrate effort. Using sonar also helps to locate baitfish that may be present on a point, as well as predatory species themselves. If you can locate the latter with sonar, then you can spend more productive time on a point. This knowledge is especially important when you're fishing large, unfamiliar bodies of water; eliminating some points and narrowing the search on others can help you to establish patterns that work elsewhere.

Casting lures around points is a common technique that is useful for many fish, especially bass, but trolling is also highly effective, as is drifting. Trolling is a good way to get lures down to fish off points, especially when there is substantial wind or current to affect cast-and-retrieve presentations. It's one of the best ways to fish the edges of points, especially those that drop off sharply. When casting around points, essentially you can cast and retrieve across points, cast to the shallows and retrieve toward deep water, or cast from shallow water and retrieve your lure from deeper to shallower water. The last approach is the least practiced but worth remembering when times are tough and especially when using deep-diving plugs and surface lures.
See: Finding Fish.

 Julio T. Buel is credited with inventing the fishing spoon; he began the commercial manufacture of spoons in 1848, but had fished with his own invention since 1821.

POISON
See: Ciguatera; Diseases and Parasites; Pfiesteria.

POLE
(1) A misnomer usually applied to a fishing rod.

(2) A fishing implement unaccompanied by a reel or by rod components, and used for making quiet presentations, primarily of bait, to specific places, some of which are not readily accessible by casting. A pole is not used for casting and there is no running line; bait is swung or dropped gently into place and a fixed length of line is attached to the tip of the pole.

Most poles in North America are made of bamboo, and referred to as "cane poles," although they may be made of synthetic material (fiberglass and graphite) and also telescopic. North American poles are commonly 10 to 15 feet in length, mainly fished from shore or bank for panfish species, but often employed from a boat. In Europe and Asia, poles may be two to three times this length (some expensive specialty poles are 60 feet long), and almost exclusively used from the bank, primarily in coarse fishing; they are made of graphite and are light in weight despite their great length.

Hooked fish are retrieved by being jerked or lifted out of the water with shorter poles and heavy line, and are led to a landing net with long poles and light line.

See: Cane Pole; Coarse Fishing; Float; Rod, Fishing.

POLING
A method of propelling a boat silently in shallow water, common to angling on saltwater flats and some rivers.

See: Flats Boat; Flats Fishing; Pushpole.

POLLACK
A European member of the cod family, similar to pollock (see).

POLLOCK   *Pollachius virens.*
Other names—coalfish, Boston bluefish, green cod, blisterback, saithe, coley.

A member of the Gadidae family, the pollock is the most active of the various codfish and has been popular with anglers. It is an important commercial species, taken primarily by trawls and gillnets, and generally marketed fresh or as frozen fillets, although it is not as popular a market fish as its cousin the Atlantic cod *(see: cod, Atlantic).* It is not to be confused with another cod family member, the Alaska, or walleye, pollock *(Theragra calcogramma),* which is not an angler target but an important commercial species, particularly in the Bering, Okhotsk, and Japan Seas. A similar species sought by anglers is the European pollack *(Pollachius pollachius).*

Pollock

Identification. Pollock are olive green to greenish brown on top and yellowish gray on the sides and belly, with silvery overtones. They can be distinguished from other members of the cod family, such as the Atlantic cod, haddock *(see)*, and the tomcod *(see)*, by three features: The lower jaw of the pollock projects beyond the upper jaw, the tail is forked, and the lateral line is quite straight, not arching above the pectoral fins. Young pollock have codlike barbels on the chin, but these are small and usually disappear with age. The European pollack is distinguished from the pollock by its lateral line, which is decurved over the pectoral fins.

Size/Age. Pollock can grow to $3\frac{1}{2}$ feet, although most adults are much smaller. The average fish weighs between 4 and 15 pounds. The all-tackle record is 50 pounds. A slow-growing fish, the pollock reaches about 30 inches at age 9. They have been reported to live as long as 31 years, but few pollock live longer than 12 years.

Distribution. These fish inhabit waters on both sides of the Atlantic, from Greenland and Labrador to Virginia on the west side, and on the east, from Iceland to northern Spain, including the Bay of Biscay, the English Channel, and the western Baltic and North Seas.

Habitat. Generally a deep or midwater fish, the pollock prefers rocky bottoms in waters shallower than those the cod or haddock prefer. They occur in depths of up to 100 fathoms, although they are found as shallow as 4 fathoms.

Life history/Behavior. The spawning season for pollock is in late autumn and early winter. Their eggs are free-floating and drift on the surface, and for the first three months, larvae are present on or near the surface. Juveniles travel in large, tightly packed schools near the surface.

Food. Pollock feed in large schools on small herring, small cod and their relatives, and on sand eels and various tiny crustaceans.

Angling. A sporting fish, pollock make powerful runs and occasionally leap and shake, providing a good fight. Angling for this coldwater species occurs year-round, but activity peaks in late fall through early spring.

Most pollock fishing occurs in conjunction with cod fishing, typically on wrecks; those far offshore tend to produce better fishing and larger specimens. Ledges, rockpiles, and other structures also produce pollock, however, and these fish are not necessarily caught close to the bottom. Many are caught well off the bottom in the lower third or near the middle of the water column, making it worthwhile to fish baits or jigs through these areas, dropping them down and fishing up through the water column while drifting.

When baits like sand eels, squid, or herring are present, pollock are susceptible to jigging. Generally, successful jigs, baits, and rigs are similar to those used in cod fishing *(see: cod, Atlantic)*.

Skimmer clams are the primary natural baits, and diamond jigs the main lure. Jigs can also be fished with a soft-plastic lure or a small bucktail rigger on a dropper line about 18 inches above the bottom lure.

POLYETHYLENE (Line)
See: Line

POMPANO
Related to the jacks, pompano are a small group of tropical species that are members of the Carangidae family. They include such outstanding food fish as the Florida pompano and such highly coveted gamefish as the permit.

See: Jacks; Palometa; Pompano, African; Pompano, Florida.

POMPANO, AFRICAN *Alectis ciliaris*.
Other names—Cuban jack, Atlantic threadfin, pennantfish, threadfin mirrorfish, trevally; Afrikaans: *draadvin-spie lvis;* Arabic: *bambo, tailar;* French: *aile ronde, carangue, cordonnier;* Hawaiian: *papio, ulua;* Malay/Indonesian: *cermin, ebek, rambai landeh;* Portuguese: *xaréu africano;* Spanish: *caballa, chicuaca, elechudo, jurel de pluma, paja blanco, palometa, pampano, sol, zapatero.*

The African pompano is the largest and most widespread member of the Carangidae family of jacks and pompano, surrounded by a great deal of confusion because until recently adults and young were classified as entirely different species. A strong fighter and an excellent light-tackle gamefish, it is a superb food fish and is marketed fresh or salted/dried.

Identification. The most striking characteristic of the African pompano is the four to six elongated, threadlike filaments that extend from the front part of the second dorsal and anal fins. These filaments tend to disappear or erode as the fish grows, although in young fish the first two of these may initially be four times as long as the fish. The body shape of the African pompano changes as it grows; starting out short and deep, it becomes more elongated by the time the fish is 14 inches long, and the forehead becomes steeper and blunter. In both young and adult fish, the body is strongly compressed, and the rear half of the body is triangular.

The lateral line arches smoothly but steeply above the pectoral fins and has 24 to 38 relatively weak scutes in the straight portion and 120 to 140 scales. Shiny and silvery on the whole, larger fish may be light bluish green on the back; on all fish there may be dark blotches on the operculum on the top part of the caudal peduncle, as well as on the front part of the second dorsal and anal fins. Young African pompano have five to six ventral bars.

Size. This species is known to attain a length of 42 inches and a weight of 50 pounds, but it can grow to 60 pounds; the all-tackle world record is a 50-pound, 8-ounce Florida fish. Twenty- to 30-pounders are common in South Florida.

Distribution. Found worldwide in tropical seas, African pompano occur in the western Atlantic, from Massachusetts and Bermuda to Santos, Brazil, as well as throughout the Caribbean Sea and the Gulf of Mexico. In the eastern Atlantic, they occur from Senegal to the Congo, with some populations existing off the coast of South Africa. In the eastern Pacific, they range from Mexico to Peru. In the western Indian Ocean, they range from the Red Sea to Sri Lanka and south to South Africa. They are also reported around Fiji and Tuvalu.

Habitat. Inhabiting waters up to 300 feet deep, young fish prefer open seas and linger near the surface, whereas adults most often prefer to be near the bottom over rocky reefs and around wrecks. African pompano may form small, somewhat polarized schools, although they are usually solitary in the adult stage.

Food. African pompano feed on sedentary or slow-moving crustaceans, small crabs, and occasionally on small fish.

Angling. An excellent gamefish, African pompano are greatly appreciated for their hard fight, stamina, and beauty. Although they look and fight much like a permit, the similarities are superficial, as these fish are not observed on shallow flats like permit and are mainly caught over wrecks and reefs, and in many places incidentally by anglers trolling or baitfishing for grouper, snapper, kingfish, and sailfish. Wreck and reef fishing for these species became more prominent in South Florida in the 1990s, as anglers identified locations that had good populations of baitfish to attract this species. Since then, targeted efforts for African pompano have borne good results. Fish are caught deep on jigs and on baits, and when attracted to the surface by chumming, they are caught on cast hooked baits, or plugs or flies.

In addition to wrecks and reefs, these fish are attracted to humps, rockpiles, ledges, and irregular bottom structures that might hold baits.

Large bucktails (1 to 3 ounces are standard), are used to jig deep, and white is the preferred color. Subtle strikes usually follow when the jig falls during the jigging motion, but making a wide-sweeping jigging motion with a tight line is

Pompano, African

African Pompano

also productive. Specialists drift over the targeted areas, jigging above structure to attract the fish away from the confines of that structure, making it easier to play the fish once hooked. Slow trolling with deep-fished live baits may also be productive.

Prodigious amounts of live baits are used as chum to attract African pompano to the surface. Anglers offer live pilchards, menhaden, or herring, and often there's action for various other species before African pompano come around. When they do, however, they are caught on live hooked baits, or cast popping plugs, shallow swimming plugs, and streamer flies or fly-rod poppers.

Shallow-caught fish make a strong first run, followed by successive runs and boat circling. Spinning and casting tackle suitable for 8- to 20-pound lines are favored, and the drag must be in good shape and the rod capable of putting pressure on a fish to keep it in check.

See: Inshore Fishing; Jacks.

POMPANO, FLORIDA *Trachinotus carolinus.*
Other names—Portuguese: *pampo, pampo-verdadeiro;* Spanish: *palometa, pampano, pampano-amarillo.*

A member of the Carangidae family of jacks and pompanos, the Florida pompano is an excellent gamefish for its size and is an exciting catch on light tackle. It is also considered a gourmet food fish because of its delicately flavored and finely textured meat. It is netted commercially and bred in ponds, and it is among the highest-priced marine food fish per pound in the United States.

Identification. Mostly silvery when alive, the Florida pompano is one of the few fish that is more striking in color after death. It then has greenish gray or dark blue shading on the back, and a golden cast to the belly and fins. Deep- or dark-water fish tend to also have gold on the throat, pelvic, and anal fins; young fish tend to have a yellowish belly, anal fin, and tail. The Florida pompano has a deep, flattened body; a short, blunt snout with a small mouth; and a deeply forked tail. Unlike most jacks, it has no scutes on the caudal peduncle. The first and spinous dorsal fin is very low and usually hard to see, whereas the second dorsal fin has one spine and 22 to 27 soft dorsal rays. The anal fin, which begins slightly farther back on the body than the second dorsal fin, has three spines and 20 to 23 soft anal rays. The Florida pompano is similar to the permit *(see),* although the permit is deeper-bodied and tends to be a much larger fish, growing to 40 pounds.

Size/Age. The Florida pompano rarely grows larger than 6 pounds and 25 inches long, and usually weighs less than 3 pounds. The all-tackle world record is an 8-pound, 1-ounce fish taken in Florida in 1984. The Florida pompano has an estimated life span of three to four years.

Distribution. Occurring in the western Atlantic, the Florida pompano range from Massachusetts to Brazil and throughout the Gulf of Mexico, although they are absent from clear waters around the Bahamas and similar islands. They are most prominent from the Chesapeake Bay to Florida and west to Texas, and are abundant in the warm waters of Florida and the Caribbean.

Habitat. Inhabiting inshore and nearshore waters, adult Florida pompano occur along sandy beaches, including oyster bars, grassbeds, inlets, and often in the turbid water of brackish bays and estuaries. They usually prefer shallow water but may occur in water as deep as 130 feet. Young fish inhabit sandy, muddy, or open beaches. Florida pompano generally form small to large schools that travel close to the shore and migrate northward and southward along the Atlantic coast, staying in waters

Florida Pompano

with temperatures between 82° and 89°F; local activity is determined by the tide and by temperature.

Life history/Behavior. Reaching sexual maturity at the end of their first year, Florida pompano spawn offshore between March and September, with a peak of activity from April through June. Females are capable of laying hundreds of thousands of pelagic eggs, and larvae grow rapidly, attaining a length of about 8 inches by the end of the first year.

Food. Florida pompano feed on mollusks, crustaceans, and other invertebrates and small fish.

Angling. Anglers pursue Florida pompano while fishing from bridges, jetties, piers, the surf, and small boats. Fishing on the bottom with natural baits is a successful method, but some anglers cast and troll small artificial lures. Because these fish are sensitive to cold water, late summer and early fall are the best times to catch Florida pompano in their northern range; they are available in Florida waters from late spring through fall in normal years, and year-round during mild winters. Runs have been sporadic and rarely sustained in the past, but numbers and availability have improved with changes in commercial netting.

Terminal tackle favored by bait users consists of two or three No. 1 or 1/0 hooks tied on short dropper loops one above the other. Sand fleas, shrimp, clams, and small crabs are good baits. The best fishing conditions are early morning or late afternoon, on an incoming high tide with light to moderate surf and clear water. The baits should be allowed to rest on the bottom for a few minutes and then retrieved very slowly. Florida pompano hit the bait hard and fast, usually hooking themselves.

Anglers who fish bays, passes, and grassflats from boats are more likely to use small jigs on light spinning tackle. The time-honored pompano jig—a round leadhead equipped with a short bucktail body—is still extremely popular with casters, but also effective are jigs with different head shapes and soft-plastic bodies. Occasionally they may be tipped with pieces of shrimp or with sand fleas, although this tactic is mostly unnecessary unless the fish are skittish or not aggressive. Sizes range from $1/4$ ounce to 1 ounce depending on depth and current.

Jigs can be fished vertically over reefs and on the edges of deep-water flats. Sandbars, passes, clam beds, and other inshore structures, including grassflats, are also targeted, often while the boat drifts and the angler casts ahead, constantly twitching the jig to give it action. Deeper fishing requires a slower movement. Before and after a flood tide are often better times.

In some places, small jigs on light line can be blind-cast by anglers wade fishing in water that is too deep to see fish; the jig should be worked very slowly. Small pink or white soft-plastic grubs on a $1/8$-ounce leadhead will do, and may also catch small snapper and bonefish.

Like all jacks, these fish have a bulldoglike disposition and make repeated strong runs, rendering them a fine light-tackle species.

See: Inshore Fishing; Jack; Surf Fishing.

PONTOON BOAT

Essentially a platform on dual pontoons, these vessels used to be known only as general fair-weather cruise-and-party craft, but have been adapted for various fishing applications, primarily in freshwater. General use includes casting for largemouth bass, white bass, and stripers, or stillfishing for the same species plus crappie, catfish, and walleye. They are also used for trolling when outfitted with the right accessory equipment.

Pontoon boats range in length from 18 to 30 feet, and use long-shaft outboard motors as their primary propulsion. For fishing, they are also outfitted with an electric motor on a front deck (center position), an electric motor attached to the main outboard so it can be directed via the steering wheel, or a small-horsepower auxiliary outboard motor next to the main motor and also connected for steering purposes.

Most pontoons sport a canopy, which can impede casting unless it can be fully retracted. High railings can also be an impediment to landing fish, and models with low railings all-around are preferable for fishing. Manufacturers of pontoon boats have taken these and other matters into consideration in fishing packages that are offered with some of their pontoon boats; in deluxe versions, that includes being fully rigged with sonar, rod holders, livewell, and the like.

Pontoon boats are best suited to calm waters. Controlling them in the wind is difficult due to their boxlike structure, and they roll atop the waves. They can be trailered but keeping them in a boat dock or marina slip is preferable.

See: Boat.

POOL

(1) A section of any flowing waterway, usually deeper than other portions and without turbulence.

Because of its depth, and sometimes breadth, the water in a pool flows more slowly than in the shallower runs and riffles, and it is where many species of gamefish are found resting or feeding. Pools vary greatly, affected by the size of the waterway and the amount of current (which depends on season, rainfall, etc.). They have varying depth, width, and length. A pool may be the size of a bathtub or a bedroom in a creek; it may be 100 yards long in a medium-sized river; and it may be several miles long in a large river that has been dredged and channeled.

In large pools the depth may vary along the pool's length. In deep pools, the bottom of the pool may be darker and/or cooler than the upper portions. A typical pool becomes shallower at the tail end because sediments carried in the current sink and build up, although this condition may be altered and moved through ice gouging. The tail of a pool may move gradually into a run *(see)* and then into a shallow riffle *(see)*. At the head of a pool, the bottom often drops abruptly from a riffle, creating a clear change from one type of water to another.

These and other factors make a pool likely to hold desirable gamefish species (including trout, walleye, smallmouth bass, steelhead, salmon, and catfish), either for security, comfort, feeding, or all of these reasons. Depending on depth, current, species, and other factors, fish may locate at the head of the pool, at the tail of the pool, or in between; fish at or close to the head of the pool are likely to be active feeders, although this is a generality. The amount of current, the presence and location of cover in the pool (boulders, deadfall trees, etc.), the type and availability of forage, and the characteristics of individual species are factors that have a bearing on when and where fish will be located in a pool, and whether it is advantageous to fish on the surface, at midlevels, or along the bottom.

Objects that offer cover enhance the likelihood of fish presence, especially if they are in deep water; and the more cover that a pool has, especially at the head and upper third of the pool, the better it will probably be. These objects may deflect current, cause eddies, create defined current edges, provide current-free holding water, and bring food to fish, so they are important. And the best cover, or the cover most strategically located, is likely to have the biggest fish.

(2) The capacity of an impoundment.

A reservoir containing the maximum amount of water that it was designed to hold is said to be at "full pool." This level is measured at the height above sea level; thus, if full pool is 290 feet, and the surface of the reservoir is currently gauged at 283 feet above sea level, then it is said to be 7 feet below full pool. This is a common gauge of water levels in impoundments; water levels are often published in local newspapers. Sudden changes may be indicative of fishing conditions; swiftly dropping pool levels due to drawdowns for energy or irrigation needs, for example, may cause fish to locate deeper.

POPPER

(1) A hard- or solid-bodied artificial fly, also called a bug or popping bug.
See: Fly.

An angler plays a fish in a long pool on this Nova Scotian river.

(2) A wooden or plastic surface plug with a concave, scooped-out mouth, also known as a popping plug.
See: Surface Lure.

POPPING PLUG
See: Surface Lure.

POPPING ROD
A term for casting rods used with revolving spool reels in saltwater. If used in freshwater, these would be called baitcasting rods or even muskie rods, but in saltwater the application is with heavy lures, usually from $5/8$-ounce up to 2 ounces. These rods range from light saltwater versions (which is equivalent to medium-heavy freshwater), perhaps used for fishing with topwater plugs, to heavier rods used in deep jigging, even though casting is not involved in the latter.

Popping rods have medium- to short-length handles, depending on application, with the latter preferred by many inshore and shallow water casters. They are matched with revolving-spool reels, often with levelwind baitcasting versions, and frequently with models having wide spools and large capacity.
See: Rod, Fishing.

POPULATION
Fish of the same species inhabiting a specified area. This term is used more often with respect to freshwater species and is slightly different from a "stock" of fish, a term that is used more commonly with respect to saltwater species and in regard to a grouping of fish usually based on genetic relationship, geographic distribution, and movement patterns.
See: Fisheries Management.

PORGIES
The Sparidae family of porgies comprise roughly 112 species, and as a group they have worldwide distribution in the tropical and temperate waters of the Atlantic, Pacific, and Indian Oceans, although a few range into cooler waters.

Porgies are similar to grunts *(see)*, but their body is even more flattened from side to side, or compressed, and high through the area just in front of the dorsal fin. As in some grunts, the eyes are located high on the head and just behind the posterior margin of the mouth. The second, or soft, dorsal fin and the anal fin are both large and are about the same shape.

Porgies are medium-size to small. Some live close to shore, others in offshore waters. They are prevalent around reefs, but some are found only over sandy bottoms; others inhabit rocky bottoms. Most species can change their colors from solid to blotched or barred and from dark to light, effecting a better camouflage. They are omnivorous and typically travel in schools. Included in the group are a number of species that are harvested for food. Many also provide good, generally light-tackle, sport for anglers. They are relatively easy to catch and, for their size, put up a strong fight.

In the United States, porgies, like grunts, are predominantly an Atlantic species off the coast. The scup *(see)* averages less than 10 inches in length but is one of the most prominent members of this family. It is valued by both anglers and commercial fishermen along the northeastern and mid-Atlantic U.S. coast. The jolthead porgy *(see: porgy, jolthead)* is one of a large group of porgies found in warm waters of the Caribbean and off southern Florida, occasionally drifting with the Gulf Stream as far north as Bermuda. Distinctively shaped, it is the largest member of its genus.

Other porgy relatives that are common in their respective regions and encountered by anglers include the most popular sheepshead *(see)*, sea bream *(see: bream, sea)*, and pinfish *(see)*, as well as the squirefish *(see: snapper)* of Australia, the dentex *(see)* of Europe, and the black porgy (*Acanthopagrus schlegeli*) of Japan.

Angling. These slightly humpbacked fish are bottom dwellers and are caught on or within a foot or two of bottom. Most porgies are landed in relatively shallow water, often 10 to 30 feet deep. Larger fish are typically taken deeper, however, and some species are located in deep offshore water.

In bays or inlets, look for porgies over a sandy or hard bottom. They also inhabit shellfish beds and the edges of reefs. Most anglers fish a two-, and sometimes three-, hook bait rig, using sandworms, bloodworms, squid, clams, and grass shrimp as bait.

Porgies are notorious bait stealers; fishing a small piece of bait, usually just enough to cover the hook, is sufficient to curtail nibbling and bait loss. Chumming is sometimes helpful for increasing the catch.

As mentioned, porgies put up a good fight for their size and are respectable battlers on light tackle. When light sinkers are used, a light to medium spinning outfit, with 8- or 10-pound line provides good sport. When heavy weights are needed because of tide, current, or depth, a boat or bay rod may be required.

Porgies are sometimes quite plentiful and can be caught in good numbers. Other times the reverse is true. In northern environs they usually become available in spring, and fishing lasts through summer. Many porgies are caught by anglers fishing the bottom for some other species.
See: Inshore Fishing.

Jolthead Porgy

PORGY, JOLTHEAD *Calamus bajonado.*
Other names—porgy; Spanish: *pluma bajonado.*

A member of the Sparidae family, which includes about 112 species, the jolthead is an excellent food fish with some commercial value, and a species that bottom-probing anglers often encounter along the eastern United States; it has been associated with ciguatera *(see),* however. The common name presumably comes from the fish's habit of using its head to bump or jolt clams or other mollusks loose from their attachments.

Identification. The high, rounded forehead gives the body a distinctive profile, typical of the genus. It eyes are large and are located high on the head. Yellowish brown, with an almost metallic luster, it may be blotched with dusky splotches or nearly solid in color, depending on the bottom over which it is swimming. Some individuals are grayish. Over each eye is a blue streak, and sometimes there are faint blue lengthwise stripes on the body. The caudal fin is lunate (crescent-shaped).

Size. Among the largest of the porgies, this species is typically 20 inches long, but it can attain a length of 26 inches and a weight of 23 pounds. The all-tackle world record is a 23-pound, 4-ounce specimen.

Distribution. The jolthead porgy occurs in the western Atlantic, from Rhode Island to the northern Gulf of Mexico, including Bermuda, and south to Brazil. It is most abundant in the West Indies.

Habitat. The jolthead occurs in coastal environs over vegetated sand bottoms and more frequently on coral bottoms between 6 and 45 meters deep. Large adults are usually solitary.

Food and feeding behavior. The diet of jolthead porgies is sea urchins, crabs, and mollusks. Small schools are often seen feeding near shore.

Angling. Joltheads are not a prime angling target, but anglers fishing for various bottom and reef dwellers sometimes catch them incidentally. They are primarily caught on baits.

See: Inshore Fishing; Porgies.

PORK RIND
A strip or chunk of pork attached to a weedless spoon or jig.
See: Jig; Spoon.

PORT
(1) The left side of a boat facing the bow.

(2) A harbor, especially one with dockage, maintenance, and launching facilities.

PORTUGAL
Spanning 91,905 square kilometers, including the Azores and Madeira, Portugal is roughly the size of Indiana in the United States and twice that of Switzerland. The westernmost country in continental Europe, it is bounded by Spain on the north and east and by the Atlantic Ocean on the south and west. Its capital city, Lisbon, has been the gateway to the Atlantic for navigators and explorers for centuries.

Portugal's primary stake to sportfishing fame, especially for visiting anglers, is not on the mainland but out in the Atlantic at Madeira and the Azores. It does offer sportfishing for local anglers along the coast and in the interior, however.

The Mainland
In freshwater, trout are the primary game species in the cooler reaches of the hundreds of miles of rivers that exist in Portugal (and are also present on Madeira). Barbel and carp are also prominent in nearly all rivers and streams. The major rivers in the mountainous northern region include the Minho, Mouro, Castro Laboreiro, and Douro; in the central region, they include the Mondego, Zezere, Alva Nabao, and Avelar.

Perch are here as well, especially in the southern part of the country; shad run up the coastal rivers from early February into July; and largemouth bass are also present. The introduced bass, known as *achigã,* have flourished, and are present in a number of waters, including Maranhão Reservoir, Vale de Gaio Reservoir, the Sado River, and the Beja and Algarve Dams, which are impoundments in the southeast on the Guadiana River.

Along the 625 miles of coast, Portuguese anglers fish for the likes of tuna, blue shark, tope, conger and moray eels, grouper, pollock, European bass, plaice, mackerel, garfish, bream, ray, and other species. The northern region generally favors colder-water species, with the area between Moledo in the far north and Oporto having the most opportunities. A number of rivers empty into the Atlantic here. Fishing ports include Esposende, Ofir, Póvoa de Varzim, Vilado Conde, Espinho, Figueira da Foz, and Nazaré.

South of this region, from Peniche on through

the Algarve region, the coast becomes rockier and broken by scattered sand beaches, and the ports offer more temperate-water fishing with big-game possibilities. Fewer rivers enter here. Fishing ports include Peniche (for the Berlenga Islands), Ericeira, Sesimbra, Sines Sagres, Lagos, Paraia da Rocha, Albufeira, Faro, and Monte Gordo.

Madeira Islands

Lying 1,000 kilometers southwest of Lisbon and 800 kilometers from the African coast, Madeira is a volcanic archipelago of four islands with a temperate year-round climate and great positioning in the North Atlantic Ocean for intercepting pelagic big-game species, especially huge blue marlin. The archipelago consists of two inhabited islands, Madeira and Porto Santo, and two uninhabited groups, the Desertas and the Selvagens, which are respectively 11 and 156 nautical miles south of Madeira.

Until the late 1980s, the Madeiras were known more for their wine production, tropical beauty, and place in early trading history than for their fisheries, even though big marlin had been taken from nearby waters. Throughout that decade, most available boats and equipment were geared toward casual tourists and inshore fishing that focused on barracuda, sharks, bonito, mackerel, and some tuna. Even today, only a handful of modern top-rate sportfishing operators exist, and facilities for visiting boaters are extremely limited. The chances of reaching the marlin grounds are not good unless one makes arrangements very far in advance.

The operators who do exist are busy during the marlin season (July through September) because the blues here have been fairly mind boggling. Some top marlin experts call this the best marlin fishery in the world. As long ago as 1980, a near-grander was caught here on rod and reel, and sporadic reports throughout the 1980s filtered out about blues weighing between 550 and 800 pounds. In the late 1980s, a 1,200-pound Atlantic blue was caught by a French angler, and bigger fish were reportedly registered by commercial fishermen, including a 1,320-pounder in 1986 and a 1,540-pounder in 1985.

Throughout the 1990s, with intensified and expert angling efforts targeting blue marlin, the catches have skyrocketed. Two developments have become apparent: a very large average size (500 pounds according to some, even higher according to others), and many fish close to or exceeding the 1,000-pound mark. Where many billfish sites talk about the potential for granders, or the two or three that have been caught over the years, this area produces many such fish in a season, and, in at least one reported instance, produced two blues exceeding 1,000 pounds in a single day. Most of the marlin are released, and most of the few that are kept are those that died during the fight. Of the released fish, some were estimated at weights between 1,100

A large bigeye tuna is boated off Madeira.

and 1,200 pounds. Just as remarkably, these monster blue marlin are almost all caught on trolled lures, the seas are calm during the billfish season, and the run to the fishing grounds is just 10 miles from the islands.

Fishing is centered out of Funchal on the island of Madeira and commences for blue marlin sometime in late June or early July, tapering at the end of September and early October. In addition to blue marlin, these waters have an abundance of bigeye tuna (some of which are large, including two current world records), plus large bluefin tuna, mako sharks, blue sharks, and hammerhead sharks. Some swordfish have also been caught, as have a fair number of spearfish. The Madeiras hold world records for spearfish, including the a 90-pound, 13-ounce fish that is the 50-pound-line-class and all-tackle record holder. The tuna fishing is reportedly best from January through April, and shark action is good from September through November.

Formed from volcanic action, the Madeiras have extremely deep water near their clifflike shores (the world's second highest cliff is here by Cabo Girao). It can be argued that the sportfishing potential here is as limitless as the depths, and the balmy climate is one that everyone finds endearing.

Azore Islands

The Azores are a group of volcanic islands due west of Portugal in the North Atlantic. Separated from Europe by almost a thousand miles, and from North America by 1,600 miles, they are volcanic mountains, rising from great ocean depths along the Mid-Atlantic Ridge. Fittingly, their shorelines are craggy and steep, but within a few miles of shore the ocean depths plunge to more than 2,000 feet.

The Azores, which are spread over more than 350 miles, are divided into three groups: the eastern group consists of São Miguel and Santa Maria; the central group consists of Faial, Pico, São Jorge, Terceira, and Graciosa; and the northwestern group includes Flores and Corvo. Sportfishing occurs out of Faial, Terceira, and São Miguel, but the bulk of the effort originates on Faial, where there is a fishing center at Horta, the island's capital. A handful of charter boats operate here, plying four significant offshore banks that lie between 10 and 45 nautical miles from port. Fishing conditions are usually good throughout the summer but are rough in winter and spring. A second fishing center is situated in Ponta Delgada, the capital of São Miguel, and big-game fishing occurs at three offshore banks situated between 12 and 25 nautical miles from port.

Much effort has been concentrated on Condora Bank off Faial. Because the bank is located along the Mid-Atlantic Ridge, the water drops off steeply fairly close to shore, and into the abyss a few miles away. When a big marlin or tuna wants to go deep here, you need more than muscle; you need a reel with loads of line capacity.

There are only a few more boats fishing these waters than in the Madeiras. Another impediment is the often heavy seas created by blustery days that make big-game trolling unfeasible. Nevertheless, the Azores have come into their own as outstanding marlin grounds. Expanded fishing efforts here since the mid-1980s have proven that there are many blue and white marlin to be caught. The blues are very big, and the whites average 80 pounds. The average weight of the Atlantic blues caught in the Azores far exceeds the average in most other—and much better known—areas. These fish weigh in at 500 pounds or better, as in the Madeiras. And the stories of granders and much bigger fish being seen and lost are not mere stories.

In the mid-1980s, the first reports of these fish were mind boggling. Commercial fishermen were said to be spotting groups of marlin. One account had it that Azorean harpooners had snared a 1,144-pound blue marlin and a 1,188-pounder. Anglers related losing monster blues, one estimated at 1,500 pounds.

In August of 1988, an angler came just shy of catching the first grander in the Azores, taking a 980-pound blue on 130-pound line and establishing a European line-class record. A published report then noted that in 10 days of angling, 15 blues with an average weight of 600 pounds were caught, including an astounding double of 650 and 500 pounds. Then, that September, a 1,146-pound blue was caught to establish a new world record on 50-pound line. Since then, more boats have joined the action, and the records have tumbled, with six line-class world records being currently taken from the Azores, the largest a 1,189-pounder captured in 1993. Scores of 1,000-pound fish have been caught, many of which were released, and one boat accomplished the extraordinary feat of catching three such fish in a single day.

One reason why the marlin are here is because the volcanic and high-rising Azores benefit climatologically from a branch of the Gulf Stream, the North Atlantic Current, which protects against extreme warmth or cold on the islands and provides plenty of forage opportunity. When the nutrient-rich water is warm enough, in the 75°F range, marlin abound. The period from May through December produces blue marlin, but July through September is best.

Other billfish that show up in these waters include white marlin, swordfish, and long-billed spearfish. Spearfish are still a bit of a mystery creature, as few have been caught worldwide, yet quite a few have been boated in the Azores. White marlin appear frequently, arriving generally before the blue marlin, but are available from May into October. At times, they are more likely to be caught by anglers trolling for tuna than by blue marlin enthusiasts, as the whites prefer more diminutive offerings that move at a slower speed. Nevertheless, offshore prospecting with lures or baits that will attract either whites or blues is the best option. Broadbill fishing is still lightly explored, although swordfish weighing up to 350 pounds have been caught here.

The Azores can offer sensational fishing for tuna. The primary target is the yellowfin, and it is not uncommon to run across these fish by the acre. Many very big yellowfins, in the 200- to 300-pound class, are caught here, particularly between July and October. Bluefin tuna are also found in the Azores, although not in the same abundance as yellowfins. Some giants have been caught, including a 974-pound 80-pound-line-class women's world record in October of 1996. But bigeye tuna are here in great quantity and in large sizes, beginning in April, and there is excellent action for these fish into June, especially off of Ponta Delgada. This is when yellowfin action picks up. Yellowfin and bluefin action heats up again in September and October, although these fish are overshadowed by the billfish at that time.

In addition to all of this, big mako sharks also frequent Azorean waters. Some 500-pounders have been trolled up unexpectedly, providing great excitement to anglers pursuing other species. Blue sharks, threshers, and several others are here as well, and such species as dolphin, skipjack tuna, and bonito are also in the mix. Inshore fishing can produce barracuda, amberjack, grouper, bluefish (several world records have been established in the Azores), and a slew of bottom species. Certainly these aren't the target of expeditions to the Azores,

> Fish do not chew their food; they would suffocate if they tried to chew, which would interfere with the passage of water over the gills, necessary for obtaining oxygen.

but by bringing some extra gear along, on a blustery day you can get into a leeward shore and still keep the lines wet and stretched.

POSSESSION LIMIT

A restriction on the total number of fish of a species or group of species that may be legally possessed by one person. In the field, the possession limit is usually the same as the daily bag or creel limit, which means that an angler may not take in a single day more than a daily creel limit. In some places, it is legal to have in possession a number exceeding a daily creel limit, for example, when the catch is stored at home in a freezer. Usually a possession limit is twice the daily creel limit, although in certain places it is more liberal than that. However, in other places the possession limit and daily creel limit at all times are the same no matter where the fish are stored.

A possession limit is a legal game regulation established by the fisheries agency with jurisdiction over the location being fished, and enforced by fish and wildlife conservation officers. Possession limits vary widely, and anglers who will be keeping fish must know the regulations that apply to both daily creel and possession limits wherever they are fishing.

See: Creel Limit; Fisheries Management; Regulations.

POTAMADROMOUS

Fish that migrate within rivers or streams to spawn.
See: Anadromous.

POUT, HORNED

A regional name (primarily in New England) for black or brown bullhead (see: bullhead, black; bullhead, brown).

POWER

The amount of pressure that it takes to flex a fishing rod.
See: Rod, Fishing.

PRACTICE PLUG

A hookless, cylindrical, plastic- or rubber-coated weight used for practice casting with spinning, spincasting, and baitcasting tackle.
See: Casting.

PREDATOR

A species that feeds on other species. Most of the fish species that are pursued by anglers are predators at or near the top of the food chain.

PRESENTATION

The act of delivering a bait, lure, or fly to a fish is an intrinsic element of every type of angling, whether casting, trolling, stillfishing, drift fishing, or jigging. Even though the term "presentation" is the one most often used with respect to casting, and especially fly fishing (as in upstream presentation, or upstream fishing), presentation is all about how objects are delivered and manipulated. Although many astute anglers are fastidious about presentation, many more are haphazard about it, even though they pay a lot of attention to lure or fly selection, to specific places to fish, and to the act of locating fish.

Good presentation begins with such obvious skills as accurate casting, using a bit of stealth, minimizing noise, and not coming right up on, over, or through areas to be fished. Stream trout anglers are among the craftiest of all people in approaching their quarry. This craftiness is largely due to the fact that stream trout, which are often found in clear and relatively shallow water, are respected for their wariness. So, anglers approach them carefully in very particular ways and try to offer flies or lures as naturally and unobtrusively as possible. Other species, especially inhabitants of stillwaters and of turbid or more cover-laden environments, do not typically enjoy the "crafty" reputation, and anglers tend to be less refined about the deliverance of their offerings, which may be a mistake.

Good presentations are aided by getting within proper casting range to make accurate casts and timely retrievals. For example, as a rule, the farther you are from specific objects that may shelter fish, the harder it is to make a really precise presentation with certain lures. If you can get close without spooking the fish, you can make a greater number of presentations in a given time period than if you were farther away, and you can be more thorough. On the other hand, if you cannot get close enough without spooking the fish, then you have to be able not only to make long, accurate casts, but to position yourself to make each one count.

In many cases, the first cast to a prospective fish lie is the most important one, so getting yourself in the best possible position is especially important. However, repetitive casting to the same spot sometimes proves more effective, but a lot of anglers who cast from boats are in too much of a hurry to do this. Making repeated presentations to cover, for example, is not something that many bass anglers, who tend to run-and-gun from one likely piece of cover to the next, do often enough. Sometimes it pays to be more like steelhead, salmon, or trout anglers, who routinely make many presentations through the same river lie before connecting with a fish. And they make exactly the same presentation drift after drift after drift, knowing that their offering has to be made at just the right depth, speed, and place time after time.

Varying the angle of presentation, however, is a good move for mobile anglers, and this is where boat manipulation skills come into play, or where wading anglers need to be patient and maneuver themselves into the proper place. When bass anglers fish cover, for example, such as fallen trees and vegetation, they have to fish it in ways that will make their lures reach the fish and will let the lures swim or be retrieved as naturally and convincingly as possible. This is why electric motors are such valuable devices. Most cover should be approached from the edges first, working deeper into it with successive casts.

The nuances of making good presentations also have to do with positioning a boat properly to drift in current or with the wind, maneuvering a boat when trolling (since this is what actually puts the lure or bait in a place for the fish to get it), and using retrieval methods for various lures. These and more aspects of presentation are discussed in many places in this book, especially under the respective lure entries.

See: Casting; Retrieving; Trolling.

PREY
A species that is fed upon by other species.

PRIEST
A short club for quickly and humanely killing a fish that is to be kept for consumption.

See: Fish Preparation—Care.

PRINCE EDWARD ISLAND
The smallest province in Canada, Prince Edward Island (PEI) is in the Gulf of St. Lawrence on Canada's east coast, separated from New Brunswick and Nova Scotia by the Northumberland Strait. Just 175 miles long and between 4 and 40 miles wide, PEI is connected to the mainland by a 10-mile-long bridge and summer ferry service. This island is the most densely settled province in Canada, with 135,000 residents, most of whom depend on renewable resources for their livelihoods.

PEI has 1,100 miles of coastline, deeply indented with many estuaries and bays. Other than barrier-beach ponds, which are found at the mouths of many streams, there are few natural lakes. There are, however, more than 800 artificial ponds, many originally constructed as mill ponds. The streams themselves are short and spring-fed; most originating from springs that discharge 7°C water in summer and winter. As a result, streams on PEI are less reliant on surface runoff and maintain good flows, even in summer.

PEI hosts a limited number of sportfish, but the numbers are deceptive. Recreational fishing here, both in freshwater and saltwater, is very good. This fact is largely unknown outside the province, excluding the island's storied tuna fishery.

Freshwater
PEI is one of the few places in North America where the brook trout, also called the speckled trout, is still king. The large input of mineral-rich groundwater and nutrient-rich runoff from agricultural land, combined with short streams and large estuaries, have created ideal conditions for brook trout. These fish inhabit virtually every stream on the Island. Sea-run trout, the fish most sought after by anglers, range up to 6 pounds.

The trout season runs from April 15 to September 15, with a generous daily limit of 10 fish. The Trout River in western PEI now has an experimental Trout Management Zone, with a shorter season, reduced creel limit, and a barbless-hook requirement.

Until mid-June, anglers most often use bait or lures to take sea trout, particularly in estuaries or ponds. The timing of runs varies from river to river, but many waters have a run of sea trout beginning in mid-June and lasting until mid-July. From the middle of June until early August, small dry flies are preferred, with large flies used in estuaries or after dark. The streams on PEI are small, and rods from 6 to 8 feet are preferred by fly anglers.

Many people enjoy fishing for trout in ponds, using baits or flies. Some ponds, however, can become overly enriched and weedy in the summer, making fishing difficult. Some ponds become too warm in summer, and angling at this time is generally less successful.

Rainbow trout are an introduced species on PEI, and only a half-dozen streams exist where they can regularly be taken. The season for rainbows is the same as for brook trout. In the winter, however, there is a put-and-take rainbow trout fishery in a few small lakes.

Atlantic salmon were once common in many PEI streams; however, overfishing and habitat degradation have reduced the number of salmon throughout the province. With habitat enhancement and stocking of salmon smolts raised in semi-natural rearing ponds, there are now five principal streams where Atlantic salmon can be angled. These are the Morell, Valleyfield, West, Naufrage, and Trout Rivers. Most of the salmon angled on PEI are taken in the Morell River, located on the northeastern side of the Island. This is the only river on PEI that is a scheduled river, and its main branch can be fished only by fly after June 1.

Although the salmon run is primarily composed of grilse, some salmon in excess of 20 pounds have been encountered. Because more than 90 percent of grilse caught on the island originate from semi-natural rearing ponds, catch-and-release is less important on PEI than in other regions where returning fish are needed to meet spawning requirements. The season extends from June 1 through late November, but the best fishing for salmon occurs from mid-June through late July. On the Morell River, many anglers enjoy trolling flies for salmon in Leards Pond, a large former mill pond. Most angling for salmon is done by wading the main river, however.

Other species found in freshwater include white perch, rainbow smelt, and eels. Perch are taken from July until September, but only in a few locations with relatively warm water temperatures. This fish was formerly restricted to warm areas, such as barrier-beach ponds, but in recent years has expanded its range to include a few artificial impoundments in some rivers.

Rainbow smelt are caught through the ice with spears in winter, although they are also fished from many wharves in late summer and autumn. Hundreds of "smelt shacks" cover the ice in estuaries and bays across PEI. Although eels have traditionally been speared through the ice in ponds and estuaries in winter, or caught by "flambeau-ers" using lights in spring, the drop in eel numbers has virtually decimated any recreational opportunities associated with this species.

Saltwater

Saltwater angling on PEI continues to be the most underutilized component of its recreational fishery. The island's many estuaries and bays, and offshore areas, offer recreational anglers excellent opportunities for a variety of saltwater species. No saltwater recreational license was required as of 1999, but a change in this policy is anticipated.

Deep-sea fishing along PEI provides good family fishing opportunities, and is a great way to enjoy beautiful coastline vistas. Mackerel, cod, and dogfish are the species most commonly caught, and numerous deep-sea charters are available throughout the island from midsummer through early autumn. Visitors can obtain a brochure about saltwater sportfishing from the provincial tourism agency.

Mackerel can be exceedingly abundant and are superb fighters if taken on a fly or even a spinning rod. There is no limit on the number that can be caught, and when runs are on, anglers can fish from wharves or near causeways, where flatfish are also taken. The commercial fishery for cod has been curtailed, but a viable recreational fishery still exists off the coast of PEI. This fishery also occurs from midsummer through early autumn, but, as is not the case with mackerel, there is a daily limit. Dogfish, a small shark, is another species of interest to the recreational angler. In autumn, dogfish can be so abundant that some commercial fishermen consider them a nuisance.

For those interested in larger fish, three species of sharks are commonly caught off the coast of PEI: blue, mako, and porbeagle. Although sharks are abundant, catch-and-release is recommended because of their low reproductive rate. Fishing for

A bluefin tuna is brought to the dock at North Lake.

these sharks generally occurs in autumn. Chum is used to attract sharks to the vicinity of the boat. Most of the blue and mako sharks top out at about 100 pounds, but the porbeagle can run two to three times this weight. Sharks of this size are excellent fighters and provide plenty of excitement.

North Lake, in eastern PEI, boasts of being the "Tuna Capital of the World," with a historical catch of many bluefin tuna in excess of 1,000 pounds. The tuna boom at North Lake took place from the 1970s through the mid-1980s but was followed by nearly 10 years with few reported tuna landings. Bluefin tuna numbers worldwide have declined, and the number of fish that can be caught is now federally regulated. The late 1990s have witnessed a return of the tuna and a subsequent resurgence in tuna charters off North Lake.

Four existing world-record giant bluefin tuna have been caught in PEI waters or by PEI anglers. Three of them weighed more than 1,000 pounds and include the all-tackle 1,496-pound world record, landed at Auld's Cove, Nova Scotia, by a PEI angler in 1979. This is the largest bluefin ever captured on rod and reel.

With PEI at the northerly migratory range of bluefin tuna, fish appearing here are, on average, at or near peak sizes. Since the mid-1990s, numerous giants in the 800- to 1,000-pound class have been caught annually off PEI. In 1997, for example, roughly 150 giants were landed in the southern gulf district (there are three districts here), and their average weight was 974 pounds; many of these were not landed by recreational anglers, however. Approximately another 330 tuna were landed in the other districts; their weights averaged between 500 and 600 pounds.

This fishery takes place from August through October, and in recent years the largest tuna have shown up in August and September. The fishery is closed when a total weight quota is reached, as all of the giants are killed upon capture and sold and shipped away, primarily to Japan. The arrangement with charter boat captains here is that tuna belong to the boat, even when caught by a client who has paid for the charter (though charter fees may be waived when a tuna is caught). These boats are otherwise used in commercial deep-sea and lobster fishing but are outfitted for the pursuit of tuna in season. Tuna must be sportfished on rod and reel on a registered commercial fishing vessel to which a bluefin tuna license is attached. The established tuna ports are North Lake and Tignish.

PROCESSED BAIT

Foodstuffs that are used to attract and catch fish even though they do not occur naturally in aquatic environments. The term processed bait is used to differentiate such items from natural baits *(see)*. Examples of processed baits include bread, dough, cheese, sweet corn, cubed meat, seeds, vegetables, and protein boilies *(see)*. Most of these are used in angling for coarse fish *(see)*, although some take a few predatory species, including trout and catfish.
See: Bait; Chumming; Float.

PROPBAIT

A surface lure with a propeller.
See: Surface Lure.

PROPELLER GUARD

A propeller guard is an outboard motor accessory for small-boat anglers who fish shallow rivers or venture into uncertain waters. Made of heavy metal and encircling the propeller, it is primarily used on 7.5- through 15-hp motors and protects the propeller and part of the lower skeg. In appropriate situations, the motor is operated in the tilted shallow-water-drive position so it will kick up when it hits an object. Some anglers have devised homemade guards, including pitchforks hose-clamped around the lower unit, but many of these devices impede high-speed operation. An alternative to propeller guards is a jet drive *(see)* outboard motor.

PUERTO RICO

Known to some as the "Land of Enchantment," Puerto Rico is an island with a strong and certainly beckoning offshore fishing reputation. The charm for anglers is a year-round fishery for blue marlin, one mostly pursued by trolling. Neither the blue marlin nor other big-game species are sought far offshore, especially along the north coast. Puerto Rico's fortuitous positioning in the eastern end of the Greater Antilles, with the Atlantic Ocean on the north and Caribbean Sea on the south, makes this possible.

Although it is a self-governing commonwealth in association with the United States, Puerto Rico is in fact closer to South America (480 miles) than to North America (1,063 miles). It lies roughly 80 miles east of the Dominican Republic, separated by the Mona Passage, and 37 miles west of the Virgin Islands, separated by the Virgin Passage.

A generally mountainous island (Cerro la Punta is the highest peak, at 4,390 feet) spanning 3,515 square miles, Puerto Rico has several small islands around its 311-mile-long coast. Desecheo is just 10 miles from Puerto Rico to the west, the popular tourist site Isla Mona ("Monkey Island") is 41 miles to the west, and Caja de Muertos ("Dead Man Chest") is the most prominent of several small islands a few miles from the southern coastal town of Ponce.

There are no significant islands to the north, but to the east lies the 51-square-mile Vieques, which is mostly a U.S. military installation and internationally known as a target and training area for the U.S. Navy. The eastern region of Puerto Rico has abundant rock formations, cays, and islands. Of principal interest is Culebra ("Serpent Island"), 17 miles to the east, which has guest houses, small hotels, restaurants, skin-diving operations, and good sportfishing. Crystal clear waters, breathtaking beaches, and coral formations are abundant, and many seabirds use the area for nesting.

Offshore

Obviously, Puerto Rico has numerous blue marlin in its waters. As well it should. Neighboring St. Thomas is generally viewed as the blue marlin jewel in the Atlantic/Caribbean, especially for big fish, and Puerto Rico is surely a close second. In fact, these two destinations are among the top locales anywhere to fish for big Atlantic blue marlin.

They do, of course, share much the same waters and are in the same migratory path for marlin. They might be spawning, or at least nursery, areas for young fish as well, as a great many small blues are seen in these waters. Puerto Rico has yet to produce a rod-and-reel grander, unlike St. Thomas, which gets more notoriety as a result. But the big fish are sure to be in Puerto Rican waters, and many visiting anglers each year try to be the first to set the grand standard.

Local boat skippers see marlin in the monster category every season, and two fish have been caught that were close to the 1,000-pound mark. One of those is the present Puerto Rican record, a 984-pounder taken in 1985; another giant blue weighed in at 980 pounds. Marlin in the 500- to 800-pound class come to the boat every season.

The trade winds can produce rough seas, incidentally, although this seldom stops the big sportfishing boats from venturing forth. Easterly or northeasterly winds, usually between 10 and 20 knots, are the rule,. Hurricane winds, of course, are another matter, and Puerto Rico was wracked hard in September 1989 by Hugo.

North coast. The currents, trade winds, deep water, and upwellings offshore from Puerto Rico all interact to create a favorable situation for pelagic species and baitfish, and especially for marlin. The Puerto Rico Trench runs parallel to the north shore of this 110-mile-long island, creating depths well beyond the reach of the most advanced sportfishing sonar. In fact, the deepest water in the Atlantic—28,374 feet—is in the western end of this abyss, approximately 75 miles from the main island.

Puerto Rico is washed by currents flowing from the Atlantic into the Caribbean and thence becoming the Yucatán Current headed into the Gulf of Mexico. The flow washes around the island to the west in the Mona Passage. It is believed that billfish migrate past the north coast and funnel by the west coast into the Venezuelan Basin. Blue marlin, white marlin, sailfish, yellowfin tuna, wahoo, and dolphin are abundant along the north coast.

Of the billfish, the blue marlin is most numerous. Blues are caught year-round, usually only 2 to 5 miles off the coast. Relatively small blues are captured between February and June. In June they begin to appear in numbers, and from July through October the fishing is unusually bountiful. The blues that remain from June until the middle of August are larger than those caught in September and October. Blues usually vary between 225 and 450 pounds in summer; however, 713- and 895-pounders were boarded in a single summer day, and a 980-pounder was caught off the north shore. The summer fishery here may be good because the blues are then the main catch rather than one of many species to be caught. At other times of the year, the catch is peppered with all the typical offshore nomads that one sees elsewhere in blue water.

A number of charter boats operate out of San Juan, the capital city, and weekend fishing is popular among local anglers. Despite relatively small fishing effort, approximately 500 blues are caught annually off San Juan alone, and twice that number are taken off the rest of the northern shores.

Such prolific results are reflected in the records of the prestigious Club Nautico de San Juan Billfish Tournament, which holds the unofficial world record for most blue marlin—190—caught in a single four-day tournament in August 1988.

More than 15 blue marlin tournaments are held annually around the island; these are sanctioned by the local sportfishing ruling body, Asociacion de Pesca Deportiva de Puerto Rico, and the country has been honored with conservation awards for its development of sportfishing regulations and conservation ethics. Nine of these tournaments are held along the northern shore.

White marlin are caught every month, year-round, but are more plentiful in April, May, and June. Whites usually range from 45 to 65 pounds, but some over 90 pounds have been caught. Sailfish occur along the north coast in October and are most abundant in November and until the middle of December.

May through July is the best period for yellowfin tuna. Anglers sometimes encounter large tuna schools during early summer months. The usual size of yellowfins is from 60 to 150 pounds, and some approach 200 pounds.

Dorado (dolphin) numbers are abundant off the north coast, especially in summer. Yet the best months for dorado fishing here are from early December through the beginning of March. The average weight is from 10 to 15 pounds, but fish of 30 to 50 pounds are not uncommon.

Wahoo fishing is especially good close to shore off San Juan in January. These fish are also abundant in late December, and available in good numbers during the rest of the year.

There is fair reef fishing off the north coast as well. This is much better in the northwestern sector than it is near San Juan.

East coast. Offshore fishing is excellent on the east coast closer to the southwestern region of the island. Here, a few miles off Humacao, is Grappler Bank, whose edges drop from 30 to 500 fathoms a mile from the bank; and Little Bank, whose edges drop from 45 to 400 fathoms. Grappler is the larger bank, and wahoo are most abundant on its eastern side. Little Bank produces tuna, dolphin, and skipjack tuna, as well as wahoo.

Although blue marlin over 700 pounds have been caught here, these banks are known as a wahoo paradise. Thirty- to 50-pound wahoo are the norm, even though several over 80 pounds are caught yearly and a few over 100 pounds have been reported from Grappler. The prime time for these fish is October and November.

There was once an abundance of sailfish near Culebra, but the large balls of sardines that attracted them to this area disappeared in the mid-1990s. A resurgence of sailfish occurred in the late 1990s, but not great numbers as before.

The reefs on this coast, in the Fajardo, Vieques, Culebra, and Humacao perimeter, provide the best reef fishing of the island. Fishing in these waters is also productive for wahoo, tuna, and other small migratory species. A full-service marina exists at Humacao.

South coast. Billfish, tuna, wahoo, and dorado are plentiful along the south coast from Guanica to Cabo Rojo. Blue marlin are caught most consistently south of Guanica and La Parguera, and often the largest blues of the year come from here.

The billfish found along the south coast are also migratory but seem to come and go with the

---

The first fishing and hunting club in the New World was Pennsylvania's Schuylkill Fishing Company, founded in 1732 along the banks of the Schuylkill River in present-day Philadelphia.

currents more than those in the north. Billfishing here begins in March and is consistently good until May; April and May are the best months.

A large run of dorado lingers here during the tropical winter months, when the water temperature is cooler and the winds stronger. These fish average 30 to 50 pounds, and several 60- to 80-pounders are caught yearly from the 100-fathom mark close to shore and up to 15 miles offshore.

Reef fishing is particularly good at La Parguera, where snapper, grouper, and mackerel are the main species. Private marinas exist at Ponce and La Parguera.

West coast. This area could be called a big-game angler's dream. Here the Mona Channel has depths to 3,600 feet and contains a line of ridges and canyons. Multiple blue marlin hookups and more than 10 strikes daily are common in peak periods. World-record dorado and wahoo have also come from this area.

There are two blue marlin runs off Mayaguez. One is in the summer and may have its origin in the run off San Juan. The larger run is in August, September, and October and may consist of fish migrating through the Mona Channel on their way to Central and South America. The larger run produces many fish from 75 to 200 pounds and provides great light-tackle fishing opportunity.

The run to the 100-fathom curve is about 15 miles from Mayaguez. The most productive blue marlin areas along the west are the Pichincho, Guineo, and Esponjas Banks, and the waters near Desecheo and Mona Islands. Marlin here average 150 pounds, and a 984-pounder is the largest yet caught. Pichincho has a series of peaks and a rapid dropoff. A sharp dropoff a mile from Mona Island's east end is excellent for blue marlin. Desecheo is prime for blues and sailfish along its abrupt dropoff from 600 to 2,400 feet.

Charter boat services are much more limited in this region than they are at San Juan.

Baits, lures, tackle. Trollers place great emphasis on watching for bait, feeding fish, and other signs that might indicate the presence of marlin. Both natural baits and lures are part of their arsenal.

Blue marlin here display a varied diet. Tuna, dorado, mackerel, and needlefish are among their fare. White marlin eat a great quantity of squid, as well as blue runners, surgeonfish, and little tuna. Sailfish feed on essentially the same forage as white marlin, plus flyingfish, which are the chief food of dorado.

The most popular angling baitfish in Puerto Rican waters is the ballyhoo, which is naturally abundant locally and used to catch all species of big-game fish. Mullet may be used for billfishing, as are ballyhoo, small barracudas, and bonito. Small dorado, tuna, and tarpon are also successfully employed. As in most big-game areas, the baits used do not necessarily reflect the actual diet of the fish sought.

High-speed trolling with large offshore lures is favored by some anglers over slower trolling with natural baits, in part to cover lots of ground while searching. These are effective, as are smaller lures used by light-tackle enthusiasts.

Generally, big-game tackle here consists of 30- and 80-pound International Game Fish Association (IGFA-class) outfits. Some tournaments mandate a maximum of 30-pound tackle. Many anglers choose even lighter tackle for dorado or billfish. Fly fishing has increased, as good numbers of fish make this method a more feasible proposition.

Inshore

With all the attention placed on marlin in the past, little has been detailed about Puerto Rico's inshore fishing opportunities. However, snook, tarpon, bonefish, barracuda, ladyfish, snapper, and assorted other species exist here, principally along the shore where there are flats and bays. In recent times, a little more attention has been paid to these resources, and even some skiff guides exist for inshore, mangrove, lagoon, and tidal river fishing

San Juan Bay is known to have large schools of tarpon, and the mangrove-lined creeks and lagoons that branch off from the bay are also prime for tarpon and occasionally snook and jacks. October through December brings schooling action from small tarpon; larger fish roam here from January through March, when 50- to 100-pounders are available. Fish to 150 pounds have been caught here, however. Some anglers concentrate on the mouth of San Juan Bay, where big tarpon swim along the edge of the ship channel. The Loiza River, and several lagoons, enter on the east side of the bay. The mouth of the Loiza is favored for tarpon and jacks after heavy rains muddy the water and draw in schools of fish to forage on bait; however, the river flows significantly only when heavy rains cause the upstream reservoir to overflow. The mouth of the Espiritu Santo River nearby is similar.

Flats and reefs on the south and east coast are generally lightly fished. On the east, Culebra Island, which is a national wildlife refuge, features good bonefishing, especially inside the bay of Ensenada Honda on the island's southwest tip. Numerous cays along the south mainland coast reportedly contain bonefish. The mangrove flats near La Parguera once harbored snook and bonefish but have suffered from netting.

PUMPING

The act of systematically raising the rod tip, then quickly lowering it while simultaneously reeling in line, in order to tire a fish and bring it to the boat. This is a key component of fighting a large or strong fish.

See: Landing Fish; Playing Fish.

PUNCTURING

A technique, usually used by fisheries professionals and occasionally by anglers, for relieving the pressure built up in the air bladders of fish that have been retrieved too rapidly from deep water and that are to be released. Puncturing is also known as venting and fizzing, and it is performed on species that do not have a pneumatic duct connected to the air bladder and that cannot expel air; these fish, when retrieved quickly from deep water, cannot naturally adjust their air pressure and cannot make rapid vertical movements. Puncturing entails the insertion of a sharp object, usually a long needle, through the body wall of the fish to let the pent-up air escape through the puncture hole.

See: Catch-and-Release.

PUPA

A resting stage in the life cycle of some insects; the larval insect is enclosed in a protective case where it changes into the adult form.

See: Insects.

PURSE SEINE

A commercial fishing net that is used to encircle a school of fish (sometimes located by spotter planes); the net hangs curtainlike and is pulled tight much the same way as a string closes a purse.

See: Commercial Fisherman; Seine.

PUSHPOLE

A pole made of wood, aluminum, fiberglass, or graphite that is used to propel a boat quietly, or to temporarily stake (anchor) it in shallow water. Probably as old as the boat and possibly older than the paddle, a pushpole of some form has been intrinsic to boat use and, even with the sophistication of modern gas and electric motors, it is today still an important element of fishing, most popularly used in the shallows of marine estuaries, bays, flats, canals, and inshore environs.

Almost any open boat under 20 feet long can be propelled by a single pushpole. Though many people associate fishing use of a pushpole with saltwater flats angling, any small boat can be poled in a situation where the water is shallow and it is desirable to quietly move along. Pushpoles are used to propel a canoe upstream against a current, glide a skiff across a bonefish flat, or muscle a bass boat through heavy weeds.

The advantage offered by a pushpole is accomplishing movement with less noise than the quietest electric motor, with no batteries to become depleted or moving parts to wear out. The disadvantage is that a person who poles cannot fish while in the act of poling; if it is necessary to continuously pole, the poler does not fish while a companion does. Pushpoles may come in handy, incidentally, for retrieving lures that get snagged on objects. Some freshwater models are equipped with a head that sports a spike for such a purpose (or pulling down a tree branch to reach a stuck lure or fly).

Features. Pushpoles are between 12 and 22 feet long, depending on the size of boat and the usual depth of water fished, with most saltwater models 18 to 20 feet. The depth of water to be poled is the best guide for how long a pole should be, but many people base length equivalent to the overall size of the boat, so the pole, when fastened along the gunwale, doesn't extend much beyond the bow and/or transom.

Pushpoles were once solely fashioned from round lumber stock, then made out of hollow fiberglass tubing similar to that used for pole vaulting in track and field athletics, as well as from aluminum. Today the basic length of a pushpoles is made primarily from fiberglass; some are made from graphite, some from a composite of graphite and fiberglass, some from wood, and a few from aluminum. Though light, aluminum tends to be noisy, is prone to eventual rusting in saltwater, and can be cold to the touch; it is less popular and primarily restricted to small-boat use in freshwater. Wooden pushpoles are still used in some places, especially in northern river canoeing; they work for light applications, but don't last long in heavy-duty use, especially when asked to propel a relatively large boat in wind and/or current. Wooden poles have always been subject to sudden breakage, and while any pole can break,

A guide uses a pushpole to quietly stalk the flats.

when you depend on a pushpole a lot, having it break can be as traumatic as losing your engine far from shore. Therefore, the majority of use has shifted to synthetic poles, primarily for durability and, in the case of graphite or composites, also for lightness. In saltwater, commercially made poles are virtually all made from synthetic materials and cost hundreds of dollars.

The diameter of a pushpole is generally from $1^{1}/_{4}$ to $1^{1}/_{2}$ inches, with the smaller diameter being better for smaller hands. A large-handed person generally needs a thicker pole to avoid hand fatigue and cramping. The main section of the pole may be one piece or multiple pieces (some are three-piece units). Aluminum models may have two sections that telescope. You can make a wooden one from $1^{1}/_{4}$- to $1^{3}/_{8}$-inch round lumber yard stock, and attach a couple of 6-inch pieces of round stock side by side to one end of the pole for a foot.

Length and material has a bearing on weight, which can range from under 4 pounds to nearly 8 pounds in synthetics, and lighter in aluminum versions (which are smallest). Graphite pushpoles are most expensive, but they tend to be lighter, which is important because even the lightest poles feel heavy by the end of a day of poling. Graphite is also more slippery than other material, and some users wear light leather gloves for a better grip. Among synthetic poles, light colors, usually a cream or off-white, are less prevalent than dark colors, mainly black. Although dark colors get hot in the sun, they are believed to spook fish less than light poles. Wooden poles are usually unpainted; aluminum poles may be painted with a dull finish that does not produce glare.

Graphite poles are usually stiffer than other synthetic poles, and this endears them to many flats guides. Stiff poles are powerful but not very flexible, which means that beginning polers find them hard to use because they seem unresponsive. The real problem is that experienced polers know how to plan and anticipate every move in advance, while less experienced or beginning polers are more reactionary, and thus rely on the flex of a pole a good deal while maneuvering. Veteran guides prefer the stiffest and lightest poles for those times when they need to pole fast; a stiff pole enables quicker movement.

The ends of a pushpole may be round and blunt, tapered to a point, or fitted with a triangular or forked foot. Usually one end has a point and the other a foot or fork, so the pole can be reversed depending on the bottom material. The pointed end is used for burying in a soft bottom—to hold the boat in position for a while or to stake out—and for poling over hard bottom. It features a silent and relatively splashless entry and exit from the water. The larger foot end is used for poling over soft bottom or mud. Feet shapes include a Y, triangle, or hybrid of the other two. A triangular-shaped foot is popular for grabbing bottom and not sinking too far into a soupy bottom, and it can also be used for paddling, since it has more surface area. Both ends may be made from different material than the basic body of the pole, and can be replaced or changed, although aluminum ends are likely to be noisy in rock or hard-bottomed areas.

Pushpoles are usually mounted along the gunwale of a flats boat, and secured with J-shaped brackets. Three brackets are required to hold long synthetic poles in place, two facing inward at the ends and one facing outward in the center. These should be situated so as to put a bend in the pushpole while it is in the brackets, which supplies the friction to keep it in place. Telescoping aluminum poles can be stored in a rod locker. Wooden one-piece poles are usually just laid down in the boat.

Poling. Poling is not difficult and is entirely a function of practice. A South Florida flats guide can pole a 16- to 18-foot skiff all day for many miles without fatigue using finesse rather than brute power. So can the weekend angler who is in reasonable shape and learns the proper technique. Proper poling is seldom a matter of muscles and brute strength, although someone who has been poling for a long time is much more proficient than someone who has just started.

The important thing to remember is that travel in a straight line requires a balance of the effects of wind and/or current. To go straight ahead in

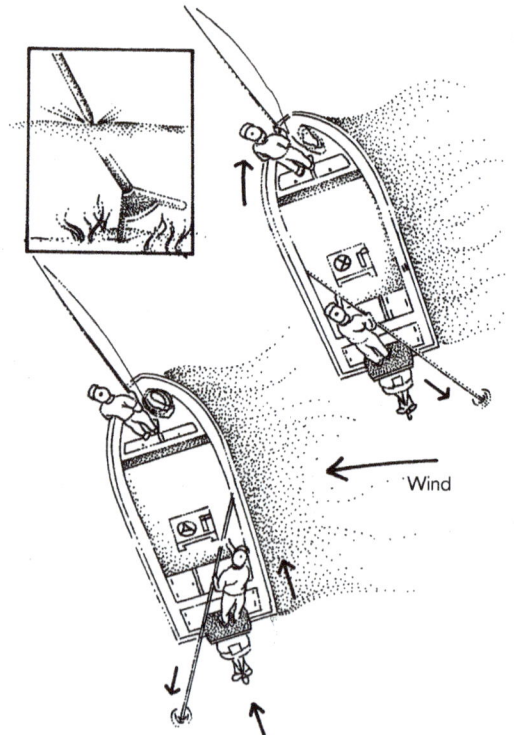

To turn the bow toward the wind, push off from the upwind side (right); to quarter with the wind instead of turning broadside to it, push off from the downwind side (left). Use a pointed end on a hard bottom and a forked end on a soft bottom (inset, top).

calm water, just push the pole straight astern. If the water is calm and there is little or no wind, the bow of the boat moves in exactly the opposite direction from the thrust of the pushpole. If that thrust is essentially parallel to the keel and straight astern, the boat moves straight ahead regardless of whether the poler is in the center or to one side. Usually, however, there's wind and/or current, and this must be countered by "crabbing" the boat against those forces in a slightly right or left turning attitude, similar to but not quite as emphatic as necessary for turning. To pole continuously in a straight line downwind, you do not need to keep switching from side to side. Angle the tip of the pole to one side or the other of the centerline to correct direction. Use short pushes when first learning and gradually you'll be able to use longer ones, walking your hands over each other down the pole as you push.

To turn left, stick the pole against the bottom off the left (port) corner of the stern and push. To turn right, the pole must be off the right (starboard) corner. The greater the pole's angle to one side or the other of the boat's centerline, the quicker the turn. Often it is necessary to push out the stern of the boat to give the bow angler a better angle at the fish; this is a modified turn which is executed by jamming the pointed end of the pole into the bottom a few feet from the stern and repositions the bow. It is especially useful so that the angler and poler are not aligned, which might be problematic for a fly caster.

If you're facing downwind and need to move quartering the wind, turn the boat to a 45-degree angle by pushing off at the stern on the upwind side, then keep the boat headed straight by pushing off on the downwind side.

Use the forked end for a soft bottom and the pointed end for a hard or in-between bottom. To prevent a pole from getting stuck in soft bottoms, twist it when completing the push to break the suction. Keep the angle of the pole high in hard bottoms to prevent it from slipping.

Staking out. Many anglers use a pushpole to keep the boat stationary if the water is reasonably shallow and the bottom soft enough. This is usually a temporary form of anchoring, and it is often done in such a way that if a strong fish is hooked, the pole can be untied and retrieved quickly to start moving as necessary. Some even carry a second shorter "stake-out" pole so that the boat can be immobilized at both ends. The long pole is usually thrust into the bottom at an angle of 30 degrees or less (from the horizontal and as low as possible to reduce the stress of bending), to also reduce the likelihood of interfering with casting, before being bent over even a little farther and tied to the boat. A strong pole will hold a boat in a surprising amount of wind and current, but if it is poorly made, or stressed too much via a sharp bend, that's the time when it will most likely fail. Before you buy a ready-made pole or blank, make sure the manufacturer stands behind its product under reasonable circumstances.

See: Flats Boat.

PUT-AND-TAKE FISHERY

The placing of hatchery-raised fish in waters where they can be caught by anglers. This term applies primarily to freshwater and refers to the stocking of fish in areas where there is little expectation of creating a naturally sustaining population of fish. Thus, the objective is stocking fish to provide recreation and food, not to enhance native populations of fish. This objective may apply to privately operated pay-to-fish preserves or farms or to public waters stocked by government agencies.

See: Hatchery; Stocking.

The Guinness Book of Records lists the longest earthworm as a South African one that reached 22 feet long when naturally extended.

QUARTERING SEA
Waves coming toward the quarter, or side.
See: Waves.

QUEBEC
Covering 523,859 square miles, Quebec is by far the largest of Canada's 10 provinces. Offering more than 1 million lakes and countless thousands of miles of rivers, it stands to reason that Quebec is also an angler's dream. More than that, the province offers a wide spectrum of angling experiences and species that would be difficult to match anywhere in North America.

A great many popular freshwater gamefish—northern pike, walleye, muskies, black bass, yellow perch, sunfish, brook trout, rainbow trout, brown trout, lake trout, arctic charr, landlocked salmon, and Atlantic salmon—abound within Quebec's borders. The potential surroundings are nearly as varied as the fish, allowing anglers to choose from a range of backdrops, including Montreal skyscrapers and distant wilderness settings in which hearing a floatplane would be a big event. Great fishing is accessible by vehicle, but if adventure is the goal, some of Quebec's waters are accessible only by air or pack trip. This province offers hidden headwater lakes, brawling rivers, and windswept tundra barrens, not to mention thousands of cottage lakes and some of Canada's largest and most sprawling impoundments.

Naturally, not every waterway teems with all species of gamefish, and certain areas are better for some species than others. For instance, muskie fishing is best along the St. Lawrence and Ottawa Rivers, whereas anglers will find the best arctic charr fishing in the rivers flowing into Ungava Bay 900 miles and more to the north. By the same token, excellent northern smallmouth bass fishing is available in the Gatineau region near the Ontario border; 600 miles to the east, the angler would be hard pressed to find a black bass of any kind. This is, instead, superb Atlantic salmon country. It's all a matter of knowing where in this vast province to go, and which locations provide the better opportunities. The waters mentioned below are only representative of the areas discussed.

St. Lawrence River Lowlands
From the last foothill of the Laurentian Range south to the U.S. border, southern Quebec offers the most diverse fishery within the province. By virtue of its population density, Quebec also has the most heavily used fishery. Transecting the region is the St. Lawrence River on its way from the Great Lakes to the Gulf of St. Lawrence. It offers variety of gamefish, high numbers, and trophy potential, especially in bodies of water like Lakes St. Francis, St. Louis, and St. Pierre, which are actually basins within the river's course, as well as Lake of Two Mountains at the confluence of the Ottawa and St. Lawrence Rivers.

Together, these four basins, as well as the Ottawa River upstream from the Carillon Dam, offer among the best trophy muskellunge fishing in North America. Fish of less than 30 pounds hardly get a second look from the region's dedicated muskie fishing fraternity, not when fish exceeding 50 pounds are being caught and released annually.

This level of success, however, is rarely enjoyed by casual anglers, as it requires specialized equipment and techniques. Although the muskie season opens in mid- to late June, few muskie anglers fish seriously here before mid-August. One reason is that muskies need most of the summer to regain the weight and strength lost over the winter and ensuing spawning period. The second is that late-season muskies are generally more aggressive; as summer yields to autumn, anglers record improved success. When weather permits, some diehards fish well into December, and specimens in the 50-pound class have been taken amid blizzards. Most muskies, in all sizes, are taken by anglers fast-trolling big plugs over shoals and ledges in 15 to 25 feet of water.

Northern Quebec offers many wilderness fishing experiences, among them brook trout fishing on the Broadback River, shown here.

Self-illuminated lures were first conceived in 1915 with "Dr. Wasweyler's Marvelous Electric Glow Casting Minnow," featuring a battery-operated bulb.

In an effort to control and even suppress introduced yellow perch, smallmouth bass, and rock bass numbers, Quebec fisheries biologists released muskie fingerlings in many lakes of the Lower Laurentians during the 1960s and 1970s. In the presence of abundant prey, the muskies quickly established self-sustaining populations and provide surprisingly good angling in bodies of water like Lakes Tremblant and Maskinongé, as well as in countless other smaller lakes throughout this cottage country. Casting a big jerkbait is the most productive method, and, although most of the fish are in the 5- to 15-pound class, their numbers more than compensate for their size.

The basins of the St. Lawrence River also consistently produce big walleye, thanks to the abundance of baitfish in the murky, nutrient-rich waters. Walleye weighing up to 4 pounds are common, and anglers targeting big walleye catch fish of 8 to 12 pounds throughout the summer. Most conventional techniques like bottom bouncing, jigging, and trolling produce results when varied according to water and weather conditions. The common denominator, however, is that the majority of bigger fish are caught in areas of some current around the islands and along the edges of the shipping channel on Lake St. Francis and Lake St. Louis. On Lake of Two Mountains, it's important to work the edges of the shoals that follow the current of the Ottawa River.

The easternmost of the St. Lawrence River basins, Lake St. Pierre has not traditionally produced many big walleye, but it does regularly yield sauger worth bragging about. These oddly marked kin of walleye occur in most waters linked to the St. Lawrence, but St. Pierre is known as a consistent sauger producer, offering a reasonable chance at a fish in the 3- to 4-pound class.

Black bass thrive throughout southern Quebec as well as in many of the cottage country lakes of the Lower Laurentian. Smallmouths are the dominant variety, and, although most are small—a 4-pounder is classified as trophy size—they are every bit as feisty as their reputation dictates. The St. Lawrence River, the Ottawa River, and Lakes St. Francis, St. Louis, and Two Mountains are all good bets throughout the summer. So are the Chateauguay River from the U.S. border to Lake St. Louis, and, east of that, the Richelieu River, Chambly Basin, and Missisquoi Bay—an arm of Lake Champlain that extends into Quebec. Lakes Memphremagog, Massawippi, and Brome, as well as many smaller bodies of water in the eastern townships along the U.S. border, also have excellent populations of smallmouths.

In the Lower Laurentians, Bark Lake near Barkmere, Tremblant near St. Jovite, Achigan near St. Hippolyte, and Ouareau near St. Donat, along with many other lakes, offer good smallmouth fishing.

Good largemouth bass fishing spots are something of a rarity in Quebec and are rarely divulged. There are fishable pockets in the weed-choked bays of Lake St. Francis, among the Peace Islands of Lake St. Louis, and also among the Boucherville Islands of the St. Lawrence River off the east end of Montreal Island. The fish tend to be in the 2- to 4-pound class, and one double that from Quebec waters is definitely worth writing home about.

Northern pike are present in most of the region's waters. A few notable exceptions, among them Memphremagog, lie in the eastern townships. Pressure on these pike is such that most weigh less than 6 pounds, although specimens twice that size are caught on occasion. Anybody looking for trophy pike stands a better chance in the more remote waters of central Quebec. This region does boast a fishable population of chain pickerel, however, especially in Lake Memphremagog, where a 3-pounder is better than average.

Although not native to these waters, rainbow and brown trout were introduced so long ago and so frequently that they have indeed taken hold. Thanks to regular supplemental stocking efforts, the fishing is surprisingly good. One of the prime areas is Lachine Rapids, a fast-water stretch of the St. Lawrence River where it squeezes around the south side of the island of Montreal. Although browns and rainbows of 8 to 14 pounds are caught there every year, a more reasonable expectation is a fish half that size. From February through April, shore fishing is productive along the south side of the rapids, but boat fishing is distinctly more productive because a larger number of pools are accessible. The rapids can be extremely treacherous, however, and anglers are advised to venture out with a reliable craft and someone who knows the water. Casting a variety of lures works well here.

Good fly fishing for rainbows, browns, and even some brook trout exists along the Chaudière, which flows from Lake Mégantic near the Maine-Quebec border north to enter the St. Lawrence River near Quebec City. Although the river is treacherous in high water, many areas are easy to wade. Fish of a pound or less are most abundant, but it isn't unusual to hook a trout of 3 pounds. Coaxing it from the currents is another matter.

Browns and rainbows have been stocked in numerous lakes in the eastern townships, the most popular of which are Memphremagog and Massawippi. Although both harbor bigger fish, a reasonable expectation is trout between 2 and 4 pounds. The most productive time is the two-week period after the late-April opening (or early-May ice out, whichever comes first), when the trout forage close to shore and can be caught by fast-trolling plugs or streamers about 4 feet below the surface close to the shoreline. The technique also produces landlocked salmon in the 2- to 6-pound range on Lake Memphremagog. Lake trout are also present in both lakes, although these fish are much more difficult to catch, especially after they've moved to deeper water. Shallow trolling works early, but by June deep trolling is the game, using lures that resemble rainbow smelt.

Lake trout tend to be more abundant in the lakes of the Laurentian playground, north and west of Montreal. Among them are Lakes Cayamant and Poisson Blanc near Gracefield, Lake Simon near Duhamel, Lake McGregor north of Buckingham, and Lake Tremblant near St. Jovite. Although the latter produces hefty lakers on occasion, it is better known for its big landlocked salmon. Biologists introduced Atlantic salmon fry throughout the 1960s, and with large numbers of rainbow smelt present as well as ideal spawning redds available on the Caché River, the fish quickly took root.

Tremblant has produced salmon topping the 23-pound mark and regularly yields fish of between 8 and 16 pounds. Smelt-imitation lures trolled close to the surface during the first three weeks of the season work well, after which deep fishing comes into play.

Despite the variety of high-profile gamefish found through southern Quebec, the greatest angling effort is expended on various panfish species. Without question, yellow perch are the most widely distributed panfish. This distribution is partly natural and partly due to human carelessness; thus, these fish are abundant all along the St. Lawrence River from the Ontario border east to Quebec City, including Lakes St. Francis, St. Louis, and St. Pierre; along the Ottawa River and Lake of Two Mountains; and in Richelieu River and Missisquoi Bay. Eastern township lakes like Memphremagog, Massawippi, and Brome are good bets all through the summer, and in the winter ice fishing season.

Most of the cottage-country lakes in the Laurentian playground also have large populations of perch, but they tend to be rather small. Lakes St. Francis, Two Mountains, and St. Pierre offer the best fish, in number and size. Dunking a nightcrawler in the pockets among the many weedbeds yields the best catches.

Where perch are present, there are apt to be rock bass, pumpkinseeds, and even some bluegills as well. The most prized of the panfish, however, is the black crappie, which is found in large schools on the St. Lawrence and Ottawa Rivers. In May, bullhead fishing is popular along waterways like the Chateauguay River. Most of the fishing occurs at night from shore. You'll find the most productive spots by looking for a collection of lights from lanterns along the shoreline.

In addition to the aforementioned fishing in southern Quebec, runs of shad and a winter tommycod fishery exist here. Atlantic shad first show up in Montreal-area waters toward the middle of May and linger for about three weeks before continuing on their migration to the spawning grounds at the base of Carillon Dam at the head of Lake of Two Mountains. During their all-too-brief stay, they provide good fishing on the Rivière des Mille Iles near Terrebonne, and on the Rivière des Prairies near the hydroelectric facility located between the Pie IX Bridge and the Papineau Bridge. Most anglers wade waist-deep and then cast small, brightly colored shad darts out into the current on light line. This is shoulder-to-shoulder fishing most of the time, but when one of these fish starts to peel line, one quickly forgets the crowd. Most of the shad weigh 3 to 4 pounds, but fish up to 8 pounds have been taken here.

Tommycod are also migrants from saltwater, but they make their spawning runs in the middle of winter after the Christmas holidays. The major spawning ground is at the mouth of the Ste. Anne de la Pérade River, which flows into the St. Lawrence about halfway between Montreal and Quebec City. Traditionally, between Christmas and New Year's, a village of some 1,200 fishing shanties is set up on the ice in preparation for the onslaught of anglers, who arrive by cars, vans, and buses. Some tommycod are caught at the beginning of January, but the prime time is usually between January 12 and 20. Few if any fish are left come the beginning of February.

These fish look like miniature cod and average between 8 and 12 inches in length; a big one runs to 18 or 19 inches. The singularly unsophisticated fishing method consists of dangling a bank of lines off a 2 ¥ 4 into a hole that runs the length of the shanty. A heavy lead weight holds each line to the bottom, and from these lines two short pieces of cord are suspended that each hold a hook baited with a cube of half-frozen liver. By monitoring the vibrations of a matchstick tied into the line at eye level, the angler detects the bites and then simply hauls up the line. Sometimes you have only one fish, sometimes two, and occasionally it's possible to haul in four fish, two clinging to each cube of bait!

The fishing goes on around the clock, but the best action is at night. The fish come in waves and, when the bite is on, hit faster than the lines can be rebaited. Periods of incoming tide seem to be most productive.

Eastern Region
Lower St. Lawrence River: Gaspé Peninsula, North Shore, and Anticosti Island. Almost all of Quebec's more than 100 scheduled Atlantic salmon rivers flow through this region. Among the most popular and perhaps best known are those of the Gaspé Peninsula, an idyllic coastal region of rugged headlands buffeted by brisk onshore breezes from the Gulf of St. Lawrence on one side and rolling lands caressed by the gentle waters of the Baie des Chaleurs on the other. The peninsula alone boasts 26 salmon rivers, among them such fabled waters as the Matapédia, Grand Cascapédia, Bonaventure, York, and St. Jean, as well as lesser-known waters such as the Patapédia, Little Cascapédia, Grande, Dartmouth, and Ste. Anne. Also found on the peninsula is the Matane, where many of today's finest salmon anglers learned to fish for Atlantic salmon, as well as a num-

ber of restored rivers. These include the Nouvelle, Pabos, Port Daniel, Cap Chat, and Ouelle.

Perhaps the popularity of these waters lies in a century of unbroken angling tradition, but it more likely rests in their present-day accessibility. With a couple of minor exceptions, Highway 132 crosses the lower reaches of these rivers, making it possible to do a complete loop of the Gaspé.

Starting in the highlands of the peninsula's interior, these streams change abruptly in nature along their short and tumultuous course to the sea. Initially their waters tumble across basalt ledges, then over boulders, and finally around freestone banks before reaching the estuaries. The habitat is well suited for the sea-run Atlantic salmon that spawn in these rivers, and the pools in which they linger on their way to the upriver redds are considered by many salmon anglers as among the most classic in the world.

Two-sea-winter salmon in the 8- to 12-pound class dominate the runs, but three-sea-winter fish of 14 to 18 pounds are a reasonable expectation on the bigger rivers like the Grand Cascapédia, York, and Matapédia. Multiple spawners on their way back to the redds a second or third time are caught every year, and these can weigh well in excess of 30 pounds. Salmon of 35 to 45 pounds stand as the record on just about every river. Some, like the Matapédia and Grand Cascapédia, continue to produce fish of those dimensions even today. One-sea-winter fish, called *grilse* and weighing 3 to 5 pounds, typically enter freshwater after the beginning of July.

Some salmon are rumored to enter the rivers in the spate waters of May before the salmon fishing season opens, but the first major runs show up in the majority of Gaspé rivers between the middle and end of June. Because the dime-bright fresh fish are most aggressive, and the water conditions at their best, prime salmon fishing time is considered to be the last week of June and the first two weeks of July, although the fishing can be good at any time of the summer, especially on a rise of water.

Although Atlantic salmon are king in the Gaspé region, brook trout also inhabit these waters. In fact, many headwater lakes of the salmon rivers provide excellent fishing for handsomely colored brookies, most of them weighing under a pound, although 2- to 4-pound fish are caught in some of the bigger bodies of water.

The sea-run trout fishing on virtually all of this region's rivers is well known to local anglers, but it is almost completely overlooked by visitors who come to pursue salmon. Sea-run trout here are brook trout that leave freshwater to gorge themselves on the abundance of the sea, returning only to spawn in their rivers, much like the salmon with whom they share the pools. When they first enter the streams, the fish are silver-flanked and possess barely discernible halos along their flanks, but after only a few days in the freshwater pools, the flamboyant markings characteristic of brookies begin to emerge.

On average, sea trout weigh a pound or two, but 3- to 4-pounders can be encountered on most rivers of the Gaspé region. On some, like the Bonaventure, York, Ste. Anne, and Patapédia, even larger sea trout are taken every summer. The West Branch of the Little Cascapédia is probably the most productive, having yielded specimens up to 10 pounds. Four- to 6-pounders are regularly seen finning in the pools. They're skittish fish, however, and duping them into taking a fly is often a difficult challenge.

Barely visible across the Gulf of St. Lawrence from the Gaspé Peninsula is the rugged North Shore escarpment. It, too, is an area noted for Atlantic salmon fishing as well as both sea trout and freshwater brookies. In fact, there is salmon fishing from as far west as the provincial capital of Quebec City all the way east to the boundary with Labrador near Blanc Sablon. The westernmost salmon river is the Jacques Cartier, site of a highly successful salmon restoration program throughout the 1980s and early 1990s. Unfortunately, because of the sharp, towering escarpment that rises virtually at the water's edge, most rivers from there east to the mouth of the Saguenay, a distance of some 100 miles, have insurmountable waterfalls within the first mile or so from the sea.

Three modest streams flowing northwest into the Saguenay have surprisingly good Atlantic salmon runs: the St. Jean, the Petite Saguenay, and, thanks to dedicated restoration efforts between the mid-1980s and mid-1990s, the Rivière à Mars. On the opposite shore of the Saguenay is the well-known St. Marguerite, accessible via Tadoussac and Sacré-Coeur. Both snake through gently rolling country, and most of the watercourse runs over gravel and sand banks. If you have any doubt at all about the presence of salmon, investigate the big holding pool in the sanctuary above the fishing sectors. In addition to salmon, this river offers excellent sea trout fishing, especially in September after the salmon season closes.

As one moves eastward along the North Shore, there are a number of worthwhile salmon rivers to choose from. The first of these is another successfully restored stream called the Escoumins, which today offers as reasonable a chance of hooking a good salmon as it did in the 1960s. Next is the Laval, a dark and brooding river due to its tannin-stained waters. Although it produces nearly a hundred salmon per season, a surprising proportion are large fish.

Several minor salmon rivers flow to the coast beyond Baie Comeau. The next notable salmon river is the Godbout—a pleasant freestone river above the gorge, a sandy river below the gorge, and a rough and untamed river in between. As is the case with most streams along this stretch, it sees the first heavy runs after the first week of June but provides good fishing as long as good water conditions prevail. The Trinite also merits a look.

At Port Cartier, there is the aux Rochers River, which is sometimes overlooked, although it shouldn't be. Inland from Port Cartier is the Port Cartier Wildlife Reserve, which offers excellent fishing for lake trout, big brook trout, and northern pike.

The Moisie, a world-famous salmon river, flows into the Gulf of St. Lawrence east of Sept Iles. Statesmen and kings, tycoons and magnates, have cast their flies over its waters in the hope of hooking one of the Moisie's legendary salmon. Fish of 20 and 30 pounds are relatively common, and much bigger ones are hooked every year but are not always landed. This is a big river that flows out of a rugged, unkempt land, so it's necessary to make the right connections to fish it.

Another excellent salmon river is the Rivière St. Jean, some 85 miles farther east. Although the salmon on average do not compare to those of the Moisie in size, they more than compensate in number. The best pools are 10 miles and more upstream from the mouth and largely inaccessible other than by boat. Advance arrangements are essential.

The road ends a short distance beyond the town of Havre St. Pierre, and access to all salmon rivers farther east is by air. Notable among them are the Natashquan, Étamamiou, Mécatina, and St. Augustin, although there are several others as well.

Between the North Shore and the Gaspé Peninsula lies Anticosti Island. Some 130 miles long and 40 miles across at its widest point, this wedge of limestone offers numerous small, quaint salmon streams. Most are small enough to cast across with line to spare, and, except in the Jupiter, the salmon tend to be in the 6- to 8-pound class. The grilse here are smaller. Most of Anticosti's rivers depend on rain and therefore offer inconsistent fishing. The most dependable is the Jupiter, followed by Rivière aux Saumons, Chaloupe, and La Loutre. Others, like the Bell, might not have a drop of water one week and yet have spate conditions and great fishing the next.

Brook trout are the only other fish inhabiting Anticosti Island. All of the rivers that are accessible from the sea have good runs of sea trout. Most have native populations of brookies, as do the few lakes with sufficient water for winter survival. An overlooked opportunity is coastal fishing for big sea-run trout near the mouths of the rivers.

Northeastern Region

The region east of the Saguenay River, west of the Labrador border, and south of the 50th parallel is essentially a remote land of endless black spruce forests and open taiga, punctuated with countless lakes and wild rivers. Moose and woodland caribou still roam without ever crossing a fence, and few people other than loggers, miners, hunters, and anglers ever venture deep into this realm. It is an angler's haven, especially for trout devotees.

Brook trout are the primary species found in virtually all the streams and countless headwater lakes. The sheer number of large and small waters throughout this region make any attempt at listing them and evaluating their fishing potential a monumental if not impossible task, but many can be described by touching on a few.

As a general rule, most of the lakes tend to be deep and tannin-stained and have sandy shorelines that drop off quickly. Brook trout are abundant in the smaller lakes as well as in the streams that etch their way south around the rounded topography of the Canadian Shield. Most of these rivers flow toward the Gulf of St. Lawrence, but those in the western portion of this region flow into Lake St. Jean and the Saguenay River.

Starting in the eastern portion of the region, the majority of the watersheds produce brook trout; some are also home to Quebec red trout, a landlocked arctic charr. A few also have landlocked Atlantic salmon, and several significant rivers have runs of Atlantic salmon, as discussed in the section on the North Shore of the St. Lawrence River. As a general rule, it is safe to say that, because of the short growing season and the poor food base in the waters flowing down out of the Labrador escarpment, the trout (both brookies and Quebec reds) that spend their lives in freshwater tend to be rather small. Sea-run brook trout, which feed in the gulf and return to freshwater only to spawn, inhabit many of these rivers as well.

Typical of the smaller North Shore watersheds is the Watshishou, located east of Havre St. Pierre. A number of tributaries gather water from the rugged interior of the North Shore highlands, flowing into and through a string of fairly large, deep lakes and finally becoming a full-fledged river dashing to the Gulf of St. Lawrence. The lower portion of this watershed is frequented by Atlantic salmon, whereas the lakes have an abundant supply of brook trout up to 16 inches and Quebec red trout up to 12 inches. Landlocked salmon of 4 pounds and more are caught both in the lakes and in the fast-water streams that connect them. Anglers occasionally catch larger brookies in the 2- to 4-pound class, especially in the lower lakes. These are thought to be sea-runs.

The larger watersheds like the Olomane, Natashquan, Magpie, and (largest of them all) Moisie, reach deep into the backcountry of the North Shore, almost to the border of Labrador. Most are scheduled Atlantic salmon rivers for at least the lower portions, but the tributaries and lakes offer a wider variety of gamefish.

An example is Lake Magpie, which is actually a widening and deepening of the Magpie River entering the Gulf of St. Lawrence roughly halfway between Havre St. Pierre and Sept Iles. About 45 miles long and barely 2 miles wide, it is fed by 27 tributaries and surrounded by magnificent rock faces that resemble coastal fiords. The lake itself is home to five primary gamefish, as well as lake whitefish.

 Most species of fish lay many thousands of eggs. Spawning walleye, for example, in extreme cases, have reportedly laid over 600,000 eggs.

Some primitive fishes from the Jurassic Period have a troutlike appearance and are believed to have been able to live in both marine and freshwater environments.

As is the case for most North Shore drainage basins, the brook trout tend to be on the small side, but abundant. The average size is 12 to 14 inches; some are caught on the lake itself, but they're most common in the numerous tributary streams. Although landlocked salmon are present as well, they're not abundant, and the fish are mostly under 2 pounds. The long-standing lake record is an 8-pound specimen.

Lake Magpie does have a good population of lake trout, and anglers can reasonably expect fish of 15 to 20 pounds. The lake record is a 26-pound fish. The northern pike fishing is notable, too, offering opportunities for trophy specimens of 25 pounds and more. Anglers report seeing large pike lying like logs on the surface of shallow bays.

Farther to the west along the North Shore, near Port Cartier, Lake Walker has a known lake trout and northern pike fishery, as well as larger brook trout. Brookies to 2 pounds are common, fish in the 2- to 4-pound range are hooked regularly, and larger individuals are taken from time to time, especially near the more remote north end of the lake.

One of the most imposing drainage basins along the North Shore is the Manicouagan River, which enters the gulf near Baie Comeau. Although much of its flow has been fettered by a series of massive hydroelectric dams, it continues to provide reasonably good fishing in the lower reservoirs and surrounding lakes. The prime spot, however, is the immense Manicouagan Reservoir some 60 miles inland. This doughnut-shaped body of water is fed by countless tributary streams, most of which provide excellent fishing for brook trout up to 2 pounds, although trophy specimens up to 8 pounds are occasionally caught in both the lake and the tributary pools.

The Manicouagan watershed has long been known for its excellent landlocked salmon fishing, even prior to the construction of dams. The fish are abundant, but they tend to be small, averaging about 2 pounds on the more remote waters. Fast trolling with silver smelt-imitation spoons in the deep bays is among the most productive methods throughout most of the summer, the exception being the occasional period of intense heat and sun. Lake trout are abundant throughout most of the watershed. These fish weigh between 6 and 8 pounds on average, but substantially bigger trout are present. Northern pike tend to grow large in the Manicouagan region, and trophy fish in the 20- to 30-pound range are liable to take trolled lures in the shallow bays. You'll need to be well equipped and largely self-sufficient for this jaunt.

Two additional reservoirs of significance in this region of eastern Quebec are the Outardes and the Pipmuacan. Both are remote and provide excellent fishing for lake trout. Trophy fish are regularly caught in the latter. Characteristically, the tributary streams and headwater lakes surrounding them offer good brook trout fishing.

In the Sacré Coeur region, a number of inland lakes provide good freshwater brook trout fishing as well as superb Quebec red trout fishing. Quebec reds rarely grow to more than a pound or so in most provincial waters, but this particular area regularly produces reds twice that size, and 4- to 6-pound specimens have been caught in the past. Lake des Sables in the Rivière des Sables watershed is a prime spot. This watershed also produces big brookies, but the same can be said for many of the drainage basins of the Lake St. Jean-Saguenay region of Quebec. Among them is Lake Poulin de Courval and its surrounding headwater lakes in the Rivière des Sables watershed. They consistently produce 3- to 5-pound brook trout, and the action on 12- to 16-inch fish is steady to the point of redundancy.

Lake du Dégelis and surrounding lakes in the Rivière Portneuf watershed also have large brook trout, and several of the lakes also produce 2- to 4-pound Quebec red trout. The Rivière Portneuf itself can be waded once the spring runoff abates. It offers good stream fishing with flies and spinners for brook trout up to 3 pounds.

Lake St. Jean and its surrounding waters are perhaps best known for landlocked salmon fishing, however. The main lake is a large round basin some 15 miles across. Although it produces good fishing for walleye up to 4 pounds, as well as northern pike up to about 15 pounds, its name is synonymous with angling for landlocked salmon, better known in this region as *ouananiche*. That's partly because since the 1880s anglers have been drawn to this body of water from throughout eastern North America and even Europe in search of the lake's feisty salmon.

Lake St. Jean's salmon tend to be small, averaging around 2 pounds, even though 4- to 6-pounders are caught from time to time. What they lack in size, they more than make up for in aggressiveness and spunk. They eagerly hit smelt-imitation lures trolled in the prop wash less than 20 feet behind the boat and, once hooked, typically jump a half-dozen times.

To experience the best fishing, it's important to follow the schools of salmon around the lake, starting in the Chambord area shortly after ice out. As the summer progresses, salmon make their way north along the western shore of the lake, passing Roberval around the middle of July and reaching the mouth of the Ashuapmushuan River toward the middle of August.

Larger landlocked salmon inhabit this region as well, but anglers must travel into the backcountry northwest of Lake St. Jean to find them. Several of the reservoirs on the Péribonka River, a major tributary to the lake, contain landlocks averaging 4 to 6 pounds, with fish pushing double digits from time to time. Farther north, in the headwaters of the Péribonka, Lake Duhamel regularly produces landlocked salmon between 4 and 8 pounds, and fish to 14 pounds have been caught. Access to the

Lake St. Jean backcountry is largely by vehicle over gravel lumber roads or by floatplane.

Central and Northwestern Regions

For a dedicated angler, the region stretching from Lake St. Jean to the Ontario border and from the foothills of the Laurentians to the 50th parallel is the realization of every dream. It has more bodies of water than one person can hope to fish in a lifetime, with countless lakes, tumbling streams, and big rivers. In concert these waters offer a variety of sportfish, including walleye, pike, lake trout, brook trout, landlocked salmon, and black bass. Best of all, the region has just the right mix of waters that are either road-accessible, reachable on foot, or accessible only by air.

As a general, although not rigid, rule, brook trout are the predominant species in the eastern portion of the region, whereas pike and walleye are most prevalent toward the west. The larger, deeper lakes of the central and western portions are home to lake trout. Landlocked salmon also do well, although they are an introduced species in the region as are, for the most part, smallmouth bass in the southwestern corner. Some of those introductions date so far back that the gamefish have established self-sufficient numbers and are considered native by local anglers.

With a few exceptions, the area contained by Highway 155 from Lake St. Jean to Trois Rivières, down the St. Lawrence River to Tadoussac, and up the Saguenay River to Lake St. Jean is brook trout country. Because much of this area is easily reached from Quebec City, a steady level of fishing pressure is exerted and many bodies of water are stocked on an annual basis. As a result, the bulk of the trout caught are in the 10- to 12-inch class. Nevertheless, on a fair number of lakes 2- to 4-pound brookies are a reasonable expectation. Among them is Lac des Neiges in Laurentides Provincial Wildlife Reserve, a lake once set aside, along with nearby Lac à l'Épaule, as a retreat for politicians and dignitaries. Stream fishing can be particularly good in the upper reaches of rivers like the Bostonnais, the Kiskissink, and the Métabetchuane.

Also in this region is Portneuf Wildlife Reserve; in addition to having quality lake and stream fishing for brook trout, the reserve offers surprising, and surprisingly good, muskie fishing. A number of lakes in the territory were stocked with this species during the 1970s, and the experiment proved more successful than anyone dreamed possible. The muskies aren't huge—20 pounders are the exception rather than the rule—but muskies in the 5- to 10-pound class are present in numbers and ever willing to take a lure or streamer fly.

To the west of Highway 155 and the St. Maurice River, there's a far greater variety of gamefish. Brook trout are still the most common species in the watersheds draining into the southwestern quadrant of Lake St. Jean, as well as the lakes in the southern drainage basins. But in the heart of the region, brook trout are banished to headwater lakes by the abundant walleye and pike in the lower waters. Many of the larger lakes also have lake trout.

Some of the best road-accessible brook trout fishing is available at Mastigouche and St. Maurice Provincial Wildlife Reserves. Most of the lakes in St. Maurice produce small fish in the 10-inch class, although bigger fish are possible for anglers familiar with the area. For instance, Lake Polette averages fish of 15 inches, yet at Lake St. Thomas, a walk-in lake, the average weight is $2^{1}/_{4}$ pounds.

In addition to good brook trout fishing in lakes such as Grand Lac des Iles, Lac au Sable, and St. Bernard, Mastigouche Wildlife Reserve also offers good fishing for landlocked salmon in Lac Sorcier. The fish were introduced during the 1960s and have established a self-sustaining population. The majority are in the 3-pound size, and fish double that are rare, but they react well in the early season to a streamer or lure trolled close to the surface.

The lakes situated northwest of Lake St. Jean, however, are more representative of the diverse fisheries of central and western Quebec. Innumerable small headwater lakes teem with pan-size brook trout, and virtually all the larger collector lakes like Nicabau, Charron, and Aigremont offer strictly walleye in the 2- to 4-pound range, and northern pike running to 15 pounds, although larger specimens are present.

In the heart of central Quebec is one of the province's most prolific bodies of water. Created in 1917 by the damming of the St. Maurice River at the La Loutre Rapids, Gouin Reservoir has a massive surface area of more than 500 square miles, most of it highly productive northern pike and walleye habitat. In fact, it is so prolific that a commercial fishery annually harvested more than 3,000 pounds of fish without any apparent impact on the stocks until it was abandoned in 1972.

Accessible by gravel lumber roads or by air, the recreational harvest falls far short of the toll formerly taken by the nets. Although trophy walleye may well swim forgotten here, in the bays, fish in the 3- to 5-pound range are incredibly abundant and provide outstanding action throughout the summer. Northern pike are plentiful in these sheltered bays, where anglers can reasonably hope for fish weighing up to 15 pounds; some larger ones are present. Gouin is accessible by fly-in to established camps, and also by a rugged drive. It is a vast lake, one that is easy to get lost on. Flooded timber, reefs, and mazes of islands make this a place to exercise great caution.

Another excellent destination for walleye and northern pike anglers is the Cabonga-Dozois Reservoir system. Created in the late 1920s by damming the Gens de Terre River at the outlet of Bark Lake and the Outaouais River at La Barrière, this immense reservoir complex is a confusing maze of islands and extended bays. The walleye, lake

A northern pike is landed on Dozois Reservoir in Verendrye Provincial Reserve.

trout, and northern pike that once teemed in Lakes Bark, Rapid, Washkega, Wagoose, and Cabonga adapted well to the vastness of their new environment; and walleye are so plentiful that, given the right conditions and the right spot, it's possible to hook fish on virtually every cast. Most Cabonga walleye weigh between 2 and 4 pounds, but larger ones to 10 pounds are taken every season.

The key to successful walleye fishing on Cabonga-Dozois waters is knowing where the fish are. From the late May opening to the end of the first week of June, look for them at the mouths of incoming rivers. After the middle of June, fish along sandy shoals, in sandy bays, and off rocky points. Most of the big walleye lurk along the edge of the stickups, the vestiges of a drowned forest.

Northern pike are so abundant, they verge on becoming a nuisance at times, but anglers who target these fish can catch many up to 10 pounds—and some specimens in the 15- to 25-pound class—simply by working the shallow bays and the mouths of tributary streams. Lake trout, on the other hand, are less predictable. Fish weighing up to 40 pounds have been caught by anglers working the shoals off Cabonga Dam with gang trolls. Smaller lakers of between 5 and 10 pounds are caught by anglers working jigs and spoons through the fast-water pool at the base of the dam itself during early summer, when water flows are at their peak.

The Cabonga-Dozois Reservoir system can be confusing and, every summer more than one party of anglers wanders into one of the many blind bays, convinced that they are in the channel back to camp, and eventually runs out of gas around nightfall. Either an experienced guide or a GPS unit is a must, as is a sturdy, deep-hulled boat of 16 feet or more, capable of withstanding sudden summer storms.

Downstream about 50 miles along the Gens de Terre River, which in itself provides excellent fishing for big walleye, is Baskatong Reservoir—an excellent road-accessible fishery for pike and walleye. The fish tend to be somewhat smaller on average than in Cabonga as a result of Baskatong's greater accessibility and heavier fishing pressure. The backcountry behind Baskatong provides a wide range of fishing opportunities for brook trout, lake trout, splake, walleye, and pike. Gravel lumber roads cut into the territory provide dusty access, but many of the best lakes are accessible only by floatplane.

Farther to the west, along the Ontario border, Lake Kipawa is known for pike and walleye, although other opportunities exist as well. Some of the finest smallmouth bass fishing in the north is available locally, especially at Lake Beauchene and adjacent smaller waters, which are south of Kipawa and southeast of Temiscaming. Smallmouths grow to 5 pounds in Beauchene, and the walleye and northern pike are good size, too. The region also has brook trout, some to 4 pounds.

To the southeast, Gatineau River country offers

more opportunity for smallmouth bass. Exceptional northern smallmouth fishing brings anglers to Lake Blue Sea near Gracefield and to Lake McGregor north of Buckingham. On average, these fish weigh less than 2 pounds, but they definitely make up for their small size in pugnaciousness and abundance. This is also lake trout country, and lakes such as McGregor, Poison Blanc, Simon, Sept Frères, and des Iles, are just a few of the better spots.

Northern Region
That part of Quebec north of the 50th parallel is an immense territory covering about 74 percent of the total land area of the province. Typically, it is remote, sparsely inhabited by barely 42,500 humans, and stretches from the boreal forests and muskegs north to the subarctic barrens, where summer is measured in weeks, and frigid winds scour the earth's exposed crust. To count and catalog the lakes and rivers of this vast wilderness would requires a lifetime of devoted service; to fish the more accessible ones would take many lifetimes.

At one time, only a small corner of the far northern region was accessible by vehicle. Now a road runs northwest from Lake St. Jean to Chibougamou, then west-southwest to Lebel sur Quévillon and Senneterre. A spur runs north from Chibougamau to Lakes Waconichi, Albanel, and Mistassini. All three provide excellent fishing for lake trout, brook trout, walleye, and northern pike. As a rule, the walleye are small, but northern pike tend to grow big, with fish in the 10- to 20-pound class a reasonable expectation. Anglers easily land pike by trolling close to the surface, but the sandy flats at the inlet of the Papas, Cheno, and Toqueco Rivers at the north end of Mistassini are ideal for casting big streamer flies.

Lake trout are abundant but small on Waconichi, although anglers equipped with the proper gear can pick up fish in the 15- to 20-pound range. Lake trout tend to be somewhat larger on Albanel, but the best lake for this species is Mistassini, where trout over 35 pounds have been taken. The majority of the lakers, however, are between 5 and 15 pounds.

The brook trout fishing is legendary. Waconichi can provide steady angling for 2-pound brookies to enthusiasts trolling small minnow-imitation plugs or casting streamers. On Albanel, the same techniques can produce fish of 3 pounds, and this lake's major tributary, the Témiscamie River, has a trophy fishery. Brookies up to 4 pounds are fairly common, and fish twice that size are logged on occasion. Mistassini also offers excellent angling for big brookies among the many islands that run like beads up its middle. A variety of techniques works, but every now and then a hatch will bring fish of 2 to 4 pounds to the surface, providing exciting surface fly fishing. The Papas, Cheno, and Toqueco Rivers at the north end offer outstanding late-summer fishing for trophy brook trout.

Although not accessible by road, LakeAssinica and several other bodies of water in the headwaters of the Broadback River are home to the famous Assinica strain of brook trout. The average pocket-water brookie here weighs roughly $2^1/_2$ pounds, but the deeper holes consistently produce 5- to 6-pound specimens. Nine-pounders are taken annually, and the past record for the area is over 10 pounds. Hardware is productive on the lakes, but fly fishing brings the most fish to hand in the river. The best dry fly fishing for big brookies occurs in July and early August. From mid-August to early September, anglers fish the spawning runs for big, full-color brookies. The region is accessible by air from Chibougamau, and it's possible to mount a float-camp expedition in the region.

Until the middle 1980s, the Mistassini region was essentially the northern limit of road-accessible fishing in Quebec. But then a new network of wide and well-graded roads, initially built to haul massive generators to the James Bay hydroelectric project, was opened, and these have provided access not only to the rivers of the James Bay region, but also to the Caniapiscau Reservoir in the heart of this northern land. Excellent fishing for pike and walleye is within easy striking distance from the town of Radisson. In fact, superb pike and walleye are taken by anglers fishing off the top of the dikes built to contain La Grande 2 and La Grande 3, although the aesthetics might be sorely lacking. Continuing eastward along this stretch, the town site of Brisay is the gateway to the vast Caniapiscau Reservoir. Despite the short growing season, this body of water consistently produces northern pike and lake trout in the 10- to 20-pound class, and larger fish are common. Trophy brook trout from 3 to 8 pounds are caught fairly regularly throughout the short summer.

About a decade after the reservoir was created by damming the headwaters of the Caniapiscau River, biologists found that the landlocked salmon grow, on average, two to three times as big here as in surrounding waters. Typically, the Caniapiscau watershed has always produced landlocked salmon in the 3- to 6-pound class, and the speculation is that the reservoir's salmon grow more rapidly on a steady and nourishing diet of abundant whitefish, enabling them to quickly attain 10 pounds and more.

Beyond the reach of roads, northern Quebec offers fishing that dreams are made of. Access is primarily by floatplane out of four major gateways: Radisson in the James Bay region, Labrador City on the Labrador-Quebec border, Schefferville on the Labrador-Quebec border, and Kuujjuaq on the shores of Ungava Bay. The Radisson gateway is mostly used to access the angling opportunities of the James Bay and Hudson Bay drainages. The rivers and lakes lying to the north of Radisson are legendary for trophy brook trout.

Typical of these is the Seal River, which flows down out of the sparse taiga through a chain of

relatively small lakes to finally reach the sea at Cape Jones, the northern tip of James Bay before it becomes Hudson Bay. Brookies in the 2-pound class are the average on both the river and the lakes, whereas fish double that size are a reasonable expectation, especially during the onset of the spawning run in mid-August. In addition, these waters also produce excellent fishing for northern pike in the 6- to 20-pound class.

Brook trout are also abundant in the rivers of the Hudson Bay coast, but arctic charr become increasingly dominant northward. One of the best-known charr fishing areas along this coastline is Richmond Gulf near the village of Umiujaq. Although the fish tend to be in the 3- to 5-pound class, they are abundant and strike readily.

Farther north along the coast is the Tuksukatuk watershed. Three- to 4-pound brookies hold in the shallows of the main river, and lake trout are caught in the same area, even on flies. In the lower portion of the river, fresh-run arctic charr congregate in the shallow runs, where they take streamer flies and silver spoons readily. The rivers around the Inuit settlement of Povugnituk, well up near the northern tip of the peninsula, also produce charr in abundance.

Across the Ungava Peninsula to the east is the village of Kangirsuk at the mouth of the Payne River. Large schools of arctic charr congregate in the saltwater just off the mouth of the river through late June and most of August, providing steady action. Most anglers cast spoons from big, stable freighter canoes, but the fishing can be equally good from shore as well when the schools swing close to land.

Tidal pools inside the river offer tremendous sight fishing for charr. Around the middle of August, charr move upriver on the Payne, and in-river fishing in fast water outshines the river-mouth fishery. In addition, anglers frequently hook into hefty lake trout in the same pools. An angler landed a laker of about 35 pounds while charr fishing in the mid-1970s. The best lake trout fishing, however, is in Payne Lake, where fish of 20 to 40 pounds cruise the shallows for prey through the short barren-land summer, and they pounce on virtually any lure cast to them. The tributary streams are home to small brook trout.

Between the Payne and Leaf Rivers to the south along the Ungava Bay coast there are about a dozen other rivers that drain the heart of the peninsula, all with their own runs of sea trout and arctic charr. The Leaf is a significant river, drawing much of its flow from Lake Minto very close to the Hudson Bay coast. Two- to 3-pound sea-run and freshwater brook trout are found in many of the pools and countless tributary streams along its 200-mile-long course, but the river fishing for charr in blazing spawning colors is the foremost attraction. Schools of charr are caught in Leaf Bay through late July, and the schools start to move up the river in August to provide good fishing throughout the month and in early September. A small run of Atlantic salmon also enters the river in August, but this is largely a hit-or-miss proposition.

Atlantic salmon runs are more predictable on the Koksoak River, which enters the southern basin of Ungava Bay at the gateway community of Kuujjuaq. Two major branches—the Larch (shown as the Rivière aux Mélèzes on most maps) and the Caniapiscau (the same river that was dammed in its headwaters to create the Caniapiscau Reservoir discussed earlier)—meet about 80 miles inland to create this river. Virtually all of the Koksoak's Atlantic salmon runs turn into the Larch River branch, then into the Rivière du Gué, and finally the Delay River. Overwintered salmon provide good fishing in the Delay in July, and fresh-run salmon reach these waters later in August.

The 250-mile-long Caniapiscau River is rumored to have some salmon, but it is better known for its excellent brook trout and landlocked salmon fishing. Anglers also land lake trout on the river itself, although the best fishing is in the many lakes drained by its tributaries. For instance, Lakes Lemoyne, Nachicapau, and Canichico—located just east of the Caniapiscau itself and linked to it by way of a short river—offer fishing for large lake trout as well as landlocked arctic charr and brook trout.

East of the Koksoak, the Whale River (listed as the Rivière à la Baleine on most maps) has a long-standing reputation for its Atlantic salmon fishing. It flows into Ungava Bay about 100 miles east of Kuujjuaq, and, in most years, salmon are present in numbers from ice out in June through freeze-up in late September. The early fishery focuses on over-wintered salmon that have not yet spawned, but by mid-July, dime-bright estuarine salmon that mature in the brackish water of the river's mouth make up the bulk of the fish. In August, they're joined by heavy runs of salmon from the Atlantic feeding grounds. As a rule, Whale River salmon average between 8 and 12 pounds, although some runs consist almost entirely of fish in the 14- to 16-pound class. The record is a 24-pound fish taken in 1976.

A short floatplane hop farther east is the Tunulik River, well known for excellent arctic charr in the pools at its mouth. During the first half of the arctic summer, most of the charr are taken just off the coast in the open water of Ungava Bay; but by the end of July, the tidal pool at the base of the first falls provides most of the catches until the end of the season in early September. The Tunulik is known for its big charr; most fish are in the 8-pound class, but trophy charr from 14 to 18 pounds are taken regularly on bright silver spoons cast into the pools. After the middle of August, the charr linger in the upriver pools of the Tunulik, where they share the water with brook trout up to 2 pounds and lake trout averaging about 10 pounds.

The next major river system to the east is the George, considered one of the top Atlantic salmon rivers in the world. Some 400 miles long, the

George sees runs of more than 10,000 salmon, and all of them pass through one of the best-known stretches of water in the world: Helen's Falls, a 3-mile-long torrent barely 20 miles from the coast. The fish generally show up in early to mid-August, and the runs keep coming until the end of September. Three-quarters of the fish are salmon in the 6- to 10-pound class; the remainder of the run is evenly split between one-sea-winter fish (grilse) and three-sea-winter fish of 14 to 18 pounds. The biggest salmon recorded on the George is a 28-pounder.

Salmon here take flies well and seem to have a special penchant for black patterns. Helen's Falls, however, is not the salmons' only resting place on their way to upriver spawning grounds. Numerous excellent holding areas reach as far as the de Pas River, some 300 miles inland.

The George also offers excellent fishing for arctic charr and sea-run brook trout, primarily from the mouth to Helen's Falls and in the Ford River, a tributary to the George just downstream from the falls. Farther inland, freshwater brookies and lake trout share the pools, and, close to the headwater, big northern pike lurk in the shallow backwaters.

The George is the last of the four scheduled Atlantic salmon rivers of the Ungava Bay region, and the remaining watersheds emptying into the eastern basin of Ungava Bay are primarily arctic charr rivers, although a sea-run brook trout fishery exists as well. Keglo Bay, Weymouth Inlet, and the Koroc River produce consistently good charr fishing from mid-July on, although open-water fishing on the saltwater of the bay for dime-bright charr is good from the time the ice goes out in late June or early July.

Northern Quebec features trophy brook trout, along with lake trout and big northern pike, in the southeastern corner of the region, along the Labrador border. Accessible through Gagnon or Labrador City gateways are Lakes Chambeaux, Ternay, Justone, Lucault, and Matonipi, to name just a handful from among the hundreds in the region. Brook trout of 2 to 4 pounds are fairly common, and fish twice that size are caught from time to time during the short 10-week season imposed by the elements. Lake trout are also numerous and vary between 5 and 25 pounds. Northern pike inhabit most of the region's watersheds, and, because of the light fishing pressure, anglers can encounter trophy fish of 15 to 30 pounds.

QUEENFISH (CROAKER) Seriphus politus.
Other names—herring, herring croaker, kingfish, shiner, queen croaker; Spanish: *corvina reina*.

The queenfish is a small croaker and a member of the Sciacnidae family (drum and croaker). Essentially a panfish-size bottom scrounger, it is not an esteemed sport or food fish, but it is commonly caught from Pacific coast piers and may be desirable as whole or cut bait for other species.

Queenfish (Croaker)

Identification. The queenfish has an elongated, moderately compressed body. The upper profile is depressed over the eyes, and it has a large mouth. Its coloring is bluish above and becomes silvery below. The fins are yellowish. This species is distinguished from other croaker by its large mouth; by the base of its second dorsal and anal fins, which are roughly equal; and by the wide space between its two dorsal fins. There is no chin barbel on the lower jaw.

Size. The maximum length of the queenfish is 12 inches, but most fish are considerably smaller.

Distribution. The queenfish is found along the Pacific coast, from Yaquina Bay, Oregon, to Uncle Sam Bank in Baja California, Mexico. It is common in Southern California but rare north of Monterey.

Habitat. Queenfish commonly inhabit shallow water over sandy bottoms in summer. They mostly occur in water from 4 to 25 feet deep but have been known to dwell as deep as 180 feet. They often gather in tightly packed schools, sometimes with white croaker *(see: croaker, white)*, in shallow sandy areas near pilings and piers, and they migrate to deeper water at night.

Spawning behavior. Spawning occurs along the coast in summer. The eggs are free floating, and newly hatched juveniles appear in late summer and fall; they gradually move shoreward from depths of 20 to 30 feet into the surf zone.

Food. Queenfish feed on small, free-swimming crustaceans, crabs, and fish.

Angling. This species is often caught as a byproduct of other bottom fishing efforts, using natural baits on small hooks. Live sardines are a common bait.

QUEENFISH (JACKS)
Other names—leathery, queenie, leatherskin, whitefish, skinny-fish, giant dart, talang queenfish, doublespotted queenfish.

Members of the Carangidae family of jacks, pompano, and trevally, the species *Scomberoides lysan* and *S. commersonianus* are together popularly referred to as "queenfish," the former generally as doublespotted queenfish and the latter as talang queenfish. Very fast moving and powerful fighters when hooked, queenfish are noted for their long runs and a dogged struggle that is often punctuated with spectacular and repeated leaps as they try to

Queenfish (Jacks)

Talang Queenfish

throw the hook. Most anglers who have hooked up to a queenfish regard the experience as one of their most exciting, light-tackle challenges. It is also a reasonable table fish if bled immediately on capture, although the flesh of large specimens tends to be a bit dry.

Identification. Queenfish have a long, laterally compressed, deep, thin body that is covered in a leathery skin with deeply embedded scales. Silvery green with yellowish reflections, it carries a series of blotches that on *S. commersonianus* lie above the lateral line, and on *S. lysan* on either side of the lateral line. Both the second dorsal and anal fins of *S. commersonianus* are sickle shaped, which distinguishes it from *S. lysan*. The soft dorsal fin of *S. lysan* carries a distinct black area not present in *S. commersonianus*. The tail of each species is deeply forked.

Size. *S. commersonianus* are known to exceed 14 kilograms in weight, and *S. lysan* 7 kilograms. The world record for the former stands at 15.6 kilograms. Most captures fall in the 1- to 5-kilogram range.

Distribution. Queenfish range across the tropical top third of Australia, from about Gladstone in central Queensland to Carnarvon in Western Australia. Although not a common occurrence, they are sometimes taken from coastal waters near Brisbane, southeast Queensland. Elsewhere, they are broadly found in Indo-Pacific waters, including the Gulf of Thailand, Okinawa, Indonesia, the Philippines, Papua New Guinea, and the East Coast of Africa. *S. lysan* also occurs in Hawaii but is unconfirmed in the Gulf of Thailand.

Habitat. Mostly taken by boat anglers, the queenfish occurs around the coral cays on Australia's Great Barrier Reef, and close in to rocky headlands, bomboras, bays, river mouths, and wharves. They are also frequently caught by anglers chasing barramundi in mangrove creeks.

Life history/Behavior. Little research has been carried out on the queenfish, and its spawning behavior is not known. Adults prefer waters with a fast tidal movement, although anglers target the top of the tide and the start of the runout when fishing in mangrove creeks and estuaries.

Food and feeding habits. The queenfish is well known for its voracious attacks on schools of small food fish. At night, it is not uncommon for schools of queenfish to swim close to well-lit areas and attack a shoal of small baitfish. They may occasionally eat crustaceans.

Angling. High-speed, heavy-duty baitcasting or spinning outfits with a 7- to 10-kilogram line are the standard for taking queenfish. Queenfish will also take most natural baits, whether live or cut fish. Ganged hooks rigged with pilchards or garfish are also popular, as is the casting and fast retrieval of strip baits. By far the most favored method is casting fast-moving surface poppers, spoons, bucktail jigs, or minnow-type lures to sighted feeding fish. Wire leaders are frequently used, especially by bait anglers, although many use a heavy monofilament leader.

Because of the queenfish's habit of feeding on bait schools close to reefs and rock formations, small-boat anglers should maneuver close to these structures to cast or troll along their fringes. Gaffs are almost invariably used for boating the fish, as only small queenfish will fit into the average net.

Fighting a big queenfish is largely a matter of ensuring that a cool head and a pounding heart work in complete harmony. Aerial displays of shaking head and twisting body are common, and care should be taken not to hurry the playing process. Queenfish tend to remain in open water rather than adopt the tactics of some species (trevally, for example) of finding the sharpest rock edges against which to rub the line. Jumping tactics will quickly tire them.

Fly anglers can approach within casting distance of feeding fish and can be assured of fast responses and tackle-testing runs. Large saltwater flies, rapidly retrieved, are the best bet.

QUINNAT
A term for chinook salmon *(see)* in New Zealand.

QUOTA
A saltwater fisheries management term for the maximum number of fish that can be legally landed in a specified time period. This limit can apply to the total fishery (commercial and recreational catch) or to an individual fisherman's share. Quotas are primarily assigned to commercial fishermen, but in cases where stocks are low and there is a significant shared catch between commercial and recreational fishermen, such as with tuna, quotas apply to both.

R

RACE
An area of disturbed or confused water caused by the clashing of currents (see) and tides (see).

RADIO
See: Communications; Weather.

RADIO DIRECTION FINDER
A radio direction finder (RDF) is an electronic device primarily used for navigation and to determine radio signal bearings. Some big-boat anglers use an RDF to scan for radio chatter from anglers and to identify the location of anglers who report being on a school of fish. If they are not having success at their own position, they may pick up and head to where others are located.

RADIOTELEMETRY
Electronic tracking of fish for purposes of research and fisheries management (see).

RAFT
An inflatable boat. When used on large vessels, including commercial craft, an inflatable boat is called a life raft. Heavy-duty rafts are used in big-river recreation, especially for whitewater boating.

RAISE (A Fish)
Raising, a term used in various forms of sportfishing, occurs when a targeted species is attracted to the lure or bait and can be seen on the surface as it pursues lures or bait that are being fished on or close to the surface. Saltwater big-game anglers are said to "raise a fish" when it comes into their trolling spread and either shows interest in a teaser, lure, or bait, or actually attacks it. If they "raised" three fish in a given day, it would mean that on three separate occasions they saw a fish (usually a billfish but also tuna) swimming with or chasing their lures, even though they may not actually have caught any of them.

Stream trout and salmon anglers are said to raise a fish when they can see one move and look at their offering, and muskie anglers are likewise said to raise a fish when they see one pursue or follow their lure on the retrieve, generally near the boat.

This term is often used in referring to fish that are difficult to catch, and to conditions in which an angler is unlikely to catch, or even see, many specimens in a single outing. This is especially true for giant tuna, marlin, Atlantic salmon, and muskellunge.

RAYS AND SKATES
The various families that belong to the order of fish known as Rajiformes are generally referred to as ray and skate, and include such groupings as sawfish, guitarfish, electric ray, stingray, eagle ray, manta ray, and skate. Among the dominant distinguishing features of this order are gill openings wholly on the ventral surface and forward edges of the pectoral fins connected with the sides of the head and situated forward, past the five pairs of gill openings; eyeballs not free from the upper edges of the orbits, as they are in sharks; and no anal fin.

Most Rajiformes are easily recognized by their form. Their bodies are flattened dorso-ventrally, and the pectoral fins extend widely and seem to be part of the body. The tail section is more or less defined from the body, the eyes and spiracles are on the top side, and the mouth and entire lengths of the gill openings are situated on the bottom side. Sawfish, however, are sharklike in general appearance. They are classified among the order Rajiformes on skeletal considerations as well as for the relationship of the pectorals to the gills and because of the absence of upper eyelids. The shape of the majority of guitarfish resembles a cross between sharklike and skatelike forms.

Some members of this order have no dorsal fin, others have one or two. Some possess a distinct caudal (tail) fin, others do not. The spiracles are larger than those of most sharks and are always located on top of the head. The majority have well-developed eyes. In a few species, however, the eyes are degenerate. Without exception, the order Rajiformes has five pairs of gill openings. Some have smooth skins; others are covered with thorny or prickly protrusions; and some have tails armed with dangerous, saw-edged spines. The shape of the teeth varies. Teeth may resemble thorns, knobs, or plates, or be sharply pointed. They may be in bands, transverse rows, or mosaic patterns. None of the members of this group has luminescent organs, but some have electric organs.

In those Rajiformes that lie on the bottom or bury themselves in the sand, the spiracles are important in the process of respiration. Water taken in through these passages courses over the

A big ray from Marco Island, Florida.

gills and out through the gill openings. Skate, however, may hold their heads slightly above the bottom when resting and take in some water through the mouth. Mantas swim more freely and inhale water mostly or completely through the mouth; they have proportionately smaller spiracles.

The members of the Rajiform clan range in size from only a few inches to giant mantas with a breadth of about 23 feet. The spectacularly armed sawfish reach a length of more than 20 feet.

The mode of locomotion varies within the group. Skate and stingray are propelled forward smoothly along the bottom by undulating the pectoral fins from front to rear. Guitarfish use their tails chiefly in swimming, with an assist from the pectorals. Mantas and eagle ray, with their more pointedly shaped pectoral fins, swim with a flapping motion of the fins or "wings," more or less resembling bird flight. In the process of swift motion, some eagle ray and mantas hurl themselves into the air, often completing a somersault, one of the most spectacular sights of the sea. Sawfish swim chiefly by lateral undulations of the posterior portion of their trunk, aided by the caudal fin and to a lesser degree by the pectorals.

All members of this order effect fertilization internally; the act is facilitated by a pair of claspers developed along the inner edges of the male's pelvic fins, in the same manner as it is in sharks. The inner edges have deep grooves, with the edges more or less overlapping, thereby aiding the transportation of the sperm into the female.

Development in the skate family is oviparous. The eggs encased in horny capsules are commonly seen washed up on sandy beaches. As far as is known, however, all other members of this order are ovoviviparous; that is, embryos develop inside the oviducts of the female until ready for extrusion. In this type of development, there is no placental attachment between mother and young.

Most Rajiformes live on the bottom or close to it and are comparatively sluggish. Some of them lie buried in the sand or mud most of the time and are poor swimmers. Skate are capable of swift propulsion when necessary, although they usually swim slowly and close to the bottom. Sawfish also spend a good part of the time along the bottom but rise to pursue fish at middepths or higher. Eagle ray are quite active and often swim close to the surface, although they feed on the bottom. In opposition to its close cousins, the mantas seem to have abandoned bottom living and spend most of their lives swimming near the surface or not too far beneath it.

Ray and skate subsist on a variety of animal food, including all available invertebrates that inhabit sandy or muddy bottoms. Eagle ray, as a group, prefer hard-shelled mollusks, while the sawfish occasionally leave their bottom foraging to crash into a school of closely packed fish. Electric ray are strictly fish eaters, sometimes taking surprisingly large prey in comparison to their size. The mantas, including the giants of the group, feed on tiny plankton, small crustaceans, and small fish. Their mode of feeding is similar to that of the huge whale sharks and basking sharks. Food is carried into the mouth by the intake of water and sifted by the so-called prebranchial apparatus, as the water passes over the gills and out through the gill openings.

Commercially, ray and skate are of little value. Small quantities are used from time to time as fertilizer and as baits for traps, although the meat from the wings of some specimens is used, and has been passed as scallops in the past. When caught along North American coasts, the great majority are released. There has historically been a greater demand for skate in northern Europe. Various ray are available in fish markets in many tropical areas, but the quantity used is small. These bottom dwellers can be a great nuisance to anglers because they take baited hooks meant for other fish. Also, they are capable of inflicting a painful wound with their serrated spines when stepped on or handled incautiously.

Rajiformes are widely distributed in latitude and depth in the Atlantic, Pacific, and Indian Oceans, including adjacent seas. They also cover a broad thermal range, from cold polar waters to warm tropical seas. The most numerous group are skate, which primarily inhabit the temperate belts of the two hemispheres. Their cousins are found predominantly in tropical and subtropical waters. Electric ray may be grouped as occupying an intermediate geographical position.

As an order, Rajiformes constitutes a saltwater group, but several species of stingray have colonized in freshwater in the lower portions of South American rivers draining into the Atlantic. They are found far up some rivers, however. Sawfish also frequently inhabit freshwater.

Although these fish are seldom sought by anglers, some are encountered or at least observed by them, especially by people fishing in shallow tropical and subtropical waters, so brief reviews of the families follow.

Pristidae (sawfish). These sharklike ray have a long snout that is formidably armored with sharp teeth along each side. They are bottom dwellers like typical ray but will rise toward the surface to slash through a school of baitfish, turning to pick up any that have been stunned or wounded. Sometimes they succeed in impaling several fish on their toothed snout; these are then scraped off on the bottom and eaten. The long snout is also used to probe into sand or mud to dig up shellfish. If molested, a sawfish turns this food-getting snout into a powerful weapon of defense and can inflict serious injury, but there is no evidence of unprovoked attacks.

Like ray, sawfish have gill slits on the underside of the body on each side just behind the mouth, and the large pectoral fins are joined broadly to the head. The body is long and slim, more like that of a shark. The four species of sawfish are cosmopolitan in distribution in warm to tropical seas, inhabiting shallow waters and straying into brackish water or even freshwater. A sizable population has become landlocked in Lake Nicaragua.

The smalltooth sawfish *(Pristis pectinata)* is commonly 15 feet long and sometimes reaches a length of 20 feet. It can weigh as much as 800 pounds. This species is common throughout warm Atlantic waters, from the Mediterranean southward to Namibia and from North Carolina to Brazil. The largetooth sawfish *(P. perotteti)*, a western Atlantic species, is similar but has larger teeth in proportion to its body. Sawfish that live in Indo-Pacific waters are the giants of the clan.

Rhinobatidae (guitarfish). Guitarfish have a distinct raylike body, with the forward part rounded or heart shaped. The snout is wedge shaped, and the tail sector is not clearly distinguished from the body. The caudal fin is relatively short and thick, but the dorsal and anal fins are well developed. The gills are on the underside of the body, which is typical in ray.

Guitarfish inhabit tropical and subtropical seas around the world and are sometimes found running up into freshwater. There are 43 species in the family. Like typical ray, guitarfish are bottom feeders, eating mainly small crustaceans and mollusks. They are ovoviviparous. Most species are 5 to 6 feet long, although the giant guitarfish *(Rhyncobatos djiddensis)* of the Indo-Pacific region reaches a length of 10 feet.

Smalltooth Sawfish

The Atlantic guitarfish *(Rhinobatos lentiginosus;* see: guitarfish, Atlantic) is widely distributed in warm waters and is especially common in the Atlantic. Its average length is 2 feet, but some reach a length of 3 feet; the females are larger than the males. The grayish brown body is covered with small whitish spots. The shovelnose guitarfish *(R. productus)* is a 4-foot species found in the Pacific from the Gulf of California to San Francisco.

Torpedinidae (electric ray). Roughly 14 species of electric ray inhabit seas throughout the world. Some live at great depths, others in shallow inshore waters. Some are as much as 6 feet long and weigh 200 pounds; others are less than a foot long. The eyes are small and functional in most species but are rudimentary or obsolete in a few deep-water forms. None of the electric ray are good swimmers; they spend most of their time partly buried in the sand or mud on the bottom and move only sluggishly. Their bodies are soft and flabby compared to those of skate and other ray, and the skin of most species is soft and marked. Development is ovoviviparous.

All electric ray are able to generate jolting charges of electricity. Any diver, swimmer, or angler who has come close to or tried to handle an electric ray knows the power of their shock. This defense protects these ray from would-be predators and delivers stunning blows to prey that would otherwise be too fleet for these slow-moving fish to capture. Ordinarily, however, these ray eat crustaceans, worms, and similar small animals that can be captured without the need for discharging electricity.

The Atlantic torpedo *(Torpedo nobiliana)*—which ranges in the eastern Atlantic from Scotland to South Africa, including the Mediterranean, and in the western Atlantic from Nova Scotia to North Carolina—is the largest of these ray. It averages roughly 30 pounds in weight, but individuals as much as 6 feet long and weighing 200 pounds have been reported. Despite its name, this fish is anything but speedy or torpedo-like; instead, it is sluggish, and therefore characteristic of the Latin meaning of the word "torpid." A related $1^1/_2$-foot-long species, *T. marmorata,* lives in the Mediterranean and along the eastern Atlantic coast from the United Kingdom to South Africa. The Pacific electric ray *(T. californica)* is similar to the Atlantic species but smaller, and it is found from British Columbia to

Lesser Electric Ray

Fifty species of stingray in six genera are distributed in warm, shallow waters around the world. A few stray into brackish water or even into freshwater. They range in size from species that measure only a foot across their wings to others that have spans as great as 7 feet. In nearly all species, the body disk—including the winglike pectoral fins—is nearly round. Although stingray feed on worms, their main diet is crustaceans and mollusks, which they crush between their flat-topped teeth. A few stingray are active and aggressive enough to catch fish.

One of the most common stingray along the Atlantic coast of North America is the bluntnose stingray *(Dasyatis say)*, which measures about 3 feet across its pectorals. It ranges from New Jersey to Argentina and is widespread in the West Indies, sometimes straying into cooler waters during warmer months. The Atlantic stingray *(D. sabina)* measures only slightly more than a foot across its wings, which are very rounded. This uniformly

Baja California, Mexico. Also small at seldom more than a foot long is the lesser electric ray *(Narcine brasiliensis)*, which ranges from North Carolina to the Gulf of Mexico.

Dasyatidae (stingray). Stingray are best known for their long, slim, whiplike tails that are armed with one to several spines near the base. When caught or stepped on, a stingray lashes its tail and invariably manages to impale a spine in its molester. Poison from glands along the grooves on each side of the spine flows into the wound, delivering additional and excruciating pain. The venom should be flushed from the wound as soon as possible, and it is best to see a doctor for treatment and antibiotics. Deaths have resulted from untreated stingray wounds, particularly when they have been inflicted in the trunk area rather than on the limbs.

Stingray generally lie on the bottom, almost completely buried in the sand or soft sediment. Camouflaged also by their grayish brown and often mottled coloration, they are almost impossible to see. Wading anglers walk slowly in a bottom-shuffling manner that usually, but not always, sends a nearby stingray scuttling off.

yellowish brown stingray is found in the western Atlantic, from the Chesapeake Bay to southern Florida and the Gulf of Mexico, and has occurred in the Mississippi River. More common than the Atlantic stingray and ranging from New Jersey to Argentina is the southern stingray *(D. americana)*, which averages about 3 feet wide. On the underside of its tail, just behind the spine, are finlike folds; above them, the tail is keeled.

The round stingray *(Urolophus halleri)* is common in the eastern Pacific, from Northern California to Panama. It measures about 1½ feet across its pectorals. In the Atlantic, from North Carolina to the Caribbean, is the closely related yellow stingray *(U. jamaicensis)*. In both species, the rounded disk is mottled with dark on a light brown background. The tail is short and stout, and the venom is extremely potent.

Stingray of one group live so exclusively in freshwater that they are usually placed in a separate

Atlantic Stingray

Southern Stingray

family, Potamotrygonidae, and are referred to as river ray or river stingray. There are 14 species in three genera of this family, and they are found in South America.

Myliobatidae (eagle ray). As a group, these are among the most pelagic of the ray, although not as completely as the mantas. They still seek their food mainly from the bottom, however, probing for shellfish and crustaceans, which they crush with their powerful flat teeth to get at the soft insides. At other times, they swim almost swallowlike through the water. Now and then an eagle ray will burst into the air in a brief, spectacular "flight."

Unlike the typical bottom-dwelling ray, the 22 members of this group have a distinct head region, with the eyes and spiracles located on each side rather than on top. A distinctive fleshy lobe, or crown, caps the front of the head. Most species have one or more poisonous spines at the base of the tail, but the spines are so short and so close to the body that they cannot be used very effectively even in defense. Eagle ray occur in all warm and tropical seas.

The spotted eagle ray *(Aetobatus narinari)* is cosmopolitan in warm seas. One of the giants of its clan, it may measure more than 7 feet across its "wings" and reaches weights of between 400 and 500 pounds. Its tail carries more than one spine, frequently as many as five. Because its snout resembles a duck's bill, this species is known also as the spotted duckbilled ray. Its wings and body are heavily spotted, earning it the name of leopard ray as well.

The bullnose ray *(Myliobatis freminvillii)*, which occurs in the western Atlantic from Cape Cod to Brazil and possibly in the Gulf of Mexico and the Caribbean, lacks spots and is considerably smaller, measuring only about 3 feet across. The bat ray *(M. californica)* occurs in the Pacific, from the Gulf of California to Oregon. Like other eagle ray, it has a special fondness for shellfish and becomes a destructive pest where oysters and clams are being harvested commercially.

Mobulidae (mantas). The mantas, also called devil ray, comprise a 10-member family that spans a wide spectrum of size, from ocean giants to species that measure only a few feet across the pectoral fins. Mantas are easily distinguished by two flexible head protrusions, called cephalic fins, that form narrow lobes, one on each side of the head. These appendages are used chiefly to facilitate the entrance of small pelagic food organisms into the wide mouth. The cephalic fins, separated widely and extending forward from the head, resemble "horns," from which the name "devil ray" originates.

Mantas lack a caudal fin. Their skin, aside from tail spines, is naked or covered with small tubercles or prickles. The minute teeth are in both jaws or in only one, in series and forming a band. The Atlantic manta and the Pacific manta have a terminal mouth (at the end of the snout) rather than one that is directed downward as in their close cousins, the

Atlantic Manta

mobulas. Development is ovoviviparous. They range in tropical to warm temperate regions of all oceans.

The giant manta *(Manta birostris)* is circumtropical and the largest species; its wing span can exceed 20 feet, and it can weigh well over 3,000 pounds. The dorsal color of the giant manta is dull, varying from dark olive brown to black. There may be a lighter patch on each shoulder and various blotches and indistinct markings. The superficial areas of coloration may be natural in some and accidental in others because the dark pigmentation is easily rubbed off. The underside of the body is white or creamy white.

The European manta *(Mobula mobular)* belongs to a genus of mantas that have teeth in both jaws and that have the mouth on the underside of the head. Measuring about 4 feet across its wings, the European manta is further distinguished by its possession of a spine, or sometimes two, at the base of the tail, as in other types of ray. This species occurs from Iceland south to Senegal but is most abundant in the Mediterranean region, and strays have occurred off New Jersey and Cuba.

In the western Atlantic, the devil ray, or little devilfish *(M. hypostoma)*, occurs from New Jersey to Brazil and is about the same size as the European manta; it has a long tail that lacks a spine. The devil ray is extremely active in its feeding habits, commonly forcing schools of small fish into the shallows as several mantas rush into the milling fish to scoop up a mouthful. This manta also easily and regularly leaps clear of water, whereas the giant Atlantic manta, because of its size, has difficulty in getting completely into the air. The devil ray usually travels in small schools.

Rajidae (skate). In skate, the dorsal and anal fins are greatly reduced in size, and the pelvic fins are deeply notched so that they appear as four fins rather than two. The pectoral fins are large and winglike, joined at the front of the head to form a shelflike snout. The tail is moderately slender. Males have long, prominent claspers used in mating.

Skate produce unusual leathery egg cases called sea purses or sailor's purses. At each of the four corners of the case is a thin projection that helps to anchor the case to objects on the sea bottom. These egg cases are nevertheless commonly washed ashore and are among the curios picked up by beach wanderers.

Skate Egg Case

Skate can dart swiftly, when necessary, using their pectoral fins in undulating motions for graceful underwater propulsion. But they are essentially bottom dwellers, usually lying quietly half buried in the sand or mud during the daylight hours and stirring to feed at night, although they also take an angler's bait during daytime. Skate are brown or grayish, commonly mottled, blending well with the bottom. When they rest, they usually fan the sand or soft sediment as they settle so that only their eyes and spiracles are above the surface. By creating suction with their body, they can cling to the bottom so tightly that they are difficult to dislodge. If forced out of hiding, they squirm and twist, frequently managing to impale a victim with their tail spine. A few species can deliver a mild shock; their electric organs are located in the tail and are connected to spinal nerves.

Skate sometimes eat fish, making their catches by darting up quickly from the bottom and then holding the fish down with their body until they can grab their victim with their mouth, which is on their underside. Mostly, however, skate feed on shellfish and crustaceans, which they secure by grubbing them from the bottom. Skate have flat, pavementlike teeth for crushing the shells. In many countries, skate are caught commercially and are prized as food.

Most skate live in rather shallow water and close to shore, but there are some deep-water species. The largest genus is *Raja*, which contains more than a hundred species found in cool to temperate waters throughout the world.

The little skate *(R. erinacea)* is the most common species along the Atlantic coast of North America, ranging from Nova Scotia to North Carolina. Also known as the hedgehog skate, it is about $1^1/_2$ feet long and weighs only about a pound. It has a row of spines along its back, from just behind the eyes to the end of the tail fin. The big skate *(R. binoculata)*, reaches a length of 8 feet. It is found from the Bering Sea and the Aleutians to Baja, California, Mexico. The more abundant California skate *(R. inornata)* averages only about 2 feet in length and has four to five rows of prickly spines on its tail; it occurs from British Columbia to central Baja California. Also notably thorny is the clearnose skate *(R. eglanteria),* which has spines on its back as well as on its tail. This species is common along the middle and northeastern Atlantic coast in summer but retreats to warmer waters off Florida and in the Caribbean in winter. It gets its name from the translucent areas on each side of its snout. The barndoor skate *(R. laevis)* is one of the most aggressive of all skate and grows to a length of about 5 feet. It is common from Newfoundland to Cape Hatteras and is often caught on baited hooks. The barndoor skate's counterpart off the coast of Europe is the common skate *(R. batis),* which is harvested commercially. It ranges from Norway and Iceland to Senegal, including the western Mediterranean.

RDF
See: Radio Direction Finder.

REACH CAST
An in-air technique for presenting a fly or mending a fly line.
See: Mending.

READING WATER
A term for watching water conditions to determine where fish may be located and how to present lures, flies, or bait to them.
See: Finding Fish.

RECORDS
The largest individuals of a particular species of fish taken by anglers, according to the characteristics or type of equipment used, the body of water, the geographic or governmental region, or other method of classification. Most official records are kept by a government or private organization by state, province, or nation, usually for the major species that are pursued by anglers, but in some cases also for species that are uncommonly caught or rare. These records are based on the weight of the fish without regard to the time it took to make the catch or the difficulty involved.

Common Skate

The most celebrated world-record catch is commemorated by the state of Georgia.

The criteria for establishing state, provincial, and national records vary widely. The equipment permitted in one, for example, may not be permitted in another; likewise, the circumstances surrounding the catch (foul hooking, more than one person handling the rod, etc.) may cause disqualification in some but not in others. Thus, there may a good deal of discrepancy between these types of records.

On a worldwide basis, records for both freshwater and saltwater species—known as world records—are kept by the International Game Fish Association *(see)* in several methods of categorization, and they are based upon defined internationally accepted rules regarding the equipment, methods, and circumstances.

The IGFA keeps these records according to line-class and all-tackle categories for fish caught on all types of fishing tackle except fly tackle; there is a separate category for fish caught on flycasting equipment. The latter is kept according to tippet class, with seven tippet strengths ranging from 1 to 10 kilograms. Line-class records correspond to the specific breaking strength of line, and range from 1 to 60 kilograms, although line-class records do not exist in the heavier strengths for species that do not attain large weights. An all-tackle record is the heaviest individual of a given species of sportfish caught on sporting tackle, using line up to 60-kilogram (130-pound) breaking strength; it may also be a line-class world record.

Certain important requirements must be met when submitting applications for world record recognition. One of the more important is the requirement that the catch be weighed on certified scales, and preferably be witnessed by disinterested parties who will attest to the weight. Another is that a sample be sent of the line used to catch the particular fish being considered for a world record; the line is tested by IGFA to determine its actual breaking strength *(see: line)*, since this may differ from the label strength. A clear photograph of the fish, with the tackle used, is also required to assure proper identification of the species.

Hundreds of world records exist, and scores of new records—usually displacing previous records—are established every year. Just as many are denied record status as are granted; denial is usually because the line is found to be heavier than the category for which the fish was submitted or because the fish was weighed on uncertified scales.

Over the years, much controversy has surrounded some records, especially ones for very popular species or species that people are especially passionate about. As a result, some of the older records, which were established before rigorous criteria and evaluation methods were adopted, have been "retired" or disallowed.

Because of media attention and/or the length of time that existing records have gone unbroken, the all-tackle records for certain species are especially coveted. These include largemouth bass, muskellunge, northern pike, walleye, striped bass, bluefish, tarpon, bonefish, sailfish, blue marlin, and black marlin.

RECREATIONAL FISHERMAN

A person who catches fish and shellfish for personal use, fun, challenge, and leisure. This broad term is primarily applied to noncommercial fishermen in saltwater who do not sell their catch, regardless of the means used to capture the fish or shellfish, provided that such means does not involve high-volume harvesting techniques and equipment. It may also apply to noncommercial fishermen in freshwater who use methods other than rod and reel to capture fish.

Technically, the U.S. Department of Commerce considers fishing to be recreational when "pleasure, amusement, relaxation, and/or home consumption or subsistence are the primary motivations." Marine recreational fishing is defined by the National Marine Fisheries Service as "any fishing in marine waters that does not result in the sale or barter of all or part of the fish harvested."

The term "recreational fisherman" is used by marine fisheries managers as all-inclusive and to delineate commercial fishermen from noncommercial fishermen. However, to the sportfishing community, this term differs from "angler," or "sportfisherman," which are both used to signify people who use sporting equipment (i.e., rod and reel) during the act of fishing and who, in theory, are not pursuing large numbers or volumes of fish species. Thus, a scuba diver who uses a speargun to "catch" fish is not an angler, but would be considered a recreational fisherman. A person who uses a rake to dig clams for personal use would likewise be categorized by marine fisheries managers as a recreational fisherman but not an angler. And a person who uses a trotline *(see)* or setline *(see)* for personal use would also be categorized by freshwater fisheries managers as a recreational fisherman but not an angler.

Furthermore, and also muddying an understanding of this term, is the fact that some saltwater anglers who consider themselves recreational anglers—using rod and reel exclusively and fishing primarily for sporting purposes—also sell a portion of their catch in states where such sales are not prohibited for certain species (dolphin and tuna especially), evidently as a means of offsetting the high cost of traveling to offshore environs to fish for those species. The sale of fish by so-called recreational fishermen is a controversial one among anglers, and causes difficulties when sportfishing interests are pitted against commercial fishing interests.

See: Angler; Angling; Commercial Fisherman; Sportfishing; Sportfisherman.

RECREATIONAL FISHERY

A fisheries management term, primarily used in saltwater fishing, referring to all aspects of the act of fishing or the harvest of fish for noncommercial purposes, under conditions in which the proceeds are released or kept for personal use and are not sold. This term includes fisheries resources, the people who utilize those resources, and businesses providing goods and services.

See: Recreational Fisherman.

REDD

A pit or trough made by female salmon and trout in the gravel bottom of rivers or streams for spawning. Eggs are laid in the redd, which is sometimes also called a nest.

RED TIDE

An area of water, frequently discolored, that is formed by accumulations of large numbers of microscopic plants or animals. These phenomena are not tides; and although some are red, they may be amber, brown, purple, or pink, or not visibly colored. A red tide may be confined to relatively small patches, or it may cover several acres or even many square miles of sea.

Red tides have been documented worldwide for thousands of years in cold temperate to tropical waters. In North America, red tides occur on both sides of the Atlantic, off Florida, and along the Pacific coast into Alaska.

Red tides are caused by dinoflagellates. These and other types of microscopic algae (about $1/1000$ inch long), collectively called phytoplankton, are plentiful (hundreds of thousands per liter of water) and serve as a foundation for the marine food web. Dinoflagellates can produce some of the most powerful poisons in nature. When certain dinoflagellates are present in higher-than-normal concentrations, a "bloom" is created that releases poison, or toxin, into the water. This poison can cause various effects; for example, it may paralyze fish, causing them to stop breathing, after which the result may be large die-offs. Sometimes, a bloom discolors the surrounding water. Some instances of red tide have been linked to pollution, but many are unrelated.

Most red tides are harmless. However, toxic red tides can kill fish and other marine animals and can contaminate shellfish such as clams and oysters. People can become ill by eating shellfish tainted with red tide toxins. Some toxic red tides cause debilitation through paralytic shellfish poisoning (PSP), a disease that is contracted by eating infected shellfish and that attacks the human nervous system; additionally, toxic particles in sea spray at the shore can cause respiratory discomfort. Although the term "red tide" is widely used to indicate the presence of poisonous shellfish, only a very small percentage of red tides cause shellfish to be unsafe. However, outbreaks of poisonous shellfish may occur when there is no discoloration of the water, or they may be caused by other factors.

REDFISH

A common term for red drum (see: drum, red).

REDWORM

Also known as a red wiggler, this is a type of earthworm (see), normally about 3 to 4 inches long, and a popular freshwater bait.

See: Natural Bait.

REEF

A mass or ridge of rock in a body of freshwater or saltwater. Rock reefs are submerged parts of land rising from the bed of a lake, large river, or the ocean; they are permanent objects (unlike a bar or shoal, which consists of unconsolidated sediment) and can be hazardous to navigation when they rise close enough to the surface. Many reefs that are in the navigational zone of well-traveled waterways are marked with buoys, but they may not be marked in infrequently traveled areas of oceans, rivers, and lakes, or in seldom-visited far northern lakes.

Reefs may be places where various forms of aquatic life find shelter and food, and they are thus attractive to many species of sportfish, such as lake trout, walleye, and smallmouth bass in freshwater and many species of jacks, snapper, and grouper in saltwater. Fishing efforts around them include trolling, jigging, and bottom fishing with bait; in saltwater, a lot of chumming (see) is done.

In the oceans, there are also biogenic reefs, which are composed of various living organisms and are called coral reefs (see); these are either

fringing reefs (close to mainland shores), barrier reefs (separated from the mainland), or atolls (surrounding volcanic peaks).
See: Inshore Fishing.

REEL, FISHING

Fishing reels are basically line management devices that are affixed to some type of rod. Their primary functions are storing, dispensing, and retrieving fishing line.

The storage function relates to the ability of the reel to contain sufficient line to allow continued fishing in the event of a tangle and breakoff, as well as to provide for sustained runs by large fish. The dispenser function is more complex; it ranges from the ideally friction-free event of long-distance casting to the action of a clutch, which allows line to slip outward under tension (called the drag; see). The retrieval function likewise ranges from the high speed recovery necessary to impart lure action to the powerful cranking power required to raise a stubborn fish away from its protective bottom structure.

Fishing reels accomplish these functions by several means. In each case, the design of the reel tends to favor one function over the others, and leads to several basic divisions of fishing reel types.

Types

Fishing reels can be divided into two major categories, depending upon whether the spool revolves or is stationary.

Revolving-spool reels. Conventional, or revolving-spool, fishing reels receive their name because the motion of the line is considered conventional; it is pulled from a spool that revolves the same way that sewing thread is taken from its spool. Such reels are mechanically straightforward; they are characterized by strong cranking power and the ability to handle heavy lines. Although revolving-spool reels hold the majority of distance casting records, they are relatively difficult to cast and require considerable skill and practice to avoid catastrophic errors.

Revolving-spool reels can be categorized as single- or multiplying-action versions. Single-action reels, which include fly fishing and mooching products, are simply spools with handles that revolve on a shaft. The spool is large because each rotation of the handle must retrieve a reasonable amount of line. However, the large spool severely limits casting distance because the energy to start the spool rotating requires unsuitably massive terminal weights. In the case of fly fishing, the reel is simply a line storage device, and the line is pulled by hand from the reel to facilitate the cast.

Single-action reels are mounted below the axis of the rod so that forward winding retrieves the line. Because of the direct drive nature of the handle, the mechanical efficiency can be excellent, and the simplicity of the design offers great reliability. The drag function—applying pressure to make it harder for the spool to permit line to flow outward when pulled by a large fish—may be as simple as using the hand to apply friction to the edge of the spool, or may include the use of adjustable mechanical friction washers.

Multiplying-action reels are commonly referred to as multipliers and today are represented by a group of products that are generally termed "conventional " reels. These have comparatively small spools that are driven by a mechanical gear train. The gear train can be disconnected to free the spool, allowing for excellent long-distance casting in lighter weight products. Spool overrun can occur, however, leading to a vividly descriptive condition of line tangle called a "bird's nest." Avoiding this catastrophe requires considerable skill by the caster.

Because the gear train consists of parallel axes for the shafts, the mechanical forces are simply constrained, frictional losses are minimal, and cranking power is superb. Likewise, the drag system is uncomplicated and extremely effective. In addition, the line is wound directly onto the spool, easing line flexibility requirements and allowing the use of very heavy lines on very small spools. Some models of these reels can be used efficiently with a wide variety of line strengths. Multiplier reels range from freshwater baitcasting reels to big-game reels for offshore fishing applications.

Fixed-spool reels. Spinning reels are called "fixed-spool" reels as well as "stationary-spool" reels because the line is dispensed from the end of a nonrotating spool. The spool axis is parallel to the rod, and the line is pulled over the spool lip when cast. Such a system does not require energy to rotate a spool, and is not subject to overrun; thus, it is extremely simple to cast and relatively tangle free.

Retrieval is accomplished by winding the line around the fixed spool with a rotating arm. Because this motion requires a 90-degree change of direc-

A wide variety of reels, with different features and capabilities, are on the market.

tion, there are mechanical losses even with relatively limp lines. Likewise, the drive gears from handle to rotating arm require a 90-degree change of direction, leading to thrust forces and mechanical losses. Fixed-spool reels thus excel in casting, even for users who are relatively unskilled and unpracticed, but are not as efficient in cranking power as revolving-spool reels.

Two types of fixed- or stationary-spool reels are widely used and very popular, especially in freshwater fishing. One features a spool that is exposed and always visible to the user, and is commonly called a spinning reel. The other features a covered spool and is commonly called a spincasting reel. The latter has convenient push-button casting operation, and a top-mounted hand position identical to that of the (revolving-spool) baitcasting reel. Individual spinning reels can typically be used efficiently with three, or perhaps four, strengths of line; individual spincasting reels can be used with only two or three strengths of line.

The features and use of each of these types of reels is described in greater detail in their specific section.

Production and Materials

The manufacture of fishing reels requires a fairly large capital investment in dies, designs, tooling, computer design/manufacturing software, and so forth. The finished product is a mass-produced item, each as nearly alike as the other. This is true as well even for limited-production items that are "machined" from barstock, which require an enormous development cost. Fishing reels are not custom-made products that can be created for individual needs and interests, although there is a substantial amount of after-market tinkering that occurs with some, particularly reels that are put to the most demanding big-game fishing uses.

Many of the components and features of reels are discussed in detail in their respective entries, but one factor that has become more variable is the actual materials used. Many manufacturers have stressed the use of metal, or the use of plastic, in their products, but a lot of anglers do not understand why or how this may be relevant. Materials may vary greatly with freshwater and lighter-duty reels, and the subject warrants a brief review here.

Metal. The metals used to fabricate fishing reels range from simple diecast alloys (aluminum and zinc) through machinable, tough aerospace alloys (hardened high tensile strength aluminum). The choice is typically determined by engineering requirements and costs.

Positive attributes of metal in reels include strength, rigidity, and durability.

For a given-sized part, metals are generally stronger than polymers; this is true even with less expensive alloys. For this reason, the internal gears of reels are almost universally metals, such as brass, stainless steel, aluminum bronze, or other alloys. Similarly, the metal body of a reel is stronger than its polymer counterpart. In the case of high-end reels, the body is often machined from a solid block or billet of metal, resulting in the strongest possible structure, without regard for cost.

Metals are also stiff, or rigid, by nature and are able to maintain precise alignment between gears, even when subject to heavy stresses. Frame distortion under load leads to gear misalignment and loss of cranking power. The losses in cranking power are actually delivered as wear to the gear train, and measurably decrease gear life. Being rigid, metals resist this distortion and power loss.

Durability is achieved through the superior wear properties of metals. Many alloys are not only used for the frame, but may double as load-bearing surfaces.

The negative attributes of metal reel bodies include weight, corrosion, and lack of shock resistance. Aluminum and its alloys comprise the bulk of metal reel components, offering about a threefold decrease in weight compared to steel, stainless steel, or brass alloys. Titanium, although extremely light, is presently too expensive and difficult to machine to be practical.

Metal reels generally require surface treatment to inhibit corrosion, particularly in a saltwater environment. This can be done to certain aluminum alloys by an electrochemical coating process called anodizing, which can be both tough and colorful (nearly any color can be permanently dyed into the coating). Almost all top-end reels with golden or flat-black finishes, for instance, use dyed anodized coatings for protection. Some reels even have anodized coatings on internal parts, such as gears. Other alloys are finished with paints, epoxy, or other bases, and, depending on quality, can give adequate corrosion protection.

Plastics/graphite. Polymer (sometimes called "graphite") reel bodies are injection-molded from a mixture of plastics and strength fibers. The polymers or plastics include ABS, nylons, and similar materials, and the strength fibers are chopped fiberglass, graphite (hence the name "graphite"), or even silicon carbide whiskers. The injection-molding process is well suited to economical mass production. Plastics should not necessarily be confused with "cheap," as in toys; plastics are structural parts of modern firearms, for example, and can withstand enormous loads.

Positive attributes of plastics and graphite in reels include economy of production, light weight, and corrosion resistance. The cost of production and raw materials is extremely economical for these products. The fabrication process is at lower temperatures than with metals, and the die lifetime generally longer; both result in a lower cost product. Additionally, the weight of such products is about two-thirds that of aluminum alloys, although this number must be modified to include metal parts such as gears, shafts, and screws, which are internal to the reel.

The largest tides occur in the Atlantic Ocean's Bay of Fundy off Nova Scotia; Tahiti, part of the Society Islands in the Pacific Ocean, has virtually no tide.

Especially noticeable is the fact that plastics are inherently resistant to corrosion and often do not require any finishing; colored fillers can be added to the polymer before molding. Note also that metallic finishes, often vacuum deposited, can be applied so that the part appears to be made of metal. The durability of the finish is a matter of quality, ranging from those of the toy industry to those in high-wear applications such as the metal-finish knobs on stereo equipment.

Negative attributes of plastics and graphite in reels include distortion and wear. Distortion results because polymers must retain a degree of flexibility to avoid brittleness, particularly at extremely low temperatures. This is because an overly rigid polymer can fracture through propagation of a crack, much like a piece of glass. The purpose of the strength fibers is to limit crack propagation, so the final mixture must be a compromise of properties. (In the case of metals, brittleness is controlled by grain structure, which is a function of the alloy and heat treatment.) Furthermore, the flexibility of polymer parts should not be regarded as entirely negative; reels made of these materials have wonderful shock resistance and will survive hard falls much better than metal reels. The most important factor in producing a viable polymer frame fishing reel is careful structural design; done correctly, the product is excellent.

Polymers have many self-lubricating properties but are fundamentally soft and therefore can wear quickly, especially through the abrasive action of sand, dirt, and grit. Again, careful designs that restrict bearing and other movement have generally succeeded in eliminating this potential problem. In firearms, for instance, steel inserts are molded into the plastic body to provide bearing surfaces.

For both metal- and polymer-bodied reels, many of the potential problems that can be negative attributes may be avoided through minor maintenance. Generally, the potentially bad aspects of a product are exacerbated through neglect, and the reel is perfectly capable of delivering good service and value whether made of metal or plastics.

Bushings and Ball Bearings

The basic task of bushings and ball bearings is to precisely support a rotating shaft with minimum friction. In revolving-spool reels and fixed-spool reels, a rotating shaft supports the handle and gear train, which the angler cranks for retrieve; in revolving-spool reels, the rotating shaft also supports the spool, and in fixed-spool reels, it also supports the rotor.

Bushings. A bushing, sometimes called a sleeve bearing, supports the rotating shaft with a smoothly finished hole and a lubricating film. The bushing material can be the same as that of the reel body itself but is typically a distinctly separate material for better wear and lower friction. The physical contact between bushing and shaft is subject to sliding of one surface over the other, so there's a need for smooth mechanical finishing and lubrication.

For relatively low loads, the body material of diecast reels is a suitable bushing material. The common diecast metal is Zamak, a zinc/aluminum alloy with good machining characteristics. Its coefficient of friction with a steel shaft (a measure of the amount of friction between the metals) is low, and a lubricating film makes it even lower. The lubricating film is required to keep the surfaces from actually touching, and must not only withstand the pressure of the contact, but retain this property at higher temperatures as well.

Bushing materials which differ from that of the reel body are used for greater loads and include such metals as brass and bronze, as well as fiber-reinforced polymers. These bushings are firmly installed with a press fit, or even adhesives, because inadvertent rotation of the bushing would disastrously wear an oversized hole in the reel body. The bushing materials are selected to optimize mechanical properties, such as abrasion resistance and low friction. The metals are often sintered from granules (much like a graham cracker pie crust), and the resultant porous structure allows either storage or free passage of lubricants, which extends service life for the bushing. Other alloys contain graphite flakes which "self-lubricate" the bushing. Polymer bushings are strengthened with chopped fibers in the matrix. A well-made bushing gives extremely smooth rotation for the operation of a fishing reel.

Ball bearings. The major advantage of ball bearings over bushings is under heavy load conditions. Under low load conditions, the difference between the two systems is virtually indistinguishable, but as the load on the shaft increases, the superior performance of ball bearings becomes increasingly apparent. Ball bearings support their load through a rolling action in contrast to the sliding contact of the bushing. The difference can be compared to moving a rock on wheels versus dragging it along the ground; the heavier the rock, the more apparent the difference between the two methods.

The rolling action of a ball bearing depends on the roundness, precision, and hardness of its components. Lubrication is of secondary importance. High quality ball bearings have extremely close tolerances or imperceptible "play," and the small ball bearings in fishing reels rotate freely when spun. Many ball bearings are sealed with precision fitted covers, front and back, to keep contaminants out and lubricants in. In all, the ball bearing is a complex structure, and the many steps required for its manufacture make it expensive. It, and the related roller bearing, are without doubt the best engineering solution to the support of a rotating shaft under load.

Most production fishing reels are designed with both bushings and ball bearings. Because of the difference in cost of the two types of support, the more expensive models contain a larger number of ball bearings, and have a longer projected service life under harder use conditions. Various cost/

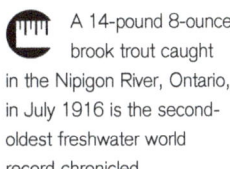

A 14-pound 8-ounce brook trout caught in the Nipigon River, Ontario, in July 1916 is the second-oldest freshwater world record chronicled.

performance tradeoffs give excellent value and satisfy the needs of all levels of anglers.

Cantilever supports. Although most rotating shafts are supported on both ends, some designs are cantilevered, or supported at one end only. Small flycasting reels are a typical example. The spool is supported on a shaft, which is cantilevered to the sideplate. The handle shaft on some conventional and baitcasting reels is another example.

In these latter cases, the flex allowed by cantilevered designs (also called set plate designs) can seriously affect performance under load because gear teeth engagement becomes compromised, and severe wear can result. The important point is that ball bearings can deliver their full capability only when the total reel design offers rigid support for all of its components. Thus, you cannot simply associate increased ball bearing count with increased quality.

Lubrication. The primary purpose of a lubricant in a fishing reel is to reduce wear. Greases are generally used in lubricating bushings, gear teeth, and sliding shafts to prevent direct metal-to-metal contact. The essential property of the grease is that its viscosity is sufficient to resist extrusion from the contacting metal surfaces by the pressure generated by heavy loads. This viscosity should be relatively independent of temperature and unaffected by water.

Suitable greases are sold by fishing reel manufacturers; if they are locally unavailable, white or "lithium-based" general-purpose greases serve well. Flake additives, such as graphite, further enhance performance but can be messy unless carefully applied, and will transfer stains to clothing.

Other flake additives include molybdenum disulfide and Teflon. Flaked molybdenum disulfide is designed for high temperature automotive disk brake service; it is messy to apply but an excellent lubricant for gears in some large conventional reels. Flaked Teflon is comparatively expensive and is used for some drag washer lubrication. The same chemical inertness that characterizes the non-stick Teflon coating in cookware also yields non-stick drag performance. It is a singular and unusual property, and leads to extremely smooth starting and stick-free drag performance, particularly in reels designed for light lines. These and other greases, however, should only be applied if the manufacturer recommends it. Some manufacturers have specific grease recommendations, or advise no greasing, so you should follow their instructions.

Light oils are intended for lubrication of ball bearings on the shaft of revolving spool reels, which must rotate freely for long casts. These ball bearings are designed to operate with a rolling action, and the light oil is intended as much for surface protection as lubrication. Grease or heavy oils inadvertently applied to spool bearings seriously degrade their performance. Such ball bearings should be washed in alcohol or acetone (in proper ventilation) and then lubricated with light oil. The oil also serves the secondary purpose of reducing bearing noise. Such oils can be used for lubricating the shaft ends, and for other light-duty uses such as baitcasting reel clutches and yokes.

If you get oil on your hands while fishing, clean your hands well to avoid the possibility of repelling fish with the odor of the lubricant when you touch lures or natural bait. In some cases, this makes no difference in fishing, but in others it can. Wipe off any lubricant on the exterior surface of a reel with an alcohol soaked rag, or use a covering scent.

See: Baitcasting Tackle; Big-Game Tackle; Conventional Tackle; Flycasting Tackle; Rod, Fishing; Spincasting Tackle; Spinning Tackle; Tackle Care, Maintenance.

REEL SEAT

The component of a fishing rod handle or butt that contains the reel.

See: Rod, Fishing.

REGULATIONS

When anglers obtain a fishing license, they should also receive a brochure, booklet, or pamphlet that details the regulations pertaining to fishing in the area covered by that license. This literature is usually a synopsis of regulations that have been adopted by law under the direction of the resource agency responsible for fisheries in that area of jurisdiction. Such regulations exist for all freshwater fishing, since licenses are required throughout North America to fish in freshwater; it is partly true in saltwater, since licenses are required in some places but not in others. Even where licenses are not required, there are still regulations pertaining to limits, seasons, angling methods, and the like, and these are detailed in some type of booklet.

Often the regulations are formidable, extensive, and perhaps confusing. Although some are straightforward and easy to understand, the trend in recent decades, as the management of people and resources has become more complex, is toward more detailed and site- or species-specific regulations. Difficult reading or not, however, these regulations are must reading for anyone who wants to fish. While most anglers realize they must know and abide by dates and limits, there are many other points that require checking. Things you may take for granted as accepted practice in one place may be against the law in another. Since ignorance of the law is no defense, you should know what the regulations are wherever you fish. Be aware that regulations vary considerably from one state or province to the next. It is a fact that some of the legal differences come from special regulations or exceptions for specific waters. It is also a fact that many regulations are difficult to enforce.

While the plethora of regulations may seem excessive and like a lot of governmental intrusion to some people, bear in mind that the reason for most regulations is to give the fish a chance and to set restraints upon people, some of whom would exercise no moderation if left unchecked. In fact, some regulations are based more upon the need (real or perceived) to control the actions of people than upon sound biological principles. It is also important to realize that many regulations have been requested or encouraged by anglers, or supported by their organizations.

No matter how stringent the regulations may be, and no matter how stringent or how difficult the enforcement may be, ethics, morality, and sportsmanship count for the most in the end, and, on this, each angler knows his or her own score.

The following is an overview and explanation of common regulations.

Licenses

Fishing licenses in North America are not federal licenses but are issued by state and provincial government agencies, which set their own fee structure. There is seldom fee reciprocity for nonresidents. The license *(see)* is usually referred to by the public as a fishing license or as a sportfishing license, but it is actually granted to people who use various means of fishing, including some methods not generally considered as sporting. These can include the use of spears, certain types of nets, setlines, trotlines, and other means.

A fishing license is not restricted to specific waters but allows an angler to fish throughout the state or province and for all or most species. The revenues received from these licenses, as well as from the sale of stamps or permits or other fees, are kept by the states or provinces and theoretically used for the management of fisheries resources. Management funds in the United States also come from a federal excise tax that is apportioned to the states *(see: Federal Aid in Sportfish Restoration Act)*.

The regulations specify who qualifies as a resident and who must have a license or who is exempt from a license (some people must have a license, but it is free). They also specify which activities are covered by this license, and they define what is meant by sportfishing for the purpose of this license; in other words, capturing fish with commercial harvesting equipment is not a means of sportfishing and doesn't qualify for a sportfishing license. A license is valid only within the boundaries of the government that issues the license. In border waters, there is sometimes a reciprocal agreement between governments honoring licenses, but in many cases, and especially in international boundary waters, there is no such reciprocity, which means that an angler needs two licenses to freely fish in waters that have divided jurisdiction (and may have to abide by different regulations when in the respective jurisdiction).

A sportfishing license is required in freshwater throughout North America, with some exceptions. Those exceptions may include people over and under a certain age, in the military, with disabilities, and members of native or aboriginal communities. A license is required of both residents and nonresidents, although the fees for the latter are greater.

The situation in saltwater is less straightforward. Some states include saltwater fishing as part of a general statewide license that is applicable to both saltwater and freshwater. Some have a saltwater fishing license that is separate from, and in addition to, a freshwater fishing license. In some places, a freshwater license may be required in tributaries and in nontidal portions of a coastal river, but no license may be necessary in the tidal portions or elsewhere in saltwater. In some saltwater environs, there is a boat license, which is a blanket license granted to the operator or captain of a boat and covering, in effect, all people who fish in that boat. The scenario is diverse, complicated by the fact that saltwater fish hinder state management efforts because they do not acknowledge governmental boundaries.

Seasonal licenses are normally valid for a 12-month period, which may or may not be on a calendar basis; they are nontransferable and nonrefundable and may not be valid until signed. There are no tests or courses required in order to receive a license, but that may change in the future; some countries in Europe have such a requirement. Licenses for nonresidents often can be bought for limited periods (a day, a week, etc.). Regulations usually require that the license be in the angler's possession when fishing and that it be shown to a conservation officer upon request. In a few states, a license must be displayed on the outer clothing above the waist, and in some it must be shown to anyone who asks to see it. In certain places, a license is not required on private waters or on farms. Many states offer lifetime licenses that are expensive when bought but economical over one's life if purchased at an early age. Combined licenses for spouses or family licenses are sometimes available, and the cost of a fishing license is usually less if purchased in conjunction with a hunting license. So-called "conservation" licenses, primarily required in Canadian provinces, have more stringent provisions for keeping fish.

Some localities may levy other governmentally imposed costs in addition to the license fee, such as a stamp. Stamps are usually issued in freshwater fishing and for particular species or to support a particular management program; the revenue derived from the sale of such stamps is used for purposes that are specific to the management of those species, instead of being put into general fisheries management coffers. Also, some places, such as state or federal parks or private preserves, require an additional license or permit for fishing; these are separate from those required by the state or provincial fisheries agencies.

State and provincial licenses, stamps, and permits can usually be obtained at tackle and bait shops, some sporting goods stores, marinas, lodges and camps, town or county clerk's offices, and at the offices of the presiding fisheries agency.

Color is a big element in fishing lures today, and as long ago as 1883, Earnest F. Pflueger was granted a patent for artificial lures coated with luminous paint for fishing at night.

They are increasingly becoming available by phone through credit card purchase.

Comparing the cost of a license with the cost of other goods (food, beverage, boat gas, etc.), and considering that a fishing license is valid for a full year and that it permits fishing for many if not all species throughout a state or province, a fishing license is pretty inexpensive. It is one of the original user fees, and for the most part, the management of both game and nongame fish is supported by the funds derived from angling licenses, with little if any financial contribution to fisheries management from nonanglers unless a small amount comes from general tax funds.

Problems. Angling without a license is the most frequent fish and game law violation. Some violations occur innocently, but the majority are made by people who should know better.

In most localities, an angler needs a license to fish on privately owned waters. Many places allow fishing in private waters without a license if you are the owner, a direct relative of the owner, or a tenant of the owner. Often the decision depends on whether the private water is stocked with public fish, has public water flowing in or out of it, is navigable, is an agricultural pond, or is stocked with fish purchased from commercial sources. In many states, regulations for private water differ from those for public water; in some cases, where licenses are not required, there are no regulations on size or bag limit, season, or manner of taking fish. In others, a license is not needed, but general regulations still apply. If a license is required on private water, it is the same license that any member of the public would buy from the appropriate government agency; this is different in some European countries, where licenses (actually permits) are granted by individual property owners.

Children under a certain age (usually 14, 15, or 16) usually don't need a fishing license, but an adult who takes children fishing may. Generally, that adult does not need a license if he or she is just supervising but does need one if he or she assists or is fishing too. The interpretation of supervision depends on the government: You may not need a license as long as you don't handle the rod while the line is in the water, or you may not be able to handle any tackle unless you are licensed. Some states consider baiting a hook to be assisting. You may need a license if you are helping children under a certain age, and a licensed adult may have to accompany a nonresident child.

Seasons

Seasons in which anglers can or cannot fish are established for certain species or for some fish in specific locations. For popular species, a closed season is usually established to protect them when they are spawning. In theory the closed season prevents too many fish from being taken and permits adequate replacement, although fisheries biologists do not agree on this issue; and it may be regarded differently depending on the fish population, the number of anglers, and the habitat. Differences in season dates for the same species exist among agencies; also, a state may have a closed season for a particular species during the spawning period but no closed season for a different species during its spawning period.

Usually those species that are abundant and for which a liberal harvest is encouraged do not have a closed season, and angling may take place on a continuous or year-round basis. A closed season may exist on a year-round basis for those species whose populations are low and in need of complete protection.

When the season opens, angling may legally begin; the start of the season, referred to as opening day, is often a very popular and eagerly anticipated event, subject to a peak of angling activity. In eastern U.S. states, the opening day of trout season, which is in early April, is a much-heralded occasion, although one that is more notable for social enjoyment than for productive angling. In the Midwest, the early May opening of the walleye season brings throngs of people to the water.

Where there are established seasons, they usually begin at 12:01 A.M. on the opening day of the season, and close at midnight on the last day of the season. With some exceptions, there are no restrictions on the hours in which a person can fish during an open season (unlike hunting), meaning that fishing is permitted at all hours of the day during the season. Exceptions usually allow fishing to begin at or just before sunrise and end at or just after sunset; these are usually established to help minimize the illegal taking of spawning fish, particularly Great Lakes salmon and trout.

Problems. One of the major causes of game law violations is the possession of fish out of season, and it is very obvious that people who possess a fish out of season have broken the law. These people usually do not have a fishing license either. Regulations not only specify that it is illegal to possess fish out of season, but that it is also illegal to fish for a species during a closed season. There are times when people inadvertently catch out-of-season species while angling for in-season species. This is not unlawful if you release them immediately. However, if a body of water is closed to the taking of all species, you cannot legally fish there out of season even if you release all fish. In some northern areas, it is illegal to fish in trout-stocked waters for any species prior to the opening of the trout season, even if the season for other species is otherwise open.

Some people deliberately catch and release certain fish out of season, under the guise of angling for species that are legal; this is a gray area that is problematic for law enforcement, since it is difficult to prove intent in court. However, there is an ethical question to fishing out of season even if you intend to release the fish, and there is the issue of adhering to the spirit of the law. Fishing prior to the beginning of the season is most common among bass anglers, and has led in some places to the establishment of special "early-season" regulations prohibiting the use of bait and permitting very restrictive harvest, or stipulating catch-and-release.

Bag/Creel/Daily Limit

A bag or creel limit regulates the number of fish that can be taken daily and is also called a daily limit. The purpose is to achieve one or more of the following: distribute the total catch among more people over a greater time period; keep populations from being reduced to such a low level that fishing is unacceptable; keep populations at a level that allows them to forage on abundant or stunted populations of other species; provide larger and (to anglers) more acceptable fish; and protect populations, if reproduction is limited, so more fish will reach sexual maturity and thereby spawn at least once.

A creel limit is commonly based on an aggregate number of specimens of one species; thus a daily limit of five walleyes means that no more than five walleyes can be kept by one angler during the period from 12:01 A.M. until midnight. It does not mean that an angler can keep five walleyes in the morning, go home, return in the afternoon, and keep five more. However, an angler could keep two in the morning, go home, come back later, and keep three more.

The creel limit is usually different for each species or grouping of fish. For example, in a recent year in Tennessee, the daily limit was 5 fish for largemouth bass, 5 for walleye, 1 for muskellunge, 2 for striped bass, 20 for rock bass, 30 for crappie, and unrestricted for bluegills and catfish. Top predator fish, which receive more angling pressure, are usually subject to more restrictive daily limits because there are fewer of them in the overall fish population and they can be more readily overharvested. Species that are not the top predators, such as bluegill, crappie, and perch in freshwater, are much more abundant than the top predator fish, and the populations of these species are influenced to a greater degree by environmental conditions. Thus, unless there is a serious problem with the population of those species, daily limits tend to be more generous than they are for predators and usually exist more as a means of preventing some anglers from being game hogs than as a means of population control.

In a similar vein, some creel limits apply to all fish that are caught, without regard to species, and all species are grouped in an aggregate amount. This is prevalent in Canadian provinces and is likely to become more popular in the future as a way to reduce the total catch of anglers in a single day. In this case, a daily bag limit of seven fish for all species might include seven of one species, or it might stipulate that no more than a certain number could be of a particular specie or species. The primary purpose here is to regulate anglers and minimize total take rather than to control specific populations of fish.

A creel limit may also have a stipulation pertaining to the size of the fish; usually the stipulation would apply to keeping a restricted number of specimens over a certain length (or size). For example, the daily limit for northern pike might be six fish, only one of which could be larger than 75 centimeters (an actual Saskatchewan regulation).

Many anglers who have caught their limit customarily continue fishing but release, or cull *(see: culling)*, their later catches. Many provincial and some state regulations specify that it is illegal to continue to catch or fish for a species once the daily limit is in the angler's possession. If an angler has a limit of five bass, for example, and then catches a sixth bass, he or she could technically be in violation of the law when holding (reduced to possession) that sixth bass, even though it is for the purpose of release, unless the regulations specifically permit this. The culling aspect of regulations is very loosely (if at all) enforced in most states, but it is more closely followed in Canada. However, in some jurisdictions, including Canadian provinces, regulations specify that an angler must stop fishing upon reaching his or her limit.

Some people think that anglers should abide by a voluntary limit equal to the existing law, whether they keep or release the fish; in other words, if the daily limit is six northern pike, the angler should stop fishing for pike once he or she has caught six of them, even if all are released. Such a notion might become a regulation, although its enforcement would clearly be difficult. In most places, however, fish that are released are not considered "taken" and do not count against the daily limit.

What many anglers fail to take into account is the fact that even when they practice careful catch-and-release, a certain amount of delayed mortality is unavoidable. This fact means that you

Crappie are among the freshwater species that often have liberal harvest limits.

still have an impact even if you release every fish that you catch. By taking a percentage of your released fish totals into account as part of your limit, you would voluntarily reduce your impact. For example, assume that 10 percent of all released fish die (which some studies indicate) and that the daily limit for a particular species is 10 fish. On a given day, you catch a total of 20 of this species, keeping 10 and releasing 10. Of the 10 released, 1 fish (10 percent) can be expected to die later; thus, your total impact for the day is a mortality of 11 fish, even though you have kept only 10 and have complied with the law. However, if you had kept less than the daily limit and released the others, your total take, or total impact, for the day, would have complied with the spirit of the law.

Admittedly this issue is really more about ethics *(see)* than fisheries management, but you can see that if an angler has a good day on the water and catches a lot of fish for which there is a low limit, even if he or she releases all or nearly all of those fish, the angler is still having an impact.

Daily limits are also associated with possession limits, which are explained later. In some places, again especially in Canadian provinces, the daily limit and the possession limit are the same. In other words, you may possess no more than one limit for each particular species at any time. This includes all fish that you have in hand, at home, in camp, and in transportation. Thus, if the limit is five walleyes and you have three in your home freezer and one in your boat livewell, then you are allowed to keep only one more walleye.

Length Limit

For some species of fish, there are no size limits, meaning that it is legal to keep a fish of any size. And in some locations, there are no size limits for any species, but simply aggregate daily limits. However, in many locations and for many species, there is a minimum legal size, largely to prevent small fish from being kept and to allow fish to grow to a size where they will have an opportunity to spawn at least once. That size is expressed in terms of length, not weight, and is measured in inches or centimeters. Where a minimum length limit exists, you must immediately release any fish of that species that is under the minimum size, and you may keep, or voluntarily release, a fish that equals or exceeds that minimum length.

It is critical that anglers understand how to measure a fish that they will keep. Measuring is done differently in some places, and it may vary with the species, especially in saltwater where some fish have forked tails. Many regulations brochures define how to determine length and illustrate it graphically. Some are rather vague, simply saying that minimum length is determined from the tip of the snout to the tip of the tail. Some can be confusing when they also refer to total length.

To measure any fish, you should lay it down, preferably on a clean, wet surface, and take the

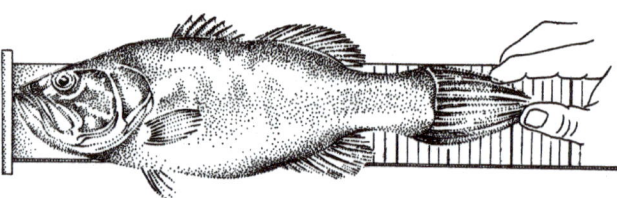

Total length is the distance from the tip of the snout to the end of the tail, as measured with the fish laid flat, the mouth closed, and the tail slightly compressed.

length measurement in a straight line starting at the snout with the mouth closed. It is helpful to have a ruler with the beginning point blunt and angled up so that the snout of the fish can be pressed against it.

Total length. Length is commonly obtained, especially in freshwater, by measuring to the end of the compressed tail. Some regulations refer to a pinched tail, others compressed, but the idea is to bring together the upper and lower portion of the tail fin, called the lobes, and measure to the longest point. This is also referred to as total length and is how freshwater fish, and saltwater fish without forked tails, are measured.

Fork length. To determine fork length, measure the straight-line distance from the tip of the snout to the center of the tail fin. This method is used for saltwater species with a forked tail; often fish with a rigid forked tail will suffer damage to their tails during transportation from fishing grounds. If they were measured on a total-length basis back at the dock, they may no longer be legal, even though they were legal when initially caught. Measuring these fish by fork length removes that problem and standardizes measurements to make it easier for anglers.

Slot Limit

A slot limit is a special adaptation of a length limit meant to encourage the protection of fish of a certain size. It can be applied in two ways. Generally a slot limit allows harvesting of fish within a defined

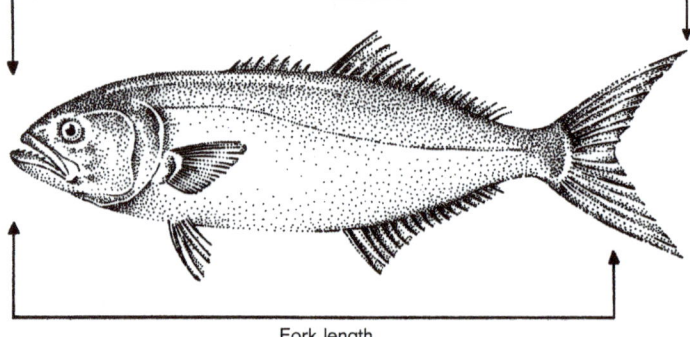

Fish are measured according to total length or fork length.

size range and prohibits the taking of fish smaller or larger than that size. For instance, if bass can be kept only when they are between 15 and 20 inches in size, then fish smaller or larger must be released immediately. Many biologists believe that a slot limit is a better way to limit catches than a minimum length limit, since it not only protects the smallest of the species but also requires release of trophy fish. These trophy fish can then theoretically be caught another day, and their return to the water helps to repopulate the species during spawning season and maintain predator-prey balance.

In less common situations, fish within a specified size range are protected, and fish within that range must be released. For instance, if lake trout between 22 and 28 inches are protected, specimens of that size must be released, but specimens smaller or larger than that can be either kept or released. Such a slot limit might be used to help protect a size or age group of fish that is underrepresented in the overall population, perhaps because of environmental factors when those fish were born.

Possession Limit

A possession limit is similar to a creel limit, but it specifies the total number of fish that can be in the angler's possession, whether the fish are in hand, in transportation, in camp, at home, on the grill, or in some combination of these. The purpose is to prevent people from repeatedly keeping daily limits and storing them for future use, thus becoming a game hog, and also to help prevent the waste of fish that have been accumulated and stored for long periods.

Possession limits are a confusing issue to anglers, and they vary, particularly between states and provinces. In some places the daily limit and the possession limit are identical. This is more common in Canada than in the United States. Where the daily limit and the possession limit are the same, you may not have more than a daily creel limit in your possession, no matter where the fish are individually stored. In a hypothetical case of a (daily and possession) limit of four lake trout, let's say that an angler goes fishing on Saturday and keeps a daily limit of three lakers. That night the person eats one, cans one, and smokes and freezes the third. The angler is now in possession of two lake trout. On Sunday the angler goes fishing again but now may keep only two lake trout total. The person keeps two and freezes them both, and has reached the possession limit. During the week the angler eats one, which reduces possession to three lake trout. The following Saturday the angler again goes fishing but technically may keep only one lake trout, even though the daily limit is listed as four lake trout.

In many states, a possession limit is equal to a two-day creel limit. Let's use a hypothetical example of a three-fish daily limit for chinook salmon, with a two-day possession limit. An angler catches and keeps the daily chinook limit on Saturday, and cans or freezes it on Saturday night. The person

This notice, posted at a Texas lake, illustrates the slot limit regulation in force.

goes fishing again on Sunday and catches and keeps another daily limit, which is stored at home that night. The person now has a legal two-day possession limit of chinook salmon in storage. If the angler goes fishing on Monday and catches and keeps one chinook salmon, he or she is technically in violation of the law, since the angler already has a full possession limit at home. But if the person ate one of the salmon for dinner on Sunday night, then he or she would be in possession of five fish, and on Monday could legally keep one more chinook salmon, but not two or three.

The possession limit may be more liberal than a two-day creel limit. However, in those places where the possession limit and daily limit are the same, a person can usually transport no more than a two-day creel limit. This regulation allows people who have been fishing at a distant location the opportunity to have in their possession more than one daily limit, but not a limit for every day that they might have been fishing.

Possession is usually defined as any means of home storage, including canned, preserved, smoked, or frozen, as well as the obvious immediate possession of fish in a boat or vehicle, or in temporary storage (at camp or trailer). Therefore, it's important to read the regulations thoroughly to understand what you may and may not do. Obviously, conservation officers or wardens are unlikely to raid your permanent residence to check for the storage of fish, unless you are a repeat violator of wildlife laws. Over the course of a season, many anglers find that they have inadvertently accumulated a few more fish than what the possession limits stipulate. This doesn't necessarily make them game hogs. Furthermore, the issue is complicated by the fact that daily and possession limits differ among jurisdictions and that anglers may visit more than one jurisdiction, and thus keep and possess fish from different places.

As noted, the purpose of possession limits is to prevent excess and to avoid waste. It is one of those areas where conscience and ethics determine a person's adherence to the limits more than formal regulations do.

Transportation

Dead fish. As much as resource managers would like you to enjoy the fish that you keep, they have no particular interest in how you store your fish or in what you transport them *(see: fish preparation—care)*. Nevertheless, there are regulations covering the state of the fish being kept while they are transported to your permanent residence, or to the place where they will be stored or consumed, and how they may be transported. This subject is referred to in regulations literature as transportation.

Increasingly, many places require that fish be identifiable when transported. Many states and provinces stipulate that you may not alter the fish in such a manner that the species would be unrecognizable. And many require that a portion of skin (often 1-inch square) be left on all fillets for identification purposes. Where there are length limits on fish, the body of the fish must usually be kept intact, except for removing the entrails and gills, so that a conservation official is able to determine the length. The fish must remain in this manner until reaching the place of consumption or residence. This restriction would preclude beheading and filleting the fish at the place of capture.

The amount of fish that can be transported is either a daily or a possession limit, but one person cannot usually transport (or store) another angler's catch in addition to his or her own, unless the other person's fish are labeled (perhaps including license number) or that person is present. The manner of storing during transportation may be regulated, too, perhaps requiring that transported fish be packaged in such a way that they can be "readily unwrapped, separated, identified, and counted," which is the exact wording of Minnesota's regulations.

Live fish. Transporting live fish is illegal in most places. This regulation prevents the introduction of those fish into other waters, which in itself is usually an illegal act, and also reduces the spread of exotic or nuisance animals or aquatic plants. Many anglers transport their catch from the place of capture to their home by keeping the fish in the boat's livewell; although this practice may keep them fresh, it may also be illegal. Bass, walleye, and panfish are especially subject to such treatment,. In the past, such treatment, where prohibited, was not enforced, but today it is a much more serious issue *(see: exotic species)*.

Methods and Equipment

The methods of fishing that are subject to regulation cover a wide gamut. Some methods are obviously illegal: using explosives and the like, trapping fish by damming the waterway or otherwise preventing their passage, stunning the fish through electric means, or using chemicals that would stun or kill. Fishing with a bow and arrow, or with a spear, as well as using trotlines, setlines, and other non-rod-and-reel methods are usually addressed in the regulations booklets but are not covered here because they are not considered sport in the commonly accepted sense of sportfishing *(see: angling)*.

Most regulations specify what is legally defined as "angling" and detail any limits on the number of hooks that can be used, as well as the number of lines. It is important to review these matters because they may change periodically or may differ by jurisdiction. Throughout Canada, for example, it is illegal to fish with more than one line, except when ice fishing. In most states, it is illegal to fish with more than two lines, except, perhaps, when ice fishing. In a few states, the number of lines is unlimited. There are usually limits to the number of hooks that may be used on a line, and a hook is defined in the regulations. In a few places, it is illegal to use wire line for rod-and-reel fishing or to use a treble hook that is not attached to a lure.

The use of chum is generally legal in freshwater or saltwater, but in many cases the legality is due to omission rather than stipulation by law. There are odd pitfalls here, though; in a few states, using corn as chum for trout is illegal, and some places make using live baitfish illegal. In Canada, nonresidents may not bring in bait. Applying scents to plastic bait or lures is not classified as chumming, but no chum or substance may be toxic, stupefying, or a pollutant. The use of scents or other chemical potions may someday be deemed an unfair advantage to anglers; these practices may then be prohibited.

Foul Hooking

Deliberately foul-hooking fish *(see: foul hook)*, also known as snagging, means hooking a fish anywhere on its body other than inside the mouth and is generally prohibited except for certain nongame species, such as paddlefish, and for some Great Lakes fish, such as salmon, during their spawning runs. However, sometimes anglers unintentionally foul-hook fish, play them, and land them. In the majority of states and provinces, an angler cannot keep fish that were foul-hooked, even if they otherwise conform to regulations, such as size. Those fish must be released immediately. Check to see whether the regulations pertain to where on the fish the foul hook occurs. Some specify that a foul-hooked fish is one that is caught behind the gill covers;

this makes sense for some species, such as bass and pike, which often take a lure with two sets of hooks, one of which may lodge on the head outside of the mouth. Bait hooks seldom manage to foul-hook fish outside of the immediate mouth area unintentionally.

Other Common Regulations

Besides the regulations just discussed, there is still a host of others that apply to angling. Make sure that you review the regulations booklets, even when you think you know what the law is because laws change and because many anglers have mistaken notions or interpretations of fishing regulations based on what they have been told by others in the past.

A common area of misinformation concerns bait. Usually, anglers may catch their own bait provided they conform to accepted methods (you can't seine gamefish for use as bait, for example) and provided that they are catching bait that is legal to be caught and/or used for fishing. There are a few important exceptions, and you should check to find out what those are. Also, be advised that in many places it is not legal to release unused bait into the water.

Regulations vary widely as to whether gamefish may be used as bait. In a few states, they may be used dead; in others, only portions of gamefish (viscera, eyes, etc.) may be used. The definition of gamefish is a key factor, For instance, bass may not be used as bait but carp may, or vice versa if the state is trying to control the spread of carp. In states where gamefish species may be used as bait, they may be possessed in size and numbers only in accordance with the fishing regulations for that particular species.

Buying, selling, or trading gamefish is almost universally illegal in freshwater except, obviously, for those who are fish farmers, possess special permits, or have commercial fishing licenses. This is a much murkier issue for marine fish. Generally, species that are classified by state law as gamefish (this has no relationship to whether sportsmen consider them to be gamefish) are considered protected and usually may not be sold by anglers. Fish that are not so classified are unprotected and may legally be sold, although there is a lot of controversy attached to this. Some so-called sport or recreational anglers have been selling some or all of their catch, especially tuna and dolphin (and before that bluefish, striped bass, and maybe other species), for many years, although it would seem that they ought to be required to have a commercial license and be classified as commercial fishermen. That has happened to a limited degree in the case of giant bluefin tuna, where quotas are established and recreational anglers or boat captains must pay a fee and obtain a permit in order to be able to sell that species. The issue of selling saltwater fish has been a hotly contested one and still remains unresolved in many states, especially those on the East Coast *(see: commercial fisherman; recreational fisherman; sportfisherman).*

Dolphin are often kept in quantity and in all sizes by anglers.

Usually you must be present when you have a fishing line in the water and you may not leave it unattended, although you can be a specified distance nearby, as in ice fishing. In some places you may not fish by trolling with a motor. In some places you may not deposit fish entrails into the water. In all locations, you may not trespass over private property.

Read the Regulations

If you have read through this entire section, you have probably noticed that the words "usually" and "generally" are employed often. This should be a tip-off that there are many different regulations and many exceptions to standard regulations, and that it is important to understand which regulations apply in the state or province where you are fishing, to the body of water that you are fishing, and to the species that you seek or actually catch.

Make sure that you read all the regulations, not just the obvious table of length and bag limits. Also read the fine print. When you do, you may find such interesting and perhaps unknown or overlooked dictums as these, taken from recent regulations booklets:

California	"It is unlawful to cause or permit any deterioration or waste of any fish taken in the waters of this state."
Kentucky	"All sportfish incidentally taken while capturing live bait with seines, dipnets, or cast nets must be released immediately and unharmed into the water."
Minnesota	"No person may have a spear in a dark house or fish house [ice fishing shanty] while angling; nonresidents may not spear from a dark house."
Missouri	"Gamefish not hooked in the mouth, except paddlefish . . . , must be returned to the water unharmed immediately."

Montana	"It is unlawful to waste any part of gamefish suitable for food."
New Hampshire	"Littering is sufficient cause to revoke your [fishing] license."
New York	"No aquatic insect nor any insect that lives in the water during any of its life stages shall be taken from waters inhabited by trout nor the banks thereof at anytime."
Ontario	"It is illegal to harm spawning grounds and nursery, rearing, food supply, and migration areas on which fish depend directly or indirectly, in order to carry out their life processes."
Pennsylvania	"It is unlawful to kill any fish and fail to make a reasonable effort to lawfully dispose of it."
Saskatchewan	"It is illegal to take more fish than the limit specifies, including fish eaten for shore lunch."
Wisconsin	"It is illegal to fish for any variety of fish in excess of the daily bag limit."

See: Catch-and-Release; Fisheries Management.

RELEASE

A release is a device that is used both to secure fishing line to some towing mechanism (downrigger cable, planer board tow line, or outrigger) and to free it from that mechanism when a fish strikes or when the angler wishes to change lures. Most releases have adjustable tension settings to allow for changes in pressure exerted by the object being towed. Most of the time, a release is used in trolling, but it can also be used for live or cut-bait fishing.

Releases are critical in many forms of trolling and present a lot of room for experimentation, as well as problems. The release must free the fishing line when a fish strikes or when the angler chooses to detach it in order to retrieve it (otherwise, the line must be brought in to manually free the line).

In downrigger fishing, releases can be attached to the weight, to the downrigger cable at the weight, and to the cable at any location above the weight. In planer board fishing, releases can be attached to the board and to the tow line at any location ahead of the board. When using outriggers, a release (also called a clip) is used on a short length of line attached to the outrigger, and generally placed midway up on the outrigger.

In all releases, the fishing line is clamped into it under variable pressure. Some feature a trigger that can be set to open under greater or lesser tension. Some feature spring-loaded jaws capped with rubber pads; how far into the pads you set the fishing line determines the tension. A release used on a downrigger cable should be small and streamlined to avoid causing drag. A release used on a sideplaner should be able to slide freely down the tow line.

With some releases used in downrigger and planer board trolling, it's a good idea to make several twists in the fishing line and place the loop into the releases. This prevents the line from slipping through without tripping the release. However, on outriggers, when fishing on the surface for big game, it may be best to set untwisted line into the release so the distance that the lure is set back can be quickly changed.

If the line has been placed properly, when a fish strikes, the line immediately pulls free of the release, which remains attached to the tow device. If the line frequently pops free of the release under rough water conditions, increase the adjustable tension. If fish strike and pop the release but seldom get hooked, the tension is too light. However, when the tension is set overly tight, small fish may not be able to free the line from the release.

Anglers can free a line attached to a release by pointing the rod directly at the release, reeling up all slack, and then snapping the rod back. Give the trailing lure a moment to rise, sink, speed up, or slow down before reeling it in, as a following fish might pounce on it when the action changes.

See: Big-Game Fishing; Downrigger; Downrigger Fishing; Flatlining; Planer Boards.

RELEASING FISH
See: Catch-and-Release.

REMORAS

Members of the Echeneidae family, remoras and sharksuckers are slim fish that have a flat sucking disk on the top of their head. They attach themselves usually to sharks or other fish—including marlin, grouper, and ray—but sometimes to the bottoms of boats or other objects. These hitchhikers take an effortless ride with their host, feeding on parasitic copepods found on the host's body and gill chambers.

Developed from the first dorsal fin, the sucking disk consists of a series of ridges and spaces that create a vacuum between the remora and the surface to which it attaches. By sliding backward, the remora can increase the suction, or it can release itself by swimming forward.

Sharksucker

On his second voyage into the West Indies, Columbus saw natives using remoras to catch giant sea turtles. When a big turtle was sighted basking at the surface, a remora with a line tied to its tail was let over the side of the boat. Typically it headed immediately for the turtle and fastened itself tightly to the turtle's shell. Then the turtle was carefully drawn back to the boat, the remora refusing to let loose.

The sharksucker *(Echeneis naucrates),* which averages $1\frac{1}{2}$ feet in length but may be as much as 38 inches long and weigh up to 2 pounds, is the largest member of the family. Worldwide in distribution in warm seas, it is gray with a broad, white-edged black band down each side, tapering to the tail. It prefers sharks and ray as hosts, and often enters shallow beach and coastal areas; it has been known on rare occasions to attach itself to bathers or divers.

Also cosmopolitan is the remora *(Remora remora),* which is common to 12 inches long and may attain a length of 34 inches. It is black or dark brown and is also found worldwide. It, too, prefers sharks as hosts. Some other species show distinct host preferences. The whalesucker *(R. australis),* for example, generally fastens itself to a whale; the spearfish remora *(R. brachyptera)* commonly attaches to billfish such as marlin.

Although often observed by anglers, remoras have no angling merits.

REPAIRS
See: Tackle—Care, Maintenance, Repair.

REPELLENTS
See: First Aid.

REPLICA TAXIDERMY
See: Taxidermy.

REPRODUCTION
A process used in taxidermy *(see)*.

RETRIEVING
An intrinsic element of angling, retrieving is the act of manipulating objects that have been cast or lowered into the water and that need to be worked by hand in order to impart fish-attracting action to them.

The keys to successful retrieval of most lures are depth control, action, and speed, all of which vary in importance depending on the situation and the lure. Achieving the proper depth is perhaps the most important factor, since you can't hope to catch fish without getting your offering to the fish's level. With many lures, the ability to achieve a certain depth is a function of the design of the lure and the way in which it is used. Action is also a function of the design, but only to the extent to which the lure is properly fished; achieving the proper action is a necessity in order for the lure to have maximum attractiveness. Speed is often the most ignored factor in retrieval and is influenced by the diameter of line being used, type of lure, current, and the retrieve ratio of the reel.

Every lure is designed to do a certain function, but that function must be coordinated with the existing fishing conditions and must be achieved through proper lure retrieval. Specific retrieval techniques for lures *(see)* and flies *(see)* are discussed throughout this book.

RHODE ISLAND
Despite being the smallest of the United States, Rhode Island offers respectable and diverse fishing opportunities. And although the interior measures only 40 miles at its widest point, the state is deeply indented in the southeast by Narragansett Bay and has 384 miles of tidal coastline. This geographic characteristic prompted its moniker, the "Ocean State," and helps explain why saltwater fishing is the primary focus of attention among Rhode Island anglers.

Saltwater
Rhode Island has among the best saltwater fishing in the eastern U.S. It possesses a convoluted coastline that ranges from craggy granite outcroppings—both above and below the water—to long, smooth, sandy beaches punctuated by inlets and backed by scores of tidal bays and ponds.

Rhode Island is a surf caster's delight, and its south-facing barrier beaches are a favorite with both striped bass and bass anglers. Striped bass are *the* fish for most Rhode Island anglers, and although no world records have been pulled onto the state's beaches, there have been many close calls. Favorite surf fishing areas for this species include Misquamicut Beach and Weekapaug Breachway (inlet/outlet), Quonochontaug Breachway and State Fishing Area, Charlestown Breachway, the outlet to tidal Ninigret Pond, the beach and outlet to Cards Pond and the Harbor of Refuge, and, in the far eastern corner of the state, the outlet to Quicksand Pond. The rock-strewn waters around West Island, off Sakonnet Point and home of one of the more famous striped bass clubs of the late nineteenth century, also offer great angling, but the public can fish this area only from a boat, as beach access is restricted.

Rhode Island is a boat angler's mecca for stripers as well, with its vast areas of inland marine waters, especially Narragansett and Mount Hope Bays and the Sakonnet River (not a river but a long, attenuated saline bay), to ply. These are protected from the elements by nearly three dozen islands and the mainland. Narragansett possesses most of the

In 1956, Sir Willoughby Norrie, Governor of South Australia, caught a 2,224-pound great white shark on rod and reel; found inside was the remains of a pet dog buried at sea.

islands; at 26 miles long and up to 12 miles wide, it nearly always provides some lee in which to fish.

Rhode Island, called Aquidneck Island by everyone but cartographers, is the largest island in the bay, almost filling it, and is followed by Conanicut and Prudence Islands in size. Bristol, too, is almost an island, separated on its north end by a few yards of dirt between the Warren and Kickemuit Rivers.

For fly rodders and ultralight tackle anglers, some of Rhode Island's most exciting saltwater fishing occurs during the "worm hatch" on Washington County's salt ponds. Beginning on the full moon in May, bloodworms emerge from the mud to mate. They appear around dusk on days when the sun's heat warms the mud; cloudy days generally do not produce large "hatches." About $1^{1}/_{2}$ inches long, the pink worms attract schools of striped bass that feed like bluegills just beneath the surface. The stripers generally range from 18 inches long to 18-pounders.

Fly anglers catch most fish on red-and-white or pink-and-yellow bucktail streamers, cast on 6- to 8-weight intermediate fly lines. Spinning tackle enthusiasts fish small, pink, soft plastic baits to match the hatch. It is critical to fish the hatch when it is just beginning around sunset; once the emergence is in full bloom, the fish key in on the real worms and become extremely selective. The most active hatches occur on the north end of Point Judith Pond, as well as on Potter and Ninigret Ponds; worm emergences have been reported in coves on Narragansett Bay as well.

With stripers in relative abundance in recent years, anglers are catching these fish within the city limits of Providence. Some of the best bass angling in early summer occurs in the city in Narragansett Bay's uppermost reaches, along the shores of the Providence, Seekonk, Warren, and Barrington Rivers.

Inshore fishing for stripers is just part of Rhode Island's saltwater story, of course. There is plenty farther out, as Block Island and Rhode Island Sounds are extensions of the Atlantic Ocean that front upon the coast. Tear-shaped Block Island is a dozen miles east of Montauk Point and 8 miles south of Point Judith. The North Rip there is a favorite for pollock, cod, and fluke anglers, especially on the south side. Inside Great Salt Pond, flounder are tops.

Rhode Island boat anglers are torn between two popular and plentiful species: blackfish, alias tautog, and bluefish. Bluefish are subject to cyclical variances, and blackfish populations have been a source of concern in recent years. At times, when blackfish are ashore in the spring to spawn, fishing for them from the beach, bridge, bank, and bulkhead is almost as good as fishing from a boat. Early in the season, however, and again in November and December, the bigger blackfish concentrate in deeper water and are taken by boaters. The largest blackfish landed within this species' range is a 20-pounder from Rhode Island waters.

Bluefish are scattered throughout the state's marine waters from late May through late November. A spot that has always produced bluefish, even during the August doldrums, is the protected water of Greenwich Bay. Elsewhere, the numerous small bays, tidal rivers and creeks, and back-bay marshes provide important nursery grounds for bluefish; in late August and September, when they have their "coming out party," snapper blues provide excellent fishing.

Ranking near, if not on, the top, is another fish that is more often pursued for its food, rather than sporting, value: winter flounder. Because of this species' popularity as a food fish, its numbers have suffered in recent times due to commercial and recreational pressures. Seasons, minimum lengths, and bag limits have been placed on these fish to halt overharvesting.

The return of fluke, alias summer flounder, has caused this species to rival bluefish as the summer's best bet. The fluke are taken on almost all inside waters, but the better fishing occurs along the outside beaches, especially near the breachways from Watch Hill to Point Judith, and along Block Island's Charlestown Beach. Most fish range from 1 to 3 pounds, but anglers have taken specimens weighing more than 12 pounds in recent years.

Weakfish, which locals call by the Indian name *squeteague,* are another possible Rhode Island catch. When squeteague are abundant, Narragansett Bay hotspots include the waters near Halfway Rock and both the east and west sides of Prudence Island, and Greenwich Bay.

The state of Rhode Island is also synonymous with big-game offshore fishing. Nebraska Shoals in Block Island Sound was once *the* place to catch giant bluefin tuna. In recent times this has changed drastically, as the baitfish upon which tuna feed changed their migration patterns. Still, every season a few tuna over 600 pounds are landed from boats leaving Rhode Island ports. The better offshore fishing nowadays is farther out, off Block Island. Here, sharks, yellowfin and bluefin tuna, as well as albacore and white marlin, are the sought-after species.

When all the warmwater marine species have headed south for the winter, cod and pollock replace them. The Cox Ledge fishing grounds, east of Block Island, still produces good catches of these species.

Incidentally, to catch what locals call a "grand slam"—a striped bass, bluefish, bonito, and little tunny in one day—fish streamers or small lures near the center and west walls of the Harbor of Refuge during the last weeks of summer and the first weeks of autumn.

Freshwater

Saltwater anglers greatly outnumber freshwater fishing enthusiasts in the diminutive Ocean State, but Rhode Island offers ample fishing opportunities to catch trout, northern pike, and a variety of warmwater fish in its streams and ponds.

Streams. The flowages in Rhode Island are not long, and they course through uneven topography. As a result, some have falls and rapids, which have been used to power textile mills and other industries. In the late eighteenth century, the first U.S. textile mill driven by water power was built in Rhode Island.

The state's premier trout fishery, the Wood River, rises in West Greenwich near the Connecticut border and flows south to join the Pawcatuck River, which separates Rhode Island and Connecticut. The Rhode Island Division of Fish and Wildlife stocks brown, rainbow, and brook trout throughout the Wood-Pawcatuck system, and small populations of wild brookies—referred to as "natives"— have managed to survive in the headwaters of such tributaries as the Falls River and the Flat River. Whether stocked or wild, trout in the Wood-Pawcatuck system have access to plenty of natural foods. Among the aquatic insects are caddisflies, small stoneflies, and many mayflies, most notably the giant *Hexagenia limbata,* which emerges on July nights. The river system's baitfish include minnows and suckers as well as Atlantic salmon fry, stocked by the state in an effort to restore the Pawcatuck's salmon run. Occasionally, there are reports of sea-run trout in the lower Pawcatuck.

Flowing from Connecticut into west-central Rhode Island, the Moosup River also receives generous trout stockings from the state. A small freestone stream with a remnant population of wild brook trout, the Moosup is an especially scenic Rhode Island river.

Several small streams throughout the state hold small populations of brook trout, but none is as rich as the little Queen River. This stream rises in West Greenwich and flows through Exeter into Glen Rock Reservoir in South Kingstown. Almost all of the land through which the river flows is closed to the general fishing public, so the state does not stock it. Access by canoe and kayak is extremely limited. For generations, the Queen's wild population of brook trout has thrived through the stewardship of private landowners.

Once one of the filthiest streams in the U.S., the Blackstone River rises in Massachusetts and flows south to Narragansett Bay in Rhode Island. Redbrick factories—relics of the Industrial Revolution and its accompanying pollution—still line the river's banks. Thanks to the Clean Water Act, the Blackstone's water is pure enough to support a run of anadromous blueback herring and stocked trout in some faster stretches, but the streambed holds several generations of heavy metals and other pollutants from industrial waste. Slower stretches of the Blackstone River hold large bass, pickerel, and carp. Access to the river abounds, as it is part of the federal Blackstone River Valley National Heritage Corridor in Massachusetts and Rhode Island.

Two other restored rivers, the Pawtuxet and the Woonasquatucket, flow through the state's most densely populated metropolitan area before spilling into Narragansett Bay. The state stocks trout on the uppermost reaches of the Pawtuxet, in the village of Hope, and the lower and slower stretches of both streams contain largemouth bass, pickerel, and carp. A survey of the Woonasquatucket also found a few native brook trout. Several stretches of the rivers near shopping malls and city buildings are lined by enough vegetation to provide pleasant canoe paddling and good fishing.

Lakes and ponds. Many of the state's ponds were built in the nineteenth century to store water for mills and other industries; the generally flat topography of the region prevented dam builders from creating very deep-water storage facilities, and most of the natural ponds in Rhode Island also are shallow. The state stocks trout in dozens of lakes and ponds—listed in the division's annual booklet of freshwater fishing regulations—but only a handful of lakes are deep and well oxygenated enough to sustain trout through the summer. They include Wallum Lake in Burrillville, on the border with Massachusetts, and Beach Pond in Exeter, on the border with Connecticut. Deep Pond, on Narragansett tribal land in Charlestown, is also capable of holding trout throughout the summer, but the state has not stocked it for several years.

The Fish and Wildlife Service also maintains a program to stock northern pike. Introduced to a limited number of Rhode Island waters in 1962, northern pike have spread through natural migration and illegal introduction to several other ponds and the Blackstone River. Anglers have caught pike as large as 35 pounds, but 10- to 12-pounders are more common. Perennial hotspots include Worden Pond, Thirty Acre Pond, and Hundred Acre Pond, all in South Kingstown; the Woonasquatucket Reservoir, also called Stump Pond, in Smithfield; Pascoag Reservoir in Burrillville; Waterman Reservoir in Greenville; and Chapman's Pond in Westerly.

There is little or no stocking of the state's other prominent warmwater and coolwater species: largemouth bass, smallmouth bass, yellow perch, white perch, redfin pickerel, chain pickerel, white catfish, brown bullhead, and several species of panfish, including black crappie, banded sunfish, redbreast sunfish, and bluegills. Large carp, goldfish, and other exotic species also inhabit some of Rhode Island's ponds.

Fishing for smallmouth bass is limited in Rhode Island. Although smallmouths as large as 5 pounds have been caught, most smallmouth ponds hold much smaller fish. The best prospects for smallmouth bass fishing include Indian Lake in South Kingstown and Stafford Pond in Tiverton. Other ponds holding smallmouths include Spring Lake in Burrillville, Tiogue Lake in Coventry, and Watchaug Pond in Charlestown.

Anglers have caught largemouth bass as heavy as 10 pounds in Rhode Island, and each year several specimens in the 5- to 7-pound class are taken. Most lakes and ponds in the state, including all of

American shad, a spring treasure along coastal rivers, make their first spawning run between ages 4 and 5 years; about 70 percent of the spawning fish will die afterward.

the reservoirs, support largemouths. Among the most interesting spots, however, are ponds with spawning runs of anadromous alewives, called "buckeyes" or "herring." Alewives spend most of their adult lives in saltwater. Around the first full moon in April, they begin running up small coastal streams to their spawning ponds. The adult alewives and their fry are an enriching food source that nourishes largemouths to become exceptionally healthy and generally large. Among the ponds where bass feed on anadromous alewives are Gorton Pond in Warwick, Brickyard Pond in Barrington, Belleville Pond in North Kingstown, and Carr Pond, also in North Kingstown, where access is controlled by the curator of the Gilbert Stuart Birthplace.

A population of landlocked alewives and other baitfish, as well as an abundance of perch and sunfish, are prey for largemouth bass on Worden Pond in South Kingstown and the two ponds connected to it by streams: Hundred Acre Pond and Thirty Acre Pond. The state has built a boat launching ramp on Worden Pond, but access to the other two ponds is difficult to obtain.

Most of Rhode Island's reservoirs also offer fine fishing for largemouth bass. These include Flat River Reservoir, also called Johnson's Pond, in Coventry; Pascoag Reservoir, also called Echo Lake, in Burrillville; Upper Slatersville Reservoir in North Smithfield; and Smith and Sayles Reservoirs in Glocester.

Many small ponds in Rhode Island offer a smorgasbord of fishing opportunities for stocked trout, largemouth bass, and panfish; among the most reliable spots—each with boat ramp access—are Carbuncle Pond in Coventry, Breakheart Pond in Exeter, and Silver Spring Lake in North Kingstown.

Rhode Island's largest body of freshwater, the Scituate Reservoir, has been closed to fishing and all other recreational uses for decades, despite its populations of largemouth bass, pickerel, yellow perch, and trout. Built on the north branch of the Pawtuxet River and commissioned as a source of drinking water in 1926, the Scituate and its five tributary reservoirs cover a total surface area of 4,557 acres in the center of the state.

RIFFLE

A hard-bottomed area of a creek, stream, or small river that is shallow and characterized by a choppy disturbed surface. Riffles have a hard bottom that isn't washed away by the action of moving water, so they are not scoured out. Riffles usually exist above a pool *(see)*, where a softer bottom has been gouged out, and may exist between pools, or between a pool and a run *(see)*, which is a generally uniform section deeper than a riffle and without the disturbed surface, yet lacking the characteristics of a pool.

Riffles may be short in distance, just 20 to 60 feet long, which is common in farm-country flows, or up to several hundred yards or more long, which is common in wide and long rivers in rocky terrain. Because a riffle is shallow, water builds at the head and rushes over it, so the flow quickens. Usually a riffle is shallow enough to produce wavy, rippled surface water, which provides increased oxygen and may also result in surface foam downstream. Most fish don't inhabit riffles or spend much time there because it is unproductive to waste a lot of energy constantly fighting current, especially swift current. Fish may move through riffles, especially those on upstream spawning migrations and post-spawners returning downcurrent, but in neither case are these fish likely to be doing anything more than passing through. Exceptions, of course, exist: If a riffle is comparatively slow and larval aquatic insects are on the bottom, then fish (like trout) may spend some time in the riffle foraging for these invertebrates.

The area above and below riffles, however, is usually more likely than the riffle itself to hold fish, either resident fish or those that are temporarily resting before migrating upstream. Small fish and other aquatic life are often disturbed, disoriented, or overwhelmed when they get into a riffle, and become easy prey at the end of the riffle where it empties into a pool. If there is a boulder or series of large rocks or other protection in a riffle, the object may have a deep pocket behind it that is out of the current and is conducive to capturing food that comes by or is washed into the pocket; in such an instance, gamefish (like trout or smallmouth bass) might reside in that specific location in a riffle.

Foreground anglers fish the top of a riffle on New York's Beaverkill River.

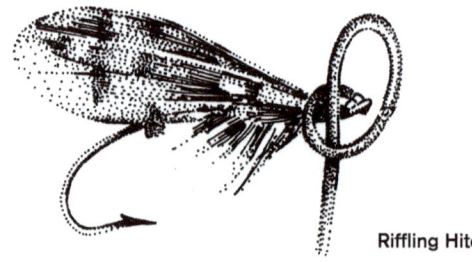
Riffling Hitch

RIFFLING HITCH

Also known as the Portland Hitch, this is a supplemental knot tied on a wet fly to plane it across the surface of a river. Used primarily in Atlantic salmon fishing, a fly with this hitch leaves a trailing wake and is very effective at attracting recalcitrant salmon. The fly is fished down- and across-stream and retrieved at a speed that causes it to leave a visible V wake; the hitch may be tied so that it sits on the left, right, or underside of the foreshank of the fly to achieve the right effect, depending on which way the fish is being approached.

The Riffling Hitch is created by making two half hitches behind the head of a fly that is already tied with a standard knot. When this is done, the tippet extends from the shank of the fly near and behind the head at an angle. Some flies are tied in such a manner as to leave extra room at the head for the hitch.

RIG

An arrangement of terminal tackle *(see);* the ready-to-fish final configuration of a lure and leader; and a ready-to-fish natural bait prepared with hook, weight, line (often wire), and other accessories.
See: Bait; Leader; Lure; Natural Bait; Trolling Lure, Saltwater.

RIGHT BANK

The right side of a river as viewed when facing downriver.

RIP

See: Tidal Rip.

RIPARIAN

Pertaining to the bank of a natural waterway, usually a river, sometimes a lake or tidewater. Riparian rights refer to the legal rights of the owner of property on a river bank.
See: Regulations.

RIPRAP

A collection of loose stones that serves as a foundation for, and to prevent erosion of, an embankment supporting a levee, dam, bridge, road, or similar man-made structure. Banks or shorelines with riprap vary greatly in length, in the size of the stones, and in the depth of the water nearby, although the riprap usually has a good pitch as it extends from above to below the waterline.

Riprap is typically found along the face of a dam, along the banks lining a tailrace, along the banks of a roadway or railroad bed that crosses water, and around the shoreline support foundation for bridges. Some species of fish are attracted to riprap banks at certain times, and the banks are especially likely to harbor largemouth bass, walleye, and catfish in freshwater because the stones provide hiding places for young fish and the food they feed upon, which attracts other species. There is usually a sharp slope to the riprap underwater, providing good depth nearby, and in many places there is also current along the face of the riprap.

RIP TIDE

See: Tidal Rip.

RISE

The visible disturbance of the water's surface by a fish that is feeding, usually on insects that are on or just under the surface. In principle, this visual disturbance, which may be the dainty sipping of a surface insect, the swirl caused by a fish that has taken food from under the surface and turned downward, or the prominent and audible splash of an aggressive strike, can apply to all forms of fish and various feeding activities that produce visible surface disruptions, but it is usually ascribed to salmonids in rivers and lakes, and to the consumption of insects. Other fish are mostly said to "swirl," even though the behavior that causes the visual disturbance may be similar. Different feeding behavior produces different types of rises, called rise forms, and these can be indicative of the food of the fish, and sometimes the size of the fish.

RIVERINE

Of or living in a river or flowing water.

ROACH *Rutilus rutilus.*

Other names—French: *gardon, vangeron;* German: *plötze, rotauge.*

A prominent coarse fish *(see)* that is widely sought by anglers, the roach is the subject of minor commercial interest. It is a member of the large Cyprinidae family, which includes minnows *(see)* and carp *(see),* and is of similar size and color to its relative, the rudd *(see).*

Identification. The roach has a somewhat cylindrical yet deep body, a moderately forked tail, a terminal mouth, and an erect dorsal fin. The scales are strongly marked, the back is gray to blue green, and the sides are silvery and taper to a white belly. The pelvic and anal fins are reddish orange, and the dorsal and tail fins are dusky. The roach may be confused with rudd (*Scardinius erythrophthalmus*); however, the pectoral fins of the rudd are reddish orange and the body is more golden brown.

Size/Age. Roach are believed to be able to live for 12 years; they grow to a maximum of 4 to 5 pounds, although the common catch is under a pound, and in some waters half of that.

Roach

Distribution. Roach are found in Europe, excluding Spain, Italy, and Greece. They have been introduced to Australia.

Habitat. These fish inhabit virtually any water, including rivers, lakes, reservoirs, and canals. The quality of the water is no impediment to their well-being, and they are equally at home in slow-flowing, still, muddy waters.

Life history/Behavior. Spawning takes place in heavy weeds in spring, when roach broadcast numerous adhesive eggs rather than construct a nest; this activity is usually accompanied by an obvious splashing commotion. The fry stay in schools and gather in large congregations, and they provide forage for numerous predators. Roach remain a schooling fish as adults, and their schools (called shoals) generally comprise similar-size individuals. Shoals of roach wander and feed in a homing area.

Food and feeding habits. Roach are primarily algae eaters, but they also consume mollusks, crustaceans, worms, and aquatic insects; most of their food is small, although larger fish consume bigger food items. They are similar to bronze bream *(see: bream, bronze)* in feeding habits, although they do not roil the water as much. They occasionally feed at the surface, and often at midlevels, but most feeding taking place on the bottom. Small roach feed at any time, but larger individuals are more active in low light.

Angling. Like other coarse fish, roach are not spectacular fighters, but they are especially popular with many Europeans, especially British anglers, and are one of the mainstays of competitive (match) fishing.

Bottom fishing with assorted baits—particularly maggots, bread, and worms—is the primary technique for roach, and this may involve prebaiting or chumming. Roach are caught at other levels, and in a variety of locations, water clarity, and current, so diverse options must be considered.

Rods from 11 to 13 feet in length, line from 2 to 4 pounds in strength, and No. 14 to 20 bait hooks are the preferred tackle. Hooked baits are fished with or without a float.

ROCKET LAUNCH

A term for the multiple-rod-holding apparatus, often part of a center console helm seat backrest, that is used to store fishing rods in sportfishing boats *(see)*.

ROCKET TAPER

A fly line with a long front taper.
See: Flycasting Tackle.

ROCKFISH

(1) A term for striped bass *(see: bass, striped)*.

(2) A diverse and important group of marine fish, rockfish are members of the Scorpaenidae family, which includes 310 species generically characterized as scorpionfish. There are roughly 68 species of rockfish in the genus *Sebastes* and two in the genus *Sebastolobus* that are found along the coasts of North America. Nearly all occur in Pacific waters. Both species of *Sebastolobus* and 32 species of *Sebastes* occur in Alaska's coastal waters, and at least 12 species range as far north as the Bering Sea.

Most of these species are important to the commercial fishing industry, which uses otter trawls to catch them, and some are important to anglers. They may also be referred to as rock cod, sea bass, snapper, and ocean perch because of their resemblance to these species or to the quality of their fillets, but the latter species are not related to rockfish. One rockfish in the Atlantic, *S. marinus,* is commonly called ocean perch in commercial markets and may also be labeled redfish or rosefish. Rockfish as a group have white, flaky meat with a delicate flavor, as befits deep-dwelling coldwater species.

Only a few rockfish species are too small to be useful for human consumption. Rockfish species are seldom marketed separately; they are generally all good to eat, but differentiating among the species—many of which are caught in the same locations and are very similar—can be difficult.

Directed fishing efforts for rockfish have resulted in overharvesting of most stocks, and elimination of some. Rockfish are extremely slow to become reproductively mature; this trait, and the tendency of many stocks to remain in one location, makes their populations especially vulnerable to overexploitation.

In addition to these factors, rockfish are deep dwellers with a swim bladder that possesses a special gas-producing and -absorbing gland. This gland changes the volume of gas in the swim bladder, which enables the fish to maintain buoyancy at different depths. This swim bladder is easily damaged when a fish is subjected to sudden changes in water pressure, such as when it is brought to the surface. The gas gland does not have sufficient time to absorb the gas in the swim bladder as the gas expands with a decrease in water pressure. Consequently, as the fish is brought to the surface, the swim bladder expands and becomes too large for the fish's body cavity and explodes out through the mouth. Countless rockfish are wasted when caught incidentally and thrown back into the water.

Most rockfish are landed in deep water by anglers using bottom fishing tactics or midwater drifting. Although commendable as food, rockfish are not known for their great battles, like salmon or tuna, or for their large size, like halibut, although the larger specimens of some species will provide good sport.

Identification. Adult rockfish range in size from 5 to 41 inches, but most species grow to between 20 and 24 inches in length. These fish are characterized by bony plates or spines on the head and body, a large mouth, and pelvic fins attached forward near the pectoral fins. The spines are venomous, and although not extremely toxic they can still cause pain and infection. Some species are brightly colored. Rockfish appear somewhat perchlike or basslike and are often called sea bass.

Life history. Rockfish can generally be separated into those that live in the shallower nearshore waters of the continental shelf and those that live in deeper waters on the edge of the continental shelf. The former comprise species that are always found in rocky bottom areas (called shelf demersal by biologists) and those that spend much of their time up in the water column and off the bottom (shelf pelagic).

All rockfish of the genus *Sebastes* are ovoviviparous, giving birth to live young after internal fertilization.

Rockfish are slow growing and extremely long lived. Black rockfish *(Sebastes melanops)*, which are a common pelagic species, become sexually mature at about 10 years of age and have been reported to reach age 40. Yelloweye rockfish *(S. ruberrimus)*, which are a shelf demersal rockfish, are a longer-lived species, becoming sexually mature around 15 years of age and living in excess of 100 years. There have been unconfirmed reports of fish at age 114.

Members of some species, such as the yellowtail rockfish *(S. flavidus)*, do not wander far and actually have an extremely strong preference for a specific site. If a fish is captured and relocated elsewhere, it will quickly return to its original home site.

Food. Rockfish feed on a variety of food items. Juveniles eat primarily plankton, such as small crustaceans and copepods, as well as fish eggs. Larger rockfish eat such fish as sand lance, herring, and small rockfish, as well as crustaceans.

Common species. The most common species encountered in Alaska include the black *(S. melanops)*, copper *(S. caurinus)*, dusky *(S. ciliatus)*, quillback *(S. maliger)*, and yelloweye *(S. ruberrimus)*.

Common species in Washington include the black, copper, quillback, and yelloweye.

Common species in Oregon include the black, blue *(S. mystinus)*, bocaccio *(S. paucispinis)*, China *(S. nebulosis)*, copper, Pacific ocean perch *(S. alutus)*, and yelloweye.

Common species in California include the black, blue, bocaccio, canary *(S. pinniger)*, chilipepper *(S. goodei)*, copper, cowcod *(S. levis)*, greenspotted *(S. chlorostictus)*, olive *(S. serranoides)*, starry *(S. constellatus)*, vermilion *(S. miniatus)*, widow *(S. entomelas)*, and yellowtail *(S. flavidus)*.

Angling. As their name implies, rockfish are found around rocky bottoms—the craggier the better—and at depths of 200 to 700 or more feet. Ledgelike dropoffs, deep rock valleys, and craggy peaks are especially good, as they contain holes and crevices where these fish can hide. In deep-water bottom fishing, it's necessary to use heavy weights or jigs to get to the bottom. Eight to 16 ounces of lead are used depending on the depths. The favored offerings are heavy metal lures, called "jigbars," diamond jigs, and similar heavy lures, often with a plastic grub or piece of squid attached. These are typically bounced off the rocks, but they can be fished up through the water column, as some species are not tight to the bottom.

In shallow water, usually under 100 feet and to maybe only 10 feet, anglers use lighter lures and multibait rigs, although this is usually where smaller rockfish are found. Herring, shrimp, worms, squid, small live fish, and strips or pieces of fish are used for bait. Some rockfish are caught near the surface and are susceptible to cast lures, even flies, although this usually occurs when the water is not rough or murky. The usual bottom rig is made up of three to six hooks above a sinker that is heavy enough to take the line to the bottom on a fairly straight course.

Because of the extreme depths fished, it takes a lot of weight and a lot of line on tackle; low-stretch lines are helpful. The bait should be sufficiently firm to stay on the hook while being chewed upon; squid are commonly used for this reason.

See: Bocaccio; Rockfish, Black; Rockfish, Copper; Rockfish, Yelloweye.

ROCKFISH, BLACK *Sebastes melanops.*

Other names—black snapper, black bass, gray rockfish, red snapper, sea bass, black rock cod.

A member of the Scorpaenidae family, the black rockfish is widely distributed in the eastern Pacific. It is an excellent food fish.

Identification. The body of the black rockfish is oval or egg shaped and compressed. The head has a steep upper profile that is almost straight; the

Black Rockfish

mouth is large and the lower jaw projects slightly. The eyes are moderately large. The color is brown to black on the back, paler on the sides, and dirty white below. There are black spots on the dorsal fin. This species is easily confused with the blue rockfish; however, the anal fin of the black rockfish is rounded, whereas the anal fin of the blue rockfish is slanted or straight. The black rockfish has spots on the dorsal fin, and the blue rockfish does not.

Size. This species can attain a length of 25 inches and a weight of 11 pounds. The largest recorded weighed $10^{1}/_{2}$ pounds.

Distribution. Black rockfish occur from Paradise Cove, California, to Amchitka Island, Alaska.

Habitat. This wide-ranging fish can live on the surface or on the bottom to 1,200 feet near rocky reefs or in open water over deep banks or dropoffs. Offshore and deep-water individuals are larger than nearshore specimens.

Life history/Behavior. Like all members of their family, black rockfish are ovoviviparous, with egg fertilization and development taking place in the body of the mother. When embryonic development is complete, the female releases the eggs; the exposure to seawater activates the embryo, and it escapes from the egg case. The young hatch in spring and form large schools off the bottom in estuaries and tide pools in summer. Adults may be abundant in summer in shallow water near kelp-lined shores, but they occupy deeper water in fall and winter. They may school over rocky reefs from the bottom to the surface and are caught at varied depths, from near the surface to 1,200 feet.

Food. The diet of the black rockfish includes squid, crabs eggs, and fish. They are occasionally observed feeding on sand lance on the surface. Salmon anglers sometimes catch this fish on trolled herring.

Angling. *See: Rockfish.*

ROCKFISH, COPPER *Sebastes caurinus.*

Other names—never die, whitebelly, chucklehead, rock cod, bass.

The copper rockfish is a member of the Scorpaenidae family and is a widely distributed, hardy species. It often appears in aquarium displays.

Identification. The body of the copper rockfish is moderately deep and compressed. The head is large with a slightly curved upper profile; the mouth is large, and the lower jaw projects slightly. Its coloring is copper brown to orange tinged with pink. The back two-thirds of the sides along the lateral line are light, the belly is white, and there are usually two dark bands radiating backward from each eye.

Size. This species can attain a length of 22 to 23 inches and a weight of 10 pounds.

Distribution. The copper rockfish occurs from San Benitos Islands, Baja California, to the Kenai Peninsula, Alaska.

Habitat. This fish is commonly found in shallow rocky and sandy areas, and is generally caught at depths of less than 180 feet; however, some have been taken as deep as 600 feet.

Life history. Copper rockfish are ovoviviparous, like all species in the genus *Sebastes*.

Food and feeding habits. The diet of copper rockfish includes snails, worms, squid, octopus, crabs, shrimp, and fish.

Angling. *See: Rockfish.*

ROCKFISH, YELLOWEYE
Sebastes ruberrimus.

Other names—red snapper, rasphead rockfish, turkey-red rockfish.

Also a member of the Scorpaenidae family, the yelloweye rockfish is known to many anglers as "red snapper," although it bears only slight resemblance to true snapper. It is one of many red to yellow species in the eastern Pacific, however, and resembles several others, making identification difficult. The large size and excellent flesh of this species make it a favorite among anglers.

Identification. The yelloweye rockfish is orange red to orange yellow in body coloration; it has bright-yellow irises and black pupils, and a raspy ridge above the eyes. The fins may be black at the margins. Adults usually have a light (perhaps white) band on the lateral line. Juveniles have two light bands, one on the lateral line and one short line

Copper Rockfish

Yelloweye Rockfish

A good rod belt greatly helps anglers fight strong fish.

below the lateral line. A large rockfish, the yelloweye is a heavy- boned, spiny fish through the head and "shoulders."

Size/Age. The yelloweye rockfish can attain a length of 36 inches and weigh up to 33 pounds. The all-tackle world record is an Alaskan fish that weighed 33 pounds, 3 ounces.

Distribution. This species occurs from the Gulf of Alaska to Baja California, Mexico.

Habitat. Rocky reefs and boulder fields, from 10 to 300 fathoms, are the usual haunts of the yelloweye. They are abundant during summer in shallow water along kelp-lined shores and are found in deeper water at other times.

Life history. Yelloweye rockfish are ovoviviparous, like all species in the genus *Sebastes*.

Food. The diet of yelloweye rockfish includes assorted fish, crustaceans, squid, and shrimp.

Angling. See: Rockfish.

ROD BELT

A beltlike device with a receptacle for holding the butt of a fishing rod and used for playing large fish while protecting the angler's lower abdomen, kidney, and groin. The primary purpose of a rod belt, which may also be called a fishing belt or a fighting belt, is to relieve the pressure that an unprotected rod butt can exert on the body while fighting a fish, especially one that takes a lengthy time to pursue, either due to its size and strength or the lightness of the tackle. Rod belts are believed to have originated with surf anglers, but are used by surf, pier, and boat anglers alike if the circumstances warrant. A rod belt is commonly used in saltwater, sometimes in conjunction with a fighting harness *(see: harness, fighting);* it is seldom used in freshwater, but may be employed by some, such as anglers pursuing giant species like sturgeon. A rod belt may be used with any type of tackle, including fly rods with butt extensions, but is most often associated with stand-up fishing *(see)* and the use of conventional and big-game tackle.

There are rod belts to suit light-, medium-, and heavy-tackle fishing. Original belts were made from leather, and some are still in use today, but most modern belts are made from highly durable synthetic materials, and some designs offer fish-playing benefit as well as personal protection. The leather models belted behind the back and in the front featured a wide reinforced area with a molded cup that may or may not have included a gimbal pin. Modern versions of the light tackle variety are essentially the same, and may have an open cup, a gimbaled cup, or an angled cup entry to facilitate rod butt placement. Putting a rod butt into the belt holder usually takes place in the heat of a battle and under a lot of tension, so it needs to be easy to accomplish.

The more experienced the angler and the more strenuous the fight, the more it is likely that an angler will prefer having a gimbal rest, which locks a gimbal-butt rod in position and allows it to pivot easily when the rod is raised and lowered. A rod that does not have a gimbal butt should be used with an open-receptacle belt. This includes most spinning rods, some conventional rods, and nearly all fly rods.

Medium-tackle belts are larger and worn lower on the abdomen, and provide more leverage. They are used with 30- to 50-pound tackle. Most feature a gimbal cup, but some do not; some models have an integrated rod butt receptacle that swivels in all directions. Heavy-tackle belts are still larger and bulky, and meant for positioning the rod butt receptacle across the thighs. These are used with 50- to 130-pound tackle and usually in conjunction with a fighting harness.

When using medium or heavy tackle in boats, it is a good idea to have a safety strap attached to the reel in case the outfit (with or without angler) gets yanked overboard, which has happened.
See: Big-Game Fishing.

ROD BLANK

The shaft of a fishing rod.
See: Blank; Rod, Fishing.

ROD, FISHING

An instrument with a handle, shaft, and reel seat, which connects a reel and line for the purpose of making a controlled presentation of bait, lure, or fly. It is an intrinsic element in all forms of sportfishing, being essential to casting, retrieving, detecting a strike, setting the hook, and playing the fish.

Effective fishing is in part determined by the use of the proper tackle for the situation; choosing the right rod is an important element of this. However, just as there are many different species of fish, diverse habitats, and methods of angling, so, too, are there many categories and types of fishing rods, each suited to a particular application. Some fishing rod manufacturers produce scores, if not hundreds, of different rods, covering a gamut from fly, spinning, baitcasting, spincasting, surf, trolling, boat, big-game, flipping, popping, noodle, and downrigger models, to name just some of the possibilities, not to mention specialized subtypes within many categorizations.

Obviously, a fly angler can't do justice to fly fishing without the right type of rod, but neither can the same type of spinning rod be used adequately in stream trout fishing as in trolling for trout with downriggers. Even when there is cross-application, some compromise must be made. Different species, special applications, and regional preferences have led to a proliferation in rods that anglers who do a variety of fishing will need. Although anglers do stretch the use of some fishing tackle, and although some rods can be used for multiple species and means of fishing, it is generally important to have the right type, length, and style of rod for a particular fishing situation. To make this choice from a potpourri of possibilities it is helpful to understand the functions, materials, features, and components of fishing rods.

Categories/Types

All fishing rods have a handle, shaft, and reel seat. The materials used for each of these features may vary. The shaft is primarily referred to as the blank; this is where the rod guides are attached, and the number and type of these vary widely. A very small number of rods do not have a series of external guides; in these, the line runs through the blank within the hollow interior and exits at the tip. Fishing rods are most commonly of one- or two-piece configuration. Some have three or more pieces; a lesser number, usually for specialty applications, have multiple telescoping sections or a telescoping butt section. Prices range widely, and though many of the specialist and top-quality performance rods are costly, high price is not necessarily indicative of the best quality and may not be synonymous with best value. Many good-quality fishing rods are to be found at midprice ranges.

The following text briefly details the most prominent different categories of rods. This information is rather generalized, as there are exceptions and special products in most categories.

Baitcasting. Used with levelwind or baitcasting reels, which sit on top of the rod handle and face the angler, this tackle provides excellent casting accuracy for the skillful user, although achieving top-level proficiency takes practice and experience. Most baitcasting rods are one-piece models, though larger, heavier duty ones may have a telescoping butt and are generally stiffer than spinning rods. Guides are usually small to medium in size, and handles may be straight or with a pistol grip, both having a trigger hold under the handle.

Spincasting. These rods are similar to those used in baitcasting and are fairly uncomplicated. The guides are mounted atop the rod, and guide rings are generally small. Reels mount a little higher on top of the rod's reel seat, and the handles feature either straight or pistol grip design with a trigger hold under the handle. Spincasting rods usually aren't as stiff as baitcasting rods, having generally lighter action for use with light lines and lures. They are made in one- and two-piece models, mostly of fiberglass, and a few are telescopic.

Spinning. Used with open-faced spinning reels that mount underneath the rod, this tackle is very popular for a wide range of fishing situations and is relatively uncomplicated. Guides are big to accommodate the large spirals of line that come off the reel spool when casting. Handles are straight, with fixed or adjustable (ring) reel seats, and both one- and two-piece models are common.

Fly. Unlike other rod types, fly rods use a large diameter, heavy line to cast a very light object.

To select a fishing rod, you should have a clear idea of your needs and the general properties of rods.

Guides are small, and rod length varies from 5 feet to 12 or 14, although most fly rods used in North America are 7$\frac{1}{2}$- to 10-footers. Fly rods are rated for casting a specific weight line; a fly reel usually sits at the bottom of the handle, but some rods have extension butts for leverage in fighting big fish.

Surf. These long rods are used for casting great distances from the beach into the surf and come in both spinning and revolving-spool reel versions. Length varies from 7 to 14 feet, though most are in the 10- to 12-foot range with long two-handed handles. They are heavy, in order to cast objects weighing 2 to 4 ounces, and guides are large.

Boat and bay. A lot of different rods fall into this catchall category predominantly devoted to saltwater fishing. These are usually workhorse products with beefy two-handed handles that accommodate conventional reels. They are generally stiff, heavy-action rods, with longer models used in pier fishing and shorter ones in boat work.

Big-game. These rods, meant for subduing the largest creatures of the sea, have the sturdiest construction. Generally short, they feature a roller guide on the tip top or throughout the blank, and sport an extra-heavy-duty handle with a gimbal mount butt for insertion into rod holders. These rods are rated according to the class of line (and reel size) they are suited for.

Other rods. Travel or pack rods are found in baitcasting, spinning, or fly versions and are three- or four-piece products (some also have telescoping butt sections). Ice fishing rods are usually very short rods with a soft tip for use around holes in the ice, mostly necessary for storing and dispensing line. Flipping rods are long (7 to 8 feet), heavy-action rods with telescoping butts that are used for making short casts in close quarters to heavy cover when largemouth bass fishing. Noodle rods are whippy 12- to 14-foot rods with guides that curve around the rod blank; they are primarily used in stream steelhead and salmon fishing for presentation and fish-fighting advantages, and sometimes in trolling. Downrigger rods are 8- to 9-foot slow-action products that are primarily found in baitcasting versions and take a long, deep bend for use when trolling with downriggers. Some other rods are made for special applications, and many manufacturers make rods designed for particular species of fish or for use with certain lures or baits (crankbait rods, worm fishing bass rods, mooching rods, and popping rods, for example).

Dynamics of the Fishing Rod

It is impossible to construct a single rod providing top performance for all types of sportfishing. This is naturally obvious to the experienced angler, but not to many beginners, who can be observed with grossly mismatched tackle. The mismatch may be in the form of reel to rod, or it may be in the form of a rod and reel combination that is too light or too heavy for a particular species of fish or method of angling. In either case, the result is less enjoyment than would be had with the proper equipment.

Although the tackle industry has taken measures to provide guidelines on balanced outfits, a lot remains to be accomplished in educating anglers about their equipment, especially rods and especially knowledge of basic nomenclature. Furthermore, an understanding of the dynamics of the fishing rod—especially how rods are used and how such use affects rod construction—is fundamental to knowing what type of rod is best for particular fishing needs, and also how to get the most enjoyment from it.

Function

Designating a rod by classifying it as being a certain type is meant to denote the intended application. Many rods today are subcategorized; for example, a baitcasting rod may be typed or labeled as a bass worming rod or a flipping stick, a big-game rod may be typed as a 30-pound-class offshore trolling rod, and so forth. Type is not completely separable from function, which is the specific task the angler wants the rod to perform.

Angling with a rod entails at least four specific functions: casting, detecting a strike or bite, setting the hook, and fighting/landing the fish. Some of these require opposite properties for optimal performance, which obviously complicates rod design.

Casting. The process of casting consists of a combination of body movements and rod action intended to project terminal tackle. The rod acts as a storage device to deliver smoothly the energy of the angler's arm, wrist, and hand, and it acts as a lever arm to increase tip velocity in the forward casting arc.

A longer rod generally casts farther than a shorter one, subject to the limitations of the individual angler's physical stature. This is because the tip velocity of a rod is directly proportional to length, although this ignores excessive bend, which tends to shorten the physical length of the rod. A higher launch velocity—the speed at which the lure, at the point of release, leaves the arc of the moving rod tip—results in a longer cast. In rods of equal length, a superior stiffness-to-weight ratio of one rod material over another provides a lighter fishing tool and thereby reduces angler fatigue after hours of repetitive use.

Stiffness-to-weight ratio is an engineering term used to quantify the ability of a material to be used effectively in structures. The higher the ratio, the larger the load that can be borne without excessive weight penalty. An aircraft constructed of solid steel, for example, would be very strong, but wouldn't fly. Likewise, a solid steel rod would be strong, but relatively unfishable by modern standards. Because some rod materials provide a distinct advantage in stiffness-to-weight ratio, they can be incorporated into longer rods to cast the same total weight of lure or bait for which a heavier rod, made of material

Rhizodontiform fishes were a highly predacious primitive fish prominent 300 million years ago; the largest fossil form possessed jaw fangs that were 22 centimeters long.

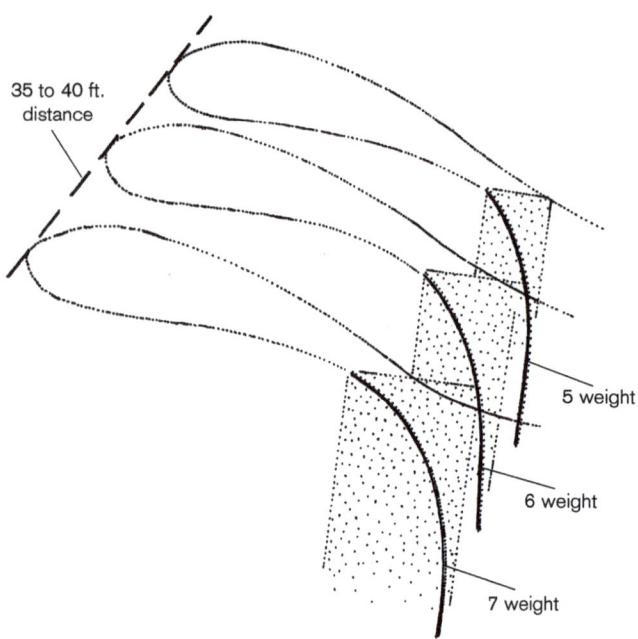

Casting distance and rod action vary with line weight. A 9-foot rod rated for a 6-weight fly line (WF or DT), balances at 35 to 40 feet.

having a less advantageous stiffness-to weight ratio, might be considered.

Another factor in the process of casting is energy storage. During a strong cast, the human muscles act in an almost explosive manner. The rod must be designed to smooth this impulse and efficiently cast the terminal rig or lure. Failure to do so results in thrown-off rigs, snapped-off lures, inaccurate casts, and backlashes (see).

Energy storage is enhanced by loss-free materials in rod construction and by rod taper. Loss-free materials are generally those with long, uninterrupted fibers with strong, mutual bonding. Ideally, a loss-free material acts like a perfect spring and returns all stored energy. Any loose ends to the working fibers, or gaps in the bonds, cause frictional losses, and the angler's energy goes into "heating" the rod rather than casting the lure. This latter case is much like bending a paper clip back and forth; it does not spring, but instead deforms and noticeably heats up.

In most fishing situations, the ideal taper for casting is very gradual, probably best illustrated by the highly developed field of fly rod design. When flexed, fly rods typically have a gradual bend from tip to butt, so that all portions of the rod assist in the storage and smooth transfer of energy from the angler to the fly line. The fly angler spends a great deal of time casting, often making delicate presentations, so it is appropriate that the fly rod emphasizes properties that are designed for casting.

Detecting a strike. From the standpoint of rod design, detecting a strike is limited to sensations transmitted by the line through the rod and into the angler's hand. Watching for line movement and noticing telltale ripples on the water are not directly involved with characteristics of the rod.

Here, the requirements for ideal rod design fortunately are aided by the laws of physics, which state that energy transfer occurs equally well in both directions through most structures. When we speak into a device, it is called a microphone; when the device emits a sound, it is called a loudspeaker. An intercom, however, uses a single device in both directions equally well. Likewise, an angler imparts energy to a lure when casting, and receives energy in the form of a vibration during a strike. A rod that casts well also exhibits great sensitivity to strikes. Thus, rods that smoothly transfer energy from angler to line and lure reciprocally transfer energy well from lure and line to angler. This property is quantified in physics as a mathematical statement called the Reciprocity Theorem.

There are some fine points to consider, however, because the strike signal can be so miniscule that fishing rod components such as reel seats and reel materials may affect the angler's ability to detect the strike. The rod, then, is not a separate entity, but rather a part of a complete system. In this regard, purposeful design of rod accouterments and reels affects optimal performance in strike detection.

Setting the hook. This is a rod function that may require a property that is opposed to those of other rod functions. An analogous example of opposing functions is a catalytic converter on an automobile; the component is not advantageous for engine efficiency, but a necessity to help provide for a cleaner environment. Rod design, too, is a balance of tradeoffs.

Ideal rod construction for hook setting requires great stiffness, so that minimal delay occurs between the strike and the angler's reaction to it. Additionally, such stiffness aids in maximizing the amount of line taken up, which in turn compensates for whatever stretch and slack may be inherent to the line being used (see: line). In this circumstance, fast acceleration is desired. Consider the situation of a fish picking up bait and the angler's reaction. In one moment, the hook is motionless; an instant later, it is moving at great speed to become imbedded in the fish's jaw.

The bass angler's worm fishing rod is an excellent example of optimal rod design for hook setting. This type of rod is designed to set the hook hard, fast, and deep. In this type of fishing, failure to "cross a fish's eyes" not only translates into a missed catch, but, in many instances, impacts on verifying whether a detected irregularity in retrieval is the subtle strike of a fish or merely the lure bumping on bottom structure.

Fortunately, the function of setting the hook can be compromised in rod design, in light of special angling techniques and advancements in the design of certain hooks and terminal tackle.

Fighting/landing the fish. This process—bringing the fish to the angler—is also essentially one of energy transfer; this time, that transfer is from the fish to the drag elements in the reel (see:

drag; reel, fishing). The construction of the rod is an important factor because it smoothes the pulsing thrusts of the fish's tail and fins, and accommodates changes in the direction and angle of the fish's runs.

In fighting a fish, there are also secondary energy losses in the friction of line bellying through the water, and in fiber bond slippage within the rod structure itself. This latter characteristic is called damping or dampening.

Damping is the process of converting vibrational energy to heat. In an automobile suspension system, for example, the task is accomplished by the shock absorbers. The energy imparted to automobile springs when there is a bump in the road is converted to heat by the shock absorber. Though desirable in some situations, damping is undesirable in others. A pole vaulter, for example, stores energy in the bending (or loading) of the pole in order to be flung over the crossbar. If a shock absorber were placed on the pole, performance would suffer greatly. Likewise, a good casting rod should not be excessively dampened.

When deflected, a properly designed rod returns to equilibrium rather quickly, instead of continuing to vibrate up and down. From a casting point of view, this is an important consideration after the rod has flexed in the forward casting arc.

To some extent, all fishing rods damp; it's a matter of degree. Rod damping helps wear down a fish. Excessive rod damping, however, can cut down casting distance because casting energy is too quickly being dissipated into heat as fiber bond slippage occurs. A well-damped rod is comfortable to use when a fish is on, just as a well-damped automobile is comfortable to ride in, compared with the ride experienced in a stiff-spring pickup truck.

The ideal taper for a rod designed to fight fish is generally abrupt. Abruptly tapered rods are usually called "fast tapers," "magnum actions," or "power rods." They are fashioned through large butt-to-tip diameter-ratio differences.

A good example of this type of rod taper is the classic West Coast albacore or tuna rod. It is characterized by being "tippy," meaning much more flexible at the tip than at the butt. When a fish is hooked, the bend of such a rod may resemble an inverted L shape, with very little deflection near the butt. The location of the bend varies according to the size of the fish and the angler-applied force exerted when pulling on the fish.

For larger fish, the bend of the tippy rod occurs downward toward the grip as well, and the rod can adjust to such a circumstance because of its thicker-walled section near the butt. On the other hand, a small fish causes a bend higher up in the more flexible portion of the rod, at a smaller cross section. A wide range of fish can be accommodated by such a rod. Furthermore, by designing in sufficient butt stiffness, this type of rod will not "bottom out," or tend to exceed its elastic limits, and the angler can exert a great deal of power against the fish. The fish-

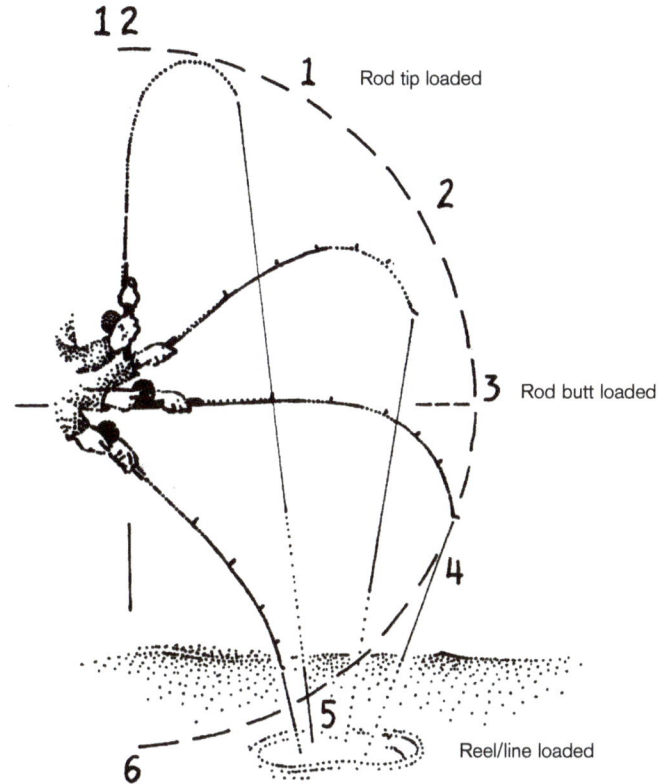

When playing a strong fish directly below your position, power is exerted when the rod is approximately between the 2 and 4 o'clock positions; this is when the rod butt carries the load. When the rod is approximately between the 4 and 6 o'clock positions, the reel and the line carry the load and the rod does little. When the rod is approximately between the 12 o'clock and 2 o'clock positions, the tip carries the load; this can be harmful to the rod and creates a situation in which the angler can do little to influence the fish.

ing conditions automatically select that particular portion of the rod cross section best suited to fight the fish.

When such a rod is cast, however, in a like fashion only very particular and limited portions of the rod act elastically to store energy. Therefore, it is a relatively poor casting instrument.

Obviously, ideal rod construction entails a number of compromises. Some of the qualities we seek in rods have similar requirements; others have opposing ones. Thus, there must always be a certain amount of give and take in designing a truly fishable rod. In most instances, the particular degree of compromise is intended to give the best possible performance for the type of rod and its function. In other words, good rod design and construction should emphasize those properties most vital to each particular type of fishing.

As noted, fly rods tend to favor casting, but at the risk of bottoming out, or exceeding the elastic limit on a truly strong fish; the exception is big-game saltwater fly rods that are very effective fighting tools but troublesome to cast unless they are of superior overall design. By contrast, the power rod

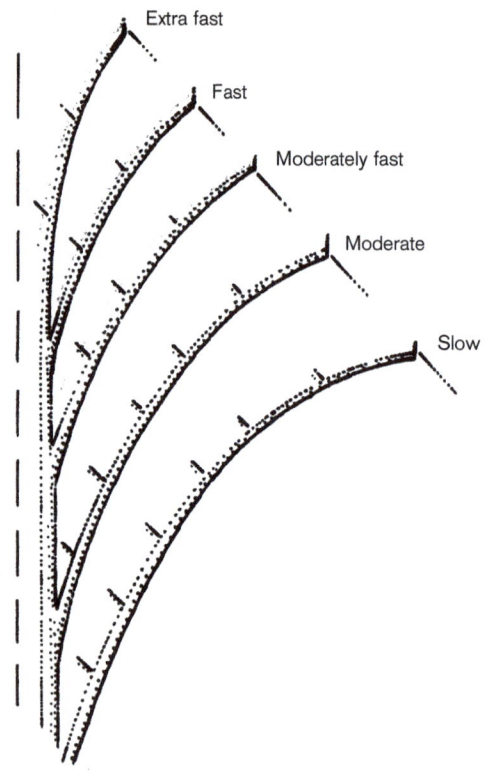

Rod Action

can quickly exhaust a wide range of fish, but at the risk of tearing the hook out of the baitfish or snapping off a lure on the cast.

Power/action. The performance and function of rods are commonly described in terms of power and action, which are somewhat nebulous terms that refer to the design of the rods based upon their construction and materials and incorporating all of the issues that have been noted so far.

In a practical sense, power is defined by the amount of pressure that it takes to flex the rod; the less pressure it takes, the lighter the rod's power. Designations are made according to an individual rod's ability to efficiently handle a certain range of lure weights and line sizes. These designations are ultralight, light, medium light, medium, medium heavy, heavy, and extra heavy.

The related concept of action denotes where a rod flexes along its blank, which is determined by the taper. A fast-taper rod flexes mostly at or near the tip, a moderate-taper rod flexes through the middle of the rod, and a slow-taper rod flexes through the butt. Specific designations include slow, moderate, moderately fast, fast, and extra fast.

Construction and Materials

Rods are mass produced by major manufacturers, but only insofar as the blanks are fabricated by large-scale methods. The overall properties of the finished product are extremely dependent on what is done to the blank after manufacture. Thus, the number, type, and placement of guides; the wrapping; and the choice and placement of handle material totally affect the end use.

Unlike the situation with reels, rod building can also be a cottage industry, and many small custom rod builders exist, most of them buying blanks from established manufacturers and custom tailoring the final product. This tailoring might be done, for example, to make an offshore casting rod suited to the build of a particular angler, or it might be done to wrap a fly rod blank with spinning rod guides to create a special river fishing rod. In addition, individual anglers purchase blanks and component materials to build rods for themselves or family members, either to suit special needs or to have the satisfaction of catching fish on a personally made rod.

A typical rod is manufactured by first cutting a cloth formed of strength fibers pre-impregnated with a bonding resin This resined cloth is normally referred to as "prepreg" by fishing rod manufacturers. From a chemical standpoint the most commonly used resin systems are phenolic, polyester, or epoxy, the latter two being more commonly employed in modern rods.

The prepreg is cut into the proper shape to provide the appropriate thickness of rod wall along the entire blank. In some rods, for instance, the butt section may utilize a wider cut of prepreg or even additional layers for a specific taper.

After it is cut into a shape, the prepreg is wound around a form called a mandrel, which is contoured to define the shape and taper of the finished rod blank. By a number of different processes, pressure and heat are applied to cure the wrapped prepreg and mold it over the mandrel. After the cure cycle, the mandrel is removed from the blank and the rod's exterior is subjected to finishing operations.

To some degree, all rod-building materials are composites. Each rod shaft consists of a strength or stress element, typically a fiber, and a bonding element, typically a resin. The stress element stores and transmits energy by elastic deformation, and the bonding element both fixes the location of the stress element and prevents the failure of one fiber from directly propagating to another.

This latter property is the principal reason why single-material rods are impractical. The failure or development of a defect would easily propagate like a crack in a windshield and the entire structure would fail. Therefore, superior construction techniques entail many small fibers to reduce the risk of breakage.

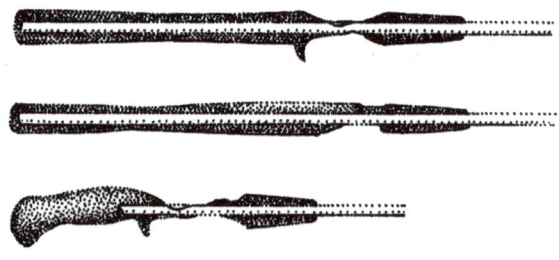

In some rods, the blank runs completely through the handle.

Another reason for using small fibers in rod construction is that it is far easier to manufacture small fibers without defects than it is to manufacture larger ones without defects. This is because fewer atoms are involved.

Bamboo. Bamboo (Tonkin cane) is a natural composite. The stress element consists of tiny fibers that distribute nutrients through the plant, and the bonding element is a material called lignin.

The principal limitations of bamboo are variations in quality and the presence of discontinuities (nodes) within the stalk of the plant. From the manufacturing standpoint, variations in the natural product, even within a single stalk or culm, necessitate an enormous amount of painstaking selection and hand work. It is labor-intensive and very costly to manufacture, which is why the very best split-cane rods are enormously expensive.

The situation with split-cane rods is much like it is in a winery. The correct circumstances and precise production control of the grapes lead to a truly outstanding wine; otherwise, the product is merely grape juice. Though capable of giving fine performance under somewhat limited conditions, bamboo is largely a material for the custom rod builder.

Fiberglass. Fiberglass is manufactured by flowing molten glass through tiny orifices in a melting furnace. The glass strands are pulled through the miniscule holes at high speeds and stretched while partially molten into fine filaments.

The glass filaments are then conditioned, coated, and woven into yarns or cloth fabrics, depending upon their intended application. The diameter and other physical parameters of the glass filaments are continuously monitored to assure a uniform product.

This uniformity was the key to successful early fiberglass fishing rod construction. The manufacturers were not only able to design rods, but were confident that quality would be uniform throughout each production run.

Uniformity also aided in developing mass-production techniques with reduced labor costs, and thereby made it possible to offer excellent fishing rods at attractive prices. Moreover, as fiberglass rod technology matured, the uniformity of the fiberglass materials permitted fine-tuning of manufacturing processes to improve the product.

One example of fine-tuning was the introduction of variations in the chemical composition of the glass melt. Of the types of glass available, E-glass, which is an alkalai borosilicate glass, is widely used because of its high resistance to water damage and its high-tensile-modulus. (Modulus is a measure of how effectively a material resists deformation. Tensile means "to pull" or place under a tension load. A high-tensile modulus material produces a stiff structure and thus aids in achieving a high stiffness-to-weight ratio. There also are other kinds of moduli, for example, compression modulus and shear modulus, which are not all independent but relate to one another.)

A higher-priced, low-alkalai, high-aluminum-and-magnesium kind of product called S-glass *(see)* can be produced with an approximately 30 percent improvement in tensile modulus. S-glass was originally developed for aerospace use but has been largely supplanted in that industry by other materials. It remains in the tackle industry as an intermediate rod material in price and performance between regular fiberglass and graphite.

Graphite. Graphite, or carbon fiber, as it is called in some parts of the world, has become a generic term. As originally developed for the aerospace industry, graphite was intended to maximize the strength-to-weight ratio, and the aim was to achieve the highest possible tensile modulus. Performance, such as in fighter planes, was more important than price. However, the proliferation of graphite products into the fishing tackle industry, beginning from high-end rods but eventually trickling down to mid- and low-priced rods, encouraged the development of a much wider range of graphite fibers, both in cost and in modulus.

The present situation requires that graphite as rod material must be evaluated in very specific terms for comparison purposes; this is hard to do because graphite has become as generic a word in common usage as "wood."

There is a further complication in that rods are frequently required to flex to a much larger angle than would be practical for an aircraft structural member; thus, another engineering quality is the elastic limit. Other complexities include the fact that most rod-building graphite fibers are used in prepreg form and proprietary processes can be used to control the ratio of fiber to resin, greatly affecting the properties of the final product. Also, the prepreg itself may consist of unidirectional, angled, or even woven graphite fibers. As a final confusion, chopped graphite fibers may be used to supplement the strength of polymers, such as used in reel seats and reel bodies.

The bottom line, however, remains delivered performance. All of this confusion aside, the "fishability" of a rod remains the final parameter; the type and configuration of the graphite fibers merely describe the fabrication method.

Graphite is produced by passing a polymer fiber, which is much like an ultra-fine monofilament fishing line, through a heated vacuum oven until only carbon atoms remain in the exiting fiber. The process is called pyrolization and is relatively expensive. The combination of advances in production techniques and substantial increases in the volume of graphite sales has lowered the price of graphite until it has become an attractive fishing rod material.

The tensile modulus of graphite runs from four to eight times that of fiberglass. Thus, a graphite rod intended for the same type of fishing as one made of fiberglass can have thinner walls and be of a more slender configuration. The net result is a significant savings in the weight of the finished rod.

Fish in captivity have been trained in various ways; as long ago as 1914, Washington resident C. W. Lange trained trout to jump through hoops, among other stunts.

A second property of graphite has both positive and negative aspects. The combination of configuration and bonding properties enhances the alignment of unidirectional graphite fibers in rod construction, so graphite rods can be designed with fibers extending unbroken from tip to butt. This construction style provides smooth energy transfer, which results in excellent casting qualities and more sensitivity than found in a fiberglass rod made from woven cloth. But there is a limitation imposed on the variety of rod tapers that can be designed with unidirectional fibers.

It is evident that the correct combination of graphite with fiberglass can produce rods with both good sensitivity and a wide variety of tapers. This process requires extremely careful design, however, and the graphite should not only be unidirectionally aligned within the rod, but also uniformly distributed around the rod shaft. Such a composite rod offers both performance and value, for it can be offered at a price between fiberglass and high-content graphite.

It is noteworthy that the percentage of graphite in a rod is not the major factor in value or performance, but rather how it is used. There has been considerable controversy over "graphite content" alone as a sales point, but such thinking has little foundation in scientific fact.

Boron. Boron is produced by the reduction of gases in contact with a heated filament. In effect, the boron is plated on the filament in the form of a coating, resulting in a fiber of great tensile strength. However, the filament (usually a tungsten alloy) is heavy and contributes substantially to the total weight of the fiber. Overall, boron fibers have a significant advantage over graphite in strength-to-weight ratio, but by themselves are not practical in mass-produced rod construction due to weight.

Because of this, boron fibers are usually employed with graphite to form composite rods and thus are subject to the same rigorous design requirements of unidirectional fiber alignment and uniform distribution around the shaft for top performance. High-boron-content tubular rods usually contain less than 15 percent boron fibers by weight, but, again, content alone does not constitute an accurate assessment of performance.

Future materials. Several interesting materials, both fibers and bonding matrices, are currently being evaluated by aerospace laboratories. However, these are exotic, both in manufacturing technology and price. For these to be worth producing, anglers would have to see a considerable performance advantage to warrant the expenditure, and/or a great reduction in manufacturing cost.

The probable future of rod construction seems to be with improved application of those materials presently used, rather than with the introduction of new materials. Advances in construction techniques, lower production costs, and perhaps sharper pricing should lead to increased sales of high-performance

Handle, guides, action, and material are all important elements in using a rod to cast, retrieve, and play a fish.

rods suitable to the varied types and functions needed in the sport of angling.

Features and Components

A fishing rod is used in conjunction with some type of reel and line and, therefore, has features and components necessary for various functions. Some are derived from the manufacturing process, such as hoop strength and spine, while others are additions that are basic to every use.

Hoop strength. Whenever a beam is flexed, its outer surfaces are under the greatest stress and provide the maximum restoring forces for returning the beam to its original shape; the central portion of the beam acts mostly to keep these surfaces spaced apart. This stress distribution holds true for any beam shape. It helps to explain the shape of the steel "I" beam used in bridge construction, for example; the outer surfaces carry the load and the central web acts to keep the outer surface apart. Likewise, the construction of snow skis consists of upper and lower strength surfaces, separated by a simple foam or cell filling.

In simplest terms, a hollow tube delivers better stiffness-to-weight ratios than a solid bar (or beam); in the latter, the middle of the object increases weight but does not contribute much to the stiffness. The logical conclusion of this is that the "best" fishing rod would be hollow, and of maximal diameter with minimal wall thickness. The ultimate examples of such a product are current production rods for specialty fishing in Asia, which have eight telescoping sections that extend to a total length of 31 feet, with a total weight of 9.2 ounces! These are production rods, and they are enormously expensive.

There are, however, complications with having a hollow rod with maximal diameter and minimal wall thickness. The first is hoop strength, which is a measure of the ability of a hollow tubular structure to resist ovaling deformation leading to inward collapse of its walls. A typical soda straw has low hoop strength and fails under bending loads by collapsing or folding in half. In tubular rod blanks, hoop strength limits the maximum diameter and minimum wall thickness attainable in mass production. There are further complications specific to rod taper, materials, and assembly techniques. Mainly though, hoop strength is enhanced by such methods as winding around the rod blank (which acts like barrel hoops), exterior mesh (which acts like support stockings), and interior fillings (which act to space the walls apart).

Winding around the rod blank can be in the form of unidirectional fiber tape, or as a cross weave in a cloth prepreg. The former can be extremely expensive and technically difficult to apply; the latter often leads to a bumpy, non-uniform rod surface. Both methods are also used to relieve the additional stresses that occur at "built-in" ferrule joints (the place where sections connect) in premium rods. Lower priced rods often enhance this vital hoop strength at ferrules by a thread wrap.

Exterior meshes, particularly those of a high-strength polyamide such as Kevlar, also enhance hoop strength. It is essential that the mesh is strongly bonded to the rod blank for best effect; think of support stockings for the legs, or of the woven mesh in garden hoses. It is further noteworthy that Kevlar and similar fibers act strongly in tension, but are soft in compression, and therefore act not as "springs," but more in the nature of damping elements. Expert fly casters have reported that Kevlar-meshed graphite fly rods cast more akin to expensive hand-built Tonkin cane rods than any other synthesized fiber.

The simplest interior filling is a solid one. Some of the earliest fiberglass fishing rods were of solid construction; they were extremely heavy in weight and slow in action, but they were virtually indestructible. They were also eventually considered unfishable. However, technology has gone full circle, and advances in rod fabrication have wedded the best of both worlds: super slender, high-sensitivity solid tips at the first 12 to 18 inches of the rod, smoothly blended into a responsive and powerful hollow tubular rear section. The bonded joint is undetectable, both visually and in performance.

Even more advanced fabrication technology has led to a tapered, precision-ground graphite core, which is used as the traditional mandrel in rod building but is left inside the finished blank for hoop strength. The rod is light, slender, yet virtually unbreakable under fishing conditions. Unidirectional fibers are exposed at the first 12 to 18 inches of the tip, giving unparalleled sensitivity, strength, and power characteristics; again, this is the best of several worlds.

In each of these latter cases, the advances in rod performance are not so much due to the materials, which are various graphite fibers, but how these materials are assembled into a rod.

Spline. The spline, or spine, is a softer direction or preferred orientation of flexing or bending for a rod blank. In other words, the rod bends more easily along one plane, which is known as the spline. This preferred orientation stems from the fabrication of a rod blank by winding prepreg cloth around a mandrel; the prepreg must have a starting and ending edge, which distresses the absolute uniformity of the blank wall and thereby defines a direction of easier bending.

Manufacturers and rod builders usually locate the spline prior to affixing rod guides to make sure that their placement is not counter to the preferred bending orientation. The spline can be located by several methods; it is typically found by gripping the rod tip, then flexing while rotating about the rod axis and noting the preferred orientation for the easiest bend.

The spline of many rod blanks can be subtle, depending on the manufacturing technology and the type of rod. For instance, rods with a Kevlar support mesh usually exhibit diminished spline characteristics due to enhanced hoop strength.

When a rod has a weakly defined spline, determining precise orientation is less important for affixing guides. An example of this would be a multi-section spinning rod. In part, this is because each section is a separate blank made by a separate process and producing a separate spline, and because the location of the guides below the rod axis becomes the dominant factor defining the bending plane.

However, for rods used with baitcasting, conventional, and big-game reels, and specifically blue water tuna rods, spline orientation can be critical because these rods tend to torque under load in even the best of cases. The guides are located above the rod axis, which is an inherently unstable situation, and incorrect spline can aggravate the tendency to torque, leading to a requirement of extra forces to keep the rod oriented vertically. The angler ends up not only fighting the fish, but also fighting the rod.

In general, however, in spite of a great deal of folklore to the contrary, spline orientation is a secondary effect and relatively unimportant. A statement such as this may agitate some custom rod builders, but spline orientation is controlled at the level of the rod fabricators, and there is little the angler can do to alter the completed rod. Additionally, advances in rod blank fabrication technology in many cases has caused the spline to be less pronounced, and therefore of diminishing concern.

Ferrules. The longest practical one-piece rod is about 5 to 6 feet in length. The reason for this limitation is that one-piece rods longer than that will not fit easily into an automobile, and the possibilities for accidental mechanical damage abound. For instance, having the wind blow a car door shut when a longer rod is carefully being maneuvered into place is disastrous. Rod manufacturers are constantly requested to make warranty replacements of rods with the characteristic creased damage of car doors and, even more common, doors in the home. (The absolute worse place for storage of a rod is behind a door; if it slips into the door jamb, it will join the Legion of Mashed Rods.) It is estimated that such accidental mechanical damage exceeds rods broken in actual fishing conditions by many orders of magnitude.

Therefore, most rods of moderate or more length are produced in several sections. (There are notable exceptions, such as the custom one-piece 11- to 15-foot products used by dedicated surf casters, who regard car-top or bumper roof racks as a necessary part of their sport.) In the distant past, these sections were produced by cutting the rod blank and joining the sections with a separate metal fitting or ferrule; the additional weight and stiffness, however, degraded the action, and most rods today are joined with integral ferrules that are part of the blank itself.

The merit of integral ferrules is obvious: no discontinuity or significant alteration of the rod action. As an example, backpacking rods for the hiker are produced as five or more sections of about a foot each, yet the assembled rod is very fishable and it requires a diligent search to locate the joints. Even better are the high-end three- or four-piece travel products that result in eminently fishable 6- to 9-foot spinning, baitcasting, and flycasting rods.

The integral ferrule is fabricated in inside and outside forms. The inside ferrule is the lightest and simplest to produce in that the lower section is made a bit larger and the tip section slides into it. The joint is ground with a precision taper, and the friction fit is sufficient for a secure grip. Many experienced anglers lubricate this joint (if not already done by the manufacturer) with beeswax, both to increase the grip and to promote smoother assembly. Do not apply the wax excessively or it will trap abrasive dirt particles; always wipe a ferrule before assembly.

Hoop strength at the ferrule is usually increased with a string wrap. The outside ferrule, in turn, is stronger because the thinner tip section is built up at the joint to fit outside the lower section. The tip section is thus as strong as the rear section, which was already strong because of the increasing rod taper toward the butt. The outside ferrule is more expensive to produce because the built-up joint requires the application of separate hoop windings on the rod blank, and each such operation increases costs. When made well, both types of ferrules deliver good service and are very fishable.

Several special products deserve distinct mention. One is telescoping rods in which the ferrules are joined from the inside. Telescoping rods are generally of three or more sections, extending to lengths in excess of 12 feet and popular for poking among bushes for species such as crappie and bream. The guides are usually of a "slip-on" configuration, always on the rod, and are slid into their correct places as the rod is extended. This process is much simpler in practice than the description. In Europe and Asia, where this style of rod is extremely popular, the guides are fitted with a plastic "stringing needle," which not only aligns but also pulls line through the guides before extension so that the rod is ready to tie on terminal tackle as soon as it is extended (you have to try stringing a 15-foot rod in a boat to truly appreciate the convenience of this accessory).

Another example is blue water rods for large fish. These conventional rods use the powerful drags of revolving-spool reels to subdue fish that easily outweigh the angler and are many times heavier than the breaking strength of the line. Because the top-side guides generate torque forces on the rod, the blanks are always of one-piece construction to prevent rotation at a ferrule.

In general, however, the ferrule is an essential part of most practical rod designs, and the convenience it provides for transport and storage far outweighs any effect on rod action.

Guides. Nearly all fishing rods have guides; this includes one tip-top guide, which is obviously at the top or casting end of the rod, and a variable number of intermediate guides, which are along the blank between the top and the handle. Of all accouterments, guides are the single most significant factor affecting rod performance beyond the blank itself. The style, height, number, spacing, and weight are all part of the guide, and therefore important parameters.

Rod guide styles can be termed either "spinning" or "conventional." Although there is some degree of universality, the basic choice that distinguishes these is large-ring bottom-mounted guides for spinning rods (as well as fly rods), and small-ring top-mounted guides for conventional rods, which are used with revolving-spool reels (baitcasting, conventional, and big-game).

Guide style includes the frame material, which includes welded stainless steel, graphite polymer, brazed wire, and others. However, the fundamental guide parameter is whether it has single or double attachment points to the rod blank, which respectively are called single- or double-foot guides.

Because casting is what spinning tackle does best, the appropriate guides for spinning rods should favor the casting function. Thus, a single-foot guide least perturbs the typical light action of a spinning rod, and is the primary choice. The single-

Manitoulin Island, a popular boating and fishing area of northern Lake Huron, is the world's largest island in a lake; it also hosts the largest lake inside another lake.

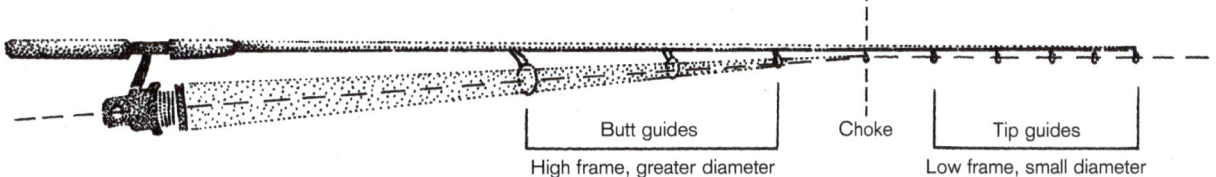

A spinning rod characteristically has the largest guides closest to the butt and the smallest guides closest to the tip. The choke guide is the intersection point where larger spirals of line funnel down when cast.

foot guide is also suitable for withstanding the forces of the line acting on the guide when subduing a large fish. These forces are directed downward, and the frame of a single-foot guide slung below the rod has sufficient strength to withstand severe tension load on the guide ring.

Double-foot construction is favored for conventional rod guides, especially for models used to subdue strong ocean species. This is because fish fighting is what such tackle does best, and the load of a gamefish on the line applies both a crushing downward force on the guide ring and frame, and a simultaneous tendency to torque or twist the rod. This latter phenomenon occurs because the line is located directly above the rod axis and is fundamentally at unstable equilibrium; when torquing begins, the lever arm for twisting increases and the condition avalanches. Such stresses require the rigid configuration of a double-foot frame (the double attachment points of the frame to the rod act in the manner of a triangle, the extremely sturdy building block of bridge spans). Light-duty baitcasting rods, such as those used for freshwater bass fishing, have a mixture of guide styles, usually double-foot guides toward the stiffer rear section and single-foot guides toward the slender tip section, which is often designed to enhance strike detection (as with jigs or plastic worms).

An important function of the guide on all rods is to prevent contact of the line with the rod blank. During a cast, such contact or "line slap" results in shorter casts due to increased friction; when fighting a gamefish, such contact is regarded as an unfavorable and irregular additional force retarding the line.

The height and spacing of guides on the rod are interactive; these parameters are mutually dependent and must be considered simultaneously. In the case of spinning rods, the line leaves the reel in the form of a cone-shaped envelope, defined by the spool diameter at its base and the tiptop at its apex. The theoretically ideal guide ring diameter, height, and spacing precisely lies along the surface of this cone because such a configuration would minimize friction and thereby lead to maximum casting distance. Although there is some disagreement about the location and effects of the lowest or first guide along this cone, most spinning rods are fabricated in a sensible manner and small departures from this ideal cone are not serious.

During retrieval of a large fish, the stress on the line is applied through the guides to the attachment points on the rod. If the number and spacing of the guides is insufficient, the stress is concentrated at these points and the rod will be bent into distinct segments instead of a smooth curve. The final result could be a catastrophic failure.

How many guides are sufficient? The optimum solution requires a compromise because too many guides leads to heavy weight, slow action, and high costs; too few lead to stress concentration and rod failure. A simple test of spinning rod design is to string the rod with monofilament line, and then lift the rod against a load to verify the quality of its design. Note that the common practice of simply wiggling the rod back and forth, or flexing the rod tip against the ceiling, reveals the rod taper but does not generally validate correct guide spacing and number.

In the case of the conventional rod, during a cast the line leaves nearly tangent to the spool

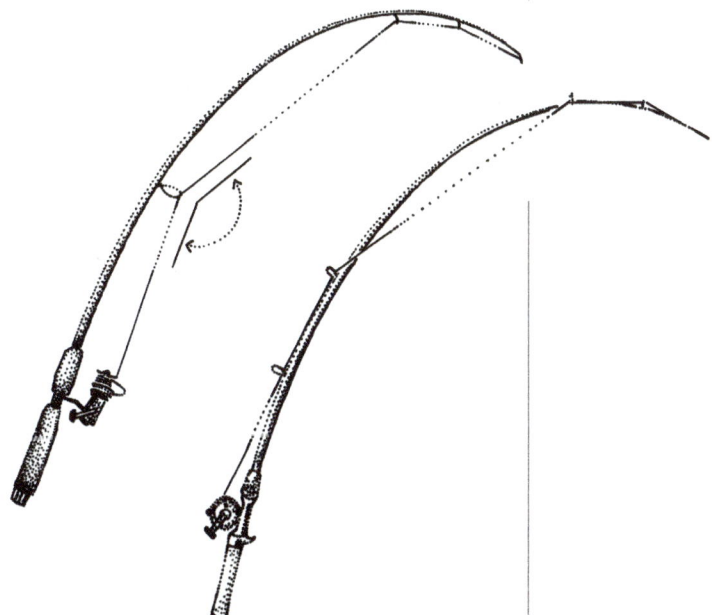

This is a greatly exaggerated depiction of poor guide placement on a spinning rod (top), where guides and line are under the blank, and on a baitcasting rod (bottom), where guides and line are on top of the blank. It helps illustrate the fact that when there is too great an angle (arrows) of line from one guide to the next, there is excessive strain on the rod and loss of power.

so that the guide rings can be relatively small. Because controlling gamefish is what conventional tackle does best, the guide configuration favors the retrieval function. During the fish fighting process, in the ideal case the guides are required to support the line above the axis of the rod. Compromises are necessary here, too, because increasing guide height reduces the number required but also increases the "lever arm" and therefore the tendency to torque. The optimum height and spacing depends on the rod action but is generally regarded as the minimum number that will not permit the line to cross the axis of the rod during maximum bend.

Although some rod designers abhor even slight contact between line and rod surface, the process of the line crossing below the rod axis certainly exacerbates the always present problem of torque. In essence, pulling the line past the rod axis is an unstable state, and the structure responds by torquing, or twisting over. The test for correct design here is the same as for spinning: thread the rod with line and check for contact under load.

Guide rings. In order to effectively confine the line with minimum disturbance, the ideal guide ring should have several properties: low weight, low friction, and high durability. Low weight is particularly important for casting applications where the additional mass of the guide can affect the action of the rod blank.

In the specific case of fly fishing, where superior casting properties for a delicate presentation are of foremost importance, the lightest of all guides, simple helixes of thin wire, are the rule. At the other end of the scale, as in blue water trolling where weight is unimportant because the rod is supported by a gimbal mount and shoulder harness, the norm is massive roller guides to minimize the friction of heavy lines and to maximize fish-fighting power. Other fishing tackle falls between these extremes. Practical guide ring materials include chrome-plated stainless steel or brass, common and technical ceramics, and various carbide and nitride compounds. These are available, depending on their configuration, in a wide range of weights.

Low friction is attained through good surface polishing, but, as usual, contradictory requirements arise from the property of durability. The wear aspect of durability concerns abrasion of the guide ring by the line; this is usually due to the action of microscopic particles of suspended sediment (quartz) carried by the line. Therefore, an ideal guide ring material should be harder than quartz, and this requirement is identical to that of a precious gemstone.

Common guide ring materials include aluminum oxide (alumina, or in its gemstone form, red ruby or blue sapphire), tungsten carbide (Carboloy), silicon carbide (SiC), titanium nitride (TiN), and zirconium nitride (ZrN). While some of these materials can be formed as a ceramic before firing, all require grinding and polishing, the same as any gemstone. This leads to a contradictory requirement: The desirable hardness property in these materials is the very feature that causes that same material to be stubborn to shape and polish. Silicon carbide guide rings, for example, typically require one week of continuous diamond dust polishing to attain a good surface finish. This manufacturing cost is naturally reflected in the finished product.

Another aspect of durability is "shock resistance," or the ability of a guide ring to withstand a sharp blow. Of the foregoing materials, tungsten carbide is reported to be the most brittle, followed by silicon carbide and aluminum oxide. Titanium and zirconium nitrides can occur in the form of solid technical ceramics, or may be applied as vacuum-deposited coatings on various substrates. The latter materials are routinely used as protective coatings on the turbine blades of jet aircraft; they may sound exotic but are extremely practical and durable. Another application of these coatings is on premium drills and cartridge case dies, where their hardness and low friction properties offer significant benefits. These are definitely guide ring materials for the near future.

The tip-top guide is a type of terminal guide ring, but its service load is substantially more severe due to increased contact and friction where the line has its greatest angular change at the rod tip. As a consequence, many rods are offered at a lower price by mounting a higher quality material such as Carboloy or silicon carbide for the tip-top ring, and using hard chrome or other materials for intermediate guides. In like manner, the stripping guide of a fly rod has the major angular change for the line (the tiptop tends to lie parallel to the line due to the combination of line stiffness and soft rod tip action), thus, its "stripper" guide is usually of higher quality than the remainder, typically the best aluminum oxide or silicon carbide. In general, the rod manufacturer is well aware of the requirements for superior guide service; its choice of materials reflects compromises on cost, quality, and perceived value.

Guide wrapping. The guide is normally wrapped onto the rod with thread, which both affixes it to the blank and serves in a decorative capacity. The thread can vary in thickness, ranging from approximately the fineness of a hair, to the coarseness of 4-pound-test monofilament, and in materials from costly silk to common spun nylon. Generally, the finer thread wraps are most highly regarded because more turns are required per linear inch, which likewise requires a higher level of craftsmanship.

Under load, the guide acts as a point of stress concentration on the rod blank, so the stiffer double-foot guide is often provided with a cushioning underwrap (called "double wrapping") to better distribute the stresses. In fact, for all types of rods, stress concentration at the guide foot is statistically the most frequent cause of failure under load; most rod breakage from a large fish is located at a site of guide attachment. This situation is further

---

Determining the number of fish that exist today is complicated by the fact that present fish species and subspecies can adapt and change within a few years.

exacerbated by the common practice of grinding the end(s) of the guide foot to knife edges to allow smooth thread wrapping.

The transparent coat of epoxy resin is the final step to protect the wrapping thread and, perhaps more important, to firmly affix the guide in place because any movement could lead to scratches on the rod blank and promote premature failure.

Once the resin has cured, the guide and wrap are now an integral part of the rod blank and affect the action. The wrap acts in the manner of an athletic support bandage, adding to the stiffness of the rod, and the weight and stiffness of the guide also affect the action. The completed rod is typically stiffer and slower in action than the unadorned blank as it was originally fabricated. Thus, proper rod design must plan for the overall effects of adding guides and wrapping.

The guide wrapping is additionally the focus of artistic expression. Its coloration can be somber or brilliant, it may be complementary or contrasting to that of the blank, it may be a single color, tiger-striped, or multi-banded; all of these are a reflection of the preference of its builder or user, and can be a source of great pride.

The acme of artistic expression is represented by the "diamond wrap" at the base of the rod blank just above the foregrip; this is a beautiful, time-consuming (expensive), and challenging bit of craftsmanship and is the hallmark of the custom-built rod. Intricate patterns are worked into the thread, and are often breathtaking in their execution. Each diamond wrap is unique and an expression of individuality. The diamond wrap is to the custom rod builder what the air brush paint finish is to the custom automobile builder. Though some may be gaudy, there is no doubt as to its vigor as an art form.

Incidentally, some custom rods have the same color combinations for the entire tackle selection of the angler: freshwater ultralight spinning through blue water trolling, all with identical color wraps. These are "matched sets," akin to the custom color striping of target and hunting arrows for the avid archer. They can be as beautiful and pleasurable to use as a set of matched and boxed sterling silver forks, knives, and spoons.

Line-through-blank rods. Because the use of guides and wrapping necessarily affect the action of the rod blank, the concept of threading fishing line through the center of a rod is as old as the first tubular rod. The absolute simplicity of eliminating not only the guides and wrapping, but torque and stress concentration points, was universally alluring. The nodal segments of early bamboo rods were drilled through, and line was inserted down the axis. The practical problems that arose were those of extreme friction, which impeded the ease of casting and the distance achieved, and caused power losses when retrieving lures, bait rigs, and fish. These problems remained with line-through-blank rods until the 1990s, with none commercially available.

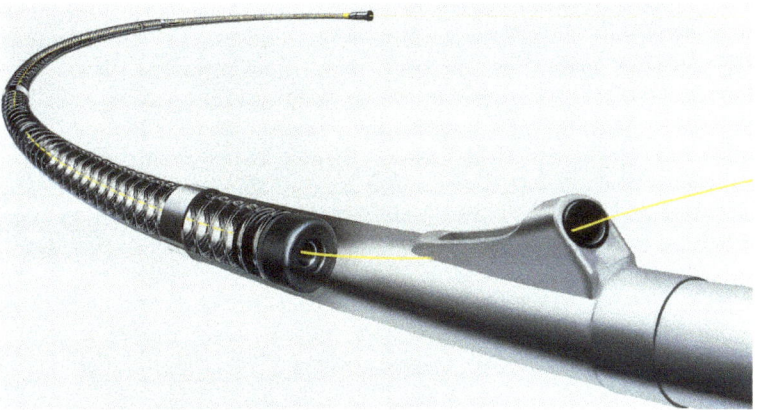

This computer-generated image depicts a Daiwa Interline rod, in which fishing line passes through the graphite blank.

The key to solving this dilemma was recent advanced technology, which precisely finished the *interior* as well as the *exterior* of the rod. These advances include internal polymer finishes and complex internal integrated structures. To date, only one manufacturer, Daiwa, has developed this for models of spinning and baitcasting rods, and these cast and retrieve as well as similar rods with external guides; in addition, they offer "perfect" bends without stress concentration, unprecedented lightness (the rod wall can be made thinner because it does not have to withstand stress concentration due to the guide foot), and torque-free characteristics.

The ability to be torque free is particular to line-through-blank rods; the fish-fighting ability is effective not only to the front, as with external-guide rods, but acts equally well for strong runs to either side. The tiptop and front section of the rod is axially symmetrical and therefore omnidirectional. Whichever direction the fish runs, the rod responds with equal bending forces. An additional benefit to the omnidirectional tiptop is that it is tangle free.

At this point, these line-through-blank products are being used primarily for freshwater fishing applications, but in time, this technology may spread to a wider range of applications.

Grips and handles. Rod grips and handles serve several functions, including comfort and control for the angler and a seat for mechanically mounting the reel.

The traditional grip material is cork because it is thermally insulating (and therefore warm in cold weather), light in weight, sensitive to vibration transmission, and provides a good grip, even when wet. Drawbacks include relatively rapid wear because of softness (cork is easy to shape but also easy to crumble), difficulty to obtain as a uniform material (it is the bark of a tree with all of the implied variations from piece to piece), and being relatively expensive in premium grades (inspection and sorting is labor intensive).

Ground and reconstituted cork, which is the equivalent of particle board, is a compromise material but is generally regarded as physically unattractive. It is used extensively in the form of rubber-bonded tape, which is spiral-wound directly onto the blank for specialty surf rods because of its light weight and durability.

Man-made handle materials include foamed polymers such as Hypalon, typically found in black but available in colors or even "laminated" configurations. These can range from foamed cylinders to molded and shaped offset pistol grips.

The choice of material is largely determined by application: cork for more finesse-like fishing and foamed polymers for rugged applications. The forces that a big-game angler applies to the rod grip would tear many materials right off the blank. On the other hand, a person casting ultralight micro-jigs would likely find the weight of polymer grips oppressive. The former needs Hypalon, the latter premium cork. Both types of grips have shapes which reflect their application; the Hypalon for the big-game angler is often a hand-filling triangular cross section to better control torquing; the premium cork for the ultralight caster is bullet shaped to better encourage the natural pointing tendency of the index finger along the rod axis for pinpoint accuracy.

The reel of the big-game angler needs not only a physically sturdy reel seat of formed stainless steel or machined high-tensile-strength aluminum, but is often supplemented by a separate accessory clamp (part of the reel) secured around the reel seat by stainless steel bolts. Angled tie rods, shoulder harness, and gimbaled butt are accessories that complete the fishing outfit, all intended to help battle the strongest species.

The reel seat of an ultralight spinning rod, in contrast, can be as simple as a few thin aluminum rings, offering not only light weight, but the convenience of positioning the reel anywhere along the handle for best balance. These rings, incidentally, should be secured not by just sliding onto the reel foot, but by rotating them several times to "bite" into the handle.

A more common reel seat is one with a threaded closure, which is regarded as more secure but suffers the drawback of fixed location. Threaded reel seats are offered over a wide range of sizes for various fishing applications. The reel seat materials for these applications are machined aluminum alloys and molded graphite (polymers with strength fibers).

In applications requiring sensitivity, the reel seat is often cut away to allow direct contact of the rod blank and reel seat so that the transmission of the most subtle strike is maximized. The choice of reel seat is determined just as in the case of the handle or grip: it should represent the combination of best comfort and utility that pleases the angler.

Some spinning rods, incidentally, do not possess either a threaded reel seat or adjustable aluminum rings, but have merely unaltered cork handles. These are expressly designed to allow the user to position a spinning reel where it feels most comfortable, using black or colored electrician's tape (preferably 1-inch width) to firmly secure it to the rod. This is preferred by some light jig users, and it is possible for anglers with sliding ring reel seats (which often don't stay put) to remove the rings and use tape to secure the reel to the handle. The main drawback to this is that the reel cannot be easily removed from the handle for storage or changing, and even the tightest manual tape wrapping may not prevent some flex or stretch in the tape at the reel foot when the rod is put under severe stress.

See: Baitcasting Tackle; Big-Game Tackle; Conventional Tackle; Flycasting Tackle; Reel, Fishing; Spincasting Tackle; Spinning Tackle; Tackle Care, Maintenance.

ROD HOLDER

A device that a fishing rod is inserted into when not being used or held by hand. Rod holders come in many forms and are made by many manufacturers. Adjustability, ease of rod removal, sturdiness and stability, and placement options are the key factors in selecting and using these accessories.

Some rod holders are primarily used for stowing rods out of the way when not in use. There are various ways to do this, depending on the design of the boat. Open boats, center consoles, and cuddy cabin craft often sport through-the-gunwale or flush-mounted holders that store rods upright. This isn't practical for many small boats, though, and horizontal mounting is preferable for some. The decks of many small boats are often cluttered with rods, and many anglers leave these to bounce freely when the boat is underway; here, a snap-in floor holder can be used to secure rods.

Holders used to contain rods that are being used—stillfished or trolled—are mounted on or in the gunwale and transom, as well as on a guard-rail, handrail, trolling board, or downrigger. Holders should be adjustable to different positions and angles, although some rod holders mounted on downriggers are not adjustable. They should beable to support a long-handled rod, a rod with a trigger grip, a spinning rod, and a heavy-duty rod with crosshair style gimbal footing. Holders should allow quick removal of the rod; some designs cause anglers to fight with the holder to remove a rod when a fish is on the line and exerting a lot of torque on the handle, which is buried in the holder.

ROD REST

A bank- or shore-planted device that supports a fishing rod being used in bait fishing and not held by hand. Rests may be used to support the entire rod or the tip section, and may hold a single rod or multiple rods.

A rod supported by a rest can be grabbed and lifted upward without having to slide or pop it out of a holder, which makes it useful when fishing

These holders keep casting rods out of the way but ready on a center-console boat.

with very light lines and floats, but impractical for fishing from a boat.
See: Rod Holder.

ROD STORAGE

Rod storage in a fishing boat takes many forms, but it is a sure bet that in most boats, except for big sportfishermen, there is rarely enough room for safely stowing all the rods you want or may need. Most anglers bring and use several rods in a day of fishing. They usually want them rigged up and accessible, but out of harm's way when not being used. When several people are in a boat, especially one in the 16- to 20-foot range, this can be a tall order. Leaving rods lying around is a poor option for fairly obvious reasons: They tend to get tangled, which makes for frustrating untangling when a rod is needed quickly, and they are subject to being broken or damaged in many ways. Rods should be secure, not bouncing around, in a moving boat, and when fishing, extra rods should not be in locations that impede fishing.

Bigger boats can use a combination of storage schemes, and open areas pose few problems for rod storage. Holding racks may store rods horizontally under the gunwales, vertically along the sides of a console, and vertically along the aft edge of a tuna tower, not to mention horizontally inside the cabin. Some open fishing boats have lockable horizontal rod storage inside floor compartments on the recessed foredeck, much like the rod-holding compartments of bass and some multi-purpose freshwater fishing boats. But in small open boats, accessible rods, especially fly rods that can't fit into upright holders, must be stored under the gunwale horizontally or along the interior sides.

Horizontal rod racks are feasible on all but the very smallest of boats (it isn't practical to stow a 9-foot fly rod horizontally along the gunwale of a 10-foot cartopper, at least not fully assembled), and you aren't going to be able to carry six rods per side in a really small boat either. But you can get many rods per side in even a 16-foot skiff with the right rack, although you may have to customize one yourself to do it. In fact, many small-boat anglers do customize their boats for rod storage purposes, and this takes on the forms of both horizontal and vertical storage, particularly in vertical systems using PVC pipe.

Properly designed and installed rod holders can contribute substantially to angling efficiency and at the same time considerably lengthen the usable life of your fishing tackle.
See: Boat.

RODE
A nautical term for anchor line.

ROE
The eggs of a female fish; also a term for a female fish with eggs.

ROLL CAST
A common and practical cast used in fly fishing.
See: Flycasting Tackle.

ROLLING HITCH
See: Knots, Boating.

ROOSTERFISH *Nematistius pectoralis.*
Other names—Spanish: *papagallo, gallo, pez de gallo, reje pluma.*

The roosterfish is a superb light tackle gamefish and a member of the Carangidae family of jacks, so named for the comb of long dorsal fin spines that extend far above the body of the fish. It has been exploited at a local level because of its excellent quality as a food fish and is marketed fresh.

Identification. A striking, iridescent fish, the roosterfish is characterized by seven long, threadlike dorsal fin spines, which are found even on young fish. This comb stands erect when the roosterfish is excited, as when threatened, but ordinarily the fin remains lowered in a sheath along the back. There

Roosterfish

are also two dark, curved stripes on the body and a dark spot at the base of the pectoral fin.

Size. Roosterfish can grow to 4 feet in length and exceed 100 pounds. The all-tackle world record is a 114-pound fish taken off Baja California in 1960.

Distribution. Endemic to the eastern Pacific, roosterfish occur from San Clemente in Southern California to Peru, including the Galápagos Islands; they are rare north of Baja California, Mexico.

Habitat. Roosterfish inhabit shallow inshore areas, such as sandy shores along beaches. Young fish are often found in tidal pools.

Angling. This inshore species inhabits moderate depths of water and fights particularly well. It will jump several times after being hooked, dive deeply, and engage in a slugfest. A good-size roosterfish, roughly 20 pounds, will make a startling first run with its dorsal comb high above the water.

Roosterfish are found in loose groups and are often spotted under working birds. They are caught by boaters who drift and troll, but also by surf anglers and those who cast from boats. Sandy-bottomed locales are good, as are bays and sections of mild surf. Smaller fish are usually closer to shore.

Trolling with strip baits, live baits, plugs, and feathers is popular; casting and live bait drifting, particularly when a group of roosterfish is located, can be particularly effective.

The tackle for these fish is often quite stout, but medium-action gear with 15- to 20-pound line has merit, and fly rods and light spinning or baitcasting gear are good choices as well.

See: Inshore Fishing; Jacks.

ROTENONE

A chemical used by fisheries biologists to poison all or a section of a lake or pond in order to kill fish. Rotenone is not known to be harmful to humans and is usually applied as a method of last resort for sampling purposes or for complete eradication of existing fish populations in order to restock the water with other species.

ROUGH FISH

A subjective and generally unofficial term for freshwater species that are not considered gamefish.

Exactly which species fall into this lump category is debatable. Species that are designated by law as gamefish do not technically warrant inclusion; however, some species may be officially listed as a gamefish in one state and not in another. Fish that are considered gamefish by general consensus do not fall under this category either; nevertheless, there are many species that a majority of anglers do not deem sporting but that a minority of anglers do.

Clearly no official listing of rough fish species exists, but on the basis of general attitudes and interest this term includes carp, catfish, bullhead, gar, buffalo, drum, suckers, bowfin, burbot, sturgeon, and whitefish *(see each species)*. Catfish, sturgeon, and whitefish probably draw a little more esteem than the others.

"Rough fish" is a term that obviously has negative connotations. This viewpoint has evolved for various reasons. Some fish, like carp, are either nonnative or their feeding and spawning behavior are such that they can be detrimental to other more highly esteemed species in certain environments. Some are less highly esteemed simply because they are more reclusive, less abundant, hard to locate or catch, scrounge for food rather than pillage, are not carnivorous, or look odd or different.

The puritanical and undemocratic attitudes that have evolved toward rough fish species have to some degree continued even in the current enlightened fishing age because highly popular species (salmon, trout, bass, and walleye in particular) have become the focus of almost faddish specialization and marketing, and because popular sportfishing literature has overwhelmingly been oriented to those fish that are perceived to be more glamorous and with greater followings.

What this means, of course, is an unbalanced approach to sportfishing effort as well as harvest, with extreme emphasis on a few top predators or highly valued food fish, and little, or no, interest, in others. That may be human nature, and it may be a cultural phenomenon. Attitudes toward neglected fish may change if the populations of more esteemed fish suffer greatly or if pursuing the less-esteemed species becomes more acceptable for other reasons (marketing, economics, food).

In the meantime, in many places, people who devotedly pursue these so-called rough fish have little competition for the resource. For those who desire to keep a good thing to themselves, this may be a good thing. However, with more interest in rough fish and with greater numbers of people pursuing them, there might be more dissemination of information and more knowledge, and perhaps opportunities for even better angling.

See: Coarse Fish.

ROW
To propel a boat using oars.
See: Boat; Rowboat.

ROWBOAT
A small craft with a displacement-type hull that is propelled by oars fitted in oar locks. The term is primarily applied to 10- to 14-foot boats, usually with a flat or semi-V bottom. Many jonboats *(see)* are called rowboats, as are many small boats available for rental at camps and marinas.
See: Boat.

RUBBER WORM
A common term for an artificial worm, few of which are made of rubber today.
See: Soft Worm.

RUDD *Scardinius erythrophthalmus.*
Other names—European rudd; German: *rotfeder*; Italian: *scardola*.

A prominent coarse fish *(see)*, the rudd is widely sought by anglers. It is a member of the large Cyprinidae family, which includes minnows *(see)* and carp *(see)*, and is of similar size and color to its relative, the roach *(see)*.

Rudd

Identification. The rudd is somewhat cylindrical yet deep bodied. It has a moderately forked tail and an upturned mouth. The scales are strongly marked, the back is dark brown, and the sides are golden brown tapering to a white belly. The pectoral, pelvic, and anal fins are reddish orange, and the dorsal and tail fins are dusky. The rudd has 8 to 9 dorsal rays, 10 to 11 anal rays, and eyes that are red or have a red spot. The rudd may be confused with the roach; however, the pectoral fins of the roach lack the reddish orange color, and the body is more silvery. It is similar in appearance to the golden shiner *(see: shiner, golden)* but is distinguished from that species by its scaled ventral keel.

Size. The maximum size for rudd is in the 4- to 5-pound range, although fish of that nature are rare. A 2-pound rudd is typically a large one.

Distribution. Rudd range from western Europe to the Caspian and Aral Sea basins but are absent from Russia; they have been introduced to the United States.

Habitat. Pools, canals, lakes, and slow-running rivers with muddy bottoms are the prime locations for rudd. They spend much time in or along the edges of vegetation.

Life history/Behavior. Spawning takes place in heavy weeds in spring, when rudd broadcast numerous adhesive eggs rather than construct a nest. The fry stay in schools and gather in large congregations, and they provide forage for numerous predators. Rudd remain a schooling fish as adults. Their schools (called shoals) generally comprise similar-size individuals.

Food and feeding habits. Rudd feed on snails, aquatic insects, and small fish, and spend a lot of time in beds of vegetation. They are largely surface feeders, but they also feed on the bottom and at mid-depths. Many rudd are observed taking food from the surface or from the underside of aquatic plants. These observations indicate where to fish.

Angling. Like other coarse fish, rudd are not spectacular fighters, but they are popular. Maggots, bread, grubs, and worms are the main baits for rudd, and most fishing occurs in or close to weeds. Fly fishing with nymphs, however, is also an option. Anglers use rods from 11 to 13 feet in length, line from 2 to 4 pounds in strength, and No. 14 to 20 bait hooks. Hooked baits are fished with or without a float.

RUFFE *Gymnocephalus cernuus.*
Other names—Eurasian ruffe; French: *grémille;* German: *kaulbarsch;* Polish: *jazgarz;* Russian: *yersh obyknovennyi.*

A member of the Percidae family of perch *(see),* the ruffe has no sporting virtue and only minor commercial value in its native European range. It was largely ignored until it was introduced into North America, evidently through ballast water discharge by transoceanic ships. Since its discovery in 1986 in Lake Superior's St. Louis River, the ruffe has been a considerable threat to the delicate predator-prey balance necessary to maintain flourishing commercial fisheries and sportfisheries in North American waters, especially in the Great Lakes. It has been reported only in Lake Superior waters but is likely to exist, or spread, elsewhere.

The species found and multiplying in Lake Superior has been identified as *Gymnocephalus cernuus.* Other members of the same genus include the striped ruffe, or schraetzer *(G. schraetser);* the Donets ruffe *(G. acerinus);* and the Danube ruffe *(G. baloni).* These are eastern European and western Asian species, native to the Danube River and tributaries to the Black Sea. The native range of *G. cernuus* is from France to the Kolyma River in eastern Siberia, and it has been introduced to England, Scotland, and Scandinavia.

Identification. The ruffe's body shape is very similar to that of the yellow perch, and its body markings are similar to those of the walleye. It has a spiny first dorsal fin connected to a second soft dorsal fin, two deep sharp spines on the anal fin, one sharp spine on the pelvic fins, and sharp spines on the gill cover. The dorsal fins have rows of dark spots, the eyes are large and glassy, and the mouth is small and downturned. There are no scales on its head.

Size/Age. The ruffe seldom exceed 6 inches in length but can attain a length of 10 inches. Most female ruffe live for 7 years but may live up to 11 years. Males generally live 3 to 5 years.

Habitat. In Europe and Asia, the ruffe occurs in freshwater and in brackish waters with 3 to 5 parts per million salinity. It exists in a variety of lake environments, preferring turbid areas and soft bottoms without vegetation. In rivers, it prefers slower-moving water. It is more tolerant of murky and eutrophic conditions than are many other perch.

Life history/Behavior. The ruffe generally matures in two to three years, and spawns between mid-April and July, depending on location, temperature, and habitat. Young ruffe have a faster growth rate than many of their competitors, and adults reproduce prolifically, which allows for quick population expansion. It is a nocturnal fish, spending its days in deeper water and moving shallower to feed at night.

Food. The ruffe's primary diet is small aquatic insects and larvae, although it may consume fish eggs. Although there is much to be determined about this fish, researchers have found that the diets of ruffe and yellow perch do not overlap much; if they did, it was feared that ruffe populations would explode and cause a decline in yellow perch, and possibly other fish species.

Angling. As noted, in North America there is no angling interest in ruffe. Where it has been located, it is illegal to fish with ruffe as bait and to transport the species dead or alive. Efforts to control the spread and impact of ruffe to other areas are urged, including being careful not to unknowingly transport the adults or juveniles in bilge water or water from bait buckets.
See: Exotic Species.

RULES OF THE ROAD
Also known as Navigation Rules, this a general term for regulations established for boats to prevent collision.
See: Boat; Navigation.

RUN
(1) A seasonal migration undertaken by fish, usually as part of their life history; an upstream migration, particularly of anadromous fish. Run is sometimes used by anglers to refer to a temporarily increased abundance of fish without respect to migratory behavior *(see: running).*

(2) A generally uniform section of a stream, creek, or small to midsize river that is deeper than a riffle *(see)* and without the disturbed surface, yet not as deep and slow-flowing as a pool *(see).* A run usually has uniform depth throughout most of its length, commencing as the depth of the tail end of a pool tapers upward and ending by shallowing to a riffle. Runs generally exist between upstream pools and downstream riffles.

Runs may also be called flats, and they vary considerably in length, depth, and width, as well as in bottom features. The bottom may have a soft sand or silt character, a mixture of sand and rock, or interspersed sections of both, as well as possess some large rocks or other cover objects. Some species of fish (or some sizes of certain species) are very

Ruffe

active in runs, especially when the flow is moderate; others visit these areas to feed but do not take up full-time residence.

(3) The behavior of a fish taking line off a reel under tension and swimming away from the angler. A fish makes a "run" when it swims any distance with a hooked bait, lure, or fly, while the drag of the reel is employed.

RUNABOUT
A general-purpose motor-driven boat, usually seating four to six people, without sleeping quarters, and used for general pleasure boating but seldom appointed with sportfishing accessories.

RUNNER, BLUE *Caranx crysos*.
Other names—hardtail, hard-tailed jack, runner; French: *carangue coubali*; Greek: *kokali*; Italian: *carangidi, carangido mediterraneo*; Portuguese: *carangídeos, xaralete*; Spanish: *atún, cojinua, cojinúa negra, cojinuda*.

The blue runner is a small, spunky member of the Carangidae family that is valued as bait for big-game fishing. It is an excellent food fish and is marketed fresh, frozen, and salted.

Identification. The body of the blue runner is bluish green to brassy, silvery, or light olive above. There is a black, somewhat elongated spot near the upper end of the gill cover, and there may be faint bluish bars on the body. A characteristic feature is the blackish shading on the tips of the tail fins. The blue runner is easily distinguished from the crevalle jack because it lacks the dark blotch found on the pectoral fins of that fish.

Size. This species usually weighs less than 1 pound and is typically 1 foot long; the all-tackle world record is an 8-pound, 7-ounce fish taken off Texas.

Distribution. In the eastern Atlantic, blue runners range from Senegal to Angola, including the western Mediterranean. In the western Atlantic, they occur from Nova Scotia to Brazil, including the Caribbean and the Gulf of Mexico.

Habitat. Blue runners inhabit offshore waters in large schools. They are occasionally found over reefs, sometimes in pairs or solitary. Young fish frequently linger around sargassum and other floating objects.

Life history. Sexually mature when they reach 9 to 10 inches in length, blue runners spawn offshore from January through August.

Food. Blue runners feed primarily on fish, shrimp, squid, and other invertebrates.

Angling. The blue runner is not a primary target of anglers, although these fish are caught incidentally by anglers trolling, casting, or fishing with bait. They are caught on small baited hooks drifted in chum lines, and are often kept as live or dead (rigged) bait for larger pelagic species.
See: Jacks; Offshore Fishing.

Blue Runner

RUNNER, RAINBOW *Elagatis bipinnulata*.
Other names—runner, rainbow yellowtail, skipjack, shoemaker, Hawaiian salmon, prodigal son; Afrikaans: *re nboog-pylvis*; Arabic: *aifa, garaeiba, gazala, mujlabah, sagla*; Creole: *carangue saumon, dauphin vert, sorcier*; Fijian: *drodrolagi*; French: *carangue arc-en-ciel, comère saumon*; Hawaiian: *kamanu*; Japanese: *taumuburi*; Malay/Indonesian: *pisang-pisang*; Portuguese: *arabaiana norte, salmao*; Samoan: *samani*; Spanish: *cola amarilla, corredores, macarela, pez rata, salmon, sardinata*; Tahitian: *roeroe*; Tuvaluan: *tekamai*.

A member of the Carangidae family of jacks, the rainbow runner does not look like other jacks because it is a much slimmer, more streamlined fish. It is also an excellent food fish with firm white flesh, marketed fresh and salted/dried. In Japan the rainbow runner is cooked with a special sauce or eaten raw and is considered a delicacy.

Identification. The rainbow runner is blue green above and white or silver below with a yellow or pink cast. On both sides there is a broad, dark-blue, horizontal stripe from the snout to the base of the tail; a narrow, pale-blue stripe immediately below it that runs through the eye; a pale to brilliant-yellow stripe along below that; and then another narrow, pale-blue stripe. The tail is yellow and the other fins are a greenish or olive yellow. The rainbow runner has a slender body that is more elongated than that of most other jacks. The first dorsal fin has six spines and the second has one spine and 25 to 27 connected soft rays. Behind this is a 2-rayed finlet. The anal fin has a single detached spine with 16 to 18 soft rays followed by a 2-rayed finlet. The rainbow runner is similar to the cobia in shape but can be distinguished by its coloring, as well as the finlets that follow the dorsal and anal fins.

Rainbow Runner

Size. The rainbow runner is typically 2 to 3 feet long, although it can reach 4 feet and 22 pounds. The all-tackle world record is a 37-pound, 9-ounce Mexican fish.

Distribution. Found worldwide in marine waters, the rainbow runner occurs in the western Atlantic, from Massachusetts throughout the northern Gulf of Mexico to northeastern Brazil; and in the eastern Atlantic from the Ivory Coast to Angola, including the areas around St. Paul's Rocks and Genoa, Italy, in the Mediterranean. They range throughout the western Indian Ocean. In the eastern Pacific, they occur from the mouth of the Gulf of California, Mexico, to Ecuador, including the Galápagos Islands; in the western Pacific, they are found near Fiji and Tuvalu.

Habitat. Rainbow runners form either small polarized groups or large schools that usually remain at or near the surface, although they can inhabit depths of up to 120 feet. They occur over reefs and in deep, clear lagoons, preferring areas with a current.

Food. Rainbow runners feed on invertebrates, small fish, and squid.

Angling. Rainbow runners are not ordinarily a target of anglers, but they are commonly caught on baits or lures trolled for other species. Fishing methods include trolling with small baits and lures, or live bait fishing. The rainbow runner is sometimes caught on heavy tackle intended for larger fish, but its fighting ability is then reduced. When hooked on light tackle, it is an excellent gamefish and a tough fighter prone to fast surface runs.

See: Jacks; Offshore Fishing.

RUNNING

A term applied to the seasonal appearance of significant numbers of fish, usually in rivers while undergoing their spawning migration, but also moving along the coast. When someone says, "The shad are running," it means that schools of these fish are known to be migrating; similarly, when someone says, "The bluefish are in," it means that numbers of bluefish are now in the area and being caught.

RUNNING DRAG

A position on lever drag (big-game) reels that allows line to slip from the spool freely without backlashing the reel; this position is reached when the drag lever is initially advanced from the freespool position.

See: Big-Game Tackle.

RUNNING LIGHTS

Navigational lights required by law to be used on boats from sunset to sunrise, in order to avoid collision. For most sportfishing boats, running lights must include red and green sidelights on the bow centerline (red to port, green to starboard), and a single white stern light visible over a 135-degree arc. There are different requirements for large vessels, and these lights must be visible when the boat is at rest, as well as when it is underway.

RUNNING LINE

A portion of a fly line behind the head that is lightweight and small in diameter, and aids distance casting by minimizing friction on the line guides.

See: Flycasting Tackle.

RUNOUT

A term for the site where shallow marsh ponds or swamps drain with falling tides or receding flood water into deeper canals and bayous. The area where the departing water drains, the runout, tends to collect certain fish species and supply them with a ready source of food, making it also a favorite target of anglers.

RUSSIA

Since the breakup of the former Soviet Union in late 1991, new countries and self-governing areas have been created and are still evolving. The vast region that was once the Union of Soviet Socialist Republics and the largest country in the world is now the Russian Federation. It still spans Europe and Asia, covering more than one-ninth of the world's land area, a region more than twice the size of China or the United States, and akin to Canada in climate. It encompasses the countries of Russia, Ukraine, Byelorussia, Moldavia, Armenia, Azerbaijan, Georgia, Kazakhstan, Uzbekistan, Kirghizia, Turkmenistan, and Tadzhikistan.

This vast area includes the world's longest continuous coastline, spanning more than 37,650 kilometers, mostly along the Arctic and Pacific Oceans; borders that face the Black and Caspian Seas; an exceptional number of rivers—many of them large, long, and prominent—that course through all regions; and many lakes, including Lake Baikal, the deepest freshwater lake in the world.

These enormous resources portend a significant freshwater sportfishery, the surface of which has been virtually untapped and little explored. The lack of infrastructure for general as well as angling tourism throughout the Russian Federation, the distance and great expense of traveling within the region, language barriers, and the state of the political and economic climate have left many questions about the actual status of the fisheries' resources unanswered. The only fairly well-developed sportfishery to date is for Atlantic salmon, and that for a relative few rivers in the northwesternmost region.

Nevertheless, Russia reportedly harbors more than 450 species of freshwater fish, of which some 20 to 30 are of interest to anglers. Chief among these, of course, is Atlantic salmon; but charr, taimen, lenok, brown trout, various sturgeon, pike, grayling, and Pacific salmon species are among Russia's coveted gamefish, although some have been adversely affected by pollution and other problems.

Although international air travel from eastern and western countries is well established, domestic travel within Russia is sometimes an adventure in itself. Flights operate to nearly every town or settlement but are sometimes problematic. Helicopters are used in many remote places, especially on the salmon rivers, but these are often subject to weather and mechanical delays. In most of Russia, roads provide very limited access to good fishing. Visitors who want to fish on their own, but who don't know the language or don't use a reliable tour operator, have minimal chance of success and would likely need an exceptional amount of time and patience.

European Region

The European, or westernmost, region of Russia is most populated and most accessible. Unfortunately, it is heavily polluted, although the pollution is localized and the region still has vast fishing potential when compared to the rest of Europe. This area contains the one fishery that is somewhat known to the rest of the world, especially to a small coterie of international anglers: the Atlantic salmon of the Kola Peninsula.

Virtually all of Russia's salmon fishing and overall sportfishing is currently concentrated in the Kola Peninsula. Some 65 peninsula rivers presently contain, or once contained, Atlantic salmon. Foreign anglers today visit only a handful of these. Among the rivers noted for their salmon fishing are the Varzuga, Varzina, Ponoi, Umba, Jokanga, Litsa, Rynda, and Kharlovka; the Ponoi has garnered the most notoriety. All provide fly fishing from camps run in cooperation with Western investors and outfitters, most are up to international standards, and all are either very expensive or extremely expensive. Because most of the peninsula is without roads or airports, chartered helicopters are often the only option for accessing many rivers. Visitors are funneled through the city of Murmansk.

Bounded on the west by Finland, the Kola Peninsula is otherwise surrounded by the Barents and White Seas. Salmon rivers in the north of the peninsula enter the Barents Sea and generally are shorter and steeper, with hearty rapids and falls and runs of shorter duration, but they also possess larger fish on average. Those rivers entering the White Sea (an arm of the Barents) are in the southern and central parts of the peninsula; they are longer and gentler in grade, void of significant falls and rapids, and generally have runs of small to medium salmon that last four to five months.

Overall, the Kola's salmon, which are plentiful and typically host an excellent ratio of adults to grilse—better than virtually all other hallowed Atlantic salmon waters—have been more or less

Salmon anglers fish the Varzina River.

accidentally saved by the existence of a large military installation on the peninsula. This institution kept civilians, prying eyes, and coastal netters far at bay, allowing salmon to migrate in and out unfettered, save for local poaching and minor local river mouth netting. The first foreign visitors fished the area in 1989, camps and more exploration soon followed, and today—not without bureaucratic headaches, poaching problems, territorial disputes, and other troubles—enough of a fishery has developed to rate this region as excellent, although some apprehension as to its future still lingers.

At least 14 of the top 20 Kola rivers have, or did have during the 1990s, established fishing camps. A high percentage of Kola salmon are believed to enter just four rivers: the Varzuga, Ponoi, Kola, and Umba; however, the exact number of fish running all of these rivers is not completely known, and modern statistics have been kept for only a decade and are subject to many variables.

The salmon season generally begins in late May or early June (the snow melts in May) and ends in late September or early October, but varies from river to river. Rivers with larger fish but runs of shorter duration end their season in early to mid-August; those with smaller fish or a second run have a longer season. The first part of the season, which experiences the highest water levels, also tends to produce the largest fish. Some rivers yield fish from 20 to 40 pounds during the spring freshet, although the high flow and rougher water conditions of some early season rivers result in many bigger fish breaking off. The early June weather can be cold, damp, and wet.

Among the north-coast rivers, the Varzina is one of the more notable fisheries. This is a swift-flowing canyon river that runs to the Barents Sea from Yenozero Lake; reaching it requires some hiking over rugged ground, but it has produced good-size salmon up to 15 kilograms that are full of stamina and tough to land. East of the Varzina is the Jokanga River. The fifth largest flow on the peninsula, the Jokanga has more than 200 kilometers of watercourse and good fishing for salmon of various sizes. Five of its tributaries—the Suhaja, Lyljok, Puiva, Tichka, Pokkryei, and Pulongi—which respectively range from 97 to 34 kilometers in length, are said to be suitable for salmon fishing as well. East of the Varzina are the Rynda and Kharlovka Rivers, both of which are difficult if not impossible to wade early in the season.

The Ponoi River, which is the Kola's largest, flows roughly from west to east through the east-central region of the peninsula and into the White Sea. It is just above the Arctic Circle, and is primarily fished in the lower 80 or 90 kilometers, as well as in it tributary, the Pornache River. The Ponoi is not only large in length, but also wide in many places. Yet it has a gentle flow that makes it easy to wade and good for anglers of all skill levels. It is restricted to fly fishing only (some rivers allow spinning and fly tackle) and catch-and-release, and has proved a fairly reliable producer. The river has been the subject of cooperative tagging for a research project.

Nearly all anglers ply the river with floating fly lines, and some fish in lower water with skated dry flies. Wade fishing is most popular, but Ponoi anglers also fish some locales from the bank and from a boat.

The Ponoi has two distinct runs of salmon: one that enters in June and July and spawns in the fall, and another that enters in mid-August, stays in the river for more than a year, and spawns the following fall. There are evidently far more fall-run fish.

The Kola's fisheries are primarily accessed through established operators who mete out one guide for every one or two clients. Pollution has not been a factor for most Kola rivers, but poaching has caused problems, and the fishing has varied in some rivers over the relatively short period during which anglers have had access. Visitors with an adventurous bent can buy a catch-and-release day license for a modest fee on most rivers, if they can find the right office and, furthermore, get to the rivers. These are not easy tasks, and do-it-yourself expeditions require time, patience, and a command of the Russian language, not to mention an understanding of the culture and local customs. The difficulties are so great that few foreigners, primarily Russian-speaking Europeans, visit fishing sites on the Kola, or elsewhere in the country, on their own. Most visitors require a local host or a reservation with an established fishing camp.

In addition to salmon, sea-run brown trout inhabit several Kola rivers, and arctic charr thrive in some of the northern waters. Pink salmon were introduced in the 1960s, and most rivers today have runs. Some of the upper rivers have excellent fishing for nicely spotted resident brown trout, which average 1.5 kilograms and may reach 4 to 6 kilograms or more. The inland lakes and rivers of the peninsula hold arctic charr, and in the southern areas there are some pike and grayling.

Atlantic salmon are also found east of the Kola Peninsula in other rivers that enter the Barents Sea, ranging all the way to the Ural Mountains. The last of these is the Kara River, which is beyond the island of Novaya Zemlya in the Kara Sea and on the western shores of Bajdarackaja Bay. East of here the arctic waters are too cold for salmon.

Thus, potential salmon waters exist along a coastline extending close to 3,000 kilometers, including the regions of Kola, Karelen, Archangels, and Komi. This broad territory has arguably the world's best current potential for salmon fishing. The area east of the Kola Peninsula is not fished much for Atlantic salmon by anglers, but includes the Pechora River, which is the largest Atlantic salmon river in the world. The Pechora is 1 kilometer wide where it enters the sea, and salmon travel more than 1,500 kilometers up the river, reportedly spawning in more than 62 tributaries. Commercial fishermen have fished it extensively in the past. The Pechora also is the only known river where both Atlantic salmon and taimen live. Other major salmon river systems in the region east of the Kola Peninsula are the Mezen, Archangels, Onega, and Dvina.

The rivers and easterly arctic coastline also harbor inconnu, which normally run to 10 kilograms, although 40-kilogram specimens have been taken.

Elsewhere in the European or western region of Russia, grayling are spread out through the area, as are whitefish and brown trout; the latter species is more prominent in the western areas and absent from the northeastern polar region. The area south of the Kola Peninsula bordering Finland is loaded with lakes and rivers, and many of these contain good brown trout fishing. Fine possibilities for brown trout also exist in the southerly Caucasus region bordering Turkey. In that same region, sea trout inhabit some rivers entering the Caspian Sea. Pike and perch are widespread in western Russia, and zander (pike-perch) are found in the southern regions; a saltwater- or brackish-water-tolerant zander reputedly exists in the northern region of the Black Sea, allegedly spawning in lower rivers and weighing up to 3 kilograms.

The sturgeon is by far Russia's largest sportfish to inhabit freshwater, and also probably its most valuable in light of the caviar resource it represents. In the European region of the Russian Federation, sturgeon are found in the Volga and Ural Rivers, which enter the Caspian Sea, and also in rivers entering the Black Sea. Recent sportfishing for sturgeon in the Ural and Volga Rivers has produced specimens up to 125 kilograms, but the numbers and sizes of the various sturgeon species have declined dramatically. Poaching for eggs and meat is a constant problem, and most Russian sturgeon are considered endangered by Western scientists.

Finally, the Gulf of Finland, which separates westernmost Russia from southern Finland and is a brackish water extension of the Baltic Sea, receives

---

The largest brown trout ever verified was a 72-pound sea-run fish caught in the Kura River, a Russian tributary of the Caspian Sea, in 1897.

the flow from many rivers and is said to contain salmon year-round. Sportfishing for salmon occurs around islands on the Finnish side of the gulf's boundary, and some large specimens are caught by casters and trollers. Opportunities for salmon and sea trout in Russian waters, along the coasts and in the tributaries—especially in the northeastern region of the Gulf of Finland near the Finnish border—are unknown.

Asian Region

Extending nearly 8,000 kilometers east of the Ural Mountains, the Asian region of Russia is immense, lightly visited, and little fished. Three salmonids—taimen, lenok, and grayling—are found throughout this region.

Several subspecies of grayling reportedly thrive here. Lenok occur in waters that range from brooks to large rivers. This species has red dots on its side like a trout, but white flesh; it normally reaches 2 to 3 kilograms but is said to range up to 6 kilograms.

The taimen is the world's largest salmonid, and Russian scientists have reported that at least one specimen weighing 96 kilograms was once taken by commercial fishermen. Taimen usually weigh 7 to 20 kilograms. They are not found on the Kamchatka Peninsula, or in the far northeastern region, and are best caught on big spoons and floating plugs—or something that imitates a mouse—and, for larger specimens, fished during the night. Fly fishing is also productive, especially for smaller fish in the clear rivers. The largest taimen are said to inhabit isolated parts of the Jakutskaya district to the east, and southward to the Khabarovsk region (the Uda River here yielded an 80-pounder to a float-camping angler in 1989), and in the region north of Mongolia, where lakes and tributaries drain into the mighty northerly flowing Jenisej River.

A sea-run taimen, called Sakhalin taimen, is reportedly found on Sakhalin Island (north of Japan in the Sea of Okhotsk) and in coastal rivers in the Khabarovsk region down to the North Korean border. Good rivers are the Koppi, Khuttu, and Tumnin. This fish has larger scales and a deeper body than its strictly freshwater relative, and the largest weight reported is 70 kilograms. There is a run in April and May and another in September and October.

Arctic charr—strictly freshwater as well as sea-run versions—range along the Asian region's unused and uninhabited arctic coast. Normally these fish weigh from 1 to 7 kilograms. Their cousin, Dolly Varden, as well as other charr, are found along the northern part of the Pacific coast.

Six species of Pacific salmon inhabit the eastern coastal rivers, though organized sportfishing efforts for them or the viability of various runs for sportfishing are little known. Chum salmon range from the Lena River in the north, which flows into the arctic-region Laptev Sea, all along the coastline to the North Korean border. The smaller pink salmon are almost as widespread as chum salmon, and also appear in the Kuril Islands. Sockeye salmon are found from the Bering Strait to the southern border. Coho salmon inhabit the northern part of the Pacific coast. Chinook salmon are mainly found on Kamchatka Peninsula. Cherry salmon, which are found only on the Asian side of the Pacific Ocean (the others range to North America), are found in the Kurils, on Sakhalin Island, and along the Khabarovsk coast, with a few found on Kamchatka Peninsula.

Rainbow trout and steelhead mainly occur on the western side of the Kamchatka Peninsula. Pike and perch exist throughout Russia's Asian region, except in the extreme Arctic, along the Pacific coast, and in Alpine areas. Whitefish are plentiful as well, evidently in several species, and several species of sturgeon inhabit the Pacific basin.

Conversion Charts

THE SYSTEM OF WEIGHTS AND MEASURES USED IN MOST COUNTRIES AND IN ALL SCIENTIFIC work is the International System of Units (SI), which is commonly referred to as the metric system. A notable and influential exception to this is the United States, where the general public, and non-scientific publications, use the U.S., or U.S. customary, system of weights and measures. Throughout the *Ken Schultz's Fishing Encyclopedia & Worldwide Angling Guide*, there is a liberal use of both metric and U.S. customary weights and measures without parenthetical conversions to equivalent weights or measures. Some anglers, especially those who travel widely and those who pay close attention to world-record fish weights and fishing line classifications, are accustomed to both systems, which are often found mixed at boat docks, fish camps, and tackle shops throughout the world. The following information is provided to help the reader make the conversion from one system to another.

U.S. To Metric Conversion Formulas

When You Know...	Multiply By...	To Determine...
Inches (in)	25.4	Millimeters (mm)
Inches (in)	2.54	Centimeters (cm)
Inches (in)	0.0254	Meters (m)
Square Inches (sq in)	645.0	Square Millimeters (sq mm)
Square Inches (sq in)	6.45	Square Centimeters (sq cm)
Square Inches (sq in)	0.00064	Square Meters (sq m)
Feet (ft)	30.5	Centimeters (cm)
Feet (ft)	0.305	Meters (m)
Feet (ft)	0.0003	Kilometers (km)
Square Feet (sq ft)	0.093	Square Meters (sq m)
Fathoms (fath)	1.827	Meters (m)
Fathoms (fath)	0.0018	Kilometers (km)
Yards (yd)	0.914	Meters (m)
Square Yards (sq yd)	0.836	Square Meters (sq m)
Statute Miles (mi) (5,280 ft)	1.61	Kilometers (km)
Nautical Miles (n mi) (6,020 ft)	1.852	Kilometers (km)
Square Miles (sq mi)	2.56	Square Kilometers (sq km)
Miles per hour (mph)	1.61	Kilometers per hour (kph)
Knots per hour	1.84	Kilometers per hour (kph)
Acres	0.405	Hectares
Ounces of Weight (oz)	28.3	Grams (g)
Ounces of Weight (oz)	0.0283	Kilograms (kg)
Ounces of Fluid (fl oz)	29.6	Milliliters (mL)
Pounds (lb)	454.0	Grams (g)
Pounds (lb)	0.454	Kilograms (kg)
Pints (pt)—U.S.	0.473	Liters (L)
Pints (pt)—Imperial	0.568	Liters (L)
Quarts (qt)—U.S.	0.946	Liters (L)
Quarts (qt)—Imperial	1.14	Liters (L)
Gallons (gal)—U.S.	3.79	Liters (L)
Gallons (gal)—Imperial	4.55	Liters (L)
degrees Fahrenheit (°F)	0.555 (after subtracting 32)	degrees Celsius (°C)

Metric To U.S. Conversion Formulas

When You Know...	Multiply By...	To Determine...
Millimeters (mm)	0.039	Inches (in)
Centimeters (cm)	0.394	Inches (in)
Centimeters (cm)	0.0328	Feet (ft)
Square Centimeters (sq cm)	0.155	Square Inches (sq in)
Meters (m)	39.37	Inches (in)
Meters (m)	3.281	Feet (ft)
Meters (m)	1.09	Yards (yd)
Meters (m)	0.547	Fathoms (fath)
Square Meters (sq m)	1.2	Square Yards (sq yd)
Kilometers (km)	3,279.0	Feet (ft)
Kilometers (km)	1,093.0	Yards (yd)
Kilometers (km)	546.0	Fathoms (fath)
Kilometers (km)	0.621	Statute Miles (mi)
Kilometers (km)	0.545	Nautical Miles (n mi)
Square Kilometers (sq km)	0.386	Square Miles (sq mi)
Kilometers per hour (kph)	0.621	Miles per hour (mph)
Kilometers per hour (kph)	0.545	Knots per hour
Hectares	2.47	Acres
Grams (g)	0.035	Ounces of Weight (oz)
Grams (g)	0.002	Pounds (lb)
Kilograms (kg)	35.2736	Ounces (oz)
Kilograms (kg)	2.2	Pounds (lb)
Milliliter (mL)	0.034	Fluid Ounces (oz)
Liters (L)	2.11	Pints (pt)—U.S.
Liters (L)	1.76	Pints (pt)—Imperial
Liters (L)	1.06	Quarts (qt)—U.S.
Liters (L)	0.880	Quarts (qt)—Imperial
Liters (L)	0.264	Gallons (gal)—U.S.
Liters (L)	0.22	Gallons (gal)—Imperial
degrees Celsius (°C)	1.8 (and add 32)	degrees Fahrenheit (°F)

Table Of Metric and U.S. Equivalent Line Strengths

Metric	U.S. Customary	Metric	U.S. Customary
1 kg	2.2 lb	10 kg	22.0 lb
2 kg	4.4 lb	15 kg	33.0 lb
3 kg	6.6 lb	24 kg	52.8 lb
4 kg	8.8 lb	37 kg	81.4 lb
6 kg	13.2 lb	60 kg	132.0 lb
8 kg	17.6 lb		

Table of Fish Weights

Metric	U.S. Customary	Metric	U.S. Customary
1 kg	2.2 lb	60 kg	132.0 lb
2 kg	4.4 lb	70 kg	154.0 lb
3 kg	6.6 lb	80 kg	176.0 lb
4 kg	8.8 lb	90 kg	198.0 lb
5 kg	11.0 lb	100 kg	220.0 lb
6 kg	13.2 lb	200 kg	440.0 lb
7 kg	15.4 lb	300 kg	660.0 lb
8 kg	17.6 lb	400 kg	880.0 lb
9 kg	19.8 lb	500 kg	1,100.0 lb
10 kg	22.0 lb	600 kg	1,320.0 lb
20 kg	44.0 lb	700 kg	1,540.0 lb
30 kg	66.0 lb	800 kg	1,760.0 lb
40 kg	88.0 lb	900 kg	1,980.0 lb
50 kg	110.0 lb	1,000 kg	2,200.0 lb

www.ingramcontent.com/pod-product-compliance
Lightning Source LLC
Chambersburg PA
CBHW040933240426
43673CB00054B/1964